ON PSYCHOSES

Paul Schilder

ON PSYCHOSES

Edited by Lauretta Bender

INTERNATIONAL UNIVERSITIES PRESS, INC.
New York

Library of Congress Cataloging in Publication Data

Schilder, Paul, 1886-1940.
   On psychoses.

   Bibliography: p.
   Includes index.
   1. Psychoses. I. Title. [DNLM: 1. Psychoses
—Collected works. WM200 S3340]
RC512.S35   1976   616.8'9   75-33517
ISBN 0-8236-4055-8

Manufactured in the United States of America

CONTENTS

III. SCHIZOPHRENIA

IV. THE DEPRESSIVE STATES

Preface

Paul Schilder's observations of the psychoses, based on his clinical experiences at the Psychiatric Division of Bellevue Hospital (New York City) between 1930 and 1940 were extensive. They embrace a wide range of organic brain disorders, alcoholism, aging, schizophrenia, and the depressive states.

In the 1970's, his observations are still appropriate. His unequaled ability to carry on psychiatric interviews with all sorts of patients was matched by his skill in giving the details of neurological examinations, in using a variety of psychological tests and procedures—some of them original—and in correlating his findings. These papers demonstrate Schilder's extraordinary ability to reintegrate all his observations into his own "constructive psychology."

This group of papers includes many contributions on the use of psychoanalytic and other psychological and biological treatment methods, including the insulin and metrazol treatments which were introduced during these years.

Between the time of Paul Schilder's first trip to the United States in 1928 and his death in 1940, he wrote, in English, over 100 papers on psychiatry, neurology, psychoanalysis, psychology, and related fields, as well as five books. Before coming to the United States, he had written over 200 papers and ten books in German.

Four of these books and a part of a fifth have been translated into English. *Introduction to a Psychoanalytic Psychiatry* (1925), the first attempt to integrate psychoanalytic psychiatry, was translated by Bernard Glueck in 1927. Two small books on hypnosis, written in 1922 and 1927—the second in collaboration with Otto Kauders—were translated by Gerda Corvin and published as *The Nature of Hypnosis* in 1956. *Medical Psychology* (1924) written as a textbook, was translated by David Rapaport (1953). Rapaport also translated parts of *Studies Concerning the Psychology and Symptomatology of General Paresis* (1930c), which he included in his *Organization and Pathology of Thought* (1951).

The first of Schilder's books written in English was *Brain and Personality* (1931a). *Image and Appearance of the Human Body* (1935), which he considered his most original and important contribution, developed from his earlier German publication *Das Körperschema* (1923a) and from his rich clinical experiences in Vienna, as well as his early work in the United States. *Psychotherapy* (1938) was the earliest critical analysis and synthesis of the many schools of psychiatric thought and therapeutic practices, including psychoanalysis. A revised and expanded edition of this work appeared in 1951. *Mind: Perception and Thought in Their Constructive Aspects* (1942b) was closely integrated with his contributions on the body image, which represented to him the ultimate gestalt of all human experiences. *Goals and Desires of Man* (1942a) was a psychological survey of life, based on his investigations of human problems. He felt that psychotherapy must be based on such studies.

He saw in these four books a unified view of the realm of psychology. He was nevertheless planning several other volumes when his death intervened, when he was 54, in 1940. Since then, an effort has been made to complete what he had started. *Psychoanalysis, Man and Society* (1951) is a collection of his sociological writings. *Contributions to Developmental Neuropsychiatry* (1964) included his writings on children and the development of primitive experiences into constructive human behavior.

Finally, there have remained his clinical papers on psychoses, neuroses, and other psychological problems. The present volume, devoted to contributions on the psychoses, contains a treatise he wrote in the last year of his life—The Psychoanalytic Theory of the Psychosis—which has not previously been published.

Publishers of his previously issued work have been uniformly gracious in granting permission to republish here.

Special thanks are due to Gloria Faretra for her devoted help with editorial problems.

Lauretta Bender

New York City
September, 1974

I

THE PSYCHOANALYTIC THEORY
OF THE PSYCHOSES[1]

[1] In addition to the literature referred to in the text, the author suggests Rickman (1927) for his bibliography of 495 titles on psychoanalysis and the psychoses; Fenichel (1931a, 1931b) for extensive bibliographies on the neuroses, perversions, and character disorders; Nunberg (1932) for his discussion of the psychoanalytic theory of the psychoses, which received Freud's direct approval; Melanie Klein (1932); Riviere (1936); Waelder (1936); and Schilder (1925, 1928c, 1931a).

CHAPTER ONE

The General Problem

NEUROSIS AND PSYCHOSIS

Freud (1921, 1922, 1924a, 1924b, 1932)[1] tried repeatedly to characterize the difference between a neurosis and a psychosis. According to his formulation (1924b), the neurosis is a conflict between the ego and the id. Libidinal tendencies are repressed by the ego under the guidance of the superego. The repressed libido regresses and breaks through in symbolic form on a lower level of psychosexual development. The symbolic representation of the infantile wish revised by the regression is disturbing for the personality and constitutes the symptom. It is obvious that the total adaptation of the conscious personality—the ego in the psychoanalytic sense— will be more or less impaired by the neurotic symptom.

In the perversions, the regressed libido similarly breaks through on a lower level of psychosexual development, but there is less symbolic deformation, and, furthermore, the ego and superego do not continue the fight against the infantile psychosexuality,

---

Unpublished manuscript.

[1] [Paul Schilder never read Freud in the English translation. His references to Freud are based on his translations of his recollection of the original writings (he prided himself on his photographic memory).—Ed.]

but comply with it. The situation may be similar in cases of so-called psychopathy, including some cases of criminality. The basic similarity between perversion and psychopathy, on the one hand, and neurosis, on the other hand, is responsible for the fact that there will be in both cases a minor impairment of the ego system and its adaptation to the outer world. Further consequences arise from the fact that the impulses tolerated by the ego system are not tolerated by society, and the individual will come in conflict with society by following the perverse or psychopathic impulse. Complicated dynamics will result from feelings of guilt and anticipated punishment in relation to the infantile drive.

In the psychosis, according to Freud (1924a), the conflict lies between the ego and outer reality. A part of reality is denied, and Freud speaks of a loss of the sense of reality.

The main difference between the manic-depressive psychosis, the neurosis, and the normal state lies in the relation between the ego and the superego: the tension between ego and superego is increased in the depressive states, whereas it is diminished in the manic phase.

The psychoses of the schizophrenic group are generally regarded as a regression to the earliest stages of libido development. The regression is brought on by repression, and the structure of the schizophrenic psychosis, according to the analytic theory, is therefore very close to the structure of a neurosis. However, the extensive regression helps impulses to emerge, which prevents the ego from functioning in its adaptation to reality. The ego is overrun by libidinal impulses and their symbolic derivatives.

The function of the ego in relation to the outer world is more severely impaired in all types of psychoses than in the neuroses. One may summarize Freud's concepts by saying that the psychosis is a far-reaching disturbance in the function of the ego. Freud himself stated, however, that even in the normal state the ego is subject to disruptions. There are rifts in its structure, and small patches of a delusional nature are imposed upon it, disrupting its continuity of function.

Comparatively little has been added to these general formulations of Freud's. Laforgue (1926) spoke of "scotomization" in which parts of the experience are completely denied. His concept, however, has a very definite and circumscribed meaning: that, in schizophrenia, denial of parts of reality is based on anal-sadistic fixations. The inner world (feces) takes the place of the scotomized outer world (father and mother).

> In the degree to which the child's libido withdraws narcissistically from his mother to his own ego, he develops an indifference towards the mother when she has become part of the outside world. He thrusts her out of his circle of interests equating her affectively with excrement. This is a hate reaction: the subject shuts himself off, repudiates his real mother and *becomes blind* towards her. This is the process which I have proposed to designate *scotomization*. It is characterized by the fact that the subject does not express hatred positively but negatively. In order to shut out mother, father and the whole outside world he shuts himself up; in order to kill them he himself takes flight from life; to castrate them he castrates himself [Laforgue, 1926, p. 476].

Hollós and Ferenczi (1925) have approached the psychology of general paresis from the point of view of Ferenczi's concept of the development of the sense of reality.

> General paresis seen from the psychoanalytic viewpoint is really Regressive Paresis. Thus we come successively to the reanimation of more juvenile and finally more infantile forms of tests of reality and of self-criticism, to ever more naïve varieties of phantasies of omnipotence, distorted through rudiments of the healthy personality (as Freud pointed out in schizophrenic grandiose tendencies), and temporarily interrupted by lucid intervals of depression in which the disorder that has taken place, is recognized at least in part through self-observation.... The colossal loss in intellectual values occasions him no more disquietude; for he has succeeded in finding in place of the lost satisfactions, those of archaic oral and anal means (greediness, soiling) [pp. 41-42].

General paresis is considered a cerebral pathoneurosis, as are the neurotic reactions following injury of the brain and impairment of its functions. "The metaluetic brain infection, by attacking the central organ of the ego function, provokes not only 'symptoms of defect,' but also disturbs, as a trauma would do the equilibrium in the housekeeping of the narcissistic libido, which then makes itself felt in symptoms of paretic mental disorder" (p. 34). Hollós and Ferenczi do not, however, attempt to give an explanation for the central phenomenon of general paresis, namely, the mental deterioration and the loss of judgment. Nunberg (1922), in a critical view, stresses with some justification that this description of general paresis reads more like a description of schizophrenia.

I have expressed a similar point of view in a communication (1922a) on the psychology of general paresis antedating the work of Hollós and Ferenczi. There is no question that regressive symptoms in the sense mentioned, are present. This regression, however, which may return to the narcissistic level, cannot be the nuclear problem of general paresis. Hollós and Ferenczi have seen this in part, too, by stressing that the deficiency symptoms of general paresis are in connection with the organic lesion of the brain. It would seem that a classification of psychosis according to psychoanalytic theory should consider these deficiency symptoms of the psychosis, as well as the symptoms that may be termed regressive.

THE EGO AND AMENTIA

In my *Introduction to a Psychoanalytic Psychiatry* (1925) I tried to come to an understanding of the function of the ego in a psychoanalytic sense, in order to arrive at a classification of neuroses and psychoses. According to Freud (1924a), the ego is the part of the personality that perceives reality and has the function of reality testing. This system is also the basis for conscious action. It is obvious that perception as such is in no way a simple function. It is built up on various levels, and even when a full perception is reached the field of perception has to be arranged in more definite units. There are, furthermore, processes of thinking, that guarantee our final relation to the outer world.

We may state that the ego is affected in the so-called organic psychosis as well as in mental deficiency. In this group belong, therefore, all psychoses connected with deteriorating processes like general paresis, arteriosclerotic, and senile psychosis, as well as deterioration in connection with brain tumor and deterioration following toxic influences. Furthermore, it will be necessary to try to come to a deeper understanding of the consequences of localized lesions of the brain that produce aphasic and agnostic signs. Of interest in this connection is that Freud, in his schematic picture of the different parts of the psychic apparatus, used some of the insights he had gained by his earlier studies on aphasia (1891).

In the types of psychoses so far mentioned, it is obviously not so much the perception that is impaired, but judgment and memory, which also obviously belong to the functions of the ego.

It is astonishing how few analytic case studies are recorded concerning Meynert's amentia, to which Freud refers. In the English literature, cases of this type are mostly described as postinfectious confusion or delirium.

The definition of amentia as such has undergone many changes. Meynert himself (1889-1890) rather uncritically used it to refer to almost every picture of confusion with hallucinations. Under the influence of Kraepelin, amentia has almost disappeared from the textbooks of psychiatry. Kraepelin (1908), showed that many of the cases called amentia were acute episodes of schizophrenia. Others turned out to be confused episodes of manic-depressive psychosis. The remaining cases were postinfectious or infectious psychoses.

Hartmann and Schilder (1923) have discussed the problem fully; we have shown that such a clinical picture exists and have defined its characteristics, although to differentiate it from other types of psychoses may be difficult. There is very little reason to include in this group the cases published by Almásy (1936). The basic difficulty in these cases lies in the undifferentiated state of the field of perception and of memory in a definite order. The capacity for perceiving definite configurations in the total field is impaired, and the difficulty extends to hallucinations, imaginations, and memory. As stated above, Freud formulated that one deals here with a conflict between the ego and outer reality. This formulation is, however, unsatisfactory. The outer world comes to us through our senses and the sense apparatus in its widest meaning. To differentiate, therefore, the outer world from the ego is tautological. It says merely that there is a conflict between the ego and the ego. There is no question that the ego function is severely impaired in this type of psychosis and that the individual realizes that such an impairment has taken place. But can one define this impairment in terms of conflict? Such a possibility exists. One might assume that the individual confronted with the tasks of ordinary everyday life will find this too difficult and will therefore regress to more primitive mechanisms of perception, memory, and thinking. This would be considered a regression that lies merely in the field of the perception. We come to the preliminary formulation that regressions may also take place in the ego mechanism as such and, furthermore, that such regression may take place in the field of either judgment, perception, or memory, or in various combinations of all three. The differentiation of ego and id is in no way definite. Any conflict in the ego system will be accompanied with and modified by id attitudes, and, accordingly, regressions in the ego will be almost regularly accompanied by regressions in the id.

One might think it superfluous to discuss these problems of organic psychosis in psychoanalytic terms, since they can be understood from the organic point of view. It is true that there are palpable organic correlates. However, the psychological understanding is something more than showing the possibility of organic defect. In general paresis, for instance, the so-called defect symptoms, the lack of judgment, and the memory disturbances are to be understood as an impairment in the function of the ego. It follows that such an impairment involves a difficulty in the relations to the outer world.

These preliminary remarks show the many complications that may arise in the psychoanalytic understanding of psychosis. We have to reckon with regressions and changes in the libido as an ego function. We have to reckon with regressions and changes in the function of the superego, and we have, in addition, to reckon with disturbances in the function of the ego. The apparatus of the ego, as far as it is concerned with perception and action in the outer world, has different aspects concerning perception in the narrower sense, in the structuralization of the world of perceptions, judgment, and memory.

Moreover, intimate relations exist between the different parts and aspects of the psychic apparatus. Regressions in the libidinal sphere, for instance, will necessarily involve changes in the superego. These changes may be regressive, parallel to the libidinal regression, or the changes may be of a reactive type. There is no question that the total personality, which involves all psychological structures, will have to make a final adaptation to the situation changed by the regressions. The psychoanalytic literature in this respect speaks also of an ego function, and Freud (1923) has introduced the term "unifying function of the ego." This concept has been elaborated by Nunberg (1930), who suggested calling it the "synthetic function," and by Waelder (1930). It is obvious that the ego in this sense is different from the ego functions we have discussed so far. On the other hand, one sees that libido regression takes place very easily in all cases in which the perceptive function of the ego is more or less diffusely disturbed, as, for instance, in organic mental deficiency or general paresis.

DEATH INSTINCT

Fundamental difficulties in understanding psychoanalytic principles were increased by Freud's later concepts concerning life and death instincts. Freud (1920) considered the libido instincts the instincts of life and the ego instincts the instincts of death. All instincts show a tendency to repetition or a repetition compulsion. This repetition compulsion is more obvious, however, in relation to the death instincts. The death instincts are self-destructive and aim at letting the individual live down his vital energies to the point of zero. According to Freud, these death instincts are silent and do not appear either in conscious or unconscious life. They appear merely in combinations with the life instincts, and diffusions may take place under the influence of regression. Others, such as Alexander (1927), believe it possible that death instincts may appear as such. Federn (1926, 1929) is of the opinion that in depressions the death instinct may come into the foreground in a pure form. Freud's concept of an instinct that does not appear as psychic experience obviously has great inherent difficulties. In fact, the whole theory of death instincts, especially in its practical applications, is not clearly defined.

Problems arise when one tries to synthesize the new analytic concept of the ego with the concept of the death instincts. It is hardly permissible to make a close connection between ego instincts (death instincts) and the ego in the psychoanalytic sense. In the previous stages of psychoanalytic theory, the connection between ego instincts serving social functions and the preservation of life and the ego was rather obvious. At any rate, Freud spoke about primary masochism (1920, p. 55), meaning the self-destructive tendencies or the death instinct. The synthesizing tendencies of the life instinct (libido) counteract these primary self-destructive tendencies, and, under their influence, the destructive tendencies are turned outward and become sadistic and destructive impulses which mix with libidinal impulses. The clinical manifestations of this fusion of the death instinct deflected to the outer world and the libido represent the various types of sadistic manifestations. One has the right to believe that these aggressive and sadistic impulses will be the stronger the more primitive the state of libido organization. Some analysts have accepted these statements of Freud's without elaborating and integrating them (Jelliffe, 1933a; K. Menninger, 1933, 1938). Menninger is even inclined to consider everything disagreeable that happens in human life, and every disease, an expression of self-destructive tendencies.

One can summarize the psychoanalytic literature on this subject up to this time (1940) as follows: Primary masochism turned outward becomes primary sadism. In depressions and in suicide, this primary sadism is turned against the self (secondary masochism). In a similar category are self-mutilations and organic diseases that are considered the expression of the drive of the individual against himself. This latter statement appears to be a poorly founded generalization. In obsessional neurosis the aggression is regarded as a confusion between life and death instincts.

I have repeatedly (1925, 1931a, 1942a) stated my opinion that there is no justification for the assumption of a death instinct and have tried to show, partially in connection with Bromberg and Schilder (1933a), that the death wish and even suicide served the purposes of life problems. I consider, therefore, the present psychoanalytic theory less satisfactory than Freud's previous attitude as expressed, for instance, in his study "Thoughts for the Times on War and Death" (1915b).

NARCISSISM

In discussing the psychoanalytic theory of psychosis, it is indispensable to consider some topics that are not important merely for the theory of psychosis, but for the theory of psycho-analysis in general. These topics are concerned with the relation of the person to the world and of the body to the world; they comprise the problems of narcissism, introjection and projection, and identification. Freud himself, and psychoanalytic theory in general, have never been in doubt that the perception of one's own body precedes the perception of the outer world. Rickman (1927), for instance, is of the opinion that the child considers the nipple part of its own body. Similar opinion has been proffered by Stärcke (1921). The most classical expression of this opinion can be found in a paper by Ferenczi (1913) on the development of the sense of ego. According to Ferenczi, the infant comes into the world with the expectation of that unconditional omnipotence promised by the wish-free existence in the mother's uterus, where he was guarded from all discomfort. When the outer world does produce discomfort, the infant wishes to regain his previous blissful situation. The wish is realized by means of hallucination—by imagining the situation. This hallucinatory omnipotence is reinforced by the outer world's response to his signs of discomfort. Gradually, as the limits separating personal wishes from reality are recognized and adaptation to culture demands more and more renunciation of narcissism, reality is recognized. The surrounding world requires from the adult, not only that he become logical, but also that he become attentive, clever, prudent, wise, and at the same time moral and aesthetic.

The underlying concept is of an entity that knows everything about its own body and derives all pleasure from its own body. It gains knowledge of the outer world by lack of satisfaction from its own body. The world is merely a product of its own feelings and experiences projected onto the outer world. This is a very sensualistic theory. It is rarely formulated in this extreme form. I have stated in a series of papers, finally collected in *The Image and Appearance of the Human Body* (1935), that the child has, from the first, a picture of the outer world. Immediately after birth the child has a relation to the outer world. According to Karl E. Pratt (1933), one finds reaction to light stimuli and to auditory stimuli immediately after birth, although some infants do not show reactions to auditory stimuli in the first three days. There is no definite proof of perception of olfactory stimuli. Taste is well developed at birth. There is, furthermore, an outspoken reaction to warm and cold. There cannot be much doubt that even in the first phases of life the child displays reactions to the outer world that far transcend the reactions in the oral zone. We have every reason to believe that the world is present for the neonate at the moment of birth. In its further development, the child shows a very lively interest in the outer world, and the interest concerning its own body is in no way more outspoken than the interest in the world. There is a parallel development concerning perception of the structure of the outer world and the structures of one's own body. It is true that the child has to experiment continually in order to find out what belongs to its own body and what belongs to the outer world. The final boundary between outer world and own body is drawn in a process of continued experimentation.

Very often, an experience ascribed to one's own body is reclassified and considered a part of the outer world, and parts that have been considered a part of the outer world are later on ascribed to one's own body. This is what the processes of so-called projection and introjection are based on. It is customary in psychoanalytic literature to consider introjection and identification chiefly under the aspect of oral incorporation. This point of view, however, is too narrow. Oral incorporation is merely one phase of the relation between the outer world and one's own body. Such statements reflect another aspect of the problem of narcissism. If the child has a very incomplete knowledge of its own body, there is no specific reason why its interest should be merely concentrated in its own body and why it should not also give interest (libido) to the outer world.

However, the problem of narcissism has many more aspects. The term itself was used at first by Näcke (1899) for those who are erotically interested in the mirrored images or pictures of their own bodies. Later on, the term was used by Rank (1927/1928) and finally Freud (1914) gave it its present connotation of love directed toward one's own body. Difficulties arise, however, even for this formulation. Freud considers the newborn child autoerotic. It derives pleasure from its erogenic zones, especially from the mouth, without any closer relation to the object as such. Freud considers these autoeroticisms narcissism only when the diverse experiences from autoerotic sources are united and form a unit. Tausk (1919) views such autoeroticisms as primary narcissism, and the narcissism in the Freudian sense as secondary narcissism. Freud never formally accepted Tausk's terminology, nor does the psychoanalytic literature contain many explicit statements regarding this point.

One has the impression that, especially in the literature on schizophrenia, the term narcissism is continually used in the sense of primary narcissism or autoeroticism. When the term narcissism is used in the Freudian sense, the opinion that schizophrenia is based upon regression to narcissism would mean that the regression goes only to a rather late stage and to an inadequately defined stage of development, for Freud has never given any specific opinion about the approximate age at which narcissism occurs. In *Beyond the Pleasure Principle* (1920), he contrasted narcissism to object libido, and not autoeroticism to alloeroticism. Generally, in psychoanalytic literature, narcissistic libido is considered all the libido directed to one's own body. Freud had said that we should not forget that there was no object in the intrauterine life and that objects could not be expected to exist in that time. E. P. Hoffman (1935) continues in the sense of Freud by saying that in the beginning of the development "there exists only narcissistic libido; by and by a maximum of object libido is reached. Ego development takes place in relation to the object insofar as the ego becomes more resistant the more narcissistic libido is turned into object libido and the more this object libido can resist being changed back into narcissistic libido" (p. 342).

The term narcissism comprises, therefore, autoeroticism as well, and it would be clearer if we followed Tausk's terminology. We formulate, therefore, that narcissistic libido is the libido directed toward one's own body. In the light of our discussions, however, this formulation leads to another difficulty, insofar as we have to distinguish between the so-called narcissistic level of development and narcissistic libido. Psychoanalytic literature generally considers a narcissistic level of development the early stage of sexual development and implies that at such earlier stages nothing exists except the experience of one's own body. I have already remarked that the earlier stages of development are not characterized by the absence of object perception, but merely by incomplete differentiation of the outer world and one's own body. On the most primitive levels, we find not only narcissistic libido, but also object libido. The situation has become the more complicated because Freud believed all tendencies to self-preservations belong to libidinal structures (1920).

To construct the psychology of the intrauterine life is of course more or less a matter of individual whim. However, we know that many motor reactions are present in intrauterine life, and we have every reason to believe that they take place in relation to changes in the surroundings—for instance, to contractions of the uterus. The fetus has, in addition, an enormous energy of growth. It is arbitrary to believe the fetus has no needs. Rank's statement (1924) that every pleasure has the tendency to reinstate the intrauterine primal pleasure is at best arbitrary and does not seem even probable in the light of the facts mentioned. We have every reason to believe that the external world exists for the fetus as well as for the newborn, although the greed of the newborn for this external world is naturally greater.

The tendency of psychoanalysts to neglect the human being's interest in the world and to overrate his interest in his own body also makes its appearance in Freud's concept of primary identification (1921). S. H. Fuchs (1937) discusses this too.[2] The whole world is taken as a part of the ego. This, according to Freud, is the earliest object relationship. It is at the basis of primary projection and introjection, forerunner of symbol formation, all of which are at the root of ego and superego formation. It is not always kept clearly apart from (secondary) identification, which can only take place if the ego already exists. Fuchs adds (pp. 286-287): "I think that we are more true to the facts and in agreement with most authors and modern views if we take the earliest stages as chaotic in the sense of a complete indistinctness of what becomes later on world and body, ego and non-ego, inside and outside, psychic and 'objective' reality. We should therefore be more correct in speaking in terms of *differentiation*. There is no need at this stage to speak of identification as a special act, because things are not yet separated and therefore need not be identified. We could thus drop the term 'primary identification'."

Hoffman (1935) says: "The primary identification takes place before the object cathexis, on the level when there is only narcissistic libido. This, however, reacts only as a whole. The stage of being satisfied is a total one as the state of the tension provoked by needs." According to Hoffman, who follows Federn (1927) in this respect, cathexis of objects can occur even with narcissistic libido. Only when the object denies the satisfaction of the narcissistic libido does it become a true object. One then not only knows that

---

[2] His paper "On Introjection" is a very complete and thorough discussion, to which this text often refers.

the object is in the outer world, but also feels it as being there. When, for instance, the infant cries when the mother leaves, it does so because of anxiety. The mother serves to maintain the economy of narcissistic libido. The removal of the mother would mean a disturbance of this economy, and therefore a threat to the whole early ego. It is therefore not object libido that is disturbed. We may speak of object libido only when the mother's leaving can take place without disturbance of the narcissistic libido economy, or without danger for the anxiety-free infantile ego.

Federn has interpreted the psychological state of depersonalization from a similar point of view. The outer world, the object, appears dreamlike and dead. The patients complain but behave as if the object appeared alive to them. Inasmuch as they take the object seriously, object libido is obviously present. The cathexis of the part of the ego that is turned toward the object with narcissistic libido is missing. Before the object is discharged from the early ego, the object has belonged to the early ego. It was endowed only with narcissistic libido. The adaptation to reality forced the ego to free the object and to differentiate ego and object. If a psychic act is to be experienced fully without ego estrangement, ego libido and object libido have to be satisfied. The ego, cathected with narcissistic libido, and the object have to meet each other. Whenever the ego is without narcissistic cathexis, estrangement (derealization) occurs. Unestranged processes lead to the normal development of the ego. Depersonalization and estrangement occur if the part of the ego that should reach the object is insufficiently endowed with narcissistic libido. Ecstasy occurs if the cathexis is too strong. Ferenczi (1913) considered every object love an enlargement of the ego.

It is in very close relation to ideas of this type that Jekels and Bergler (1934) consider the experience of love as reintrojection of the object into the ego. They find behind the loved object only the own ego. It seems that this later formulation has moved pretty far from Freud's (1914) rather clear-cut distinction between object libido and narcissistic libido. However, one must acknowledge that the nucleus of the idea of this later development is to be found in the general tendency of psychoanalysis to focus on the body rather than the world, and to underrate the value of experience in relation to the external world. The relation between the external world and one's own body is extremely complicated. One is easily inclined to consider this relation static, and fail to emphasize the continuous give and take between world and personality.

PROJECTION

It is our task now to study the processes of give and take. This is also called projection and introjection. Fuchs (1937) describes projection in the following terms: "Own unconscious tendencies are ascribed to other persons often after transformation especially into the opposite." He adds: "Again the great variety of forms of projection must be considered. The early attribution of inside experiences to outside objects is also termed 'projection'. Perhaps the term 'exteriorization' would better be applied here. If the fundamental conception of original unity of ego and world would be accepted, this would become unnecessary" (p. 293). Fuchs discusses introjection in terms of an instinctive incorporation into the mind. The term is still often used vaguely for any inclusion into the mind according to the original conception. More and more, however, it is used to designate the instinctive nature of such an intake, which was, phylogenetically speaking at any rate, a real eating-up. He recommends restricting the term definitely to the latter meaning, and, in particular, to the act of inclusion into a mature ego system, resulting in identification.

Before we enter into the discussion of these concepts it is important to keep in mind that Freud (1915c) has characterized unconscious thinking (system ucs.) by condensation, displacement, timelessness, and substitution of the outward reality by the inner reality. This latter process has also often been characterized as projection. Nunberg (1932) in his text—which is approved by Freud—characterizes projection by saying, "We are constantly transposing inner processes into the outer world, for the psychic apparatus refers every perception, whatever its source, to the outside world" (p. 41). Children and tribes of primitive development have, according to him, particularly strong mechanisms of projections since they endow the inanimate world with human qualities. In discussing the substitution of outer reality by inner reality, Nunberg mentions that, early in development, there is no sharp borderline between the outer world and the inner world. He states that to some degree they are identical in the suckling and in the primitive. Only later on does man learn something about the outer world and become capable of differentiating inner experiences from it.

These preliminary remarks show that there are obviously many different things that can be projected: (1) A part of one's own body is projected onto the outer world. For instance, a crippled patient of mine sees all other persons as crippled. (2) A sensation like pain is projected onto another person. Freud reported about a dreamer with toothache who in the dream experienced freeness from symptoms and saw somebody else afflicted with the pain instead. (3) A whole series of events might be projected onto some other person. For instance, an old lady who has urinated into her bed asserts that a man had come during the night and urinated into her bed. In such an illusion she projects not only her urination but also her wish that a man should visit her in the outer world of reality. (4) One's own inner experiences might be projected onto other persons. For instance, when one falls in love and thinks the love object has fallen in love with oneself.

We may therefore summarize that the experience of one's own body, sensations, images, memories, feelings, wishes, and emotions of all kinds might be projected onto the outer world. They may be projected without changing the quality of experience. However, an inner experience may be projected onto the outer world as a perception. A perception may be projected onto the outer world as a sensation or as an image. The projection can take place onto the inanimate world or onto persons. We have furthermore to consider that, during the projection, the content may undergo transformation, condensation, or symbolization. If one keeps these few principles in mind one will be aware of the enormous variety of phenomena. And even these remarks do not cover the multitude of the possible phenomena. When the obsessive-neurotic patient asserts that his thoughts are not his thoughts, this is obviously the first step toward a projection. In more extreme cases the patient may feel that his thoughts are put into him by an evil spirit, and, finally, in schizophrenia the patient may say that somebody else has put these thoughts and emotions into him. To the hypochondriac, his own psychological problems appear as sensations in his body. We may speak here, too, of a projection. Hypochondriacal sensations may also be experienced as influences coming from others. The complications can be very far-reaching, as in the case of the schizophrenic who thought that visual images and memories remaining after a visual impression were transmitted to an unknown person who later on sent them back to her.

It is impossible to come to a deeper understanding of the whole problem of projection if we do not make some preliminary remarks about the way an individual experiences himself in relation to the external world. The individual experiences his psychic experiences as his true self. The body is not the central self, but is experienced as peripheral in relation to the inner experiences. We experience the external world as independent from us. There is a world in close contact with ourselves and one with little contact. Sensations are closer to our central self than the body, and there are differences in the various sensations with respect to their nearness to ourselves. Pain and sexual sensations are, for instance, nearer to ourselves than a mere touch or a sound. Imagination and memories can be nearer or further in relation to the central self according to their emotional values. One might be entitled to call projection every psychic tendency that removes something from inward to more outward layers of experience. Special attention should be given to the projection of psychological complexes that relate to one's personality as a whole. One may project experiences based on identifications with other persons whom one has incorporated into oneself, such as the "voice of conscience," which is the introjected father-mother.

One may, furthermore, project one's previous stages of development onto another person. This occurs in homosexuality when a love object is chosen who is identical with the picture one has of one's earlier stages of development. One may, furthermore, project one's superego in a more diffuse way, as happens in patients suffering from alcohol hallucinosis. We may speak, therefore, about personality projection, in general, and superego and developmental projection, in particular.

One should not stretch the term of projection too far. The external world is not a projection of our own experiences. However, projections continually modify our experiences and impressions of the outer world. One should keep in mind that in early stages of development the individual does not perceive the world according to the reality of his own body or his own sensations and images. Individuals are always conscious that they are in the outer world, but they might be very unsure which parts belong to their own body or inner experience and which belong to the outer world. It is easy to point to experiences accessible to all of us in which such an uncertainty is present. After turning on a rotating chair or after any other vestibular irritation, one is not sure whether one is turning oneself or the outside world is turning around one. The zone of indeterminacy, as we may call it, plays a much greater part than we usually think. The problems of activity, passivity, aggression, submission, sadism, and masochism can be understood only on the basis of orientation. The turning of destructive impulses from oneself to the outside world, and vice versa, belong in a similar category. When there is a drive, it does not matter so much whether it is directed primarily toward one's own person or toward the other person. There are therefore continuous fluctuations between the realm of the person (body and inner experience) and the realm of the outside world. Projection and introjection are in continuous interplay.

To the concept of projection of one's own body and one's own feelings and sensations belongs, as counterpart, appersonization. To the personality projection and superego projection belong, as counterpart, the various types of identifications. The various attempts to compare projection with discharging and ejecting secretions and excretions from one's own body is, however, no more than an analogy, for there are decided differences in the psychological structure of the image of defecation. For instance, in the cases of Stärke (1921), Van Ophuijsen (1920), and Bender (1934a), the feces are identified with the persecutors; in Bibring's case (1929), however, the persecutors are the buttocks of the patient. I would explain this by the fact that the excretions, feces, urine, semen, saliva, milk, still retain some relation to one's body and the process of defecation may therefore blend with the process of projection, which is based on the principle of indeterminancy of the relation of body and world.

INTROJECTION

The individual is aware from the earliest stages of development that there is an outside world and that there is a body with sensations, representations, and feelings. However, there exist also masses of experiences that are neutral in relation to both. It depends on the total situation whether an experience is to be attributed to the body or to the outer world. With these remarks we have already approached the problem of introjection. According to the definition of S. Kovacs (1912) "introject means associate with one's own ego complex" (p. 317). Fuchs (1937) calls introjection an instinctive incorporation into the mind. When we compare this with the remarks on projection, however, it will immediately be seen that Kovacs' broader formulation covers the ground in a much better way. We may merely specify that whatever he calls "ego complex" comprises the body, sensations, body function, representations, emotions, and strivings. The term appersonization means the adoption of a part of other people's emotions, experiences, actions, and body parts into one's own personality. We should speak of identification only if there exists a tendency to take over the role of another personality as a whole. It is often true that identification expresses itself on the surface by taking over only one part of the experiences of another person, as, for instance, in Freud's example (1921, p. 134) of the sergeant in Wallenstein's camp who had learned to clear his throat in the manner of the general in order to express his wish to be like the general and to enjoy the same esteem the general received.

When small children see other children play with toys, they often go to the toy and repeat the action they have seen the other child perform. They do not intend to be like the other child, but merely to enjoy the same activity. This would be an instance of appersonization. An individual who considers an inanimate part of the outer world a part of his own body or personality introjects these objects. Clothes very often are felt as part of one's own body. A movement that is perceived in the outer world and felt as directed against one's own body should also be called introjection. One of my patients complained that she felt the sweeping in the street as performed on her genitals. When patients have the feeling that dirt on the street is brought to their mouth, one deals again with introjection. One of my patients felt his penis was lying on the street and crushed by cars or taken away by dogs. The dogs and the cars are in this case brought nearer to the body. Of course, one could just as well say that these body parts are projected into the outer world.

Clearly, it may be difficult in an individual case to discriminate between projection and introjection (cf. Ferenczi, 1912; Fuchs, 1937). This difficulty is of an intrinsic kind and is due to the fact that projection and introjection are phenomena belonging to the zone of indeterminacy between subject and object. The pathological state brings back the primary indeterminacy that is preserved in such borderline phenomena.

One can also understand all the phenomena described so far in terms of space. It is questionable whether one should consider a widening and an extension of the body image as projection of the body into space or as introjection of space into the body. One might, for instance, very well say that the patient who feels a part of her body lying around has merely lost the cohesion of her body image in space. Furthermore, many phenomena can be understood as a contraction of outer space; as, for example, when one of my schizophrenic patients complained that he felt the sex parts of people in the street near his mouth. Body space and outer space contract and expand according to libidinal problems. One cannot think of projection and introjection simply as opposites, for this neglects the complications of the real psychological facts.

Projection and introjection serve adaptation. One can call them defense mechanisms, or one can also call them attempts at new adaptations. Whenever processes of this kind go on, they are connected with other forms of unconscious mechanisms, such as condensation and transposition. One can call anxiety the motor of every development (M. Klein, 1932), but this is a very arbitrary enlargement of the concept of anxiety. One can also say that any present difficulty, such as anxiety, leads to defense mechanisms. Defense mechanisms include forgetting, condensation, symbolization, projection, introjection. These mechanisms, however, often do not pertain to the present; the present difficulties provoke regressions which Freud (1900) has described as three-fold: namely (1) to other parts of the psychic apparatus in general, (2) to previous experiences, and (3) to previous modes of thinking. During regression, introjection and projection and other unconscious mechanisms take place.

IDENTIFICATION

The term identification needs further discussion. Introjection may merely mean the centripetal movement from outer to inner circles of experience. It is obviously one-sided to think that introjection is merely patterned after oral introjection, which is the prevalent analytic opinion. Psychoanalytic literature has been giving increasing emphasis to the importance of respiratory introjection. One might also keep in mind that taking an object into one's hand, or embracing, might be another pattern of introjection. It should be remembered that it is a general function of the organism to bring something near to it and to incorporate it in various ways. The oral function is obviously one part of this general tendency. It is probably much more correct to speak of the general function of taking in (introjection) and of giving out (projection). The general muscle function of the body serves the same principle, approaching an object and retreating from an object, pulling to the body and pushing away from the body. One sees again the enormous general importance of the problem of introjection and projection. It is rather interesting to observe that introjection is to a great extent taking something from others into oneself (appersonization and identification), whereas projection of one's own experience onto the inanimate world is not uncommon.

Identification is, of course, a form of introjection of particular importance. Identification means to take over the role of another person by unconscious mechanisms, the other person thus becoming incorporated into one's personality. Such identification may take place in all psychic spheres. One may identify oneself with a person who enjoys sex more freely (identification in the id). Of particular importance are the identifications that take place in the ego. Such identifications take place in both parts of the ego. We build up our superego (ego ideal) by identifications with beloved persons. In depressions, we may identify ourselves with love objects of whom our moral personality does not approve. We might speak in an analytic sense about identification in the ego.

It is further customary to differentiate so-called hysterical identification from narcissistic identification. It is difficult to justify the term narcissistic identification. It was originally used by Freud (1917) in relation to the depressive who has chosen his object according to his own image. Later on he identifies himself with this object, which he has chosen because of the similarity to himself. Although Freud states that this takes place in depressions, none of the case reports in the literature shows these features in a clear way. We would, furthermore, have to ask whether one is really entitled to speak of narcissistic identification even if the person with whom one identifies has some similarities with one's own personality. Narcissism in such case would mean love for one's own person. The term narcissism would obviously be more appropriate for identifications on the primitive level in which other persons are not recognized in their full individuality.

For instance, a patient I described in *Seele und Leben* (1923d) claimed that a child of her sister's was her own because she had her sister's nature. She also claimed that every sexual intercourse was her own and, furthermore, if somebody sang, "I have to sing too." It is characteristic of such identifications that the person with whom one identifies oneself is not fully appreciated. Accordingly, identification of this type may sometimes be difficult to differentiate from mere appersonization. Nunberg (1930) and Fenichel (1926) regard narcissistic identification as complete and identification in neurosis as incomplete. They have hardly made the correct approach to the problem.

According to my formulation (1935), identification is only possible when preceded by an object relation. The identifications will therefore be different according to the object relation. We should, accordingly, distinguish between a pregenital and a genital identification. Full identifications occur on the genital level. The genital level corresponds, according to Abraham's formulation (1924), to a fuller appreciation of the love object. We may suspect that such an object relation precedes even the identification in the ego in depressions, which, according to my opinion, is not always present. The classical instance for identification takes place with the parent of the other sex in homosexuality. It is known that this form of identification ends the relation to the love object. Similar identifications take place in the boy's relation to his father or to his male teachers. In all these instances, some relation to the object with whom one has identified oneself still remains. In homosexual identification, however, the erotic part of the relation has been finished. In the other identification mentioned, taking the place of the father or teacher in one's unconscious mind divests the object relation of some part of its power. It is good to keep in mind that complete identification is an ideal, which in reality is never reached. Freud himself has stated repeatedly that there is in every object relation a tendency to identification. Especially at the height of any heterosexual relation, the individual has the tendency to identify himself with the love object. We may assume that such a tendency to identification is indeed universal. Whomever we see, whomever we meet, we take into our own personality by identification. This process, however, is merely a partial and tentative one. We immediately afterward restore the object to its full existence as an independent entity. The supplementary process of projecting ourselves into others is going on at the same time. This is a definite dynamic interplay which is basically dependent on the level of object relations reached. In the identification of the homosexual, the depressive, and the son, this dynamic process has been terminated, or has been fixated, instead of retaining its flexibility. It is, furthermore, probable that this identification takes place in relation to all psychological systems, although in various degrees. In this sense we may talk about a static identification when the dynamic process has come to an end. We also have to consider that a tendency to identification may be of great dynamic value and determine important behavior, or may remain dynamically unimportant. I would come, therefore, to the following classification of identifications:

1. Identification with objects incompletely appreciated
2. Identification with objects more or less fully appreciated
   a. with a love object similar to oneself (depression)
   b. with a love object of different sex (homosexuality)
   c. with an important person in one's own development
3. Developmental identification (parents of the same sex, teacher, leader)

Identifications of any type should be further differentiated in terms of their degree of reversibility, which may be static or dynamic. We may make the preliminary assumption that identifications in neuroses and psychoses will be more static than identifications that take place in the so-called normal, where, with the exception of developmental identification, a high degree of flexibility will be preserved.

As mentioned above, identifications can also be differentiated according to their relation to the part of the personality predominantly involved: ego, superego, and id.

Furthermore, we have to consider which of the reverberations of the identification process are in the body and which are the somatic and libidinal correlates. At the present time the opinion prevails that identification has its fundamental basis in the process of oral incorporation. Fenichel, however, (1931b) is of the opinion that there is an anal, epidermal, respiratory, and ocular intro-jection in addition to the oral one. Simmel (1930) speaks of an oral incorporation as earliest object relation before a difference be-tween inside and outside experience exists. Weiss (1926, 1932) adds an important point to the discussion when he stresses that the identification does not mean merely a destruction of the object, but also a resurrection of the object within ourselves. I do not think it justified to stress oral incorporation as the only physical correlate. Hárnik (1931, 1933) has especially emphasized the importance of the intake of air. The mechanism of identification is one in which the total body participates.

We will hardly understand these processes unless we are aware that, even when one introjects, appersonizes, or identifies with another person, there is still a genuine interest in the persis-tence of a world outside of oneself. However, this is not the point of view of Freud and the majority of analysts.

SUPEREGO

Freud (1923) has stated that the ego ideal, which he also calls the superego, is built up by identifications. The concept of the superego is a great advance beyond the formulation of Alfred Adler (1907, 1917) who spoke about the "directives," the guiding-plan in the life of human beings. The connotation of the superego stresses the relation to the persons who bring us up, and it is invaluable. Some analysts at the present time are questioning the value of this concept, although they have never made clear what the real objections are (compare, for instance, Horney, 1937). In Freud's first studies, no definite attempt was made to study the finer structure of the superego and its development. In my *Intro-duction to a Psychoanalytic Psychiatry* (1925) I have formulated the idea that the ego ideal has a very complicated structure. This is not only in connection with identifications with various persons, but also because of the relation of the ego ideal to libido development. Identifications on the lower levels will obviously provoke an ego ideal different from that formed at the higher levels. There is therefore not only a horizontal organization of the ego ideal, but also a vertical one.

> New characteristics come to light constantly in the beings who surround us. A given person's characteristics are apperceived differently by the newborn and by the one year old and three year old, than they are by the five and ten year old, and by the adult. "The ego ideal" which develops out of the identifications with a given person continually reconstructs itself anew in various ways, although of course all the "ego-ideal" constructions, for instance, which spring from the mother-identification are held together by a common bond. But one must at the same time maintain that the identifications of a given age-period should in some way show common features and accordingly we would defend the general point of view that the "ego-ideal" constructions show a vertical stratification in accordance with the stage of developmental organization attained. . . . [The different persons with whom the child identifies itself possess common characteristics.] Thus, for instance, both the father and mother identifications will contribute to the idea in the child's ego-ideal construction that one must not soil himself with feces, must not play with feces, and the like. In other words, every identification will possess certain features in common with others. It is especially the more general requirements of society that become in this manner deeply engraved in the individual [Schilder, 1925, pp. 15-17].

Melanie Klein (1932) is of the opinion that the superego is already introjected in the oral-sadistic phase. The child wants to expel and eject it. Because the introjected object belongs to such an early level, it is considered particularly dangerous, and the individual tries to get rid of it by projection. Organs, objects, feces, and the object that has been introjected are put at the same level as external objects, and this anxiety spreads to a multiplicity of objects. Klein stresses the sadistic character of the early superego and also sees the continuous dynamic process from introjection to superego and from superego to projection (ego projection).

Conflict

The discussion of the structure of the superego was necessary in order to have a basis for the discussion of the general theory of psychosis. The question immediately arises what all the processes we have so far merely described actually mean. The answer is that they serve the aims and needs of the individual. The individual deviates from the simple approach to reality when reality becomes too difficult or complicated. In other words, in the beginning there is this difficulty or a conflict, making impossible any satisfaction from the situation. If the individual does not want to stand the discomfort of a given situation and does not want to try to change the situation by action, he will revert to previous ways of adaptation. In analytical terms, we speak of regression, characterized by Freud (1900)[3] in a three-fold way: "(a) *topographical* regression, in the sense of the schematic picture of the ψ systems which we have explained above; (b) *temporal* regression, in so far as what is in question is a harking back to older psychical structures; and (c) *formal* regression, where primitive methods of expression and representation take the place of the usual ones. All these three kinds of regression are, however, one at bottom and occur together as a rule; for what is older in time is more primitive in form and in psychical topography lies nearer to the perceptual end" (p. 548).

It should be remembered that according to Freud the psychic process in general runs from the perceptive end to the motor end. It is constructed like a reflex apparatus. The perceptive system is entirely lacking in memory. The memory system is the basis for associations. In the hallucinatory dream, the excitation does not communicate itself to the motor end of the apparatus, but to the sensory end. The dream has thus a regressive character. If retrogression takes place in the psychic apparatus, the complex act of ideation has to return to the raw material of the memory traces. In regression, therefore, the thought is broken up into its raw

[3][In a passage added in 1914—Ed.]

material. The hallucinations of hysteria and paranoia, as well as the wishes of normal persons, correspond to regressions, i.e., to thoughts transformed into images. Freud also indicates that this regression makes it possible for the raw material of memory to be rearranged, or, in other words, all kinds of transformations, symbolizations, and condensations take place.

Accordingly, one has to expect that, in the majority of cases, projection and introjection will also change the material in the sense characterized above. I may mention an old observation of mine, that an individual with a crippled arm who projected his deformity onto other persons saw not only the arm but also the legs crippled in other persons. This gave him the consolation that he was not as severely affected as they were. One sees the multiplicity of motives that go into every projection. The case just mentioned has another significance: the patient did not, during the projection, lose the knowledge that he was crippled himself. It is quite common for an individual to retain some knowledge that what is projected is also a part of himself. One may raise the question, for which reason does regression and its consequences—introjection and projection, condensation and symbolization—take place. Following Melanie Klein, English psychoanalysts have somewhat oversimplified the problem. For them, anxiety is the sole cause for the repression that leads to retrogression. This concept is in one point in accordance with the statements of Freud, who considers the ego the source of repression. He furthermore considers anxiety a danger signal of the ego (1926, 1932). Alexander (1927) has taken a similar point of view. However, there is no question that these processes are continually modified by the superego and its demands.

The ego that, according to Freud, Alexander, and others undertakes reality testing and repression, is not merely the perceptive apparatus but a complicated organization, which Freud has described in *The Ego and the Id* (1923). In order to come to a theory of psychoses, it is necessary to go further into the description of the ego in the analytic sense. The nucleus of the ego system is the perceptive apparatus, including motility. There is, furthermore, the function of the ego as the final organizer of the diverse tendencies of the ego and the id, in which feelings of guilt play a very great part.[4] In addition, the ego has complied with the necessary demands of the reality. I have mentioned before that there is a part of the superego that is reinforced by a great number of identifications and is in very close relation to the function of the ego. There is no denial that anxiety and guilt play a very important part in its organization and its function. The objective situation may present difficulties. These difficulties may lie in the outside world or in the body with its incomplete physical endowment. In the subjective sphere, helplessness and perplexity correspond to the objective difficulty. Anxiety and guilt are not the only reactions to a difficult situation.

I come, therefore, to the formulation that defense mechanisms in general and regression in particular take place when the situation is too difficult. The difficulty in the situation may not only promote anxiety and guilt, but also helplessness and perplexity.

---

[4] Glover (1932b), who separates various ego nuclei of oral and anal character, offers a concept at variance with Freud's.

CHAPTER TWO

Organic Psychoses

DEMENTIA AND AGNOSIA

We are now prepared to turn to the more specific problems of psychosis. We start with that of organic psychoses, which one might call diseases of the ego in the proper sense. One such organic psychosis is general paresis, which has been explained by Hollós and Ferenczi (1925) as a loss of libido with reference to the brain. They speak about the cerebral pathoneurosis and neurotic reactions following injury of the brain. However, they exclude from their consideration the so-called defect symptoms. Here, we are primarily occupied with the so-called defect symptoms in judgment and memory. In my studies on the symtomatology of general paresis (1922a),[1] I have shown that the judgment and the memory function of general paresis cases is impaired in a specific way: Patients see details instead of the whole. Total perception is not differentiated and articulated into its parts. The single parts are condensed with each other and transformed. Images and connotations are substituted by related ones, which are either subordi-

[1] [Parts of this chapter were translated by David Rapaport and appear in his *Organization and Pathology of Thought* (1951)—Ed.]

32

nated, coordinated, or superordinated. Thinking that occurs without any specific preparation does not lead to a deeper satisfaction, but remains flat. Whereas the results in normal thinking are continually compared with reality (trial and error method), the tendency to corrective process is not present in dementia. Primitive tendencies come into the foreground; almost every assertion of other persons is believed (heightened suggestibility). The individual gives credence to every one of his associations (confabulation). Preconscious wishes come into the foreground. The individual wants to play the leading part. Wish and reality are insufficiently differentiated, and there are tendencies to take every story literally, as if it were a real event of historical character, and to give everything a happy ending. There is not much doubt that this basic experience of so-called dementia is closely correlated to organic disturbances in the brain function, especially in the cortical function. It can be characterized as regression to a more primitive function of the apparatus of thinking, judgment, and memory. Although it is difficult to assume that this deterioration could be connected with an actual psychological trauma, there are nevertheless some cases of general paresis where minor actual difficulties might be a signal for regression in the ego. That such an actual minor difficulty can have such an effect is, however, not explicable by psychological methods, and further psychological assumptions would be purely speculative. Moreover, in many cases of general paresis, no actual difficulty precedes the regression in the ego. It is characteristic for the uncomplicated pictures of dementia and confabulation that the material used in the productions is not of a deep unconscious character, but can be characterized as preconscious, evidencing some similarities to puberty fantasies.

I may immediately add that in specific incidents of perceptive experience, organic lesion provokes very similar disturbances. In my *Introduction to a Psychoanalytic Psychiatry* (1925), I have characterized, following Pötzl (1917), optic agnosia in the following way: "(1) Comprehension is delayed. (2) In connection with this delay the general outline is perceived first, the general category, the 'sphere.' (3) Within this general category reverberate associated concepts or impressions; at times also the thing wanted, which does not break through, but is even thrust aside. (4) The delayed product becomes blended with factually unrelated impressions. (5) The spatial arrangement is also open to criticism. (6) Training causes a diminution of the disorder. The patients fail more readily in the face of a propounded problem than when they are left to their spontaneity" (p. 99).

These remarks make it clear that even the single agnostic reaction is dependent upon the difficulty of the present situation. Actual psychological causes, however, cannot explain regression in the perceptive sphere.

Although it may be difficult to establish this in detail, one can safely say that the performance of judgment and memory found in general paresis cases and the disturbance in perception found in agnosias and of speech in aphasias are regressions to a more primitive type of functioning. This regression takes place merely in the realm of what I have broadly called the perceptive ego. One can characterize psychosis of this type psychologically as follows: (1) The actual cause, if present, is insignificant in itself and does not give any direct understanding concerning the regression. (2) All the characteristics given for the so-called primary process of experience (Freud) are also present in regressions in the perceptive ego. (3) The primary process is applied to conscious and preconscious material; no deeper personal material is involved. (4) Changes can be understood as regressions in the perceptive ego. (5) The processes of projection and introjection and identification take place on conscious and preconscious material in the realm of perception, memory, and judgment. All these processes give a greater security and importance of the ego, which, at the same time, gives up some of its adaptive function.

This description is valid for all types of mental deficiency and organic deterioration, but it is also true of organic memory disturbances of the Korsakoff type of disorientation in space and time, confabulation, and difficulties in retention.

This description, however, is incomplete. Patients who experience a regression in the perceptive ego experience their loss as
Hollós and Ferenczi and myself have emphasized. They are still
capable of comparing their present functioning with the functioning of the past, and experience this as a terrible impairment,
comparable to castration. General paresis, with the castration
anxieties related to luetic infection and all the consequences of
such an anxiety, leads to deep-going regressions in the libidinal
sphere as well. The puberty wish-fulfillments inherent in dementia
facilitate access to deeper lying material to which the libidinal
regression tends. Libidinal regression is, as mentioned, activated
by the severe impairment in connection with the manifold castration anxieties in the widest sense, which combine with the
anxieties connected with the threat to the body in general. Hollós
and Ferenczi speak about the pathoneurosis of the brain; however, it seems more appropriate to talk about fears in connection
with the loss of one's mental capacity. Libidinal regressions are
further facilitated by the fact that the perceptive ego control is
diminished. For this reason, far-going regressions also easily take
place in cases of mental deficiency. On the basis of libidinal
regression, projection and introjections of all types can take place
very easily.

These few remarks do not exhaust the whole field of psychosis with organic determinants. Kardiner (1932) has written a
study on the epileptic reaction and has shown that the epileptic
attack involves a severe threat to the ego. This ego, however, is no
longer purely the perception ego we have been discussing. Other
parts of the ego organization are involved in the severe threat. The
psychology of sleep phenomena can be understood as well from
the point of view of libido theory as from the point of view of
cerebral pathophysiology. Lesions of the cortex promote changes
in the ego. In lesions of the subcortical region, especially the
periventricular gray, psychological changes occur that have relations to libido and libidinal regression. Falling asleep and
dreaming are, after all, in connection with the sleep center of the

periventricular gray. When one falls asleep, previous ego attitudes emerge. The different parts of the ego separate, and the ego loses its differentiation. Isakower (1938) and Grotjahn and French (1938) have studied catalepsy after air injection into the brain from a similar point of view. We may again stress the concept that deep-lying personal material comes more strongly into the foreground the less the organic disturbance affects the perception ego and the more it affects the sleep and vegetative functions of the individual. Further discussion of these problems can be found in the studies of Goldstein (1939).

CHAPTER THREE

Schizophrenia

CHILD PSYCHOLOGY

The interest of psychoanalysis has rightly been devoted chiefly to the psychoses of the so-called functional type, schizophrenia and manic-depressive psychoses. We start with a discussion of schizophrenia. I have said that organic psychoses are characterized by regression to more primitive states of the perceptive ego, accompanied by a different distribution of libido. In schizophrenia,[1] we deal with regression in the libidinal sphere, and we have to expect that changes will also take place in the ego. If we consider schizophrenia regression in the libidinal sphere, we assume a pathophysiological structure akin to the one we find in neuroses: There is an actual cause, a difficulty in the present situation; the libido

[1] *Definition of Schizophrenia.* Schizophrenia is a complex of empirically determined mental symptoms, the presence of which indicates that deterioration in the sense of emotional dissociation will be the final outcome. Acoustic hallucinations and primitive sexual contents play the outstanding part. The inability to cope with simple life situations follows and expresses itself partially in a distorted motility. The final deterioration contains the same elements. There are indications of an organic process in the sphere of perception and motility and in the vasovegetative system. Hereditary factors are involved. Clinical pictures of this type occasionally end in recovery. Psychotherapy has a limited influence on this organic process. [Found in Schilder's unpublished and undated notes—*Ed.*]

37

fails to find any outlet; and regression to prior stages of libido development takes place. To which stages the libido regresses depends on the points of fixation.

The extent of the regression determines the clinical picture. It is therefore essential to appreciate the stages of early libido development. Rather sharp differences exist in the psychoanalytic literature regarding the early stages of libido development. Riviere (1936) and Waelder (1936) have formulated the different viewpoints. Riviere's approach is based on the work of Melanie Klein (1932) and reflects the general attitude of the English psychoanalysts, who believe that projection and introjection play a very important part from the earliest stages of development. These are in close relation to defense mechanisms and anxiety. The child's anxiety is, according to Riviere, due chiefly to the helplessness concerning its inner powers, namely, its destructive impulses. The child needs the object in order to project onto it the bad ego filled with displeasure. The object seems to be less dangerous than the destructive powers within. The individual wants to take the good objects into himself by introjection. The nuclei of the early ego consists, according to Glover (1932b) and Riviere, of oral and anal impulses of particular cruelty.

According to Melanie Klein, the child wants to attack, not only with its muscles, but also with its excreta—urine and feces. It not only attempts to devour, to bite, and to eat the other person, but also to scoop them out, to take away the inside of their bodies, or to destroy them by poisonous feces and urine. In return, the child feels attacked in a very similar way by outside objects. These dangerous objects are introjected and continue their destructive activities inside. Melanie Klein acknowledged, however, that the child also wants to appreciate good objects and that it tries to restitute good objects outside and inside. (Compare the previous remarks of Weiss, 1932.) The child wants to bring the object into existence again in a magical way.

Waelder points out that the methods by which Melanie Klein and her followers reach their conclusions are less reliable than the usual psychoanalytic technique. He furthermore doubts whether the aggressive tendencies of a child are present to the degree that

Melanie Klein asserts. He also insists, rightly, that individual life experiences, especially the Oedipus complex, are of greater importance than appears in the studies of Melanie Klein.

One will indeed have many doubts concerning the formulations of Melanie Klein and Riviere, especially when one is of the opinion that it is not justified to assume that the child has no access to the outward reality. One may, however, take the following for granted: (1) The zone of indetermination between the body and the world is more extensive in early childhood. (2) Mechanisms of projection and introjection combined with mechanisms of appersonization and identification are of particular importance. (3) The child has a very lively relation to the outer world in a positive sense. It wants objects in the outer world and appreciates them. This reaction is present from the very beginning. (4) The child is very much dependent on help. It may often feel deserted, and experiences deprivations with violent counter-reactions. (5) The positive and negative reactions of the child will be of more or less outspoken and primitive motor character. (6) There are strong aggressive tendencies in the child. (7) Although the oral zone is of particular importance, other zones of the body like the anal, respiratory, and skin cannot be neglected. (8) The child experiences the inside of its body as merely containing the food and the objects taken into its body.

Melanie Klein and Glover have talked about the psychoses of children and have spoken similarly to Abraham (1911) about mania and depressions. (In contrast to Abraham, Melanie Klein refers to the earliest stages of development.) They talk, furthermore, about megalomania and paranoid positions. It is obviously necessary to be careful in one's approach to the comparison between childhood attitudes and the psychoses.

Omnipotence

It is the current psychoanalytic opinion that the neonate feels omnipotent. Omnipotence would therefore be a correlate to the earliest stages of libido development. I have shown previously that the infant in the earliest stages of development is in no way devoid of interest in the outer world. The newborn does not know more about its body than about the outer world and does not love its body more than it does the world. It is true that in these early stages of development the child may have the impression that the outer world can be changed very easily. At other times the obstacles must appear insurmountable. The child may therefore have at times the feeling of omnipotence; at other times it will feel completely helpless and threatened with annihilation. This period will therefore be characterized by swings between feelings of omnipotence and feelings of complete helplessness.

Since human beings generally have the tendency to assert themselves in the world, the feeling of omnipotence may prevail and may be heightened by the child's having just been threatened by annihilation. Good and bad concerning the outer world, as well as concerning its own person, will be exaggerated. Later on, the child will be more clearly aware that its powers are negligible compared with the powers of the parents, and the feeling of omnipotence will be either transferred to the parents or retained as magic property. The omnipotence will finally be transferred to visible and invisible gods. The child's own omnipotence as well as the omnipotence he attributes to others, is always in contrast to his real feelings of helplessness in the face of danger. It is interesting that the most outspoken ideas of grandeur are to be found in puberty fantasies and the corresponding megalomanias of general paresis. In both cases one can easily prove that there are compensations and overcompensations of anxieties, insecurities, and shortcomings. They have a rather complicated structure, insofar as a comparatively good perception of the world blends with more primitive tendencies. In contrast, the megalomanias of the schizophrenic are of a more magical and symbolic type and resemble in this respect the world of the child. At a special phase of development, the child tries to overcome its helplessness by the assumption that it is invested with magical powers. This stage is not by any means the most primitive stage of development. It is based upon the child's acute awareness that it is not capable of mastering the situations with which it is faced. One understands that all the neurotic and libidinal conflicts inherent in the parent-child relation find their expression and preliminary solution in ideas of grandeur.

Very similar considerations are valid for depressive ideas of self-depreciation and smallness (micromania). Psychoanalysis, it is true, generally does not assume that the young child feels particularly small and helpless, although it emphasizes the helplessness of the ego. One has the right to assume that in early childhood the child vacillates between a feeling of utter helplessness and abandonment and power and well-being. Instead of assuming that the child in the first few months of its life is megalomanic, it seems much more plausible to assume that there is a greater lability in the appreciation of one's power and security than in the adult. Melanie Klein assumed, indeed, that children of very early age show not only manic but depressive pictures. As long as such statements are not taken in the sense that one deals with a complete analogue of the psychotic picture, they are at least more justifiable than the assumption of bliss and omnipotence in early childhood. One should also not forget that in depressive states there is not only self-accusation but also generally a feeling of satisfaction that one is capable of such a self-depreciation. At the same time, the individual increases his self-esteem by accusing himself of such far-going crimes. In every micromania there is a megalomania, and in every megalomania there is a micromania.

Since, as I have stated, the idea of grandeur is an over-compensation for defeat and dismembering, one might as well ask what the difference is in ideas of grandeur and self-depreciation in the various types of psychoses. In schizophrenics we deal with a general primitive stage of subject-object relations out of which the magic parent emerges. The ideas will therefore be in close relation to such primitive differentiations. In depressive psychosis the fear of being cut to pieces will be outstanding. At the same time, the individual will accuse himself of enormous aggressiveness, especially in the oral sphere, culminating in ideas such as uttered by one of my patients that she had taken in and devoured the whole world and then excreted it through her anus. Her vagina was also an instrument of destruction, in which penises and children were crushed to pieces. The depressive-psychotic patient, however, will differentiate objects better than schizophrenic psychotics do. In general-paretic cases, the general structure of these ideas will correspond more to the ideas of manic-depressive patients. Two factors will modify them: (1) The consciousness of infection with lues and the impairment of intelligence will provoke a particularly strong castration complex, a particularly strong dismembering motive, and a particularly strong consciousness of the impairment of the body. (2) These ideas will find an easier access to consciousness and will be further exaggerated by the impairment of judgment, i.e., an impairment of the reality function.

HYPOCHONDRIASIS AND WORLD DESTRUCTION

Hypochondriacal ideas are often to be found in the beginning of schizophrenia. They correspond to a greater insecurity in the differentiation of body and world. It seems that the subject is no longer so sure whether every part of the body really belongs where it is. One could, in a way, say that the hypochondriac organ is already partially projected into the outer world, and it is only one step from there to the feeling that enemies have stuck something into the body. The Freudian interpretation generally insists that this hypochondriasis is due to an overloading of the organ with narcissistic libido. Such an organ overloaded with libido will be given attention, which may express itself even in a somatic way in swelling and edemas (see Nunberg, 1932) which is almost a preliminary to the expulsion of the organ. There is no question, however, that the situation is much more complicated. One often sees that the hypochondriac's symptoms start in the part of the body that was given particular attention by love objects. It may also happen that such symptoms occurred because they have been seen in a love object. Contrary to the opinions of Freud, we might therefore say that the hypochondriac organ is an organ that has been and still is in particularly lively contact with the surroundings. This is therefore one of the instances where one can also speak about projection and introjection.

Melanie Klein (1932) and Susan Isaacs (1935) consider the organ that is the seat of hypochondriac sensations an introjected wild animal or persecutor, which now attacks the individual from the inside. The idea seems plausible; but only Isaacs gives evidence that seems to be convincing. It is true, however, that, in hypochondriac symptoms in schizophrenia, the thought is easily added that these phenomena are provoked by hostile influences from the outside. A patient described by Schilder and Sugar (1926) complained that the persecutors not only stuck knives and hammers into him, but that these were made either from half-digested food or from feces. The patient complained that the feces of others, which he called "gripps" (neologism for grip), were smeared into his anus. He furthermore complained that not only the food but also the inner organs were taken away from him. This is almost a complete circle of introjection and projection. It was not possible to find out the infantile determinants of these delusional and persecutory experiences in the patient, since he was dissociated.

Depersonalization can also be one of the early symptoms of schizophrenia. Patients experience the outer world as unreal, and themselves and their thinking as automatic and mechanical. One may venture the opinion that the individual has psychic conflicts that prevent him from accepting a fully differentiated world, and libido interest is taken away from the world as well as from the ego (in the common sense). Although Federn (1927) has explained this in terms of narcissistic libido's being taken away from the ego boundaries, one can probably arrive at a much simpler formula by saying that the individual no longer dares to fully experience his own body and the world. He gives up both of them and retains his full interest merely in observing his incapacity. This is therefore an incipient tendency to destroy the world and oneself, the destroyer remaining as the supreme observer. One understands that similar pictures may also occur in depressions. There is some relation between the depersonalization pictures and the nihilistic delusions of depressive states.

Depersonalization pictures have no relation to the fantasies and delusions of the destruction of the world to which Freud

(1911) has drawn attention in the analysis of Schreber's case. Schreber did not acknowledge human beings as real human beings, but considered them carelessly made. Freud explains this as a withdrawing of libido from the world to one's own self. However, many schizophrenics experience not only a destruction of the world but also a destruction of their own body. The libido explanation is therefore too simple. It is much more probable that the individual is aware that he has lost the power of distinguishing between the world and his own body and is therefore watching himself with his previous personality, sinking back to a state of incomplete perception of the world.

REGRESSION IN THOUGHT AND LANGUAGE

The phenomenon of depersonalization suggests that, while one part of the world and the ego sink down to a primitive level, there is another part of the personality watching this sinking down, or, in other words, the previous personality retains a part of its cathexis. This seems to be a formulation of great importance, and one to which we shall return. There is a varying of the type of relation between the parts of the personality that have regressed and those that have not regressed. We may speak of a regressive index which increases with the amount of regressed tendencies. We have also to take into consideration the depth of the regression. When a regression has taken place, it may or may not be reversible, so we may speak about the reversibility of the regression. Without these additions, the term regression may lead us astray. In normal thinking, regressions are of fundamental importance for every type of creative thinking. These regressions are easily reversible. Moreover, these regressions go back to a point of fixation, but the point of fixation does not retain libido. We may speak in this respect of the avidity of points of fixation. I have advanced the theory that every thought starts in a primitive way in the "sphere"—in undifferentiated, unconscious thinking. From there, a developmental process takes place, progressing from the lowest to the higher stages of development until the clear-cut thought is reached. The development of thought makes use of the characteristics of the primary psychic processes as characterized by Freud (1923). Regressive thinking is characterized by the fact that the individual is not capable of leaving the sphere of regressive thinking. Fenichel (1931b) offers a similar formulation.

I would refer the reader to some formulations I have given at other occasions concerning the language and thought of schizophrenia [see Chapter 20]. Freud has suggested that the difference between the conscious and unconscious idea is not that they are different records of the same content situated in different parts of the mind, but that the conscious idea comprises the concrete idea plus the verbal ideas corresponding to it, whereas the unconscious idea stands for the thing alone. A patient mentioned by Freud complained that her lover was pretending something (*verstellt sich*) because he stood in church at first in the one and then in the other place (*stellt sich um*). Freud explains this by saying that, in schizophrenia, primary process (condensation, symbolization, etc.) takes place merely in words.

It seems to me, however, that the formulation I have given above conveys the situation better and avoids the awkward assumption that the fundamental sign function should be absent in the unconscious.

STUPOR AND NEGATIVISM

Catatonic stupor has been repeatedly explained as a simple regression to the narcissistic level where the individual is merely interested in his own body and not in the world. Such an interpretation can hardly be maintained if one believes that the primitive stages are not without objects, but are characterized by a primitive attitude toward the world. Indeed, the catatonic stupor reveals merely an attitude of indifference concerning the world, of giving up. Very probably, this indifference is closely related to a feeling of self-sufficiency, which basically is the feeling that somebody will take care of one's needs. Such an attitude may culminate in a stupor, which may be connected with catalepsy. Catalepsy, however, also expresses confidence in others whom one lets do with one's own body whatever they want to do with it. Very closely related to catalepsy is so-called automatic obedience, indifference to pain, and, finally, the tendency of the schizophrenic to give in completely to postural tendencies. Here belong two symptoms I have observed together with Hoff (1927): The schizophrenic gives in to his postural tendencies of divergence—the outstretched arms and the posture that occurs after turning the head. One can easily turn the schizophrenic around his longitudinal axis by putting a hand on top of his head and twisting it slightly but persistently to one side.

A further type of schizophrenic reaction is a leveled and diffuse defense against everything that is done to him. This defense may be purely muscular (negativistic tension), but also may be connected with an extreme degree of fear and anxiety. Characteristic of such a reaction is that the patient reacts in the same way to everybody who approaches him.

I may mention here that although many of these symptoms can be explained on an organic basis, this in no way devaluates the psychological influences. Even a lesion of an organic structure must express itself in attitudes that can be understood in a psychoanalytic way. The same can be said about the many perceptive disturbances in schizophrenia, especially the distorted vision and the many distorted experiences relating to the body, its form, consistency, and heaviness.

PSYCHODYNAMICS

I have approached the symptoms of schizophrenia as if they were isolated. They can be understood, however, only if one takes into consideration the total configuration and the psychogenetic development. For this reason, delusion has not been discussed as an isolated symptom. It might also be mentioned that all the symptoms that have been mentioned are not merely in the sensory, motor, and intellectual spheres, but are also accompanied by more or less outspoken vasovegetative phenomena, which have been particularly emphasized by Nunberg (1921). One is perfectly justified in assuming that schizophrenic regression is connected with an insurmountable difficulty in the present situation. In all carefully analyzed cases of schizophrenia, especially in the Schreber case, such is obvious. I furthermore point to the cases of Kubie (1937) and Zilboorg (1930). The actual conflict usually corresponds to the total situation in which the attitude of the individual is of very great importance. We may generally say that the actual conflict will have to fit the point of fixation. One could perhaps also humanize the term "point of fixation" by saying that it is a past situation of great importance. From this formulation it is immediately obvious that there can never be merely one point of fixation; there will always be a multiplicity of fixation points. Of greatest importance is the point of fixation that corresponds to the deepest regression, if it has at the same time a great avidity. The deeper we come in this series of regressions, the more difficult it is to understand the total situation. Furthermore, we may assume that the organic factors will become more important the nearer we come to the deeper level of regression. We may generally say that the deepest point of regression determines the type of neurotic or mental disturbance, whereas the secondary points of fixation are of fundamental importance for the variations of symptomatology.

The actual difficulty in the schizophrenic case is often in connection with the turning points of life. The individual has the task of progressing from childhood to puberty and beyond. His failures in these tasks are connected with very specific problems. These specific problems are not exhausted by the problems of the reorganization of the primitive forms of sexuality into postoedipal sexuality. There are, in addition, the many problems with which the ego is confronted at this time. As Anna Freud (1936) has pointed out, a part of the symptomatology of puberty in general can be understood from the point of view that the individual, frightened by the enormous increase in sexual tendencies, withdraws. At the same time, the individual also has to reorganize and test his superego positions. In the narrower sphere of the ego he has to test his motility and to reorganize motor impulses. All the problems of aggression may come into the foreground, as a consequence. Other important general tasks occur in connection with childbirth and with involution. These general physiological turning points express themselves in psychological problems, which are of course only understandable in connection with the actual situations of the individual's life. We find, therefore, that the manifest causes of the outbreak of schizophrenic symptoms are the first love relation, a difficult love relation in general, the attempt to come to some heterosexual adaptation, or problems connected with the first failure in school—which are experienced as hostility of the teacher—or a conflict with a union or an employer. In most cases one might say that the actual cause is either frankly sexual or has pretty obvious heterosexual or homosexual latent meaning. In contrast to depressive and manic pictures, conflicts in connection with money or with career are met comparatively rarely.

The difficulty of the present situation forces the individual to regress to the point determined by the fixation. It is almost impossible to determine the processes leading to fixation in cases of schizophrenia. One may suspect, especially when one studies schizophrenia in childhood, that the child may feel at the mercy of extremely strong aggression. Some of this aggression is of the type described by Melanie Klein. The individual fears dismemberment or a complete dissolution either by dangerous food, dangerous secretions and excretions, or dangerous attacks in which oral tendencies may be of particular importance. The child tries to defend itself by similar methods. Since this is a very primitive level, the borderline between the individual and the world appears to be very indefinite. There will be a constant interplay between projections and introjections. Because childhood schizophrenia starts at the age between three and a half and four, we have the right to assume that the point of fixation is to be found at an earlier level of development. It is arbitrary whether one wants to find this point at the age of one month or of two years. At this early stage, to which the regression leads back, the superego is necessarily of great primitivity. Many analysts would not even speak about the superego at such early ages. It is obvious that the very early libido situation will also be very primitive. The catatonic pictures that occur correspond to a complete giving in to outer forces or to an undifferentiated refusal of all approaches from the outside world in the form of negativism. There will also be primitiveness in hyperkinetic counteraggressions, leading to pictures that are even choreiform, or automatic rhythmic without a deeper relation to the object (hyperkinetic catatonic pictures). In the perceptive world there will be not only hallucinations and experiences of being influenced, but also distortions in the form of the objects and in their consistency. These points will have to be discussed in more detail in connection with special symptomatology.

It has to be kept in mind that an individual who regresses to this deep level still retains the pattern of his higher development, and, furthermore, the higher stages of development always retain some amount of cathexis. The individual, even in his deepest regressions, does not have the same psychoanalytic organization as the individual who has never reached the higher levels of development.

This regression may occur rather suddenly in acute schizophrenic pictures, when an individual may remain overwhelmed by the breaking through of the primitive attitudes we have described. In other cases the regression may be acute but partial. Then we may find, for example, severe hypochondriac symptoms in a person who has otherwise retained many adaptations. In the majority of cases we may expect that the symptomatology is the result not merely of regression but also of the counterreaction against regression.

One might say that the regression leads to the appearance of primitive anxieties and fears of destruction, which the English authors call infantile feelings of guilt. One would then be inclined to consider a primitive anxiety and guilt feelings as the real primary symptom. However, when these anxieties and guilt feelings occur at an early stage they already find some tendency to be defended against, and, here, introjection and projection are of paramount importance. One might even call the motor signs described primitive defense mechanisms. I am at any rate inclined to believe that the formulation of anxiety and guilt as the only primary symptoms is too narrow. There are feelings of bewilderment and insufficiency that must have an enormous importance. It is arbitrary to call all these experiences anxieties. Furthermore, anxiety and guilt cannot be merely experiences of feeling. The individual takes an attitude in a specific situation. This attitude is a motor attitude. One should keep in mind that the early situation to which the individual regresses is a situation in the full sense of the word, in which a specific reality is met with a specific behavior. One may call this specific behavior a defense reaction of a primitive type, but the situation and the defense are doubtless a unit. We have to differentiate from this the defense reactions the individual takes because there is always a part of him that has not regressed at all or not regressed so deeply as to reach the primary fixation point. It is this part of the personality that starts a defense against deep regression. Defenses of this type will be more outspoken when regression is less acute or when the acute regression has subsided. Freud (1896) has shown that the greater part of schizophrenic symptomatology can be understood from the point of view of restitution mechanisms.

In many cases, regression does not take place at once, but is gradual. The individual has to resign his heterosexuality and take up homosexuality and go from there to levels of undifferentiated object relations, which makes necessary a reorganization concerning his whole attitude toward the world. Although we may talk about a gradual regression, it is characteristic for the schizophrenic and for the paranoiac group that from the beginning this regression has a direction toward the most primitive level of development. Rickman is generally correct when, in his excellent survey of the psychoanalytic theory of psychosis, he characterizes the mechanisms of paranoia in the following way: "repression of homosexual impulses; return of the repressed dealt with by projection; regression from sublimated homosexuality to narcissism; decomposition assisting repression" (1927, p. 352).

I would stress that the paranoiac has the tendency to regress to the narcissistic level of fixation whenever he encounters any libidinal difficulty in the actual situation. This difficulty may arise from the demand of the heterosexual attachment. One of my patients overcompensated immediately on this level by running around during the night seeking a bride. Voices followed him, calling him a homosexual. Others feel at this stage of development that all women are attracted to them. We have every reason to believe that even when regression is to the homosexual level the individual tries to defend himself, using secondary points of fixation as grips to adhere to when threatened by gliding into the abyss of "narcissistic" regression. The overemphasis on primitive stages of development is present before the first defense mechanisms start. In the closest study of single cases, one sees that regression takes place to secondary points of fixation or, in other words, to situations of emotional importance that have taken place during libido development. In every such situation the battle is renewed, in which the superegos and the egos of the different developmental phases try to restore an adaptation comfortable for the individual.

Freud (1911) has described how Schreber defended himself against his increasing homosexuality. Projection takes place, the beloved person becomes a persecutor who hates, and the individual feels assured that he himself does not love the persecutor. It is a complicated interplay between projection and introjection. In other cases, the paranoiac may be a homosexual from the beginning. However, due to regression to the narcissistic stage and the breaking through of primitive impulses, the object relation has the tendency to regress to a deeper level and has to be restored by complicated projection mechanisms to a level compatible with the less regressed parts of the personality. We may summarize by saying that in schizophrenia and in paranoia the individual has from the beginning a tendency to regress to the narcissistic libidinal level. The regression, however, halts at secondary points of fixation. The individual tries to remain on a higher level and at every stage of regression uses the mechanisms of projection and introjection in order to come to a better adaptation. To understand these processes completely, one has to keep in mind that every regression in the sphere of libido is paralleled by a regression in the structure of the superego. Libido and superego are not isolated, and one has to keep in mind that the final arbiter for regression and reorganization is the total personality.

We may speak analytically about the ego function in these psychoses. This ego, however, is not the perception ego, but the ego with the synthetic function of mediating between reality (perception ego), the superego, and the id. Nunberg (1930) has justly emphasized that in paranoiac cases this synthetic function of the ego is even increased and that the individual uses a particularly large amount of reasoning in order to maintain his equilibrium and his paranoid system. It is good to keep in mind that every libidinal change will necessarily have repercussions in the ego. We do not have reason to believe that we deal with independent changes in the ego organization in the psychoanalytic sense in cases of schizophrenia. If, therefore, Zilboorg (1930) and Alexander (1931) try to find the basis of schizophrenia in difficulties in the ego organization, their statement has to be qualified. One should say merely that every change in the libidinal situation means the necessity of a reorganization by the synthetic function and this reorganization will be the more difficult the deeper the regression has been. One should, at any rate, contrast the changes in ego function, especially the changes in the perception ego in organic brain diseases to the qualitatively different ego reactions in schizophrenia.

The previous experiences and the fixations of the higher levels determine not only the type of regression, but recovery as well. When the deepest level of regression has been reached, the individual will still feel the urge to return to more advanced levels of libido development. When the individual has had anal fixations in early childhood, these will be reached first during recovery. The next step may be in relation to homosexuality. Also, during the process of restitution, projection and identification will go on continually. If the individual is not capable of reaching the objects themselves, he might try to establish a relation to the words that represent the objects. This process will be facilitated by the fact that the differentiation of sign and object is incomplete at the lower stages of development. If the patient is not capable of maintaining his superiority in handling objects, he may show his mastery of words by creating neologisms or by using a manneristic speech (cf. Nunberg, 1930).

It is the general psychoanalytic understanding that the individual intends primarily to regress and is merely forced by reality to maintain higher object relations (Freud, 1922). However, in my opinion, individuals have a real urge, not only to regress, but also to progress, or they have a thirst not only for enjoyment but also for reality. Whatever the final theoretical implication may be, the fact remains that the symptomatology of schizophrenia and paranoia can only be understood as a continuous interaction between regressions and restitutions to higher levels of development. In paranoiacs we find the tendency to regorganization particularly strong. We might therefore characterize the different pictures according to the degree of reorganization. This will be partially in connection with the regressive quotient. When the regressive quotient is low and the higher forms of libido development retain a sufficient amount of cathexis, we may expect paranoiac pictures. The final picture will also depend upon the activity of defense mechanisms against the experiences of the lower levels. We therefore explain the variability of schizophrenic symptomatology in the following way: In addition to the deepest point of fixation in the narcissistic level, which is present in all forms of schizoprenia, there are secondary points of fixation at the various levels of libido development. In every case of schizophrenia and paranoia, the primitive narcissistic level is reached. However, when the quantity of libido reaches the narcissistic level on its way to regression, we speak about a low narcissistic regressive quotient. Furthermore, we suppose that in schizophrenia and paranoia the narcissistic fixation is based upon a rather great avidity or low reversibility. The regression can be acute or chronic. However, from the beginning of the chronic regression the process is characterized by the tendency to regression to the narcissistic level. Defense mechanisms take place against the breaking through of libido of the various regressive levels. The activity of this defense is probably dependent on a low regressive quotient. There may be, however, another factor of activity of defense which is incompletely known.

It is understood that the defense mechanisms are dependent upon the level of development, and when a regression to the deepest level of development has taken place in which it is possible to deal arbitrarily with the world of reality, we have the right to speak, with Laforgue (1926), of "scotomization." Laforgue has justly pointed out that at this stage anal and sadistic impulses will participate very strongly in the denial of reality.

This brings us to a final theoretical problem. In my discussion, I have not tried to distinguish between death instincts and libido. There is no question that different types of aggressiveness belong to different levels of development. One will therefore say, in the sense of Freud, that at the lowest stages of development a diffusion of instincts will play a greater part. I am speaking chiefly about aggression, and leave it to the reader who believes in death instincts to change the terminology. If one accepts Freud's theory, it will be necessary to keep in mind that the narcissistic level in which we are chiefly interested is a state in which death instincts are of enormous importance. This contradicts the customary formulations.

One more addition is perhaps advisable. According to my view, schizophrenia is what one would usually call an organic disease, and many of its perception difficulties and motor disturbances can even today be characterized from an organic point of view (cf. Vowinckel, 1930). This organic process not only can be understood from a psychoanalytic point of view, it can also be influenced in some degree by psychoanalytic therapy. This influence may merely change the secondary points of fixation and may not extend to the deepest roots. However, we have reason to believe that under certain—as yet only vaguely defined—circumstances an influence on the primary points of fixations (the organic process) may be possible.

I have not made a detailed distinction in these discussions between the different forms of schizophrenia and have spoken of paranoias in a sense similar to Kraepelin's when he speaks about paraphrenias. These cases and the Kraepelinian paranoia in the narrower sense are very closely related to schizophrenia and share their common clinical significance.

One often hears about schizoid psychopaths and schizoid reactions. I do not regard these cases as belonging in the group of schizophrenia. They may have a secondary point of fixation in the narcissistic sphere; however, this will be a point of little avidity. In addition, the regressive quotient regarding the narcissistic level will always be lower than even the mildest form of schizophrenia and paranoia. Generally speaking, psychotic reactions in psychopathic individuals and hysterias will always be characterized by much higher regard for fully developed reality than the psychosis in the narrower sense. When a person has a hysterical amnesia, his relation to the world will basically be of a high psychosexual level.

Shock Treatment

A few words are necessary about the newer treatments of schizophrenia with insulin and metrazol, the so-called shock therapy. Bychowski (1937) and Glueck (1936) have tried to come to an understanding of this therapy from a psychoanalytic point of view and, especially Bychowski (1937) and Schatner and O'Neill (1938), point to the greater amount of transference these cases develop by the treatment. More analytic material may be gained in this way. They seem to think that one deals chiefly with a release of unconscious material with the help of transference, thus explaining the cure. Jelliffe (1937) has stressed the death threat to which these individuals are exposed. Orenstein and I (1938) [see Chapter 26] have shown that the treatment as such increases the transference, but does not release material from the lower levels. The confusion that follows the convulsions and is prevalent during and after the insulin shock is of an organic type. If one tries any psychological interpretation one would have to stress that the individual has gained the impression that he has been so fundamentally threatened that he is grateful to those around him for having survived and gains a great amount of interest in the fully integrated world. At the same time, the primitive world and primitive fears lose their importance. It is almost as if the schizophrenia and its psychological contents were superseded by the organic disease and the recovery from it. This might be a reflection of the organic processes that occur during the treatment. We deal with a severe organic impairment of the brain (probably chiefly anoxemia). This impairment is followed by an organic reorganization that may blot out the aberrations due to the schizophrenic process. At any rate, it is remarkable that the psychological material that comes to the foreground during insulin and metrazol treatment is basically of the same impersonal type as the material appearing in organic diseases of the brain.

CHAPTER FOUR

Manic-Depressive Psychoses

We turn now to the general theory of manic-depressive psychosis. The psychoanalytic interest in manic-depressive psychosis started with the work of Freud (1917), who stated in his paper on "Mourning and Melancholia" that the self-reproaches of the depressive patient are directed primarily against the love object which has been chosen according to the similarity to oneself (narcissistic object choice). This object is introjected, forms a part of the ego, and is now exposed to the onslaught of the superego. In many depressive cases great hostility against the love object still remains, and very often the self-reproaches are reproaches directed against oneself because of one's own hostility. In both cases, one may speak about the turning of aggression toward oneself. However, the superego that directs hostility against the ego and the object introjected into it is itself built up by identification with aggressive objects. It can be seen that one deals with a rather complicated situation.

My own experiences make me rather doubt whether an introjection of the love object into the ego takes place in every case of

57

depression. The majority of depressive cases live in constant fear of the aggression of persons around them. I am inclined to believe that the most important point in depressions lies in the fact that the aggressive tendencies and the subject's fear of aggression by others is increased. It is true that this is very closely related to oral aggression, but it is obviously not justifiable to put so much stress on oral aggression as to neglect the other components of aggressiveness. It is interesting that, after Freud's preliminary remarks that the choice of the love object in depression is a narcissistic one, further emphasis has been put upon this point. My own experiences do not show that the depressive case chooses his love object according to his own image.

Rado (1928b) has introduced a valuable idea by stressing the fact that the depressive case wants to regain the love object by confessing his guilt. One indeed very often has the impression that the depressive case wants to be released from punishment by others, since he punishes himself severely anyhow. In their dreams, depressive patients very often re-experience scenes of bliss and contentment. Rado sees the prototype of the depressive situation in the withdrawal of food and the breast from the suckling.

Whatever part oral components may play, Gero (1936) emphasizes justly that the oral relation of the suckling means much more than merely oral satisfaction. It reflects the closeness of the body, of the mother, and a particular protection in addition. To be fed, to be at the bosom of the mother, means to be at peace with the world and to be loved by the world. It also means that one can freely love the world. My own observations have shown me that the interest of children in sucking periods in the nipple and the breast is small compared to the interest they have in the mother's face. It is almost, as Lauretta Bender and I have paradoxically formulated, that it is not the breast that gives the food but the face. At any rate, even if one stresses the importance of oral libido, one should not view it too much in isolation. Even the depressive case recognizes that a well-organized object might be cut to pieces. For the paranoiac, the dismembered object is basically another multiplicity of persecutors, since every piece turns into a persecutor. The object is reduced to many dangerous pieces, which are only partially appreciated as belonging to the inside of the body, like feces. The persecutors are due to the introjection of partial objects. We might say that the depressive patient in spite of his cruel and destructive impulses still has a closer relation to the object than the paranoiac and the schizophrenic. One may bring this in connection with the fact that the depressive case does not regress to the same primitive level as does the schizophrenic.

The projection and introjection mechanisms are indeed more restricted to relations to specific persons than to human beings as such, although the reactions against these specific and well-characterized persons are deeply destructive. Some appreciation for the person as a person still remains. One may say that the indeterminate zone in the depressive case concerns well-characterized love objects and the self (and their bodies), whereas in the schizophrenic case the indeterminate zone is between one's self, one's own body, and human beings in the world in general. It is true, however, that the relation to the other person is a deeply destructive one and repeats the relation between the superego and the ego. In addition to oral regression, anal regression is also present in the depressive case. One of my patients felt particularly clearly that she had devoured the whole world and what existed in the outer world was merely the product of her digestion. The object is expelled into the world and kept there as a hostile influence. This is, according to Abraham (1911), the first ambivalent stage of anal development.

I have mentioned before that the self-depreciation of the depressive case contains the claim to particular grandeur. He merely claims destruction and hate instead of love for himself and others. The inhibition of the depressive case is the denial of his aggressive impulses and also of his lively interest in the world, and of his wish to participate in everything. The self-denial of eating, extending into the organic sphere (lack of salivation and gastric secretion), is the denial of a strong oral wish, which is not merely the wish to devour, but also the wish to participate in the world. The anxiety of the depressive case is not only the fear of being dismembered or having the love object dismembered, it is also the fear of losing the love object. The depressive, in spite of his regressions, shows in every stage of the psychosis a fundamental, deep appreciation of the love object that expresses itself in the high organization of the severe superego.

Zilboorg (1930) and others have talked about the particular strength of the superego in schizophrenics. Such a formulation, however, is misleading. The superego of the schizophrenic is on a primitive level and shows a lack of organization. The superego of the depressive case is highly organized. The theory that in suicide one kills the introjected love object, i.e., one's own ego, comes from Freud and is built up in a fashion similar to the theory that the self-reproaches of the depressive are primarily directed against another person. The difficulty in this theory, which has many obviously true elements, lies in the fact that it does not explain the energy of action. It has to be supplemented by the idea that there is a good deal of energy in the ego and a rather strong organization of the ego to make such action possible. Although suicide is not rare in schizophrenics, it has by no means the same significance as in depressives. Karl Menninger (1933, 1938) has varied Freud's formula of the interchangeability between subject and object in suicide, but adheres to Freud's basic conception. If one speaks about diffusion of destructive impulses in depressions, one should keep in mind that the destructive impulse is then later on brought into close relation to a highly organized ego and superego system. The depressive patient has developed a strong Oedipus complex and has organized accordingly a strong superego. I think the fixation in the oral and anal spheres and the fixation concerning aggressions toward persons with the ideas of dismembering are in no way more important than the strong development of the Oedipus complex and the superego. We deal, therefore, with the two primary points of fixation to which other secondary points may be added.

Some further remarks may be added. Depressive cases experience time as standing still because they deny themselves activity. Many of them complain that the tortures to which they are exposed will last until eternity. This means, of course, that basically they want their activity and destruction to go on forever. One might justly say that behind every depressive psychosis lies much of the expansive psychology of the manic patient.

MANIC STATES

Behind every manic phase there is a depression (cf. Blalock, 1936). This is a formulation often found in psychoanalytic literature. Manic patients complain continually about the injustices done to them. At the same time, they profess to be very happy. One can almost see that the more they complain about their painful experiences the happier they become. Both factors explain two variations in the symptomatology frequently observed. There is the paranoid picture, which Helene Deutsch (1933) has explained by saying that they continually neglect the disagreeable and humiliating aspects of their lives (cf. Lewin, 1937). The manic patient does not want to acknowledge that deep down he is afraid that he is hated and wants to answer this hate with hate. At the same time, quite in the same way as the depressive case, he has before his eyes the possibility of a deep human relation. In reality he continually gropes for the objects on a genital level. However, because of the hate wish he has experienced, he is not capable of giving continued interest to his love object, and his experiences fizzle out. He would like to be capable of changing the world, but the world overwhelms him and his reaction remains disorganized. He seems to allow himself everything and seems to be free of scruples. The tension between the ego and the superego seems to have disappeared. He starts to love his body, his eating, and his defecating. He feels strongly, however, the doubt remains that he might not be fully appreciated. He does not expect full appreciation from others and is not ready to give it. There is no question that there are manic-depressive pictures in which clinically the manic and depressive phases are absent. Basically, however, manic features are present in every depression and every manic picture involves a depression. It is true that manic-depressive patients sometimes show neurotic trends, especially of obsessional character, at intervals, although it does not seem to me that this is as frequent and regular as the psychoanalytic literature, following the lead of Abraham (1911), generally assumes. A strong development of the superego nevertheless does lead to a rigidity that often resembles the character trends of the obsessional neurotic patient.

The clinical question whether the depressions of the involutional period belong in the same category as the depressions of the manic-depressive group is not our concern. Involution as such increases the fear of destruction of the body. Accordingly, the aggressive, destructive, and paranoid trends are more outspoken in involutional depressions. In my opinion, these are manic-depressive patients who merely experience their involution very strongly and bring it in connection with the depressive tendencies characterized above.

Generally speaking one should stress the fundamental difference between the structure of schizophrenia, which is to be understood as a regression to one primitive level, and manic-depressive psychosis wherein we have to reckon with two fundamental points of fixation of equal value.

Abraham (1911) has tried to formulate the conditions under which the psychogenetic sequence leads to a manic-depressive psychosis: (1) Constitutional increase of oral eroticism; (2) special fixation of libido at the oral stage of libido organization; (3) severe injury to the childhood narcissism—weaning is often psychically traumatic in these cases, so that they suffer from a sense of desertion; (4) imperfect attainment of the phallic stage of libido organization, with distortion of the Oedipus situation; disappointment at this stage causes a regression to the oral-sadistic stage, hence a permanent association of love relationships and destructive oral impulses. These factors lie dormant until, in later life, there comes (5) a frustration in object relationship or anything which, by weakening the ego, incapacitates it in its permanent task of repression. Between attacks, melancholics do not attain full object love; though the tendency to incorporate the object and to destroy it is in abeyance, ambivalence and a measure of hostility remain. This is Rickman's (1927) review of Abraham's survey. I have offered a more flexible formulation.

CHAPTER FIVE

Toxic Psychoses

I have already mentioned mental confusion in the introduction. It is well to keep in mind that mental confusion is an organic type of reaction (from the point of view of not only the psychiatrist, but also of the psychoanalyst) which shares with the organic type of mental disturbance the fact that its actual causes are insufficient to explain the regression that takes place merely in a sphere having to do with the utilization of perception into *gestalten* used for action. One finds in this perceptive sphere the same condensation and transformation we have seen in organic cases—mechanisms characterized by primary process. However, the parts of the personality affected in mental confusion are not as far away from the nucleus of the personality as the processes in general paresis and agnosia. More personal elements concerning perception, memory, and thoughts undergo changes in the picture, and even emotional processes are disturbed. Still, the deep emotional problems of individuals are only touched by implication, and, accordingly, the resulting pictures are not as indicative of libidinal development as the pictures observed in neurosis, in schizophrenia, or in manic-depressive psychosis. There is very little analytic material available on this topic aside from the paper by Hartmann and Schilder (1923). It is analytically of great importance that the individual is aware of these difficulties, compares them with his previous functioning, and feels very deeply hurt by his insufficiency. Perplexity results. The individual feels helpless and deeply impaired, and this often provokes infantile feelings concerning the castration complex in its widest meaning. It might be better to say that the individual experiences a fundamental impairment of his whole body, of which the mental functioning is an integral part. It has been mentioned that Almásy's (1936) cases are not cases of amentia.

Delirious pictures that have many things in common in mental confusion have been discussed more often from an analytic point of view. Kielholz (1926) and Tausk (1915) discuss alcoholic delirium. Obviously projections take place also in the part of the ego concerned with the elaboration of perceptions. The hallucinations may even have phallic and anal significance (the rats and mice and snakes in delirium). Although, delirium tremens is less a personal affair than is neurosis, Kielholz could show that the associations of a patient with alcoholic delirium point to an increase of homosexual components, of narcissism, and of voyeurism. The persons nearest to the alcoholic are changed into animals. They very often appear in multiplicity, since the drunkard is closely connected with the group in which he lives. Some of the toxic psychoses contain more and more personal elements and reveal more and more personality problems. Some of them can almost be read like a dream. We might generally characterize toxic psychosis as having two components: (1) Regression in the sphere of higher perception and the dependent functions of representations and memory, and (2) a dreamlike quality of experience in which the personality problems may find their expression as in a dream or fantasy. These components may appear in different mixtures in different toxic and delirious psychoses.

Some special remarks are necessary concerning alcohol hallucinosis, the voices of which Freud has justly characterized as projection of the superego onto the outside world. The superego is based upon identifications. One might also say that the voice of conscience is projected onto the voices that come from people outside who talk to each other. This is of great interest as an instance of a circular movement, or projection and introjection. The introjected persons represent the social reality in which the patient has lived in his early childhood. The objectivity of this reality is stressed by the fact that the voices speak to each other. In spite of its toxic character, alcohol hallucinosis is fully accessible to psychoanalytic understanding. The superego projected outside is of a particularly cruel character. The patients are threatened with castration and dismembering. Many are also afraid of being deprived of the inside of their bodies (Bromberg and Schilder, 1933a). Often, homosexual elements are outstanding. Regression in alcohol hallucinosis and regression in schizophrenia are very closely related to each other. There is no clouding of consciousness and no confusion. The avidity of the point of fixation is obviously completely due to the passing toxic influence, and it is at the present time difficult to define from the psychoanalytic point of view. At any rate, with the disappearance of the toxic action, the picture of chronic alcoholism that remains is not distinguishable from other types of chronic alcoholism.

This leads to the problem of drug addiction which lately has been studied by Rado (1926) and Glover (1932a). This topic does not in the strict sense, belong in our discussions and is therefore merely mentioned in sketchy form. Since Freud and Abraham it is accepted that homosexual strivings play an important part in the psychology of drug addiction, although there are many other components to be considered. Rado speaks particularly about the increase in oral tendencies and the wish for an alimentary orgasm which is in some way the infantile pattern according to which the intoxication is formed. He and Glover justly emphasize the strong feelings of guilt and depression that precede and follow the intoxication and point to a close relation between alcoholism and drug addiction, in general, and manic-depressive psychosis.

According to Curran (1937), who has studied alcoholic women, alcoholics do not find sufficient contact with other persons when they are sober, in spite of their strong wish to be close to other persons, especially of their own sex. Their social insufficiency is very marked. They show very little interest in the opposite sex and their sex contacts are very unsatisfactory. Interest in one's own body and bodies of persons of the same sex is common. This picture is often the result of a long development in which special attachment to the parent of the same sex plays a very important part. There seems to be a strong interest in the genitals, which expresses itself in the fear of being hurt. The struggle for social recognition is clearly expressed in the hallucinatory experiences. The individual fights continually under the threat of a severe superego with primitive tendencies.

It seems that this complicated psychogenetic structure is based upon a closer relation to persons and a better appreciation of the social reality than we find in psychotics. The picture corresponds more closely to neurosis and, even in the terrifying threats of alcohol hallucinosis, some closer relation to a highly developed reality is preserved. One sees, especially in alcohol hallucinosis, that the toxic influence merely discloses personality problems in the language of projection. This is the type of toxic psychosis that comes nearer to the psychosis of the so-called functional type—schizophrenia and manic-depressive psychosis.

CHAPTER SIX

Summary

The survey given here remains incomplete. Several points can nevertheless be made. To oppose neuroses and psychoses is not correct, since psychoses have structures very different from each other.

1. In psychoses of organic type, the functions of perception, judgment, and memory are impaired in an impersonal way. The organic lesion corresponds to a regression in functions fairly far removed from the core of the personality experienced as such. In all these psychoses, primary process operates on impersonal material. The regression can be explained only incompletely by a difficulty in the present. There is no definite motive for regression. However, the resulting picture is a regression. Analytically, we may call this type of psychosis primary disturbances of the ego or, better, of the perception ego. In these psychoses the relation to what Freud calls the outward reality is primarily disturbed.

2. Mental confusion comes near to this type, although the higher order of perceptive configuration and imagination is disturbed. The possibility is offered that individual problems may be expressed in the psychosis. In other words, dreamlike attitudes and dreamlike pictures may open access to the deeper layers of the

personality. In this group, too, the actual psychic cause is not sufficient to explain the regression to the lower level, and, furthermore, there is only a scant possibility of comparing this regression with experiences at lower levels of development. Only in alcohol hallucinosis can the psychosis be understood as a regression in the superego structure and in social adaptability, combined with regressions to homosexuality and dismembering motives.

3. In schizophrenia and in manic-depressive psychoses we have a sequence understandable from a psychogenetic point of view—the regression is initiated by a difficulty in the present situation and is libidinal in nature; however, the libidinal regression involves regression of the superego as well, and of the parts of the ego that are close to libidinal structures. It is therefore justifiable to speak in these cases about id and superego regressions. The regression is initiated by an act of the ego, and the ego has, therefore, a relative intactness.

4. In schizophrenia we deal with a regression to primary narcissism, with introjection and projection of primitive structure. This regression goes hand in hand with primitive forms of aggressiveness—death instincts, according to Freud. The picture is understandable only from the point of view of an interaction between various points of fixation and a combination of processes of restitution with processes of regression.

5. Manic-depressive psychoses are, according to the formulation of Freud, based upon a changed relation between the ego and the id. They are characterized by a regression to the state of oral libido, and to the human dependencies connected with it. This stage has its own introjection and projection mechanisms, different from the introjection and projection mechanisms of schizophrenia. These individuals are capable of outspoken genital object relations.

6. For the understanding of psychoses one has to take into consideration: (a) On which level of psychosexual development does the point of fixation lie? (b) Are there several equivalent points of fixation? (c) What amount of libido is bound to a specific point of fixation in relation to the total amount of libido (regressive quo-

tient)? (d) Are there secondary points of fixation? (e) What is the avidity of the point of fixation, namely, the capacity of the point of fixation to hold the regressed libido? (f) A point of fixation is a previous life situation of importance; it can by principle be defined as well from the point of view of the id and of the superego and from the point of view of the synthetic function of the ego (not from the point of view of the perception ego).

7. Regression can take place in every sphere of experience, in the organic sphere as well as in the so-called functional sphere. Regression is characterized by the so-called primary process, which corresponds to the activity of the unconscious (system ucs. as characterized by Freud).

II

ORGANIC BRAIN DISORDERS AND PSYCHOSES

CHAPTER SEVEN

Asymbolia for Pain

In 1927, we observed a patient with sensory aphasia who would have hurt herself severely if left alone. She pushed against her eyes everything that came into her hand, heedless of the pain she thus inflicted on herself. When we studied this patient more carefully, we found that she did not react to pain, or only in an incomplete and local way. There was no real defense action. Sometimes there was a local withdrawal; the patient's facial reaction was one of slight pain. When exposed to a strong faradic current, she showed pain reactions but not a real defense. She never became angry at the examiner, and even seemed to derive some pleasure from the pain. Sometimes she took a needle and stuck herself deeply with it. The patient perseverated in actions once undertaken. The perseveration and the sensory aphasia almost disappeared, whereas the changed attitude toward pain persisted. The patient also did not appreciate threatening gestures and was insensitive to loud noises and sudden flashes of light.

An autopsy was performed, and the brain was examined in a Weigert series. There was a small vertical lesion in the anterior

Appeared originally in *Archives of Neurology and Psychiatry* 25: 598-600, 1931, Erwin Stengel, co-author.

part of the left second frontal convolution. Another lesion started in the left capsula externa, and continued to the basis of the gyrus longus insulae. The anterior of Heschl's transverse convolutions also showed a lesion, but the medial parts were more seriously affected. The upper part of the first temporal convolution was also affected. The gross lesion was found in the gyrus supramarginalis, especially in its basal parts, but there were also softenings in the medullary parts of the gyrus angularis.

The clinical symptoms had pointed to a lesion near Wernicke's region. Since there were no symptoms attributable to the gyrus angularis, we believe that there may be a center in the gyrus supramarginalis, a lesion of which makes appreciation of pain and danger impossible.

Two other cases seemed to confirm the localization of the symptom in the anterior part of the lower part of the left parietal lobe. In one, two tumors were present, one in the left side of the frontal lobe and the other in the upper part of the left side of the parietal lobe and in the gyrus supramarginalis. In the second case, asymbolia for pain was observed after the removal of a tumor of the left parietal region. It can be considered as proved that a lesion on the parietal lobe is the cause of asymbolia for pain.

Our cases make it probable that the gyrus supramarginalis is the most important point in this lesion. This localization, however, has not yet been definitely proved, since in our first case a slighter lesion of the gyrus angularis was also present, and in the other cases the tumors did not allow exact localization. It is remarkable that seemingly a lesion of a part of the brain between the centers that regulate the attitude toward language (gyrus temporalis) and those that make it possible to construct properly a picture of one's own body (gyrus angularis and adjoining occipital region) should provoke asymbolia for pain. Pain must in some way be brought into connection with recognition of the postural model of the body in order to be appreciated fully.

In some of our cases there was not only a dulling of the appreciation of pain, the pain reaction also was insufficient, without being definitely apraxic. Every asymbolia for pain is connected with an incapability of reacting fully to pain. Asymbolia for pain is in some way a phenomenon akin to apraxia, although, characteristically, only in this distinctive field of reaction to pain and danger. It is known that the upper parts of the gyrus supramarginalis have an especially close relation to eupraxia.

In most cases the condition is spread over the whole body and is different from the disturbances of perception of pain in cortical lesions described by Foerster (1927) and others. In some cases the sensitivity of the lower part of the body is greater than that of the upper part.

We have observed ten cases up to the present time. That such a common symptom has for so long escaped the attention of examiners is probably due to the erroneous opinion that the symptoms are disturbances in attention; our patients, however, were very much interested in pain. In six of our cases, typical sensory aphasia was present. One patient showed difficulty in finding the right words. In two, the sensory aphasia was slight and disappeared quickly. One presented difficulties with speech. In five cases, we have seen the asymbolia for pain disappear. The disappearance of the asymbolia for pain parallels the disappearance of the sensory aphasia. Two of the patients said that they could remember that the pain had been inflicted, but that they did not feel it. Slight apraxic disturbances were present in one of the cases. In two of the cases, the postural reflexes were strongly increased. The apraxia usually became evident only in actions directed against the patient's own body. Two of our patients showed perseverational tendencies in connection with the asymbolia for pain concerning actions. These were cases in which lesions of the frontal lobe were found at autopsy.

In our experience we find that all types of lesions may be the cause of the symptom—softening, hemorrhages, tumors, syphilis, and fractures of the skull. We have therefore come to the conclusion that a lesion in a particular region of the left parietal lobe makes it impossible to build up a full perception of pain. It is not only the deficiency that is significant in asymbolia for pain, but the attitude to the pain. It is in this remarkable respect that the disturbances described here, as investigations by L. Bender and Schilder (1930) [see Chapter 21] have shown, closely resemble the reactions in a particular group of catatonic cases; but it seems that in the catatonic cases the lack of the reaction to pain has a closer connection with the individual problems of the patient.

CHAPTER EIGHT

Posture with Special Reference to the Cerebellum

Evidences of Decerebrate Rigidity in Animal and in Man

The description of decerebrate rigidity by Sherrington was an important event in neurology. Sherrington (1907) observed, in 1896, after a transsection through the midbrain between the anterior and the posterior corpora quadrigemina, an increased tonus of the extensor muscles of the neck, the back, the tail, and the legs. All the muscles that secured the erect position of the animal were overinnervated. It is the function of standing that appears in such a way. Richter and Bartemeier (1926) have shown that in the sloth, an animal in which the normal attitude is that of hanging from trees with flexed limbs, decerebrate rigidity is a flexor rigidity. Muscular tension in connection with decerebrate rigidity is a special one. Sherrington discovered the shortening and lengthening reaction of muscle. The muscle adapts itself to any length given to it without

Appeared originally in *Archives of Neurology and Psychiatry*, 22: 1116-1126, 1929.

77

change in tension. Liddell and Sherrington (1924) also described
the stretch reflex or myotatic reflex, an increasing tension when
the muscle is passively stretched. Magnus and de Kleijn (1912) have
shown that in the decerebrate animal a change in the position of
the head provokes regular changes in the tonus of the extremities
and the trunk, which they termed "*Lage* reflexes," reflexes of position. These postural reflexes are partly in connection with the
position of the head in relation to the trunk (neck reflexes). Such is
the typical picture of decerebrate rigidity. However, Schaltenbrand (1929) and others pointed out that there may be variations
in this picture; there may be flexor rigidity instead of extensor rigidity (Beritoff, 1926), or the Magnus and de Kleijn reflexes may be
absent (Bazett and Penfield, 1922). A similar decerebrate rigidity
may be obtained by sections made through deeper parts of the
brain stem. Even sections through the medulla oblongata provoke
a similar picture if the section is made above the calamus scrip-
torius.

It is difficult to find a true analogue to decerebrate rigidity in
man. One finds such pictures mostly in cases with gross destruction or compression of the brain stem. Here, however, the arms
are often not in extension but in flexion. The Magnus and de Kleijn
reflexes may be absent. Pronation and extension in the arms may
be found. The legs are in extension. If there is no shortening and
lengthening reaction, one should not speak of the condition as
decerebrate rigidity.

Walshe (1923) considers typical hemiplegia a close analogue
of decerebrate rigidity, and the interesting experience of Russell
Brain (1922)—that a quadrupedal attitude in hemiplegic persons
changes the flexion contracture of the arms to an extension contracture—seems to point in the same direction. But in hemiplegia
the shortening and lengthening reaction is not present, at least not
in the same way as in decerebrate rigidity. The stretch reflex plays
a much more important part. One may identify the characteristic
elastic residence of hemiplegia with the stretch reflex. Simons
(1923) and Walshe (1923) have found the Magnus and de Kleijn reflexes in hemiplegic patients. The arm toward which the chin is

turned shows an increased extensor tonus, whereas the flexor tonus of the opposite arm increases. These changes, however, can often be obtained only by provoking associated movements, and the latter are present only in cases in which a tendency to such movements exists. The results of the change of the position of the head in space are rather uncertain. Although Pette (1925) reported positive observations, Hoff and I (1927) have often missed the Magnus and de Kleijn reflexes in older hemiplegic persons. They are at least not constant in older arteriosclerotic patients. Simons' material consisted chiefly of younger people with traumatic lesions of the brain. When the reflexes are present in older people, they are less marked than in younger people.

The differences between hemiplegia and decerebrate rigidity are so great that there is no justification for identifying the two states. Schaltenbrand considered as decerebrate rigidity not only hemiplegia, but the rigidity of paralysis agitans. But this theory presents a marked difficulty. The stretch reflex is, at least in some cases, not well marked (although a stretch reflex does exist in some cases, see Schilder and Gerstmann, 1920). The position of the limbs in cases of paralysis agitans is different from the position in decerebrate rigidity. In typical cases of paralysis agitans, there is a semiflexion in all joints. As a rule there are no righting and postural reflexes. There is also no reason to consider the muscular state of Parkinson's disease or of a parkinsonian case an analogue of decerebrate rigidity.

In my own experience, I have observed a close resemblance to decerebrate rigidity in persons whom I etherized. One sees in them an extensor tonus in all extremities, and the arms show a considerable degree of pronation, but so far I have not obtained Magnus and de Kleijn reflexes. After all, experiences with man show that an absolute analogue to decerebrate rigidity does not exist. An organism in which the pyramidal tract plays such an important part is too unlike organisms in which the pyramidal tract is of only little importance. One must therefore describe the clinical facts as such, and one cannot always reckon that identification with physiologic experiments will be possible.

POSTURAL AND RIGHTING REFLEXES IN ANIMAL AND MAN

The decerebrate animal has retained the possibility of standing, but it no longer has the possibility of retrieving a lost position.
It has lost the righting reflexes. The animal with righting reflexes
brings the head back into the normal relation to the trunk and
brings the head and trunk back into the normal position in space.
According to Magnus (1924) and Rademaker (1926b) the righting
reflexes have an important center in the red nucleus.

(a) *Neck Reflexes.* Magnus has observed postural as well as
righting reflexes in normal animals, and these reflexes are also present in human beings. Schaltenbrand (1925) saw them in children,
but he thinks that in the normal adult the neck reflex has disappeared completely. Hoff and I (1927), however, found that in
about 90 per cent of normal adult persons passive turning of the
head influences the arms as well as the trunk. Turning the head to
the right, for instance, provokes a deviation of the outstretched
arms and of the trunk to the right. The right arm rises, whereas the
left arm remains either in the same horizontal plane or sinks a
little. The subject must close his eyes during the experiment. One
deals here with a neck reflex that resembles a postural as well as a
righting reflex.

(b) *The Pronation Phenomenon.* There are also some other
postural reactions in normal people. If a person stretches his hands
in a position of strong supination (with the eyes closed), pronation
sets in, the extent of which varies in different people. The subjects
are not aware of the pronation. There is a tendency to go from the
inconvenient posture of supination to a more convenient position
of a minor degree of supination.

(c) *The Divergence Reaction.* Another reaction of this type is
the divergence reaction. If a normal person stretches both arms
straight forward, the arms will diverge in a more or less pronounced degree. Only if the arms are outstretched so that they are
at an angle of from 45 to 60 degrees outward from their parallel
position does no divergence take place. Also, no outward movement can be observed if only one arm is stretched forward and the

other hangs down. The divergence reaction and the pronation tendency are the expression of a tendency to a comfortable and "normal posture." This tendency is at least closely akin to the postural and righting reflexes.

(d) *Persistence of Posture.* Another experiment I shall stress is a phenomenon in normal people that I call persistence of posture. If I passively raise or lower the arm of a subject who has stretched both arms forward, with closed eyes, 60 degrees above or below the horizontal line, leave the raised or lowered arm in this position for twenty seconds, and then request the subject to put the raised or lowered arm at the same height as the quiet arm, the moved arm stands above or below the quiet arm. The distance varies between two and ten cm. I emphasize the fact that the reaction has nothing to do with the persistence of muscular tension. It is a persistence of postural influences. The subject knows nothing about his mistake, and the erroneous posture of the limb becomes for him the normal posture. If, for instance, the raised arm is brought passively to the same level as the other arm, the subject feels as if the quiet arm was higher and the moved arm lower. In other words, the postural scheme of the body is distorted in such a way that the position is felt as the normal position the limb would reach when following the muscular tendency. The true normal position of the limb is now felt as a position different from the normal position in a direction opposite to the direction of the persistent tone. The postural model of the body is therefore changed, while the persistent tone goes on. The position of the limb into which the muscular tendency tries to pull the limb becomes the normal position of the limb, and all other postures are now judged in relation to this normal position.

The same is true for all other types of tone that are in connection with postural tone, the tone of the righting reflexes or, in brief, the tone of the Magnus and de Kleijn reflexes. If, for instance, from a homolateral cerebellar lesion the right arm shows a tendency to go upward and both arms are placed passively at the same height, the patient will perceive his right arm lower than the left one. If there is an outward tendency when the arms are put in a parallel position (passively), the subject will gain the impression that the right arm stands more inward than the left one. The tone of persistence of posture can be taken as a model for postural activities. It is always present in normal people and is absent only in about twenty per cent of the cases of paralysis agitans and parkinsonism. It is also absent in those groups of cases which often show a lack of other postural and righting activities as well. I have failed to find the persistence of posture in one case of symmetrical pallidal lesion and in one case of a tumor of the midbrain.

(e) *Reflexes in Extrapyramidal Lesions.* In Parkinson's disease and parkinsonian cases, turning of the head has no effect at all. Sometimes it seems as if the arms and trunk would deviate in the same direction in which the head is turned. But careful investigation shows that the limbs and the trunk are carried out with the head in a mechanical way by the rigidity. A normal person, when getting up from lying on uncertain ground, such as on a springy mattress, feels uncertain and makes use of a more infantile way of getting up, by turning his trunk around. Most patients with paralysis agitans are not able to make use of these primitive righting reflexes; they get straight up from a mattress without turning around. The postural and righting reflexes are not absent in all cases of paralysis agitans and parkinsonism. Two phenomena here described are always present in the parkinsonian cases: the pronation phenomenon and the divergence phenomenon. There is, however, a peculiarity about the divergence phenomenon in cases of paralysis agitans. It is obtained only if one fixes the elbow joints rigidly with bandages. If one does not do so, there is a marked convergence of the stretched hands, a sign that has proved of diagnostic value. It is worthwhile remarking that tonus of paralysis agitans and parkinsonism does not influence the postural scheme of the body; it is different from the tone in the righting reflexes and in the postural reaction we dealt with in this paper.

Comment. In normal and pathologic cases, one should study the following reactions: (a) the reaction to turning the head; (b) the divergence reaction; (c) the pronation phenomenon; and (d) the persistence of tone.

POSTURAL AND RIGHTING REFLEXES IN CEREBELLAR DISTURBANCES

(a) *The Cerebellar Reaction.* In cerebellar cases the neck reflexes are increased on the side of the lesion. One can see this clearly in cases of hemichorea, in which there is at least a strong cerebellar component. In rare cases the neck reflexes are so increased that there results a spontaneous rotation around the longitudinal axis (André Thomas, 1916; Hoff and Schilder, 1927; Gerstmann, 1926). If, for instance, the head is turned to the left after a cerebellar lesion on the right, the trunk and arms may deviate in a paradoxical way to the right. There is here an increased tendency to turn to the right in the presence of a lesion of the right side of the cerebellum.

(b) *The Pronation Tendencies.* Wilson (1922) has drawn attention to the fact that cerebellar patients often have shown an increased pronation and has brought this observation in relation to the pronation posture of decerebrate rigidity. Hoff and I have stressed the fact that this is an exaggeration of the normal tendency. Gierlich (1920) expressed the opinion that supination is phylogenetically a younger function than pronation. In pyramidal lesions one also finds the pronation tendency. This pronation tendency, however, occurs in connection with a change not only in tone but also in strength. One therefore comes to the conclusion that the cerebellum helps in the assumption of an uncomfortable position, which is at the same time a phylogenetically younger position.

(c) *The Bárány Test.* Bárány's past-pointing test (1907) probably belongs in the same group. Goldstein (1927) has emphasized that most cerebellar patients point outward. This is an exaggeration of the divergence reaction. If one examines with the divergence test one finds that the divergence is better marked on the side of the cerebellar lesion. Whereas in a normal person the outward deviation is to be obtained only when both arms are stretched forward (and not when only one arm is stretched forward), in cerebellar cases the deviation also takes place if only one arm is stretched out. This deviation, as Fischer and Wodak (1924) have emphasized, is the basis of past-pointing. Past-pointing is the result of a tonus that interferes with active movement. A cerebellar lesion increases the outward tendency of the whole half of the body. Turning the head to the side of the cerebellar lesion increases the outward tendency of the arm to a considerable degree. Often, the elevation of the arm is also increased. It also happens sometimes that turning the head to the opposite side will provoke an increased outward tendency of the affected arm. I speak of this, then, as a unilateral paradoxic reaction. As I have pointed out, these different types of cerebellar hypertonus influence the postural model of the body. When only the outward movements of the arm are increased, one deals with an anisosthenia (André Thomas) or, as I prefer to say, with an anisotonia.

In cerebellar cases, one finds also another interesting homolateral phenomenon of anisotonia. If a cerebellar patient is lying on an even support and the healthy leg is brought into semiflexion with the heel resting on the support and the patient is asked to place the other leg in the same position, he imitates in such a way that the knee on the side of the cerebellar lesion is higher than that on the healthy side. That is not hypermetria. The same mistake is made if the leg on the side of the lesion is brought to an extreme degree of flexion and the subject is asked to imitate the semiflexion of the other leg. The leg on the side of the cerebellar disease will be in a state of hyperflexion again, as compared with the other leg. One is therefore dealing, not with hypermetria, but with anisotonia. The lesion of the cerebellum makes the flexion prevalent. In the lower extremities the cerebellum protects the influence of the extensors and is opposed to the influence of the pyramidal tract. I want to emphasize that the patient knows nothing about his trouble; if the leg on the diseased side is passively brought into the same position as the other one, the patient will feel that the leg of the diseased side stands lower than the other. One reaches the general conclusion that the tonus of this cerebellar symptom influences the postural model of the body. It is difficult to say whether or not these disturbances of tonus are in connection with a special localization of the lesion. The facts point to a different localization in the vermis (trunk) and in the hemispheres (extremities). Goldstein denied that there is ever a cerebellar lesion with which only the leg or arm is affected. The problem is not yet settled. I have seen localized muscular disturbances of a type different from the one here described, but in this case no autopsy was made and it was impossible to exclude a lesion of the medulla oblongata. That the cerebellum has some connection with postural reflexes was originally pointed out by clinicians, especially Goldstein. Afterward, Rademaker (1926a) adduced experimental facts that give the same evidence. No one believes today that the primary reflex arc of tonus goes through the cerebellum. But the cerebellum has a great influence on this primary reflex arc.

Comment: Rademaker (1926b) denied that a cerebellar lesion can ever provoke loss of tonus. From the point of view of a clinician, I emphasize the possibility that loss of tonus can occur in cases of cerebellar lesion. Patients who have no palsy let the hand sink at the joints whether the hand is supinated or pronated. There is an incapacity to maintain the posture of the hand against gravity. Those patients, too, do not react with sufficient resistance against passive movements—for instance, shaking. I have also seen patients in whom Bárány's ear irrigation test did not provoke past-pointing and deviation, and patients in whom the fall reactions were absent. I believe, therefore, that the function of tonus can be inhibited by cerebellar lesions.

One also finds marked changes of postural tonus in cerebellar lesions. One cannot suppose that such a complicated organ as the cerebellum has only one function; besides the postural changes of tone, one finds hypermetria and hypometria (bradyteleokinesis). Intention tremor is only one type of this insufficiency of the cerebellar brake system. Not enough is known about the localization of these symptoms. I am inclined to relate them to the nucleus dentatus-ruber system. I believe that the imitation phenomenon, which can often be found in cases of combined sclerosis, perhaps has a relation to the spinocerebellar tracts. But all these problems are still unsettled. Another cerebellar system has to do with the classic symptoms of Babinski's and Jarkowski's (1921) asynergia, consisting in a lack of coordination between the active motor tendencies of the arms and legs and the innervations of the trunk. That is a disturbance quite different from the one described here. I believe also that adiadokokinesis is an expression of this mechanism. I consider it, according to my investigations (Gregor and Schilder, 1913), a kind of central myasthenia.

But whatever the theoretical aspect of these problems may be, I stress the practical and diagnostic value of the following symptoms: increased divergence (deviation test); pronation phenomenon; increased righting and postural reflexes; paradoxic bilateral or unilateral deviation; the imitation phenomenon. Finally, I stress the fact that the change of the postural tone changes the postural model of the body (Goldstein's opinion also should be compared).

In tabes, one sometimes finds one or another of these symptoms, either in connection with the fact that the loss of afferent impulses changes the function of the postural apparatus, or in connection with some primary changes in the postural apparatus and the cerebellum. Little is known, however, about the changes in the postural apparatus in tabes, although clinical facts emphasize that not only is there a loss of coordination, but there are also characteristic changes in the postural apparatus.

The primary reflex arc of the postural apparatus is under the influence not only of the cerebellum. I have described with Hoff (1927), and partly also with Gerstmann (Schilder and Gerstmann, 1920), a syndrome occurring after a lesion of the parietal-occipital lobe (gyrus angularis or field 19 of Brodmann). In these cases I found not only increased postural and righting reflexes but also spontaneous turning of the body around the longitudinal axis. In these cases changes of the postural model also occurred, and optic hallucinations were present. The postural tone also influences optic perception. (Goldstein's opinion should be compared with this, too.)

Goldstein and Riese (1923), Zingerle (1926), and Fischer and Wodak (1924) have found similar movements and changes of perception in normal people who were given the order to follow their motor impulses freely. Many investigators have suspected that in these experiments psychogenetic factors might play an important part. Indeed, it is not easy to distinguish between voluntary impulses and postural reflexes in normal persons. But the results in organic cases show clearly that there is at least some truth in the experiments of Goldstein and others. The phenomena that I have described here are by no means psychogenic. They have been proved valuable from the point of view of diagnosis. The problem of tone and posture is complicated. The results are not final, but I consider them a beginning of an important investigation.

CHAPTER NINE

Turning Tendency
and Conjugate Deviation

REPORT OF A CASE

J. B. D., a linotype operator 25 years old, was admitted to the
Henry Phipps Psychiatric Clinic of the Johns Hopkins Hospital on
December 18, 1928 in a delirious condition following an exploratory craniotomy. During the past five years the patient had had
attacks of left frontal headaches which became progressively more
severe; some of them were accompanied by dizziness. During the
same time he also had a feeling that the left side of his neck was
stiff, hot, and swollen. In April 1928, he began to have attacks of
unconsciousness lasting for one to two minutes, with general
rigidity of the muscles, flushing of the face, and "staring eyes." He
would usually bend forward or to the right side, clench his fists,
and press them against his body. His head frequently would turn
slowly from one side to the other "as if he were looking for something." After an attack, he gradually regained consciousness

---

Appeared originally in *Journal of Nervous and Mental Disease*, 71: 260-267,
1930, O. Oedegaard, co-author.

within a few minutes; during this time he was confused, walked around, seemed to hear and see imaginary people, and talked to them. The attacks were preceded by a "melancholy state." He had these from two a day to three in a week. There was always complete amnesia for them.

In October, 1928 he had a more severe attack lasting for five to ten minutes, during which time he was unconscious, cyanotic, and had labored respiration. His whole body was tense. His head turned slowly from one side to another, and he had slow flexion and extension movements of his arms and legs. He bit his tongue, but was not incontinent. Following this attack he was unconscious for half an hour. In addition to the attacks, he had occasional double vision and frequent headaches, particularly before and after attacks. Frequently, he heard voices from behind—but always corrected himself when he turned around and saw that nobody was there. His memory (especially for recent events) gradually became poorer.

His family history was essentially negative, his past life uneventful. There were no evidences of lead or alcohol intoxication. He was of average intelligence and had never had fits of any kind.

On admission to the hospital, December 4, a complete physical and neurological examination—including visual fields, eyegrounds, and vestibular tests—gave negative results. Wassermann reaction was negative in blood and spinal fluid. Air injection showed a possible defect in the filling of the left ventricle and some shadows in the right hemisphere. An exploratory craniotomy in the right parietal region gave no evidence of brain tumor.

Following the operation, his general condition was good. His temperature was normal except for some slight elevation from December 9 to December 12, 1928, and his pulse was of good quality. He vomited only occasionally on the first two days following the operation. Mentally he was very drowsy, unconcerned about everything, and responded poorly or not at all to questions and orders. At times he mumbled senseless remarks to himself (such as "beings sent to Hell"), yet apparently understood what was said to him most of the time. He was very restless—at times resistant—and had to be spoon fed. He voided in bed all the time.

At least once (December 13) he had an attack of unconsciousness which, according to his wife, was exactly like his previous ones.

On admission to the clinic on December 18, he was drowsy and indifferent, grasped most questions fairly well but with obvious effort and difficulty. His attention fluctuated—he was distractable and unable to concentrate on a topic for any length of time. He talked freely but rather slowly. At times his sentences were mixed up, and occasionally he perseverated. He was in a rather shallow, indifferent mood, with bewilderment as the outstanding trait. He was also slightly euphoric at times. His facial expression was empty, and he showed a peculiar lack of interest in everything. He was disoriented for time and place, but grasped the situation of being a patient and asked the doctor to help him. His memory was poor, especially with regard to time relations and recent events; his retention was poor. To tests for calculation, general information, etc., he gave some good and some senseless answers. He had some insight, talked about having been in a delirious state and having difficulty in understanding.

Neurological examination on admission showed: The deep reflexes were completely absent—abdominal and cremasteric reflexes were active but no plantar response could be obtained. The sensibility was apparently intact for touch (he was not very cooperative). Reaction to pain was not obtained from the arms, while over the rest of the body it was decreased. His vision was apparently disturbed, he frequently acted as if he was blind (bumped into things, etc.), but at other times he was able to read ordinary print. (An adequate examination was impossible, due to his mental condition.) Motility: When he lay on his back there was a constant marked deviation of the eyes to the right and frequently a deviation of the head to the same side. The left leg usually was crossed over the right. There was marked general restlessness, consisting mainly in a turning to the right of the entire body about a longitudinal axis. It usually started with the head and took place rather slowly but with considerable force, reaching from 90 to 180 degrees. This turning was most marked when he was aroused by examinations or questions, or when he moved spontaneously; it was, for instance, apparently impossible for him to sit up in bed without some turning of the body to the right. This turning occurred even during conversation when he was in good contact. The turning was less marked when he was lying on his abdomen. Sitting on a chair he turned to the right, making short stepping movements until the back of the chair made further turning impossible and he would very nearly fall off the chair. Standing up he showed the same tendency but more markedly. He also walked sideways (or obliquely) to the right, at times almost in a complete circle, always making short steps. When his head was passively turned, his entire body would follow immediately with great force, almost 180 degrees. This neck reflex was most marked to the right side, but was also very definite to the left. No turning of the head or body could be obtained by any change in the position of the extremities. As a rule the deviation of the eyes was more marked during the turning, but occasionally it was not present at all. The coordination of his arms and legs seemed fairly good, but movements were rather slow and at times awkward. He showed a special difficulty in sitting down and getting up from a chair. He would make repeated efforts to get up, but the movements of the trunk were not adequately supported by movements of the legs, and he could not get up without help. His gait was slow and unsteady, and his steps were short. Frequently, he swayed to one side, mostly the right. At times, he would suddenly fall either forward or to the right; it was as if there was a sudden loss of muscle tone starting in his neck. He showed a definite apraxia; given a pack of cigarettes with one cigarette half drawn out, he fumbled with it for two to three minutes before he got it out. Asked to light it, he fumbled around with the paper matches in a planless way and tore the package in two, and finally rubbed a match on the cover in a place other than the correct one. He could not put on his shoes and had difficulty in holding a newspaper in the correct manner.

At one time during the examination he became more restless, with a very marked and forceful turning tendency—then he got pale, lost consciousness, and developed a definite rigidity of the face, jaw, neck, and arms. It lasted for about one to one and a half minutes—then he sat up in the bed and urinated on the floor. After this attack he was more quiet (seemed somewhat exhausted), but the motor phenomena remained essentially the same.

During the following days the deviation of the eyes disappeared and was replaced by a slight and inconstant tendency to look downward with a bending forward of the head. The turning tendency to the right also diminished, but at the same time the patient developed a similar tendency to the opposite side. These new phenomena were most marked on December 22. He did not turn much in bed, but standing up he would occasionally turn about 360 degrees to the left. He also had a tendency to walk to the left, occasionally in a complete circle of two or three meters diameter (circus movements). The neck reflexes were not very marked, but stronger on the left side. There was no deviation of the legs and only occasionally a slight deviation of the head to the left.

In the next couple of days all these motor phenomena disappeared—a normal neck reflex persisted. At the same time he gradually cleared up somewhat mentally and his vision became very much better. No further attacks were observed, but he complained of severe headaches. His apraxia disappeared (that of the trunk was last), and his sensibility to pain became normal over the entire body, including the arms. When he was discharged January 7, 1929 (at the request of the family) he was drowsy, disoriented to time, and had a marked memory defect for recent events. There were no abnormal neurological signs apart from complete absence of all deep reflexes.

Laboratory findings: Blood count—normal (no evidence of lead poisoning); urine—negative; Wassermann—in blood and spinal fluid—negative. Other findings in the spinal fluid could not be evaluated, as there was considerable admixture of hemolyzed blood; this evidently was due to the craniotomy.

The diagnosis in this case is rather difficult. The whole development made a brain tumor seem probable. The auditory hallucinations pointed to the temporal lobe, although very likely not only auditory but visual hallucinations were present. The report of the relatives made it seem probable that attacks of the same kind as were observed in the clinic were also present before admission. We therefore did not think that the neurological picture observed was the result of the operation, but considered it the result of the tumor, and only reckoned with the possibility that the general injury of the operation made the symptoms more pronounced. We would also connect the loss of all deep reflexes with this operative insult.

Foerster (1923) has shown that Brodmann's cortical field 19 has to do with production of a conjugate deviation to the opposite side, and Wenderowič (1928) described deviation of the eyes with hallucinations as the result of an irritation in this field. Previous writers have been inclined to place the center for conjugate deviation of the eyes in the angular gyrus. It is therefore justified in this case to suppose a lesion of Brodmann's field 19. The deviation in this case (increasing during an epileptiform fit) is an irritation phenomenon—we therefore assumed a lesion on the left side. This diagnosis fits well with the fact that the patient has had left frontal headaches and a queer paresthesia in the muscles of the left side of the neck.

The apraxia pointed to the parietal lobe, and the optic trouble made it probable that the neighboring parts of the occipital lobe were affected. The disturbances of pain perception have already been discussed [see Chapter 7] and point to the same regions.

The reason for publishing this observation is that a tendency of turning around a longitudinal axis is connected with conjugate deviation. One might say that the deviation has irradiated from the center for conjugate deviation to the neighboring centers for turning of the trunk. Very likely the connection between the two phenomena is closer than one would suppose, in view of the slight mention of it in the literature. The importance of the crossing of the legs as a symptom of turning tendency should be noted.

According to Hoff and Schilder (1927), in almost every normal person turning the head provokes a turning of the arms and the body to the same side: neck reflex. But a spontaneous turning around the longitudinal axis is due to a lesion or irritation of the same cortical field that is responsible for the conjugate deviation. (It can also be due to cerebellar lesions.) Rothfield (1928) has published a case with turning tendency and believes that a lesion of the thalamus was responsible, but in his case the tumor also involved the parieto-occipital region.

When a conjugate deviation is accompanied by a strong tendency to spontaneous turning, then there must be either an excitation of the neighboring centers for the trunk or of the primary center of Magnus and de Kleijn—or of both. Hyperactivitiy of the latter is in this case indicated by an increase of the righting reflexes to both sides, with predominance of the right.

It is of importance that the turning in our case occurs with taking short steps, as in the observations by Hoff and Schilder (1925b), Gerstmann (1926), and Kauders (1925). The latter case also offers an interesting similarity to ours in that the turning came in epileptiform fits. The hallucinations in our case are also easily explained in connection with these cases. Most of them had hallucinations on the side to which they turned.

In our case it is remarkable that the turning tendency is so closely related to other motor impulses (it increased whenever he moved)—and this in an apathetic individual where many of the higher motor impulses were absent.

It might also be mentioned that a tendency to bending forward with deviation of the eyes downward was noticed in our case, and, furthermore, occasional sudden loss of muscle tone, with swaying to the right side—symptoms that have not up to the present been described in parietal lesions.

We do not think the patient's apathy can be explained only as a consequence of general brain lesion. In our case the period of excitation, with turning and conjugate deviation to the right, was followed by a period when the turning was more pronounced to the left. One could speak of a period of inhibition, or exhaustion of the centers involved in the turning to the right. When this change took place, the conjugate deviation disappeared. The connection between the two symptoms is obviously not an absolute one. The turning of the trunk is due to independent neighboring cortical centers, through which the impulse is carried to the primary centers of Magnus and de Kleijn. The turning to the left was less marked than that to the right. As far as we know, our observation is the first where this change from excitation to exhaustion was observed.

The patient showed his turning tendencies very markedly while walking, and when he walked more rapidly even showed typical "circus movements," a rather unusual symptom. Halpern (1928) has collected the literature concerning this symptom. Our observation shows that these circus-ring movements occur when there is a turning tendency and, at the same time, an impulse to walk forward—they seem to be a result of the interference between these two impulses.

Without any apparent loss of sensibility as such, the patient showed a deficient reaction to pain, which may belong to the "asymbolia for pain" described elsewhere [see Chapter 7]. We believe that this symptom points to a lesion in the posterior portion of the supramarginal gyrus. In an observation by Schilder (1928c), the pain asymbolia was (as in this case) confined to the upper part of the body.

The patient's apraxia was of a peculiar type in that it was especially marked in the actions of sitting down and getting up. This persisted after the apraxia of the hands had disappeared. His motor difficulties are probably due in part to his general apathy, but are based on apraxia, so that this observation supports the opinion of Hoff and Schilder (1927) that the parietal lobe is the region where the righting reflexes are integrated in the general system of praxia.

CHAPTER TEN

Motor Phenomena
During Nitrogen Inhalation

Himwich, Alexander, and Lipetz (1938), reasoning that the effects of insulin and metrazol treatments in cases of schizophrenia are due to a common factor, namely, the production of cerebral anoxia, introduced nitrogen inhalation therapy. They have already described the manifestations occurring during this type of treatment. We are interested in more detailed observations of the neurologic phenomena evidenced during this procedure, especially the motor sequence.

The procedure of Alexander and Himwich (1939) was initiated at Bellevue Hospital by Green and Adriani (1940), who have reported on the clinical findings. The technique, except for minor variations, is essentially the same. The apparatus consists of an anesthesia mask, which is connected in series to a canister of soda lime and a breathing bag. The oxygen is supplied by means of an ordinary gas machine, and the nitrogen is delivered from a large tank of commercial gas. The carbon dioxide is removed by the

Appeared originally in *Archives of Neurology and Psychiatry*, 44: 10009-1017, 1940, Alexander Levine, co-author.

soda lime, thus reducing the discomfort of the patient. The apparatus is first filled with pure oxygen, and when the patient has had a few breaths, nitrogen is run into the mask, gradually displacing the oxygen. In the meantime, frequent readings of the blood pressure and pulse rate are taken.

The treatment is generally continued until severe motor phenomena are present and the patient is deeply unconscious. In most of the cases the procedure did not take more than two minutes, which is a somewhat shorter period than that required in Himwich's method. On occasion, however, the treatment was continued up to four or five minutes and in some cases was extended to ten or fifteen minutes. This prolongation was made possible only by reducing the oxygen content of the inhalation mixture more slowly or by occasionally adding small amounts of oxygen.

The following description is valid for the short and the somewhat longer treatments. It will be necessary to add a comment on treatments that were prolonged to ten or fifteen minutes, because here the phenomena were qualitatively and quantitatively different.

Short Treatment

The motor sequence exhibited by patients undergoing the relatively short nitrogen inhalation therapy may be divided into four more or less distinct phases, which tend to overlap.

Stage of Restless Movements: This stage started shortly after the inhalation of nitrogen began. Usually, the first thing to occur was a restless moving of the lower extremities, consisting chiefly of crossing and recrossing of the legs. This was sometimes associated with slight flexion at the knees. Often, the patient would rub his feet and legs together. Inward and outward rotation of the legs was also common, together with plantar flexion and extension of the toes and feet. One frequently had the impression that the patient tried to stop these movements and therefore pressed the legs against each other in an attempt to fixate them. These movements occurred soon after the diminution of the oxygen content of the inhalation mixture was begun. It was interesting to note that some patients who had previously had several treatments showed these restless movements as conditioned reflexes the moment they were wheeled into the room, before nitrogen inhalation was started. At the time when the restless movements appeared, ankle clonus might be present. This became more apparent as the treatment progressed. Patellar clonus was rare. The clonus was not well sustained and had the characteristics of clonus seen in cases of paralysis agitans, with a tremorlike quality, as compared with that of pyramidal-tract origin. The patients were still able to count at this point. Pupillary changes occurred at about the same time. The pupils became large and reacted sluggishly to light. With the progression of the treatment the pupillary reaction became still worse. The clonus, the restless movements, and the pupillary changes appeared approximately at the same time, although one may precede the others.

It had been noted that, in this and in the two following stages, any attempt to elicit the abdominal and plantar reflexes tended to increase the motor phenomena. It may be mentioned that during the entire course of the treatment the abdominal reflexes were persistently present and Babinski, Oppenheim, or Rossolimo signs were never obtainable.

Myoclonic Phase: This followed the first stage. Myoclonic twitches occurred around the mouth, in the flexors of the arms, in the extensors of the knees, and in the flexors of the foot. These twitchings were usually irregular and were often associated with a myoclonic dorsiflexion of the big toe.

Rhythmic Phase: The myoclonic twitches increased and approached a rhythm consisting of symmetric extension of the knees and feet. This might become alternating, so that it appeared as if the patient was stamping his feet. Occasionally, the myoclonic twitches might resemble coarse tremors. Toward the end of this stage the pupils became fixed to light in middilatation. At this point many patients closed their eyes violently, and there was a great deal of resistance when an attempt was made forcibly to separate the eyelids. Conjugate deviation of the eyes occurred in either a horizontal or a vertical plane, with slow rolling movements in any direction.

Tonic Phase: The myoclonic twitches became more tonic in character. They became prolonged and finally melted into each other in tonic postures. In the upper extremities one usually saw, at first, flexion of the elbows, with extension of the fingers, and flexion of the hands. A grasp reflex might be present, but it was transient and of low intensity and was not common. In many cases the flexion was combined with abduction and raising of the arms. Occasionally, the flexion was followed by an extension of the arms, with pronation and abduction. The shoulders were pulled downward. The extension sometimes preceded the flexion.

In the lower extremities the common posture was one of extension and abduction. Later there might be some flexion in the knees and hips, with dorsiflexion of the feet. This might be more marked on one side than on the other. One or both of the lower extremities might be raised in the air, extended at the knee, and flexed at the hip. At the height of the extension, arching of the back occurred, with retraction of the head, producing a complete picture of decerebrate rigidity, with extension and pronation of the extremities. At this point the Magnus-de Kleijn reflex was obtainable. Turning the head usually produced chin-arm extension and occiput-arm flexion. The lower extremities as a rule did not follow suit. Sometimes a paradoxic response was obtained during this maneuver, with chin-arm flexion and occiput-arm extension. Now the pupils were greatly dilated and did not react to light, and the eyes remained fixed in one position.

Recovery: Usually at this point pure oxygen was given. The tensions continued, and sometimes one obtained the impression that the extensor rigidity of the lower extremities changed to the flexor type. However, a careful checkup showed that when extensor rigidity had persisted under oxygen deprivation it changed to flexor rigidity before oxygen was administered. It seemed that the change in the phases may be facilitated by the administration of oxygen. The situation in the upper extremities appeared to be similar.

A few seconds after the oxygen was given, the rigidity changed to myoclonic twitches and the myoclonic twitches changed to rhythmic movements and finally to restless movements again. In other words, there was then a transition from phase 4 to phase 1, in reverse order. The ankle clonus appeared immediately after the severe rigidity, which had caused it to disappear, was relaxed. It was more easily obtained in the recovery stage than in the first four stages. In the same way, the pupils and the ocular movements returned to normal in the reverse order. In the majority of cases the pupils quickly returned to normal. Occasionally, the pupillary reactions became sluggish when pressure was applied to the abdomen.

It should be emphasized that during the entire procedure the reflexes were slightly increased and that at no time was a Hoffman, Babinski, Rossolimo, Oppenheim, or Chaddock sign elicited. The abdominal reflexes were obtainable as long as the tensions in the abdominal muscles did not prevent their appearance.

The patients retained the capacity for counting up to the beginning of the rigid state. There were never any aphasic difficulties. They were able to pronounce clearly and distinctly. This was likewise true after awakening, at which time they had no difficulty with the Visual Motor Gestalt (Bender) and Goodenough Draw-a-Man tests. The unconsciousness seemed to last a comparatively short time. The patients were emotionally unchanged after the treatment was over. A few became incontinent of urine during the tonic phase. Most of the patients vigorously denied that they had been unconscious at all. Some of them stated that they had a choking sensation under the mask, with difficulty in breathing, while others denied this.

The short treatments and the treatments of medium length were similar, except that in the latter the sequence of events was spread over a somewhat longer time. The individual differences that occurred in the patients were not marked. However, each had his specific pattern, which was repeated with every treatment.

In one case, neurologic signs did not develop and the patient passed into a flaccid state, so that treatment had to be interrupted before tonic phenomena appeared. In the treatments that followed, a slight variation in technique was sufficient to evoke a typical tonic response.

Prolonged Treatment

The neurologic picture during the long treatment differed considerably from that just described. The restless movements began at about the third minute of treatment and lasted for about three minutes. The tensions and the myoclonic twitching were less dramatic, as if the same amount of muscular tension were spread over a longer period. There was a tendency on the part of the patient to become completely flaccid and to lose the abdominal reflexes. The same was true for the patellar and Achilles tendon reflexes, although the latter were generally more resistant and persisted for a longer time. The plantar reflexes might disappear completely, but were never replaced by the Babinski toe responses. A Hoffman sign was occasionally observed, but this was variable.

In this procedure the tonic phase was not observed at the termination of the treatment. Instead, there was a tendency toward flaccidity at this point, so that decerebrate postures did not occur. When more oxygen was given, rigidity might occur and the reflexes return.

In one case, it was observed that the hands became completely anemic and cataleptic. This condition, however, was restricted to the hands and seemingly was the result of local anemia. At times the hands showed tetanic postures.

After pure oxygen was given, the twitches and the restless movements recurred in the reverse order. The unconsciousness in patients undergoing this treatment was deep. They remained confused afterward and showed a changing attitude toward the environment. The pupillary disturbances persisted for some time. In one instance, aphasia was observed immediately after the patient awakened. At the termination of the treatment psychologic changes were noted. One patient showed a negative transference to the physician, characterized by aggressive and resistive behavior; another patient began to call for her mother. Because of the dangerous systemic reactions occurring during the long treatment, the number of patients was limited to two. The results therefore have no statistical value and are preliminary.

Observations of this kind are interesting, because knowledge of the results of cerebral anoxia is still limited. Studies have been made on human subjects in whom the carotid arteries were ligated. Fetterman and Pritchard (1939) and H. Wortis (1936) have reported such cases, in which hemiplegia, aphasia, convulsions, and deterioration of personality were shown clinically. However, such a procedure obviously produces much more than cerebral anoxia, because there is interference with the circulation and with the removal of waste products. Moreover, there are other factors to be considered, such as vascular anomalies, previous pathologic changes, and reflex activities.

Careful studies were made by Courville (1936) on narcosis produced by nitrogen monoxide. Again, however, certain difficulties are encountered because of the narcotic effect of the anesthetic. His findings are remarkable for the amount of severe cortical degeneration. This corresponds to his observation of convulsive seizures and signs of implication of the pyramidal tracts, such as the Babinski reflex, in most of the cases. Aphasic manifestations were present in some of the cases.

The method used in animal experimentation consisted chiefly of eliminating the circulation to the brain. Grant, Weinberger, and Gibbon (1939) showed that cats subjected to periods of circulatory arrest up to five minutes and ten seconds recovered entirely within 24 hours and remained normal throughout the survival period. A group of cats in which circulation was arrested for from three minutes and 25 seconds to five minutes and 45 seconds showed motor weakness for from two to seven days, which then disappeared. However, the behavior of the cats became permanently altered. They showed marked apathy and indifference. Animals subjected to circulatory arrest for from six minutes and seven seconds to seven minutes and five seconds remained in coma for a number of hours and showed tonic spasms, clonic convulsions, bouts of intense hyperactivity, and profound evidence of cerebral cortical damage. Cats with circulatory arrest for longer periods remained in coma for many hours and had tonic and clonic fits, decerebrate attitudes, paralyses, spasticities, and gross tremors.

Pathologically, the animals subjected to the longest periods of circulatory arrest compatible with life showed marked disintegration and necrosis of the cortex, with involvement of the basal ganglia, thalamus, hypothalamus, and geniculate nuclei. The pons, medulla, and spinal cord appeared normal except for degeneration of the pyramidal tracts. With the lesser degrees of anoxemia, the basal ganglia and the cortex were involved, while, finally, the brains of cats that showed permanently altered behavior during life presented diffuse areas of nerve-cell degeneration, seen chiefly in the cortex, the other nerve structures appearing to be intact.

The oxygen need of the central nervous system is obviously not the same in all parts. Alfred Meyer (1927) found that there is a higher rate of oxygen consumption for the cerebellar cortex than for the cerebrum, as well as a high value for the cornu ammonis. Gerard (1938), experimenting with guinea pigs, found that the respiratory rate of the medulla is hardly one-third as high as that of the cerebrum. At the lower end of the scale is the cervical sympathetic ganglion, which can resist anoxemia for almost one hour, while the neurons in the central nervous system become electrically quiescent a few seconds after the nutrient artery is clamped. The survival time—that is, the duration of anoxia after which revival with oxygen is possible (measure of reversibility)—was found to be as follows: motor cortex, fifteen seconds; corona radiata, twenty seconds; geniculate body, fifteen to 30 seconds; cerebellum, ten seconds, and medulla, 50 seconds. Even if one takes these statements for granted, they have not been proved to be correct for man. Furthermore, it is not known whether the rate of oxygen consumption determines the onset of the clinical symptoms.

Our observations show that the motor phenomena occurring during nitrogen inhalation therapy do not present any of the characteristic signs of implication of the pyramidal tracts. The persistent absence of the Babinski sign is remarkable in this respect. We must stress that the myoclonic twitches and the rhythmic movements present are often associated with more or less isolated dorsiflexion of the big toe. However, this is a phenomenon with an extrapyramidal basis and has been already observed by the Vogts (1922) as such. The abdominal reflexes remain unaltered throughout the treatment. Furthermore, aphasic signs and convulsive seizures were not observed during the short treatment. The absence of these criteria indicates that definite damage to the motor sphere was not present. This does not, of course, exclude the possibility of involvement of the cortical region. It may be possible to postulate the presence of a lesion in the premotor area in connection with the restless, rhythmic, and myoclonic movements, although association of these phenomena with striopallidal or midbrain structures seems more probable. One may still assume that cortical damage liberates these activities, but such an interpretation seems to be much more arbitrary than the statement that the phenomena observed in these cases are related to the functions of subcortical mechanisms.

After the appearance of tremors and myoclonic movements, the treatment terminates in a picture of decerebrate rigidity. The elimination of the cortex alone is not sufficient to provoke such a picture, which generally appears only after there is an interruption in the brain stem below the level of the red nucleus. The sequence of the motor events and the symptomatology speak strongly against the idea that the cortex is attacked first. The restless movements, the tremors, and the myoclonic movements certainly do not have the character of phenomena occurring after cortical lesions.

This is, at any rate, what immediate observation shows. On comparing these observations with those of Courville in cases of narcosis induced by nitrogen monoxide, one might say that Courville found predominantly cortical lesions. Still, the Babinski sign, convulsions, aphasia, and changes in the abdominal reflexes were observed. Phenomena of the same type are present in patients given insulin and metrazol, during insulin coma, and after awakening from metrazol shock [see Chapters 26 and 27]. One might say that, according to Himwich, Frostig and their coworkers (1939), cerebral anoxia is of fundamental importance in such cases. Insulin hypoglycemia produces cerebral anoxia by limiting the supply of dextrose to the brain. It has been shown that the brain metabolizes only dextrose and that in the absence of this the oxygen uptake is diminished (Himwich, Bowman, Wortis and Fazekas, 1939). The metrazol shock treatment produces cerebral anoxemia by interfering with respiration during the convulsion (Gellhorn, 1938).

If anoxia is the basis of these reactions, however, it must differ from the anoxia in our cases. Metrazol certainly has other effects, as is true of insulin. There are probably quantitative factors as well as factors of distribution of the anoxia. The hemoglobin saturation of the blood during metrazol convulsions may be as low as 40 per cent. The figure is still lower during nitrogen inhalation. This consideration, that the distribution of the anoxia in time may change the picture considerably, gains greater probability when one considers that the long nitrogen treatment certainly has different qualitative effects. Not only is the motility picture different, but the changes in consciousness during and after treatment are much more outspoken. Nevertheless, it is not probable that the picture observed during insulin and metrazol treatments is due merely to anoxia, even when one considers the difference in sequence and distribution of oxygen deprivation.

Fraser and Reitmann (1939) have come to the same conclusion regarding metrazol shock. In a study of the effects of short periods of severe anoxia induced by nitrogen inhalation, they commented on the lack of convulsive phenomena and the differences in the neurologic manifestations as compared with those occurring during metrazol treatment. They concluded that anoxia is not to be regarded as the most important mechanism of the action of metrazol.

There is loss of consciousness at the height of the nitrogen treatments of short and of medium duration. On awakening, the patients are amnesic for this loss of consciousness. They awaken immediately after the treatment is terminated and do not show any deep confusion. Disturbances in the gestalt function and the Goodneough drawing, which appear after treatments with insulin and metrazol, do not occur here. The short loss of consciousness comes on much later than the motor phenomena. One might postulate that the loss of consciousness is due to cortical involvement, but it seems more probable that subcortical factors play at least a partial role.

The psychologic changes occurring after the short nitrogen treatment are practically nil so far as transference is concerned, whereas they are outspoken after insulin and metrazol [see Chapter 28] therapy and also after the long nitrogen treatment. At present, it is impossible to understand the neurologic basis for these differences. We, at any rate, are inclined to believe that subcortical, subthalamic, midbrain, and even medullary factors are responsible for the changes in consciousness. Nevertheless, this point may be argued.

An extensive literature exists on the effects of low oxygen tension on psychologic functions (McFarland, 1938). Barach and Kagan (1940) at Bellevue Hospital have studied the effects of breathing an atmosphere containing thirteen per cent oxygen. The patients showed emotional disturbances and drowsiness. At present one does not know enough about the neural basis of psychologic processes to justify any conclusion, but there are correlations between subcortical lesions (subthalamic and in the walls of the third ventricle) and the sleep function. The deeper degrees of unconsciousness may even be related to structures in the medulla. The absence of the tendon reflexes during the prolonged nitrogen treatment is probably of spinal origin.

It is our contention that short and acute oxygen deprivation affects, primarily, subcortical motor functions and spreads from subcortical to cortical structures. This may partly explain the changes in consciousness. We should be inclined to say that the absence of abdominal reflexes, the appearance of the Hoffman sign, and aphasic manifestations in the long treatment are due to spread to the cortical structures, and we should at the same time assume that the spread takes place to the medulla and the spinal cord.

Pupillary abnormalities often precede any other phenomena during nitrogen inhalation therapy. M. Bender (1945) has produced pupillary dilatation by stimulation of the frontal cortex of monkeys. It seems more probable to us that the pupillary changes present in our cases, however, were due to the effect of anoxia on the brain stem. Since we discuss the pupillary changes in detail in another communication, we shall not elaborate further on this point [see Chapters 22 and 23].

It is interesting that the restless movements are semivoluntary and can be provoked as conditioned reflexes. A subcortical neural background is certain to be present here. One probably deals with complicated interactions between an organic nucleus of subcortical character and the reactions of the total personality. This phenomenon is somewhat characteristic for a large group of motor reactions that have not yet been studied sufficiently. They correspond to a phase sometimes observed during insulin treatments, in which wild mannerisms of a similar type may be found.

SUMMARY

The neurologic phenomena occurring during nitrogen inhalation have been described. During relatively short periods of cerebral anoxia produced by this technique, the motor sequence may be divided into four phases: the stage of restless movements, the myoclonic phase, the rhythmic phase, and the tonic phase. With the administration of oxygen, recovery takes place, and there is a transition from the fourth to the first phase, in the reverse order. At the height of the treatment there is loss of consciousness, for which there is amnesia on awakening. No sequelae follow this procedure.

When the nitrogen inhalation is prolonged up to from ten to

fifteen minutes the manifestations are different. Then there is a tendency toward flaccidity, with elimination of the tonic stage. The state of unconsciousness is deeper and the patients remain confused and show psychologic changes. Signs of involvement of the pyramidal tracts (Hoffman sign and absence of the abdominal reflexes) and aphasic difficulties occur only during the course of the long treatment.

These findings differ from those in other types of cerebral anoxia, such as that occurring during nitrogen monoxide anesthesia, hypoglycemia, and metrazol treatment of schizophrenia. We wish to stress the absence of any reliable signs of cortical involvement during short periods of nitrogen inhalation, such as convulsions, aphasia, and evidence of implication of the pyramidal tracts. The probable subcortical character of the manifestations has been discussed.

CHAPTER ELEVEN

Paraphasic Signs in Diffuse Lesions of the Brain

We are accustomed to consider aphasic speech disturbances merely from the structural point of view and to separate them strictly from psychogenic speech disturbances that occur in cases of neurosis and schizophrenia. However, in this problem as in others, the relation between psychogenic and organic factors has not been justly appreciated. The similarity of slips of the tongue to paraphasias has often been mentioned. Kraepelin has repeatedly emphasized the similarity of dream language to sensory aphasic speech disturbances.

When we deal with a sensory or motor aphasic patient, we have to keep in mind that his speech is not the result of the lesion, but is the expression of his total previous experiences, which, by virtue of the organic lesion, express themselves in a more primitive way. It is true that in aphasic speech difficulty personal problems find only a more or less incomplete expression. It is charac-

Appeared originally in *The Journal of Nervous and Mental Disease*, 82: 613-636, 1935, Frank J. Curran, co-author.

teristic of every disturbance in the organic sphere that the more individual problems of the personality remain unchanged and that only the "tools of the personality" are affected; as a result, the expression of the personality is merely changed in the less individual spheres of life. That paraphasias take place in organic cases is the result not of the individual's problems, but of the organic defects that hinder the correct expression. Nevertheless, the type of mistakes a paraphasic makes is largely due to his individual experiences.

In our opinion, the idea that the aphasic disturbance is a disturbance in symbolic thinking has received too much emphasis (Head, 1926). On the other hand, on should not forget that with the two outstanding types of aphasia, clear-cut changes in the impulses take place. In the motor aphasic, we find a decrease, and in the sensory aphasic, we find an increase in speech impulses. In Head's classification, motor aphasia corresponds to verbal aphasia and sensory aphasia corresponds largely to syntactical aphasia. These impulses are not impulses for speech only, but for action in general. The amount of impulses will, of course, deeply influence the total picture, but especially the paraphasias. Quantitative studies concerning the relation between disturbances in impulses and speech disturbance in the narrower sense have never been made. The impulses, however, depend very much upon the total state of the patient and upon his previous personality. Cases must exist in which the borderline is narrow between speech disturbances due to personality problems and those of organic type due to generalized or localized lesions. It may be suspected that the less severe the local lesion is, then the more prominent will be the psychogenic functional aspect and the aspect appropriate to the diffuse lesion of the brain.

These remarks were written after our experiences with toxic psychoses and head injuries had repeatedly pointed to this problem.

CASE 1

G. S., a 44-year-old male admitted to Bellevue Hospital January 7, 1934 and discharged February 10, 1934, was arrested because of alcoholism. On admission, he was in a stupor. Occasionally he mumbled, "I am all right. I have had a glass of beer. I have been here all day." His pupils reacted sluggishly to light.

On January 8, his temperature rose to 104°F. He was restless, confused, got out of bed. He had stiff neck, was hyperesthetic, the pupils were fixed to light, a right Babinski was present.

On January 11, the patient was delirious, moderately cloudy in his consciousness, disoriented, jolly, made good contact. When his reflexes were examined, he said, "What are you doing that for? Let me alone." Marked hyperesthesia was noted all over the body; there was tendency to resistance with rigidity all over the body but especially in the right arm. There was a tendency toward a grasping reflex. Abdominal reflexes were absent. Deep reflexes were normal. No Babinski or Oppenheim was present. Spinal tap was bloody in all three tubes. Temperature was between 101 and 102. Patient talked continually. He spoke about everyday life details. He had slight aphasic signs and, when pinched, he said, "Please don't do that. It is a natural feeling. It is mine."

On January 12, a left-sided ptosis appeared. Weakness of both recti interni and weakness of the left rectus superior were seen, the left pupil reacted more sluggishly than the right, and neck rigidity had increased. An operation over the left fossa media was recommended. A large clot was found and removed on January 13.

This case had, as the operation showed, a subdural hemorrhage over the left temporal region. There was no question but that he must also have had widespread minor lesions in the brain, due to the severe head injury. Before the operation, the clouding of consciousness was so severe that the question of whether he had paraphasic signs could not be decided. After the operation there were clear-cut paraphasias. Thus, he said on January 19, "I got that knocked away a couple of years ago." He called the eyebrows "hairs." On January 25 he called a cigarette "Cigaroot." When shown matches, he said, "It sounds like Canarsie, that's it," and he added in a flighty way: "Buy a couple of clams and you get a glass of beer for nothing." When a nail file was shown to him, he said, partially perseverating: "That is for the watch."

Sometimes it was not so clear that one dealt with paraphasias. When asked what kind of place he was in, for example, he answered: "This here is supposed to be like a straightening out place, a place that is really down and out. You know in good times. You know what I mean. Do you think I like to be here?" At another time he called a red stamp a green stamp. When his eyes were touched, he said: "Don't touch it, it is not good for you, it is not good to feel into it. I will tell you what I done." He called the eyes "glimmers." "Put your glimmers on—leave them on."

The patient usually understood simple questions. In the foreground of the clinical picture were the excitation, the euphoria and flightiness. It was very probable that the wrong choice of words was partially in connection with these factors. It was difficult to evalute his enormous energy in speech impulses. They were probably due not only to general factors but also to the lesion of the Wernicke region. A stilted choice of words thus resulted from a combination of the localized disturbances and the general factors. For example, he called the physician a "celebrity," or he called the hospital "a straightening out place," or, when asked to name the little finger, he answered: "I am no pugilist." His choice of words led to other queer expressions. When he was asked to name a nail file, he said: "Why a guy showed me that already —slide into it—I always give a break—why do you want to give it away—take it home with you." Similarly, he called the cap of a nurse an overseas cap and he called the nurse a double-header. A severe organic head injury had resulted in the patient's having memory disturbances of a Korsakoff type.

We conclude that a slight sensory aphasia did not severely impair the construction of sentences, but may have led to stilted expressions and the choice of words that seem to be playfully and willfully out of the ordinary. Such a speech disturbance could occur particularly when there was a strong drive to talk, partially in connection with the lesion of the Wernicke region and partially with general factors due to a head injury.

We have observed many similar instances in head injuries, and we consider this speech disturbance a rather typical one. We have observed a particularly interesting instance in the case of right-sided head injury, the case history of which follows.

CASE 2

W. F., a bricklayer, aged 45, was admitted to the surgical service of Bellevue Hospital on March 26, 1934, and transferred to the Psychiatric Department on April 5, 1934. He was found unconscious on the street. He had been drinking and, during a quarrel, had been pushed or struck, falling to the ground.

On the day of admission he was comatose and no history was obtainable. Positive findings included hematoma over left parietal region; slight laceration of scalp; alcoholic odor of breath; pupils in middilatation, irregular, fixed to light; old blood in and about lips; small laceration of left cheek; spasticity of right extremities with right deep reflexes hyperactive but with plantar flexion; fibrillary twitchings of muscle of right upper extremity; spinal tap showed bloody spinal fluid in all three tubes.

During the next few days he was alternately comatose and very excited—very profane, restless, requiring restraints; asked and tried to get out of bed. On March 27, 28, and 29, he had fever of 101°F.

On April 6, patient was drowsy but could be aroused by painful stimuli. When awakened, he became very noisy. He was disoriented and complained of headache in the anterior part of his skull. He said, "I want to go home. I want to lay in bed and stay home. I want to go home and stay there. (What is this?—ring.) It's a Dutch ring, will you give me a drink of something? (What is this?—pen.) All right. That's a new kind of ounce, a pen writing something—gimme a piece of something."

Physical and neurological examination revealed a poorly nourished, drowsy, white male. Both arms were flexed. There was no cooperation for cerebellar tests, no abnormal involuntary movements. Patient appeared to use right side more than left. The left side was less sensitive to pain, and did not move even when he experienced pain on this side. Left pupil was larger than right and reacted more sluggishly to light. Left disc was blurred. Right fundus was hyperaemic. Neck was stiff, but there was no definite Kernig. There was a left facial palsy of central type. Bilateral Babinskis were present. Patellar reflexes were active and equal. Ankle jerks were not obtained. Left abdominal reflex was less active than the right.

Manometric examination of spinal fluid showed initial pressure of 220-240 mm. of water, which on jugular pressure rose to 540 mm. Colloidal gold was 0—0. Blood and spinal Wassermanns were negative.

On April 7, patient became progressively more drowsy. Pulse was 56. Right craniotomy was done. Tense, bulging intact dura was found. On opening dura, brain bulged out. A small amount of clotted blood with yellow serum was evacuated. Laceration of brain was seen at the lower interior pole of the right frontal lobe. Blood clot was removed.

Patient was still very restless and uncooperative, constantly trying to get out of bed. He had to be kept in restraints. He talked in a rambling, incoherent manner. He was disoriented. There was a marked memory impairment for recent and remote events. He showed a tendency to confabulation. He had no memory for recent operation. He was incontinent.

On April 18, he said, "Well, I feel pretty fair. Like everything else, I could feel better. I have headaches. My only trouble is that I have a little trouble with my eyes and my bowels don't move right. No, I have no trouble with my head. I haven't had a skull fracture. (Why the bandage?) I don't know why. My head is all right. Still, all in all, it would need a little bandage if necessary, if I were employed again—any kind of position would require a bandage, laboring or driver's helper."

Patient was much more alert in the next few days and much more cooperative. He talked in a relevant, coherent manner. He still had an amnesia for his recent injury and was insistent that he had had no injury to his head and could give no adequate information for the bandage on his head. He was fairly well oriented. He did poorly on memory tests. His pupils reacted promptly, they were equal. There was no Babinski and no neck rigidity.

On May 5, the patient said: "I feel good. I've been up but I don't want to stay up too long. I've been in here five weeks. I had a bad head. I believe I had an operation performed on my head. I'm coming all beautifully but I still have headaches once in a while. This is May 4, 1933, no 1934. This is Bellevue. You're a doctor here. I'm 45. I was born in 1889 in New York. Married in 1904, over 25 years ago. I got married at age of nineteen. F.D. Roosevelt is President. Before him Hoover. N.Y. Mayor is LaGuardia. Before him were O'Brien and James Walker. Governor is Lehman. Before him was Al Smith." (100—7?) "93." (8 x 9?) 80 something.

"I understand that my mind wasn't clear. Because of the accident a loss of memory—but after a while I recuperated and my memory marched back. I do not remember having an operation. My eyesight isn't so good yet. When I started to read—it's a strain on my eyes. I had a brain concussion at least seven years ago and my eyes were affected."

Patient was alert, quiet, cooperative. He talked in a stilted, formalistic fashion at times. When urged to get up and walk, he got up for a few minutes and then lay down again, complaining of being weak. He was well oriented. He showed no definite trends. He did much better on formal memory tests. He had no recollection of his accident, the operation, or for a few weeks after the operation. He gave a history of old head injury seven years ago. In walking, patient tended to swerve to the left and assumed a rather queer gait, holding neck stiff. According to his wife, he has walked this way since the accident seven years ago. There was lordosis of chest. He swung both arms widely. No neck rigidity was present. There was good power in all limbs. He showed a positive Romberg.

Examination by psychologist was made on May 7.

On memory tests: Excellent parrot repetition of digits in forward order. He did eight correctly. He was unable to do more than four in reverse order. More than the average number of syllables were recalled when given in sentence form. Recall of paragraph —much confabulation and loss of central ideas. Information—

personal, intact. Score lowered by retarded speech. School (old associations) very poor. Learning new associations, about 35 per cent of normal. *Calculations:* Successful only with the simplest processes. In three minutes gave no response to 59 from 100. Did easy change problems quickly. *Drawing:* Primitive tendencies in space orientation. Concepts immature. He retained design if not too complex. If time of recall was lengthened and design hard, elaboration and confabulation entered. *Assembling of parts into wholes:* Ship, absurd; manikin—six years. Unable to rearrange pictures to tell a story as it should be, although he made up a story to fit the arrangements as he made it.

X ray of skull, taken May 10 , showed evidence of a craniotomy in the right parietal area. There was an irregular fissure involving the left temporal bone from the mastoid process to vicinity of the sella turcica.

On May 8, patient was asked to define certain words. (What is a puddle?) "To my knowledge a puddle is a space, a spot, some sort of thoroughfare. You make a—you can't overcome—you meet with a similar accident or carry your natural limbs across, but it's accidental in a way but the incorrect way. That makes it really accidental, but otherwise a mistake that can be overcome if you would keep your sense and get about yourself and the incorrect way running straight so it would never happen."

(What is love?) "I will tell you really that means everything in the right sense. It means everything, that is, I mean the thing since that is what I mean. The only way that anybody that you have, that one may, the word 'love' that they use judgment and common sense right to the minute, from the start to the end. I consider that a wonderful helping device. It all depends how the certain individual who loves you, stands by your side and helps you in every way. I call that a helping device, that it goes over in the real sense. When a certain individual makes that a certain way it is excellent for her or for the gentleman and it proves a success and I call that really a success."

(Do you think you are talking in a sensible way?) "In conversation with any person I should say, I should imagine, I should say

I am talking plenty sense. The individual with whom I am contraversing, I am trying to come to an agreement with the individual to give him the benefit of my conversation and to really have an impression in his own mind that my conversation is given in the way it was all the time."

(What is religion?) "Religion is in general a wonderful something you really live up to that is, going to the church as a Catholic or Episcopalian. There is different ways of explaining that. There is people that has different meanings to religion. The meaning of religion is living up to the word religion strict and right into your actual faith. But it really means faith and living up to the faith right up in your standard. The standard should be 100 per cent."

On May 12, patient was asked to name eyebrow. He said, "Not an eyelash, but an eyebrow. They protect the ball of the eye —according to the way you use the naked eye when you are traveling. (Difference between a child and a midget?) That's really appealing to me, that's odd. A midget stays in one position. A child advances rapidly regardless to health. (Difference between a lie and an error?) An error is something that happens accidentally, but a lie is not accidental. (Are you right handed?) Truthfully speaking I am right handed. But in the line of sport the left hand becomes sensational."

When examined two months after his discharge, on July 16, 1934, he said: (What is love?) "Well, my idea of this explanation of that, this is my idea to—everybody may not approve of this idea, considering this information between myself and the physicians. This idea of love that's a cooperating idea between two individuals. That really doesn't signify or mean the homing problem but outside of the homing problem. That is, in real friendship. Very excellent and positively, positively it makes things according to your listening to it and your reading it off to me, it may not meet with my approval, and I approve of it but I sincerely hope it will do. There is no question about it, my opinion and my idea is I certainly can see that it meets with your approval. (Do you know what a puddle is?) Oh, a puddle, as I should imagine that an adjusted affair, somehow or another, something that is in a position to take considerable time to remove it. You have some utensils to do it. (What is a puddle?) My impression is that it is something that has to be removed. But it would take favorable utensils to remove it. Something that has to be in mechanical shape and form. That's counting an instrument."

(How long is it since you left here?) "Well, Doctor, I left here in May. (What date?) I just can't recollect. I should imagine—this is July—it's about six weeks. (What have you done since then?) I have not been doing anything in line of employment. It seems to be very hard to secure just at present in conditions. As far as that is concerned I have done a little of this light labor, and of course the biggest wasn't extraordinary but satisfactory. (How did you happen to come here?) Well, Doctor, truthfully spoken, I will explain it to you how this really became a serious problem. Not it happens that I can memorize—to be exact on the memorandum— a man I know, that is as a friend I know for the past ten years, were having a conversation is discussing a sport problem. Of course, it was like everything else. We became involved on this sport problem and of course, he did not seem to meet with my explanations in the different line of sports, in discussing the affairs of the different people connected with it, baseball. I know of him as far as personality and character, he is marvelous as far as that is concerned. I didn't just ordinarily push him like that. It was only in fun, or fooling, as I can explain it. I took this sudden fall and, of course, my head struck the other automobile and the license plate, which resulted in this injury."

(Was it a severe injury?) "Well, Doctor, I wouldn't say that positively but it was only on the idea of thinking, which I believe. (What kind of treatment did you get in the hospital?) Oh, you mean in the hospital here? Well, Doctor, as I can say, it was wonderful, wonderful. (What was done for you?) There was a sort of, I should really say, operation performed. (What kind?) An operation in regards to keeping the sense of mind always together, not for me, as I can truthfully say, and not to imagine, but really to say or believe, to keep the sense in the mind. (Were you actually operated on?) Oh, yes. (What part of the body?) That I cannot say. I will say this, that I was sort of out of form as far as consciousness."

Left pupil was still dilated. Pupils reacted promptly to light. Deep reflexes were equal and active. The abdominals were active and equal. There was no response to plantar stimulation.

On July 17, when asked to write definition of "frustrate" and "midget," wrote: (frustrate) "Something to Study Personal and Make a Clear Success of this one. Meaning of this said word or it Does Create Confusion. (midget) Actor in Person Performer in Height and size."

The flightiness of the previous case was in this patient substituted for by a queer sort of circumstantiality. The patient found it impossible to end a sentence. He had to correct himself again and again. It was very difficult for him to come to a final conclusion (see especially productions of May 8). This was noticed particularly when he gave definitions. Quite probably his stilted expressions were the result, not only of the localized lesions in the right temporal and frontal lobes, but also of his entire personality. It is remarkable that he could express himself precisely in concrete questions, for instance, concerning baseball players. One may ask whether a left-sided lesion of minor character is not present in this case, too, or whether a right-sided lesion may not provoke pictures of this kind when there is also a more diffuse lesion of the brain. He had an injury of his head six or seven years ago. At any rate, the close similarity of such a speech disturbance to schizophrenic speech disturbances was startling.

However, even in the queer way he gave a definition of a puddle, he never overstepped the boundaries of everyday life. Compare with this three definitions given by a far-progressed schizophrenic woman of 35 years of age. She says: (puddle) (1) "Is a drop of water of Scotch—a rosebud—and soon it goes into four roses to be big enough for a battleship. Ask Einstein, he knows more about it than I do. (2) Mud and water makes most water. (3) That's where the transformation of an ugly duckling into a swan."

CASE 3

H. M., 45 years old, was admitted to Bellevue Psychiatric Hospital October 14, 1933 and discharged November 16, 1933. A brother stated that she had been drinking all her life and had been taking bromides every time she became intoxicated. We had no knowledge of whether or not she had ever taken barbitals. According to a friend, she had been taking twenty to 25 tablets of bromide a day during the previous few weeks. The family history was negative.

On the day of admission the patient stated that she took bromides for her nerves. Her speech was slurred, she was confused and disoriented. She said, "I drank some whiskey; they gave me bromides; I haven't been feeling pretty good; he told me our source is just a source." She showed a forced type of crying. There was an impairment of perception and comprehension.

The physical examination showed that she was toxic, the tongue was coated, a few erythematous macules were present on the left foot and on the left patella, with acne-form eruption on the face. Heart and lungs were negative. Pulse and temperature were normal in the beginning but rose to more than 101°F. on the 24th and 25th and was still elevated on the 26th. The pulse went up to 100°F. The patient appeared dehydrated. Neurologically, the patient showed in the beginning sluggish reaction of the pupils, tremulousness of the tongue, speech difficulties of paraphasic type, but the speech was also slurred and bulbar. The abdominals were absent. There was a left Hoffman and tenderness in the calves; otherwise neurological findings were normal. There were no barbitals in the urine. On October 20, there were 450 mg. of bromides per 100 cc. of blood and on October 25, 263 mg. of bromides per 100 cc. of blood. On October 30, 259 mg. of bromides were found in 100cc. of blood. Blood Wassermann was one plus.

On October 16, the patient said, "I have been taking bromides three months altogether. Don't you think the bromides are beautiful? (What are these?—flowers.) Bromides. (What color?—red.) Bram—scarlet—scarlet bromide. (What is that?—wall.) Fish color. No color. (What color is my hair?) En—the conditions and the productions and conductions. (What is this?—pencil.) It is a piece of brown pencil. It is a pencil. It smells very badly—from firt —disease. I am 34. I am from lisem . . . ."

On October 23, patient said, "I have been away and naturally like two luminaries. They think they are pretty smart."

The patient talked continually. Speech was slurred. Her face had an empty expression. She put her legs on the table. She correctly named her nose and her eyebrows. When asked to name her thumb, she said, "You shake hands with it—shoe," grasped her shoe, and finally said, "thumb," patted the hand of the examiner and said, perseverating three times, "thumb—thumb—thumb." The patient was hyperprosectic and brought details of the outer world into her spontaneous speech.

When a pencil was put in her hand, she wrote in a micrographic way, illegibly but with clear perseverations, changing the direction, and said, "It means anything—nothing—but you write that to my brother." When ordered to copy a figure, she said, "It will not do you any good. You can't prescribe it. You lose your sign." The patient wrote very quickly, and her micrographia was partially due to the increase in speed of writing.

On October 25, the patient was still subdelirious, confused, and showed a cloudy sensorium. It was possible to get her attention for only a few moments at a time. She showed a tendency to perseverate and transform words. She was asked, "How are you feeling?" She said, "Otherwise I am being cold—I am feeling very cold. (How are you?) If I didn't feel so terribly occurilia why—a—well, I imagine that would be the work—don't you have an ocracular-oraculla absolutely. (Where are you?) I think now—I feel very—well, let me get off here—let me get off there that sprinkler. (Where are you?) Something sortly I thought it was for sportly. (Day of the week?) It's a startly—it isn't startly me. (When shown dollar bill, says:) Protograd. (Day of week?) Now I think—it's 18th. (Shown dollar bill) A dollar bill. (Shown five fingers) Five dollar bill. (Shown two fingers) Two dollar bill. (Shown fountain pen) Fountain pen."

On October 31, patient was shown a cover of *Cosmopolitan Magazine* with picture of girl and was asked what was on the picture. She replied, "I think it's a pretty nice looking picture, don't you. You could go for that yourself, couldn't you? (What is this magazine?) I think it's a Cosmaport—Costapotal—I can't say it, my teeth are out—Cosmopolitan. (Shown picture of bottle of beer —what is it?) Picture of bottle of ketchup. Beer—I am not a beer drinker I think that's why. Would you beer—would you draw beer red? (Picture of Camel cigarette advertisement with girl in red evening clothes is presented to her.) You have me admiring this just looking at it just getting an impression—well I suppose a girl admiring a ball game using a particular brand of Camel—cold either—no coal or Camel—she is evidently doing something. (Shown very colorful illustration of a woman, a young girl, a young boy and a bull dog, books and fruit—what do you think of the picture?) There's nothing to think about. (Picture?) Cake of fruit there—and some books. (What else?) I see a girl with something around her fingers here—looks like something here—something metal to brush with. (Points to flowers.) Something like a flowering pot—the boys and the girls are flushing—with a hose like. (Where is hose?) The only place the game—where the hose would be—what walk out of the—wall would have to be taken for granted really."

She generally walked about in an aimless fashion, mumbling to herself incoherently. Her general stream of talk was free and voluble with a tendency to rambling and flight of ideas. Her capacity for attention was still not very good but much better than previously; the patient was no longer in a subdelirious state, but she showed more of a Korsakoff Syndrome, with confabulations, marked retention impairment, and recent memory defects. The mood was generally very amiable and friendly. Patient was engaging in her manner, but inclined to become tearful abruptly without apparent provocation. She still showed a marked difficulty in speech coordination, which resulted in quasi-paraphasic talk with literal, as well as verbal transpositions, but at times she was distinctly dysnomic. When shown colored as well as black and white illustrations and photographs, she showed an inability to grasp the general import of the picture. She picked out occasional details, but even then elaborated in a confabulatory manner upon the character and purpose of the details and then showed a flight of ideas.

During the next week the patient cleared up considerably, and her only remembrance about the psychotic episode was that she thought she was hanging upon a pier out of the water and was in danger of drowning. "Maybe it was because I was in a continual bath." She had no memory of the actual happenings on the ward and did not recognize her handwriting. It was not possible to get a deeper insight into her personality structure. She had had a high school education and was moderately promiscuous. She worked as a telephone operator and said she drank because she was unhappy with her husband.

This case was one of bromide intoxication. She was certainly confused. She had difficulties in perception and picked up only details. She was distractable; she confabulated. It is difficult to separate the speech disturbances from the perception disturbances, but she had doubtlessly paraphasic signs. She used new words, as for instance, "luminaries," and at times her speech was almost completely paraphasic. She said, "But I told you slippers and you and how you wear other drapes—it is rather overcustomed—or friend to friend." She called the thumb "you shake hands with it—shoes." There were also clear signs of perseveration. Her handwriting showed these same characteristics.

She also showed the same difficulties in ending sentences as did the previous patient. When asked, "What do you think of the general situation?" she replied, "What do you think of the general situation—you don't think so good—in what position—you know all the trigonomists—you offer them pretty well to us—don't you?" The speech disturbances broke into her thought processes. She said: "I never saw a bull dog eating pieces of tulips—did you? I suppose it is supposed to be silly—bit—it's silly—a boy eating a piece of tulip—it's ridiculous—you do hesitate—naturally—when you are used to your teeth every day. When I talk now I evidently go too fast for my own mind—don't you think so?"

The general mood of amiability and the increase in speech impulses were characteristic of the paraphasic patient. Confusion and speech disturbance were coordinated. They influenced each other. The use of queer and stilted expressions was also manifest here. We deal again with a slight lesion of the Wernicke region in combination with a general disturbance. The resulting picture was not very different from some of the speech disturbances occurring in schizophrenics. We consider disturbances of this kind as rather typical for a group of toxic psychoses.

Wuth (1927), Sharpe (1934), Diethelm (1930), and Levin (1932), writing on the subject of bromide intoxication, mention nothing about such speech disturbances.

Dimitz and Schilder (1921) have seen a similar picture in acute encephalitis, with delirium, and, occasionally, in alcholics. I (1928b) have described cases in which a toxic infectious psychosis was coupled with paraphasic signs. The following case shows a rather similar picture of the same problem.

CASE 4

E. P., age 45, a graduate nurse, was admitted May 15 and discharged May 29, 1934. She was brought to Bellevue Hospital from her residence because she had become noisy, excited, and had acted as if she had had a stroke.

Her husband gave the history that she was first taken ill four years previously, at which time she was very erratic and flighty. After being kept at home three months, she was put in a private nursing home where she remained eighteen months. There she was quiet, depressed, heard voices at times, thought she was getting radio messages from the bed springs. Since then she seemed normal, but insisted on living away from her husband because he had put her in a hospital.

On the night before admission, while waiting at her cousin's home, she began to laugh hilariously. Her mouth became twisted and then she could make only guttural sounds. The husband added that she used to have convulsions before being sent away, when she would froth at the mouth and be unconscious for a time, although tongue biting and incontinence were not noted.

On admission, patient stated: "I want to see my sister-in-law. I should not have done it. I don't know what girl name was. Her doctor—my sister come about ten o'clock. She wanted to wait until the train came."

Physical examination revealed the pupils to be slightly irregular, they reacted sluggishly to light. Heart tones were of good quality, rhythm was totally irregular. Electrocardiogram showed auricular fibrillation. Lungs were clear. Abdomen was negative. Knee jerks were equal and active. There was a suggestive Hoffman on the right. Positive Babinski was present on the right. Speech was aphasic. Patient had difficulty in naming parts of her body and following directions. Blood Wassermann was negative. X ray showed moderate enlargement of the heart. Enlarged heart suggested presence of double mitral heart disease.

When interviewed on the ward later in the day, she said: "I live now 425 Lexington Avenue. (It says 591) Yes. No, I said 591. (How old are you?) 27—45. I am 26. I was born in '28. No, never had any children. (Mother and father not living?) In 1928 my mother was buried in Whiting, Indiana, and my father was buried in Bayview. (Name of the place?) Yes. Bellevue. Today is 13—May—28. I will be 40 years in May. (What month is this?) This is 1934."

(Why are you here?) "Why I don't know. You see my husband—I have been separated for about a year. I just moved the 23rd of May—and then my sister lives at 1425—no, she is 225 West 46th Street and her name is Mrs. McDermott. (Why in the hospital?) Why I don't know. And my sister and her husband came about eleven o'clock. Dr. N. came and wanted me to agree to disagree—he wanted me to disagree. He want me to take this chest off and I don't know—I don't believe in it. You see, I am studying now for two—years Christian Science. (What kind of work do you do?) Well, I am studying singing—in May 29, 1921 I married. I was in the French Hospital in 1934. (You were in a sanitorium?) No, well, that's a mistake—no my sister—he took me—I don't know what the name of it. (Since you are out you

want to live by yourself?) Yes, because—he doesn't know—he said
it was a fatigue—a fatigue—my husband said so—I don't want to.
If he took me—if he said over there—I have stayed there 1925—in
1925—in 1913—now that's where I studied in French Hospital in
1934 I am telling you—in 1934 and Miss Jordan—Miss Jordan is
there—because I don't want to live with him, not after he's agreed
to give me that place. This woman doesn't know anything about
Christian Science."

When told to put her left hand on her left ear, she did this
correctly. She was told to put her right hand on left and did this
correctly. She correctly placed her right hand on her nose. When
she was asked to show the little finger of the left hand, she said:
"Left finger—it is the finger right hand. (Thumb) The thumb.
(Index finger) The finger—the pointer. (Middle finger) This is the
third. (Ring finger) The fourth. (Ring finger left hand) It is the
finger for my wedding ring and my engagement ring—it is the
fourth finger for the right hand. The right hand for the left—the
right hand is for the left. (Thumb left hand) The thumber—t-h-u-m.
(Index finger left hand) It is the third finger. (Little finger) This
is the third finger of the left hand—the left hand—moving it
up (correct). (Index finger) This is the left finger—left finger.
(What way am I moving up?) Down (correct). (Thumb) Thumb—
down—up, I mean (correct)."

At times patient was slightly euphoric, at other times somewhat irritable. Conversation was sometimes a confused jargon.
She was repetitious. She was oriented at times; at other times appeared bewildered, incoherent. No delusions or hallucinations
were elicited.

On May 21, the patient stated: "I don't know why I am here.
It's my sister. A girl ran right out and got a doctor. This is Bellevue, 21st Street, May 1934. I haven't been sick. I don't want to live
with my husband. His home is in Massachusetts. He goes there
three or four days a week. I'm going to earn my living.

"This stuff is a mesmerism of hypnotism. He won't give me
any money at all. I've been studying to take voice. He doesn't
want me to do that. It's very fully, the idea of going away for three

or four days. He refused to let me draw out $1000 to pay the insurance. It's $80. It's $3000 you see. It's $2000. It's $3080—$38.50—that's my rent $5. I have steam heat, electric, I can live in two rooms."

(Voices?) "No, I did not hear voices. Not at all. (Were you in a hospital before?) No. (In Brooklyn?) No, my husband elected—he went and followed up the fire escape—he brought me to 183. (Why?) He first brought me there and she opened the doors. (Radio from the springs?) No, never at all. That woman just kept me there and thought that was science and health. I don't know who I was there."

Patient was still very circumstantial. She expressed trends against her husband. She had no insight into her recent acute illness. She denied hallucinations.

On May 28, patient stated: "Some place in Massachusetts there is a sanitorium for people who are interested in science but you have to be a member or have to have different people sign or some such reference for this. He brought me to this place—103 Gates Avenue, Brooklyn. She locked me into a top room with a skylight. I must have stayed there about a year. I was awfully surprised when I saw the papers were dated December 25, 1931. (Why were you surprised?) The people had sold the house and gone to Long Island and left me there. My husband came and brought me food after two or three days. Then a plumber came and opened the door and opened it—said he wanted to know what it was. I just got out the door and down the steps and out."

(What is a puddle?) "I should think the Ku Klux Klan."

(Believe in God?) "I believe in one Supreme Power—we just know it—we feel it. I know that I have been getting along very well and doing very well but my husband was not at all interested in Christian Science—I was and that is the whole nutshell of it. He was a Catholic and I was turning Christian Scientist. The soul is an expression of the thought of God. What could hold us up unless the One Mind held us up? God gives us good food. If you will live right and think right, you will find you will be well provided for—it is up to man to know how to pick it up."

Patient was elated. She talked in a queer, circumstantial way.

Patient wrote hastily, erased, made mistakes, wrote "hs" instead of "is," and did not find the right words. When told to draw a picture of a man, she said: "I can draw flowers. I never drew a picture of a man. (What is the difference between a child and midget?) Midget is prenatal care. (Lake and river?) Lake is usually salt water—I mean the other. River is usually salt water—lake is not salt. River is usually narrow—it usually connects with cities. Lake is usually wide. (The Mississippi River is wide.) There are five rivers—there are five different lakes. (Difference between a lie and an error?) A mistake is when people usually make that mistake. An arrow is directed among a lot of people. For instance if a man came out and gave a talk about Democracy or Roosevelt —he could swing the people. Lie is deliberate—is very very wrong as records prove. Error is a lie against truth. (Difference between a bush and a tree?) When a bush grows, it just grows right down and a tree grows up. A bush—you take the currant bush—any kind of a bush that doesn't grow up—lilac tree of course, sometimes grows up to the trees. We have had them about three feet high at home and I have seen them as high sometimes as an oak tree."

She repeated very complicated sentences correctly and wrote dictation very well. She wrote rapidly and did not make the same mistakes as in spontaneous writing. At this time she showed paraphasias in writing and disturbances in thinking and she talked in a stilted way.

This was a patient who seemingly had a psychosis of a schizoid type. It could not be decided definitely whether this was a schizophrenic episode or a schizoid reaction. It may have been in connection with the heart disease, but the schizoid reaction remains. The patient apparently had remained schizoid in her personality. She had a stroke, followed by a slight sensory aphasia. Her definitions showed the same queer and stilted character we have seen in the other cases. For instance, she said: "A lecture is a subject telling about a certain subject—the theory and the publisher. (What is perfunctory?) That is a subject—it explains progression. (Frustrate?) The question which is not electioneer—is pertaining to the lecture—K-r-u-is Latin isn't it? It means a subject just when you work out the principles of the subject. Perhaps in urine analysis or something like that. (Envelope?) You write up people and put an envelope in—it is a folded page. I have studied all the languages."

One sees here again the perseveration, the roundabout way of expression, the influence the wrong speech has on the thinking processes. This was shown, for example, in her definition of brunette. "Is usually blond, blond, complexion and hair, usually blond complexion." Her writings showed the same characteristics. When definition of puddle was asked for in writing, she wrote "mixture of thoughts, muddled water, other sand—with in his" and continued writing spontaneously, "puddle, mixture, ice cream soda, chocolate and vanilla soda." The patient showed a great urge in writing, she was rather macrographic, in contrast to the previous patient who showed micrographia.

The disturbances at the time her aphasia improved were particularly interesting. It is possible that the patient's schizoid character partially influenced the way in which she expressed herself in the aphasia. On the other hand, we must say that the slight aphasia led again (perhaps with the help of personality factors) to stilted expressions and roundabout ways of talking.

This case leads almost to the threshold of schizophrenic speech. We therefore conclude that a slight sensory aphasia due to a particular lesion of the brain can lead to speech disturbances in which the stilting of expressions, mannerisms, and perseverations play the outstanding parts. Instead of the full-blown paraphasia we find the use of unusual words which may lead to unusual thoughts. The slight paraphasias will be particularly noticed when there is a strong urge to speech, with elation and a general increase of impulses. A similar effect will occur under the influence of a general confusion and schizoid personality; such factors may increase the wrong choice of words. The influence of such speech disturbances on the thinking process is particularly great. In all the cases mentioned, the mannerisms and the stilting remained nearer to the everyday life and did not lead as far in the realm of the personality as do the schizophrenic speech disturbances, in which archaic structures are more noticeable. It is true that the combination of aphasic disturbances and schizoid personality in confusional states may diminish these differences.

Kleist (1934) has pointed to lesions of the temporal and occipital region which provoked thought disturbances similar to the schizophrenic thought and speech disturbances he called "paralogic." He has spoken about paralogias in which, instead of the correct representation, a wrong one is reproduced or only part of it comes into the consciousness, or else the representations are fused. This disturbance, which is akin to paraphasias, is a disturbance in process of thinking and representing before the final verbal formulation is made.

In an earlier paper, Kleist (1914) had already pointed to the similarity of the neologisms in aphasics and schizophrenics. One of his patients called the fin of a fish "Schwimmflugel" (swim wing) and a lamp "Flammenlampe" (flame lamp). Kleist's ideas are further expanded in the papers by Adolph Schneider (1927) and Fleischhacker (1930). Schilder and Sugar (1926) point to the similarities and differences between schizophrenics and aphasic speech disturbances. The formulations of Carl Schneider (1925) are certainly too schematic. He concludes, for instance: "In aphasia the speech disturbances are always in the form of incomplete construction and there are no tendencies to citatory speech and no derailment due to the flight of ideas" (p. 251). A paper of Walter Riese (1928) is of special interest from our point of view. He reports about a case who has no insight into his defect. This patient calls an electric lamp "Leuchtlampe" (illuminating lamp). A voluminous book he calls "Tiefakt, eine tiefaktige Sache" (deep act, a matter of deep act); he calls a stethoscope "Ohrpuffer" (ear pusher); he calls an open pair of scissors "Scherenschwung" (swinging of scissors); he calls a bunch of keys "schwarzes oxydiertes Taschentuch" (black oxidized handkerchief). Riese emphasized that these reactions show the character of primitive language. They named in a more naïve way the perceptive details of the object. They were therefore less abstract than the language generally used. Riese was inclined to believe that these naïve reactions were only possible when the patients were not aware of their speech defect, and he believed that such reactions occurred as a result of lesions of the corpus callosum. Our own cases could not, of course, be used from the point of view of localization, but it was true that our patients also had no appreciation of their speech disturbances. Their approach, too, remained naïve.

We are inclined to believe that impulse disturbances that manifest themselves in micrographia and macrographia may be one of the factors responsible for the lack of insight into their defects, since such impulse disturbances are commonly found in sensory aphasia cases. In these sensory aphasia cases, insight was lacking.

It was of particular importance to compare Riese's remarks with some of the conclusions of William A. White (1926). "The language of schizophrenia is of a lower order of abstraction than normal adult language. . . . The thinking and the speech of a schizophrenic while of a lower order of abstraction nevertheless make use of words which we are accustomed to use to express a higher order. This discrepancy is one reason why such language is so hard for us to understand" (pp. 412-413).

SUMMARY

Our findings point to the importance of aphasic signs in seemingly confused utterances in toxic psychosis and allow at least a preliminary approach to these psychoses from the point of view of brain pathology. We wish to emphasize the importance of general factors of an organic nature, as well as personality factors in these cases of speech disturbances due to localized lesions of the brain. We also describe a particular type of speech disturbances after head injury. We believe that speech disturbances of minor degree coupled with impulse disturbances have a deep influence on the thinking processes in general lesions of the brain of traumatic and toxic origin. Although the speech disturbances observed are not identical to schizophrenic speech disturbances, an inner relation doubtlessly exists and points to the possibility of an organic nucleus for schizophrenic speech disturbances.

CHAPTER TWELVE

Experiments in Repetition and Recall

We have studied the problem of memory by what we think is a new method. We read a short story to our subjects and ordered them to repeat the story again and again until they were exhausted and refused to continue.

This technique was suggested by the experiments of Karsten (1928) on psychic saturation, such experiments having been previously suggested by Kurt Lewin. A similar technique has been used by F. Hoppe (1933) on suckling babies and by Anna Freud (1930) on menstruating women. Karsten directed her subjects to draw fence pickets on sheets of paper until they lost all desire to continue the work. The qualitative analysis revealed the following features:

> At the beginning, the side of a page constitutes a unit of effort. Later a dissolution of the original configuration occurs, variability in performance being prominent in the final stages. Concurrently, errors and loss in quality appear, and eventually the task loses its meaning.

Appeared originally in the *Journal of Genetic Psychology*, 51: 163-187, 1937, Frank J. Curran, co-author.

The work not only becomes disorderly and loosely connected, devoid of definite boundaries and termini, but breaks up into little independent fragments. A larger whole has disintegrated.

Although Karsten has also used more complicated patterns, the task demanded from the subject remains simple. Furthermore, no problem of memory was involved, since the subjects had a pattern before them and the pattern was so simple that it was not liable to be forgotten. Our own experiments deal less with the problem of exhaustion than with that of retention and recall. We were interested to learn which parts of a story would appear when repeated recall is demanded after one exposition.

After various stories had been tried out, we used for the principal part of our investigations the following story:

Olaf Nelson—died here—today—of burns suffered—when a match ignited—his grass skirt—in a hula dance comedy—during the American Legion—convention.—District Attorney—Brown—announced —that he would file—manslaughter charges—against Mr. Moore.— Moore—lighted—a cigarette—and tossed away the match.—Brown interviewed—fifteen witnesses—who said Moore—deliberately tossed—the match to Nelson's costume.

This story, which, as the dashes indicate, consists of 24 items, was read slowly and aloud to the subject once. The subject was instructed to listen carefully and to repeat the story as often as he could. He was told: "We want to see how often you can repeat the story before getting exhausted." We used 21 subjects. They were either medical students or student nurses or patients who had come to the hospital in a state of acute excitement or intoxication, but who had recovered at the time the test was taken. One case of organic memory disturbance, one Korsakoff case, and one schizophrenic case were used for comparison. We did not study the results merely from a qualitative point of view; we checked, in every repetition, whether each of the 24 items was (a) correct, (b) changed, (c) absent, or (d) whether other items were added. After we had finished the qualitative survey we were able to use a more elaborate scheme for tabulation, which has been applied to seven protocols. In two of the normal cases and in the Korsakoff case, both methods were applied. The following scheme was used:

1. Number of words of the story
   a. In the original story
   b. In last repetition
   c. In present report
2. Number of added words
   a. To original story
   b. To last repetition
3. Number of omitted words
   a. From original story
   b. From last repetition
4. Phrase substituted by similar phrase
5. Phrase added to story
6. Added phrase expressing merely attitude of subject
   a. Impatience
   b. Disgust, uncertainty
   c. Jokes
   d. Rebellion
   e. Gabby or talkative attitude
7. Substitution of word which is a synonym (A) or is similar (B)
8. Substitution of a word which has a more general meaning
9. Substitution by a more specific word
10. Substitution by a more common word
11. Substitution by a less common word
12. Perseveration
13. Emotionally stronger
14. Emotionally lighter
15. Deprecation
16. Colloquialism (vulgarity)
17. **Substitution by a more moral word**
18. Substitution by a less moral word
19. Newly added words which do not substitute other words
    a. Change in individual names

20. Items omitted
21. Perseveration of mistakes
    a. In individual names
22. Correction of mistakes
    a. In individual names
23. Reappearance of omitted words
24. Reappearance of omitted sentences
25. Changes in the place (location) of a word: ante-
    position (A), postposition (B)
26. Reversal between two items

When a change fell into two categories, the more important
one was tabulated. The title of the story was read to the subject,
but no reproduction of this was asked for.

We reproduce one of our protocols taken from a healthy
twenty-year-old woman, E. S.

First trial: "Olaf Nelson died today because of serious injuries
he received when his costume was set afire. It was during a hula
dance comedy given by some convention that a Mr. Moore lighted
a cigarette and threw the match away. The D.A. interviewed
about fifteen people who said that Mr. Moore purposely threw the
match at Mr. Olaf's grass skirt, Mr. Nelson's grass skirt. The D.A.
is bringing some charge against him."

Second trial: "A Mr. Olaf Nelson died last night from serious
injuries which he received when his grass skirt caught afire at a
hula dance comedy given by some big convention. The D.A. questioned the guests, and about fifteen of them said that a Mr. Moore
had deliberately thrown a match at Mr. Nelson's grass skirt after
Mr. Moore had lighted a cigarette. Charges are to be brought
against Mr. Moore."

Third trial: "A Mr. Olaf Nelson died last night from serious
injuries [pause] after [pause] his grass skirt which he was wearing
caught afire. I know the story, but I just don't feel good, that's
why I'm hesitating. I've served six days here and I want to go
home. I came here voluntarily. The D.A. interviewed the guests

and fifteen of them said that a Mr. Moore deliberately threw a match at Mr. Nelson's grass skirt. This all took place at a hula dance comedy given by some convention. Charges are to be brought against Mr. Moore."

Fourth trial: "A Mr. Olaf Nelson died from serious injuries received when the grass skirt which he was wearing caught afire. The D.A. interviewed the guests and fifteen of them gave the same story. They said that a Mr. Moore, who had thrown the match after lighting a cigarette, had thrown it purposely at Mr. Nelson's grass skirt. This all took place at a party, at a hula dance comedy given by a convention. So charges are to be brought against Mr. Moore [speaks slowly with long pauses]."

Fifth trial: "Again? A big Swede [jocularly]—a Mr. Olaf Nelson—died last night from serious injuries received when his grass skirt which he was wearing caught afire. Fifteen of the guests told the D.A. that a Mr. Moore deliberately threw a match at Mr. Nelson's grass skirt. Charges are to be made against Mr. Moore. This all occurred at a hula dance comedy given by some convention. That's all."

Sixth trial: "A Mr. Olaf Nelson died last night from serious injuries which he received when his grass skirt which he was wearing caught afire. The D.A. questioned the guests and fourteen of them said that a Mr. Moore threw the match deliberately at Mr. Nelson's grass skirt. Charges are to be made against Mr. Moore. This all occurred—the accident occurred—because it might have been an accident—at a hula dance comedy given by some convention. That's all."

Seventh trial: "A Mr. Olaf Nelson died last from serious injuries received when the costume which he was wearing caught afire. The guests told the D.A. that a Mr. Moore deliberately threw a match at Mr. Olaf's grass skirt. Charges are to be made against Mr. Moore. The accident occurred during a hula-comedy given by some convention."

Eighth trial: "Enjoy yourself. I don't care. Write from now to doomsday. I'm getting a little bit nuts from this. Maybe they're trying to make a mental case of me, even though I'm not one. . . .

But I'm getting a kick out of it just as much as they are. A Jew named Freedman is a darned pest always giving me tests [good humoredly]. A man—a Mr. Olaf Nelson died last night from injuries received when the costume he was wearing—fifteen of the guests told the D.A. that a Mr. Moore deliberately threw a match at Mr. Nelson's costume. The charges are being brought up against Mr. Moore. This—the accident occurred in the midst of a hula dance comedy given by some convention. That's all. Satisfied yet?"

Ninth trial: "A Mr. Olaf Nelson died recently from severe burns after his costume caught afire by a match thrown carelessly in his direction. The guests told the D.A. that a Mr. Moore threw the match purposely at Mr. Nelson's costume. Serious charges are being made against Mr. Moore. The accident occurred during a hula dance comedy given by some convention. 'S all."

Tenth trial: "A Mr. Olaf Nelson died last night from serious injuries received when his costume caught afire. The guests told the D.A. that a Mr. Moore threw a match purposely at Mr. Nelson's costume. Serious charges are being brought against Mr. Moore. This all occurred at a hula dance comedy given by some convention."

Eleventh trial: (She goes to window) "A Mr. Olaf Nelson died recently from serious burns which he received when his costume caught afire. The guests told the D.A. that a Mr. Moore threw the match purposely at Mr. Nelson's costume. Serious charges are being made against Mr. Moore. The accident occurred during a hula dance comedy given by some convention. 'S all."

Twelfth trial: "A Mr. Olaf Nelson died recently from serious burns which he received when his costume caught afire. The guests told the D.A. that a Mr. Moore purposely threw a match at Mr. Nelson's costume. Series charges are being made against Mr. Moore. The accident occurred during a hula dance given by some convention."

Thirteenth trial: The next day the subject said: "Mr. Olaf Nelson died. I will draw you a picture instead." Subject drew the head of a woman and refused to go on with the Nelson story.

TABLE 1
QUANTITATIVE CHANGES IN REPETITION

	Comparison with Original Story				Comparison with Preceding Repetition			
	Number of Items				*Number of Items*			
Trial	correctly repeated	changed	omitted	added	correctly repeated	changed	omitted	added
1.	6	14	4	2				
2.	5	15	4	1	6	12	3	1
3.	5	13	6	8	14	4	2	7
4.	4	16	4	3	15	6	6	2
5.	6	11	7	6	12	6	3	4
6.	5	14	5	5	14	3	2	3
7.	4	13	7	3	13	7	4	0
8.	3	13	8	8 + 13	13	6	1	5 + 13
9.	2	14	8	5	11	10	13 + 4	4
10.	4	12	8	2	14	6	3	0
11.	5	11	8	3	13	5	0	1
12.	4	12	8	1	17	1	1	0

Table 1 immediately confirms our qualitative results and gives them a more definite shape. It can be seen that material not available for one repetition may be available for the next repetition. The comparison of items correctly reproduced in the different repetitions shows that continuous changes take place. It is of interest that the number of omitted items shows changes only in the first seven repetitions and that after the eighth repetition the number of omitted items remains constant. It is also noteworthy that after an emotional outburst at the eighth repetition the number of additions decreases steadily. It is furthermore interesting that the subject tends to cling to her version of the story and of the nineteen items produced in the eleventh repetition, seventeen are correctly repeated in the twelfth repetition, only one is omitted. We can conclude that a rather active process of continuous change and testing comes to a relative rest and that a stabilized pattern occurs after the eighth repetition. The number of words omitted from the original story increases at the third repetition, but remains almost constant after the fourth repetition. At the twelfth repetition the number of omitted words is only 41 whereas the number of omitted words in the tenth repetition was 47. The number of added words goes up with the emotional outburst at the eighth repetition, but decreases considerably toward the end of the experiment. In the last repetition, only six new words are added and seven words of the previous repetition are omitted. Of the other categories of the general scheme, nine and ten are particularly interesting. Substitutions of words by words that are more specific are infrequent in comparison with the substitution of common words. Perseveration is encountered much more often toward the end of the series. Changes in the location of words are common. Words that have been omitted may reappear at any time.

A second protocol may confirm our opinion that we do not deal with chance results in the first protocol.

R. W., a normal subject, age 27 shows the following results:

(1) "Olaf died here today while doing a hula dance from a match touched his skirt. The D.A. something—"

(2) "Olaf died here today while doing a magic dance, from a match that touched his skirt. The D.A. said he has witness."

(3) "Olaf died here today while doing a magic dance, from a match that touched his skirt. The D.A. says he has witnesses for something."

(4) "Worlof died here today while doing a magic dance from a match that touched his skirt while dancing for some kind of society or something."

(5) "Some District Attorney or something. Worlof died here today while dancing a magic dance from a match that touched his grass skirt."

(6) "Worlof or Orlaf died here today while doing a magic dance from a match that touched his grass skirt. Some kind of D.A. or something."

(7) "Gracious—Orlof, whoever he is, he died here today—no —yes—while doing a magic dance—no—yes—a match touched

his grass skirt. From a burn—I didn't say that before. He was at a charity ball. The D.A. said something about witnesses. Twelve witnesses."

(8) "Orlof died here today from a burn while doing a magic dance from a match that touched his grass skirt. That's as far as I can go. I can't get in that about the D.A. and the twelve witnesses. I'm usually good at remembering things." (Subject interrupts continually to tell about troubles.)

(9) "I have to laugh. Orlof died here today while doing a magic hula-hula dance from a match that touched his grass skirt. Now, that's as far as I go—D.A. and twelve witnesses— charity organization."

(10) "Orlof died here today from a burn while doing a magic hula-hula dance from a match which touched his grass skirt. The D.A. says that he has twelve witness as far as I can remember."

(11) (Sulks) "Orlof died here today while doing a magic hula-hula dance. The D.A. says he has twelve witnesses."

(12) "Orlof says—Worlof died here today while doing a magic hula-hula dance. The witness says he has twelve witnesses." (Subject weeps.)

On the following day, without repetition of the original story, she said: "Orlof died here today while doing a magic hula dance from a burn which touched from a match which touched his grass skirt. And the D.A. said he has twelve witnesses that saw him burned."

Omitting the qualitative analysis, we proceed with the discussion of Table 2. It is characteristic that, whereas in the first four repetitions only two items were correct, the number of correct items from the fifth to the eighth repetition was three, and that in the ninth repetition even four items were correctly reproduced. At the eleventh and twelfth repetition the number of correct items dropped again to two, but rose the next day to three. The number of omissions was least in the seventh and tenth repetitions. Also, this subject had a greater tendency to stick to her story, and the number of items taken over from the one story to the other rose to nine in the eighth and ninth repetitions. The drop in the last two repetitions was evidently due to the emotional factors that pro-

TABLE 2
QUANTITATIVE CHANGES IN REPETITION

| | Comparison with Original Story | | | | Comparison with Preceding Repetition | | | |
| | *Number of Items* | | | | *Number of Items* | | | |
Trial	correctly repeated	changed	omitted	added	correctly repeated	changed	omitted	added
1.	2	5	17	2				
2.	2	7	15	1	8	1	0	3
3.	2	7	15	3	9	1	0	1
4.	2	4	18	5	6	1	4	4
5.	3	5	16	3	6	1	3	3
6.	3	6	15	4	8	1	0	2
7.	3	8	13	10	7	1	2	11
8.	3	6	15	5	9	1	8	3
9.	4	4	16	5	9	2	3	3
10.	3	8	13	3	7	3	2	2
11.	2	6	16	0	7	0	4	0
12.	2	4	18	4	6	0	2	1
	NEXT DAY				WITHOUT REPETITION			
13.	3	8	13	6	7	2	1	6

voked her crying. It seems that her emotions destroyed the comparatively stabilized pattern she had reached between the eighth and tenth repetitions. The number of words omitted from the original story remained quite constant, but the number of added words continually decreased. Substitutions of words by words with a more general meaning were common, as were substitutions by words that are more common. Individual names were changed. Sometimes more moral words were used, sometimes synonyms. Perseveration of mistakes played an enormous part.

DISCUSSION

When the story had been read to the subject, an impression must have remained. This impression was the basis for the recall. According to our experimental procedure, all recalls had to go back to this primary impression. We may call this impression the memory trace. It is easy to see that each recall is different from the preceding one. We may form the opinion that the trace remains constant and that every recall brings different sides of the trace into appearance. It does not seem very likely that the trace should be stabilized. It is much more probable that the trace itself undergoes an organization and that the recalls merely register the organization that takes place. It is true that the experiences of psychoanalysis make it very probable that traces have a much greater stability than one usually supposes. The psychoanalytic method can unearth traces based upon experiences in very early childhood. Memory consists, as Freud has emphasized, of two different systems, one system retaining the trace in its original form, the other system consisting of an elaboration of the original trace by condensation, displacement, and symbolization. Experimental studies by Schilder (1924) have led to identical conclusions. The great persistence of original traces also appears in experiments in hypnosis in which seemingly forgotten material can be brought forward. The trace and its recall can be separated from each other, but only artificially. It depends upon the total situation which part of the memory material can be utilized. We therefore come to the conclusion that in our experiments we dealt not only with changes in recall, but also with changes in the organization of traces. Our experiments clearly showed that a change in the trace from repetition to repetition did not consist merely of a fading of the trace and the lessening of its efficiency. Again and again in our protocols, words and sentences not available at a previous recall became available at a later recall. Even from one day to another an improvement in recall often took place. The change was insufficiently described by the mere hint of quantitative changes in the trace. It is true there were some general characteristics. The greatest loss in the efficiency of the trace often occurred in the beginning, during the first, second, and third recall. However, even the first recall showed signs of a very active mental process. Phrases were substituted by similar phrases, words were substituted by synonyms, by more general or by more specific terms, and by words that were more or less common.

All shades of emotion were expressed in the series of recalls in the choice of words. It was obvious that a total personality was involved in the processes of the organization of phrases in which the verbal formulation played a very important part. With the continuation of the recalls, it became obvious that once the individual had organized a trace, he had a decided tendency to stick to this organization, which seemed to originate from his particular attitude. The right columns of our tables clearly show this. We may speak about perseveration. In all our protocols the subject tended to come to a relative stabilization of the process of organizing the traces. It is obvious from our protocols, especially from the right columns, that the activity of the organization diminished and the changes became rather stabilized. A definite pattern was formed. This pattern was only relatively, not absolutely stable. It seems that the individuals were willing enough to go on with repetitions until this pattern was reached, and that their unwillingness to go on was very closely related to a definite formation of the pattern. The emotion and the organization are simply two sides of the same fundamental process that leads to saturation. We deal with a process of great activity, which in our opinion, reflects what is going on with every trace. The memory traces in these experiments also very clearly showed the forces paramount in verbal development and verbal formulation. We found an outspoken tendency to substitute specific and rare words by more common words. There is a leveling tendency in language.

We were interested in comparing the results obtained in normals with the results obtained in pathological cases. It is obvious from Table 3, which represents the record of a schizophrenic girl, how little interest the patient had in the material offered to her. After the third repetition, no item of the story was utilized, not even in an altered way. The patient still remained interested in her own production and 40 items were taken over from her third repetition to her fourth repetition, but eventually she did not even maintain interest in her own story. We reproduce the first and the fifth repetition.

TABLE 3
QUANTITATIVE CHANGES IN REPETITION

	Comparison with Original Story				Comparison with Preceding Repetition			
	Number of Items				*Number of Items*			
Trial	correctly repeated	changed	omitted	added	correctly repeated	changed	omitted	added
1.	0	9	15	20				
2.	0	0	24	46	0	0	9	44
3.	0	5	19	53	24	5	24	21
4.	0	0	24	112	40	5	5	39
5.	0	0	24	48	8	8	66	16
6.	0	0	24	25	0	0	32	18

First trial: "Mr. Moore has deliberately let a match toss away and set five or six people on fire. That was in San Francisco. I believe he's still in jail yet. I believe that Mr. Moore the District Attorney ordered the investigation to keep him in jail for tossing a match and setting a bomb and killing so many people. I can't memorize that. It's impossible. I'm giving my statement as far as what you said."

Fifth trial: "I don't even know the man. I am just guessing in my own mind. What's the idea of doing this? Just to pass the time. I don't know any more he is out of office six years. I remember the train, the bomb and he being arrested three hours after. He was seventeen years in jail. Oh yes, I think he was married. I believe on account of the people accusing him it was because of his wife and home. He was a pretty young man when he went in, but he is pretty old 'bugger' now, but still he is able to hold a job in the bank and support his family. No more now. I have to beat it."

This is a clear-cut instance of someone who was less interested in the recall of the trace than in expressing her own emotional trends.

More relevant to the topic are the results in cases with memory disturbances on an organic basis. We add a protocol of a

42-year-old woman with severe memory disturbances of an organic type. The nature of the organic process from which she was suffering could not be ascertained. The patient showed no tendency to confabulation. The story had to be read to her twice before she could be induced to repeat it.

(1) "Olaf Nelson died from burns from a lighted match from his skirt."

(2) "Olaf Nelson died from burns from a lighted match from his skirt."

(3, 4, 5) Repetitions are identical, in spite of the urging of the experimenter.

(6, 7, 8, 9) Repetition "from his skirt" is substituted by "to his skirts."

After the ninth repetition, the patient complains: "It is hard to repeat it when you merely hear it."

The patient is now ordered to read the story herself aloud.

The tenth repetition, however, is still identical.

At the eleventh repetition, the patient adds, "Moore died from the burns of a match lighted in a dance comedy hall."

(12) "Wilson, what's his first name, Olaf, Odolf Wilson died from burns from a match that lit his skirts."

(13) "Odolf Wilson died from burns of a match that lit his skirts in a comedy dance hall."

(14) Identical.

(15) Identical, but omits "in a comedy dance hall."

(16, 17) Identical to 15.

(18) "Olaf Wilson died from burns from a lighted match to his skirts."

(19 to 24) Identical.

(25) The examiner tells her, "Take your time, tell the whole story." The patient repeats and adds, "That occurred in a comedy dance hall." Asked whether her report is correct, she says: "Wilson comes in somewhere."

(26, 27) Identical to 24.

(28) She adds, "In a comedy dance hall." Urged whether the

story is complete, she adds, "Who is this; who was produced; manslaughter; he was charged with manslaughter?"

(29) Identical. Patient adds, "I was thinking who was charged with manslaughter. Wilson was it, was it not? He was the cause of the matches; manslaughter that is more of a hit, more of a fight."

The patient was given an hour's rest and then repeated the story as follows:

"Adolf Wilson died from burns that set his skirt on fire. It occurred in a dance hall. (How did that happen?) He evidently had something explodable about his clothing. The matches exploded and the skirt got on fire. That occurred in a dance hall academy. (What did the other people say?) Wilson was charged with manslaughter. (Who charged him?) Officials I presume." (The patient did not think she had memory defects.)

Because the technique of examination had to be changed in this case, we have refrained from tabulating it. The perusal of the protocol shows that the same processes that go on in the normal are present in the pathological case, but in exaggerated form. It is particularly obvious in this case that a definite pattern was prematurely formed and then kept with a great tenacity, but individual names, words, and items were also radically changed. It is also obvious that it depended on the circumstances how much of the existing traces could be utilized by the patient.

We come to the conclusion that the pattern formation present in the normal can be accelerated in cases of organic memory disturbances. Many of the other changes are qualitatively identical with the changes that take place in normals, but are more outspoken. We have also studied in detail several cases of Korsakoff's psychosis, one of which is tabulated (see Table 4) in that this patient had retained only very little of the original story, but after the sixteenth repetition one item was still correct and two were changed. A great productivity in producing new items is obvious when one looks at the number of items added in the left column.

TABLE 4
QUANTITATIVE CHANGES IN REPETITION

| | Comparison with Original Story | | | | Comparison with Preceding Repetition | | | |
| | *Number of Items* | | | | *Number of Items* | | | |
Trial	correctly repeated	changed	omitted	added	correctly repeated	changed	omitted	added
1.	1	2	21	46				
2.	0	1	23	25	0	3	40	21
3.	1	1	22	22	12	4	15	5
4.	0	1	23	22	10	2	16	7
5.	1	2	21	33	10	2	9	29
6.	1	2	21	18	11	1	23	11
7.	1	3	20	17	11	1	7	10
8.	1	1	22	27	7	4	13	16
9.	0	1	23	21	7	3	15	12
10.	0	2	22	16	3	4	16	7
11.	1	2	21	12	3	3	9	7
12.	0	2	22	16	9	6	5	8
13.	1	2	21	17	9	6	1	10
14.	1	2	21	14	9	5	7	4
15.	1	2	21	22	10	3	3	14
16.	1	2	21	20	8	5	5	8

The column on the right side shows that the patient had a greater tendency to stick to the items he had invented himself.

Here is a part of the protocol.

First trial: "A man named Nelson attended a hula dance and while there lighted a cigarette. After taking a puff of the cigarette he deliberately threw the remnant of the partly smoked cigarette into the crowd—not deliberately. He misjudged the direction where he stood and the outer edge of the spectators. What happened, I don't know. How would you finish it? The police were called, who sent hurried calls for ambulance and those badly burned were rushed to the hospital. The man who threw the cigarette butt was taken to the station house for examination for insanity. His name he said was John Nelson, age 38, living at . . . and . . . I am making this up, father of three children."

Third trial: "Harry Nelson, 28 or 38, is under arrest today charged with throwing a lighted match butt into a throng of spectators. I have said that before. He was held for examination as to insanity. He is a well-known resident of his community. . . . I have said that before."

Ninth trial: "In repeating for the third time under protest. Harry Nelson, twenty years old, a resident of the district was arrested for throwing a lighted butt into a crowd of spectators . . . I am unable to say word for word what I said into further versions of Nelson's act. I have made a note."

Eleventh trial (The patient protests again, vigorously, against continuing): "John Nelson is under arrest today charged with throwing a lighted cigarette butt and match into the midst of a nearby crowd gathered to listen to him or to another lecturer."

Fifteenth trial (The patient protests again, vigorously): "In Bellevue Hospital the doctors are more crazy than anybody else in the observation world. John Nelson, 28 years old, a resident of this neighborhood, is arrested today, charged with throwing a lighted cigarette butt and match into a crowd of spectators. Today he is held under arrest and held for observation."

After the sixteenth repetition the patient again protests vigorously. (Do you like to tell the same story twice?) He continues after a pause of ten minutes and repeats the story as follows: "John Nelson, age 28, under arrest today charged with throwing a match into a crowd of spectators. He was held for police and observation" (the patient is a newspaper man).

Studying such a protocol carefully, one will find that traces are formed by these patients too. In the different trials, different parts of the traces are utilized. The pattern formation is fairly obvious. In some of his previous protocols, pattern formation was overshadowed by a wealth of new details invented by him, but recognizable, too. The variations and swings, the antepositions, postpositions, and substitutions found in the normal can be found here, too, but the swings here are more outspoken. Perseveration so closely related to pattern formation plays an important part. It is obvious that we deal in this case, too, with a very active process of organization. This organization is much more determined by the individual attitudes of the patient than by the character of the material. We know from other studies that in cases of this type a tendency exists to remove from a story everything that might be offensive. These cases tend to like a happy ending. Furthermore, the individual experiences are mixed with the objective pattern. Any attempt to characterize such a process simply as a difficulty in retention is clearly erroneous. One deals with processes of organization that are, in comparison to the normal, accelerated and exaggerated. One gets the impression that the processes organizing the trace are less controlled and more under the influence of the individual attitude of the patient.

CONCLUSION AND SUMMARY

We have read a story once to a number of normal and pathological subjects and have asked them to repeat the story until they were exhausted and refused to go on. In addition to omission of words and items, a number of other changes were observed. These changes were not merely due to the fact that recalls were demanded, they indicate a process of the organization of traces. The change in the trace from repetition to repetition did not consist merely of the fading of the trace. One deals with a very active mental process in which the total personality and its problems are involved. The organization of a trace that has been developed has the tendency to persist, and a relatively stable pattern is formed. When the pattern is formed, individuals become unwilling to go on. The emotion and the organizations are merely two sides of the same fundamental process, which leads to saturation. The processes described are probably processes which take place in every trace and are of importance for the understanding of changes in the use of words.

In cases of organic disturbances in the memory function, the processes or organization of the trace are accelerated and exaggerated. They are less controlled by the trace as such and more under the influence of the patient's individual attitude. These disturbances cannot be understood merely as defects in retention and in old memories.

CHAPTER THIRTEEN

Psychic Disturbances
After Head Injuries

The symptomatology of head injuries has been studied more carefully from a neurological than from a psychiatric point of view
(Glaser and Shafer, 1932). Strauss and Savitzky (1934) have
spoken of the neurological side of this question, and Winkelman
and Eckel (1934) of the histopathology. Since Adolf Meyer's
important paper (1904), no detailed study of psychosis after head
injuries has appeared in the English language. In the German
literature, papers by Berger (1915) and Pfeifer (1928) contain
important material.

The following study is based on 35 selected cases of head injuries which I have observed in the psychiatric wards of Bellevue
Hospital. Only serious head injuries have been considered. The
acute phases have been the special object of my attention; the
chronic sequelae are considered merely for comparison. The total
number of cases that have been observed is, of course, much

Appeared originally in *American Journal of Psychiatry*, 91:155-187, 1934.

larger. The present study has no statistical purpose, and is concerned chiefly with the question of symptomatology and psychophysiological mechanisms.

A. R., 34 years old, of Italian extraction, was struck on the occipital region with a blunt instrument on March 22, 1933. He was found in a stuporous condition. It is not known how long the unconsciousness lasted. After awakening he was resistive and delirious. At admission he complained of headache. When urged to speak he replied: "This is the carabinieri department; I can't tell you the day; this is Mac Kee." His temperature was 104 and his pulse a little accelerated. The X-ray examination of the skull was negative. The spinal fluid was bloody and contained crenated cells. The thyroid was enlarged, and there was a slight exophthalmos. There was rigidity of the neck and slight resistance against passive movements. The tongue deviated to the right. On the left side there was a Babinski and an Oppenheim reflex. There were no other neurological signs. The skull, especially in the occipital region, was sensitive. In the next few days the temperature subsided. The patient remained confused and bewildered. He was rather torpid and did not talk spontaneously. There was urinary incontinence. On April 22 he showed fundamentally the same picture. He appeared bewildered and had to be prompted to speak. He complained about headache. "Maybe I got a cold. I was in my house before I came here. I am here two or three weeks. We are going to pay. We shall not do anything about it."

He knew his address, but did not know the date. He recognized simple pictures when they were exposed for a sufficiently long time.

A series of pictures were shown to him tachistoscopically. These were the pictures that Ross and I (1934) have shown to normals and comprise the Binet-Simon incomplete human figures. In addition to these was a picture of a boy with one leg missing, a boy with one arm missing, a picture of a woman with one breast missing, a female figure with three arms, and a female head with three eyes. Whereas the normal person recognized these pictures mostly correctly when the time of exposure was below 1/25 of a second, the patient said, when the Binet face without nose was exposed one-fifth of a second: "Is like light; like A.B.C.: I see, but they go out; I see a picture, just like a boy." Two repetitions provoked the same answers. At the time of exposure of half a second, he said: "She has only one eye." This is an answer one gets from normals when the exposure is very short. They then transpose the defectiveness from one part of a picture to another part. In his answer to the subsequent exposures, he made, in an exposure time of one-fifth of a second, the same mistakes that normals make at much shorter exposure time. When a boy was shown whose right arm was missing, he said, after three exposures: "That is the same boy with the leg (boy with one leg only had been shown before). He is just standing up; the legs and the arms are good this time." He expressly stated that he had two arms and two legs. He persisted in the description when the picture was shown for one second, and even imitated the posture of both arms, imagining the missing arm in the same position as the one present. When he looked at the picture in a prolonged exposure, he finally said, "He has only one arm." When the picture of the woman with three arms was shown to him, he made grave mistakes in the exposures of one-fifth, one-half, and one second. When the picture was finally shown to him, he still said, "She has two arms," making in this lengthened exposure the same mistake the normal makes in shorter tachistoscopic exposure. When asked again about the picture a few minutes later, without a new exposure, he said, "It was a naked girl picture. She had three arms." Summing up, we may say that he had difficulties in tachistoscopic perceptions, even of those pictures he could recognize otherwise. In complicated pictures he made the same mistakes that the normal makes in tachistoscopic exposure.

On the same day, he was given the gestalt test, which has been introduced into psychiatry by L. Bender (1938). Plate 1 shows the gestalt test forms the patient has to copy. The figures on the left half of Plate 2 show his reaction at the height of his confusion. The figures at the right show his performance when the

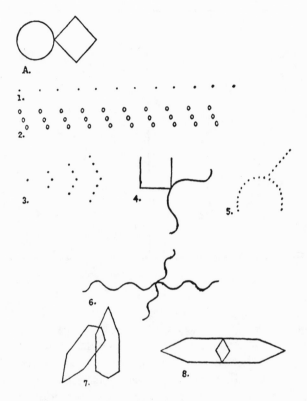

PLATE 1

confusion was improving. At the height of the confusion the patient very often changed rectangular figures into circles or ellipses
(figure A, 7,8). Points were changed into short lines (1,3,5). The
direction was changed (2). Angles were changed into straight lines
(3). Gestalt principles come out in a very primitive and almost exaggerated way (3,7,8). In figure A the patient emphasized the
gestalt principle in a primitive way by connecting the two figures
with a line. The gestalt principle was overlooked (4). With the improvement (right side of plate) the change in the direction was still
present (2,3), the gestalts were simplified (4,8). The patient drew
the figure of a man in a very primitive way.

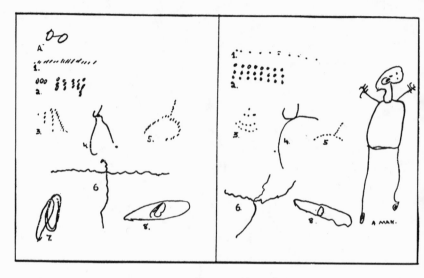

PLATE 2

Wertheimer (1923) has shown that the figures reproduced are not seen as senseless arrangements of details, but as characteristic gestalt forms. There are no irregular dots, but a series of triplets (figure 2). Figure 5 is seen as half of a circle with an elongation, and not in any other way. All of the figures reproduced are typical gestalt figures that are perceived as such. Bender has shown that one gets valuable information if one orders persons with mental deficiency or schizophrenia to copy these gestalt tests. Very often the gestalt figures are not reproduced as such or the forms are brought down to a lower level. Simple gestalt principles may become exaggerated. In other instances the gestalt principles are overlooked. Motor execution is clumsy and awkward. One may generally say that the visual-motor gestalt patterns are on a very primitive level, and in this elementary sphere we find disturbances that must deeply impair the primitive basis of orientation.

On the 28th of April the patient showed qualitatively the same picture, but he had improved so much that an extensive psychometric and memory test could be given. The following results were obtained: On memory tests answers were given to all personal questions, but the reliability of responses could not be checked. Information about current events was very inferior. He varied in replies to questions of school information. The score was 50 per cent of the normal. In repeating the alphabet, he rushed through, omitting several letters. In counting numbers backward (20 to 1), he repeated several numbers, but responded accurately in 39 seconds (normal is nine seconds). In rote memory of digits he gave four forward and three backward (four to seven-year performance). His rote memory of logical material was below six years, and in his logical memory for long passages he made no score at all. His identification of objects was correct. He was able to describe pictures at the seven-year level, but could not interpret their meaning adequately. Visual attention was about five years or less on Knox cubes. On army designs his score was zero. In formulating new associations there was much confusion, and he made a gross score of thirteen. Perseveration was marked. He read below a fifth-grade level and afterward could remember nothing of what he had read. He was disoriented, claiming he was in the city hall, and gave the wrong date. In perception tests, he perceived data, but could not synthesize. His emotional reactions were dulled. He was agreeable and uncomplaining, and his facial expression was of a vacant stare. There was no insight into his failures in the tests. In the Wells memory test, he attained a score of 45 per cent; with the Pintner Patterson, he scored at the level of five years. In the tests with the mare and foal, manikin, ship, and with the Knox cubes, his score was that of five years. His copying of the diamond resembled an elliptical outline. In a retest eleven days later there was no improvement except that the confusion was diminished. In the Goodenough tests (drawing the figure of a man), he scored at six years. In the gestalt tests there was a marked improvement. For two months after this there was no further improvement.

This observation represented a typical picture of the confusion that follows a severe head injury. It was a real confusion of the organic type, characterized by an inability in the perceptive sphere and an inability to coordinate the data of perceptual experience. The tachistoscopic examination points to the conclusion that the perceptive processes were slow and incomplete. The gestalt test, ship test, manikin test, showed the difficulty in coordinating parts into a whole, in developing the simple and primitive gestalt into definite structures and giving them the final direction. A similar basic disturbance exists in the memory. The disorientation was due basically to the difficulties in the perception and gestalt functions, but beyond these we have a deep disturbance in the emotional attitude, which we cannot measure.

These investigations are not concerned with the neurological picture. But it is worthwhile mentioning that the period of unconsciousness is very often followed by a period in which a negativistic resistance is coupled with varying muscular tensions. It seems that the deep clouding of consciousness is coupled with a negativistic attitude, which is psychic as well as neuromuscular. It is remarkable that the serious trauma did not find any psychic representation. The patient did not know anything about his head injury and blamed his headache on a cold.

More complicated from a pathogenetic point of view is the following observation:

B. R., 46 years of age, was admitted to another hospital on April 10, 1933. He had been found unconscious on the street. After his admission he had an epileptic convulsion. On the 11th he showed a left facial weakness and a Babinski on the right side. There was blood in the spinal fluid and fissure fracture of the squamous portion of the right temporal bone, the line of fracture extending for a distance of three and a half inches. There was ecchymosis of the left eye and old blood in his right ear. On admission to Bellevue Hospital he was restless and confused. His orientation was poor. He had a temperature of 106, respiration 32, blood pressure 100/70. According to the relatives, he had been drinking steadily for the last three months. On April 22 he said, "I am 32 years old. In the paper I am 45, but I am a little over 32. I will be 33 on the fourth of July. Yes, I was doing some drinking lately. Yes, I was in the army. I did not get enlisted. This place belongs to the City of New York. I do not want to put myself in the wrong. I know one way, I do not know the other. I really don't think anything is the matter with my leg. [One of his legs had been amputated.] This doctor was talking to me this morning [incorrect]. This is a club. I just don't know exactly the name of it. I got in here before. Yes, occasionally I have fits. I have them more when I am not eating correctly." On April 25 and 26 he was still disoriented but did not show any signs of confusion. He said he fell on his head ten days ago; that he was unconscious for not more than ten days. Later he said that he was in the hospital three days. He made contradictory statements concerning the accident.

The psychological examination showed the following results: In his vocabulary he scored at the fourteen-year-old level. In the manikin and the ship tests he scored nine years, one month; the profile test nine years, five months; Knox cubes seven years, and the army design test six years, nine months. In Wells memory test he obtained a quotient of 67. He reproduced the marble statue test with only slight relevancy. The analysis of these tests showed a vocabulary score of low-average intelligence. His present level of functioning is still lower. This is due chiefly to the disturbance in all phases of orientation and his memory disorder. His score of personal information was 34 per cent; in new associations, 40 per cent; in digits backward, 40 per cent; in manikin, ship, and profile tests, 70 per cent; in digits forward, 100 per cent; in identification of objects and memory for sentences, 100 per cent. There was a marked perseveration of mental and motor acts. His comprehension was slow, and adjustment to a shift of ideas was even slower. He could easily be encouraged to confabulate and was only vaguely oriented as to time. He was consistently amiable and cooperative.

In a retest on May 10 he showed a marked improvement in orientation and in memory function. Visual test scores involving attention were still low, although higher than before. Logical memory for a long passage was poor, and rote memory for digits backward was much impaired. Gestalt tests and tachistoscopic tests were given April 23 and proved completely normal.

This case is not quite so clear from an etiological point of view. Epilepsy and alcoholism complicated the picture, but the patient had no psychosis before, and his serious head injury was proven by the X rays and the blood in the spinal fluid. The head injury was probably the leading etiological factor, although the alcoholism may have contributed to the final elaboration of the picture, especially as it concerned the patient's mood and emotional attitude. But the psychosis as a whole is a post-traumatic psychosis. The patient seemingly had only a short confusional state, which was followed by a state of clearness with memory disturbances predominant. There were no difficulties in perception and none in the gestalt functions and visual-motor patterns. The disorder was that of a rather clear-cut Korsakoff picture. In the German literature (Bürger-Prinz and Kaila, 1932) there is a tendency to doubt the possibility of memory disturbances without perceptual difficulty. Our case shows that these doubts are not fully justified. Störring (1931) has taken a similar point of view. Memory, perceptive function, and gestalt function are to a large degree independent of each other. Moreover, logical reasoning was certainly less impaired in our patient than memory, although one hardly ever misses defects in judgment in Korsakoff cases with regard to their confabulatory material (Pick, 1915; Gruenthal, 1923; Hartmann and Schilder, 1925). At any rate, we can draw the conclusion that a head injury can be followed by the Korsakoff picture without perceptive difficulties. I have observed identical pictures following head injuries without the complication of epilepsy and alcoholism. The Korsakoff psychosis is, according to Pfeifer (1928), an almost regular occurrence in psychosis after head injury. The following case shows a very similar problem:

A. G., 44 years old, was found unconscious on September 24, 1932. There was a fracture through the occipital bone, extending to a distance of three inches, and a fracture in the left parietal bone. The bones were not depressed, nor was the intracranial pressure increased. The spinal fluid was bloody in all tubes. There was a fresh hemorrhage in the right fundus. The upper lip was lacerated and blood came from the mouth. Babinski was present on the left side. He complained of severe headache and was dull. During the next days he was restless, noisy, and resistive. On October 3 he said, "It is a railroad hospital. I am here one day and a half because of a cold. Yesterday I was in Reading." He gave the date correctly. He did not know there was a fracture of his skull and forgot about this half an hour after he had been told. On October 5 he remembered all that had occurred at the time of the injury. He related that he had been hit by an automobile, with a friend who was injured. The two of them started to chase the automobile, but could not get it. Then he went home. His wife called the doctor, and he was brought to the hospital. Psychological tests showed that his comprehension score was six; information thirteen, which was about the average. In Wells memory test he scored 62 per cent. He improved in comprehension and memory in the course of the next day, but sometimes confused elementary facts. The rote memory for digits was poor. On October 19 he said, "I feel fine today. I am 27 days in the hospital. They picked me up on the street." He then gave seemingly reliable details about the way he was run over. There was a history of mild alcoholism.

Here, confabulations did not run parallel with the defectiveness of memory. It is a point of interest that after a while the patient showed some knowledge of the accident, but he distorted it in a confabulatory way, becoming the active hero. When he was near complete recovery, he finally remembered the accident. The patient reported by Hartmann and Schilder (1925) reacted in a similar way following severe head injury.

The following case shows the independence of confabulations and memory disturbances:

J. T., 59 years of age, was found unconscious on his doorstep on March 4, 1933. His scalp was lacerated and the spinal fluid was

uniformly bloody. On March 5 he said, "I came from New York—
you say I came in an ambulance. My head hurts. I don't know
what happened to me. I guess I got hit somewhere, but I don't
know where." He was poorly oriented for time. The pupils reacted
sluggishly to light and there was a bilateral Babinski. On March 11
he said: "I was out yesterday. I went downtown to see my boss. I
want fresh air." On March 15 he said, "I have seen you before
somewhere. I can't hear because of an accident. On the back of a
truck something fell on my head. I was out one night. I was working when I came back here. I am 64 years old." On March 17 he
said, "I am here one day. I was out for a walk twice." In the tachistoscopic examination he needed longer exposures than the normal,
but his descriptions were generally accurate. Only when the
woman without a nose was exposed 1/25 of a second, he first said,
"I don't think she got a mouth," and later on, "she just got a bit of
a nose." In the following days he gave an accurate description of
the accident. He was unloading a truck and a box fell on his head.
But there was no possibility of checking the truth of this. The
Babinski reflex was still present. He still continued telling that he
had been out and saw his boss, worked, etc. In the Wells memory
test he scored 110; the repetition of the marble statue story
showed a low average; his score in the ship test was fourteen; in
the army design, seventeen years, six months. On April 6 he still
repeated his confabulations, but accepted corrections, and from
then on retained full insight. There was a history of alcoholism in
this case. His confabulations were probably connected with the
head injury. The confabulations persisted at the time the memory
was intact.

The following case shows a minimum psychic disturbance
consisting of a persistent amnesia for the time before the accident:

Betty O., 20 years old, was admitted on June 19, 1932 after
she had been knocked down by a backing taxicab. It is not known
whether she was unconscious. She had a fissure fracture through
the right parietal bone, and another line extended into the

squamous portion of the temporal bone and from there into the base. There was blood in the spinal fluid. A Babinski was present on the left side. She gave a wrong address and at first said she was fourteen years old. The next day she was fully oriented but uncooperative and said, "I felt sick all day long. I want to go to sleep." She did not know how she came to the hospital or what had happened, and complained about headache. There was no insight. On the following day an attempt was made to bring back her memory. She remembered that she left the store where she worked in order to get a bathing suit. She did not know how far she went or where the accident happened. Her remembrance ended abruptly at the time she left the store. In the following days and weeks, repeated attempts were made to bring back her memory. Suggestion was used, and hypnosis was tried, but it was not possible to bring her into a deep state of somnolence. Even medinal did not help in the hypnotic attempts. When the patient left on July 11, the amnesia still persisted. She had never taken alcoholic drinks.

The case histories reported so far give us insight into the two fundamental symptoms that occur after head injury. The clouding of consciousness with confusion, and memory disturbances. Clouding of consciousness has always been observed in the cases that come to the psychiatric wards. Primarily, the state is one of unconsciousness. Our data about its duration are incomplete. In many of our cases it changed into a state of deep clouding, with restlessness and attitudes of resistiveness which were partially psychic but also had an organic component. When the patient could be made to speak, there was clouding of consciousness and disorientation in space and time. This state is hardly ever completely absent, it may last a long time as in the first case described. When it lasts longer, a deep bewilderment and helplessness may be present. Tachistoscopic examination shows that the patient needs a long time to come to any perception. The perceptive function as such is retarded. In addition to the retardation in perceptive function, a difficulty exists in synthesizing primitive impressions into a unit. Complicated pictures are not at all understood. There is a

deep-going basic disturbance in the gestalt functions. Visual-motor
gestalt patterns show a very primitive structure. Points are distorted into short lines. Angles are straightened out. Diamonds are
turned into elliptoid figures. There is an inability to use the right
directions. The gestalt principles may be exaggerated in a primitive way. The gestalt may be degraded to a primitive level or the
gestalt principle may be overlooked completely. The perception
and the gestalt difficulties certainly contribute to the disorientation
and are basic for the helplessness and the confusion. They may
improve gradually. In many of the cases reported here, the stage
of confusion subsided quickly. The perceptive difficulties and disturbances in the gestalt functions are then only present in a minor
degree and may finally be completely absent. The difficulties in
the performance tests, in the ship tests, in the manikin tests, generally run parallel to the gestalt tests and the tachistoscopic tests,
which allow a deeper analysis of the disturbance.

During the confusional state, memory and judgment are impaired, but impairment of the memory, especially for recent
events, is more outspoken. When the perception and gestalt-function disturbances subside, the picture of a Korsakoff psychosis remains, which was especially clear in the second case reported here.
The perceptive and gestalt disturbances may then be completely
absent. The confabulatory element does not run parallel to the
memory disturbance and may even be present when the memory
has come back to normal. Although alcoholism was a complicating factor, in some of the reported cases alcoholism is in no way
a necessary factor in the genesis of the traumatic Korsakoff syndrome. In all of the cases reported, there is a particular amnesia
concerning the accident in the confusional state as well as in the
Korsakoff state. The amnesia can be complete, later on a vague
knowledge concerning the accident may exist, based partially on
reports of others, but this knowledge is very often distorted in a
confabulatory way. In some cases, this part of the amnesia may
clear up; in others the amnesia is persistent. The amnesia for the
accident may be the only lasting psychic symptom. The resistiveness of the amnesia, its persistence, are in contrast to hysterical

amnesias and also to amnesias that are due merely to alcoholic intoxications. The return of the memory of the accident very often occurs through a confabulatory stage.

Whereas the confusional state is characterized by a mood of helplessness and bewilderment, the Korsakoff state very often shows a mood of serenity and mild euphoria, in spite of persistent headaches. Irritability was present in the last case reported. It is astonishing how little the patients are concerned about their head injuries. They do not appear in dreams. It is another outstanding part of this confusional state and that of Korsakoff psychosis that the psychic material that appears is rather impersonal. In the average case comparatively little of the previous personality appears in the psychosis. It is as if an impersonal province of the psyche was affected.

Although the foregoing descriptions give an adequate picture of the majority of cases, they are in no way complete and do not cover all the possibilities. Changes in the mood sometimes occur as in the following case:

Rose de F., 40 years old, was admitted November 8, 1931 and discharged December 11, 1931. She was brought from a general hospital with a history that she had walked out into a dark road in front of an automobile. She received abrasions of the right forehead, buttock, and knee. The spinal fluid was bloody. The X ray was negative, as was the Wassermann in the blood and spinal fluid. She was at first resistive and restless. On the 9th she stated: "My name is Rose F—, and my mother's name is Amelia. No, I don't live on Third Avenue. I am 39 years old. I felt sick. I came here myself. This is Fordham Hospital. I am sick about six months. I have pain in my chest. I have neuralgia. My head aches. I had trouble with my mother." The day, she said, was "October," and when asked the year, she remarked, "Can't you look up on the calendar?" The patient was depressed, complaining, confused, and disoriented. She was unable to give any reliable information about herself. The pupils reacted sluggishly to light. She said, "It was an accident, about a week ago, I don't remember when. It was on

Fordham Road. Henry wanted me to work. They took my wages. Maybe it was in church. I said a prayer. Finally I found myself in a hospital. No, I'm not working. That's the trouble, I am not working. I told them I was going to see my boss, instead of going to 21st Street. They know I was working at brassieres, they wanted me to press." She rambled in her description of her previous occupation. She knew it was now November, 1931 and that she was in Bellevue. "I don't know how I got hit. My mind is like a blank. I **know it was on Fordham Road.**"

On November 16 she was very restless, threw herself about, and seemed sort of frantic, not knowing what to do with herself. Her speech was rambling, disconnected, apparently involving numerous personal difficulties which had preceded her injury. She had no clear memory of the accident itself. She was emotional and showed a patchy amnesia. The left pupil was larger than the right. On November 20 she said, "I still feel dizzy. I was born in 1890. I am 40. This is 1900. I do not see double." There was a slight weakness of the right sixth nerve. There was a tendency to sinking of the left arm and flexion of the left elbow. The fingers were hyperextended and the little finger abducted.

On December 1 she was still very much mixed up, though she gave the proper date and said correctly that she had been here three weeks. She said she felt better, but was not able to say how. She talked in a very rambling way about difficulties at home. She claimed that her mother was a crazy invalid, but gave no specific information. She never completed a thought and never answered a question directly. In this way the patient showed no improvement in the three weeks she had been here, but she did appear quieter and her facial expression was less strained. The gestalt test showed disturbances of the same qualitative character as in the first case reported, but of lesser degree. On December 11 she continued dazed and unstable. She complained constantly and had a strained, harassed, unhappy facial expression. The pupils were dilated, the left a little more than the right. There were slight athetoid movements of the left hand. Her speech was disconnected and rambling, and there was still a tendency to mull over old emotional problems and confuse them with her present difficulties. She seemed to have real insight in understanding what had happened to her. When taken out of bed she complained of pain and tenderness in her limbs.

This patient showed a decidedly depressed mood. She was not only dazed, but worried. She carried over her everyday preoccupations into the post-traumatic psychosis. She had memory disturbances and showed minor disturbances in the gestalt tests, changing angles into a straight line and exaggerating primitive gestalt principles. But it remains questionable whether the depressive mood was the immediate result of the head injury or only the expression of her previous mood.

A more common type is the following:

G. U., 28 years old, was admitted to the prison ward of Bellevue Hospital charged with technical homicide. He had been driving in an intoxicated state and turned his car over. One of his friends was killed. He himself suffered a fracture of the right and left hands and laceration of the left eye. The spinal fluid and the X-ray examinations were negative. The pupils were dilated, and there was a Babinski on the left side. He thought the accident had happened about three months ago. At first he said that someone hit him over the eye, but immediately afterward said that the mother of the dead friend had dropped any charges. He said he did not know who was driving the car. He was disoriented for place. He was almost elated and talked continually in an excited way, repeating monotonously that he wanted to go home and asking when this would be allowed. His Wells memory quotient was 71. His score in the ship test was seven and in the manikin test ten years, four months. There was no outstanding deterioration. The information score was twelve. The marble statue and grocery tests were below average. In the tachistoscopic examination he differed slightly from the normal.

Here, too, we deal with a case where the changes in the mood were outstanding. There was an empty excitement with monotony and without any real flightiness. The excitement was mixed with elation. He was a young man and, previous to the psychosis, of an outgoing personality.

This leads to the case of a young girl, eighteen years old, who was described as very sociable and friendly before the accident. She was admitted on March 6, 1933, two weeks after being knocked down by a truck and receiving lacerations of the scalp.

The full history of the accident was not available, but it is reported that her unconsciousness lasted 36 hours. There was nystagmus and bloody spinal fluid, but the spinal pressure was not increased. In the surgical wards she was irritable, restless, noisy, and violent. On admission to the psychiatric ward she described the accident, but this was not a genuine memory, only a repetition of what she had been told. Memory disturbances of other types were not present. In her emotional attitude she resembled postencephalitic children. She asked continually in a monotonous way to be taken home, and was pestering in her attitude. Her mood was jocular, but her jokes were superficial. She said she would give whiskey to the physician. She also cried very easily. "Doctor, I like you. I like you, darling." She tried to kiss the physician, and said: "I have a party at home. Doctor, sit on the chair." In the following week her restlessness subsided, but her mood remained empty. She had no definite disturbance in perception or in tachistoscopic examination.

I have observed an almost identical case in another young girl. The emotional state in these cases is an emptiness or monotonous excitement coupled with elation and lack of insight.

There is another group of cases in which sensory aphasic difficulties play a great part.

H. E., a Belgian, 41 years old, was admitted to another hospital on March 15, 1932 in a condition of stupor. According to the police record he had fallen from a staircase and had resisted the officer who wanted to help him. A fracture of the parietal bone was revealed by the X ray. The line of the fracture extended into sagittal suture and another line into the lambdoidal suture. There was laceration of the scalp, bloody spinal fluid, and blurring of the discs with elevation of two diopters. He became noisy and uncooperative and was sent to Bellevue Hospital. The spinal fluid was then xanthochromic. On the 21st he said in a rambling way that he drank some wine, fell on the staircase, hurt himself on the skull, and went to a policeman. He did not remember that he had resisted the policeman. He told about his whole past, and said that his wife left for France on March 13. He thought it was now April 12. He identified the thumb correctly, called the index finger the interior; the little finger the ring finger; and the ring finger the wedding finger. Later he called the index finger the exterior finger. He was very amiable, but somewhat excited. There was still blood in his right ear. On the 23rd, he said, "I know you now. (Have you seen me before?) A couple of times [incorrect]. (Do you know this lady?) I never saw her before. You see so many nice girls in New York you have to know each one better so you have to talk to each other. You will be a difficult professor. The questions that you propose have to be two at once. It has to be negative or positive." He gave the date as March 30. "If my English is not perfect, I don't want no pity and no excuses. (What picture did I show you?) It was about a man with a head all smashed to pieces" (incorrect). He had also forgotten what he had for lunch, and did not know the time of day. He complained continually about severe headaches, but he was elated and talkative.

On the 25th the memory disturbance had disappeared. He was still very amiable and talkative and somewhat manic in his mood. His skull was still sensitive. He no longer had difficulties in naming complicated objects. But the next day he said, "What do you think I accomplished today, the first and second speak within a beautiful car. I didn't know I was doing it. It was a DeSoto. The field was wet. It was foggy weather." In the next days he did not show any aberrations except his talkativeness, restlessness, and a hypomanic mood. The optic discs were then entirely clear. According to his report and to the report of his friends, he was always an amiable and easygoing person; he had calmed down considerably when he was discharged on April 10. When seen several weeks later he impressed one as a pyknic body type, definitely cyclothymic personality, with a tendency to elation.

The hypomanic picture in this case, which was observed after the head injury, is definitely an exaggeration of trends that were present in him before the accident. The severe headaches did not impair his elation. He showed slight amnestic aphasic signs. It is possible that a lesion near to the Wernicke region may have contributed to the general attitude of talkativeness and elation. Memory disturbances were present only at the beginning.

In another case, T. B., 45 years old, sensory aphasic signs were much more in the foreground. He had the euphoria, the lack of insight into his defectiveness, and the optimism characteristic of this localized disturbance. But his disorientation at the beginning was probably due to the general disturbance in connection with the head injury.

The following case is more interesting:

A young man, 27 years of age with one year of college education, while under the influence of alcohol at a party, fell over the bannister to the floor below, alighting on his head. He was brought to the hospital in a stuporous condition which persisted for several days. X-ray examination showed multiple fractures at the vault of the skull on both sides. He showed bilateral Babinski reflexes, and on the fourth day he developed right-sided convulsions with paralysis of the right side of the body, including the face. A diagnosis was made of laceration and hemorrhage in the left motor region, and five days after the accident he underwent a decompression operation of the left frontoparietal region, which revealed laceration and maceration of the underlying brain. There were multiple subdural hematomas and intraparenchymal hemorrhages. The dural vessels were tied, part of the dura was cut out, free blood and blood clots and macerated brain tissue were removed. The remaining brain looked blue and contained many hemorrhagic areas. However, he improved immediately, and in a few days there was no right hemiparesis and no recurrence of convulsions or other neurological deviations. As he began to speak he showed a severe sensory aphasia with the following features: He was restless and noisy, especially at night, but always euphoric. In his manic behavior he talked continuously in a facetious strain with many paraphasic mistakes. He was unable to name objects and showed a finger agnosia. He understood with difficulty any commands or questions, whether spoken or written. He also showed paraphasic mistakes in writing. When asked to count to ten he said: "1, 2, 3—any goddam thing. All right, who can't count to ten. I would do it. Anyone could. 2—. It must be very . . . same goddam thing. Where did you get that nice one [referring to the stenographer]?" He wrote a letter to his mother: "Dear Mother, I am wanting meeting. I am myself leaving meetings. I am feeling fine." Subsequently he improved very much and went home after one month, although still somewhat euphoric and showing some paraphasic mistakes in talking and writing.

The case was carefully followed and came to an almost complete recovery. He proved to be hypomanic in his temperament, even when healthy. Before the accident, he was known as a practical joker and was extremely sociable and popular. He was very much interested in money and his mother. These were the two outstanding topics at the time of his post-traumatic psychosis. The head injury and sensory aphasia, therefore, increased tendencies that were in the structure of his personality.

My material does not contain acute cases with predominant motor aphasia. I have seen a case two years after the accident in which there was an old depression of the skull and an occipital lesion. There was right hemiplegia and a mixed aphasia, predominantly motor. This patient showed an irritability and a tendency to depression and moodiness, which is so characteristic in motor aphasia. He also had a hypochondriacal attitude toward his defectiveness, of which he was always conscious.

There are also other localized lesions that may provoke a characteristic mental attitude.

R. B., 44 years old, was admitted to the hospital on November 20. According to his wife, he was a war veteran, drank rather heavily, and then commonly looked for trouble. Five weeks previously he had come home bloody, with his head split open, but had not shown any mental aberration. The day before his admission he had a convulsion. On the day of his admission he was excited. "I am not right in the head. No sir, about three weeks I can't bring it out. There about three weeks, a while, one time, I would like to go to work. See if you can get my wife so that she can talk." He perseverated in his speech. The Wassermann in the blood and the spinal fluid was negative; but the fluid showed a trace of globulin and eleven cells. The pupils reacted to light. On the right side the abdominal reflex was absent, and there was an Oppenheim reflex. He made queer movements with his right arm and right leg. He grasped and pointed with the right arm. A right hemianopia was present, and he did not react to pinching of the right side. The eye grounds were normal. Pulse was 66. On the 25th he was more clear. He could name objects and said, "I do not come close enough to objects with the right arm." There was an astereognosis on the right side. He complained: "It feels like grease in my right hand." On November 28 he said, "The right side is on the right; the bad side hurts me; the east side, the left side is good." He perseverated: "The bad side is the right side. It is not any good for me." He did not name objects, nor did he read or write. He did not use the right side. On November 30 he could be made to write, but said "B" and wrote "R." He copied the word "angel" as "anga." Instead of the word "promoted" he read "promotes." He complained about blurring vision on the right side and of queer feelings in his right arm. He lost objects placed in his right hand. He was still astereognostic. Sometimes he felt that he held something in his right hand even when there was nothing. It was as if he "would have a baseball in his right hand." On the right side he heard people talk about him. He complained that he felt something in his right leg when he moved his left leg. The tonic tensions in his right arm had disappeared and also the queer movements he had made, but he still had a tendency to try out movements with his right arm. He reported now that three years ago he had trouble with his right toe. Lately he has also had pain in his right knee. In the next few days he became more clear. The aphasic signs completely disappeared, and the sensibility in the arm was now intact. The patient was quiet, he kept in good contact, and showed no hypochondriacal trends. Later on he was readmitted because of quarrels with his wife. At that time there was no hypochondriasis nor evidence of any organic disturbance.

In this case one deals with a lesion of the parietal lobe (astereognosis) and an aphasia, which is described as parietal type. The optic tracts are also certainly affected. But I mentioned the case not so much because of its interesting parietal symptomatology as because of the hypochondriacal attitude which the patient had toward his defectiveness, which is in some way a counterpart of the parietal nonperception of one's own defectiveness. It is more than probable that the preceding troubles the patient had with his right side played some part in the picture. The alcoholism may also have played some part, but the acoustic hallucinations appeared only on the right side. We have a hypochondriacal attitude toward the defect of the right side of the body and the space corresponding to this right side of the body. The localized lesion he suffered from the head injury has therefore a decided influence on the general attitude and mood of the patient. His previous experiences and the alcoholism are important factors in the picture.

In spite of the fact that I have described a good number of cases, I do not think that more than an outline can be given concerning the changes in the mood after head injury. We notice a general tendency toward resistiveness immediately after the accident. Bewilderment, apathy, indifference with euphoria (especially in the Korsakoff cases) may follow. In a group of cases, more definite changes in mood, such as depression and worries, may be in the foreground. In other cases there may be an empty excitement similar to mania, but more monotonous and emptier. Encephalitis-like monotony and a tendency to pester are found in a group of head injuries in young people. In other cases the picture may more resemble manic states. In cases where paraphasias and sensory aphasias are present, euphoria, manic attitudes, optimism, and lack of insight into the defectiveness may prevail. Moodiness and a strong feeling for their defectiveness has to be expected in cases with motor aphasia. In a case with parietal lobe symptoms, a hypochondriacal attitude has been observed. But, whatever the moods may be, confusion and memory disturbances have always been present in the cases studied here. It is difficult to decide which of the symptoms are due to the general lesion of the brain and whether attempts at localization can be made.

We should not forget that general lesions of the brain also show clinical pictures of systematic character. Cerebello-pontine symptomatology dominates the picture of multiple sclerosis even when the lesions are spread all over the brain and spinal cord. In epidemic encephalitis, the clinical picture is more characteristic and more systematic than the histopathological changes. The same is true concerning general paresis. We are inclined today to consider even a general disturbance in consciousness from a point of view of localization. We know that localized lesions of the third ventricle provoke sleep and a deep disturbance of consciousness. Breslauer-Schück (1917) showed that it is at least probable that lesions in the medulla oblongata can provoke deep clouding of consciousness. The periventricular gray has a regulating function concerning consciousness, and we have the right to suppose that disturbances in the ventricular gray have at least some influence on the genesis of unconsciousness and the clouding of consciousness. Forster (1918) and Reichardt (1904) point to the fact that lesions of the occiput more often provoke loss of consciousness than injuries to other parts of the brain. Pfeifer (1928) believes that, in concussion, the cortical region is put out of function by anemia. But I do not think we have the right to neglect the undoubted regulating function of the ventricular gray on the cortical function. It is more than probable that unconsciousness and clouding of consciousness are due to a disturbance in the cooperation between the ventricular centers of consciousness and the cortical apparatus.

We should keep in mind that in sleep and in the dream and in the psychic changes that accompany lesions in the infundibular region, the psychic material that comes to the surface is of a much more individual character than the psychic material emerging in the cases reported here. The hypothesis is possible that the proximal parts of the ventricular gray have a closer relation to the personal psychic material, whereas the gray of the fourth ventricle and the aqueduct deals more with the impersonal side of consciousness. Gamper (1928) has even attempted to connect the memory disturbances of Korsakoff cases with the lesions in the gray of the third ventricle and in the corpora mamillaria, but his material is taken from alcoholic encephalopathy cases in which, according to the findings of L. Bender and Schilder (1933) [see Chapter 14], cortical lesions are also present. It is not very probable that the subcortical changes are sufficient to provoke the serious disturbances in the gestalt function. But the subcortical apparatus doubtlessly contributes to the genesis of the confusion and probably also influences the other parts of the post-traumatic pictures. I do not think that memory disturbances and impairment of judgment of the organic type can occur without lesion of the cortical sphere. But the pictures vary according to the drives and moods in the amount of confabulation, and it is probable that subcortical factors play a part here.

The mental confusion of the head-injury cases has its definite characteristics in comparison with the mental confusion in toxic and postinfectious states. I would venture the hypothesis that, besides the different localization of the lesion in the ventricular gray and the difference in the severity of this lesion, the more serious and anatomical changes in the cortical lesion of brain-injury cases may be of some importance. We are completely at a loss when we try to interpret the retrograde post-traumatic amnesia from the point of view of localization. Psychological factors certainly are insufficient to interpret the phenomenon. The clinical picture shows definitely that the amnesia lies deeper in the organic sphere than the psychogenic amnesia. Its way to recovery is not only more arduous, but also qualitatively different.

There is no question that changes in consciousness carry with them a particular mood and emotional attitude. The mood of resistance is organically bound to awakening from deep stupor. The bewilderment and helplessness characterizing the following phase, Symonds (1932) calls "Post-traumatic stupor." It is less flexible than the bewilderment and helplessness of the toxic cases. We do not know yet which conditions are apt to prolong the phase of stupor or which conditions lead to the excitement, which in the beginning is brutal and senseless, and later on becomes more differentiated. Allers (1916) has described an apathic syndrome after gunshot injuries of the head. Pfeifer (1928) is inclined to correlate this with frontal lobe lesions. Our clinical material does not give definite hints in this respect. The X-ray findings in our material very often show fissure fractures of parietal bones, but the fissures in the vault do not give a definite indication of the place of the lesion in the brain. Basal fractures very often cannot be seen in the X ray. At any rate, we have to reckon with disturbances in mood, which are strictly organic and may be due either to the generalized or local injury to the brain. I am inclined to believe that subcortical lesions play an important part in those disturbances of mood that resemble postencephalitic pictures. Ziehen (1910) has observed character changes in children after commotion which are reminiscent of the character changes in postencephalitic children. I have pointed to the tendency to hypomanic pictures in cases of sensory aphasia [see Chapter 11]. In some of the cases not mentioned here, pain asymbolia was present [see Chapter 7]. Strictly localized lesions in the cortical sphere may therefore contribute to the general emotional attitude. But I have emphasized that the individual life history and the emotional constitution are of equal importance.

The hypochondriacal attitude in one of our cases was due to a parietal lobe lesion. Pfeifer mentions that he has seen the catatonic phenomena nine times among 63 cases of frontal lobe lesion, but they were outspoken only in three cases. In the one case of our series that showed catatonic phenomena, the connection with the injury could not be established beyond doubt. True, we know that catatonic phenomena may be on a cortical as well as a subcortical basis. We may generally say that the psychic symptoms after head injury can be brought into connection with so-called generalized lesions, with subcortical lesions, and with localized lesions in the cortical region.

The pathological findings are sufficient to give a general idea of the basis of the pathogenesis we have discussed. We found, for instance, in one of our cases that survived several days, a marked diffuse congestion of all parts of the cerebral cortex and brain stem associated with universal perivascular hemorrhages. In many places there were small cleavages in the tissue filled with red blood cells. The hemorrhages appeared to be most severe in the area surrounding the ventricles, but they were also present in other parts of the brain stem and hemisphere, remote from the ventricles. The mammillary bodies are also involved. But we also find in such brains, as Symonds, especially, emphasized (1932), other lesions as contusions, and small foci of destruction of myelin and ganglion cells. I do not intend to discuss the finer anatomy, but would refer to the papers of Pfeifer (1928) and Rand and Courville (1932). The latter describe the changes in the glia.

The periventricular changes deserve a special comment. In 1887, Duret described hemorrhages in the wall and in the surroundings of the aqueduct and the fourth ventricle. He expressed the opinion that the spinal fluid was under increased pressure due to the influence of the head trauma and injury to the narrow canal system. General opinion confirms Duret's statement. Stengel (1927) and Rosenhagen (1932) have seen similar changes in cases of tumor. In sixteen tumor cases, Rosenhagen sometimes found extensive fresh hemorrhages in the brain stem. These could even be seen macroscopically. Wilson and Winkelman (1926) found gross pontile hemorrhages in traumatic and in tumor cases. I cannot think that Duret's hemorrhages and the periventricular hemorrhages generally can be without influence upon the psychic symptomatology. One has to consider that there is a very similar pathology and even hemorrhages in encephalopathia alcoholica, which has so many points of resemblance with the pictures observed after head injuries. It is true that the lesions are generally more closely confined to the ventricular system in the alcoholic cases than in the traumatic cases. I have not mentioned the increase of intracranial pressure after head injury in these pathophysiological discussions. Subdural, epidural, and subarachnoid hemorrhages may contribute to this. In other cases, the brain tissue changes as such may provoke the increase in the pressure. But there is no definite relation to the seriousness of the picture, and the symptoms are not due to the pressure as such, but rather to the damage it does to the tissue. Whatever part the increase in pressure may play in the symptomatology in cases of head injury, our pathophysiological considerations retain their significance.

I have discussed, so far, rather typical psychoses after head injury. The connection between head injury and psychosis is less obvious in the following cases and certainly much more complicated:

S. B., nineteen years of age, was admitted to the psychiatric ward of Bellevue February 6 and transferred to a state hospital on February 23. According to the report of relatives he was always well and did not show any peculiarities in his behavior. There was no history of psychosis in the family. He was out of work and drank occasionally over the last three years. A month ago he was hit over the head. The examination showed him to be of asthenic build and having a Babinski on the right side. The spinal fluid was xanthochromic and under increased pressure. The left eye was bruised.

He made all kinds of monotonous movements with his hands, dancing, grimacing, and singing in a monotonous way. His whole attitude was very manneristic, and his facial expression was one of bewilderment. It was impossible to come in close contact with him. He collected saliva in his mouth. He whispered, "Lord, oh Lord." He was apprehensive and seemingly reacted to hallucinations. He rolled out of bed, grasped his camisole, and said, "I will hold him 'till he sleeps, that black bastard." He grimaced wildly, and his movements were almost choreoathetotic. On February 17 he grasped at everything. There was a slight expression of suffering in his face. On February 18 he was overactive, sang, drew his legs up in bed, and, holding them in a cataleptic attitude, wiggled his feet sideways in a rhythmic way. On February 23 he was manneristic, showed stereotyped movements, and sang a great deal.

There can be no question that this patient had suffered a severe head injury. But whether this cataleptic picture was merely the expression of the injury or whether it was not merely elicited by the injury is impossible to decide. We are generally at a loss when we are unable to prove the memory disturbances and the confusion of the organic type. But even if the psychosis should be in closer relation to the injury, we should not forget that the personality and constitutional factors may also find their expression in the psychosis. On May 23 he still showed a catatonic picture, according to the report of the state hospital to which he was sent.

Still more doubtful is the connection between psychosis and trauma in the two following cases:

J. M., 24 years old, had an accident on October 4, 1930. Fifteen bricks had fallen on him from a distance of 22 feet. He was unconscious for a short time, but went home. He was dazed for several days, and then began to behave peculiarly. He acted as if he were broadcasting and spoke irrationally. He drank perfume and said he had lots of money. Examinations of the blood and spinal fluid were negative. The X ray showed no pathology. On December 6 he said: "I tried to get down on myself. The doctor gave me an injection on the left to bring the tongue to the left side. The tongue in the middle means a man's love. The voices sent over the radio were the voices sent by the good Lord above. I am a mortal sinner. I am worried when away from my people. It is just the same for me because I am a fighter. I am an inventor, the discoverer of science."

He was occasionally cataleptic and remained in stiff postures.

On December 9: (How do you feel?) "I feel perfect. The whole bunch of us feel fine at the present time. Don't just look serious when I announce this: The world looks very short. You know Leopold? Shake hands. I am the right link of the new world, if it could be a possibility. I was hit by bricks on the top of the head and also on the back. I was dazed for a few moments, and then I got up and walked to the office, and there was fellow by the name of George who asked me if I wanted to go home. I refused him, and I went into the office, and I also refused to have the doctor stitch me up. (What about your tongue?) On this side it stands for a woman. When I put it on this side it means I am a little c.s. This is what you call a prick, and this is what you call the right wing. (Patient accompanies this with movements of the tongue to different parts of the mouth.) To tell the truth, I am friendly. You are Jewish. You are also Jewish. You are Jewish too. This means you have a place to go, and you may be a Rabbi in a synagogue or else a physician."

He was elated and admonished the physician not to put his tongue on the wrong side. In May 1933, according to a report from the state hospital, he showed a typical schizophrenic picture with hallucinations. He had withdrawn more and more and then showed deterioration, which progressed steadily during the following three years.

The following case shows a similar problem:

H. W., 35 years old, was admitted to the wards on March 23, 1933. According to the history of friends, he was hit on the head on March 6 with a piece of lead pipe by someone attempting to rob him. It is not known whether he was unconscious, but the next day he began to talk in a confused manner, was excited, violent, and threatened to kill his relatives. At admission he showed a recent laceration of the left frontal-parietal region. The fundi were normal. The spinal fluid and X-ray examinations were negative. He was combative, assaultive, noisy, impulsive, ran about the ward unclad, and expressed ideas of grandeur. He had auditory hallucinations. He remarked: "I came here to see the world. My name is written in the sky, we are going to die. I am going to cut your head off, the world is coming to an end at three o'clock. I am the most powerful man in the world. Give me a cobra and I will cause it to lie down. I have the power of tongues, God speaks to me and gives me power. I hear people talk to me when I am alone. They call me Son of God and Prince of Priests. They say that I am crazy, but they said the same thing about Jesus Christ."

It seems doubtful whether in these last cases the head injury had more than a psychological significance in the outbreak of the psychosis. Probably we deal in both cases with acute schizophrenic pictures.

The following case offers another interesting problem:

M. G., 22 years old, was admitted on March 11, 1933. She had fallen from a window, which she was cleaning, and was admitted to the surgical ward on February 25, 1933. Her sensorium was clouded. There was a fissure fracture of the right frontal and parietal bones. The Wassermann was negative, and there was no blood in the spinal fluid. The family history was without significance. Little things preyed on her mind. She mourned for a year when her father died. Nine months ago she had a baby. After she had weaned it, she was depressed and occasionally said that she did not want to live. A short time ago there had been a fire in the apartment house. On the ward the patient was apprehensive and misinterpreted her surroundings continually. She was restless, noisy, excited, screamed, and was overtalkative. "Don't let them hit me. Don't let them touch me. I see what they are doing. I was nervous lately. You're harming me. You're murdering me. Murder, murderer. Give me a chance. They are not bringing me back to health. I am afraid. I imagine it was just a little curse on me, falling out of the window. It was just my religion. Nobody put the curse on me of falling out of the window. I felt I was going to be tortured. A few months I am upset. I found it a little hard to take care of the baby. I felt depressed about it. It was hard to stay in. The baby was not so well. It was an accident. I was cleaning a window and felt a little dizzy. I did not know what happened. I never tried to kill myself. I felt like I was going to be tortured."

On March 12 she said: "Please don't let them touch me and hit me. I see what they are doing. My son is nine months old. I was very nervous lately." The patient continually made remarks about the physician. "I know what I am here for. You are going to kill me. You torturers. You lay them down and medicate them. I know you are going to kill me anyway. I weaned the baby after the third month. I want to live if I am given a chance. I look on you as murderers. You torture me. What have I done to deserve this? Why don't you kill me at once? I told my mother to see me until I die. How can you bear to torture another Jew like that?"

The picture in this case is that of a typical agitated depression. Aggressiveness was outstanding. The psychosis had developed after head injury, which was followed by a state of confusion. One may say that the patient was depressed before. It is not probable that the patient made a conscious attempt to suicide. Unconscious factors probably played a part in the accident. Nevertheless, the mental picture changed after a definite skull fracture. Sadistic trends and excitement were then in the foreground. These were constitutional factors. There may have been a beginning depression. This is only one of the instances where individual experience and psychic constitution are deciding factors for the type of psychosis after head injury. I do not think it is merely by chance that we deal with the picture that belongs to the manic-depressive group. I have already discussed the relation of manic constitution to subsequent manic pictures after head injuries. Head injury and manic-depressive psychosis seem to be more closely connected than head injury and schizophrenic pictures.

Wagner-Jauregg (1889), Stransky (1911), and Ritterhaus (1920) believe in a direct causal relation between manic-depressive psychosis and head injury. I believe in a more indirect connection, as shown in the cases reported here. In my experience of many years I have never seen a case of manic-depressive psychosis in which the head injury was the only etiological factor. But the head injury in these cases certainly does not act merely as a psychic trauma; it has an organic consequence for the elaboration of the psychosis.

Epileptic attacks from head injuries cannot be discussed here. In some of the cases reported here, epileptic attacks had only a symptomatic significance and were without influence on the picture of the psychosis.

A few remarks are in order regarding the relation of psychosis after head injuries to alcoholic psychosis. In a comparatively large number of our cases, alcoholism was a complicating factor. It is true the alcoholic exposes himself more easily to the traumatic situation. In addition to that, we have to assume that the periventricular gray in the alcoholic is attacked by the alcohol and so becomes predisposed or slightly changed. One may suppose that the possibility of hemorrhages, especially around the ventricular system, is greater in the alcoholic. But the symptomatology of the psychosis after head injury in the alcoholic and nonalcoholic is practically identical. There are many common features between the psychoses with encephalopathia alcoholica and the post-traumatic psychoses, such as the clouding of consciousness, the resistiveness, the confusion, and the memory disturbances. I do not intend to discuss the differential diagnosis in detail. But the similarities in the clinical pictures point to pathophysiological mechanisms, which are based on the severe disturbance in the ventricular gray in connection with cortical lesions.

This study is primarily concerned with the acute psychotic pictures after head injuries. The following case histories merely illustrate the connection between acute and chronic cases:

J. J., 34 years old, was admitted to Bellevue Hospital on March 20, 1933. He had been knocked down by a train. The diagnosis of a concussion of the brain was made. The X ray was negative. The left pupil was wider than the right. At first there was a Babinski on the left side, but in the next days this became bilateral.

He complained about dizzy spells, had an asymmetrical face, and swayed in Romberg position to the right side. There was no nystagmus. Bárány's reaction was exaggerated. There was tremor of the eyelids. When a mental test was made on March 31, 1933, he showed a mental age of eleven years, one month. He was slow, almost confused, and showed a wide scattering in the test. The memory score in the Wells test was 57. Re-examination in the course of March showed an increase in the mental age of one year and two months. Rote memory was still below normal; logical memory improved; memory quotient improved by sixteen points. The most remarkable improvement was noted in the association tests. He still complained about headache. During the night he occasionally heard people calling him by name.

I mention this case merely in order to show the persistence of disorder of the memory and of the intellectual functioning and the variations in these that may occur.

Another case shows yet another side of the problem:

E. C., 29 years old, was admitted on March 22, 1933. In 1929 he had received a fracture of the skull. He was on the running board when an automobile hit his car. The head injury was followed by unconsciousness and stupor. At the time, he exhibited symptoms of manic-depressive psychosis. The X-ray examination of the skull showed a fracture of the right parietal bone. In addition, he suffered a fracture of the right maxilla, which caused severe pain. On February 4, 1933 he developed severe pain in the head, which was followed by disorientation and coma. He showed complete anosmia, impairment of taste, and vertigo. An encephalogram showed fairly large, asymmetrical ventricles and large basal cisterns, indicating a mild degree of cortical atrophy which was chiefly on the left side. He was depressed and anxious concerning his condition. His memory and attention were impaired, but there was good intelligence and insight. When he returned home from the Neurological Institute he went away, and did not inform his wife of his whereabouts, and was later brought to Bellevue Hospital. "I just came back from Pennsylvania. I have been in the mountains. The climate up there, the weather conditions and everything else is so much better than in New York. I just left the city. I was worried about myself. I used to have plenty headaches. Weather conditions in New York are not so good for me. It is not merely weather conditions, perhaps it is just the hustle and bustle of the big city. I was not missing, I just went away. Of course I knew where I was going. I went on my own free will. Of course I should have told the police department. (The patient is a policeman.) I felt 100 per cent better when I was down there. I don't think my wife knew it. I didn't want her to be worried. She knows I can take care of myself." He was unstable and irritable. In a mental test he showed superior intelligence and was above the average in memory test (102 per cent). Gestalt tests were normal.

This case is mentioned in order to show that emotional disturbances may remain after the disappearance of the memory disturbance. The patient, who was previously normal, well adapted, and did not show any hereditary traits, afterward showed the picture of an unstable and irritable psychopath. I may mention in this connection that after the malaria treatment of general paresis, mental deterioration may be completely absent, but the patients may show similar emotional instability as was seen in the following case:

E. O., 35 years old, was brought to the Bellevue Psychiatric Hospital on April 3, 1933. On August 18, 1932, he had been attacked by six men. He was struck on the back of the head with a telephone and was knocked down and for a time was unconscious. His scalp was lacerated, but there was no bleeding from the nose, mouth, or ears. The laceration of his scalp was closed with one stitch, and he was sent home. After the accident he was unemployed. He complained about attacks of dizziness; then he saw double and had headaches. There was an impairment of memory. The physical examination at that time was negative. He was nervous and under increased tension. He was admitted to another hospital on November 17, 1932 and remained there until December 7, 1932. During this stay he complained of dizziness, headache, and pain in his back. He claimed that he imagined things. At times he seemed to be confused; he said he saw two men in the hall watching for an opportunity to take him out, that he could not sleep because the Reds were after him. They had pursued him for the past few months, and would get him. They had tried to poison his dog and would get his family. On November 28 he still held the same delusional ideas. The blood Wassermann was negative.

The wife stated at his admission that the patient had been depressed during the past twelve months and had threatened suicide. He had attacks of dizziness and trembling. He was afraid that somebody was after him, and saw strange people in his room at night. The patient himself reported that he had been hurt by Communists. Since that time he was afraid of everybody. "I can't trust nobody. Somebody wants to grab me at the neck. I don't see how it can be true how anybody can do it to me. Sometimes I see people looking at me. I hate to go to the subway or elevated. I am afraid of getting pushed off. I can be talking to someone and my mind goes blank. Sometimes I hear as if there were two people talking of me. My house is all boarded up—windows and doors. Sometimes I see someone in my bed, and when I swing around quickly I don't see anybody." The patient did not show any evidence of mental deterioration or organic memory disturbance. The X ray of the skull was negative, and there were no neurological findings.

This case, in which there is no evidence of fracture of the skull or subarachnoid hemorrhage, shows a paranoid and hallucinatory picture. But the emotions connected with his ideas of persecution are of psychogenic type. The way in which he gave his narrative and his reactions were too dramatic and did not show deep emotion. His complaints were too demonstrative. The picture is psychogenic. In decided contrast to the other cases reported, the terrifying scenes during the night and his hallucinations are in close relation to the traumatic scene. The case qualifies in this respect as a traumatic neurosis, in which, according to Freud, the traumatic event comes back in dreams and fantasies (cf. Kardiner, 1932). We may draw the general conclusion that the psychological attitude in serious head-injury cases is fundamentally different from the attitude in traumatic neurosis. Whereas in the organic case the accident is forgotten or is remembered without any terror and even with some satisfaction, the traumatic neurosis shows the tendency to relive the traumatic scene with terror connected with the original event. This differentiation is, of course, schematic. Further clinical studies should be made. Even if the last case reported should have slight organic changes in the brain, which may facilitate the neurotic reaction, there is still a sharp difference in the attitude toward the trauma in the predominantly organic or neurotic case (Jelliffe, 1933b).

The various interrelations between head injuries and the previous personality have been carefully studied by Kretschmer (1919) and Gordon (1933). The latter points to the structural damage that may lead to late degenerative changes. According to him, the paranoid pictures and the changes in mood are the result of the disturbance in the dynamics of mental life, and the old somatic trauma is not a direct etiological factor in the development of the psychosis. But we should not forget that the injury to the brain can also change the individual's emotional attitude in a direct way. This becomes especially clear in the epileptoid and epileptic cases, which have not been discussed here. The late psychotic picture may be partially due to the direct changes in the emotions, but the head injury, and the headache and dizziness it causes, may also have a similar significance as the day reminiscence in the genesis of a dream. The head injury may act, therefore, as an organic as well as a psychogenic factor.

Summary and Conclusions

1. In 35 selected cases of serious head injuries in which either the X ray proved fracture of the skull or the spinal puncture, subarachnoid hemorrhage, or both signs of serious traumatism were

present, the state of unconsciousness with complete relaxation was very often followed by a state of deep clouding of consciousness and a general resistiveness. This attitude is partially psychic and partially based on organic neuromuscular components.

2. In the next stage there is clouding of consciousness and far-reaching disorientation in space and time. Deep bewilderment and helplessness may be present. (a) Tachistoscopic and clinical examinations show that the patient needs a long time to arrive at any perception. The perceptive function as such is retarded. There is also difficulty in synthesizing primitive impressions into a unit. Complicated pictures are not understood. (b) The gestalt function is deeply impaired. Primitive structures appear in the visual-motor gestalt patterns. The perception and gestalt difficulties disturb the basis of orientation. (c) The central personality, feeling its inability, reacts with helplessness and confusion. (d) The same basic disturbance finds its expression in the ship test, the manikin, and the profile test. (e) Memory and judgment are likewise impaired, but impairment of the memory, especially for recent events, is generally more outspoken. (f) It is probable that the clouding of consciousness, the perceptive difficulties, and the disturbances in the gestalt function are partially independent from each other, although they may influence each other and are closely interrelated. (g) Memory disturbance and impairment of judgment always accompany the perception, gestalt, and consciousness disturbances. The impairment of judgment is less pronounced than the memory disturbance.

3. The period of this disturbance can be short, but can also last for several weeks. It may develop after a free interval.

4. When the perception, the gestalt-function disturbance, and the clouding of consciousness subside, the picture of a Korsakoff psychosis remains. In some of the Korsakoff cases the perceptive and gestalt disturbances may still be present. But the absence of clouding of consciousness differentiates these pictures from the picture described in the second case, T. R., and the perceptive and gestalt disturbances can be completely absent. The confabulations do not run parallel to the memory disturbance, and can be

present even when the memory has returned to normal. The memory disturbance is chiefly a disturbance in retention. Impairment of judgment especially concerns the correlations of the data of memory.

5. Although alcoholism was a complicating factor in some of the reported cases, it is in no way a necessary factor in the genesis of the traumatic Korsakoff picture.

6. The psychic material that appears in the confusional state (post-traumatic stupor of Symonds) is rather impersonal and has generally little connection with the previous structure of the personality.

7. The post-traumatic confusion is a confusion concerning perception and synthesis of impersonal material and is well characterized in comparison with the toxic confusion in which the synthesis, perception, and gestalt are affected in their more personal aspects. The post-traumatic confusion, therefore, may be characterized as confusion of the organic type, which primarily affects the ego in a psychoanalytic sense (perception ego of my own nomenclature).

8. Amnesia concerning the accident is the rule both in the confusional and in the Korsakoff state. The amnesia can be complete and can be retroactive for a shorter or a longer period. Later on, a vague knowledge concerning the accident may come back, partially based on reports by others. But this knowledge is very often distorted in a confabulatory way. In some cases the amnesia may clear up, in others the amnesia is persistent. The amnesia concerning the accident may be the only lasting psychic symptom. The resistiveness of the amnesia is in contrast to hysterical amnesia and also to amnesias that are due to mere alcoholic intoxications. The regaining of the memory of the accident is very often preceded by a confabulatory stage.

9. Frequently, the patients are not concerned about their head injuries.

10. The mood after the accident is very often characterized by resistiveness. Apathy and bewilderment may follow. Indifference with euphoria are common in Korsakoff pictures. In some

cases, depression and worries may be in the foreground. In others, excitement similar to mania may occur, but this is more monotonous and empty. Postencephalitic monotony and pestering were found in a group of head injuries in young people. In other cases, the picture may have more resemblance to manic states. In cases in which paraphasias and sensory aphasias are present, euphoria, manic attitudes, optimism, and lack of insight into the defectiveness may prevail. Moodiness and a strong feeling for their defectiveness has to be expected in cases with motor aphasia. In a case with parietal lobe symptoms, a hypochondriacal attitude has been observed.

11. The changes in the mood can be attributed to a variety of factors. (a) One is the general reaction pattern of the brain. Confusion as such, coupled with perceptive and gestalt difficulties, carries a particular mood. (b) The Korsakoff psychosis also carries with it a typical mood. We deal with changes in mood due to the organic state. This organic state may be due to a so-called general injury of the brain. (c) It is possible that some kinds of blind excitements and manic states belong in the same category. (d) One is inclined to bring the encephalitic-like pictures in connection with more subcortical, midbrain, and diencephalic lesions. (e) The localized injuries of Broca's and Wernicke's region bring with them characteristic changes in mood. (f) Parietal lobe lesion may carry with it a hypochondriacal attitude.

12. But in the changes of mood after head injury, not only are the impairment of generalized and local organic patterns of importance; the constitutional emotional temperament (manic or depressive) likewise finds its expression, as well as the personal fate and the complexes that are reflected in the mood.

13. We may expect that constitutional attitudes and personal, acquired patterns have more opportunity to come to the foreground when the traumatic state is less severe or less acute. Unconsciousness and death certainly do not show many individual trends.

14. Even the so-called general symptoms of brain injury can justly be considered from the point of view of localization. Multi-

ple sclerosis, epidemic encephalitis, general paresis, and brain tumor certainly involve the whole brain. But the clear-cut clinical pictures still show a systemic character.

15. The changes in the ventricular gray are partially responsible for the changes in consciousness, and participate in connection with the cortical lesions in the final elaboration of the disturbances in memory, judgment, and in the Korsakoff pictures.

16. Special emphasis is laid upon the diffuse congestion of all parts of the brain associated with universal perivascular hemorrhages. The hemorrhages are especially severe in the areas surrounding the ventricles. The hemorrhages around the fourth ventricle and the aqueduct (Duret) deserve special attention. Other foci of destruction are due to immediate damage and not to hemorrhage.

17. Similarity in the clinical picture of alcoholic encephalopathy and post-traumatic psychosis is regarded as due to similar pathology as it concerns the periventricular and cortical lesions. The possibility is discussed that the periventricular and cortical damage through alcohol predisposes to traumatic changes through head injuries.

18. My material does not offer any proof for the genesis or traumatic origin of schizophrenia, but catatonic symptoms may be a sign of local lesion, and a head injury may, from a psychological and organic point of view, be an eliciting factor.

19. Head injuries may directly provoke manic pictures and probably also those of depression, but they are not the exclusive cause of manic-depressive psychosis. They can change mild depressive pictures through organic and psychogenic ways into those that are severe.

20. Impairment in memory and judgment may constitute chronic pictures after head injuries.

21. Emotional disturbances and changes toward schizoid, psychopathic, and epileptoid trends may be the final outcome of the organic disturbance.

22. In minor head injuries, the traumatic scene has a definite significance. It may be relived again and again in dreams, halluci-

nations, and fantasies, and may be interwoven with paranoid attitudes.

These few remarks cannot give more than a preliminary idea of the importance of this subject, which has not only practical interest, but also important theoretical aspects that should be studied more carefully. Only if we increase our theoretical knowledge shall we be able to do justice to our patients.

CHAPTER FOURTEEN

Alcoholic Encephalopathy

Acute and chronic alcoholic intoxications produce a variety of
clinical pictures which are fairly well differentiated from each
other. This paper will deal principally with the so-called polioencephalitis haemorrhagica of Wernicke. This condition may be
associated with polyneuritis, and there are many associated but
atypical pictures, at least if one considers Wernicke's (1906) classic
description. More recent investigations, especially those of
Gamper (1928), Ohkuma (1930), and Neuberger (1931), disclosed
the relation of polioencephalitis to other alcoholic psychoses. In
the classical picture of polioencephalitis the following characteristics have been emphasized: ocular palsies, deep clouding of consciousness, asynergia, and toxic changes. Alcohol has been shown
to be important in the etiology, but Oppenheim (1923) and Neuberger have found that influenza and other conditions may produce the same picture. Small hemorrhages in the ventricular gray
areas and around the oculomotor nuclei were found long ago in
cases of chronic alcoholism by Raimon (quoted by Oppenheim,

Appeared originally in the *Archives of Neurology and Psychiatry*, 29: 990-1053,
1933, Lauretta Bender, co-author.

1923). As Schroeder (1930) has suggested, there is no encephalitis in the proper sense, but degenerative changes occur in the blood vessels and are associated with hemorrhages. Lüthy and Walthard (1928) and Ohkuma (1930) believed, however, that an inflammatory process may also be present. Gamper (1928) claimed that a Korsakoff syndrome was often present in such cases. As is to be expected, polyneuritic signs are often found with lesions of the central nervous system such as are present in Wernicke's polioencephalitis. Pseudopellagrous lesions of the skin have been observed in patients with chronic alcoholism by Klauder and Winkelman (1928) and by Boggs and Padget (1932). This is an interesting association not mentioned in the German literature, except that Kumer (1931) observed some endemic cases of pellagra among alcoholic patients. A number of our cases have also shown these cutaneous lesions. This raises the more general question of whether the polioencephalitis, as well as polyneuritis, may not be an expression of a general trophic change, or whether the trophic changes may result from lesions of the vegetative centers of the central nervous system and thus be an expression of a vegetative polyneuritis.

We shall not attempt here to deal with other interesting types of chronic alcoholic disturbances, although we may mention that Schilder (1930a, 1932a [see also Chapter 16]) has shown that lesions of the striopallidum and substantia nigra in chronic alcoholism are evidenced by flexor contractures in the outstretched arms with convergence at the elbows. These changes may be associated with alcoholic tremor, but may also be independent of it. In acute and chronic alcoholism one may also see pictures that closely resemble paralysis agitans. The various neurologic problems offered in delirium tremens cannot be considered here. These may include striopallidum and midbrain syndromes as well as the well-known cerebellar syndrome.

An analysis of the present series of cases, which were studied in Bellevue Hospital, has led us to make a classification into five clinical groups. The first of these comes nearest to the classical picture of polioencephalitis haemorrhagica superior, with clouding of consciousness and changing rigidities in the limbs as character-istics. In the second group, cerebellar disturbances are more promi-nent. The third group closely resembles acute catatonia in both mental and neurological features. In the fourth group, the delirious features are more marked, the neurological features less so. In the fifth group, polyneuritic signs are associated with various polioen-cephalitic signs.

I. Alcoholic Encephalopathy with Clouding of Consciousness and Changing Rigidities

Case 1. Clinical History. A man, aged 45, had been drinking heavily and neglecting himself completely for several weeks before admission to the hospital. He answered questions briefly at first, but immediately became drowsy. His speech was slurred. There was deep clouding of consciousness, with marked restlessness at night. He continually grabbed at objects; he pulled at his shoes and tried to catch things. There was no psychic resistance, and he showed an increased reaction to pain. He tried again and again to get up, but fell back, and there was a dissociation between the activities of the limbs and the trunk. There were no lasting rigidi-ties, but a frequently recurring and changing resistance to passive movements. Often, when the legs were extended and flexed he continued the movement rhythmically. There were restless move-ments of an athetoid type, together with Dupuytren's contractures of the fingers. The neck and jaw were stiff against passive move-ments. There was paresis of the right internal rectus muscle. Pupil-lary, conjunctival, and corneal reflexes and the eyegrounds were normal. Arm tendon and abdominal reflexes were present and equal; the left patellar reflex was also normal, but the right one was diminished; both Achilles reflexes were absent. There was no Babinski reaction on either side. There was no change in the clinical picture in the next few days. The changing rigidities were always present. Death occurred eleven days after he was admitted. Post-mortem examination showed pneumonia of the left lung, a pial edema, and congestion of the brain.

Summary and Comment. The characteristic lesion was a ventricular ependymitis,[1] with an underlying vascular disturbance which invaded all the ventricular gray masses.[2] Similar lesions were seen on the surface of the brain, but they were less severe. The optic nerve was also involved. Diffuse fatty changes were present in the nerve cells of the cortex. Three principles seemed to be involved in the localization of the lesions: (1) All surfaces of the central nervous system closely associated with the spinal fluid were affected, especially where there was a tendency toward stagnation of the fluid. Thus, the ventricular system, especially about recesses and pockets, was more involved than the surface of the brain. (2) Nuclear areas were more prone to lesions than adjacent. white areas. This was seen both in the cortex and in the brain stem. (3) Visceral nuclear areas seemed more vulnerable than somatic or cortical nuclear areas.

The outstanding clinical features were: (1) clouding of consciousness with delirious features, (2) a tendency to rhythmic movements, (3) athetoid movements, (4) changing rigidities, (5) grasping and groping, (6) paresis of the right internal rectus muscle, (7) asynergia between the legs and trunk, and (8) increased reaction to pain.

The lesions in the brain were so widespread that it is difficult to correlate accurately the clinical and anatomic findings. But it is probable, as we shall show later, that the clouding of consciousness was associated with lesions of the ventricular gray area; the rigidities and athetoid movements with lesions around the nucleus of the eighth nerve, the subthalamic region, and the substantia nigra and putamen.

Case 2. Clinical History. A woman, aged 48, was transferred to Bellevue from another hospital on June 21, 1931 with the

---

[1] The term ependymitis is used here, not in the sense of an inflammatory process, but in the classic sense of a reactive process in the ependymal glia cells.

[2] [The details and illustrations of the histopathologic and neuropathologic studies have been omitted—Ed.]

history that her husband had died three months before and that she had taken to drink. She had complained of gastritis and melancholia; for three days she had been in bed and had refused to get up; in general, she was very negativistic. She did not answer questions. She had a dazed expression, and her eyes rolled about without fixing on anything. She responded to painful stimuli only slightly, by restless movements. There were changing rigidities in the limbs. Her temperature was 101 F.; no pathologic condition was found in the heart, lungs, or abdomen to account for the fever. She had a tense expression of pain on her face and was blindly resistive to all examination procedures. The neck was rigid; the pupils were irregular and small, the left being fixed to light and the right one nearly so. The tendon reflexes of the arms were present and equal, but the knee and ankle jerks were absent, as were the abdominal reflexes. The Kernig sign was present on the right. Lumbar puncture showed clear fluid without increased pressure; it contained no cells or globulin, and the Wassermann and colloidal gold reactions were negative. Urinalysis gave negative results.

The following day she was more stuporous, did not talk, moaned, was resistive, was unable to swallow, and showed a complete ophthalmoplegia. Temperature was 104 F., but there were no foci of infection, and the medical consultant related the fever to the cerebral disturbance. She died on this day. The anatomic findings at autopsy were: chronic mitral valvulitis, calcification and arteriosclerosis of the aortic valve leaflets, fatty infiltration of the liver, chronic interstitial hepatitis, chronic diffuse nephritis, and congestion and edema of the brain.

Summary and Comment. The outstanding clinical features were: (1) marked clouding of consciousness, (2) changing rigidities, (3) reduction in impulses except negativistic ones, (4) ophthalmoplegia, (5) impaired reactions of the pupils to light, and (6) rapid febrile course. The changes in the brain were diffuse but very acute, being most severe along the floor of the ventricles and the base of the brain and optic chiasm. In general, the lesion had the same characteristics and distribution as that in case 1, but it was more severe and more acute, and there was a more generalized disturbance of the brain as a whole. Concerning the localization of disturbances, the same may be said as for case 1. The pupillary changes may have been correlated with lesions in the floor of the aqueduct and the surface and base of the midbrain, in accordance with Ingvar's (1928) findings.

Case 3. Clinical History. A chauffeur, aged 37, was brought to the hospital on a charge of disorderly conduct on June 9, 1931. He had been drinking heavily for two years and steadily for six or eight weeks, but had stopped eight days before. After that he had had hallucinations of people walking about his room, had misidentified relatives, and had been confused. On admission he was dull, confused, resistive, unsteady, and tremulous. His speech was thick and incoherent.. The pupils reacted sluggishly to light. The tongue was beefy and tremulous. He was clumsy, ataxic, and all his movements were tremulous. The tendon reflexes were present and equal, the Babinski reaction negative. Examination of the heart, lungs, and abdomen gave negative results, as was the Wassermann reaction of the blood and spinal fluid. The colloidal gold curve with the spinal fluid was 12210000; the total protein was 6.25.

On June 12, he was dull and tended to perseverate his first response to any command. Speech was slowed, slurred, and thick. He had difficulty in swallowing. He was unable to walk without support and showed extrapyramidal rigidity. Nystagmus was noted, but cooperation was poor for ocular movements. The pupillary reactions were sluggish. On June 13 he was dull, not talking, but fumbling with the bedclothes in a delirious way. He was incontinent. The pupils were dilated, unequal, and reacted poorly to light. There were partial bilateral ptosis, bilateral abducens weakness, and failure of convergence, associated with staring and some tendency for the eyes to wander upward. He would turn his head rather than his eyes when he wished to look to either side.

There were changing rigidities and convergence tendencies in the arms, with an increased defense reaction to pain.

On June 15, the patient's expression was blank; he made rotary movements of the head and held his hands in the air as though whirling a string; there were awkward pseudo-athetoid movements of the hands. He looked straight ahead with only slight movements of the eyes to the right, showing an external ophthalmoplegia. Pupillary reactions were prompt. There were resistance and rigidity of the neck, and rigidities of the arms that increased with tensions, especially in the arm-shoulder muscle group, and the same was true of the thigh group. The tendon reflexes were brisk in the upper extremities and normal in the lower; plantar reaction was normal. There was a positive support reaction in the lower extremities. On June 18, he was more apathetic, showed a complete ophthalmoplegia, and a grasping reflex, and was beginning to show bulbar and respiratory difficulties. He died on June 19. Autopsy performed the next day showed anthracosis of the lungs, congestion of the stomach, fatty infiltration of the liver, hypertrophy of the bladder, hypertrophy of the prostate, and congestion and edema of the brain.

Summary and Comment. There was a severe ependymal reaction of the whole ventricular system, with an irregular marginal involvement of the surface of the cerebrum, cerebellum, and brain stem, such as the upper surface of the quadrigeminate bodies. Besides this, the ventricular gray masses were involved, especially in the medullary nuclei and the level of the pons, but less in the midbrain, and again severely in the third ventricle, including the mammillary bodies and the central parts of the thalamic and caudate nuclei. The lesions were characteristically an ependymitis and marginal gliosis, with an underlying increase in the vascular bed, congestion, hemorrhages, and an extensive invasive and reactive gliosis.

The outstanding clinical features were: (1) clouding of consciousness with delirious features, (2) serious troubles with speech and with the impulses, (3) increased reaction to pain, (4) severe ophthalmoplegia, (5) changing rigidities, (6) a grasping reflex, (7) pseudo-athetoid movements, (8) a positive support reaction in the lower extremities, and (9) asynergia of the trunk.

This case adds further evidence of the same kind as in our previous consideration of the localization of disturbances. The support reaction and grasping reflex were probably in connection with the lesions in the same apparatus that produced the changing rigidities. The lesion in the folia of the cerebellum and the roof of the fourth ventricle accounted for the asynergia.

Case 4. Clinical History. A man, aged 35, was admitted on May 15, 1931 on voluntary application and stated that he had been drinking heavily. He said: "I was here a few months ago. This time I drank for six nights. I began vomiting last night." He complained of gastroenteritis. He knew the date. His pupils reacted to light. On May 23, he presented deep clouding of consciousness and did not talk. He had a rigid face, a tendency toward sucking, and a grasping reflex. The pupils were narrow but still reacted to light. He could not move the eyes to either side or upward completely, so that he usually looked downward; he could not converge. There was stiffness all over the body, which was like a resistance. All movements were awkward, and he remained in queer athetoid postures. Tendon and abdominal reflexes were present and plantar reflex was normal. There was an exaggerated reaction to pain all over the body, with especially strong retractions of the legs when the plantar reflexes were examined. The skin on the extensor surfaces of the hands showed a desquamating pellagroid lesion. The internal organs were normal. The Wassermann reaction with blood and spinal fluid was negative. In the right eyeground, below the disk was a large fresh hemorrhage. The patient was restless at night. On May 25 his speech was slurred and bulbar in type. He sometimes looked to the right side with both eyes. He was a little more active. Caloric stimulation of the ears did not produce any reaction. Touching of the lips provoked immediate pouting. There was rigidity in both legs, with some degree of catalepsy. The left great toe was held in the Babinski position. Tensions in the arms and legs were associated with a support reaction. Throughout, he spoke only occasional words. On May 28, he said: "There is only one toilet. See what they are doing." On June 8, he could get on his feet, but showed retropulsion. He was anxious to obey commands, but tended to hold postures, and showed a resistance against passive movements. He usually looked straight ahead, though the eyes sometimes showed spontaneous movements to either side, associated with a horizontal systagmus. On this date, convergence was possible, but upward movements of the eyes were still impaired. Pupillary reactions were prompt. When shown a picture of a girl, he said, "It is a monkey," thus showing difficulty in the apperception of pictures. His speech was slurred. He said: "There is nothing the matter with me; I came in this morning. I am in the observation ward. This is January, 1928."

By June 12, the cutaneous disturbances had cleared up. He now talked continuously. He still showed stiffness and pseudo-athetoid movements in the hands. There was a strong flexor tendency in both elbows. There were only partial difficulties in the ocular movements. He was transferred to the Manhattan State Hospital on June 17, 1931. Following is a report received from there: "Incontinent of urine; unable to feed himself; speech practically unintelligible; markedly deteriorated; psychomotor activity increased; restless; dysarthria of speech. There was very little emotional display. At times it seemed as if he might be reacting to auditory hallucinations. Tremor of facial muscles. Positive Gordon Holmes reaction. Atrophy of the limbs. Nystagmus present. Speech thick and scanning. Wassermann reaction of the blood negative; Kahn test negative; colloidal gold curve 0000000000. Patient showed marked asynergia of extremities, head, and trunk. There was marked ataxia in the finger-to-nose test, a constant wagging tremor of the head and occasionally of the left arm and leg. Pupils were unequal and sluggish. There was a primary optic atrophy. Speech was dysarthric and slurred. Deep reflexes were all active and brisk. Plantar response difficult to elicit because of hyperkinesia. On September 3, he showed emotional instability and was tearful; there were marked coarse movements of the hands and legs. The pupils were equal and reacted well to light. On October 5 he was quiet, kept shaking his head from side to side, and was constantly coughing and masturbating; the sensorium was defective. On October 9 he died. The diagnosis was alcoholic psychosis, Korsakoff, delirious type. Cause of death, chronic alcoholism; hemorrhagic alcoholic encephalitis; contributing cause of death, bronchopneumonia."

Summary and Comment. Clinically there were: (1) clouding of consciousness with delirious features, (2) grasping and sucking reflexes, (3) complete ophthalmoplegia except for upward movements, (4) absence of vestibular reactions to irrigation of the ears, (5) bulbar speech, (6) changing rigidities, (7) athetoid movements, (8) support reaction, (9) convergence reactions in the arms, (10) increased reaction to pain, (11) pseudopellagrous reactions in the skin, (12) retinal hemorrhages. It is of interest that at the state hospital atrophy of the retinal disks and pupillary disturbances developed. There were apparently also additional cerebellar signs. In this case the encephalopathy led to death after six months. Otherwise the case is typical. It is of especial interest that fresh hemorrhages were observed in the retina; they are probably comparable to the hemorrhages seen microscopically in the central nervous system in the other cases studied.

Case 5. Clinical History. A man, aged 42, who was brought to the hospital on May 28, 1931, had always been well until the preceding winter, when he had pneumonia. After that he felt weak and started to drink. On admission, he was tall, emaciated, shaky, and tremulous, and showed a pellagroid rash on both hands. The pupils were unequal; the left reacted to light better than the right. He showed tensions all over the body which were similar to resistances. The Wassermann reaction of the blood and spinal fluid was negative. On June 3, he said, "I'm all right—all right." He could not name objects. A few days later he said, "This is some place in Harlem." He picked at imaginary objects and was confused. It was impossible to get more than a few words from him. There was no true aphasia, but difficulty in getting out the words and a seeming lack of impulse for speech were noted. After June 8 he did not talk at all. After considerable desquamation, the pseudopellagrous lesions on the hands were replaced by an atrophic skin. There continued to be irregular tensions in all extremities that looked like resistances. The hands assumed awkward athetoid positions. When the arms were passively extended they diverged at the shoulders and converged at the elbows. He had a marked sucking reflex and a marked grasping reflex, especially in the right hand. The hands were held completely stiff when passive movements were made with the arms. Stiffness in the legs was even more marked. There was an increased reaction to pain shown by a marked retraction of the legs when the plantar reflexes were examined. The facial expression was rigid. The tendon reflexes of the arms were normal, but the Achilles reflexes were not elicited, possibly owing to the tensions. He was always grasping in a semidelirious way. The ocular movements, pupillary reactions, and eyegrounds were normal. In the next few days he became more restless and the grasping tendencies increased. The hands remained in the air in queer stiff athetoid postures. The mouth was held half open, with the head retracted and the eyes wide open. He sometimes acted as though he had hallucinations. He died on June 14, 1931.

Summary and Comment. The symptomatology in this case showed: (1) clouding of consciousness with delirious features, (2) sucking and grasping reflexes, (3) difficulty in bringing out words, (4) changing rigidities, (5) athetoid movements, (6) increased reaction to pain, and (7) pseudopellagrous changes in the skin with subsequent atrophy. The case is remarkable because there were no signs referable to the eyes.

Case 6. Clinical History. A woman, aged 31, who was admitted to the hospital on June 28, 1931, was violent and excited.

She said that she had been drinking for about a week. She said, "I have heard people talking. I can't hear what they say. I saw my husband this morning. I have had some trouble, but I can't tell you because it doesn't concern you." She had visual hallucinations and was disoriented for time and place. The eyelids were slightly ptotic. The pupillary reactions were prompt. She made very quick, jerky movements, especially in the shoulders, but there were no muscle spasms. She had grasping tendencies, especially with the right hand. Tensions similar to voluntary tensions sometimes occurred and made her rigid. Sometimes she displayed something similar to cataleptic tendencies in the legs. Pointing positions with both index fingers were often seen. Achilles and patellar tendon reflexes were absent, as were the abdominal reflexes. There was soreness of the muscles of the calves of the legs, with an increased reaction to pain. On July 2 the pupils were stiff and all ocular movements were poor; she was able only to make a few nystagmoid upward movements. There was a slight rigidity of the neck, which was changeable. There were rhythmic movements of both hands. The Wassermann reaction of the blood and spinal fluid was negative, as were also other spinal fluid tests. The patient died on July 5, 1931.

Summary and Comment. This case showed: (1) clouding of consciousness with delirious features, (2) ophthalmoplegia, (3) grasping tendencies, (4) changing rigidities, (5) tendencies to rhythmic movements, (6) quick jerky movements, and (7) an increased reaction to pain. The case is significant because of the quick jerky movements, which occurred in a picture otherwise similar to that in the preceding cases. Later we shall describe cases in which these movements were the dominating feature.

Case 7. Clinical History. A man, aged 46, was admitted to the hospital, on March 13, 1931 with a history of severe alcoholism. He was rambling, incoherent, confused, and disoriented; he said, "My name is Ryan [not true]. I have been drinking at the hotel. I am just beginning to get overcome. It is overcoming me. I don't think I am much of anything. I am at Center Street." It was difficult to get an answer from him; he gave his name incorrectly and was slow in obeying commands. The facial expression was rigid, but the pupils reacted promptly. He recognized simple pictures but not more complicated pictures. All tendon reflexes were present and normal. The plantar reflex was negative, but the Hoffmann reaction was positive on the left and there was a transient ankle clonus on both sides. There was some tenderness in the muscles of the calves of the legs. When rhythmic movements were started, he tended to continue them. When he stood up, he swayed and fell backward. There were many changing rigidities in the limbs. Sometimes it was almost impossible to make any passive movements. He had a tendency toward paradoxical contractures and sometimes assumed athetoid postures. He grasped in a delirious way. He did not move when placed in bed, and lay immobile without covering himself unless directed to do so. He showed support reaction in both legs, but sometimes the stiffness in the knees would not disappear when the toes were bent. There was a general tendency toward stiffness in both legs. The extensor rigidity diminished in the next fortnight, but did not disappear entirely. He confabulated, saying, "I was here yesterday. I was watching the dead men. They were all over the bridge. I was on a rampage drinking whiskey for two months. It is a wonder I didn't get killed. I'm not safe here either. They are likely to come for me any minute. Those men are in the gang." The patient died on March 25. No post-mortem examination was made.

Summary and Comment. This case showed: (1) clouding of consciousness with delirious features, (2) a Korsakoff picture, (3) changing rigidities, (4) athetoid postures, (5) a support reaction, (6) asynergia between the trunk and legs, (7) a positive Hoffmann sign and ankle clonus, and (8) neuritic tenderness. In this case there were signs of a lesion of the pyramidal tract. Toward the end of the observation period the mental picture approached a Korsakoff psychosis.

Case 8. Clinical History. A man, aged 48, was transferred from another hospital on June 5, 1931, with a diagnosis of dementia paralytica. The Wassermann reaction of the blood was negative. Nothing was learned of the previous history. He was friendly but disoriented, and said: "You are an inceder—that's an investigator—I am inceptor. She is helper for in the incinerator. I am 38; my father is 52; my mother 42." Sometimes he showed ability to carry out complicated commands, but readily became confused. Sometimes he stammered badly. The pupils were small and practically fixed to light. He could not converge the eyes. The tendon reflexes were normal all over the body. There was no plantar reflex. He fell back when put on his feet and showed many changing rigidities in the limbs. On June 11 he was friendly, stammering at the beginning of words, but talked fluently. He said he was at Fordham Hospital and was sure that he had seen the examiner on the day before, which was not true. He was suggestible to confabulation. When asked the difference between a child and midget, he said, "There is something to it." When asked the difference between a bush and a tree, he said, "One grows and the other one ceased growing." A few minutes later he had forgotten both questions. Pupillary reactions were prompt and the ocular movements normal. The facial expression was rigid and there were slight changing rigidities in the arms. There was some tendency to grasp, but no groping. The outstretched arms showed a tendency to convergence at the shoulder and flexion at the elbows, the right more so than the left, and also changing rigidities of an extrapyramidal type in the legs. There was a marked asynergia between the trunk and the limbs, and the trunk was drawn backward. Patellar and achilles tendon reflexes were lively. There was an extreme defense reaction against pain when the plantar reflexes were tested, and, in general, pain produced an exaggerated reaction.

On June 13, the patient was transferred to the Manhattan State Hospital. They gave the following report: "When admitted he was feeble, deteriorated, and completely disoriented. His pupils were sluggish to light, but reacted fairly well in accommodation. Knee and ankle jerks were present and active; speech was slurred.

The blood Wassermann reaction was negative with alcoholic antigen; two plus with cholesterolized antigen; Kahn test, two plus; spinal fluid, negative to all antigens; colloidal gold curve 11122210000. On June 21, he was in poor condition and incontinent. His answers to questions were incoherent and irrelevant; he reacted to auditory hallucinations; he was disoriented and remote and recent memory were poor. On July 8, the knee jerks were exaggerated, the pupils fixed and irregular in outline, and the speech thick. He showed a marked mental deterioration; he was unclean in habits, and required spoon feeding. He died on July 28, 1931."

Summary and Comment. This case showed: (1) a psychic picture akin to a Korsakoff psychosis, (2) disturbances in speech akin to stammering, (3) a variable pupillary reaction to light, (4) difficulties in ocular convergence, (5) asynergia, (6) changing rigidities, (7) a marked support reaction, (8) a grasping reflex, and (9) increased reaction to pain. The ocular signs were relatively insignificant.

COMMENT

The most constant feature in the clinical picture is the clouding of consciousness, which may be of different depths. Usually in the course of the illness, the clouding increases as the general condition becomes worse, or the clouding subsides as the patient improves. With the clouding of consciousness delirious features always occur, together with grasping and groping. The mental confusion is accompanied by disorientation and difficulty in the perception of objects. The patients cannot differentiate well pictures shown to them, especially more complicated ones. There are also difficulties in the integration of the various impressions in perception. With the lessening in the disturbance in consciousness, the mental picture tends to become more like that of a Korsakoff psychosis. However, a typical Korsakoff psychosis did not occur in any of our cases. Probably clouding of consciousness and delirium are two different psychopathologic entities. It is known that clouding of consciousness as such is due chiefly to a retardation in all psychic processes, including those dealing with perception. The essence of confusion is a failure to come to a full perception. Objects are perceived only in parts and incompletely or, when the whole is perceived, it is not possible to differentiate it into its parts. The different parts of perception are mixed together, and this is true of mental images as well as of object perception. The internal and external worlds are not well separated from each other. However, the mechanism of confusion is not identical with the mechanism of hallucination, although hallucinations occur more readily in the presence of confusion. In the cases described, the clouding of consciousness played a much greater part than in the usual cases of mental confusion, such as occur in the toxic psychosis that Meynert called amentia (Hartmann and Schilder, 1923; Mayer-Gross, 1924). On the other hand, the inability to grasp a complicated perception is less pronounced in our cases than in postinfectional confusional cases. The picture has some similarity to delirium tremens, in which a moderate degree of confusion is associated with a strong tendency toward hallucinations. In our cases, hallucinations do not play such an important part. To summarize, we may say that the mental picture is dominated by clouding of consciousness, in which the difficulties in perception play the most important part, while difficulties in the integration of perception play a less important part, and hallucinations the least of all.

In a short differentiation of Korsakoff psychosis from delirium, it may be said that in Korsakoff psychosis the difficulties in the integration of material in the past, or memory, are more pronounced than in immediate perception. There is no clouding of consciousness. Instead of hallucinations, one sometimes finds an active tendency toward confabulation, which essentially means a mistake in the differentiation synthesis of the memory material. In cases 4, 7, and 8 there are features akin to the Korsakoff psychosis, but the outstanding feature is the clouding of consciousness, which may be combined with rhythmic movements passively initiated. This phenomenon was especially noted in cases 1 and 6.

Other phenomena, which are probably in close connection with the clouding of consciousness, are grasping, groping, and the sucking reflex. Grasping and groping are phenomena of considerable interest. They are known in delirium tremens in connection with hallucinations, when the patient grasps at imaginary or real objects. Careful observation shows that this grasping is autonomous and not based on either perceptions or hallucinations. But still the grasping and groping lie on a psychic level. Pointing also plays an important part on a psychic level. I have observed the case of a person who first hallucinated objects, then pointed at them, and finally tried to catch them. Genetically, pointing is a mitigated grasping. One points when one cannot touch the object, and touches when one cannot grasp the object. In its essence, every kind of pointing is a grasping. Besides the psychic level of pointing and grasping, there is a physiologic level for the same phenomenon. Schuster and Pineas (1926) have studied this phenomenon carefully, and in this country Freeman and Crosby (1929) and Davis and Currier (1931) have published articles on the subject. We are not interested here in the question of whether this phenomenon arises from lesions of the striopallidum or frontal lobe; it is probable that lesions in either area may produce it. It appears that both physiologic and psychologic levels may be integrated together. The grasping in delirium tremens may have a purely neurologic basis, which initiates or modifies the psychic attitude. Betlheim (1924a) has shown this interaction of the two levels in an illuminative case. The physiologic basis of pointing has been emphasized by Goldstein and Boernstein (1925). Grünbaum (1930) has described the pointing reflex, and maintains that it belongs to the same group of phenomena as grasping and groping. Groping is in some way between pointing and grasping. One of our cases (case 6) showed the tendency to assume pointing positions with the index finger. It seems possible that these primitive tendencies come out when there is clouding of consciousness. The clearness of consciousness seems in some way to have an inhibitive effect. But besides this general influence, there appears to be a special apparatus, destruction of which brings grasping and groping to the surface. The same is true of the sucking reflex, first described by Wagner-Jauregg in advanced dementia paralytica. Betlheim (1924b) has shown that it may also occur when there is a lesion of the gyrus supramarginalis associated with an apraxia of the face.

Thus, it appears that grasping, groping, pointing, and sucking have a neurologic apparatus at various levels. The findings of Gamper (1926) show that there must be at least medullary and midbrain centers for these activities. Striopallidal influences are also acting, and there are probably cortical centers in the frontal lobe as well as in the supramarginal region. These are in addition to general cortical influences, which may or may not be working on the level of psychophysiologic integration.

As our anatomic findings show, there are widespread lesions of the central nervous system, and it is difficult to say which particular lesions are at the base of the clouding in consciousness. The most constant area of lesion is in connection with the ventricular gray matter, and it seems probable that these lesions play a part in the genesis of the clouding. It is also probable that the effect of such a lesion in the ventricular gray matter would not be so far-reaching if there were not also disturbances in cortical function. At any rate, cerebral function as a whole is impaired, not only by the toxic and anatomic disturbances, but also by functional influences arising from the injured vegetative centers. Kleist (1926) has often emphasized that there is a chain of centers of consciousness which extends from the medulla oblongata to the posterior wall of the third ventricle. It is more than probable, according to von Economo (1929) and Schilder and Weissman (1927), that also the more proximal parts of the ventricular gray areas, especially the base of the third ventricle and the subthalamic region, have something to do with the regulation of consciousness.

Clouding of consciousness and its anatomic and functional basis may be partly responsible for the grasping, groping, and pointing on the psychophysiologic level of integration. But in case 1 especially, we also observed lesions in the striopallidum. Little is known about which particular brain-stem center has to do with these activities. Since there are lesions in the brain stem, we have to reckon with the possibility that the apparatus for grasping, groping, and sucking is impaired in various points of its organization.

The next group of phenomena to be considered are the changing rigidities, athetoid movements, and asynergias between the limbs and trunk. The rigidities are of a special type and to our knowledge have not been described before. It is sometimes difficult to differentiate them from an active resistance, and they are changeable in appearance, but certainly are not due to a psychic influence alone, although psychic influences may play an important part. Active movements are also awkward and stiff and lead to queer postures in which the patient sometimes appears almost cataleptic. The athetoid movements are probably closely related to these changing rigidities. There is usually not a definite tendency to flexion or extension. It is true that the legs are mostly extended and there is a greater tendency to flexion in the arms, especially at the elbows. The flexor tendency at the elbows definitely links these rigidities with the convergence phenomena (Schilder, 1930a) [See Chapter 17] in alcoholic patients and with the paralysis agitans picture. The athetoid movements of the fingers sometimes show some relation to pointing and grasping. Another important feature in these rigidities is that they show a definite relation to the support reaction. When, for instance, the toes are bent upward, the legs become completely stiff and cannot be bent at the knee. Flexing the toes make the legs immediately flexible, and the stiffness disappears. Apparently this is a particular type of tension reflex, although the localization of its center is not possible at present. The most probable hypothesis is an association with the tonus centers near Deiters' nucleus and the substantia reticularis. In this particular group of cases, the subthalamic region and the striopallidum are also involved, as well as Deiters' nucleus and its neighborhood. Certainly the latter are important centers of tone, but in our group of cases, in which the tensions are so prominent, the lesions are more widespread.

Kleist (1927a, 1927b) and his pupil Straus (1931) have pointed to the instinctive resistance, which they associate with thalamic lesions. The phenomenon was observed in ten cases of arterio-

sclerotic softening. But in all of these cases the putamen was involved as well as the thalamus, and in some cases other parts of
the brain were also involved. Kleist emphasized the similarity of
this phenomenon to an automatic negativism minus a general
negativistic psychic attitude. The phenomenon of negativism he
called counterfixation. It is a resistance to change in posture
brought about by a muscular tension that increases with the effort
of the examiner. From an introspective point of view, this counterfixation is an instinctive resistance and is connected with a particular feeling reaction. Kleist pointed out that the same phenomenon
is seen in focal lesions of the brain, as well as in psychosis. But in
focal brain lesions the instinctive resistance is chiefly reactive,
while in psychosis it is more spontaneous. He was of the opinion
that such a counterfixation is also directed against gravity. Mayer-
Gross and Reisch (1928) have observed similar phenomena, which
they call preparedness to resistance. With hemiplegia, the phenomenon occurs on the nonparalyzed side. Kleist and Mayer-Gross and
Reisch drew attention to the common coincidence of this phenomenon with grasping and groping, and claimed that the primary
center for its integration lies in the medulla, but Mayer-Gross and
Reisch also believed that it may be released as well by lesions in
other parts such as the thalamus. Straus pointed to the similarity
between the support reaction and the negativistic resistance, and
showed that it is characteristic of the support reaction that it occurs
only when the hand or foot is passively hyperextended or dorsi-
flexed, whereas the tension rigidity disappears when the hand or
foot is brought in the opposite relation to the arm or leg, but he
inconsistently stated that the support reaction occurs only when the
patient is unable voluntarily to relax the muscles. The support
reaction and instinctive resistance are certainly not identical, as
Mayer-Gross and Reisch claimed. In our cases the support reaction
was present without the resistance.

When we try to correlate the findings in our cases with the observations of Kleist and Mayer-Gross and Reisch, we find two outstanding points: (1) The psychic factor in resistance is much more
prominent in our cases than in the purely neurologic conditions

described by the other investigators; (2) the rigidities are very changeable and spontaneous; these changing rigidities could be elicited when the patient acted against resistance. Our patients also showed spontaneous athetoid movements. Our findings were in many ways similar to conditions that are present in catatonic states. This problem will be more fully discussed in connection with the next group of cases. It is difficult to know whether all of these phenomena are release phenomena or irritative responses arising directly from the injured areas presumably responsible for them. It should also be noted that it is possible that the clouding of consciousness and the underlying physiologic factors may increase the tendency to these tensions, as we have often observed that they increase the tendency toward instinctive resistance. Clouding of consciousness acts partially as a psychic factor. The outward world becomes more threatening and more dangerous, and a greater resistance against any interference from the outside follows. There are also certain physiologic factors that underlie the phenomena of clouding and that may be responsible for the muscular tensions, but, even so, the central changes in the tonic apparatus are certainly more significant.

Of course we do not think these tensions are found only in alcoholic encephalopathy. We have observed two arteriosclerotic cases in which similar tensions were present. Here is a brief history of one case.

A man, aged 60, showed marked arteriosclerosis and gave a negative history for alcoholism. When admitted to the hospital on May 25, 1931, he had a rigid facial expression, held his mouth half open and the lower part of the face was flaccid. He held his hands in a rigid position and had a strong resistance against opening them. There were negativistic tensions in the arms and rigidities in the hands, partly following the support reaction. He showed rigidity of the neck, which was partially voluntary. The pupillary reactions were prompt. The patient walked with small steps and remained in awkward positions. He did not obey orders or imitate postures. He had a grasping tendency and a sucking tendency. He showed a strong defense reaction to pain. On May 26, he lay in bed with the eyes closed and assumed queer postures. He showed changing rigidities in all limbs. Sometimes he suddenly changed position—for example, raising the left arm with pointed fingers— and remained in this position stiffly for a while. He did not talk. On May 28, he showed rigidities, partly of a voluntary type, and sometimes assumed a pointing position with the fingers. There was a strong grasping tendency. The fingers remained cataleptic in positions given to them, but especially if placed in a pointing position. He was transferred to a state hospital on June 1. The following report was received from there: "He was restless, especially at night, insisting on getting out of bed and walking around. He took only milk and was entirely incontinent. He lay in bed in the daytime in a stuporous state, and reacted to stimuli by crying. If the arms were raised from the bed, he held them there for a long time. There were no spontaneous movements, except to resist when stuck with a pin. He kept his eyes shut and his mouth open. His facial expression was vacant. He resisted an attempt to open his eyes. He occasionally carried out simple commands, but most of the time he paid no heed. At times he uttered a few words, usually in an unintelligible manner. He never emerged from the stuporous state in which he entered the hospital, but became more and more comatose, and died on June 31, 1931. Diagnosis: Psychosis with cerebral arteriosclerosis. Cause of death: cerebral hemorrhage."

Another case was in an arteriosclerotic person with epileptic attacks. In still another case, a catatonic picture followed an injury of the head without a fracture of the skull. Here, the psychic influence on the rigidity was especially strong.

It is remarkable that clouding of consciousness does not diminish the reaction to pain, but that, on the contrary, all of our cases showed an exaggerated response to pain with an especially vivid defense reaction. This comes out especially well in the response to the stimuli for plantar reflexes, which call forth an exaggerated flexion of the whole leg. There is probably an impairment of the inhibitory mechanism for the reaction to pain, just as there is an inhibition in the primitive reactions for sucking and grasping, but this phenomenon is probably also related to the increased tendency to muscular resistance. Mayer-Gross and Reisch observed hyperalgesia on the side homolateral to a capsular lesion among the cases they reported, and Schmidt (1918) observed that in about half the cases of hemiplegia there is an increase in the sensitivity of the skin and of the deeper tissues. Babinski and Jarkowski (1921) found hyperalgesia on the side of the paresis as well as on the other side.

Asynergia, or the dissociation between the movements of the legs and the trunk, is one of the common symptoms in our cases. Asynergia is well known as a cerebellar sign. In our cases coming to autopsy there were lesions on the margin of the cortex, in the folia overlying the ventricles, and in the roof of the fourth ventricle. We shall later discuss cases in which the cerebellar symptoms are in the foreground, and show that asynergia is associated with these lesions, especially of the dentate nucleus. It is also possible that the clinical appearance of the dissociation between the trunk and limbs is partially due to the rigidities. At least, the stiffness makes the falling of these patients more impressive. Thus, it is possible that the rigidities cover a part of the cerebellar symptomatology. Typical intentional tremors were not observed in any of our cases.

The support reaction was first described by Rademaker (1926b) in animals whose cerebellum had been removed. Later, Schwab (1927) found it in human beings and showed that it occurred with lesions of the frontal and temporal lobes. Its actual localization is not known. Our material suggests some relationship to the tensions, and perhaps even that such tensions are necessary for the support reaction. Both positive and negative support reactions were observed. When the patient's legs are in a state of tension and the toes are pushed down, the tension relaxes. If there were only a resistance in the common sense, one would expect an increase in tensions under these conditions. The support reactions are therefore more than an expression of the tensions. Whether the cerebellar lesions are sufficient to explain their occurrence is

doubtful. They seem to be related to lesions in the tonus apparatus, as we have already discussed.

Many of our cases showed marked disturbances in speech.
There were bulbar dysarthrias, difficulties in bringing out words,
lack of impulses, and troubles akin to stammering. The speech
troubles observed here are most like those seen in diseases of the
extrapyramidal tract. Disturbances in muscle tone are partly responsible, and it is possible that lesions in the nucleus of the tenth
and twelfth nerves play a part.

From time to time we have observed other signs of widespread lesions in the central nervous system. One case showed a
positive Hoffmann sign and ankle clonus. In other cases more definite signs of a lesion of the pyramidal tract may be found. Various
neuritic signs may also be present. Optic atrophy developed in one
patient who lived a relatively long time. Histopathologic changes
were noted in the optic nerve in two of the cases coming to
autopsy. Oculomotor signs are, of course, due to lesions in the
nuclei of the oculomotor nerves, which are located in a vulnerable
position in the gray areas about the aqueduct and also in the
fasciculous longitudinalis posterior. It is remarkable that in case 1,
paresis of the right internal rectus alone was present, and that
signs of ocular paralysis were absent in case 5 in spite of the otherwise evident severity of the lesion. In case 8 there were difficulties
only in converging the eyes. Other cases usually showed a diver-
gent palsy. In two cases, only upward movements were preserved.
Fixation of the pupils to light and other serious disturbances in the
pupillary reactions were observed. This subject will be discussed
again later.

In cases of chronic alcoholism one is not dealing only with a
disease of the central nervous system. The patients are always extremely emaciated. Sweating is common. Elevation of the temperature without a toxic process is observed again and again.
Pseudopellagrous changes in the skin of the hand are seen. The
whole digestive tract is diseased, and the patient has a coated
tongue, digestive disturbances, and diarrhea. Retinal hemorrhages
are noted. It may be supposed that there is a general disease of the

organism which expresses itself all over the body, or even that the changes elsewhere are primary and the changes in the brain secondary. It is possible that there is an intermediate cause related to the liver and digestive tract that is significant in the genesis of the cerebral lesions. Since we have not as yet made special investigations in this direction, we shall not discuss this hypothesis at present. Gamper (1928) called attention to the fact that the lesions involve the centers for the vegetative functions of the whole organism. All of the patients in this group died. In some cases death occurred suddenly and after a short interval, while other patients lived for six months, in which case there might be improvement at first. In the grouping of these cases we were guided by the clinical picture and learned only subsequently that the pathologic findings further justified the classification. The clinical picture is therefore highly characteristic, as is also the pathologic picture. The lesion is widespread, especially along the ventricular surfaces but also on the external surfaces, and hemorrhages play an important part, in contrast to other groups in this series, as will be seen shortly. The term polioencephalitis haemorrhagica superior, as Schroeder (1930) pointed out, is not justifiable. There is no inflammatory process and, as we shall show, hemorrhages do not always occur. However, for this group the term encephalopathia or polioencephalopathia haemorrhagica would be justified.

II. CASES IN WHICH THE CEREBELLAR SYMPTOMATOLOGY WAS PROMINENT

Case 9. Clinical History. A man, aged 39, was admitted to the hospital on June 22, 1931, with a history of heavy drinking. At the time he showed poor pupillary reactions and impairment of ocular movements so that when he tried to look upward or sideways the eyes moved only downward; convergence was also unsatisfactory. The eyegrounds were normal. The right arm showed an outward deviation, which increased when the head was turned to the left. The hands tended to supinate spontaneously, and turning the head to the left also increased this. Furthermore, when the arms were extended in front and the head was turned to the left, the right arm moved inward and upward, while the left arm moved outward with a tendency to flexion at the elbow. There was a marked cerebellar tremor of the right arm, but almost none of the left. The tendon reflexes were present in the arms, while the patellar and Achilles reflexes were absent. There was soreness of the muscles of the legs and of the arms. The Babinski reaction was negative. There was weakness of the legs, especially in the upper part, and on the left this weakness was mixed with a cerebellar tremor. The patient displayed great difficulty in sitting up, owing to the weakness of the trunk muscles and an asynergia between the trunk and the limbs. Turning to the left in the turning chair produced none of the usual reactions; turning to the right produced only an inadequate nystagmus and subjective dizziness. Pseudo-pellagrous changes were present on both hands. He showed a hallucinatory psychic picture. He did not know how long he had been in the hospital and thought that he was in the Jefferson market. He said, "Five of us escaped. Were you up to see my sister? You are Mr. Barnes, aren't you? I saw you in the Bronx. It is May, 1931 or 1932. Yesterday I was a strong man pushing big heavy trunks, and now I am so weak." He made jokes when pictures of children were shown to him, and said, "It is cows jumping over fleas." No clouding of consciousness occurred until just before death on June 29. There was no post-mortem examination.

Summary and Comment. This case showed: (1) no clouding of consciousness in the beginning, but hallucinations and confabulations, while clouding of consciousness gradually developed toward the end, (2) severe ophthalmoplegia, including convergence difficulties, (3) absence of the normal vestibular reaction to turning, (4) marked cerebellar signs, including lateral deviation of the right arm, (5) tendency to flexion at the elbow, but no other tensions, (6) peripheral neuritis, with weakness in the trunk and upper part of the legs, (7) pseudopellagrous changes in the skin of the hands. The case differs from those of the previous group in that tensions do not play an important part. Only flexion in the elbow was present, which is a reliable sign of extrapyramidal tract disease. The cerebellar signs that were present were intention tremor, deviation of the right arm, and a paradoxical reaction of the outstretched arm or a deviation to the left side when the head was turned to the right. Hoff and Schilder (1927) have shown that this paradoxical reaction is a cerebellar sign. The absence of the usual reaction to turning on the turning chair is probably due to a lesion in Deiters' nucleus and its neighborhood. We have found similar impairment in this reaction in other cases as well, but not all of our patients have been examined by the Bárány methods. The following case shows an interesting dissociation in the Bárány reaction. The case is important because it offers some hints for the localization of these reactions.

Case 10. Clinical History. A man, aged 51, was admitted on December 12, 1929 after having had trouble with walking, and pains in the legs for five or six months. He was in an intoxicated state, tremulous, and picking at the bedclothes as though he were grasping small objects. He said, "I want to get the color of that shirt. There is brown paint in my sleeve." On December 17 he was delirious, picking at things, and refusing to eat. He had difficulty in recognizing pictures, usually noticing only parts of them. He said, "It is in the monthly bulletin. It gives you information. If you are sick, they send you a doctor after three days. I am here in my father's house. I only came in here today. I was in St. George. There is the recording angel." When he tried to stand, he fell to the left and backward. He could not look to the left or right, but only upward or downward; convergence was preserved. During the following days convergence contractures developed. Both pupils reacted poorly to light. Movements of the jaw were extremely awkward. Irrigation of the ears did not produce a nystagmus on either side, but did produce the usual deviations in the arms and trunk. When the arms were outstretched, they diverged strongly at the shoulder, with flexion at the elbow. There was a spontaneous turning of the trunk to the left. When the head was turned to the left with the arms outstretched, the left arm went higher. He also had a strong pronation tendency, a slight intention tremor, a bradyteleocinesia, and a slight adiadokokinesis, more marked on the left side. Tendon reflexes in the arms were normal. Marked awkwardness was displayed in the hand grip. The legs showed a slight intention tremor, especially on the left. Patellar reflexes were weak, but the other reflexes in the legs were normal. There were no signs of neuritis. He died with signs of insufficiency of the heart on December 20. The Wassermann reaction of the blood and spinal fluid was negative, and the spinal fluid was otherwise normal. Post-mortem examination showed bronchopneumonia.

Summary and Comment. Neuropathologic studies showed ependymitis and subependymal vascularization in the ventricular gray matter for the whole length of the ventricular system, which were more severe in the floor of the ventricles but present also in the roof, as in the quadrigeminate bodies, the dentate nucleus, the vermis of the cerebellum, and the lateral thalamic nuclei. It was most marked in the fourth ventricle along the recess beneath the restiform body, thus especially involving the nucleus of the eighth nerve; also in the floor of the aqueduct, involving the nuclei of the oculomotor nerves, and in the floor of the third ventricle, involving the mammillary bodies. The surface of the cerebrum and cerebellum showed less involvement, with some fatty changes in the nerve cells. The margin of the brain stem showed some gliosis.

Clinically, this case showed: (1) a delirious picture with moderate clouding of consciousness, (2) falling to the left and backward with spontaneous turning of the trunk to the left, (3) strong divergence of the arms, (4) bradyteleocinesia and adiadokokinesis, (5) intention tremor, (6) pronation tendencies, (7) no tensions except the convergence reaction at the elbows, (8) conjugate palsies of sideward movements of the eyes, with preservation of convergence and gradually developing convergence contracture of the ocular muscles, (9) inadequate pupillary reaction to light, and (10) failure of nystagmus on caloric stimulation of the ears, with the usual deviations of the arms and trunk.

Some of the neurologic problems in this case deserve discussion. There was, for instance, a double paralysis of the conjugate movements of the eyes. Oppenheim (1923) has connected this phenomenon with a lesion of the fasciculus longitudinalis posterior on both sides. Although in our case there was no evidence that this tract was injured directly, we may suppose a disturbance in its function, since the areas about it and nuclear masses associated with it were injured. Clinical examination showed that we were not dealing with a weakness of the muscles, as such, inasmuch as the patient was able to use the internal rectus muscles for convergence. Gradually, a convergence contracture developed. According to Brunner (1927), the absence of nystagmus from caloric stimulation of the ears is due also to a lesion of the fasciculus longitudinalis posterior. According to him, this experimental nystagmus is absent when the nuclei of the ocular muscles are destroyed, when both fasciculi longitudinales posteriores are destroyed, or when one of these tracts and the arcuate fibers of the opposite tract are injured. It is interesting that in this case the deviation of the arms and trunk was present following caloric stimulation of the vestibular nerve, while nystagmus was not. This shows that the pathway for the reaction of the trunk and arms to vestibular stimulation is different from the pathways for nystagmus. Deiters' nucleus showed considerable injury in this case, but was not entirely destroyed. Perhaps its partial preservation accounts for the preservation of the trunk and arm movements, or perhaps the pathways for the body movements are not dependent on Deiters' nucleus.

It is easy to connect the histopathologic findings with the clinical cerebellar signs. The dentate nucleus as well as other parts of the roof of the fourth ventricle, including the center of the cerebellum and its vermis, were involved in the lesion and apparently more so in this case than in the cases of the previous group. Also, in this case the thalamus, subthalamic region, and putamen were less extensively involved. The reactive glioses and proliferative changes in the vessels were more marked than the hemorrhagic responses. It appears that we were dealing here with a process that in some way was a little different in localization, less widespread, and less severe than in other cases. This difference may account for the absence of tensions and rigidities and also for the fact that the clouding of consciousness was less severe.

The case also offers some interesting data relative to the problem of pupillary disturbances in alcoholic patients. There was a severe impairment of the pupillary reaction to light, whereas the reaction in accommodation was preserved. We may therefore say that the patient displayed Argyll Robertson pupils. It has already been mentioned that pupillary changes in cases of alcoholic encephalopathy are not common; even incomplete Argyll Robertson pupils are rare. The genesis of the pupillary disturbances in these cases is from lesions in the nuclei of the intrinsic ocular muscles or in the pathway that connects the optic nerve with them. The diffuse nature of the lesion in our cases forbids a definite localization, but it may be recalled that Ingvar (1928) showed by means of comparative studies that the fibers concerned in the Argyll Robertson phenomenon pass over the surface and base of the midbrain to the nuclei of the ocular muscles and are thus most likely to be involved in submeningeal or marginal lesions such as are seen here. The lesions in the floor of the aqueduct offer a further explanation for the pupillary changes in alcoholic patients. In our experience, pupillary disturbances are common in acute alcoholism, although these changes are not extensive or long-lasting and, according to Schilder and Parker (1931) [see Chapter 22], resemble the pupillary disturbances observed in catatonic patients; however, it would appear that in acute alcoholism the alcohol attacks similar parts of the brain.

III. Cases Resembling Acute Catatonia

Case 11. Clinical History. A man, aged 31, was admitted on November 11, 1929 with a history of having been a heavy drinker for many years. When admitted, he was delirious, groping and pulling, and smoking imaginary cigarettes. On November 15 he was very confused and made queer grimaces. Speech was halting. He was very restless. He walked with a broad base, was stiff and shaky, and fell backward. There was a tendency for the limbs to suddenly become stiff, and all movements were occasionally interrupted by myoclonic jerks. The arms were flexed. All other neurologic findings were normal. The Wassermann reaction was negative. The skin was dry. He said, "Yes, yesterday you showed me a magazine. It was gruesome. It had a girl's name. (Where are you?) I trust to fate where I am. In the bone—in the bone—jackass. I watch the sky. (Don't you see any difference since you are here?) It is lighter and bluer. (Where are you?) Oh, near Germany, France, Germany—from 1917 to 1940. (Where are you now?) I was since then without consciousness, but I know that every minute I was inside and outside hospitals. What uniforms do the people wear: moustaches, revolvers, or what?" He named simple objects and grasped them firmly. If his arms were rhythmically moved, he continued the movement alone. On November 18 he was very aggressive. He was jerky in all movements and tossed about in bed. He was very noisy. He knew where he was, but his thought processes were very disconnected. His emotional reactions changed suddenly. On November 19 he jumped up and down in bed and rolled from one side to the other. He pushed his head rhythmically from left to right and backward and forward, or held his head in queer postures, staring at the ceiling. Speech was inarticulate. He said, "You are stuck now. The idea is the first. You went through everything." His temperature rose to 101.3 F. and on November 20 it rose to 104 F. He was excited and restless at this time, opening and closing his mouth rhythmically and showing rhythmic movements of the lips. He snapped at objects and continued grasping, but there were no tremors. There were changing rigidities in the legs, which sometimes changed into rhythmic movements of flexion and extension. He died on this day. No autopsy was performed.

Summary and Comment. Clinically, this cased showed: (1) far-going dissociation in thinking and also, probably, disturbance of consciousness, (2) a tendency toward rhythmic movements, (3) motor restlessness and myoclonic movements, (4) a grasping reflex, (5) asynergia, and (6) changing rigidities. The psychic changes were predominant. The extent of the dissociation in thinking was more outstanding than the clouding of consciousness. In the neurologic picture, the absence of oculomotor signs is remarkable. The case differs from those in the group with changing rigidities in that myoclonic movements were present.

Case 12. Clinical History. A man, aged 42, admitted on October 13, 1929, had been a heavy drinker throughout his life, but lately had drunk more than usual; he had not been able to work for three months. Two weeks before admission, he heard voices and said that he wished to die. On admission, he was sullen and disoriented for place and time; he soon stopped talking, and shouted out suddenly as though he heard voices. His facial expression was stiff, tense, and staring. The pupils reacted less well to light than in accommodation. The eyegrounds were normal. He often remained in cataleptic positions. He was continuously grasping but not in a delirious way. The fingers were often held in an outspread position, and the little finger was often hyperextended at the proximal joint. When walking, the trunk was drawn backward. He showed a swaying, cerebellar ataxia. The abdominal and Achilles reflexes were not obtained, but the patellar reflexes were present. The Wassermann reaction was negative with the blood and the spinal fluid. The colloidal gold curve was normal; there was no increase of globulin or cells in the spinal fluid. He said, "This is a hospital. Governor Whalen has killed all the Jews. Darling, darling, come! The doctor has sent me here. I drink hard liquor, gin. I am God." He suddenly sat up and became restless. (What do the voices say?) "Many things. The truth lies. (Who are you?) God." On October 16 his speech was disconnected. He threw himself out of bed. He said, "Are you a citizen?" He hid under the sheets and apparently had hallucinations. He often failed to answer questions. Tensions frequently appeared suddenly all over the body. On October 18 he said, "They shot me just now," and made wild defensive movements. On October 20, while walking, he suddenly stiffened and fell back. There were athetoid movements in the hands, and the small finger was abducted. He had sudden outbursts. On October 24 he assumed queer postures, grasped the arm of the examiner, and clung to him. He showed no negativism. On October 26 there was a pill-rolling tremor of the right hand, with variable rigidities in all limbs. He shouted, "There —there they come here—here—there!" He blew out his lips. He died on October 29.

Summary and Comment. The same brain lesion seemed to be present throughout the ependyma and subjacent gray centers along the ventricles in this case as in the others, but it was limited more to a glial ependymal reaction and there was less extensive vascular disturbance.

Clinically, this case showed: (1) clouding of consciousness with extensive dissociation in thinking, (2) a tendency toward rhythmic movements, (3) athetoid and cataleptic postures, (4) changing rigidities, restlessness, and sudden movements, and (5) a grasping tendency. This case is almost identical to the previous one. The psychosis was dominated by extensive dissociation in thinking. There is a marked similarity between these cases and acute catatonic pictures; the motor signs, however, are of a more massive and neurologic type. The rigidities link this group definitely with the previous one. The absence of oculomotor signs corresponds with the fact that there are fewer histopathologic changes in the ventricular gray matter.

Case 13. Clinical History. A man, aged 45, who was brought from home by his wife on October 10, 1931, had been drinking heavily for many years, had been unemployed for two years, and for two weeks had been overtalkative, obscene, restless and belligerent, and was losing weight. On a previous admission, in 1928, he had recovered in five days from an acute alcoholic confusional state. At that time he had been restless, picking at the bedclothes, tremulous, requiring restraint, noisy, yelling for a knife, euphoric, and disoriented. On the present admission, he was euphoric, disoriented, and had confabulatory hallucinations. He was emaciated and decrepit. The pupils were moderately dilated and practically fixed to light; ocular convergence was poor. There was a fine tremor of the hands. Within a few days he became worse. He was resistive, restless and tremulous, and showed an occupational delirium. He gave irrelevant, incoherent replies and acted as if he were responding to auditory and perhaps visual hallucinations. He appeared anxious, kept his fists clenched, and usually maintained queer postures. Physical and neurologic examination at that time revealed: normal fundi, practically fixed pupils, normal ocular movements, tremors of the facial muscles, a beefy, excoriated, tremulous tongue, increased and changing rigidities in the limbs, especially the legs, active deep reflexes, and absent abdominal reflexes. The Wassermann reaction of the blood was four plus. Examination of the spinal fluid on two occasions showed a negative Wassermann reaction, no cells, no globulin, and a colloidal gold curve of 0001210000. At this time he said: "If you hurt me, God damn you, I will kill you! All my bones are broken. (Why don't you sit straight?) That is what you are supposed to do to save your life. Papa, pray for me. Oh, my daddy, stop crying now." On October 27, he twisted one side of the bed linen and said that it was a pile of iron. He blew out his cheeks and showed some rigidities and stiffness mixed with resistance. On October 29 he said, "My tobacco and eyes. I was down there. You told me to go down there and get a drink of water." He grabbed things, closed his eyes, made himself stiff, and was restless. He appeared to have hallucinations. He showed tensions of a voluntary character. He had great difficulty in getting up and, when put on his feet, fell backward and made his legs stiff. He showed considerable resistance to passive movements, and all active movements were very clumsy. On October 31, he had wide pupils that reacted variably, but at times were practically fixed. He made only inarticulate sounds. There were changing rigidities all over the body, but more so in the legs, which were usually held in flexor contraction. When put on his feet, he sank down at the knees. There were jerky movements and tremors of the hands. He seemed to have hallucinations and to be almost delirious, staring and pointing about. On November 4 the mental picture was practically the same. He confabulated rather vividly. He lay in bed most of the day talking to himself and imaginary persons, or singing. He was disoriented and showed impairment in recent and remote memory. His attention, however, was sharp, for he promptly answered all questions directed either to him or to other persons in the room. Upward movements of the eyes were limited, but he looked downward fairly well. Convergence of the eyes was lost. The facial expression showed anxiety. There were some flatness and an occasional twitching of the right side of the face. He would lie in bed with the legs drawn up, flexed at the knees and turned to the left. There was increased tonus in all muscles of the body, especially of the legs. He responded vividly to pinching of the lower extremities. The palmar surfaces of the hands and plantar surfaces of the feet showed a fine desquamation of the superficial layer of the skin. He perspired excessively, was emaciated, had a severe diarrhea, and was incontinent. He died on December 1, 1931. The post-mortem findings were: syphilitic aortitis, perihepatitis and congestion of the liver, congestion of the spleen, syphilitic interstitial orchitis, pial and arachnoid edema of the brain, general emaciation, and decubital sores.

Summary and Comment. The lesions were typically an ependymitis along the ventricular system and marginal gliosis along the surface of the brain and the brain stem, with some tendency toward invasive gliosis, which was most marked along the recesses of the ventricles or the depths of surface convolutions and with a predilection for vascular injury to the adjacent gray masses, especially those connected with visceral functions. There was also some reaction in the meninges and the choroid plexus. It is interesting that we can safely say that the syphilitic infection had not invaded the brain and that the pathologic changes found were definitely due to alcoholism and not syphilis, so different are the two types of lesions.

Clinically this patient showed: (1) moderate clouding of consciousness, but with extensive dissociation in thinking; he gave the impression of having vivid hallucinations but not in the sense of occupational delirium, (2) a tendency toward pointing and grasping, (3) asynergia, (4) changing rigidities in which the psychic element played the important part, (5) severe dissociation in motility, with quick jerky movements, (6) pupillary disturbances, but no other ocular signs, (7) increased reaction to pain, and (8) profound vegetative disturbances. In this case the psychic changes were again in the foreground. The absence of oculomotor signs is again noteworthy. The rigidities were more intermixed with psychic elements than they were in the first group of cases. This case was more chronic than the two others of this group, for the course lasted more than six weeks. The outstanding histopathologic feature was the predominance of the glial reaction. It is of interest that we were able to demonstrate lesions in the spinal cord as well.

Here again we deal with a special group of cases. Whoever has seen such cases will be impressed by the apparently vivid hallucinations and by the wild reaction to the hallucinations. Consciousness is not as clouded, but the utterances are nevertheless all abrupt and disconnected. The similarity to severe acute catatonic states is evident. There are many signs of dissociation of a catatonic type in the motility. There are aimless blowing of the lips, tightening and stiffening of the body, the assumption of queer bodily postures, and catalepsy; in some cases, a tendency toward rhythmic movements. But these psychomotor movements are still dependent on underlying neurologic factors. There is a marked grasping reflex, and the tensions, although under the influence of the psyche, are definitely similar to the tensions in the first group of cases. Support reactions were not observed. Increased pain reaction was absent in one case and not adequately tested in another. In addition, there were jerky movements very similar to the myoclonic movements seen in acute epidemic encephalitis. It appears that these are irritation phenomena—that there are psychic changes that influence the muscular response and muscular responses that influence the psyche. The neurologic signs are more diffuse and directed more toward the psychic side. The similarity of the picture to an acute catatonic psychosis is certainly a feature of great general importance. These cases differ considerably from the classic picture described by Wernicke. There is a complete lack of oculomotor signs, and the histopathologic picture shows a predominance of glial reaction with a minimal amount of hemorrhagic reaction. Thus, the group may be looked on as a fairly well-defined entity in the cases of alcoholic encephalopathy.

IV. PROLONGED DELIRIUM ASSOCIATED WITH NEUROLOGIC SIGNS

Case 14. Clinical History. The patient, aged 36, a brother of the patient, case 4, was admitted on October 10, 1930, with a history of heavy drinking and of having been drinking steadily for three weeks. Two days before admission, he imagined that bears were chasing him. On admission, he was drowsy but nearly oriented. Two days later, he had vivid hallucinations and said, "I see three girls lying down and three fellows in white—a whole bunch of kids coming to me. There is a nurse. Everything is moving around." He became completely delirious. He pointed to the wall and said, "This human being and that one is holding me back." He moved his fingers restlessly, plucking at the bedclothes from time to time, and picking. He was constantly grasping and groping. There were rigidities in the arms, with convergence mixed with resistance. There was a support reaction in all extremities, but, in spite of this, a tendency toward semiflexion of the legs. Pupillary reactions were sluggish; speech was slurred. There was a serious cerebellar asynergia. The tendon reflexes were all normal. On October 27 he said, "I made a trip with an air ship last night. I am back in the hotel now. The bed is under me. I don't know the number of the room. I met you on 24th Street. There is an old man with whiskers coming." Examination of the blood and spinal fluid gave entirely negative results. He was transferred to a state hospital on November 20, still having hallucinations, but at times was normal for a few hours. He was discharged from the state hospital on April 4 and later reported to our dispensary, where he was found to be clear mentally and showed only a slight awkwardness in motility.

Comment. This is a typical case of delirium. It is mentioned here partly because the patient was a brother of a patient whose case was reported in the first group, and partly because in the picture of prolonged delirium there were signs that were essentially identical with the neurologic signs in the first group, though milder in degree. The signs were the varying tensions, the asynergia, and the support reaction.

It should be emphasized that there is some relation between the different types of alcoholic psychosis. In a case of prolonged delirium one will find resemblances to the symptomatology of the encephalopathic cases. But in spite of this, there are different nosologic entities. It would be of interest to study the neurology in cases of delirium tremens from the point of view developed here. There are not only differences between the different groups, but similarities that point to a similarity of lesion in all alcoholic psychoses. It is not clear why in one person alcohol produces a delirium, in another an alcoholic hallucinosis, and in a third an encephalopathia. Neither is it clear why, in the first two groups of this series, we dealt chiefly with a picture of delirious type, with clouding of consciousness, while in the third group, that having catatonic features, there was a predominance of hallucinosis with disconnection in thinking.

V. Alcoholic Polioencephalopathy Combined with Polyneuritis

Some of the cases of group I showed a mixture of neuritic signs with signs of lesions in the central nervous system. We shall now report cases in which the neuritic signs played a more important part. In some, the neuritis was the predominant feature.

Case 15. Clinical History. A woman, aged 46, was admitted to the hospital on May 6, 1931, from her home, with the statement that she had been sick for a month, owing to drink, and that she had spasms that started from a pain in the head and imagined that she saw things. She had started to drink six years before, and drank every winter until she reached a condition similar to the present one; the husband sent her to the country for the summer, where she was away from liquor and regained her normal health. Once, three years before, she had more hallucinations than at present, but she had never been so weak in the legs or had convulsions until three days before admission. She was emaciated and toxic. There was a pellagroid dermatitis on the dorsa of the hands. All nerve trunks and muscle bellies were tender, and all deep reflexes were hyperactive. The pupillary reactions were adequate, but there were seemingly paralyses of all ocular movements, except for up-and-down movements. Irrigation of the ears did not produce the reaction of nystagmus. Speech was slurred and bulbar in type; the tongue was edematous and tremulous. She gradually lost the power to swallow. There was rigidity of the facies, which progressed in a day or two to facial muscles that resembled choreiform movements. She was constantly grasping and groping for things, picking at the bedclothes, and resisting every effort to examine her or to care for her. The movements were jerky and athetoid. She was incontinent, confused, and disoriented, had visions of dolls dancing on the mantelpiece, and heard imaginary undifferentiated noises. She complained of dizziness. At times she was fearful, screaming, and fighting blindly. She died on May 14. No post-mortem examination was made.

Summary and Comment. This case showed a delirious picture with: (1) clouding of consciousness, (2) paralysis of ocular movements except for up-and-down movements, (3) absence of caloric nystagmus, (4) choreiform and jerky movements, (5) grasping and groping, and a grasping reflex, (6) bulbar speech, (7) peripheral neuritis chiefly shown by pain and tenderness, and (8) pellagroid dermatitis. The similarity to cases in the first group is obvious.

The neuritis is evident from the nerve tenderness. There was no paralysis or diminution in reflexes.

Case 16. Clinical History. A girl, aged 28, was transferred from another hospital on January 21, 1931, with a diagnosis of Korsakoff's syndrome and polyneuritis. On admission, she was disturbed with hallucinations in the visual and auditory fields, disoriented, and ataxic. Her past habits had been irregular. It was generally believed that she drank a good deal, both socially and by herself; the exact amount or nature of the alcohol was not known. For several months previous to admission, she had become run down, failed to eat regularly, and complained of weakness in the legs; she vomited food and was depressed. She was poorly nourished; the body everywhere was hyperesthetic and tender, especially over muscle bodies and nerve trunks, more particularly in the lower limbs. She also complained of numbness and heaviness in the legs. Pupillary reactions and all ocular movements were normal, and there was no nystagmus. There were constant fine tremors in the facial muscles and tongue, and unsteadiness of head movements. There were ataxia and coarse tremor of the arms, with choreiform involuntary movements and queer rigidities and postures. The tendon reflexes in the arms were hyperactive. There were weakness and loss of power in the legs, with absent tendon reflexes and muscular atrophy, all of which progressed during the course of the illness. She was under observation for four months until death occurred. The heart, lungs, and abdomen were normal on repeated examination, except for a low-grade endocervicitis which responded to treatment. All laboratory tests, including examination of the spinal fluid, a Wassermann test, chemical analysis, and culture of the blood and urinalysis, gave negative results. She showed an irregularly elevated temperature, sometimes septic in type, which was accompanied by a normal leukocyte count. From time to time she passed into a state of shock without apparent cause; then the temperature dropped suddenly, and she became cyanotic and nearly pulseless, but she always responded to stimuli. She was incoherent, rambling, emotionally unstable, especially irritable, with frequent hallucinations and confabulations, inattentive, and uncooperative. The clinical picture did not change much in the course of the next four months, except for a progressive weakness and atrophy in the legs, progressive inanition in spite of every effort, including a diet of a high vitamin content and blood transfusions, to help her gain strength, and a loss of emotional coloring and intellectual alertness in the mental picture, with a decrease in hallucinations and confabulations. On January 23, she said (What are you doing here?): "I live with my husband —what do you think—I live with other men? You let those people talk and torture me and keep it up. You took a chicken off my family. I had a chicken at home. (I shall tell you a story.) I shall be delighted to hear it. Why the Hell did you come to my room when you didn't know me on Wednesday? When I was crying and throwing my face and ribs, I asked my mother not to take me home. She didn't want to take me home. They were all scheming me. Once you looked into my eyes." On February 5 she said, "I don't think it was ham—I didn't eat any ham. (Do you know who I am?) Yes, I know who you are. You know that I know who you are. (What is the difference between a horse and a jackass?) I don't know your name. I suppose I am a jackass. Don't bother me. I don't mean nothing. I never did. I don't—are you trying to get rid of me?" At this time her hands showed a coarse tremor and were very restless. She was irritable, had a distressed expression, and said, "Oh, my God." On February 9 she said, "Oh I got my hand on it. I didn't put it on there purposely." There were many small movements of the fingers, like coarse tremors, but sometimes individual fingers would jerk suddenly. By this time the legs were entirely paralyzed and very sensitive to touch. The tendon reflexes of the legs were entirely absent. She was easily excited and had difficulty in breathing. She died on May 31. The autopsy was limited to the head.

Summary and Comment. The localization of the lesion was the same as in the other cases, namely, along the ventricular ependyma and surface of the cortex and brain stem, but it was more chronic and less invasive and was characterized mostly by ependymal and marginal gliosis and little or no underlying vascular reaction.

Clinically, the case showed: (1) a delirious picture in which inhibition and akinesia later played an important part, (2) a peripheral neuritis, especially in the legs, with paralysis, (3) rigidity and tendencies toward queer postures in the arms, and (4) severe vegetative disturbances, leading finally to death. The chronic progressive course in this case was remarkable. There were some features similar to those of group I, but the neuritis was the most prominent part of the picture. It was an interesting mixture of a severe polyneuritis and an incomplete encephalopathy similar to the condition in the other cases.

Case 17. Clinical History. A woman, aged 44, had been in another hospital for several weeks and had been taken home recently by her husband. He stated that she had drunk for years, and for about two months before admission had been unable to eat or to walk and seemed to be losing her mind. At the other hospital she did not improve and was not well when he took her home. On admission on January 19, 1931, she was disoriented, apathetic, and unable to cooperate. She answered most questions with her name, but said, "It is a very complicated matter. I am at 144th Street." She was hypersensitive all over the body, especially in the legs. Both arms were very weak. In extension, the left arm extended to pronate and converged at the shoulder, while the right arm raised itself and diverged. There were extreme weakness and hypotonia in the legs so that she could not stand. Patellar and achilles reflexes were absent. There was no Babinski reaction. There was nystagmus on both sides, but more on the right. The patient also had difficulty in moving the eyes, but lateral movements were more difficult than convergence. The left pupil was larger than the right; both reacted promptly. The optic fundi were normal. The Wassermann reaction of the blood and spinal fluid was negative, and all other tests of the spinal fluid gave negative results. In the next few days the nystagmus changed, showing a rotatory component, with the quick movement in the counter-clockwise direction, and also a vertical component. She sometimes remained in cataleptic attitudes. Irrigation of the ears did not provoke any nystagmus, past pointing, or deviations of the arms or trunks. Her utterances were abrupt and disconnected. She said, "I feel like punching you in the nose. (Why?) Oh, I just feel that way. (Is that the kind of girl you are?) You mean is that the kind of a girl I turned out to be. I feel like fighting. (Where are you?) Still in the synagogue. (What are you doing there?) Looking at you. (What year is it?) Nineteen-fourteen—now here he comes with the questions." On January 29, there were rigidity of the neck and drowsiness. She died on February 1. There was no post-mortem examination.

Summary and Comment. Clinically, there were: (1) a Korsakoff psychosis, (2) marked polyneuritis all over the body, (3) nystagmus but no reaction to caloric stimulation of the ears, (4) difficulty in lateral movements of the eyes, and (5) some tendency toward cataleptic postures. An atypical Korsakoff's psychosis and polyneuritis were in the foreground in this case, but there were also signs pointing to a lesion in the central nervous system similar to that in the foregoing descriptions.

Case 18. Clinical History. A woman, aged 42, was transferred from a medical ward, to which she had been admitted on March 16, 1931, with a complaint of difficulty in walking for two months. She had weakness in both legs, with loss of reflexes and sensory disturbances up to a definite level at the third lumbar segment. There was also weakness of the upper extremities, with exaggerated reflexes. There were nystagmus in all directions, disturbance in speech, and psychic troubles. She complained that she had not had a bath in ten days, that the physician gave her morphine in her dining room, that a colored man pulled her toe, and that her husband and everybody were all singing and having a good time. All serologic tests of the blood and spinal fluid were negative. She was transferred to the psychopathic division on

March 25, where she was found to be confused—especially at night—confabulatory, and disoriented. She said, "I would like to go to the hospital and have my knees operated on." There was spasticity of the right arm, with hyperactive reflexes and a positive Hoffmann sign. The left arm showed tremor. She lay in bed with the legs flexed and complained bitterly of pain and tenderness in them. The Achilles and patellar reflexes were absent, nor was there a Babinski reaction. She had difficulty in stretching her legs and could not move her feet. There were: a slightly stiff neck, nystagmus to both sides, slurred speech, and a stiff facial expression. The eyegrounds were normal. Four days later she was oriented. She said, "Doctor, if you could answer the question for me why I am here and I had a million dollars, I would give it to you. I went to church yesterday. (Are your legs all right?) Yes, I have a peculiar way of dressing. After I have my bath, I always put on my shoes and stockings first, and then I take a walk around the bathroom and kitchen and start to dress. I have been doing that more so since my legs are so bad." The patient was unable to walk, but there had been some improvement in the paresis. There was improvement in the arms too, but the facial expression was still stiff. The nystagmus was disappearing, and on April 1 the Hoffmann sign had disappeared. From that time on there was steady improvement until she was discharged on April 27, when she was almost free from symptoms with the exception of hypersensitivity, especially in the legs. Before discharge she admitted drinking regularly. Subsequent efforts to follow up this case were not successful because the patient moved from her former address.

Summary and Comment. This case showed: (1) neuritic paralysis of the legs with unusual distribution of the sensory disturbances, (2) confusion of a toxic type, (3) spasticity and increased reflexes in the upper extremities, (4) nystagmus, and (5) bulbar speech. It was evident from the history that we were dealing with an alcoholic neuritis, but there were also signs of lesions of the pyramidal tract and bulb.

Case 19. Clinical History. A woman, aged about 49 years, was admitted on February 21, 1931 with a statement from relatives that she had been on one of her periodic drinking spells for the previous three weeks. She complained that her feet were in straps and that adhesive tapes were around the tips of her fingers. She continually tried to remove these tapes and picked imaginary threads from her body. She was confused, disoriented, and mis-identifying. She had crying spells. She was unable to walk. On ad-mission, she said, "There is a nail on the top of my foot. I don't drink. My husband is here; he can tell you. My fingers feel as if there were needles in them. Please take my stockings off. (She had none on.) I will be 75 in April." She had an alcoholic facies. Her voice was high pitched, with a peculiar intonation. The retinal disks were injected. The pupils reacted sluggishly to light. There was a quick nystagmus to the right; on the left the nystagmus con-sisted chiefly of the slow component. There was good convergence of the eyes, but she had difficulty in keeping the eyes to the left. She lay in dorsal decubitus, unable to move herself to either side although she could use her arms. The lower limbs were held in a frog position with the knees flexed and rotated outward and the soles together. She was unable to move the proximal segments, though she could move the toes freely and the foot to some extent. All deep reflexes were absent. There was definite weakness in the upper extremities, with moderate atrophy of the interosseal mus-cles, involuntary movements of the hands and wrist, and a pill-rolling position of the hand. Careful examination of the sensibility was not possible. Pain did not seem to bother her much anywhere. She said, "It feels like meat, like food." When a cross was drawn on her hand with the examiner's finger, she said: "It feels like the button on a coat. I think it is the button from your vest." When a cross was drawn on her hand with a pin, she said: "It feels like the edge of an iron burning me. It's like a cord. It's like sheepwool." When asked if she knew that she was paralyzed, she said: "I got up about four-thirty and I got my daughter's lunch and all of a sudden there was a numbness in both hands. I would like to know what that smell is you put in my eyes. I will tell you how I know. There was a young girl and she had two doctors and I stayed with her until the doctors came. They weren't in the room very long when they put this stuff in the room. (Where were you yesterday?) I was out this morning. I walked to church and I came home with the lady. (But you are paralyzed.) I asked you if you would take me and you said if you felt good you would." She was very inattentive. When shown the picture of a silver fox, she said, "I say that is out in the woods. It looks like those white lions." She did not change much in the next few days, and died of bronchopneumonia on February 27. There was no post-mortem examination.

Summary and Comment. This case showed: (1) delirious features, (2) severe peripheral neuritis, and (3) nystagmus and impairment of lateral movement of the eyes. The neuritis was the predominating feature, although the nystagmus suggested a lesion of the brain stem as well.

Case 20. Clinical History. A man, aged 52, was brought to the hospital on April 8, 1931, after having been found on a floor uttering incoherent babble and betraying the existence of auditory and visual hallucinations. He had an alcoholic breath. He admitted drinking excessively. On admission he was dull, shaky, and tremulous. He said, "I am a little nervous. I have been here before. I am a little nervous. I was a little drunk. My mother died and my two brothers—no, I take it back—my mother's brother—they are dead all right. I didn't hear things, but somebody in this hospital stole $5,000 from me. (What is the date?) It is the 14th day of January, 1878—no, that's my birthday—it is 1931. I was home yesterday, seeing my mother and two brothers." He was silly and euphoric, and did not understand his present situation. He had a flaccid face, with tremors of the lips and irregular pupils that responded sluggishly to light. He was apraxic in the use of his tongue, and, when he tried to move it, there were associated movements in the muscles of the face. He had great difficulty in opening his mouth. He was emaciated; the skin of his hands was dry and scaly, especially between the fingers, and there was edema of the ankles. The spinal fluid was normal in all examinations, including the Wassermann reaction, which was also negative with the blood. During the next few days hallucinations continued and he was restless. On April 14 he said, "I had a nervous breakdown. To tell the truth I lost my brothers and my mother. Four people are dead in my house. I was home last night and I was home this morning." His expression was dull and his reaction euphoric; he continued to confabulate. He showed marked polyneuritis, with ptosis of the eyelids, weakness in all extremities, absent tendon reflexes, tenderness all over the body, and a bilateral foot drop. On April 15 he was oriented for place. He said, "I didn't go out today, and I am tired. I will go out every day and get some fresh air." He confabulated at suggestion. He bent down to pick up imaginary glasses, and said, "I am going to be operated on for my throat." He fumbled with the bedclothes and was always grasping at things. He also had a grasping reflex. Even the grasping was ataxic. He made rhythmic movements of the right leg and showed an intention tremor of the hands. He tended to supinate the arms, and showed weakness on pronation. There was marked atrophy in the muscles of the hands, and a wrist drop was present. He made many small meaningless movements with the fingers and tended to hold the hands in cataleptic positions from time to time. He had a staring expression with no pupillary disturbances, but with some difficulty in sideward movements of the eyes. The pseudopellagrous erythema of the hands and feet persisted, producing ulcerations of the toes. During the next few days all the symptoms progressed. He said, "I am pretty good. I am in Norwood, New Jersey. I got up late this morning. I am in my home. The train is the best thing for me to go over." He had a tendency to perseverate, recognized objects, obeyed commands, and made many delirious movements. The emaciation had become more marked; the atrophy in the lower extremities had progressed; the tendon reflexes remained absent; definite paresis of the abducens muscle had developed on the right and less definitely on the left; the pupillary reactions had become poor, the right one being nearly

absent. On April 23 gangrene of the toes of both feet had dev-
veloped. He died on April 29. There was no post-mortem examination.

Summary and Comment. This case showed: (1) a delirious
picture with later Korsakoff features, (2) marked polyneuritis, (3)
grasping and groping tendencies and a grasping reflex, (4) cataleptic attitudes and athetoid movements of the hands, and (5) pellagroid changes in the hands and feet, which progressed. The catalepsy and the psychosis pointed to a lesion of the central nervous
system in addition to the polyneuritis.

In all of the polyneuritic cases discussed so far there was definite evidence of a process in the central nervous system such as
was found in the other groups of cases. In case 15 the signs of lesions in the central nervous system dominated the picture, so that
this case links the two groups together. In case 9 there was a
marked neuritis in connection with the demonstrated lesion in the
central nervous system. Rigidities in the arms, catalepsy, and a
tendency toward athetoid movements were rather common in
most of the cases. But in case 19 there were only the nystagmus
and impaired lateral movements of the eyes to suggest the central
lesion. In case 17 the absence of caloric nystagmus and difficulties
in ocular movements were the most significant features, although
there was also spontaneous nystagmus. There are two cases in the
group with marked pseudopellagrous changes in the skin of the
hands and feet. All cases showed a psychosis in which clouding of
consciousness played some part. In other cases there was confusion; in some of these, as the confusion tended to subside, a picture was left that was akin to a Korsakoff psychosis. In case 18
there were signs of a pyramidal tract lesion. Signs of such a lesion
also played some part in the following case.

Case 21. Clinical History. A man, aged 50, was transferred
from Harlem Hospital on February 3, 1931, complaining of a
tingling sensation in the legs and arms and being unable to walk by

himself. He said he drank heavily, that someone was after him to take his money. He stated: "I feel fine, only I can't move my hands. I don't know why. I guess I am paralyzed." He now denied that he thought someone was after him. Orientation at this time was good. He had paralysis of the right arm, especially at the shoulder, but retained ability to flex the forearm. The left arm showed more power than the right, but was also weak. The tendon reflexes were sluggish. Gait was staggering, with a positive Romberg sign. Achilles and patellar reflexes were hyperactive on both sides, and there was a bilateral Babinski sign. There was a definite heel-to-knee ataxia. Pes cavus of both feet was present, as was tenderness of the muscles and nerve trunks. Pain sensation was intact; the patient was even hyperesthetic. In both lower limbs a pinprick was felt as electricity spreading upward, but on the fingers and dorsal surfaces of the hands a prick was felt as a light touch. Postural sense in the fingers was lost. Otherwise he was also hyperesthetic in the upper limbs. The pupils were a little irregular, and the reaction of the right one to light was defective. There was a bilateral partial ptosis of the eyelids. Serologic tests of the blood and spinal fluid were completely negative. Toward the end of February, atrophic disturbances developed in both hands, and the skin over the backs of the hands became broken, coarse, and covered with a fine brownish-white desquamation. Examination of the urine, blood, and internal organs gave negative results. Electric reactions in the muscles, even in the paralyzed ones, were normal. The patient began to improve rapidly in March and was discharged on March 17, with only some weakness in the arms and a persistent Babinski reaction. An effort was made to locate him in December, 1931, but he could not be found.

Summary and Comment. This case showed: (1) severe polyneuritis without mental symptoms, (2) bilateral nystagmus, (3) bilateral partial ptosis, (4) a persistent Babinski sign, and (5) pellagroid changes of the skin. Again, the clinical symptoms give evidence of a cerebral lesion, such as was found in the encephalopathic changes of the central nervous system that accompany the polyneuritis. Almost any possible combination of neuritic and encephalopathic lesions may occur. We shall not attempt here to discuss alcoholic neuritis. The common coincidence with pellagroid changes of the skin may be mentioned again. Nystagmus and changes in the Bárány reactions are common in cases of this group. The one case coming to autopsy showed that the changes in the central nervous system are of a chronic progressive type.

Problem Cases and Further Questions

In order to show the great variety of questions involved, we report the history in a case of alcoholic neuritis with an unusual trophic disturbance.

Case 22. Clinical History. A man, aged 61, was admitted with a history of chronic alcoholism. He complained of loss of sensation in both hands. Physical examination showed edema of the hands and atrophy of the skin with blisters and redness. There were also erythema and edema of the feet. The cardiovascular-renal system was normal. The Wassermann reaction and chemical composition of the blood were normal. Neurologic tests showed paralysis of both forearms, with slight atrophy of the interosseal muscles. The electrical reactions showed a slight quantitative diminution. The tendon reflexes in the arms were exaggerated. The reflexes were otherwise normal. The pupils reacted normally to light. The patient was disoriented for time and showed an organic type of confusion. In the next few days the trophic disturbances in the hands and feet increased. There was edema of the hands. The left foot showed a laceration over the dorsum of the toes and a diminution to sensitivity for pinprick. The vessels were palpable and seemed to be of good quality. The skin of the hands appeared like roast beef on the dorsal surface and was thick and unyielding on the volar surface. The interossei and digiti quinti muscles were wasted, and there was weakness in all finger movements. The power of extension was better than the power of flexion. There was a glove type of hypalgesia for pinprick extending to the middle of the forearm. Both hands showed a livid bluish color. The hands were tremulous, and there was convergence of the outstretched arms.

Summary and Comment. This was a case of demonstrated neuritis, with trophic disturbances of the hands and feet. According to the history, the etiologic factor was alcohol. This was probably a special type of neuritis in a senile person. Evidence of vascular disturbance that could cause the trophic disturbance was absent. The patient subsequently improved and was discharged.

The following case is reported because of its similarity to tabes dorsalis.

Case 23. Clinical History. A woman, aged 58, was admitted on January 26, 1931. She said, "I feel all upset. I am afraid I am going to die. I had a nervous attack four or five days ago." She confessed that she drank a good deal. She was disoriented, agitated, and depressed. She moved her hands restlessly, picking at her hair. The optic disks were pale. The pupils were small and reacted sluggishly to light. The tendon reflexes of the arms were normal. The outstretched arms showed marked convergence at the shoulder and elbow, and there was tremor of the hands, but no other disturbance in the motility of the upper limbs. The lower extremities showed marked loss of power and hypotonia, especially in the muscles acting on the knee joints. Power at the ankles was better, but she could not stand or walk. The heel-to-knee test was performed in an ataxic manner, with the big toe held in the Babinski position. The tendon reflexes in the lower limbs were absent. The knee joints were enlarged like those in a tabetic knee. Roentgen examination showed some exostosis of the articulating surfaces. She was constantly making small movements with the feet, usually abduction. The sense of posture in the toes was lost. Sensibility was impaired in a stocking formation to the upper third of the leg. When a line was drawn on the foot with a pin, she said, "It was something wet or something. It was just one point like a dot."

When two parallel lines were drawn, she said, "I feel something sticking in my foot." When three parallel lines were drawn, she felt it as "one mark." When a line was drawn on both feet, she felt it only on one foot. When two spots were touched on the left foot, she felt three spots. When a cross was drawn on the left foot with a pin, she felt two or three burning spots with a long aftereffect. When a cross was drawn on the right foot, she felt a circle. The Wassermann reaction was negative with both blood and spinal fluid. The colloidal gold curve was flat, and the spinal fluid was otherwise normal. Psychically, the patient showed impaired orientation and slight mental deterioration. She was transferred to a state hospital on January 31, 1931. A report from that hospital stated: "She was in a restless state, voluble and displaying distractibility, with fluctuation of mood; she claimed that she was unable to walk due to numbness and stiffness of the legs, and complained of dizziness. The biceps and knee jerks were absent; the Babinski reaction was positive on the left side. Eyegrounds showed early retinal arteriosclerosis. The Wassermann reaction of the blood was negative. The general condition improved, and in June she was able to leave her bed without assistance; in July she was up and about and was noted to be oriented in all spheres, although recent memory was somewhat defective. She was paroled on September 7 and reported on October 2, when she was still weak and unsteady on her feet due to residual alcoholic neuritis, but she denied any further use of alcohol since discharge."

Summary and Comment. This patient showed a picture suggestive of tabes dorsalis. There was even enlargement of the knees, suggesting a tabetic arthropathy, but there was no syphilitic history and serologic tests were negative. She was alcoholic and recovered. There were disorientation, convergence of the arms, and a tremor of the hands. Thus, this was not a case of tabes dorsalis but of alcoholic neuritis in which the spinal cord was also involved. Also in a case of Korsakoff's psychosis with polyneuritis of certain alcoholic origin, we have found disturbances of sensibility that were similar to those reported in this case. Stein and von Weizsäcker

(1928) considered these changes typical for central (spinal cord or higher) lesions of the sensory pathways. To what extent the spinal cord is involved in alcoholic neuritis is an interesting question. We found histopathologic changes in the spinal cord in case 13. We hope that in later investigations we shall be able to consider this question more fully.

The following case is of interest because it simulates syphilis of the central nervous system, with special midbrain symptomatology.

Case 24. Clinical History. A woman, aged 29, was brought to the hospital on June 7, 1931, with the statement that she had been drinking for a week. She was drowsy, lethargic, too weak to walk, maudlin, tremulous, and smelled of alcohol. On June 8 she said, "I get drunk about once a month; this is March." She was stuporous, confused, and disoriented. She was well nourished but dehydrated. The internal organs were normal. The pupils were small, but reacted to light. On June 9 she was worse; she could not be aroused and responded very slightly to pressure on the supraorbital nerve. The pupils were unequal, the left being larger than the right, and did not react to light. The tendon reflexes were present and equal; there was no stiffness of the neck, and the Kernig test was negative. She was incontinent. On June 11 she could be awakened, and it was discovered that she had left facial paralysis and ptosis of the left eyelid; the left pupil was constricted and inactive to light, and there was limitation of ocular movements on this side. The biceps reflex was absent on the left, and the left hand grip was weak. The knee jerks were absent bilaterally, but the Babinski response was negative. A spinal tap was done on June 12 and gave negative results in all examinations, except that the colloidal gold curve was reported to be 433221000. The spinal tap was repeated on June 22 and gave entirely negative results. On June 17 she was brighter, but there were still ptosis of the left eyelid and weakness of the left side of the face; the left pupillary reaction was incomplete and the tongue deviated to the left. There

were flexion tendencies, especially in the left arm. The tendon reflexes in the arms were present. There was no Hoffmann reaction,
but a positive Meyer reaction was present on both sides. The
patellar and Achilles reflexes were absent, as was the Babinski
response. There was a slight soreness of the calf muscles of the
legs. On June 23 she said, "I went out last night to buy a pair of
stockings. (How much did you pay?) Ninety-eight cents. (What
color were they?) I always buy black. I know you are a jollier. What
is the use of living if you can't get a laugh?" When she tried to
walk and was unable to, she said, "I can't walk without my
shoes." She tended to fall backward and showed some retropulsion. Ptosis of the left eye persisted. There were nystagmoid movements on looking to the left, and upward and downward movements of the left eye were impaired. The pupillary reaction was
sluggish in the left eye but prompt in the right eye. Both arms
showed strong flexion at the elbows, the left more than the right.
There were no other types of rigidity in the whole body and no
troubles in sensibility. On June 29 she was showing improvement,
although she complained of double vision; she still had nystagmus
on looking to the left, and the left pupil was a little larger than the
right and still reacted sluggishly to light. However, the ptosis had
improved. She was oriented and no longer confabulated. She was
discharged on July 7, apparently recovered. On December 15 a
social worker visited her home and met her coming from a speak-
easy under the influence of liquor. She dragged her right foot and
kept the left eye closed (ptosis); when she talked, there was an evidence of slurring. The neighbors said that she was nearly always in
this condition.

Summary and Comment. In this case, with a negative Wassermann reaction, we found: (1) Korsakoff type of psychosis, (2)
ptosis of the left eyelid, (3) an incomplete reaction to light in the
left pupil, (4) flexor tendencies especially in the left arm, (5) absence of patellar and achilles reflexes, (6) tenderness of the muscles
of the legs, (7) a tendency toward retropulsion, and (8) no disturbance in tone. Until it was known that the serum was normal, we

thought we were dealing with a case of cerebrospinal syphilis. A closer study of the course of the disease made the diagnosis of an atypical case of alcoholism certain. There were a history of alcoholism, the Korsakoff psychosis, and the neuritic signs. Besides this, the patient showed midbrain symptomatology, with ptosis, impaired ocular movements, and increased flexor tendencies, all on the left side Hoff and Schilder (1927) consider the absence of persistence of tone a reliable sign of midbrain and striopallidal lesions. There was also retropulsion. In this case the alcoholism had caused a rather unusual symptomatology. Apparently the variety of neurologic symptoms that can be produced by chronic alcoholic intoxications has been underrated. The neurologic symptomatology is extremely variable; still, it is evident that it always centers about symptoms that are due to the characteristic neuropathologic findings in the central nervous system.

COMMENT ON THE NEUROPATHOLOGIC FINDINGS

In all seven cases reported here in which neuropathologic studies were made, as well as in several others not included in this report, the same fundamental principles in both localization and type of lesion have been demonstrated.

The first principle is that the lesion always occurs in parts of the central nervous system that are adjacent to spinal fluid spaces, such as the surface of the ventricular system and the surface of the brain and brain stem; in other words, the lesion is always marginal. Furthermore, the lesion is usually more severe where the spinal fluid flows least freely. Thus, when it occurs on the brain surface, it is most often in the depths between the convolutions. In general, however, it is more severe in the ventricular system than on the outer surface of the brain and brain stem. In the ventricles, it is most severe around pockets and recesses. Within the fourth ventricle, the lateral recess beneath the restiform body is an area of predilection, consequently involving the nuclei of the eighth nerve. Severe lesions are also common about the aqueduct of Sylvius and in the depths of the floor of the third ventricle, about the hypophyseal recess, including the mammillary bodies and the optic chiasms—which are doubly exposed both by their relationship to the floor of the third ventricle and by the recesses about the base of the brain. These data suggest that the spinal fluid contains the noxious agent. Of course, the problem is not so simple, but if it were, what might one assume this agent to be? Is it the alcohol itself? It is known that alcohol may be found in the spinal fluid after heavy drinking. Dobrovizky (1929) has shown that alcohol, or at least some related reducing substance, may be present in the brain substance in persons who have died of acute alcoholism; he stated further that it is present in largest quantities in parts of the brain that he assumes from clinical analogy to be most affected—namely, in the cerebellum and vegetative centers. The earlier views of von Monakow (1905) suggested that alcohol in the blood reduced its oxidation powers and also attacked the lipoids of the nervous system, especially the myelin, thus assuming that this was the cause of the alcoholic neuritis. Although we have not as yet made an exhaustive study of the peripheral neuritis, the distribution and type of the lesion within the central nervous system do not argue for this sort of disturbance. Neither is there any evidence of atheromatous changes in the vascular system as a result of circulating alcohol. On the other hand, in many patients with chronic alcoholism an encephalopathy does not develop. The question may be raised whether the cause is the alcohol per se or some contaminating substance it contains. Recent experience in some parts of the United States with the so-called ginger paralysis following the use of fluid extract of ginger as an alcoholic beverage, has led to investigations, with the result that Smith and Lillie (1931) have found that a contaminating substance, triorthocresylphosphate, is responsible for the neuritis of the lower limbs, reaching the peripheral nerves from the circulation and producing a lesion which ascends to the anterior horn cells. So far, however, there has been no evidence to suggest such an associated poisonous agent in the alcoholic encephalopathies that have been occurring in chronic alcoholism, at least from the time of Gudden and Wernicke up to the present, and in all parts of the world.

The fact that the pathologic lesion does not come to a standstill when the alcoholic intake is withdrawn, but shows a remarkably progressive tendency sometimes for weeks or months after the drinking has stopped, with fresh hemorrhages and reactive gliosis and proliferative vascular changes together with a progressive clinical picture, argues for a secondarily derived toxin, such as might arise from the pathologic state of the alcoholic liver or from disturbed absorption through the atrophic mucosa of the gastrointestinal tract. These are all involved but fascinating problems open for further work. Frequently, in our cases, changes were found in the spinal fluid, with a positive globulin reaction and a slight change in the colloidal gold curve, such as 0011211000, with a negative cell count and negative Wassermann reaction. It is reported that a pathologic lipemia is present in alcoholism (Feigl, 1918; and Bang, 1918). Whether this has any connection with the frequently reported lipochrome changes in the nerve cells (Carmichael and Stern, 1931), certainly nearly always present, as well as with the frequently occurring corpora amylacea, is doubtful. However, the fact that these changes are similar to those found in pellagra, especially in the so-called pseudopellagra associated with chronic alcoholism, reported by Klauder and Winkelman (1928) and Boggs and Padget (1932), raises the question of a possibly associated or secondarily induced avitaminosis, as suggested by Wechsler (1932). In what way these conditions may be related to the lesions of the vegetative centers of the spinal cord and midbrain, as has already been suggested by Orton and Bender (1931) in similar conditions, is a problem we hope to work out in the near future [see L. Bender, 1934b].

If we consider the lesion as marginal, it includes the marginal gliosis of the outer surface and the ependymal gliosis of the ventricles and in both cases is productive and reactive, suggesting an irritative process. The marginal gliosis about the brain stem and spinal cord is usually only a few decimeters in thickness, is invasive, and of the astrocytic type. It is prone to follow connective tissue trabeculae. On the surface of the cerebrum the lesion invades the brain along the pial intrusions and also sometimes produces irregularities or hummocks on the outer surface. It is usually limited to the first cortical layer where the reactive cells are astrocytic in type, but occasionally a cytoplastic gliosis is also seen in the second and third layers, together with swelling of the microglia and oligodendroglia. When the surface of the cerebellum is involved, the lesion is very patchy; there are a glial scarring, with retraction of the outer layer, a loss of Purkinje cells, and some invasion of glia cells in the corpuscular layer. Gamper (1928), who studied sixteen brains and reported findings similar in many ways to ours, emphasized the lack of pathologic changes in the cortex. It is true that the cortical nerve cells and deeper layers of the cortex are remarkably free from pathologic disturbances, but the marginal lesions were practically always present in the cases we studied. The marginal gliosis seems to be the explanation for much of the involvement of the optic nerve, which may be looked on as a narrow evagination of the central nervous system. The lesions concerned in the peripheral neuritis are not explained in the same way and will not be considered in this report. The ependymal reaction is the most marked and characteristic part of the glial pathology. It is both reactive and invasive. It tends to narrow the lumen of the ventricles and aqueduct, and produces an irregular surface with glial hummocks and ependymal pockets. There is also a subependymal wall of gliosis that tends to invade the reticulum. Between the outer ependymal wall and this invasive wall there is a loose mesh of glia fibers containing a coagulable fluid, possibly amylogenous in nature. This somewhat schematically presents the first principle in the localization and type of the lesion, which is, briefly, a marginal and ependymal gliosis.

The second principle is probably dependent on the vascular bed that is related to these marginal surfaces. Thus, on the outer surfaces the small invading pial vessels bear the brunt of the lesion. Also in the spinal cord of one case in this series in which lesions are reported, the lesion was found to be directly connected with the distribution of the central branches of the anterior medial spinal vessels that enter the spinal cord through the anterior raphe and immediately terminate about the central part and lateral horn of the spinal gray matter. The invasion of the lesion into the brain stem from the ventricles is also associated with the vascular bed of this region, although its direct connections are not so clear. Whenever there is any lesion deeper in the brain, such as in the thalamic nuclei, it is always by way of the invading blood vessels. In fact, aside from the ependymal and marginal gliosis, the lesion seems to be primarily a vascular one. There is congestion which, in the most acute cases, may be the most general reaction and may extend some distance into the brain tissues. There are characteristically numerous small hemorrhages about the small vessels, discovery of and emphasis on which led Wernicke to call the condition encephalitis haemorrhagica superior. There are also conspicuous capillary budding and vascular organization, and proliferative changes in the vessels involving both the endothelial and adventitial layer of the vessel walls. We did not find marked regressive changes in the blood vessels, although they have been remarked by others (Bouman of Utrecht, 1931; Ohkuma, 1930; Spielmeyer, 1922). The vascular lesions have the same distribution as the glial ones in general, but invade more deeply. To some extent they are found on all surfaces of the central nervous system—the cerebrum, cerebellum, brain stem, optic nerve, and even the retina—but they are most marked within the brain stem along the ventricles. The vascular changes and the marginal and ependymal gliosis are apparently not directly dependent on each other, because in the more chronic cases the gliosis may occur without much vascular reaction, as in cases 12 and 16, while in the more acute cases the vascular reaction may predominate, as in cases 1, 2, and 10; in case 3 there is still another type of reaction, shown by a specific gliosis characterized by a greater reaction of the interstitial glia cells, both astrocytic and cytoplastic, with some areas of actual destruction of tissue but without much vascular disturbance. The localization of the interstitial gliosis, however, is the same as the vascular lesion in the other cases.

This brings us to the final principle underlying the distribution of the lesion, and that is a tendency toward a specific electivity for gray masses and especially for the vegetative gray masses that surround the ventricles. All of the white areas of the brain or the myelinated tracts, with the exception of the optic nerve, are remarkably free from lesions. Even in the pontile region, where the vascular disturbance invades the reticular formation, it tends to stop short at the white tracts, such as the fasciculus longitudinalis posterior, almost as if the myelinated tracts presented a barrier to the progress of the invasion. This is a contradiction to the long-accepted belief that the myelin sheaths are particularly vulnerable to alcoholic intoxication. The subcortical layers are never involved. But for that matter the cortical gray layers show a relative immunity to the disease as compared with the vegetative gray areas of the ventricular system, for which the lesion appears to have a high grade of selectivity. Many investigators (Wernicke, Oppenheim, Gamper, Ohkuma, and Neuberger) have recognized this, but none has sufficiently recognized all the conclusions that may be drawn from these findings. The most severe lesions are found in the floor of the fourth ventricle, including the nuclei of the eighth to the twelfth nerves, and in the periaqueductal gray masses, including the nuclei of the ocular muscles, and finally in the floor and walls of the third ventricles, including the various vegetative nuclei of the thalamic and hypothalamic regions. The predilection for the mammillary bodies has been noted by many, but it is probably only the result of the location of these bodies at a vulnerable point at the base of the brain and the floor of the third ventricle, and furthermore because they have a rich capillary bed. That the lesion invades them from the periphery is seen in case 15, which was the most slowly progressive case in our series; yet the lesion is still limited to the periphery, leaving the center of the bodies free. But in the more severely acute cases, the lesion has fairly well destroyed these bodies and invaded the hypothalamus, and in some cases even the corpus striatum, as in such cases it also invades the corpora quadrigemina and the roof of the fourth ventricle, including the dentate nucleus of the cerebellum. Hiller (1928) has called attention to the vascular distribution as the basis for the electivity of the lesions in the central nervous system, and, although it obviously plays an important role in this condition, it does not tell the whole story, just as it does not explain why in different diseases vascular beds are elected.

Of particular interest is the fact that although the nerve cells nearly always show some slight lipoid changes, as emphasized by Carmichael and Stern (1931) and many others, actually the nerve cells and fibers are left remarkably intact, even in regions in which the severe vascular and glial changes occur. It is true, especially in the mammillary bodies, that nerve cells are apparently destroyed by the high degree of vascular organization, but even in this case normal cells may be seen between the budding capillaries. The absence of any inflammatory response is also remarkable.

There still remains the question why there is the difference in extent, at least in the distribution and severity of the anatomic response, with a different clinical picture in persons with apparently similar alcoholic histories. Tsiminakis (1931), who reported three cases and spoke of an alcoholic affinity for certain parts of the central nervous system, nevertheless claimed that there is no correlation between the lesions and the clinical picture. Our studies show, however, a very close correlation, as has been brought out by the clinical discussions. In summary, we need mention only that three cases, which showed the most severe lesions starting on the margin of the brain, brain stem, and especially the ventricular system and invading the visceral gray centers, especially in the medulla, midbrain and hypothalamic regions, had before death already been classified together as representing a clinical picture with deep clouding of consciousness and changing rigidities, etc. Furthermore, the case that showed the most striking cerebellar symptoms showed lesions penetrating most deeply into the roof of the ventricular system, including the dentate nucleus, the corpora quadrigemina, etc. Cases discussed under the heading of acute catatonia showed a more or less active and invasive response consisting mostly of the marginal and ependymal gliosis alone.

Since we do not deal with an inflammatory process, it would be better to substitute the term encephalopathy for encephalitis. One may call the cases described here alcoholic encephalopathy or alcoholic polioencephalopathy. The term haemorrhagica is only appropriate to part of the cases, such as those reported in connection with our group I. We believe that our study gives a clearer understanding of the term "wet brain." At autopsy there was usually subpial edema. It is, of course, in no way characteristic, and a more careful study of the phenomenon is necessary. The histopathologic and anatomic facts, at any rate, fit in with the experimental studies of Howe (1932) which have shown that injections of alcohol into the blood or local applications on the brain produce hemorrhages and edema on the surface of the cortex.

Summary

1. cases with changing rigidities in the foreground

Among the cases described by Wernicke (1906) as polioencephalitis haemorrhagica superior, we have separated a group in which the changing rigidities are in the foreground of the neurologic picture. These rigidities are characterized by their changeability and their tendency to increase when passive movements are performed. They are partially phenomena of resistance, as the psychic phenomena of resistance are inseparable from the neurologic picture. They are often accompanied by athetoid movements, and phenomena of grasping and groping are present with the grasping reflex and the sucking reflex. Positive and negative support reactions are common. Disturbances of speech are often observed. Oculomotor signs and pupillary changes are common but not essential. Optic atrophy and retinal hemorrhages have been observed. Asynergia is a typical feature. Clouding of consciousness and disturbances in sleep are present in every case. Delirious features may be present. In some cases the clouding of consciousness may fade and leave a mental picture similar to Korsakoff's psychosis. There is marked increase in the reaction to pain. Vegetative disturbances, with emaciation, elevation in temperature, sweating, and trophic disturbances in the skin of a pseudopellagrous type are observed and lead to death in from two days to six months.

Histopathologic examination shows a lesion of the ventricular gray masses starting from the medulla oblongata, reaching through the third ventricle and involving especially the corpora mammillaria. Also involved are the substantia nigra, the subthalamic and thalamic regions, and the putamen. There are also lesions in the superficial layers of the cortex. The lesions are characterized by hemorrhages, proliferative changes in the small vessels, and a marginal glial reaction in which astrocytes prevail. All surfaces of the central nervous system closely connected with the spinal fluid are involved, but more especially where there is a tendency toward stagnation of the fluid. Nuclear areas are more prone to lesions than adjacent myelinated areas, with the exception of the optic nerve. The changing rigidities and similar phenomena, such as athetosis and disturbances in speech, are probably due to lesions of Deiters' nucleus and the adjacent tonus centers, and perhaps to lesions in the region of the hypothalamus, thalamus, and striopallidum. But it is also probable that the disturbance in consciousness is a factor. The phenomena of grasping, groping, pointing, and sucking have their origin in the medulla, midbrain, striopallidum, and cortex, with psychophysical integration playing a part. They can be produced by lesions at various levels. The changes in consciousness and delirious features are due to lesions of the centers of consciousness in the periventricular gray masses extending from the medulla to the third ventricle. The support reaction and the asynergia are due to lesions in the cerebellum, but lesions of the tonus apparatus may also play some part. The increase in the reaction to pain is due to disturbances in the centers of consciousness, but there are also more direct brain-stem factors involved. There is a possibility that some of the vegetative symptoms are secondary to changes in the vegetative centers in the ventricular gray areas. There are also unquestionably somatic disturbances in metabolism.

2. CASES WITH CEREBELLAR SYMPTOMATOLOGY

Among the cases of alcoholic encephalopathy, was a group in which the cerebellar symptomatology was in the foreground of the picture. Two of these cases showed marked oculomotor signs, and the reaction to caloric stimulation of the ears was impaired in both cases. Rigidities were not conspicuous, as in the former group, and the clouding of consciousness was less severe. Histopathologic examination in one case showed less severe vascular disturbances than in the other group, but the lesion had penetrated more deeply into the roof of the ventricles and aqueduct, invading the dentate nucleus of the cerebellum. The anatomic findings offer a possibility of interpreting the Argyll Robertson pupil and the double conjugate palsy observed in one case.

3. CASES RESEMBLING ACUTE CATATONIA

In this group the symptomatology is chiefly that of an acute catatonic picture. In the psychic picture, dissociation and hallucinations are prevalent. Clouding of consciousness plays a less important part. Rigidities are closely associated with resistance of a psychic type. Athetoid movements of a partially psychic character are present. Grasping and groping, and especially pointing, are common. Asynergia is observed, but is partially influenced by tensions and psychomotor activity. In the histopathologic picture a glial reaction is most prominent, with some indication of a more widespread toxic disturbance in the cortex. The theoretical interest in these cases lies in the fact that they link some of the psychomotor signs of catatonia with the rigidities that are due to localized lesions of the type described in group I. The jerky movements are probably an expression of an irritation of the tonic apparatus, which is also responsible for the changing rigidities.

4. PROLONGED ALCOHOLIC DELIRIUM

In one case there were observed asynergia, tensions of varying degrees, and support reactions. These symptoms point to an encephalopathy of a mild degree.

5. CASES OF ENCEPHALOPATHY COMBINED WITH A NEURITIS

Seven cases were studied in which there was a mixture of neuritic and central nervous system signs. The cerebral symptomatology may dominate the picture, and the neuritis may be indicated only by the painfulness of the deeper tissues; or, at the opposite extreme, there may be only nystagmus and slight ocular signs to suggest lesions of the central nervous system associated with a marked polyneuritis. Signs of a lesion of the pyramidal tract may be present. In the majority of cases there was a tendency toward queer postures, athetoid movements, and even jerky movements. Pseudopellagrous changes in the skin were present in three cases. Clouding of consciousness, when present, was usually of minor degree, but all variations to a typical Korsakoff picture may be observed. One case showed no psychic changes during most of the period of observation. Chronic progressive glial changes, with the same localization as in the other groups, were found in one case. Although none of the patients in the first three groups survived, two of those whose cases were reported in this group recovered. In these two cases the signs of disturbances in the central nervous system were not marked.

6. PROBLEM CASES

Three problem cases of changes in the central nervous system are discussed: (1) the case of a senile person with alcoholic neuritis associated with peculiar trophic changes in the hands and feet, (2) a picture resembling tabes dorsalis, and (3) a picture of unusual midbrain symptomatology. The variety of the neurologic symptomatology of chronic alcoholic intoxication has thus far been underrated.

Neuropathologic Problems. The lesions always occur in parts of the central nervous system adjacent to the spinal fluid and are most severe where the spinal fluid flows least freely, especially in the ventricular system. There is a tendency toward a specific electivity for gray masses and especially for vegetative gray masses along the ventricles. The data suggest that the spinal fluid carries the noxious agent. The different clinical groups described show a corresponding difference in the anatomic localization and the type of the lesion, so that we are inclined to recognize at least four different groups: (1) cases with a prevalence of changing rigidities, (2) cases with cerebellar features, (3) cases resembling acute catatonia, and (4) cases associated with polyneuritis. Because the lesion is not inflammatory or primarily hemorrhagic but is characterized by a marginal and ependymal invasive and productive gliosis with an underlying proliferative vascular lesion, we suggest the name alcoholic encephalopathy instead of the classic name polioencephalitis haemorrhagica superior of Wernicke.

CHAPTER FIFTEEN

Paralysis Agitans Pictures
in Alcoholics

There is little question but that the coarse tremor of the alcoholic
may be regarded as a midbrain phenomenon. We do not yet know
the final localization of this tremor. Even the symptomatology of
this tremor is not sufficiently described. One sees types in which
the tremor is coarse and irregular. In some cases it is of the
swinging and regular type of paralysis agitans. But it usually does
not have the typical localization. In the cases I have seen, it was
mostly a tremor in the hands.

One type of alcoholic tremor is especially interesting. It is
found in chronic alcoholics who are under an acute intoxication.
They have violent jerks and shakiness all over the body. It is an
irregular coarse tremor, especially in the big joints and in the head.
This tremor is so violent that the patient cannot lie in bed. Patients
of this kind usually suffer very much. They are very restless. They
beg for something to relieve their shakiness and restlessness. The

---

Appeared originally in the *Journal of Nervous and Mental Disease*, 76:586-588,
1932.

amount of tremor is dependent upon psychic factors. We do not
know yet what these differences in tremor mean. At any rate, the
tremor points to a midbrain or striopallidal lesion.

Schilder has pointed out another midbrain phenomenon—a
marked tendency to convergence of the outstretched arms [see
Chapter 17]. This tendency to converge is based on a flexor
contracture in the elbows. It is often combined with the tremor but
is independent of it. One sees it in acute as well as chronic alcoholics,
and also in alcoholic delirium. In alcoholic hallucinosis it is comparatively rare. One sees that the phenomenon often passes with the
acute intoxication. I have considered this phenomenon a midbrain
or striopallidal phenomenon.

I may add that Hoff and I (1925b) have already recorded that
postural reflexes are very often diminished when a delirium tremens has passed. One deals again with a similarity to paralysis
agitans pictures.

When one sees a great number of heavy alcoholics, one will
find a great number of cases with a rigid face. The characteristic
facial expression of the chronic alcoholic is due partly to the
rigidity of the face, partly to the vasomotor and trophic changes of
the skin. In a number of cases one finds that the persistence of tone
is diminished or absent. Hoff and I (1927) have shown that the
absence of persistence of tone is a very reliable sign of a midbrain-
striopallidal lesion.[1]

I may mention here the awkwardness one finds so often in the
motility of the chronic alcoholic. This awkwardness may be partly
due to the same mechanism, although there probably are other
mechanisms involved too. The difficulty in crossed movements
especially (left hand to right ear and vice versa) probably has to do
with the cortical centers for praxia.

In a limited number of cases, one sees pictures in which the

[1] When a subject brings his arms parallel forward (with closed eyes), and one
arm (M-arm) is raised 45 degrees above the horizontal line and stays there for 30
seconds and the subject is ordered to bring the M-arm down to the level of the arm
which has remained quiet (R-arm) the M-arm is not brought down to the level of the
R-arm, but stops several centimeters above. This phenomenon is present in every
normal. We have called it persistence of tone.

resemblance with paralysis agitans is striking. I report short abstracts of the histories of two such cases.

James B., 45 years old, was transferred to Bellevue Hospital on January 27, 1931, with a diagnosis of acute alcoholism. Speech was slurred. He said that he drank a lot of whiskey. He was drowsy. His face was very rigid and unmoved. He blinked rarely. His arms showed a marked rigidity and were a little cataleptic. He had difficulties in sitting up. Pupillary reactions and reflexes were normal. His movements were very slow. His face was seborrheic. He breathed deeply and slowly. The next day his drowsiness was diminished, he was depressed, cried in a childish manner, said that nobody cared for him, expressed fear that he would die, made slight mistakes in imitation, complained that his wife always accused him of going with other women. Neurological signs had not changed. When he was out of bed he stooped in a typical paralysis agitans posture. In the next two days the rigidity diminished, but he was still awkward and had slight cataleptic tendencies. Whereas previously there had been a convergency of the arms, there was now a marked divergency. He was still awkward and had difficulties in crossed movements. Persistence of tone was practically absent. On the third of February he was talkative, genial. The blinking was still rare. The left pupil did not react for a short while. Wassermann of blood and spinal fluid was negative. Patient was discharged on February 6 without neurological signs.

Edward L., 40 years old, was admitted on February 21 with anamnesis of heavy chronic alcoholism. His memory had not been good lately. Patient was tremulous, answered in a slow way, was restless and irritable. In the following two days he was delirious, restless, noisy. On February 25 he showed a coarse tremor of both extremities; sometimes of head and body. The outstretched hands showed a definite convergency, especially the right one. There was a hypertonia in the arms. The left hand dropped a little. He bent his head forward slowly. His body was rigid when he tried to walk. His feet were in extension. There was a rigidity in both legs.

He had a tendency to retropulsion. His face was rigid. His calves were sore. The pupils reacted very poorly and were more than mid-wide. Both feet showed a tendency to paradoxical contracture. All muscles had a tendency to rigidity when passive movements were made. At the time of dismissal on March 1 the neurological signs were present in a diminished way. The patient had cleared up considerably psychically.

Both cases show marked signs suggestive of paralysis agitans, one case especially in the upper extremities. This type is the more common one. Seemingly, chronic alcoholism affects the midbrain and the striopallidal system.

Gatzuk and Hoff (1930) have made interesting experiments which confirm this point of view. They found that chronic alcoholics often react to an acute experimental intoxication with alcohol (26 grams) with a diminution or disappearance of the persistence of tone. The same effect cannot be obtained in normal persons, and they draw the conclusion that chronic alcoholism sensitizes the midbrain-diencephalic centers. I may point out that, in our material of heavy chronic alcoholics and also in one of the cases reported, the persistence of tone was absent too.

CHAPTER SIXTEEN

A Specific Motility Psychosis in Negro Alcoholics

Statistical studies (Haven, 1932) show that the rate of alcoholic mental diseases among Negroes in New York State in 1922 was higher than among native whites but lower than foreign-born whites; but in 1929 to 1931, the rate among Negroes was twice as high as that among native whites. Despite this, to our knowledge, no attempt has been made to differentiate the clinical picture as it appears in Negroes from that commonly observed in whites. Our clinical experience at Bellevue Hospital leads us to believe that the commoner alcoholic psychoses, viz., delirium tremens, Korsakoff's psychosis, alcoholic hallucinosis, and encephalopathy, show no difference in Negroes as compared with white people. We have, however, observed one interesting group of cases in Negroes that show distinctive psychological and motility disturbances.

These cases are not particularly common, for we have observed only seven such cases in Negroes at Bellevue Hospital. We have also

Appeared originally in the *Journal of Nervous and Mental Disease*, 90:1-17, 1939, Sam Parker and Herman Wortis, co-authors.

seen one case in a white individual which could be likened to this group. Our report contains in addition one case of schizophrenia complicated by alcoholism with the motility disturbance very much akin to that we shall describe below.

Case 1. A 49-year-old American Negro was admitted to Bellevue Psychiatric Hospital on July 28, 1936. He was brought to the hospital by a patrolman who had rescued him from the lake in Central Park. The patient stated that he had attempted to drown himself because he had committed so many sins that he wished "to meet the Lord and get absolution." His past history was entirely normal except for a fractured skull two years before. The patient's wife revealed that he had been drinking very heavily for the past five years, but that his behavior had been quite normal until one month before admission, when he began speaking about people trying to hurt him, and saw imaginary objects—usually animals.

Physical examination on admission revealed a well-developed, well-nourished adult male Negro who was toxic, dehydrated, and tremulous. He was fearful, apprehensive, and reacting vividly to visual and auditory hallucinations. His physical examination was otherwise normal except for jerky nystagmus on lateral gaze.

Throughout his hospital stay his behavior was peculiar. He would throw himself on the floor, crawl about on his hands and knees, rock back and forth in his chair, and at times would bang his head forcefully against the wall. There was a constant tendency toward retropulsion, the patient falling backward across the beds and against the wall, but rarely hurting himself. He manifested peculiar counterclockwise, circular movements. He would walk up and down the ward constantly, never in a straight line, but would move forward by turning completely around his longitudinal axis. He was overactive, overtalkative and, despite the frightening content of his delusions and hallucinations, he maintained a cheerful, almost playful attitude toward the other patients and his examiners.

His postural reflexes were of a very primitive type. There was a marked tendency to divergence of the outstretched arms. When the head was turned to one side, the chin arm raised considerably, and usually the patient would continue to whirl about his longitudinal axis. When the head was pulled backward, the whole body turned to follow it.

Blood and spinal Wassermanns were negative, the colloidal gold curve was flat, X rays of skull were normal. Bromides were absent in the blood and there were 20 mgms. of luminal in 1000 c.c. of urine.

A sample of his productions follows:

(How do you feel?) "I feel pretty miserable, doctor, they go kill me. (Who is going to kill you?) They go kill poor me. (What did you do?) I guess I done the whole world wrong. (Want to have your picture taken?) I got no need for pictures now myself, but it might be all right for the world, but it is too late for me.

(Who makes you bang yourself like that?) "I see that gentleman in there (another patient). He makes motions and I have to do them. They go kill me ... people go beat me up. (Who is he?) According to the papers, they go kill me ... they go have me killed, that's all. (Why?) I don't know, I guess I possibly may not be the man like I should be and I have to give up. I haven't lived as a man should live. I been slack in several things. I was a slacker in the army. I was naturally scared. (What else?) I don't know nothing else that I done so much wrong. They put me to work on a project and I got sick and laid off and they can have some of that against me, that I didn't stand up and come. (Date?) The 12th. (Of what?) I don't know, sir, I tell you the truth. (Month?) July. (Year?) 1936. (Know what hospital this is?) Bellevue. (How many times here?) Seems like this is about the third time I was here. (How many days now?) About ten (sixteen days), and I don't think I have sleep five hours since I been here.

(Whale story) "I don't believe I could do it ... John Smith was on a boat sailing from Los Angeles, California and ... (What was on the boat?) I can't remember ... that I can't tell you ... Anyway, he fell off the boat and a whale swallowed him leaving a trail of blood.

(9 x 12?) "I don't know. (9 x 5?) I could tell you ... 50. (Spell

horse) H-o-r-s-e. (Maybe) M-a-d-e-y. (Hear voices?) I hear voices of people now, talk about go kill me and go slay me and burn me. (Take off your sex parts?) Yes, sir, and cut my ears off and skin off my head and fingers and legs and I don't know sir what all. I don't think they will leave nothing but I hope my soul will be saved in heaven.

(Why do you bang your head against the wall?) "I really don't know what that come from . . . super power or what causes me to do that. (Is it natural man's or God's power?) I don't know sir. (Why don't you do it now when you talk to me?) Same control that makes me stop and talk to you is same control that makes me do that.

(See visions?) "I see something you might call the visions, I see different mens and animals and then animals and I don't know what else. (What kind of animals?) Just kind or manner of thing.

(What shall we do with you?) "You got me as I am, you have to take me. The life I have lived. I hope and trust in God; and hope any sins will be forgiven. Other people will bang my head against the wall. If ever I become a sensible man, it will be in another world.

(Can night watchmen fly?) "I don't know whether I can fly. I couldn't say. (You were on the floor yesterday barking like a dog, do that again.) If I get the feeling, I can do it."

All during the above interview the patient was pleasant, amiable, and smiling.

His gestalt studies showed evidence of disorientation and confusion, and were typical of the organic group. There was a reversion to primitive loop formations.

On August 26, 1936, he was discharged to a state hospital, although still toxic and tremulous and still lacking complete insight into his hallucinations. A follow-up letter to this hospital resulted in the following reply received on January 11, 1937:

"We wish to inform you that the diagnosis made in this case is Korsakoff psychosis. He is resistive, destructive and self-condemnatory. He becomes easily upset in reaction to hallucinations, misidentifies physician and people around him, is unaware of current events, historical happenings, and shows marked memory defects."

We deal here with an alcoholic psychosis with clear-cut and definite motility disturbances which in many respects reminds one of the manneristic "faxen-syndrome" of the schizophrenic. Throughout, there appear to be elements in the picture which remind one of the practical joker. It should, however, be noted that this picture of playfulness and mannerisms is painted on a serious organic background. The motility disturbances included propulsion and retropulsion, spontaneous turning around his longitudinal axis, and primitive postural reflexes. The picture is similar to that occasionally seen in catatonic schizophrenia.

Case 2. A 40-year-old American Negro was admitted to Bellevue Psychiatric Hospital January 11, 1931. He was transferred from a general hospital where he had been taken by a friend, who said that the patient had attracted a crowd on the street by loud talking and peculiar conduct. His behavior continued "peculiar" on the wards of the hospital, and he was transferred to our service. On admission, the patient was oriented as to time and approximately oriented for place. He gave a history of alcoholism and expressed ideas of reference as well as auditory hallucinations. He said, "Yes, I hear them saying lots of different things. It has been going on for about two weeks. They all treat me with the cold shoulder. They were cracking jokes about me, and it got me worried."

Physical examination revealed a well-developed and fairly well-nourished adult male Negro who was toxic, tremulous, dehydrated, and appeared to have lost much weight. The heart was moderately enlarged to the left and there was a blowing systolic murmur at the apex which was not transmitted. Signs in the right chest were suggestive of pulmonary abscess. Pupils were equal, somewhat irregular, and reacted only moderately well to light. Extraocular movements were normal, there was no nystagmus, and the fundi were normal.

Physical examination was otherwise entirely normal. Blood and spinal fluid serology were completely negative.

On the sixth day in the hospital, patient's temperature rose to 101 and remained irregularly above normal, but below 101, until February 5, when it again returned to normal and remained until February 17, when he was transferred to a state hospital. On January 14 (patient's third day) he appeared duller, confused, and unable to concentrate. On the 15th, he was not accessible, but sat up in bed staring straight ahead and humming to himself in a singsong fashion. He resisted physical examination. On January 17 the patient was again accessible; he spoke coherently, told of his drinking escapades, admitted that he was seeing angels and devils, and acted very frightened. On the 21st the patient said, "I am the guy what swum across from Norfolk. I got my head ... my hair cut. (Where were you yesterday?) Didn't I get operated on yesterday?" He was very unsteady on his feet at this time and showed marked tendency toward playfulness, smiling and grinning almost continuously despite his fearful delusions. Occasionally, however, he would become apprehensive for several minutes at a time, and during these periods he would become resistive and his whole body would become rigid. He was dull, wandered around the ward in a confused manner, and occasionally verbigerated in a playful manner, saying "Wuff-wuff-wuff." At other times he would gaze straight ahead while standing rigid. Immediately following this he would lapse into a playful mood, go through shadow-boxing motions, rock back and forth, and tend to turn about his longitudinal axis in a counterclockwise fashion. His pupils on this occasion were small and fixed to light. On the following day, he suddenly said, speaking of himself in the third person, "Some man got him, got Coleman." On January 24, while being demonstrated at staff conference, he kept himself rigidly extended throughout and had to be supported lest he fall. He began to wave his right arm rhythmically and flexed his left leg. At the same time, fishlike movements with his mouth were noted. Throughout the whole procedure he remained mute. If unsupported, he tended to fall back across the bed in a rigid position. He was not resistive, and his facial expression was flat throughout this experience. The following morning he became excited and disturbed and, when restrained in bed, tended to bounce up and down in rhythmic fashion. He still remained mute. On January 26 he was still in constant movement when not under the influence of sedatives. He tended to move his head in a circular fashion and again waved his arms about his head, but was not resistive. While his motility disturbances were growing more and more marked, he himself was becoming more and more accessible. On January 29 he was still catatonic and rigid, but he had become much more resistive and was obviously reacting to hallucinations. He brushed off the bed and said, "Get those fellows away from here. Take that away." On February 3 he said he had been in the hospital for about four months, but in general he was clearer and much more accessible. He still exhibited a tendency toward catalepsy, the right pupil was fixed to light on this occasion, and the left reacted only slightly. When allowed to stand up, the tendency toward retropulsion and turning on longitudinal axis was more marked than ever. On the 10th of February he said, "They placed charges against me, one for being crazy and the other for being half man and half woman." He was still confused and disoriented for time and place. On this occasion his pupils reacted to light and accommodation. On the following day, however, they were again practically fixed to light, but later in the day began to show change of reaction, reacting better when patient's mental condition was clearer and showing a tendency to become sluggish or fixed when he became more resistive or catatonic.

A follow-up letter from the state hospital, to which this patient was sent, states:

"He was admitted to this hospital on February 17, 1931. At that time he was unable to give a clear account of the onset of his illness. He was disoriented for time, place and person, but remembered going to Bellevue because of chronic alcoholism.

"Physical examination: Pupils reacted sluggishly to light and accommodation. Knee jerks were increased. Blood pressure was 120/72. His urinalysis was negative. Complete serology for spinal fluid was negative; blood Wassermann was plus minus with alcoholic antigen and two plus with cholesternized antigen; Kahn was three plus; and two sputum examinations were negative for T.B. X ray showed findings suggestive of lung abscess at the right base. Internist examination was also suggestive of lung abscess of right lower lobe, right chronic otitis media, and chronic gingivitis and pyorrhea.

"On March 16, 1931, the patient was noted as being bed-ridden and poorly nourished. He had to be fed and cared for in every way. He answered questions by saying, "I don't know." He was disoriented in all spheres; remote and recent memory were poor; retention and immediate recall were poor.

"On May 15, 1931 the patient's physical condition was noted as being critical. He was running a temperature and showed extensive involvement of the base of the right lung; over this area breath sounds and moist rales were heard. There was much purulent expectoration. Mentally he was still confused and disoriented. His condition became progressively worse and he died on May 16, 1931.

"The cause of the death was lung abscess. The mental diagnosis: Psychosis with other somatic disease."

Compared with case 1, the confusion in this case was much deeper, but it may be that the severe organic illness (lung abscess) to which this patient eventually succumbed was a contributing factor. In the motor picture, his catatonia and rigid postures were again more outspoken than in the previous case, although he was not nearly as playful, nor was the tendency toward spontaneous movements around the longitudinal axis as continuous as in the previous case.

Case 3. A 44-year-old American Negro was admitted to Bellevue Psychiatric Hospital June 28, 1931 after an alcohol bout of several days' duration. On admission the patient was confused, practically comatose, and unable to cooperate for physical examination. A short while after admission he cleared somewhat, rambled in his speech, and spontaneously expressed delusions of persecution. He said, "They were trying to kill me in the case. The fellows that sell it to me. It is all scratched." On June 20, he was still confused and somewhat paraphasic in his speech: (What town is this?) "This is Savannah....Oh, it's New York. It's 1899. (What building is this?) 242. (How long have you been here?) 1899. (What do you do?) Peddle crabs . . . I sell water . . . milk . . .this thing like Aprils. . .you know Aprils. (Shown a fountain pen and asked what it was.) That is April. (A pencil) Aprils. (Erasers) That is rubber. (Asked the time: seventeen minutes to eleven.) Twenty-two to nine." (Put your left hand to your right ear.) Patient puts left hand to left ear. (Cross your fingers.) Patient puts his hands over his ears. (Cross your fingers.) Patient continues holding his hands over his ears, then puts them on the side of his face and begins to hit his head. (Show me your hands.) Patient puts out both hands. (Cross your fingers.) Patient turns his hands over, showing the back, and continues to do this in a rhythmic sort of fashion which gradually merges into athetoid movements.

When his hands were lifted to test for catalepsy, the patient stood up. He did not react to painful stimuli anywhere on the body, and spontaneous movements were all rhythmic and of a stereotyped character.

Physical examination revealed a well-developed and fairly well-nourished adult male Negro who was toxic, tremulous, and mildly dehydrated. Pupils were large, round, equal, and reacted well to light and accommodation. Extraocular movements were normal, there was no nystagmus, and the fundi were normal. The outstretched tongue showed evidence of recent bruises and cuts, and was tremulous. The heart was enlarged to the left, and there was a blowing systolic murmur over the apex, and a ringing second aortic sound. Blood pressure was 160/100. The liver was somewhat enlarged and percussed two fingers below the costal margin. There was pretibial edema bilaterally. Neurological examination was entirely normal except for a right Babinski sign. Lumbar puncture performed on July 8 revealed clear fluid under normal pressure with no increase in cells, negative globulin reaction, and completely normal serology. On the 2nd of July he showed an elevation of temperature to 101, but this returned to normal three days later. On July 3, he showed marked difficulty in articulation, and at times speech was definitely paraphasic. He showed a tendency to transpose, repeat letters, and change syllables—e.g., instead of repeating "particular" he said "paracookoo." When asked to write "electricity," he made unintelligible spiral scratches and showed some tendency to primitive reversion to loops. On July 7 he was still dysarthric and answered questions in an irrelevant fashion. When shown bread, he said, "It is dessert." When asked to repeat the word "wife," he said "hife." His general reactions continued dull and apathetic, but at about this time, he began to show a tendency toward sudden changes in posture. He would make himself stiff and catatonic and show a tendency to fall backward, manifesting muscular tenseness and stiffness in his entire body that were not quite extrapyramidal nor yet of the voluntary resistance type. His face maintained a stiff blank expression, and he tended to remain mute. On July 13, 1931 he was transferred to a state hospital where he died nine days later.

This picture resembles the catatonic cases of alcoholic encephalopathy described by Bender and Schilder [see Chapter 14], although the willful and playful component in this case is much stronger than in the cases we described there.

Case 4. A 34-year-old American Negro was admitted to Bellevue Psychiatric Hospital April 18, 1931 from a general hospital. He had been transferred to Bellevue because of his "refusal to eat, mental and emotional dullness, and tendency to sit stupidly in his bed and stare straight ahead." On admission, he complained of headache, pain in back, weakness, and loss of weight of two months' duration. In addition, his spells of vomiting had forced him to discontinue working several times, and he had begun to talk and think with great difficulty for some time prior to admission. Physical examination was entirely normal, as were also his laboratory examinations. He was clear and coherent, but appeared depressed and somewhat retarded. His mother gave a history of chronic alcoholism. He also gave a history of previous hallucinatory experiences of a persecutory type. His general appearance revealed that he had lost much weight recently, and he appeared somewhat drawn.

On April 22 the patient appeared bewildered, apprehensive, and was obviously hallucinating again. When told by the examiner that he could not go home, he said, "Well then, please don't let them kill my mother while I am here." On this occasion it was noticed for the first time that while sitting up in bed, the patient showed a tendency to fall backward suddenly, or to sway from side to side, as if in a sudden hypnotic trance. Throughout, his face remained blank and unmoved. When taken out of bed, he showed some tendency toward propulsion and retropulsion. On April 24 the patient developed a paranoid-hallucinatory state. He continued depressed and appeared even more toxic than previously. April 25 he began to experience somatic ideas of a hypochondriacal nature—e.g., he said, "I have got a grasshopper in my throat. I know it because I feel it." On the 29th he appeared somewhat clearer, but began to express ideas of a religious nature. He said, "I want to go home. I feel all my sins are gone. I have been saved. I was saved this morning by Jesus Christ through the Holy Ghost. I can feel it all through my body." Immediately after the interview, the patient fell backward to the floor as if in a hypnotic trance. When asked what happened, he said without any change of facial expression, "When I gets tired, I just got to lay down." On May 8th patient was still hallucinating, depressed, retarded, and physical and neurological signs were unchanged. He said, "I get tired and my head doesn't seem to be able to govern my body and then I just falls right over." His facial expression continued dull and fixed. He continued in status quo until May 13, when he was transferred to a state hospital. The following is quoted from a letter received from this hospital December 28, 1931:

"He was admitted to this hospital May 13, 1931. He reacted to auditory hallucinations and admitted having had delusions of poisoning directed against his wife. He was approximately oriented and gave a history of excessive drinking. His physical examination showed: The pupils were equal and regular and reacted fairly promptly to light and accommodation. His blood pressure was 146/82. His reflexes were hyperactive. His speech was slurring. Eyeground examination was negative. The serology was negative. Neurological examination was entirely normal except for a slight speech defect. X rays showed an old depressed fracture in the left frontal region.

"On May 16, 1931, the patient was noted as answering questions rather slowly but in a fairly coherent and relevant manner. Emotionally, he was rather dull and apathetic; he admitted paranoid ideas against his wife, and stated that he struck her. He admitted drinking but denied visual and auditory hallucinations. At this time he was fairly well oriented; his remote memory was poor; his recent memory was good. Retention and immediate recall were poor, as was his general knowledge. Subsequently, he showed no tendency to be resistive or assaultive. He frequently complained of pains in his stomach.

"On August 13, 1931, the patient was noted as being cooperative. He showed no disorder of stream of thought. Emotionally, he was superficial. At this time he denied trends but admitted experiencing hallucinations about a month previously. He was well oriented and showed no memory impairment. His physical condition was good.

"On September 9, 1931, the patient was discharged to the care of the Medical Examiner's office to be returned to South Carolina. The diagnosis was Alcoholic Hallucinosis, condition improved."

The psychiatric picture in this case resembles very closely the one noted in case 3; in the motility sphere, the tendency of this patient to let himself drop is the outstanding point. He showed no tendency toward rigidities and there was no spontaneous turning around the longitudinal axis. He improved after a short stay in a state hospital. His present whereabouts are unknown.

Case 5. A 49-year-old American Negro was admitted to Bellevue Psychiatric Hospital July 9, 1931. On admission he was confused, disoriented for time and place, and manifested an organic type of deterioration with practically no comprehension and insight. Throughout the examination he smiled continuously in a silly fashion and without apparent reason. He talked in a rambling and at times disconnected fashion. On July 10 he said, "I didn't do it on the floor . . . give other bishop this morning . . . I must have been it . . . drunk instead of being . . . twelve . . . or was it after twelve . . . (What is the color of my hair?) I live at 85 North Pearl . . . up town . . . Pearl Street, Albany . . . this is Albany now . . . (What place is this?) This is the place . . . or temple . . . I ask you if it is a house or a temple? (What temple?) Jesus' temple. (When is the 4th of July?) . . . I will have to find out. (How old are you?) I am going to travel to the 4th of July. (What part of the country were you born in?) North side."

Physical examination on July 10 revealed a well-developed, fairly well-nourished adult male Negro who was toxic, tremulous, and moderately dehydrated. Physical and neurological examination were entirely normal except for the following positive findings: There were bilateral Babinski, Oppenheim, and Rossolimo, with bilateral ankle clonus. In both sitting and standing position the trunk and head definitely leaned to the right with the chin turned somewhat to the left. There was a tendency to fall to the right and backward in either sitting or standing position. When left to himself in the middle of the room, the patient showed definite retropulsion with a tendency to circle counterclockwise. The retropulsion was in very short steps. Also noted was spontaneous, coarse tremor of the right side which most resembled a Parkinsonian tremor. The bladder was distended and overflowed. There was no elevation of temperature at any time. Complete examination of the blood and spinal fluid was entirely normal, as was the serology. The history given by a long-standing friend, as well as by the patient's wife, was that of chronic alcoholism. There was no history of convulsions, trauma, or infectious disease. July 14 the patient was still confused and disoriented, and continued to smile in a senseless fashion. There was a tendency to walk on his heels, and his gait was definitely spastic. The pyramidal tract signs persisted. July 18 the patient was somewhat clearer mentally, but still continued to smile in a silly fashion. His gait was much better;

of the pyramidal tract signs, only the Oppenheim and ankle clonus were still definite, but the tendency toward retropulsion was still present. July 23 he was still disoriented and the mental picture was essentially unchanged, but he appeared brighter. He still showed tendency to lean toward the right when the arms were outstretched, and the pyramidal tract signs were again obtained. July 29, 1931 he was transferred to a state hospital. A follow-up letter December 28 gave the following information:

"On admission he was well oriented and talked in a polite manner. It seemed to him that recently people were against him. Physical examination revealed: Blood pressure 104/58. His blood and spinal fluid Wassermanns were negative. Neurological examination showed that the abdominal reflexes were rather weak but present; the knee jerks and ankle jerks were considerably exaggerated, and there was ankle clonus on both sides. It appeared that the previously marked pyramidal tract signs were clearing up.

"On August 1, the patient was agreeable, cooperative, and answered questions relevantly, but was often contradictory. He showed no sensorial or intellectual defects, denied auditory and visual hallucinations, and expressed no paranoid trends. He improved rapidly and, on November 5, 1931 was paroled. Diagnosis: Alcoholic Psychosis, Confusion. Condition: Recovered."

In the motility field this case displayed characteristics of the group; namely, retropulsion, awkwardness, motor playfulness, and the tendency to turn spontaneously around the longitudinal axis. This case was not very severe and apparently ended in complete recovery.

Case 6. A 31-year-old American Negro was admitted to Bellevue Psychiatric Hospital July 6, 1931 after having attacked a police officer on the street. When questioned about this, he said, "The officer didn't beat me up so I had to beat him up." During the ambulance ride to the hospital, he gazed fixedly at the officer he had beaten up, smiled fixedly, and said "I will do everything you tell me, Mr. Law." He admitted chronic alcoholism.

Examination at this time revealed a well-developed, well-nourished adult male Negro who was toxic, tremulous, and moderately dehydrated. He was disoriented for time and place, and expressed delusions of persecution with religious coloring, as well as auditory hallucinations. His general physical condition was good. The blood Wassermann was plus minus on two separate occasions. His mental status throughout his hospital stay was unchanged, except that on occasion his pupils were practically fixed to light, and it was noticed that on these occasions patient would become stiff, rigid, and out of contact with his environment. At such times he was inaccessible to questioning or prodding, and would perspire profusely. He was discharged to a state hospital July 15, 1931; a follow-up letter on December 28 gave the following information:

"On admission he was mildly excited and somewhat confused regarding the cause of his hospitalization. He admitted drinking. Physical examination showed knee jerks and ankle jerks to be absent. The urine showed albumin. His blood pressure was 138/96.

"July 21, 1931, the patient was noted as being neat and tidy and caring for his personal needs. He answered questions in a fairly relevant and coherent manner. He stated that he was happy and satisfied, but he reacted to auditory hallucinations. His orientation was good and he showed no memory defects. His retention and immediate recall were good, and his attention and mental tension were fairly adequate.

"August 4, he was noted as denying auditory hallucinations. He showed rapid improvement, and on August 31st there was no disorder of stream, his emotional reaction was adequate, he denied hallucinations, and admitted excessive alcoholism. On September 20, 1931 he was paroled for a period of one year. Diagnosis: Alcoholic Psychosis, Parnoid-Hallucinatory Episode of Confusion. Condition: Recovered."

This case had fewer motor symptoms than did the other patients, but there were still mannerisms, facetiousness, and attacks of sudden stiffness. He also showed catatonic pupillary reflexes. The case ended in complete recovery.

Case 7. A 33-year-old Irish-American was admitted to Bellevue Psychiatric Hospital April 15, 1930. He was a heavy drinker and there was a marked incidence of alcoholism in the family. About two weeks prior to admission, he was said to have begun to act queerly, brushing imaginary things away from before him, and talking irrationally.

Physical examination revealed a well-developed, fairly well-nourished adult white male who was toxic, tremulous, and moderately dehydrated. He was reacting vividly to auditory and visual hallucinations. April 25, the patient developed diarrhea, became very toxic and dehydrated and, despite all efforts to combat his illness, it progressed. He was very awkward and jerky in all his movements. He spontaneously executed rhythmic scratching and rubbing movements, and when pinched or pricked with a pin, he reacted to pain in a very exaggerated manner. When tickling gestures were made before him, he became wildly excited. Ticlike movements frequently appeared in his shoulders, and he had periodic attacks during which he became red in the face, assumed a terrified expression, and became cataleptic all over. During these attacks he would shout and scream. He rolled his head from side to side continually. His talk became very facetious, although appropriate emotional facial expression was lacking. He continued alternately playful, facetious, restless, and confabulatory, and when excited by tickling gestures, he became ataxic. When the neck and arm postural reflexes were tested, he continued to turn spontaneously around his longitudinal axis.

We were unable to control his diarrhea despite appropriate medication. By the middle of June he was noisy, screaming, shouting incoherently, and there were choreiform movements of the entire body. Gradually he became more and more jerky, his temperature continued to rise, and his general condition became worse. He became delirious and responded to auditory and visual hallucinations. He died July 11, 1931. No autopsy was obtained.

This 33-year-old white Irish-American chronic alcoholic presented a picture in which confusion and persecutory delusions were in the foreground. In the motor sphere the picture was somewhat similar to, although not identical with, that described in our Negro cases. The mannerisms and facetiousness were much less outspoken, and the rhythmic scratching movements and exaggerated reaction to pain and tickling were very much more marked. The diarrhea complicated the picture and undoubtedly contributed to the unfortunate outcome.

Case 8. A 34-year-old American Negro was admitted to Bellevue Psychiatric Hospital August 23, 1935, reacting violently to both auditory and visual hallucinations. He was also confused and disoriented as to time and place. Physical examination revealed a well-developed and fairly well-nourished adult Negro male who was toxic, tremulous, and somewhat dehydrated. Examination otherwise was entirely normal. August 25, the patient was seen for the first time by one of us. He was smiling continually and had a happy, contented expression on his face, but was mute. He was able to stand upright, but after a short while he tended to fall backward against the wall, never hurting himself. Despite his difficulty in standing, if he were ordered to get up and walk, he was able to do so without trouble. There was no spontaneous rigidity and no tendency to turn around the longitudinal axis. There was slight divergence of the outstretched arms, and in turning the head to the side, the chin arm rose. Laboratory examination was entirely normal.

The patient improved steadily, and September 5 he was discharged on contract to his wife. There were no further evidences of hallucinations at this time, and the patient had insight into his previous hallucinations. The motility disturbances had disappeared entirely.

Disturbances in the motor sphere were essentially those of retropulsion; there was no catalepsy and no turning around the longitudinal axis. The postural reflexes were moderately catatonic in type. This case was of a milder variety and resulted in complete recovery.

Case 9. A 22-year-old American Negro was admitted to Bellevue Psychiatric Hospital November 7, 1934. He had been discharged from the same hospital four days previously with a diagnosis of alcoholic hallucinosis with catatonic features. On that occasion the patient had entered the hospital toxic, confused, disoriented, but not hallucinating. There was a heavy odor of alcohol on his breath. His picture was complicated by waxy flexibility and a tendency suddenly to assume awkward postures. On November 3, 1934, he was no longer confused, and was oriented for time, place, and person. The catatonic features had disappeared. He was discharged to his mother's custody.

At the time of his second admission it was stated by the patient's family that he had again begun to act peculiarly, although he had not been drinking at all since his discharge. He wandered about the street gesticulating with his hands and feet and making funny faces at other people. This time he was clear and oriented, but he showed a peculiar quiet elation; he grinned, smiled, and paid little attention to the examiner, although it cannot be stated that he was negativistic, nor was he irritable. He showed a tendency to maintain awkward postures, suddenly became cataleptic, and then tended to turn spontaneously around his longitudinal axis. He showed no reaction to painful stimuli. His pupillary reactions were changeable, and, at the time of patient's most marked rigidity, his pupils tended to be fixed. There was a marked divergence of the outstretched hands, and when the patient's head was turned to one side, the chin arm rose, and on occasions the patient continued to whirl about his longitudinal axis.

Gestalt test showed schizoid features in that his figures showed a combination of high maturation levels and primitive tendencies. Figures 3 and 4 also showed a splitting of the parts; otherwise his figures were rather stiff.

The laboratory examination was entirely normal except that the patient had a four-plus blood Wassermann.

He was discharged to a state hospital December 1, 1934, with a diagnosis of dementia praecox, catatonic type. A follow-up letter from the state hospital yielded the following information:

"During the initial interview at this hospital, he would laugh in a silly manner, repeat every question before answering, and was evasive, retarded, and circumstantial at all times. He made many facial grimaces and jumped out of his chair and walked around the room for no apparent reason. He tended to minimize his alcoholic history, denied auditory hallucinations, and his productions were irrelevant and incoherent. He was disoriented for time, place, and person, but his recent and remote memory were good. He had no insight into his condition and his judgment was impaired. A spinal fluid Wassermann was negative in reaction while the blood Wassermann was four plus.

"To date, the patient is disoriented for time, place, and person. He is argumentative, intensely antagonistic, sarcastic, unfriendly, seclusive, and indolent. His productions are rambling and disconnected. He is quiet and well behaved for a few days and then becomes loud, boisterous, disturbed, and profane. His insight and judgment are still defective."

There was a history of alcoholism here, but the final analysis, including a follow-up letter from the state hospital, concurred in the opinion that alcoholism was merely incidental to his personality disintegration and not the causative factor. The rigidities, playfulness, catalepsy, and turning around the longitudinal axis remind us very much of the pictures described above in alcoholics. The primitive postural reflexes and also the pupillary changes have been described in Negro schizophrenics. In this case one also has a feeling that organic factors play a large role in the motility disturbances, but the outspoken signs are much less evident.

The similarity between catatonic schizophrenia and the alcoholic Negro of the specific group which we are describing is rather marked.

DISCUSSION

We feel it proper to consider the seven cases we have observed of alcoholic psychoses in Negroes with characteristic features in motility a specific group. In all the cases, there is a history of severe and long-standing alcoholism. The age of the cases averages about 40. The clinical picture is characterized by severe hallucinations of a persecutory character. There is very often an element of dissociation. In the majority of cases the sensorium is somewhat clouded, and in the more severe cases clouding is even deeper. Memory discrepancies are also present in most of the cases, but in the acute stages of the illness they are obscured by the mental confusion. The hallucinatory content corresponds to the customary alcoholic hallucination, although the sexual content is less marked. In the presence of more or less severe clouding of consciousness, the cases cannot clearly be classified as alcoholic hallucinoses, but remind one rather of the pictures Bender and Schilder (1933) have observed in hallucinatory and catatonic alcoholic encephalopathy [see Chapter 14].

The cases present obvious signs of a severe cerebral process. The transitory rigidities change to cataleptic postures and vice versa. Retropulsion and falling backward are present in one form or another. The backward falling is sometimes associated with rigidity and sometimes with a hypotonic flaccidity. There are rhythmical iterations in the movements of the extremities and the face, also obvious increase in the divergence of the outstretched arms, in the neck reflexes, as well as in other postural reflexes. In the majority of the cases, we have also observed a tendency to turning about the longitudinal axis, which increases to whirling activity (case 1). In two cases there were changeable pupillary reactions. In one, there were motor paraphasias, and an occasional mutism was observed in several of the patients. On the basis of these descriptions, one might feel one is dealing with a somewhat monotonous and severe organic picture. It should be emphasized, however, that all the symptoms described are quite changeable in character and often give the impression of voluntary exaggeration, mannerism, and playfulness. Case 1 whirls objects and bumps his head against the wall, while others let themselves flop in the manner of malingerers and hysterics. There is an atmosphere of silly playfulness that one might characterize succinctly as a sort of

Ganser syndrome. Ganser-like remarks may occur even in the patient's language. Notwithstanding, this playful picture is drawn upon a sinister organic background. Indeed, the prognosis of these cases is far from good, two of them having died, one persisting in a severe Korsakoff state, and in another a milder form of deterioration was present at discharge. In three cases, which were less severe clinically, recovery was complete. We are inclined to the impression that somatic complications in the two cases mentioned above were secondary to the organic brain disease.

We have mentioned the fact that in our extensive material we have seen but one similar picture in a white man. Moreover the playfulness was much less marked in his case than in the Negro patients. He had a special reaction to tickling. This patient died during a subsequent admission, but there was no autopsy.

Our findings make it clear that we deal in these cases with an organic brain process due to alcoholism. It is worthwhile mentioning that none of our cases showed pseudopellagra. Apparently these cases constitute a special type of alcoholic encephalopathy closely related to the hallucinatory and catatonic type in which the preliminary histopathological examination shows prevailing glia reactions and no changes in the vascular apparatus. We find it remarkable that in such a severe brain disease, the racial factor appears to be so significant. It should be emphasized that, in contradistinction to these cases, the classical pictures of encephalopathy have been observed in about the same proportion among Negroes and whites on our service at Bellevue Hospital. The picture we describe here is therefore not the typical picture of encephalopathy among Negroes, but is a specific type of encephalopathy among them. Since we have had no opportunity for histopathological studies, it is impossible at this time to speculate about histopathological processes and their localization in this group. We might assume a widespread process, especially involving the postural apparatus and affecting similar brain centers as are responsible for catatonic disturbances. It is of great interest in this regard to compare our cases with the picture of case 9, in which the catatonic phenomena were combined with alcoholism in a Negro. Besides the similarity in the motor sphere, this patient showed the changeable pupillary rigidities that, according to Schilder and Parker [see Chapter 22], are so characteristic of Negro catatonics and have also been observed in two of these cases.

We conclude, therefore, that there exists a specific type of alcoholic encephalopathy among Negroes, characterized by clouding of consciousness, hallucinations, mannerisms, and playfulness in the psychic sphere. In the motor sphere, the mannerisms are paramount and imitate the "faxen-syndrome" of schizophrenia. Rhythmic iteration, retropulsion, falling backward, rigidities, increased divergence of the arms, and turning about the longitudinal axis occur in colorful and varying combinations; although it appears as if the patients exploit the motility in the service of practical joking, they are obviously forced by an inexorable motility disturbance into their psychomotor attitude. It is probable that the racial factor is of importance in determining the final pattern.

Summary

1. Seven cases of a specific syndrome of alcoholic encephalopathy in Negroes have been observed.

2. The cases are characterized by: confusion and threatening auditory hallucinations in the psychic sphere. The motility imitates the "faxen-syndrome" of schizophrenia and appears in a playful and manneristic fashion. Nevertheless, the definite organic signs of iteration, retropulsion, falling backward, rigidity, and turning about the longitudinal axis are woven into the pattern.

3. The disease can lead to death or deterioration; milder cases may recover.

4. Only one similar case was observed in a white man.

5. We have observed a similar picture in a schizophrenic Negro who was also alcoholic. The organic features in this case were merely indicated.

CHAPTER SEVENTEEN

Convergence Reactions in Alcoholics

When the normally healthy person (eyes closed) stretches his arms parallel before him and tries to keep them quiet, the arms tend to diverge (divergence reaction of Hoff and Schilder, 1925a, 1926, 1927). The reaction mentioned is absolutely constant in healthy individuals. It is dependent upon the bilateral extension of the arms. Prior to our communication, Fischer and Wodak (1924) described as the "spontaneous deviation reaction" movements of the extended arms that occurred when the subjects examined were instructed to give free rein to whatever impulses for movement arose. With this method, they obtained varying results, i.e., both divergence and convergence. The instructions given by Fischer and Wodak introduce an uncontrollable element into the examination and thus make the reaction unsatisfactory.

Cerebellar lesion increases the outward tendency of the arms to such an extent that even when only one arm is extended, there is a lateral deviation of the limb (deviation reaction of Bárány). This

---

Appeared originally in the *Journal of Nervous and Mental Disease*, 71:1-3, 1930.

reaction is based primarily upon movement in the shoulder joint. Cases of cerebellar lesion in which, instead of the lateral deviation, there is also a convergence (in the shoulder joints) are rare. There can, nevertheless, be no doubt that they occur. Of the cases of this latter type recorded in the literature, I should like to mention only the cases of Gerstmann (1926). One could also speak about an "inward deviation."

This divergence of the outstretched arms with eyes closed can, however, be overcome by another phenomenon, which we have described as the convergence reaction. This reaction consists in a flexion of the outstretched arms at the elbow, and causes the hands to be approximated. This phenomenon is also, in its slighter manifestations, dependent upon the bilateral extension of the arms, and appears even in those forms of Parkinsonism that, with other methods of examination, have shown no flexion tendency of the elbows. As further experience has demonstrated to us, this reaction is a sensitive sign of early or residual Parkinson encephalitis. Whether it is due to a lesion of the midbrain in encephalitis, or whether damage to the striopallidar system is at fault, is a question that cannot be settled. That it is, however, not simply the opposite of the divergence reaction, but a true convergence at the elbow joints which may not always be grossly apparent is easily demonstrated when one fixates the elbow joints by the application of a splint. When this is done, the divergence reaction becomes apparent again, and we see that it has not been abolished by the encephalitis. Whether conditions leading to the abolition of the divergence reaction exist at all is not known. To date we are acquainted only with increases in the divergence tendency.

The convergence can also occur on one side only, but even then it is enhanced by the extension of both arms; indeed, the unilateral sign often becomes visible only upon bilateral extension of the arms. In a case of Stengel's (1927), in which there were midbrain hemorrhages due to pressure directed along a certain line (metastases in the brain), the reaction was present on one side only. In such a case, the reaction is an important midbrain symptom and serves, in cerebellar or angular tumors, as an indication that there is a proximally directed progress of the growth or at least as an indication of a proximally directed pressure. In two cases of angular tumor, the convergence reaction was present on the side of the more marked cerebellar signs. Both cases presented further symptoms of midbrain damage. Cerebellar disease as such, however, does not produce convergence of the arms.

There may be circumstances that make it difficult to differentiate the convergence reaction in this sense from a slight pyramidal paresis. The convergence phenomenon is not, however, related to the paralysis. It does not react to turning of the head, whereas our experience hitherto has shown that the convergence found in slight pyramidal lesions always reacts strongly to head-turning in the opposite direction. First a marked sagging or sinking of the affected arm occurs and, secondly, an increase in the convergence.

With this view in mind, the convergence reaction can be exploited as a valuable sign in mesencephalic or striopallidarnigral lesions. From this point of view, we have given closer attention to the appearance of the convergence phenomena in alcoholism. Observing the extensive number of alcoholic cases of the Bellevue Psychiatric Hospital, it has been found that the tremor occurring in acute or chronic alcohol intoxications is very frequently combined with convergence of the arms. The convergence is not always equally marked on both sides, nor is there a definite reason for this at hand. The position of the head never has any influence on this convergence phenomenon. There are also cases of tremor without convergence and some with convergence but without tremor. The convergence (and the tremor) pass with the disappearance of the acute alcoholic intoxication, and in some cases the reaction disappears entirely, permitting the normal divergence reaction to appear in full strength.

This convergence phenomenon is also present during abortive alcoholic deliria. It is often so marked that it hides even the increased divergence tendency. It is present along with the cerebellar symptoms found in delirium tremens and the general increase of postural and righting reflexes Hoff and Schilder (1925b) have described.

The convergence phenomenon in acute and chronic alcohol intoxication can be considered an indication of a midbrain lesion. Hoff and Schilder (1925a) have pointed out (also Zingerle, 1926) that the postural and righting reflexes are often at first increased in delirium, and that they are diminished after the delirium or even absent. We wrote: "Just how the increase in postural and righting reflexes occurs in delirium tremens is a difficult question to answer. One could lay it to the cerebellar damage which is at least probable in alcoholic delirium; but it might just as well be due to an initial irritation and consequent depression of the primary reflex centers." The convergence reaction is doubtless an indication of a primary lesion of the tonus apparatus in the midbrain, but it cannot be denied that the phenomenon might be due to a damage of the striopallidum.

CHAPTER EIGHTEEN

Organization of Memory Traces in Korsakoff's Syndrome

Karsten (1928) studied psychic saturation by directing normal subjects to perform simple drawings, such as fence pickets, and simple designs continuously until the subjects were completely exhausted and refused to go on. She found dissolution of the original configuration in the course of such an experiment. The drawing became disorderly and loosely connected, devoid of definite boundaries and broken up into little independent fragments, and the larger portions were disintegrated. Curran and I have studied verbal material with a similar method and found evidence of organizing forces and active processes during repetition of the recall of a story told once to the patient [see Chapter 12]. In cases of organic memory disturbances, the evidence of acceleration and exaggeration of organizing processes was striking.

A series of patients with Korsakoff's syndrome were examined during this investigation. L. Bender (1938) collected a large mass

Appeared originally in the *Archives of Neurology and Psychiatry*, 39: 482-487, 1938, Lauretta Bender and Frank J. Curran, co-authors.

of material concerning the copying of gestalt patterns, first used by Wertheimer under various conditions, and was able to trace the development from early childhood of the ability to draw these gestalt figures. The following characteristics of visual motor patterns were found in cases of the Korsakoff syndrome associated with alcoholic and traumatic psychoses. There is a correct grasp of the figure as a whole and its orientation on the background, with a tendency to some reversion to primitive responses and bizarre confabulations of parts of the figure without interference in the structure of the gestalt; there may also be perseverative tendencies due to major impulses.

In the aforementioned investigations it had also been shown that there are forces in the memory of normal persons that tend to accentuate gestalt principles. A gestalt pattern drawn the day after exposure showed, for example, separation of two parts which either touched or crossed each other, or completion of incomplete figures.

We decided, therefore, to study the forces of organization in perception and memory in cases of the Korsakoff syndrome by using the method of repetition in copying gestalt patterns. Seven cases were used for this investigation. We used three figures employed by Bender in her Visual Motor Gestalt Test (1938), figures 3, 4, and 5 (see Plate 1, p. 155). When the patients were requested to draw these patterns over and over again, the following changes took place:

1. In the first copy of the patterns in figure 3, dots might be replaced by crosses, circles, and numbers, as described by Bender (1938). During the repetitions these changes might become progressively outspoken; instead of points, there might finally emerge primitive vortices of almost one-half inch (1.27 cm.) diameter. Plate 3 shows these developments (copies 1, 3, 8, and 23 are reproduced). The patient had before him, after the first copy, only his own immediately preceding attempt.

In the course of this development there was not only a change in orientation, but complete reorganization of the pattern. It may be seen, however, that the whole development had an inner logic.

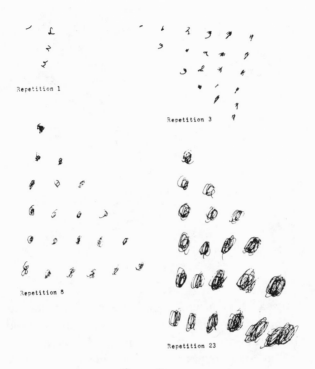

Repetition 1

Repetition 3

Repetition 8

Repetition 23

PLATE 3

2. In another case the points were immediately replaced by small ellipses and circles, but in the further copies a dot was again put in the middle of each circle (Plate 4).

The gestalt principle of this figure (figure 3), which consists of three parallel, angular lines, was preserved insofar as the angular lines were retained as units; they tended, however, to become straight lines, and finally the straight line was replaced by a curve. This development took place even when the patient saw his previous performances.

Further changes in the series showed a marked tendency to contract the figure, and the patient now tended to link his small circles so that the whole ground was filled. This tendency to contraction to fill the space became progressively more marked. The

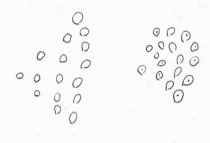

PLATE 4

result is the same whether the patient's previous drawings are hidden from him or not, but the development is hastened when the patient has to depend entirely on memory. It is important that the patient subjectively experiences the inner pull. The patient may ask in the course of this endeavor, "Do you want them changed or not?" The development can be seen in Plate 4.

3. Similar observations were made concerning figure 4. In the first copy by three patients, A, B, and C, the curved position was simplified only a little. In the eleventh copy of patient A the rectangle was elongated and the curve simplified. After the eleventh copy, the patient turned the page and had no figure before him. From the twelfth to the 24th copy the rectangle was closed and progressively elongated (Plate 5). One sees here three important principles: (a) simplification of curves, (b) horizontal elongation, and (c) tendency to closure.

4. In another case, patient B, the tendency to closure appeared gradually. It was at first incomplete and later became complete. The patient, realizing the inner pull of the figure, asked, "Shall I close it?"

In this case there was a decided tendency to flatten the curve.

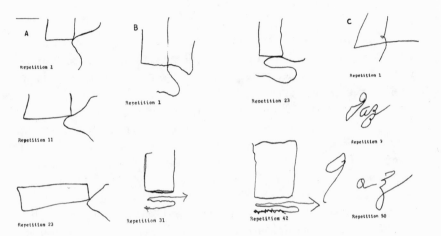

PLATE 5

The tendency became progressively stronger from one repetition to another. At the same time, the curve was separated from the open quadrangle, and, in addition, there was a progressive pull of the curved line to a position below the bases of the pattern. One may speak here of progressive dislocation. There was also a progressive tendency to mark the beginning and the end of the curve (figure 4 by patient B in repetitions 31 and 42).

5. In another case of the Korsakoff syndrome, the gestalt of figure 4, patient B, was disrupted completely, as Plate 5 shows. The curve with one vertical line of the quadrangle seemingly suggested a letter to him. This letter became definite only after the third repetition; then, in the following repetitions, he changed the gestalt completely into a word, as seen in the ninth repetition. In the next 40 repetitions he retained this word, but separated it into single letters from about the 50th repetition on. When one gestalt principle was discarded, another was put in its place. The development of this new gestalt was gradual.

6. Another patient transformed the pattern of figure B progressively into that of a staircase. A new organization was built up from parts of the previous organization.

Comment

As Bender (1938) has shown, in Korsakoff's syndrome there is a tendency to substitute for the simple geometric units confabulations in the form of letters or numbers from the banal material of everyday experience, as well as a tendency to go back to more primitive patterns. Our investigations with repetition of drawings show that even in the cases in which the first production does not show regression to the more primitive pattern, subsequent repetitions will reveal it. The circle, the vortex, and the curve are form principles that dominate the gestalt drawings of children up to the ages of four and five. The same may be said concerning the tendency to closures, filling the figure, and separation of gestalten and the subsequent rigidity of the gestalt principles. Our experiments show further that one deals indeed with field forces and principles of organization. These field forces are obviously present from the beginning. They come into clear relief through repetitions. They are so strong that in some cases they force the patient to produce them even when he still has the original pattern before him, but they have a more decided effect on memory material. Experiments of this kind show decidedly that an attempt to understand an organic defect merely as a defect is futile. The person with an organic defect is seemingly more than normally at the mercy of field forces and tendencies to organization, which, as Bender's experiments on representations and memories have shown, are also present in the normal person. These field forces tend to simplification and rigid organization of the field, until a stage is reached having similarities to the processes of organization as they take place in the child of four or five years. Although the basic principles of organization are identical in the various cases studied here, variations exist: In one case the curve becomes merely more primitive; in the second it is more flattened, and in the third it becomes transformed into a letter. The action of the field forces is, therefore, determined not merely by the characteristics of the figure as such, but by individual attitudes. It is important that when a field force has once made its appearance it acts with great consequence through the whole series of pictures produced. The organic disease not merely destroys but allows the liberation or emergence of forces otherwise kept in check. One cannot understand the psychology of the Korsakoff syndrome if one considers merely the obvious difficulty in retention of memory. One deals not merely with the fading of traces, but with a new type of organization of the traces. Curran and I (1937) have come to similar conclusions, on the basis of studies with verbal material [see Chapter 12].

From a practical point of view we have found this method useful in the differentiation of organic and psychogenic disturbances in memory.

Summary

In seven cases of the Korsakoff syndrome the patients were requested to draw a gestalt pattern repeatedly. In such a series of repetitions, instead of the perceived dots, crosses, circles, numbers, and vortices may be produced. Patterns not only are changed in orientation on the background, but may be completely reorganized. The tendency to curves instead of angles may come into appearance. Figures may be contracted or expanded and elongated, especially in the horizontal plane. Curves may be simplified, flattened, or reorganized into staircase patterns. The tendency to closure may become increasingly obvious. Parts of the figures may be progressively dislocated. Adjoining configurations may be completely separated from each other. These changes take place in perceptive as well as in memory patterns and represent reversion to a primitive type of organization in the perceptive field. They are the expression of strong field forces which have been liberated by the organic process. The psychology of the Korsakoff syndrome cannot be understood merely from the point of view of the fading of memory traces. There is a different type of organization comparable with organizations in childhood and, under special conditions, in the normal person.

CHAPTER NINETEEN

Aspects of Old Age and Aging

The psychiatric pictures occurring in old age can be understood only if one takes the psychology of aging into consideration. The psychiatrist observes that human beings between 40 and 50 start to think about the coming of old age. There is the gradual change in appearance; the hair may start to gray, and there may be a feeling of a diminished capacity for physical work. In women, the menopause is generally considered the end of one period of life and the beginning of a less desirable period. The individuals may feel that their erotic value is diminishing. If life has been satisfactory and there is a prospect of continued emotional and social security, they will feel that their values as personalities have not diminished and that they can still enjoy the importance their experience and social power bestow upon them. When, later on, the impairment of sensory functions and motor performances become undeniable, and when the decline in memory functions and creative mental capacities also becomes obvious to the individuals themselves, they may be easily resigned to looking back on the experiences and achievements of the past. They may still feel sure of their inner value in

Appeared originally in the *American Journal of Orthopsychiatry*, 10:62-69, 1940.

relation to their families or surroundings in general. We may expect that some will be unable to stand their losses by age, and may then revolt by complaining. Others will answer to the deprivation by giving up completely and, finally, there will be a group who will try to find compensation in a fantasy world which may be a revival of the past, and which may deviate in one or the other direction from reality. We may speak about two phases in aging and call the first, the phase of libidinal rearrangement, the second, the phase of organic impairment.

Modern psychiatry is accustomed to view psychotic manifestations not as queer additions to the so-called "normal" personality, but as specific aspects of psychophysiological developments, which, in essence, are identical in the normal and in the pathological case. We may therefore classify the psychoses of aging persons in two large groups. The first group does not show "organic" changes. There are no definitely abnormal autopsy findings in the brain. Clinically, we do not find an impairment of intellect and memory. Two main subgroups can be differentiated: depressive pictures and paranoid pictures. Of less importance are the chronic manic pictures (Wertham, 1929).

The second group is the organic group, which can be differentiated according to several principles. One may differentiate the forms with localized defects from the forms with generalized and diffuse defects. However, the aphasias and agnosias due to localized lesions are not so much the concern of this discussion. One may also differentiate presenile deteriorations from senile deteriorations. To the presenile group belong Alzheimer's and Pick's diseases and, in some sense, Huntington's chorea. To the senile group would belong senile deterioration as such. Furthermore, there belong here the arteriosclerotic deteriorations and the psychiatric pictures to be observed in patients with vascular hypertonia (Krapf, 1936). The psychiatric literature of these problems is very extensive (see Henderson and Gillespie, 1927; Bleuler, 1924; Kraepelin, 1908; Spielmeyer, 1912; Rothschild, 1937).

We are not so much interested in the much discussed clinical question of whether the depressive pictures of the involutional period are part of the manic-depressive group or whether they constitute a specific group. I am of the opinion that they belong to the manic-depressive group and that their specific features are due to the general problems of involution and aging. During involution the individual feels that his body is impaired. He reacts to this with fear and anxiety. The difficulties of the tasks of life, sexual and otherwise, frighten him. The individual compares his present body image with the past one, and feels that he has lost. He also compares his present mental self with his previous mental self.

The physical disturbances connected with aging, especially with the menopause, may increase the strength of the feeling of general impairment. In milder cases this may lead to pictures of the so-called "neurasthenic, hypochondriac type," in which the connection with an actual difficulty is very obvious. In more out-spoken cases, the anxiety in connection with the waning of the body and of the libido is overwhelming, and depressive pictures result. There will be an overwhelming fear of death, which may finally lead to a desire for death. However, projection soon ensues, and the individual will experience the threat of annihilation from the outside. This threat may be directed specifically against the sex parts (castration complex), which are experienced as the essence of life, which is about to be taken away. Patients may also be afraid that the insides of their bodies may be taken away. These ideas of impairment of the body may be transformed into a general fear of being robbed. The idea of being robbed of money comes into the foreground. I come, therefore, to the conclusion that the depressive pictures of involution are dominated by the fear of impairment of the body function in general, and of sex especially.

They may culminate in a general fear of death. Death is experienced in cases of this type as slow or fast dismemberment. This complex may be combined with acute anxiety or with inhibition. These primary fears and anxieties are met by two defense mechanisms. One is projection, as mentioned above. Depressive pictures of involution often show this projection mechanism. However, the individual may also try to regain his lost youth in fantasies and increased sex tension. This change, however, will be immediately followed by an increased feeling of guilt and by projection, and the sexual threat will then be experienced as coming from outside. The persecutors of these cases may then represent the increased sex danger, although they may also represent the dangers of decaying sex. Furthermore, in some of my cases, I have gained the impression that the persecutors represent the endangered parts of the body which have been projected into the outward world and retain their relation to the individual by coming back as persecutors. So-called "atypical pictures" may result from such an interaction between projection and reintrojection [see Chapter 30]. Melanie Klein (1935) has stated that the dismemberment motive plays an important part in the depressive case. She correctly states that the depressive continues to care for, and worry about, the object. These worries are not present in the paranoiac in whom the object, cut into pieces, becomes merely a multiplicity of persecutors, every piece growing into a separate persecutor. However, in the senile and presenile depressions, the persecutor may indeed be a part of one's own body, which has become an independent threat. It should not be denied that, in all these cases, relations to love objects persist. However, these love objects may not be appreciated in full, but only in parts. We thus come very near to some of the formulations of Abraham (1924), who attributed an important role to the tendencies of the depressive not to love the individual as a whole, but merely parts of him. There is no question but that there is a continuous complicated interplay between projections and introjections going on in these depressive cases. The introjections are identifications and appersonizations. The projections throw either parts of the individual's body into the outward world, or parts of persons or total bodies previously introjected. There is no question that the enormous aggression of these patients, which is partially in connection with the fear of decay, provokes feelings of guilt and a tendency to self-punishment, which may lead either to inhibition or to aggressive action against the self. I cannot in such a general discussion go into details of the psychoanalytic theory of depressions. It should merely be stated that in involutional depressions, anxiety and fear of dismemberment play a greater part, in connection with the general characteristics of the coming age. This is particularly obvious in patients who, after several depressions in earlier life, suffer a new attack in the involutional or senile period. It is obvious that we also have to search in involutional depressions for the infantile determinant of the psychosis and, furthermore, for the constitutional and character problems involved. Titley (1938) has characterized the prepsychotic personality of patients with agitated depression as rigid, stubborn, overconscientious, and meticulous. "A rigid ethical code, proclivity for saving and extreme reticence, coupled with markedly sensitive and anxious trends, recurred throughout." It is interesting that not only the depressions of later age have a more chronic course, but also the manic states (Wertham, 1929).

Although I have tried to characterize these pictures from a clinical and psychological point of view, I do not doubt that these psychoses have a biological background that is closely related to the involutional processes occurring in everyone.

I have observed a psychosis after cataract operation in a woman of 53, in whom very similar mechanisms were prevalent (Schilder, 1923c). In connection with a general fear of involution, she feared she would be cut to pieces; she received presents which were taken away again. Not only she herself, but others also were treated in this way. She was also persecuted by rats, which obviously represented parts of her own body. However, this was a psychosis of hallucinatory type.

This case leads over to paranoid pictures, the second group of so-called "functional, involutional psychoses." These cases have been described under different names: involutional paranoia (Kleist, 1913); involutional paraphrenia (Serko, 1919). Even the authors with predominantly clinical interests stress the fact that sexual motives play a major part. There are jealousy, rape, delusional marriage, complaints about indecent suggestions and attacks. There is no clear-cut dementia, but the individuals are often pedantic, cling to details, sometimes become circumstantial, and generally are not very productive. Delusional and hallucinatory elements may be present; delusions are systematized to various degrees. In my opinion, the typical cases of this group are characterized by their definite and clear-cut relation to the outward world.

A 73-year-old woman, for instance, is well preserved physically and is not only very keen in observation, but also displays a particular care in drawing the gestalt figures (L. Bender, 1938), and also draws a flower pot very well. She was married, and has been widowed for a long time; her sex life has been rather inconspicuous within normal limits. In her opinion, age doesn't count; it's the mentality. She was never afraid of old age. "Why fear death? It's just a putting over." "I have a spiritual background in a practical way." "I never felt that I was stout; I never dieted." However, the patient feels that it is not nice to be stout. Several years ago, she said, a reducing machine was installed in the house, but now this machine has been changed into an electric machine which provokes vibrations in a woman, who, in turn, excites men sexually. She thus becomes an object of attraction to men. For this reason she has to keep her vagina covered, so that men cannot put their electricity in her sex parts.

The machine by which she is attacked is obviously in very close relation to the state of her own body. It seems, thus, that this patient has solved the problems of death and aging in a rather perfect way.

In senile paranoia, the problem of aging and death is solved by projection.

We turn now to the organic impairments of old age, and it seems advisable to classify them according to a new principle, namely, whether the involution is predominantly in the parenchyma or in the blood vessels. The involution of the tissues can be of the special type of Huntington's chorea, involving not only the cortex, but also the basal ganglia. In senile involution in the proper sense, one finds an increase in the pigment of the ganglion cells and, finally, degeneration of the ganglion cells. There is also the characteristic thickening and form change in the fibrils in the cells, as described by Alzheimer, particularly outspoken in cases of Alzheimer's disease. We find atrophy of the brain tissue in general, including the glia, particularly in Pick's disease. There are, in addition, other changes in the glia, in which the cells may become large and pale. There are, furthermore, the argentophil plaques which are also found in Alzheimer's disease, and about the origin of which opinions are divided. Most probably, we deal with a degeneration of cells and glia, with subsequent changes in the colloidal state of the surrounding tissue. One may state generally that Alzheimer's and Pick's diseases merely show two sides of the aging process with particular clarity. Both diseases are comparatively localized.

These remarks were made merely as a basis for the clinical discussions. It is not necessary to discuss in detail the histopathology of the arteriosclerotic and hypertensive states, with their subsequent tissue changes of stasis, necrosis, and malacia. From a clinical point of view, it is possible to differentiate the types of involution. Krapf (1936) has found twilight states and episodic emotional fluctuation to be characteristic of the hypertensive psychosis. There are personality changes, consisting of a lack of adaptability in regard to all mental processes. The arteriosclerotics show, according to Krapf, Korsakoff pictures and dementia, sometimes connected with local symptoms. Although depressions may be present, they are rather colorless. In Alzheimer's disease, the symptoms come at an earlier age; the local signs, although not very clear cut, are more in the foreground. They are not only aphasic and apractic, but also striopallidar. Pick's disease involving particularly the frontal lobe, starts with frontal lobe symptoms: hilarious hyperactivity, and lack of affective control. This is followed by increasing apathy and lack of spontaneity (cf. Mayer-Gross, 1938). Kahn and Thompson (1934) have shown that the clinical diagnosis of Pick's disease is possible. Cases in which the Korsakoff syndrome and the difficulties in retention are more in the foreground have also been called presbyophrenia.

One may generally state that the important characteristic of all these psychotic pictures is mental deterioration. Even the confusional states of the hypertensive show a difficulty in the perceptive and intellectual function akin to deterioration. It is true that one can differentiate the dementia of senile or presenile cases from other types of deterioration. The changes in the personality are generally not as severe and abrupt as in general paresis. The individual retains his social relations in a better way. Scheid (1933) has collected and discussed the literature pertaining to this point. It is, furthermore, possible to point to some differences in the perceptive functions between Pick's disease and the other forms of deterioration (Goldstein and Katz, 1937). Moreover, in Alzheimer's disease, the changes connected with the focal lesions may color the basic picture of deterioration, despite which, it is possible to give a general picture of this deterioration. There are the increased difficulties in intellecutal function which are an exaggeration of the changes in simple senility (Miles, 1935; D. Wechsler, 1939). One gets the best access to these problems by studying the gestalt function, the Goodenough test, the drawings and clay work of senile persons. In the gestalt tests one sees the reappearance of primitive gestalt forms with an exaggeration of gestalt principles.

An 81-year-old woman has almost completely lost the sense of gestalt function. Her attempt to draw a human figure ends in scribbling; her clay work is on a somewhat higher level. However, she cannot determine whether she has made a bug or a bird and adds numerous excrescences which she calls wings. She drew a donkey with two heads.

A 72-year-old man says, "I would like that people would consider me as young. Sometimes I feel old and sometimes I feel young. Sometimes I feel old when I look into a mirror and see my teeth, and I have no teeth." His attempts to draw a picture of a man are of a particularly primitive character.

One can generally sum up as follows: cases with deterioration show a return to primitive gestalt principles. This return may be very far-going and even imitate forms which have been seen in aphasics. In the more severe grades of deterioration, we find very primitive clay work. Patients make a cigar by simply rolling the clay, they make simple forms, call it a pipe, arrange small globules around it, and say, "These are the ladies on the roof watching me smoking my pipe." (Concerning the clay work, cf. Bender and Woltmann, 1937.) In the drawing of a man, and generally in the drawing of pictures, primitive-form principles appear, with simplifications, repetitions, distortions, omissions. The finished product may change its meaning continually. The psychology of memory disturbances in the Korsakoff psychosis having been discussed so often, it may be sufficient to say that the primitive distortions are also to be found in the memory material.

I have shown in my study on psychoanalytic psychiatry (1925) that the memory disturbance is also connected with the breaking through of more primitive material. The stories that patients repeat are rebuilt to suit their emotional needs. They become the dominant figure and hero of every story. This is also true concerning the memory disturbances of the senile, which do not consist merely in distortions and condensations, but also allow the patient to live out many of his infantile strivings and desires.

We may generally say that we find in seniles not only a reversal to primitive forms of perceptive and intellectual experiences, but also a return to uninhibited emotions and infantile and juvenile desires.

Are these release phenomena due merely to the impairment of perception, memory, and judgment? Similar pictures may be found in senile patients who do not show very definite disturbances in the perceptive and intellectual spheres. We may assume that libidinal regressions are not merely facilitated by the intellectual impairment, but are deeply dependent upon the regression of the emotional personality. This regression probably takes place not merely in the so-called functional, but also in the organic sphere (Scheid, 1937). The emotional factors in senile deterioration have only rarely found sufficient attention (Jelgersma, 1931). Old age is characterized by the increasing consciousness of decay and the fear of approaching death. G. S. Hall (1923) has given a dramatic description of this. However, there are forces at work that overcome aging and approaching death in a psychological way. One patient says, "I think they all go backwards when they get to a certain age, but I don't." This patient answers the question, "Are you strong?" with, "Not so extra; I go out once a week." The 85-year-old L., who can hardly walk, says she feels healthy and doesn't want to get stout. In the colony where she lives, an old man helps her in walking and brings her sandwiches. "Maybe he wants to make me. He is not as old as I am; he is only 70." "I don't want to be any younger; I want to live until God calls me." The patient complains that the nurses in the colony treat her badly and persecute her. A 76-year-old woman says, "If you have something to eat you are happy; if not, you are unhappy." She says one shouldn't think about death. "One has time enough to die." A 65-year-old man says, "I feel healthy and strong; I am happy." "I never think of dying; I want to live to about 80." One may compare such optimistic remarks of demented patients with the remark of a 55-year-old, automobile mechanic, who is well preserved and comes in merely because of drinking: "I always think of death; I am an auto mechanic; death lurks at every corner; I think especially of it when I am driving."

Generally speaking, the apprehensions and fears of the presenium and early senium are overcome with the deterioration. These patients may feel happy and strong again, revive heterosexual wishes, or may at least feel gratified by oral satisfaction. The fear of being poor, of being robbed, or of being persecuted may persist and may act as a constant stimulus to escape into a state of greater happiness. The aging and the senile may even try to get renewed satisfaction in a sexual approach to younger people. However, in the majority of cases, this approach to youth will remain in the realm of daydreaming, fantasy, and confabulation. There are indications that these regressions follow the pathways through which the individual has gone in childhood, adolescence, and adult life. We may expect a revival of the Oedipus situation in all its variations. There are psychic compensations in senility. When the individual is no longer capable of enriching or maintaining his relations to the outward world, he regresses to infantile situations and looks from there to new possibilities. One may state that the senile still lives in a very real world. He has a definite relation to time and space, though the objective facts of time and space are distorted. Even when the senile regresses, he regresses differently from the schizophrenic. He does not go back to a magic world, but remains in a world that fulfills the strivings and desires he had in adolescence and manhood.

Rothschild (1937) finds no direct anatomical correlation between the findings in senile brains and the degree of deterioration. He is inclined to believe in general compensatory factors of physical character. However, we know very little about this. I still believe that an improved histopathological technique will make the correlations between clinical pictures and histopathological findings closer. At any rate, the psychiatric study of senility shows clearly that, whatever the difficulties of age and aging may be, there are compensatory psychological mechanisms which relieve the individuals from anxieties and guarantee psychological satisfactions.

III

SCHIZOPHRENIA

CHAPTER TWENTY

The Psychology of Schizophrenia

In every field of scientific research it is advisable from time to time
to review the facts, assumptions, and theories and to evaluate
them anew. Such an endeavor concerning the psychology of
schizophrenia is the more advisable because insulin shock therapy
and metrazol therapy have, besides their doubtless practical value,
great theoretical interest, for they have faced the schizophrenic as
an organism with new tasks.

One is entitled to say that the modern psychology of schizophrenia is based upon the efforts of Freud (1891, 1894, 1896, 1911,
1914, 1924a, 1924b), Bleuler (1911), Jung (1907, 1912), and their
associates. One should not forget that Bleuler's and Freud's approaches are in many respects opposed to each other. According
to Eugen Bleuler (1911), the basic disturbance of schizophrenia is
an organically determined change in the associations. Manfred
Bleuler (1931) characterizes the disturbance in the associations in
the following way: (1) Two unrelated ideas in the patient's mind
are connected. (2) Several different ideas are combined by condensation. (3) Symbols are liberally used. (4) General notions are used

Appeared originally in the *Psychoanalytic Review*, 26:380-398, 1939.

instead of concrete statements. (5-6) The associations are often determined by alliterations and "mediate" associations. In mediate associations, the train of thoughts is determined by unimportant partial identities in the material.

On the basis of this organically determined primary disturbance, the complexes have a freer sway, and secondary symptoms like hallucinations, autism, and negativism appear. It is difficult today to judge such a theory. Nobody any longer believes that one can do very much with the concept of an organic disturbance in associations. These are very mechanical ideas. Thinking is not a chain of associations, and, even when an organic disease of the brain exists, we cannot understand the resulting picture merely from the point of view of a destruction of memory material, but have to ask in what way the thought processes have changed. Is the individual contented with preliminary solutions? Does he think it is necessary to give the same care to his thought processes as before, and is the whole process of the evolution of thoughts not prematurely interrupted? It should be considered a principle of modern psychopathology that we should ask not only which functions the individual cannot perform, but also in what way he solves the tasks put before him. In other words, to chalk up the defects of thinking in general paralysis, for instance, does not teach us very much about the psychology of dementia. I have studied the psychology of general paralysis from this point of view (Schilder, 1930c). Bleuler's merits lie in the careful psychological study he has made of the many manifestations of schizophrenia and in the overwhelming evidence he has presented concerning the psychological determination of the majority of schizophrenic manifestations.

It is true that Jung, as well as Abraham (1924), made basic contributions before Bleuler. Jung has shown better insight into the fundamental problem, for he studied psychological problems with psychological methods and did not consider psychological manifestations dependent upon primary disturbances in association. From this point of view an old controversy between Jung (1912) and Bleuler (1910) concerning schizophrenic negativism is remarkable.

Jung justly defended the thesis that negativism is an attitude of re-flection and not a consequence of difficulties in associations. With this, we come to the basic psychoanalytic concepts of schizo-phrenia.

As early as 1896, Freud gave attention to the psychogenesis of paranoia. In the later development of his ideas, greater emphasis was put on the regression to homosexuality, and finally the formu-lation is reached that the schizophrenic gives up his relations to objects—the other persons around him—that he withdraws libido from objects and concentrates it on his own body as narcissistic libido. On the way to this regression from object relations to narcissistic self-love, the stages of infantile sexuality are revived in reversed order until, finally, in the catatonic stupor the individual is interested only in his own body, and the world loses importance to him. Discussion of these conceptions can be found in the work of Nunberg (1920) and Schilder (1931a).

Difficulties arise concerning the concept of narcissism. The underlying assumption of psychoanalysis that the perception of one's own body takes place prior to the perception of the world is erroneous, as my extensive studies on the body image have shown (1935). Direct observation of children shows that the child has to gain by trial-and-error experimentation a picture of its own body. Furthermore, it is incorrect to state that the child has no interest in the outside world. The investigations of Canestrini (1913) have shown that the child has sensual perceptions and interests immedi-ately after birth, and the records of child development show clearly that the development of the child is a continuous process, and has the intention of mastering the world as well as its own body. Gradually, a clearer picture of the world and its various configurations and the picture of one's own body, the body image, emerge. The German term for configuration is *Gestalt*, and the German word *Gestalt* primarily means the configuration of the body. The psychoanalytic literature correctly differentiates pri-mary from secondary narcissism, indicating that the knowledge of one's own body has to be developed. Freud offers a psychological explanation for schizophrenia. He fully recognizes that the psychological understanding of schizophrenia does not imply that it is not an irreversible organic disease, and he thus avoids the mistake of Adolf Meyer (1906, 1922) who draws, from his understanding of the schizophrenic, the false inference that schizophrenia is not an irreversible organic disease.

It is customary these days to say that one should not discuss such problems because there is in any case no borderline between organic and psychogenic. Such a point of view, however, does not take into consideration that the so-called psychogenic processes are obviously organic processes of a definite order and that the so-called organic processes are psychogenic processes of a definite order, too. The psychogenesis of a neurosis is different from the psychogenesis of, and the psychogenetic factors in connection with, organic diseases. The organic processes taking place during a neurosis are very different from the organic processes in senile dementia or general paresis. Later psychoanalytic concepts emphasize that regression does not take place in the libidinal sphere, but postulate disturbances in ego formation (Zilboorg, 1930; Alexander, 1931). The psychoanalytic concept of the ego is sufficiently vague, however, as to deprive such a general statement of any real value. It is obvious that a severe disturbance in libidinal attitudes cannot be an isolated event in a psychological organization. The system of adaptation based upon libidinal identifications has to undergo changes. If one calls this system of adaptations, and the defense mechanisms of all kinds, the ego, there cannot be any doubt that ego disturbances are present whenever there are changes in libidinal development. If one includes, in the definition of the ego, an emphasis on the perceptive apparatus with its motor possibilities, specific proofs are necessary if one wants to ascertain that this perceptive apparatus is disturbed in schizophrenia. I shall try later on to characterize the disturbances in the perceptive apparatus observed in schizophrenia.

When one studies any case of schizophrenia, it is easy to see that a regression in libidinal development has indeed taken place. We see the patient thrown back to very primitive attitudes. He is thrown out of heterosexual relations, clings to them and tries to overcompensate, falls back into homosexual levels and cannot even tolerate homosexual relations, fights against them, projects them, hallucinates, feels persecuted, and builds up the impression that the whole world revolves around himself as its center. In these stages, the schizophrenic feels he is beautiful, strong, the center of attention, and everything concerning himself gains a particular importance. It is obvious that he ascribes this importance to the fact that he is loved by everybody. Many years ago (Schilder, 1923b) I saw a patient who considered every sex pleasure occurring in the world as her own sex pleasure. Her jealousy concerning her sister was obvious, and the psychosis started with the usurpation in fantasy of her sister's sex pleasure and child. Since then, I have often observed similar mechanisms. The patients experience orgasms in a telepathic way and think that these orgasms are broadcast for public knowledge; the others participate in the orgasms. These patients believe they are loved by everybody, they are in particularly close relation to other human beings, but this relation to other human beings has become leveled, and is not an individual but a diffuse reaction. The previous personality of the patient may either accept such primitive experiences as a blessing, or consider the bliss as rather doubtful and start to defend itself against it and to experience it as persecution. The acceptance may be verbal or in the field of sensation, or the patient may express this state of extreme gratification in action. He may become mute, quiet, and ecstatic, and everyday life actions become more or less unnecessary. One of the basic schizophrenic attitudes is, therefore, the diffuse erotic relation to all other human beings, which may express itself genitally or otherwise.

Schematic psychology has seen in earliest childhood (or in uterine existence) an uncomplicated state of satisfaction to which the persons around the child become contributors. One may generally be skeptical concerning all formulations that are too simple. At any rate, in schizophrenics one sees not only the state of bliss, but also other very different primitive attitudes. One is the attitude of indifference. The individual feels that it is obviously not worthwhile to show any particular strivings. It is very probable

that this indifference is closely related to a feeling of self-sufficiency, which, basically, is the feeling that somebody will take
care of his needs. Such an attitude may culminate in a stupor
which may be connected with catalepsy. However, the catalepsy
also expresses confidence in another whom one lets do whatever
he wants to do with one's body. Very closely related to the catalepsy is the so-called automatic obedience, the indifference toward
pain, and, finally, also the tendency of the schizophrenic to give in
completely to postural tendencies. Here belong two symptoms
Hoff and I (1927) have observed: the schizophrenic gives in to his
postural tendencies of divergence of the outstretched arms, and
also to the postural tendencies that occur after turning the head.
One can turn the schizophrenic around his longitudinal axis easily
by putting a hand on the top of his head and twisting it slightly but
persistently toward one side. He starts whirling around his longitudinal axis.

A further type of schizophrenic reaction is a leveled and diffuse defense against everything that is done to him. This defense
may be purely muscular (negativistic tension), but it may also be
connected with an extreme degree of fear and anxiety. Characteristic of such a reaction is that the patient reacts the same way to
everybody who approaches him.

Whereas we do not know any organic reason to account for the
first reaction described (the indifference), the catalepsy, the automatic obedience, the changes in the postural reflexes, and, finally,
the negativistic reactions have clear-cut relations to mechanisms
in the central nervous system, which, according to our knowledge,
are accessible only to so-called organic agents. This, of course,
does not change our opinion that we deal with primitive psychological reactions; these primitive reactions, however, are based
upon organic changes in the central nervous system.

It is much more difficult to come to a psychological explanation for the hyperkinetic catatonic, where the organic relations are
easier to define. Motor parallels to hyperkinetic acts can be found
in the organic states of alcoholic encephalopathy and of hypoglycemic excitement. From a psychological point of view, the

neglect of the structures of the world, the reversal to primitive rhythmical forms, iteration, and symmetrical movements are most outstanding. One would, at any rate, stress that one deals again with actions in a world that is not differentiated and not clearly defined. Consequently, blind aggression and destructiveness follow.

In the majority of cases of schizophrenia, we meet less extensive disturbances in thinking and perception than those I have described so far.

With regard to the perceptual difficulties of schizophrenics, Allers (1909) has come very close to the problems we are particularly interested in here. He has pointed to changes in the perception of schizophrenics, and from various points of view has helped to an evaluation of the metamorphoses and distortions in perception observed in schizophrenia. These are distortions concerning the perception of the outside world, and also in perception of the body. In many respects one is entitled to say that the somatopsyche, in the sense of Wernicke (1906), is particularly affected, or, in my terminology, changes in the body image prevail. My own investigations have led me again and again to such a conclusion, and lately the work of A. Angyal (1935, 1936a, 1936b, 1937) points in the same direction. L. von Angyal (1936) also speaks of the interparietal syndrome occurring in schizophrenia. The parietal syndrome as worked out by Gerstmann, Hoff and Schilder (1925) and Pötzl and Herrmann (1928) and quoted by Schilder (1935, p. 35) consists chiefly of the change in the perception of one's own body, and agnostic and apractic phenomena. Gurewitch (1932) has pointed to the importance of the syndrome for understanding the symptomatology of schizophrenic and toxic psychosis. Many of these phenomena have a close relation to observations made in mescal and hashish intoxication, in which disturbances in the parietal occipital function have been proven by the investigations of Mayer-Gross and Stein (1928). One may doubt whether the syndrome observed in schizophrenia is really identical with the parietal occipital syndrome. Whereas the purely organic syndromes show very little connection with the patient's history, the schizophrenic syndrome

shows rather clearly an inner relation between the picture and previous experiences, and the symbolic meaning of many of the complaints is obvious. On the other hand, one cannot deny that the
parietal syndrome in schizophrenics has many features that can
hardly be explained otherwise than by an organic change of the
underlying brain mechanisms. I think these phenomena have the
more importance, since it is very difficult to conceive of them
merely as regression in the common sense. One may, however,
point to the schizophrenic's general uncertainty concerning the
perception of his own body and of the world, which is somewhat
analogous to early stages in ontogenetic development. The pain
insensitivity of the schizophrenic studied by L. Bender and myself
[see Chapter 21] is fairly closely related to the relative insensitivity
to pain observed in younger children.

The thought processes in schizophrenia have always received
a great amount of attention (Vigotski, 1931). Thought development and language development are so closely related to each
other that it seems necessary to discuss them together. A few
words are required concerning the general theory of language.
One is justified in saying that language is a sign system that points
to definite objects, which Ogden and Richards (1923) call "referents." Although the sign system is far from being completely reliable in the so-called normal adult, it is still less reliable in the child
and in the schizophrenic. One of the most important difficulties in
thought functions of schizophrenics lies in the fact that the sign is no
longer considered a sign but, under the strong influence of instinctual drives, is taken for an object. In Pavlov's experiments (1927),
the salivation occurs after the light or sound signal (sign). In other
words, the dog reacts to the signal as if it were the object it
signalizes. The dog reacts, therefore, to the sound as if it were the
food. Similarly, the schizophrenic reacts to anything that was once
connected with an important love object as if the love object as such
were present. The schizophrenic does not differentiate a signal from
the referent. Accordingly, for him the word is the same as an object,
and by analyzing the word one learns something about the object
the word signalizes. One of my patients, asked what the acting

principle in the world is, answered with "the words." "One can improve one's existence by words. One can influence buying and selling, and one can ruin people by the word 'ha-ha.' Sometimes two or three words are so powerful that one can devitalize several people. There are strong and weak words. One can also take out the words and provoke misfortune and disease. There are also daring and hearty words. One can find out by them who has done a certain thing." The patient thinks that words lose their value by use and have to be cleaned and scoured in order to regain their potency. Good words like la-la contain other words, sometimes even ninety thousand. The patient treats words as a chemist would treat complicated substances. Magic thinking, so common in schizophrenia, takes, under the influences of strong emotions, the sign for the referent. However, when the schizophrenic differentiates sign from referent, the signs are undifferentiated.

In the beginning of conditioning, a sign similar or partially identical or connected with the primary sign might provoke the salivation. When one starts to condition a dog to the sound of a tuning fork, any sound may mean that food will come. Not only the tuning fork of the specific wave length with which the conditioning was undertaken, but the tuning fork of any wave length and even the ringing of a bell, provoke the salivation. I conditioned human subjects to electric shocks with light signals. One of my subjects, turning on the electric light at home several hours after the experiment, had a disagreeable expectation that the shock might follow. Signs are inexact in the beginning. Signs vaguely related to each other may provoke the same reaction. The words father, strength, power, God, potency may point to the same basic situation, the same referent. In schizophrenia, signs are insufficiently differentiated and are substituted for each other.

We find the same lack of differentiation in the referents, the material of schizophrenic thinking. I have previously (1920) tried to show that in every thought of any human being a gradual constructive process takes place [see also 1942b—Ed.] The biological urges, needs, and tendencies strive toward a clear insight into the relations between objects and try to come to an understanding of the relation between signs and objects. Thinking is at first generally oriented—the subject decides what is useful or dangerous. By continued experimentation in thought and action, the individual substitutes the pluralistic and general connotation by symbolizations and condensations, until finally a definite insight into the structure of the object is reached. Condensations and symbols are stages in the development of thinking and indicate that the final result is not reached. The formal analysis of schizophrenic thinking and actions shows that the individual has not reached a full development of thought. I have called this background of the normal experience in which the development of thought and language takes place "the sphere" (1924). In schizophrenia, thinking remains in the "sphere" or, in other words, the thinking of the schizophrenic is comparable to the background of the thinking of the so-called normal. The newer investigations by Vigotski (1931) can be interpreted in the same way. The thought and language process of the schizophrenic is arrested, and he tries to reach satisfaction in a world of incomplete differentiation. It is as if the schizophrenic says "this fully differentiated world of yours is much too difficult and dangerous, and therefore I content myself with a more primitive world." The disturbances in the thinking of paranoiacs are basically the same as the thought disturbances that I have characterized, but they are limited to more specific experiences. The paranoiac as well as the schizophrenic may even cling to some parts of reality, in thinking and action, and may show a particular clinging to reality in order to reassure himself that he is still capable of mastering the world. From this point of view, the drawings of a paranoid schizophrenic of my observation are remarkable in that the love for detail is obvious. It is important to keep in mind that the patients try again and again to come to fully developed thoughts and they may even succeed, but they cannot keep their grasp on the reality. Schizophrenic thinking is a continually moving drama.

The emotional and thought difficulties of these patients deeply influence the perceptive sphere, far beyond the measure we may ascribe to the parietal occipital insufficiency. One also has to understand the hallucination from this point of view. L. Bender's gestalt studies (1938) are of particular importance. I repeat her conclusions and demonstrate to you some of the typical responses of schizophrenics:

> The dissociation that occurs in schizophrenia in the optic motor patterns, as they are illustrated here, may be said to depend on the last expressed general tendency, but not by a simple reversion back to any one even level of development in any regular way. The general principles of the basic intellectual level of the given person are always retained, even in advanced schizophrenia, but there are dissociations in this or that part of the sensory motor pattern. As it is here demonstrated, it may be expressed as a change in the rate or direction of movement in a part or a whole of the pattern in one or two basic directions. Thus, there may be a disorientation or spatial separation of a part by a movement in the radial direction on the horizontal plane (most often) or by a rotatory or vortical movement to an angle of 45 degrees. This may take place in some integral part of the picture, thus exaggerating the principles of gestalt or totally disregarding such principles, or it may involve the whole of the figure. There are also tendencies to revert to other more primitive principles, such as by perseverations, carrying over from one form into the next, changing dots to loops, fragmentation, representing dotted lines as wavy lines, micropsia and accentuation of the horizontal plane, and to avoid crossed and angulated forms, as well as failure to integrate the whole field or properly relate some one or more parts to the whole [pp. 102-103].

Gestalt drawings of schizophrenic children are particularly instructive. I demonstrate such drawings, which were collected by L. Bender (1938, p. 105). Francine is capable of copying gestalt figures, but reverts immediately from this developed perceptive world and adds loops and extensions until the primary pattern is completely destroyed (See Plate 6; compare with figure A, Plate 1, p. 155). In every one of her gestalt drawings one can see how she shrinks back from the world of clear-cut forms. It is interesting that she often attempted to tear up the drawings she had made. The reversal to primitive forms comes out with particular clarity in one of her abstract drawings in which the primitive formal principles are clearly expressed. In describing parts of one of her

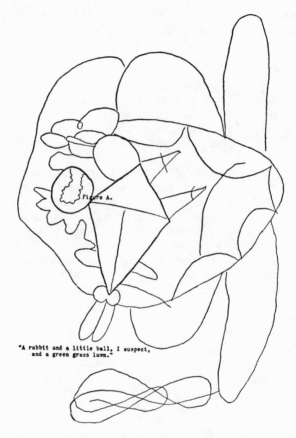

"A rabbit and a little ball, I suspect, and a green grass lawn."

PLATE 6

other pictures, she says: "This is a roni, but not a macaroni." Our studies concerning the Goodenough drawings in schizophrenics [see Chapter 28] showed characteristic drawings in adult schizophrenics in which primitive formal principles blend with a more realistic approach.

I have so far given a static description of the symptomatology of schizophrenia under a unified point of view. However, we haven't yet talked about the central attitudes and about the emotional life of the schizophrenic. It will come as no surprise to find the same primitive tendencies found in the perceptive, motor, and conceptual spheres also in the emotional sphere. A process of going back to primitive experiences, with continual attempts to regain reality and, furthermore, without any definite impairment of the fundamental motor, sensory, and conceptual functions, is characteristic for all these disorders. It is not my task to repeat the psychoanalytic formulations and descriptions concerning the emotional processes and libidinal structure in schizophrenics.

Sinking down to the deepest level of libidinal development, the schizophrenic clings to those stages of his development where he had strong infantile experiences and retains some of his object relations in the heterosexual, homosexual, anal, urethral, and oral spheres. When he tries to come back to reality, he uses the same object relation as steps of the ladder to come back to his previous heights of adaptation. One of my patients, for instance, whose childhood was dominated by a powerful father by whom he felt threatened, kept this relation to his father in symbolic form even in the depth of psychosis. By identifying himself with his father, he regained the feeling of power, and finally gained full access to reality through an elderly woman who substituted as the kind mother for him. At the age of four he had strong anal experiences which, in the psychosis, facilitated a homosexual anal attachment to a male nurse, who helped him considerably. The schizophrenic psychosis is a continuous interplay between steps forward and an adaptation to love objects on a higher level, the tendency to overcome failures in love relations by increased object relations, and a helpless sinking back again to deeper libidinal levels. Parallel to the difficulties in libidinal adaptation, far-going changes in the structure of the ego ideal, the superego, make their appearance. Primitive tendencies to self-punishment may appear, and, in the attempt to regain the world, the superego may display particular force. Still, it is not difficult to find out that the superego has also reverted to primitive levels, although there are continued attempts to regain a differentiated superego.

Even this description does not answer the fundamental question—what was the psychodynamic sequence in the psychogenesis of schizophrenia? I belong among those who believe that schizophrenia is an organic process in the sense described above. However, this organic process is of great lability, obviously continually modified by psychogenetic sequences, and we have the right to ask for the structure of a psychogenesis even if an organic process should reflect itself in the psychogenesis.

It is obvious that the simple solution proposed by Adolf Meyer (1906, 1922) and Campbell (1935) cannot be considered satisfactory from the point of view of psychogenesis. There is nothing specific in the conflicts which they claim as the origin of schizophrenia. Such conflicts obviously exist, and the validity of their description cannot be denied. However, nowhere does it become evident why such a conflict should not have led to a simple neurosis instead of to such a severe picture. If one wants to come to a psychogenetic understanding, other mechanisms have to be invoked. The banal conflicts cited by Meyer and Campbell have a causal influence only insofar as they provoke earlier conflicts of deeper character. According to earlier psychoanalytic formulations, these earlier conflicts would lie in the narcissistic sphere. Such conflicts, however, are difficult to define, and they have not been proven empirically.

Zilboorg (1930) and Alexander (1931) assume early libidinal conflicts which prevent clear-cut ego formation. The discussion of any individual case would fill a volume. I can only point to my own experiences in cases successfully treated psychotherapeutically in which experiences occurring before the fourth year indicate that the children were exposed to terrible threats from their parents. In one of my cases, the earliest remembrance, going back to the age of three, is that of threatening shadows which the boy tried to propitiate by offerings of small pieces of sugar and buttons which he valued. In another of my cases, threats emanated from the mother and continued through the later childhood. In another case, an enormously strong father appeared like a wild animal, and the threat of evisceration was forcibly brought in the foreground when the insides of herrings were torn out. It seems that the continually reinforced threat of annihilation leads the child to attitudes of withdrawing which are not only outspoken in the libidinal sphere but also in the sphere of action and adaptation. The child no longer dares to maintain the higher forms of libidinal adaptation. He builds up the consciousness of his own powerful personality, but doesn't dare to test it. Instead, he develops the primitive defense mechanisms described above. The experimentation and the danger lead then to an incomplete differentiation of external world and body (hallucination and delusion), to hypochondriacal ideas (the hypochondriac symptom is an incomplete "projection"), and to the disturbances in thinking and language and motility described above. These primitive forms of sexuality are accompanied by equally primitive structures of the superego and ego ideal. They are in a continuous state of change, as if the processes of identification must be repeated again and again. There cannot be any question that the difficulties in the psychological formulations are due to the fact that the psychological structures involved are of a very primitive character such as are encountered in so-called organic processes.

One might hope that the analysis of schizophrenic children would lead to a clearer insight. However, schizophrenic children are rare, and no complete analysis has been published so far. Melanie Klein (1932) once reported the analysis of a four-year-old schizophrenic, but she changed this diagnosis later on and spoke merely of psychotic positions in childhood in which the child feels particularly threatened by the "bad objects" in himself. No definite psychogenetic factors could be elicited in the schizophrenic children studied on the children's ward of Bellevue Hospital by L. Bender; however, a dissociated cruelty repeatedly appeared, as, did the complaint of being rejected and attacked by the parents. It seems that it is possible to arrive at least at a consistent theory of the schizophrenic symptomatology from a psychological point of view. However, it must be conceded that the empirical material is not sufficient, especially concerning the psychogenesis.

One might hope to come to a better understanding of schizophrenic psychology by studying cases which have been treated by insulin shock (Sakel, 1935; Sakel and Potzl, 1938) or metrazol

(Meduna, 1935, 1936, 1937). I may start by saying that I am convinced of the efficiency of both treatments on the basis of our experiences in Bellevue Hospital [see Chapters 26, 27, 28; also J. Wortis, 1937a, 1937b; Wortis et al., 1937]. The degree of this efficiency, however, has yet to be determined. Observations of several years will be necessary.

In addition to our clinical observations of the phenomena during insulin and metrazol treatment, we have utilized L. Bender's visual motor gestalt test (1938) and the Goodenough test (drawing the picture of a man). In the moment the patient started to come under the influence of insulin and became drowsy, difficulties in perception appeared. The gestalt drawings of a patient, B. Y., who seemingly did not go into deep coma may be mentioned first (see Plate 7). When the patient drew figure 3 of the gestalt test, angles were substituted by curves, dotted lines by uninterrupted lines. A series of circles was substituted by a straight line in figure 2, and angular figures were substituted by loops in figure 7. There was also the tendency to closure of open figures in figure 4. In another case that showed a manneristic syndrome during hypoglycemia, the two parts of figure A, a circle touching a rhomboid, were separated from each other and an enormous tendency to perseveration was obvious. When the patients come out of the insulin coma the same phenomena appear. In the confusion that follows the convulsion provoked by metrazol, the phenomena were identical in character. Perseverations were perhaps a little less outspoken.

The patients under the influence of hypoglycemia and those with confusion after the induced convulsion regularly show aphasic disturbances of the character of anomia. The anomia is more outspoken concerning the parts of the body than for objects in the outer world. I come, therefore, to the conclusion that the phenomena observed during these treatments are of the type observed in severe organic toxic lesions of the brain and different from the phenomena observed in the course of schizophrenia. The material appearing in these cases is independent from the personal experiences of the individual, and only occasionally does one see sexual

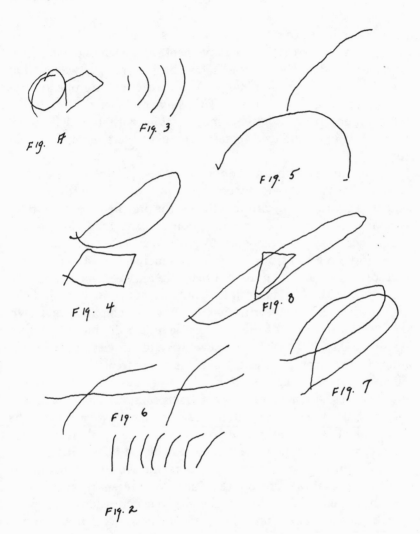

F19. 7

F19. 3

F19. 5

F19. 4

F19. 8

F19. 7

F19. 6

F19. 2

PLATE 7

complexes coloring the paraphasic mistakes. However, it is true that during the insulin coma, which is slower in development and disappearance, schizophrenic material may combine with the signs of organic confusion. The symptomatology may also become more complicated in many other respects, time-sense disturbances, changes in the perception of movement, and even depersonalization may appear. The general statement is correct, however, that the phenomena in insulin and metrazol treatment are phenomena of so-called organic confusion. They have no inner relation to the schizophrenic psychology, but may combine with it, which occurs more often in insulin treated cases and even there, comparatively rarely.

Our studies with the Goodenough test [Chapter 28] lead to very similar conclusions. Incompleteness and perseveration, difficulties in coordinating different forms, the prevalence of primitive-form principles (from a perceptive point of view) are also present here. There is also the tendency to come closer to the perception of the world. One can study the gradual emergence of the complete picture of the human figure in a hebephrenic case when emerging from the metrazol fit. He is at first only able to draw lines and circles, progresses to very primitive figures in which parts are drawn over again. In many of the pictures there is a double set of eyes (Case B). Case F shows the perseverative tendencies in the beginning and the incompleteness. Case H is a case treated with insulin. Figures drawn during the shock show perseveration and gestalt disturbances. A complete series of emergence, after the coma was terminated, shows features identical with the emergence from the metrazol fit. In another case treated with metrazol, wavy lines were drawn when the patient came out of the coma. Incomplete loops are preseverative attempts to draw the eyes. It is worthwhile mentioning that the schizophrenic attitude, present from the first, becomes even clearer due to the organic confusion. It is also worthwhile to realize that the process of emergence is not continuous, but goes on in different steps and what is gained in the one step may be lost in the next.

Of particular importance are the phenomena of emotional relations to the physicians when the patients awaken from their state of unconsciousness and confusion. They show an increased attachment to the persons around them and show a more or less outspoken transference with more or less outspoken manifest erotic trends which show both homo- and heterosexuality. It seems that the recovery from the coma for which the patients are grateful increases their possibility for forming emotional relations to the world. It is as if the patients now have the conviction that the threat coming from the world can be overcome. Jelliffe (1937) has spoken of death threat as the basis for the curative effect of these treatments. His formulation is correct insofar as he describes what is going on in the psychological sphere. However, we have to assume that these psychological attitudes are the reflection of deeper lying physiological problems. In psychological formulation, if there is a death threat it is different from the one produced by situations. A psychological study of these cases shows, at any rate, that schizophrenia and psychological treatment and insulin and metrazol treatment lie in different psychological spheres: the treatment lying in the sphere of "perceptual organic psychology" and the disease lying in the sphere of "organic emotional psychology." If we try to understand the effect of the treatment from a psychological point of view, we may say that the construction and reconstruction process is going on in organic layers and that during this reconstruction the emotional difficulties prevalent before lose their importance. It is as if the psychophysiological organism would now have more important things to do.

Sakel (1935) and Meduna (1935) have emphasized that amnesias take place and are partially responsible for the psychotherapeutic success. However, the amnesia present after the metrazol injection clears up regularly, and, although as in other schizophrenics the remembrances of the insulin or metrazol treated cases are incomplete, true amnesia is never present. I think, therefore, that the authors have so far overrated the importance of memory problems for the understanding of the experiences of the treated cases.

I have repeatedly stated that neither the metrazol nor the insulin treated cases gain a deeper insight into the problems of personality. On the contrary, many cases in which, during the psychosis, some degree of psychoanalytic insight is present, lose this psychoanalytic insight when the "recovery" has taken place [see Chapter 26]. The metrazol case who often shows some degree of elation which borders on the hypomanic after the treatment is finished, is in this respect not different from the insulin-treated case. This becomes particularly obvious when one starts the psychotherapeutic work when the organic treatment is finished, as I have done. I have found that the patients do not gain psychoanalytic or psychodynamic insight after the treatment. However, they come to an objective insight, they know that they were sick, they know that they had delusions, hallucinations, and unfounded fears and anxieties. There cannot be any question that the treated case at the end of the treatment is not psychologically much better adapted than he was before the treatment started. I do think, therefore, that these cases generally need psychotherapeutic help. Whether this psychotherapeutic help has any definite effect in preventing relapses cannot be ascertained at the present time. The "cured" schizophrenic, however, needs further help in his psychological problems. There are cases on record of patients who have remained cured without psychotherapy, but we do not know enough about their deeper psychological adaptation.

Summary

We have come to a unified attitude concerning schizophrenic psychology (cf. Benedek, 1935; Association for Research in Nervous and Mental Disease, 1928; Fenichel, 1931b). The schizophrenic threatened in early childhood withdraws into more secure positions. He tries to heighten the importance of the strength of his own personality. Furthermore, he uses primitive methods of defense, either by giving in to immobility and catalepsy or by negativism. He may also use the technique of violent attack. He does not dare retain higher forms of object relations. Primitive types of libidinal development occur. In addition, we find primitive stages of ego-ideal development. The primitive attitude also appears in the formation of language and thought processes. Symbols, projection, renewed identifications belong in this sphere. The primitive threat is revived by dangerous situations of everyday life. The threat of being destroyed leads to outbursts of aggressiveness which appear particularly clearly in the schizophrenia of children. Many of these manifestations of primitive motor defense and obedience have close relations to organic brain mechanisms. However, the perceptive faculties and the motor faculties are disturbed in a sphere that is not the same as in gross lesions of the brain.

During and after metrazol and insulin shock, aphasic and confusional states occur of clear-cut organic type. They were studied with the help of the Bender gestalt tests and the Goodenough test. The phenomena belong to another order than the phenomena in schizophrenia. After the insulin shock and after the metrazol convulsion the patient has an increased capacity for transference. It is as if he felt that he is safe now from a psychological point of view and would form a better relation to the world and would consider a psychotic experience of no importance. One may speak with Jelliffe of "a death threat overcome," if one keeps in mind that this death threat comes from the depth of the organism and is a reflection of organic occurrences. At any rate, the individual reorganizes his attitudes in connection with the physiological reorganization in the organism. Amnesia plays an unimportant part in the psychophysiological reorganization. The individual gains by the treatment an objective but not a psychodynamic insight into the occurrences of the psychosis. He may need, at any rate, psychological help, although we do not know yet whether this psychological help can prevent relapses. At any rate, psychological help does not seem to be essential for the immediate curative effect. Schizophrenia can be understood, at least in some degree, from a psychological point of view, and we may state that the organic process of schizophrenia is modifiable in some degree by psychological methods. The organic methods of treatment are at the present time even more effective, and it is to be hoped that their psychological analysis will help us to a deeper understanding of schizophrenia and will improve our psychotherapeutic and organic approach.

CHAPTER TWENTY-ONE

Unconditioned and Conditioned Reaction to Pain in Schizophrenia

Nearly every textbook of psychiatry mentions that the reaction to pain in catatonics is incomplete or absent. Stransky states in his *Textbook of Psychiatry* (1905) that the response is inadequate. It has also been described that when catatonics are stuck in the tongue with a pin they rarely withdraw their tongue, but offer it again and again to this more or less painful procedure. Nevertheless, the literature contains only occasional remarks about the problem of the reaction to pain in schizophrenia, and it has never been carefully studied. Our interest in this problem has been aroused by a series of cases described by Schilder and Stengel (1928a, 1928b) [see also Chapter 7] in which the pain reaction all over the body was more or less incomplete in connection with gross lesions of the brain due to arteriosclerosis, trauma, cerebral softening, tumor, or syphilis. Many of these cases showed sensory aphasia. Apractic phenomena of a minor degree were not uncom-

Prepared by Lauretta Bender and Paul Schilder while Research Assistant and Visiting Lecturer (respectively) at the Henry Phipps Psychiatric Clinic, Johns Hopkins Hospital, Baltimore. Appeared originally in the *American Journal of Psychiatry*, 10: 365-384, 1930.

mon and, in some, the postural reflex tendencies were increased. From the clinical symptomatology, a lesion in the region of the gyrus supramarginalis seemed probable.

The first of these cases came to autopsy and showed, in addition to a small lesion in the frontal lobe, a softening in the gyrus longus insula spreading to Heschl's transversal convolution and the adjoining part of the temporal lobe. The process continued into the medullary substance of the gyrus supramarginalis, especially in its basal parts and reached also into the gyrus angularis. Two tumor cases, one studied post-mortem, the other by operation, confirmed the localization in the parietal lobe, especially in the gyrus supramarginalis.

All the cases showed the following characteristic features: The patients did not react at all, or only incompletely, to pinpricks, blows with hard objects, and faradic current. Sometimes there was a local reaction by partial withdrawing, but never an efficient escape or defense reaction. An expression of pain was often present. Some of the patients offered themselves readily to pain and even inflicted it upon themselves. Their utterances often hinted at some perception of pain, but this perception was certainly not adequate, and the reaction was by no means purely apractic. The patients also reacted very incompletely to threatening gestures or other dangerous situations.

We have studied a series of catatonic cases in a similar way in order to get a fuller description of the pain reactions of the schizophrenic than has appeared in the literature up to the present. It seemed of especial interest to see if it would be possible to build up a conditioned reflex to pain in stuporous cases. For this purpose we made use of a very simple apparatus, consisting of a simple induction coil, two dry cells, a small light, and two electrodes so placed on a board that the hand rested on them, with the palm of the hand touching one and the tips of the fingers the other. After the patient's hand was placed on the electrodes, the light was flashed as the signal stimulus, or, in unattentive patients, the skin of the forehead was touched. The signal lasted about two seconds and was immediately followed by a strong electric shock, and after several such signals and shocks, the signal alone was given or it was followed by the buzzing of the faradic apparatus without the current's passing through the electrodes.

Sixteen cases were examined by this method, some in the Henry Phipps Psychiatric Clinic of Johns Hopkins Hospital and some in the Springfield State Hospital at Sykesville, Maryland.

Before considering the conditioning responses, we shall give a general description of our patients' reaction to pain. Patients in whom catatonic symptoms were not strongly expressed often reacted in a way that was not very different from the normal. Cases with stupor but without marked tension often showed no reaction to pinching, pinpricking, and moderate striking with the handle of the percussion hammer, but when the electric current was used they withdrew rather quickly and energetically (as in Cases 5 and 6). Patients with marked tensions often reacted to prolonged pinching by squirming of the pinched hand. Sometimes the squirming spread from the hand to the elbow, but rarely to the shoulder. There was usually no general reaction except for occasional sighing or change in respiration, or even tears in the eyes, or a stiffening of the body. It was characteristic of all the reactions that the patients never actively attempted to escape or defend themselves.

The general response was one of attitude rather than action. The local reaction never led to a real relief of pain. It is remarkable that in some of the cases (Case 9, for instance), the sudden strong electric shock provoked a quick active withdrawing each time. The reaction is thus different from the patient's reaction to a prolonged pain like pinching. In the electric experiments, this was seen clearly in the conditioned and unconditioned reactions. When the hand was pressed against the electrodes, there was squirming, which spread only to the next joint, and an increased athetoid play of the finger and a tendency of the fingers to crawl away from the electrodes. Gradually, a queer, stiff posture of the hand developed, the fingers stiffly bent in partial flexion, in what we will call the arched position. In Case 12 the fingers were so rigidly extended that only the fingertips touched the electrodes, the thumb and little finger being adducted so that a spiderlike picture of the hand was produced. If, after several electric shocks, the hand was pressed down on the electrodes by the examiner, then the hand alone would fly back when the pressure was released, either with its distal or proximal part, and would remain two or three centimets from the plates. There was a marked resistance in the hand alone to being pressed against the electrodes. Thus, the hand is acting like a part separated from the rest of the individual, who is not acting at all. In Case 14 the individual fingers acted in a similar way. We thus have the phenomenon of isolation of the different parts of the limbs. Especially remarkable was the extent to which the patients, after the shock of discontinuation of the pain stimulus, returned very nearly to their previous positions. This may be due to the tendency of not acknowledging the active movement and the consequent annulment of it. In one case (13), when the electric current was on and no constraint was exerted, the patient returned sixteen times for the shock. It may be that in some cases the patient seeks to repeat the experience of pain. The submission to the examiner may also play a part. When we summarize, we find the following features:

1. The reaction is often retarded and incomplete.

2. The reaction is influenced by the quality and strength of the stimulus.

3. The reaction may be limited to a tonic squirming one.

4. The squirming is usually local, at the most, spreading only to the next joint.

5. The phenomena of arching of the hand, spider position of fingers, and rebound of isolated hand or fingers, and increased athetoid movements of fingers are outstanding types of reactions.

6. The reaction may be an expressive stiffness of the whole body.

7. Emotional reactions and changes in breathing may be present.

8. Effective pushing back or escape do not occur in cases with marked motor phenomena.

9. The complete or incomplete return to the disagreeable stimulus is a common feature.

Although a better understanding of these phenomena will be possible in connection with the consideration of the conditioned reaction to pain, we may say now that the most striking feature is that the defense of the individual no longer seems to be integrated. The pain is not appreciated in the sense of the life situation, but as a local disagreement or something going on in the bodily sphere. The normal person would perhaps react in a similar way when inflicted by a pain coming from a disease against which defense is not possible. But even so, his expressive reactions would be more closely connected with his whole personality and would probably be directed more against the pain. Disintegration in the pain reaction of our patients is also evident in that the reaction is confined to an isolated part of the body and that the reaction is less one of defense than an expression of attitude. The pain reaction is therefore a local and a passive one.

In the discussion of conditioned reactions, one must not forget, as Schilder (1929b) has pointed out, that conditioned reflexes are responses to a total situation which cannot be separated into its single parts. Bechterew (1912) emphasized that attentiveness has some influence on the development of conditioned reflexes. In the normal subject, the determination to stand the disagreeable stimulus and to show one's own strength plays the most important part. We cannot expect the same cooperation from our patients. It is often necessary to coax the patient into continuing the experiment. Even then, the signal is often sufficient to break through this superficial and reluctant determination.

The following protocol demonstrates this:

Protocol, Case 1. A young married woman of 29, who has shown symptoms of schizophrenic psychosis for several months. She had a haughty, withdrawing mannerism and facial expression and either refused to shake hands or did so very coldly and stiffly. After the first shock she withdrew her hand sharply, rubbed it with the other hand, looked at both examiners with a cold smile, and said that she didn't think it was necessary to have a shock like that just for fun. She refused to try it again, professing a lack of interest in the experiment. After much urging she did replace her hand reluctantly on the electrode. She withdrew it hastily after the light alone had flashed. She then was very much annoyed and, when asked why she withdrew her hand when there was no shock, said with obvious displeasure, "One can have reasons for doing things without explaining everything." She insisted on returning to her ward.

In several other cases, the patients could not be induced to repeat the experiment. But it is noteworthy that in one (Case 2), conditioning had already taken place after one shock because, a little later, the light alone was flashed and the patient appeared frightened and shrank away.

In the following case it is interesting that such a response occurred in a patient who showed an incomplete reaction to the other types of pain:

Protocol, Case 3. A young woman of 27 who has been in a state institution for seven years with schizophrenia. At the onset of her psychosis, she had to be constantly guarded because of a persistent tendency to self-mutilation. Now she was uncommunicative, was very shy and self-conscious, always looked away from the examiner, and all her movements were quick and darting. When the skin of her forearm was pinched, she sometimes did not respond at all or else showed a quick response, which, however, was neither energetic nor complete. She sometimes brought the other hand toward the place that was being pinched, but never pushed away, or she pulled down at her sleeve with quick little inadequate movements. When asked to put her hand on the electrode, she started to do so quickly and just as quickly started to pull it away again. She looked away rather than at the light. After the first shock she withdrew her hand sharply and cried out, and by no means could be persuaded to place her hand on the electrodes again.

Case 4 also showed such a reaction, although the other pain responses were of the squirming type. Also seen was a marked dissociation between the local reaction and the general reaction, such as is common in many of these patients.

Protocol, Case 4. A young woman of 29 who had been in a catatonic stupor for about a year. She was cared for in bed where she was resistive, uncommunicative, and spoon-fed. After the first shock, she withdrew her hand and cried out and would not permit her hand to be replaced on the electrode. Her resistance was by squirming movements of the arm and stiffening of the body, but there were no normal defensive movements from the other hand, or defensive cries, etc.

Protocol, Case 5. A Jewish boy of 24. He had been catatonic for about four years. When studied in Phipps Clinic a year before, he showed marked stiffness, mannerisms, etc. In the recent examination he was more flaccid. There was no resistiveness in jaw or neck or any of the muscles, and only a slight tendency to catalepsy. There were catatonic pupillary responses, absent deep reflexes, and a tendency to reiteration, especially of requests given by examiner such as, "Sit down," but usually no response to questions. He had a rigid, staring facial expression. After the first shock he withdrew his hand sharply with an exclamatory "Oh," but started to replace it. After five shocks, the local response became less and replacing more complete, so that finally he practically left his hand on the plates, but then suddenly jumped up saying in his low, slow, monotonous voice, "I got to go home," repeating this several times. After some urging, he returned, sitting on the edge of the chair and replacing his hand in an arched position. Through six more shocks, he withdrew very little and diminishingly so, always replacing, but the arched position of his hand became more pronounced. He became more tense, and there was a tendency for the hand to crawl off the electrode so that he missed the shocks. Urging did not persuade him to keep it in place. When asked if it hurt, after a considerable delay, he said slowly and monotonously and without expression, "Damn right, it hurts," and then jumped up saying, "Goodby," which he repeated again and again, even after he was persuaded to sit down and try it some more. Then he was given the signal stimulus (a touch on the forehead), and there was seen only a slight movement of the head. After three more shocks he was given the signal stimulus and the buzzer without the shock. He lifted one finger a little from the electrode, but replaced it promptly. Thus he showed less of a local response, which tended to diminish, and more of an emotional summing up.

Protocol, Case 6. A brother to Case 5, age 23, who has been in state institutions with schizophrenia for four years, showing delusion and hallucination, seclusiveness, mutism, refusal of food, constrained attitudes, posturing and grimacing, stereotyping, laughing and talking to himself. During examination he frequently laughed inappropriately and showed an increase in righting and postural reflexes. When the skin of his forearm was pinched, he grimaced in an exaggerated way, but showed no local or defense responses. After the shocks, he always showed a marked withdrawal of the hand to the opposite side of the body and sometimes gave a little exclamation. At first he always replaced the hand himself, later this had to be done for him. After four or five shocks he would not look at the light, and, even with much urging, only momentarily and with much scowling and grimacing. He never showed any unnatural position of the hand, and withdrawing was always in a natural way. Because of his inattention to the light, he was not conditioned to it, but when the signal light and buzzer without a shock were given, he withdrew his hand. His response was less of the catatonic and more of an emotional type.

It is of interest that in Case 5 the local reaction of rather natural withdrawal diminished while, at the same time, he refused to continue with the experiment. That his reactions were rather natural is the more interesting because this patient had been examined a year before by Schilder and his responses to pain were then of the local and squirming type. Nevertheless, conditioning was possible in spite of his general attitude. The reaction of his brother (Case 6) is similar, except that he did not show the general resistance against the experiment. The result of the conditioning was therefore clearer. He tried to defend himself by not looking at the light.

In the two following cases, conditioning developed much more definitively.

Protocol, Case 7. A woman of 43 who has been in a state institution for ten years with a paranoid type of schizophrenia. She showed no unusual mannerisms or behavior, but talked continuously of her "water disease" and the "wall people" who talk to her. After the first shock she withdrew her hand and cried out and had to be urged to replace it. She complained that her arm might become paralyzed, but after a little argument agreed to try the other hand, and throughout the experiment shifted back and froth from right to left. After each of six shocks she always withdrew her hand, grasping and remonstrating, but always immediately replacing the other one. The seventh test was the signal light only, after which she withdrew and jumped a little, but laughed at herself and quickly replaced her hand. The experiment continued in this way for some time. She always laughed at herself when she withdrew after the light only and without a shock, making some excuse such as, "A miserable feeling makes me do it when I don't really feel anything." "It's a prethought." "You cross the bridge before you come to it." Occasionally when there was no stimulus, she withdrew her hand when the usual period of time had elapsed. After the experiment had continued for a while, she began to cry a little and attempted to hold the reluctant hand on the plate with the other one, but she never attempted to get away from the experiment and afterward expressed the opinion that she felt better and she believed that if she could get used to it, it would make her "water disease" better.

Thus, this patient excused herself when she withdrew without a real shock, as Schilder's (1929b) normal subjects did. It is of interest that not only the light but the plates and the time were signals, and provoked the conditioned response. She showed the same conditioning whether she used the right or the left hand.

Protocol, Case 8. A young woman of 23 who for a few months had shown delusions, random and inappropriate speech, and an inadequate and inappropriate response to the environment. She initially expressed a lack of interest in the experiment, but finally put her hand on the electrodes. After the first shock she withdrew her hand, gasping a little and drawing away with her body as a whole, but after some urging she replaced her hand. The light alone was flashed, and she withdrew her hand, thus showing that she was already conditioned. The response was with the hand alone. The conditioned response occurred a second time, but failed a third. After another shock she responded as she did at first and then again gave a local response to the condition stimulus. After that, she tended to withdraw her hand as soon as she saw the light and before the shock. Throughout the rest of the experiment she responded only with the hand and always remained conditioned for three or four signal stimuli afterward. From time to time she interrupted the experiment by quickly unscrewing the four screw caps that connected the apparatus by wires to the plates, throwing them at the examiner, saying, "Here are your four screws with four tails making television," (Caps are marked "Tel") and also continually complaining about Johns Hopkins Hospital which, she says, is "filth and slime." After 25 stimuli (including the signal stimuli when not accompanied by the shock) she began to hold her hand on the electrode in a very stiff position with her fingers overextended and thus tended to hold them above the one electrode unless watched and urged to keep them in contact. She became more and more reluctant to replace her hand, from time to time, shifted to the left. Once she told the examiner to put his hand on the electrode himself, but more often she told him to look at the light himself. For conditioning, either the light alone was adequate, or the light and buzzer, or the mere touch of the electrodes and the lapse of the usual period of time. After the experiment, she spoke of every nerve of her body being hit by steel, by Johns

Hopkins Hospital, illustrating by tapping her fingers on the table like a Morse code.

This patient had to be coaxed into putting her hand on the electrodes. The first shock had a conditioning effect that lasted an unusually long time. After a greater number of experiments, she tried to escape the shock by stiffening her hand. She shifted from the right hand to the left. Whereas her reaction to the first painful experience was a more general one, later on she reacted only with her hand. Also, in this case, the mere touch of the electrodes was conditioning. The last two cases show rather clearly that conditioning is dependent upon the general attitude and, where a strong determination to expose one self to the shock is not present, the signals provoke the condition reaction very easily. Many different stimuli may then act as a signal, not only the electrodes themselves, but even time.

Protocol, Case 9. A woman of 37, who had been under institutional care for twelve years with schizophrenia. She was a small, asthenic woman, constantly distracted by auditory hallucinations, smiling and grimacing to herself and showing some slight athetoid movements in her hands, especially the left. She was cataleptic and showed increased postural and righting reflexes. Her response to pain was very interesting. If she was pricked with a pin, there was a slight local withdrawing of the hand but no general response or defense, and she continued to smile, though she looked away and offered the hand again. If the skin of the forearm was continuously pinched, she did not withdraw at all, but looked away and only withdrew the arm after the pinching had ceased. If the knuckles were struck with the handle of the percussion hammer, she did not object, and each time the little finger rose to anticipate the blow. Again, when told to give her right hand so it could be pricked with a large pin held out in preparation, she lifted her left hand a little as though to defend herself, but pushed the right in front of it to be struck. When asked, she always admitted that she felt the stimulus. She was very cooperative with the electrical tests

and again and again replaced her hand on the plates without remonstrating at all, receiving more than 50 shocks. After the first
shock, she gave a slight exclamatory cry of "Oh." This never occurred again. During the first twelve, she slightly withdrew her
hand and immediately replaced it smiling. After that she was often
not attentive to the light and looked away to the right. When re-
monstrated with about this, she frequently insisted that the light
had not flashed. On the 22nd stimuli, the shock was omitted, only
the signal light was flashed; she withdrew her hand incompletely,
and when this was repeated on the 27th, pointed to the light saying, "It flashed." She usually made a similar comment when the
light flashed without a shock. When she was urged to watch the
light she seemed to be able to do so, but the position of her hand
had changed. It had taken the arched position, and there was a
constant playing of the fingers on the electrodes so that no one of
them remained in contact for more than an instant. When remon-
strated with about this, she said, "It does it." When her hand was
pressed down on the electrode there was a marked rebound phenomenon as soon as the pressure was relieved. Conditioning occurred, first, as a slight movement in the little finger as soon as she
saw the light and before the shock. Soon she became strongly conditioned, and after a single shock she withdrew five or six times to
the signal light alone. When the light was no longer sufficient, she
still responded to the buzzer alone. The condition reaction and
withdrawing were never as strong as the real one. She withdrew
more slowly and almost questioningly. Whether the examiner was
standing near the apparatus or away from it made a difference in
her response. If he was away from it, her hand remained more
quietly on the electrodes, when he approached it, the slow inces-
sant playing of the fingers began. If her hand was placed on the
bare board of the apparatus, in no way in contact with an electrode, it would lie quietly, but if the light was flashed there was a
slight movement in the fingers, and then, if the buzzer was heard,
she quickly withdrew her hand from the board, and replaced it.
This recurred five times, though the response was less each time
and, finally, did not occur. If the hand was then replaced on the

electrodes, the slow playing of the fingers again occurred; she avoided looking at the light and showed a response both to the light and buzzer. Eighteen days later the patient was demonstrated before a clinic. She placed her hand on the electrodes as requested, but immediately the athetoid movement of the fingers playing on the electrodes occurred, which increased when the examiner stepped over to the apparatus, and there was a sharp withdrawal when the light alone was flashed.

In this case we find only a local reaction to pain. To the electric shock, she first reacted generally and later only locally and in an inefficient way. Her tendency to go back to the stimulating plate deserves comment. It is seemingly in connection with her general tendency to cooperation and obedience. Her defense consisted partly of not looking at the light. In this respect she reminded one of Case 8, who told the examiner that he should look at the light. In this case the arching of the hand and associated phenomena played an increasingly greater part as the experiment proceeded. It was certainly a local conditioning. It finally became a local defense reaction. The local conditioned withdrawing was at first a partial one. The touch of the electrodes brought out an increased athetoid playing with the fingers in addition to the arching. It was interesting that after a while the conditioning became very marked. She was even conditioned when she put her hand on the bare board. Thus, it would appear that she had not completely analyzed the whole situation. The situation is less differentiated into its parts than it is in a normal person. The general reaction in this case did not correspond to the local conditioning. It appeared that the return to the electrode was in some way a distrust in her own movements. She undid her own actions. This is similar to what one may often see in negativistic cases in which both the position that is given by the examiner and their own movements are annulled. She still showed strong conditioning after eighteen days.

Protocol, Case 10. A young woman of 24, whose illness began two years ago with depressive features and delusions of reference. For some months she had been stuporous and mute, retaining saliva, urine, and feces, and requiring tube feeding. She was examined four times. She was always uncommunicative, lying stiffly with eyes closed. She showed muscular resistance, especially in the jaw and neck but also in the other muscles. There was an initial increased resistance to passive extension and some catalepsy.

In the first examination she showed a general response to the first shock by a quick inspiration and quivering movement of head, neck, and arm, but she did not withdraw. This response diminished with the next three shocks and became limited to a tremor of the fingers on the electrodes. After the fifth shock she showed conditioning by tremor in the little finger after the signal stimulus (touch on the forehead) before the shock. With the eleventh shock the current was increased to maximum. She quickly withdrew her hand with an expiratory cry, but immediately put it back. After the second shock of this sort there was a tendency for the fingers to crawl off the electrode as soon as they had touched it again. Subsequently she would hold the tips of her fingers just above the electrode and not keep them in contact until they were pushed down several times. There was a conditioned response to the signal stimulus in the thirteenth test, in which she drew up her little finger but replaced it again quickly. On the fourteenth, a similar stimulus was given, to which she failed to respond. After this she did not always replace her hand after a shock, but permitted it to stay in position when it was placed there for her.

In the second examination on the next day she withdrew sharply and showed considerable emotional response after the first shock. The second test was the signal stimulus only, to which she showed conditioning by withdrawing her hand and increasing her respiration. She received a shock for the third and fourth tests and then showed increasing arched position of the hand and athetoid playing of the fingers on the electrode. She showed slight incomplete withdrawal movements after the eleventh and twelfth, which consisted of the signal stimulus only, and, in the eighteenth, a quick withdrawal even after the mere lapse of time without any stimulus. With the 22nd, she showed partial withdrawal after the signal stimulus alone and a complete withdrawal as a result of a fortuitous noise that occurred a little later.

In the third examination seventeen days later, she showed a marked response both by withdrawal and by emotional demonstration after the first shock. She at once replaced her hand, but, as soon as it touched the electrode, showed a conditioned response by withdrawing and catching her breath. This recurred four more times but with diminishing strength. Simply touching the board or any other part of the apparatus did not produce the response. If her hand was pressed against the electrode, there was a marked rebound phenomenon when the pressure was released. When the forehead was touched, there was a pronounced quivering of the whole body and a quick withdrawal of the hand. This was repeated twelve times with a similar response, though there was a tendency to delay the response and to withdraw the hand a shorter distance each time. In the 22nd test, after the initial shock, touching the dorsal surface of the left hand also caused a withdrawal of the right hand from the electrode, showing the tendency of spread of the conditioning from the primary point of stimulus to a distal part. This failed the next time, but touching the left cheek resulted in a withdrawing movement of the hand. This failed the next time, while touching the forehead still called forth responses several times, and when this was exhausted, touching the forehead and buzzer was twice successful in producing the conditioned response. In all, 30 conditioned responses occurred after the single initial shock. Then another shock was given and simply leaning over the patient in preparation to touch her caused a withdrawal. After the conditioning had been exhausted with this shock it could be reproduced very strongly by the examiner's saying, "Now I will give you a shock after I have touched you." The withdrawal, which was extreme, occurred only after she was touched. After a third shock, it was surprising that the patient at first showed no conditioned responses. However, the examiner had stepped a little away from the apparatus. As soon as he stepped back to the apparatus and put his hand on the button, there was a return to strong conditioning. This was in spite of the fact that the patient had her eyes closed and appeared to be unobservant. A final shock was given at the end of this examination.

In the fourth examination, three days after the third, the patient was immediately examined for conditioning in lieu of the last shock of the previous examination. She responded strongly to touching of the left hand, cheek, forehead, and buzzer and responded in all 35 times. Conditioning was always exhausted first in distal parts, such as the left hand, and last to the original signal, touch on forehead, and buzzer. But when exhausted in the distal part, this could be again re-enforced, although more weakly, by using the original signal once.

In this case the same attitude may be observed as in the previous one but her fear of the electrode is sufficiently great to temporarily prevent her from returning all the way back to the electrodes. And she showed a defense reaction by the crawling off of her fingers when her hand was placed on the electrodes. Next, the isolated hand struggled against being put back on the electrodes. In the second series of tests, the conditioning appeared much more quickly. Local defense by arching and athetoid movements occurred. In the next series a few shocks had a very strong conditioning effect. Not only the primarily touched part of the skin (forehead) was effective in this way, but also the touch of the skin of a remote part of the body (other hand). When the whole situation did not make it probable that the shock would occur, the signal stimulus alone did not provoke a reaction. This shows that there was obviously an appreciation of the situation in this seemingly stuporous patient. The conditioning lasted several days. It was stronger from the primarily touched part of the body than from the other parts of the body. When the conditioning from the distal parts was exhausted, that from the forehead was still possible. The spreading and nondifferentiation in the original area is remarkable and shows a lack of appreciation of this part of the situation. The distal signal may get its conditioning effect back again after the proper signal is once more given. The conditioning effect of the signal can be re-enforced by verbal interpretation, which, therefore, must be comprehended by the patient.

The athetoid movements and the arching and the rebound made the experimenting difficult in the cases already mentioned. In *Case 11*, a young man in a stuporous condition with stiffness in the jaw but without marked stiffness in other parts of the body, this local phenomenon made the experiment impossible. After the first shock it became more and more difficult to make his hand stay on the electrode. The hand alone would withdraw, and there were athetoid snakelike movements of the fingers; finally, the resistance spread to the elbow, and he had a frightened look. After nine shocks it was no longer possible to keep his hands on the plate and the experiment was therefore discontinued.

Protocol, Case 12. A young man of 30 years, who had been in a catatonic condition with some early tendency to remissions for thirteen years; for about five years he had been in nearly the same condition. He walked on his tiptoes with a marked tremor of the legs; the arms were flexed at the elbows and the hands held in stiff, contorted position. His neck was extended stiffly back, his shoulders were held high and his face had a rigid masklike expression. He drooled continuously. He was stiff and cataleptic. His right pupil was smaller than the left, and both showed a catatonic light reaction. Pinching the skin of the forearm called forth no response. When we attempted to place his hand on the electrode, it was found to be very stiff and to show the rebound phenomena. After a shock he withdrew his hand and replaced it, but it became increasingly stiffer and with his fingers held rigidly in a spiderlike position until, finally, it was supported on only one or two upright fingers. It was found that by clamping the thumb under the board the hand could be held in contact with the electrodes, but even so he soon managed to hold the hand just above the electrode. After about twenty shocks he showed less and less local response or withdrawal of the hand and more general response, in that the tremor which was before most marked in the legs now appeared in the arms and hands and he became generally more tense. There was no conditioning to the signal stimulus (touch on the forehead) and the buzzer without the shock after twelve shocks, but on the 23rd there was an evident increase in general tension and tremor and again on the 28th, 31st, and other subsequent ones.

In this case the marked local reaction is certainly some kind of a conditioning. By clamping the thumb under the board he could be made to suffer the shock. Thus, the thumb and the rest of the hand do not act in a coordinated way. The spiderlike position of the hand is a new type of defense. This case is one of the few in which local conditioning did not occur. Instead of the local reaction, the general stiffening appeared, which is probably more of an expression than a defense.

Protocol, Case 13. A woman of 58 who had been catatonic since her menopause. She was mute and stiff and showed muscular resistance but no catalepsy. When she was pinched, there was no local response but a general complaint, turning her body away from the examiner, turning her head away, showing a distressed facial expression, making little complaining noises and lifting the other hand, but making no adequate defense.

After the first shock, she quickly withdrew her hand but partially replaced it showing an expression of distress and slight sounds of distress and tightening of the whole body. In replacing her hand she held it in the arched position, and when the light only was flashed, she shrank with her whole body a little but did not move her hand. This was after a single shock and occurred a second time also. After another shock, the light alone again produced the same response. After suffering a shock she first withdrew her hand a very little and returned it, then she cried a little and brought the other hand toward the apparatus, drawing her body together, thus, after the local response was over, a general response which, however, was inadequate was brought into play. The same response was repeated a number of times, except that the arching of the hand became more pronounced. When the light and buzzer alone were used, there was a general shrinking of the body and contraction of the shoulders but no local response. As

the shock was repeated several times, the local response diminished until finally she simply lifted the tips of her fingers a little and
replaced them so quickly that she often got a second or even a
third shock, at the same time showing a progressive shrinking and
drawing together of the body. Then for awhile she did not remove
her fingers at all, so that she received a rather prolonged shock
each time. At the same time her respiration was increasing and she
became more tense. On the 46th stimulus the current was run
through the electrodes continuously and she withdrew and immediately replaced her fingers fourteen times, each time receiving
a shock; she was slower in replacing it the fifteenth time, then her
fingers crept slowly toward the plate until finally touching it the
sixteenth time; then they were held just off the electrode indefi-
nitely and did not change this position when the buzzer stopped.

We have in this case, too, the arching and the stiffening. The
local response gradually became less and less. The tendency to return to the previous position was so great that she got several
shocks when the current was kept on for a longer time. One can
hardly avoid the opinion that there was some active interest in the
pain. Throughout the whole experiment every painful stimulus
produced an expressive stiffening, as did the signal stimulus. It
was not possible to condition her for a local withdrawing.

Protocol, Case 14. A woman of about 50, who had been
under institutional care for nearly 25 years, most of which time
she was in a catatonic stupor with occasional intervals of excitement. She could walk, although very slowly and stiffly, and she
showed some cooperation, but did not speak. Her hair was worn
short and ragged by stereotyped movements of her hand over her
head She was very stiff and tended to remain in cataleptic positions. She showed a marked muscular resistance but also some
sensitiveness against resistance. There was negativism in the jaw,
vasomotor disturbances in the extremities, and absence of the deep
reflexes. She was examined in two interviews. In the first, an effort
was made to condition her to the light, but she was not sufficiently

attentive, so the signal stimulus was changed to a touch on the forehead, and after ten or eleven shocks there was evidence of a slight twitching in the thumb or little finger after the signal stimulus alone. Her response to even the strongest current was remarkably slight, a very little withdrawing of the hand, which was then immediately replaced. She never gave any general response. There was a tendency for the hand to assume the arched position in the course of the experiment and for the fingers to crawl off the edge of the plate, and each time her hand was replaced the fingers were a little nearer the edge of the plate. Two weeks later she showed the same general picture. After the first shock there was a quick withdrawal of her hand but no general response. But then it was difficult to persuade her to keep her hand in contact with the electrodes, for she held her fingers just out of contact. If they were pressed down, there was a sharp rebound phenomenon when the pressure was released. If the pressure was limited to only one finger, the rebound phenomenon occurred in only this one finger. Finally, her hand was held against the electrode and the resistance against the examiner's hand was noted. With each shock there was a strong local reaction in an effort to remove the hand, but no general response. She tended to overextend her fingers, and her resistance to having her hand held against the electrodes increased in this way, extending only as far as the elbow. On the fifteenth stimulus there was evidence of increase in resistance in the fingers after the signal stimulus (touch on the forehead) and before the shock. On the 22nd, only the signal stimulus was given, and she responded with slight resistance in the fingers. After her hand had been held in position for 30 tests, she permitted it to remain there without pressure and showed a quick lifting of the fingers after the shock with replacement, but after this there was an increased playing of the fingers on the electrode. On the 24th, the signal stimulus was given and the buzzer sounded without the shock. There was a slight movement in the hand. Her hand was then held forcibly against the electrodes while the current was kept on continuously. She at first struggled against it in her hand only and her face showed a slight expression of displeasure. But she soon ceased to struggle, and her facial expression became calm, and, after the pressure was released from her hand, she did not remove it from the electrodes but continued to accept the strong electrical stimulus. She showed no response whatever to sharp blows on her knuckles with the handle of the percussion hammer or to pinching the skin of the forearm.

In this case we obtained only the arched position and a slight local response, but conditioning was nevertheless possible. In the second series the local rebound phenomenon was from the start much stronger, but it is of interest that the local resistance disappeared in the course of the experiment. The local conditioning was always incomplete.

Protocol, Case 15. A woman of 58 who had been in the state hospital for 32 years in a condition alternating between catatonic stupor and excitement. At the time of examination she was in a stupor without stiffness but some catalepsy. To the shock she responded by a withdrawal of the hand at the elbow but no general response. Arched position and rebound phenomena were developed. She showed conditioning twice after six shocks by a slight movement in the hand after the signal stimulus.

Protocol, Case 16. A woman of 28 who had been in a catatonic stupor for four years. Because she would not place her hand on the electrodes, the electrodes were pressed against the dorsal surface of the left hand as it was held up in the air, the arm flexed at the elbow. At first there was no general reaction but only a local contraction of the stimulated muscles. After the fifteenth, there was a slight withdrawal and something like sighing and crying. After about the twentieth, she showed a conditioned reflex (to touch on the forehead) by a slight withdrawal of the hand and increase in body tension. This also occurred on the 30th, but on the 31st she did not respond to the touch and sound of the buzzer (without a shock). She thus showed a very incomplete reaction to pain—a slight general sign of discomfort and a slight local reaction. There was a definite careful replacement of the hand whenever it was removed.

These last two cases do not show any particular new features. The conditioning was always incomplete.

In all cases mentioned here, conditioned reactions to pain could be provoked if the patients lent themselves to the experiment. In some of the cases the local defense made the experiment difficult on account of arching and spiderlike position of the hand, athetoid movements of the fingers, crawling away from the plates, and the rebound phenomenon. In Case 16 although the general negativistic tendency was a technical obstacle, conditioning was possible. The arching itself may be considered a conditioned reaction to the touch of the electrodes which tended to induce the individual to a quick or squirming withdrawal, but either the order of the examiner or the determination of the patient kept the hand back. The arching was therefore the expression of two conflicting tendencies. One of our patients (7) held her one hand down with the other one. In normal people the same tendency appears either as a stiffening or some action preparatory to the quick withdrawal after the shock has come. The arching is thus rather a complete expression of an ambivalent reaction. The athetoid movement and slow crawling away from the plates belong in the same category.

The conditioned pain reactions were partly local and partly general. In two cases (12 and 13) there was only a general conditioned response. In Cases 14 and 15, the conditioning reaction was partly a local one. In a special group are Cases 1-5. They did not show a general reaction of conditioning in the common sense, but a determination to stop exposing themselves to the shock; this played the exclusive part in 2, 3, and 4 and was the most important factor in the departure in the first case. In one case (5) a long summation process was necessary before the final resistance against the continuation of the experiment took place. The local reaction was either a complete one, as in Cases 7, 8, 9, and 10, or an incomplete one, as in Cases 14, 15, 16. The incomplete reaction consisted in lifting one or two fingers. In Cases 9 and 10, the incomplete reaction preceded the complete one. In Case 10 this was true of both the general reaction and the local one.

The signal for the conditioned reaction was the original stimulus, the light, or the touch on the forehead. But also touching distant points of the skin, the touch of the electrodes, and even of the board by the subject's hand, and the lapse of time, could take the place of the signal stimulus. These facts show again that the stuporous condition and the change in the attitude result in an incomplete analysis of the situation. Cases 7 and 8 were cases of schizophrenic disturbance in thinking, while other cases were stuporous conditions. On the other hand, especially in Case 10, the experiments showed an appreciation of some details of the situation one would not have expected. We agree with Bechterew (1911) when he says that the method of conditioning patients shows us something about their mental state that we cannot get by any other method. Refusing to continue the experiment, arching, rebound phenomena, athetoid movements of the fingers, playing about over the electrodes are also responses to the situation that are in close relation to the experience of the shock. If it is not a conditioning in the proper sense, it is at least the remembrance that is acting and a preparedness to meet the shock. It is remarkable that in the cases of deepest stupor the response becomes a more and more local one. It is as if only a part of the body were reacting to the anticipated pain. Here our results concerning the actual pain agree with our results concerning the "remembered pain." We point again to the fact that many of our patients show a purely local reaction. It has to be remembered that when the normal individual is exposed more and more often to the stimulus the response becomes more and more a local one. Thus we provoke a reaction more and more dissociated from the whole personality. The same is true in experiments with animals. But in these patients the reaction to the signal belonging to the previous painful situation is still more dissociated from the whole personality than the local reaction of the normal. The reaction was either general and undifferentiated and expressive, or local and dissociated. Kempf (1918) emphasizes that such local responses are on a segmental basis. We would rather point to the popular division of the body into hand, arm, and elbow for such a response than to the segmental relationship.

From the point of view of the theory of conditioned reflexes, our experiments show to what extent complicated psychic attitudes are significant in these responses. These experiments on pathological cases are thus as revealing as those on normals, relative to what is going on during the conditioning.

The problem that interests us most is the problem of the reaction to pain. In Cases 1 to 8 the importance of the individual's general attitude was clearly seen. They reacted in different ways because they were different personalities with different attitudes to the experiment. In Cases 9 to 16 there was another factor, which, however, was also present in the previous ones, and that was the dissociation of the motor reaction. It is noteworthy that the latter group belong clinically to the purely catatonic type of picture. There is, of course, the question whether we have to consider these particular reactions only from the point of view of a change in the attitude or whether we have the right to suppose that these different attitudes have also to do with a change in the function of the brain. The resemblance between the above-mentioned asymbolia for pain in cortical lesions and the reactions in our catatonics seems to be more than a superficial one. In both, we find dissociation of the defense. Certainly also the brain lesion does not destroy the appreciation of pain and the response to it, but provokes only a less integrated perception and reaction. One may point also to the resemblance between the return of our patients to the stimulus and the way in which the organic cases often return to the pain, which is perceived but not appreciated in the right way.

It may be that the dissociation in the organic cases is less changeable than in the cases here described, but there is enough in common in the two types of disturbances to justify the opinion that in the catatonic cases, too, the dissociation is in connection with a change in the function of the brain. The clinical facts do not allow us to draw any conclusion about whether this changed brain function results only from the general psychic attitude, which tends to decentralized reactions and to the loss of interest in an action of a correctly integrated and differentiated structure, or whether there are primary changes that coalesce with the changes coming from this general attitude. One might suppose either that attitude and primary organic change would tend in the same direction or the psychic disturbance might be partly provoked by the change in the integration. It is even impossible to say whether the changes in the attitude to pain in our cases involve the same apparatus in the brain or only some parts which are in more or less close relation to the suggested supramarginal apparatus.

Pain is an important factor in all our life situations. Change in the attitude toward pain indicates a deep change in either the general psychic response or in the apparatus which serves in the integration of attitudes to the life situation.

CHAPTER TWENTY-TWO

Pupillary Disturbances in Schizophrenic Negroes

Pupillary disturbances in catatonic patients were first described by Westphal (1907, 1921, 1925). He observed that the pupils showed "seemingly irregular changes in their reaction to light, ranging from a prompt reaction to absolute rigidity, frequently with sluggishness, but always with changes in form." He also found that the pupillary reaction in convergence was often preserved. Loewenstein (1927a, 1927b) showed that the so-called Redlich phenomenon of the pupils can also often be observed in catatonic patients. Redlich (1908, 1921) was the first to describe the fact that in epileptic persons strong muscular exertion sometimes provokes pupillary rigidity, but he was also able to demonstrate that similar muscular exertion in other patients also diminishes, and even abolishes, the pupillary reaction to light. He interpreted the phenomenon as the effect of the muscular strain. Loewenstein considered the emotional factor connected with the muscular exertion

Appeared originally in the *Archives of Neurology and Psychiatry*, 25: 838-847, 1931, Sam Parker, co-author.

the basic cause of the pupillary phenomenon. Shortly after West-phal's discovery, E. Meyer (1909) was able to provoke a diminu-tion and an abolition of pupillary reactions to light by means of pressure against the iliac point. Muscular exertion and iliac pres-sure often provoke mydriasis and even a change in the shape of the pupil. According to Westphal, the pupillary changes in catatonic patients are generally combined with mydriasis. Because of their inconstancy, Kehrer (1923) called these pupillary phenomena "spasmus mobilis." In some cases, however, the phenomena per-sisted for a considerable time, and Westphal described cases in which pupillary rigidity was the regular state for considerable periods, interrupted only occasionally for transient periods by good pupillary reactions. According to Koester (1927), if the pu-pils are frequently examined over a long period, the frequency of these changes in catatonic persons is found to be about 34 per cent. Other authors, however, have not found such a high percentage of changes. Reichman (1913), for instance, found marked pupillary changes in eight of 215 cases examined, but six more were added when Meyer's method was employed. W. Menninger (1928) found marked disturbances in the pupillary reaction to light in 25 per cent of 400 patients examined over an extensive period of time.

According to the wide experience of Schilder in the Viennese psychiatric clinic, even the smaller percentages quoted by Mennin-ger and Reichman are much too high if one considers only the pa-tients available for observation in a psychiatric clinic. Only two cases of marked pupillary changes in catatonic persons were seen in the course of several years at the Viennese psychiatric clinic; a report of one of these cases was published by Hartmann (1924). In such a department the patients cannot, of course, be observed for any great length of time, and it is possible that the difference in frequency may be due partly to the difference between acute and chronic cases. Long observation of a single case, however, offers a better opportunity for recording the phenomenon because the pupillary disturbances are sometimes present for only a short time and then disappear.

We examined the patients of Bellevue Hospital systematically for pupillary changes. We found that in the course of three months there were only two cases of marked pupillary changes, in the sense already described, among all of the white schizophrenic patients admitted. Among Negro schizophrenic patients, however, we found a number with marked disturbance of the pupillary reactions, although the number of Negroes is less than ten per cent of white patients. Among twelve schizophrenic Negro women, there were six with distinct changes in the pupillary reactions and, of twelve schizophrenic men, five showed similar pupillary disturbances. We considered as positive only such cases in which the sluggishness and incompleteness of the reaction were marked. In all of these cases the signs of Meyer and of Redlich were positive to a greater or lesser degree. From a methodologic point of view, it must be noted that the Negro's pupil is more difficult to study than that of the white person because of the dark color of the iris. The patient's resistiveness to the examination sometimes makes it still more difficult. Perseverance and great care at repeated examinations are necessary.

Another difficulty is presented by the fact that the psychiatric diagnosis of psychosis in Negroes is in many respects not always easy. There is a primitive type of motility with tendencies to rhythmic movements. The emotions of Negroes are also decidedly more difficult to understand. Religious content and ecstatic experiences are common even in healthy Negroes, and superstition of all kinds is widespread among them. Many symptoms that are of use in the diagnosis of schizophrenia in a white person are useless and even misleading in making a similar diagnosis in Negroes. Furthermore, syphilis is a common disease among the latter. The blood and spinal fluid were examined in most of our patients, but we know that there are certainly pupillary changes in syphilitic cases in which tests of the blood and spinal fluid give completely negative results. It may be said by some that the catatonic pupillary disturbance is so different from the syphilitic pupillary change that a differential diagnosis can easily be made. As we shall discuss later, we cannot approve of such a statement, for if the syphilitic pupillary change is not complete, the disturbances already described are common also in the pupils of syphilitic persons. We shall return to this problem later. In spite of all these difficulties, however, one can be sure that in mental conditions in Negroes that belong to the schizophrenic and, especially, to the catatonic type, pupillary changes of the character described by Westphal are common.

We may emphasize that among the schizophrenic cases with pupillary changes that we have observed, catatonic symptoms prevailed. In the negative cases, paranoid symptoms were predominant. Thus far, we have not seen pupillary disturbances in the paraphrenic cases.

The pupillary changes in our cases may be described as follows. Usually the pupils are mid-wide or somewhat larger. We have not seen pupils that were extremely dilated. In one of the cases to be reported, there was marked narrowness of the pupils, but such cases are the exception. The reaction to light is generally better than the reaction in accommodation, but in some of our cases even the latter reaction was absent. Changes in the width of the pupils are common. The pupils usually remained regular in shape in our patients, and, even in those that manifested irregularities, the deviation was comparatively small. In all of our patients, the pupils retained reaction to pain and dilated when pain was provoked. The impairment of the pupillary reaction to light varied from sluggishness to complete rigidity. From our material, we have taken only the cases that showed at least marked sluggishness. Iliac pressure and active muscular exertion, with the exception of one case reported, either had no effect on the width of the pupils or made them somewhat wider. In one case the pupils narrowed. We did not find a positive Redlich or Meyer phenomenon without changes in the spontaneous reaction of the pupils to light. We found that the Meyer phenomenon was never present without the Redlich phenomenon and vice versa. In rare cases, active muscular exertion or iliac pressure may improve the pupillary reactions, but even in such cases, with the same method on other occasions, we found a definite impairment of the pupillary reactions. Frequently, the pupillary reaction to light may change in the course of one series of examinations. One must only be careful not to flash the light too often because even in a healthy person this may lead to impairment of the pupillary reaction. In many of our cases the impairment was observed to be essentially the same on the two sides, but frequently there was a marked difference in the reaction of the two pupils. In some cases, an examination on the following day revealed a complete reversal of the reactions in the left and the right sides. We present abstracts of some of the more interesting cases.

REPORT OF CASES

Case 1. A man aged 22, an American Negro whose family history revealed a trend of nervousness and emotional instability, was the fourth of nine children. He roamed a great deal and loved to remain by himself. He had previously been arrested for disorderly conduct. He was admitted to Bellevue Hospital after stealing a car and subsequently colliding with a streetcar. In the hospital he showed sudden outbursts during which he attacked other patients. He reported that for many years he had heard the voice of his mother and that spells were cast over him. On June 23, 1930, he said: "I'm saving everybody in here. I'm King Bee. The officer put his cap on my head and made me king, and I saw it through the screen. He made me captain. I came out of the White House this morning. I will certainly go East this morning." He hit two patients in the eye on this morning. In explanation, he stated that they waved their feet and made his feet go to sleep, and that they also laughed at him. He spoke of leprosy in the room. He showed an unmoved facial expression. The pupillary reactions were prompt.

On June 28, the pupils were almost rigid, especially the right one. They were not more than mid-wide. For the past few days he had complained that people laughed and spat at him. He had not, however, again been aggressive. He was quiet and more seclusive at this time and lay near the window. Half an hour later, the pupils were markedly dilated and reacted poorly.

Comment. We report this case because it shows particularly how, in a patient with apparently normal pupillary reactions, a sudden change or even a disappearance of the reactions can occur.

Case 2. A man aged 36, an American Negro with not very dark skin, was brought to Bellevue Hospital on May 1, 1930, after having been found on the street saluting in a military manner and shouting that he was a delegate for the Elks. He said that the lights were giving him signals. According to his brother, he was a heavy drinker, but the brother could say nothing about the onset of the present illness. The patient said that the people at "the building" started clawing at him for using three fingers, and that one of them asked him why he used them. Then, he said, "she broadcasted" and told everybody about his using those fingers and that they called him bad names. He said that the people who worked in his building wanted to get him out of his position; they had picked on him for the past few months and had watched him in the building and on the street. "I began to learn a little science about dreams. I'm always going to places in my sleep and have different things shown to me. I'm not a scientist, but I can understand such true things. I'm always guided by my mind." He was silly, rambling, talkative, and disconnected.

The pupils were small, irregular in outline and practically fixed to light. The spinal fluid was clear, under normal pressure, and showed no globulin reaction, no increase in cells, a negative colloidal gold curve, and a negative Wassermann reaction. The Wassermann reaction of the blood was negative.

On May 2, he was pseudocataleptic, moved his mouth in a fishlike manner, and said, "I'm directing you. That's the other street and this is the cross street. I'm standing on the square. I teach wisdom here. Some people abuse me and kick me around." The reaction of the pupils to light was incomplete on both sides, but the convergence reaction was much better. A little later the pupils were wider and reacted almost normally to light. When the patient squeezed the physician's hands, however, the pupils became very narrow and absolutely fixed to light. Iliac pressure had the same effect. In the course of the next few days there was no change in the pupillary reactions and the patient became somewhat more resistive.

Comment. This case was noteworthy because of the narrowness of the pupils. When they were small they became rigid; when they were wider they reacted well. It is remarkable that active and passive pressure provoked narrowness of the pupils and an absence of the reactions. Clinically, the case was one of typical schizophrenia with some catatonic symptoms.

Case 3. A woman aged 25, a British West Indian Negress, was admitted to the hospital on May 13, 1930 after having been picked up in the street in a disturbed condition, overtalkative, and expressing religious ideas. The day after admission, she said: "I think I been under the spell since I began to love a man. Then he put his family watching me. The Blessed Mother said to me, 'If you talk too much the people in St. Mark's Church will get you. They will set a trap for you.' " The patient said that she heard the voices while the mission was going on. The pupils were dilated and reacted well to light. On the following day, she said the Blessed Mother had brought her to America to save America. The pupillary reactions were changeable in both eyes and sometimes almost absent. Active muscular exertion, as well as passive abdominal pressure, provoked almost absolute rigidity of the pupils to light, and they simultaneously became somewhat wider. The face had a vacant expression. In the course of the next three days, the mental condition cleared up; the patient became quiet and cooperative, and the pupillary reactions became normal. Bodily, she was of a dysplastic type. The blood and spinal fluid were normal in every respect.

Comment. In this case there was an acute paranoid condition, which disappeared within a short time. The clinical classification remains unclear. We report the case in order to illustrate how transient reactions, either schizophrenic or schizoid, may be connected with pupillary changes. In the next case, the diagnosis of schizophrenia was clear-cut.

Case 4. An American Negress, aged 22, was admitted to the hospital on June 13, 1930, with a statement from her husband that she had lost her way a year previously and had seen and talked with devils. She had recovered from this attack shortly afterward. For a week prior to the present admission, she had been depressed and uncommunicative, smiling to herself in a silly manner. The day before admission, she had prayed a great deal. She remained uncommunicative, but obeyed orders and requests. She was slow to give up passively assumed postures and sat stiffly, but was not negativistic. She would suddenly clap her hands.

The pupillary reactions were prompt even on muscular exertion. On the day of admission to the hospital the patient showed marked catalepsy but obeyed orders well. She showed a marked reaction to turning of the head. The pupils were wide, but did not react well to light, the left being almost stiff. The reactions were the same on abdominal pressure and changed frequently in character. On June 17 the right pupil was almost rigid, while the left reacted somewhat better, the reactions, however, were still changeable. The patient continued to be cataleptic. On June 18 the pupils reacted promptly, but the mental symptoms had not changed appreciably.

Comment. We report this schizophrenic case to illustrate that changes in the mental picture do not run parallel with changes in pupillary reactions. The case also showed that the right and left pupils do not always react in the same manner.

Case 5. A very dark-skinned British West Indian Negress, aged 31, was first admitted to the hospital on April 28, 1930, five days post partum, because she had become excited in the obstetrical ward of another hospital and reported visual hallucinations of two babies. Her physical condition was essentially normal; the patient rested quietly, expressed no hallucinations or delusions, and was taken home by her husband after three days. Four days later, on May 28, 1930, she was readmitted to the hospital with a statement that she had become depressed, thought she was going to die that night and had become very religious. She moaned continuously and said, "Please don't take my life, doctor. I'm innocent of it all now. The Lord look down. The people on the street said I belong to the State. I heard them saying I'm a bum and a dirty dog and you got me here to die like a dirty dog. You all said I went with Dr. T. I thought I had a black and a white baby, but I never went with no white man." She was excited and resistive to examination.

The pupils were mid-wide, the right a little irregular in outline, and both were stiff to light. Two days later, she was still moaning, overtalkative, apprehensive and shouting, "I will never do it again." The pupils were still almost rigid. A week later, she was much quieter. The right pupil was practically fixed and irregular in shape. The spinal fluid was found normal in every respect. Subsequently, the patient became more and more dull and stiff in her emotional life. The depression practically disappeared and was replaced by stupor, so that the diagnosis of schizophrenia was more evident. The pupillary disturbance had suggested this diagnosis at a time when the clinical picture alone was more distinctly that of a depression. This was a case of schizophrenia combined with pupillary changes developing post partum.

In order to increase the extent of our statistical material, we examined eleven Negro men and fifteen Negro women (all schizophrenic) in the Manhattan State Hospital. Dr. I. J. Furman, medical superintendent of the hospital, aided us in this study. Four of the eleven men and twelve among the fifteen women manifested pupillary disturbances. These patients were examined only once or twice. Most of them had been in the hospital for over two years. These patients, as well as those in Bellevue Hospital, included both American and West Indian Negroes. There appeared to be no difference between the two groups, although the number of our cases may be too small for any definite conclusion.

COMMENT

Of course, the question arises whether the pupil in Negroes does not show a greater tendency than that in white persons to the phenomena of Westphal, Meyer, and Redlich. Our investigations among Negroes give no basis to this opinion. We found but one psychopathic Negress with pupillary changes of the type under consideration, but similar phenomena have also been observed in white persons. Westphal found pupillary changes in a case of traumatic neurosis whenever he discussed the question of withdrawing the compensation. We have not thus far seen similar changes in manic-depressive Negroes.

This leads directly to the question whether the pupillary disturbances described by Westphal and by us are characteristic of schizophrenia. Westphal said they are not. He observed the phenomenon in a case of traumatic neurosis, pointed to the possibility of similar changes occurring in some cases of hysteria, and described identical states in cases of epidemic encephalitis. Nielsen and Stegman (1926) observed a normal person with signs of vegetative imbalance who manifested pupillary rigidity from time to time. Kehrer (1923), too, did not think that these changes are specific evidence of catatonia. We found similar changes in every pupil having a slightly impaired reaction or in which a previous damage to the pupillary reaction could be proved. It is convincing in this respect that in patients of any kind who have received scopolamine hydrobromide, hyoscine, homatropine, or morphine, either hypodermically or as eye drops, the restitution phase shows phenomena that are identical with the pupillary changes described in our schizophrenic patients. The reaction in these phases is changeable and sometimes disappears completely when the patient exerts active pressure or is pressed at the iliac point. This is equally true of the narrow pupil following administration of opium or morphine as when atropine or hyoscine is used. This experience makes it all the more necessary to make sure, in the diagnosis of pupillary changes in catatonic patients, that they have not received one of these drugs.

Alcohol may have a similar effect on the pupils. Among alcoholic patients with delirium and hallucinosis, we found many in whom similar phenomena were present, although absolute rigidity was rare. In alcoholic hallucinosis, the emotional state of the patient appears to have something to do with the pupillary disturbances. One patient with epilepsy and strong emotional disturbance manifested a state of marked muscular tension when he left his bed. The pupils became rigid, although at other times they reacted well. The stiffening of the muscles coincided, in this case at least, with the pupillary changes. It may be mentioned also that in the pupils of syphilitic persons having incomplete or only slightly impaired reaction, the reaction to light may be found changeable and subject to influence in the same manner as in catatonic patients. The experience of Westphal respecting the pupils in persons with epidemic encephalitis is identical with our own.

The material cited might lead to an impression that the so-called catatonic pupillary disturbances are due to a slight organic or toxic damage of the pupillary apparatus. Such an interpretation would not, however, explain the fact that similar changes can be found in purely psychogenic cases. There must be pupils that constitutionally react in a different manner to emotions and to the conditions of the Meyer and Redlich phenomena. In this respect, it is noteworthy that the sister of the patient described by Hartmann (1924) was examined by Schilder at a time when she presented a typical neurasthenic picture. There was no sign of a syphilitic infection, and the Wassermann reaction of the blood was negative. She showed rather well-marked changes of the pupillary reactions, but they were not as distinct as those of her sister. At that time, the mother developed hypochondriac delusions of a paranoid type, but her pupillary reactions were prompt. This observation proves the importance of a constitutional factor for the genesis of catatonic pupillary changes. The sister of one of our Negro patients also had defective pupillary reactions.

We do not doubt that investigations of a greater number of cases will show that pupillary disturbances among catatonic Negroes are more common than they are among white persons, but the constitutional racial element alone cannot explain the difference. It is probable that the constitutional factor is of a somatic rather than psychic type. Loewenstein (1927a, 1927b) was able to show by graphic methods that there are different constitutional types in respect to the pupillary reaction to light among normal persons, and that some of these types are more closely allied to the catatonic reactions. Redlich (1921) remarked that his phenomenon can also be observed in normal persons to a slight degree.

In addition to the constitutional factor, however, there must be an additional psychic or toxic factor. We are inclined to believe that a psychic element alone is hardly sufficient. Westphal and Hartmann noted that pupillary changes frequently do not run parallel with changes in the psychic picture; our experience corroborates this. If there were only a psychic factor, one would have difficulty in explaining the individual differences in two pupils. A psychic factor, nevertheless, plays some part. Frequently, one observes that the first iliac pressure or the first muscular effort has a greater influence on the reaction of the pupils than do later trials (see also Loewenstein, 1927a). Not infrequently, also, one sees that the first reaction to light is less than later reactions. It is especially true that almost identical psychic pictures sometimes are, and on other occasions are not, accompanied by pupillary disturbances (this also occurs in white persons) that hinder us from placing the psychic factor in the foreground of our interpretation.[1] We conclude, therefore, that the disturbances in the pupillary mechanisms described here are based on: (1) a constitutional factor; (2) the organic state of the pupillary apparatus, due either to a lesion or to a toxic influence; this may include any change in the muscular state or in the state of the sympathetic nervous system; (3) the psychic factor. In the psychogenic cases, factors 1 and 3 operate together. In catatonic cases, factors 1 and 2 are probably of greater

---

[1] We have not discussed the genesis of the Meyer and Redlich phenomena. That the psychic factor plays some part in both seems certain. But we are inclined to believe, with Redlich, that the muscular exertion as such has some specific effect. The Meyer phenomenon involves the functioning of the sympathetic or the parasympathetic nervous system.

importance than factor 3. Factors 2 and 3 are effective in the cases of syphilis or of intoxication with alcohol, scopolamine hydrobromide, etc.

Westphal was of the opinion that the phenomena described by him and by us are due to striopallidal lesions. He pointed especially to the pupillary changes in postencephalitis. We do not think that the same interpretation is admissible for all cases of spasmus mobilis of the pupils. We believe that a great deal of study will be necessary in order to find out which pupillary apparatus is affected in a given case. A definite proof of a striopallidal influence on the pupils has not yet been presented.

Summary

Pupillary changes in catatonia are much more frequent in Negroes than in white persons. A constitutional factor appears to be essentially responsible, and it is probable that this factor concerns the pupillary apparatus as such. Pupillary changes of the so-called catatonic type may be observed in any pupil that is affected by a toxic or an organic lesion of a slight degree. We found them particularly in cases of intoxication with alcohol, scopolamine hydrobromide, and morphine. The phenomena are due to a coincidence of constitutional, psychic, and toxic anatomic factors.

CHAPTER TWENTY-THREE

The Effects of Drugs
on the Catatonic Pupil

The catatonic pupil first described by Westphal in 1907 is usually in middilatation or a little larger, with a varying response to light ranging from a prompt reaction to absolute rigidity. The reactivity of a pupil changes from moment to moment. One examination may reveal a sluggish response, more marked in one pupil than in the other, while a subsequent examination a few seconds later produces an entirely different picture—there may even be a total lack of reactivity. This variability is likewise true concerning the size and equality. Because of this inconstancy, Kehrer (1923) aptly called the pupillary phenomena "spasmus mobilis".

These pupillary disturbances are not characteristic of schizophrenia only. Westphal observed similar findings in a patient with traumatic neurosis and in patients with epidemic encephalitis. The phenomenon is also frequently associated with syphilis and alcoholism.

Appeared originally in the *Journal of Nervous and Mental Disease*, 96: 1-13, 1942, Alexander Levine, co-author.

The clinical observations of Koester (1927), Reichmann (1913), and W. Menninger (1928) have been described [in Chapter 22], together with observations of pupillary anomalies in eleven out of 24 schizophrenic Negroes and the greater incidence of these changes in colored people.

In addition to these conditions in which pupillary changes are found, certain mechanical procedures can influence the state of the pupils. The Redlich phenomenon of the pupil is an example of this. Redlich (1908) was the first to observe the fact that in epileptics, strong muscular exertion sometimes provoked pupillary rigidity. Moreover, similar muscular exertion in other patients also diminished, and even abolished, the pupillary reaction to light.

This particular finding can be easily demonstrated by having the subject use active pressure. If he squeezes some object, such as the examiner's hand, and the pupils are examined at the same time, it will be noticed that usually some degree of dilatation of the pupils occurs, together with a diminution of their light reactivity. In our own investigations we found that, in a large series of cases, every individual tested demonstrated this reaction. It could be obtained whether or not the pupils were originally average or pathological, as long as some reaction to light was present. It appears that the degree of disturbance provoked depends on the amount of active pressure used. It was noted that active pressure still further decreases the reactivity of the catatonic pupil and may abolish it completely.

Similarly, E. Meyer (1909) was able to provoke a diminution and abolition of the pupillary reactions to light by means of pressure against the iliac point. This sort of passive pressure also produces a dilatation of the pupil. In our patients it was not a frequent finding in individuals with average pupils, but was more common when pre-existing anomalies of the pupils were present. We found that when pressure on the abdomen was used to elicit the Meyer phenomenon, the most desirable place was over McBurney's point.

The question arises of how to interpret these findings. Redlich believed that the pupillary changes produced by exertion were the effect of the muscular strain. Loewenstein (1927a, 1927b) felt that the emotional factor, present during exertion, was the basic cause. Westphal attributed the phenomenon of catatonic pupil to strio-pallidal lesions, pointing to the frequency of pupillary changes in cases of postencephalitis. On the other hand, in an attempt to explain the pupillary variations occurring in psychogenic as well as irreversible organic states, we put forward constitutional, psychic, and anatomic-toxic factors as coincidental causes. We felt that the psychic factor played some part in both the Meyer and Redlich phenomena and agreed with Redlich that muscular exertion had some specific effect. The Meyer sign was somehow related to the functioning of the sympathetic or parasympathetic nervous system.

In order to gain further insight into this problem, we have studied a series of patients, in whom the pupillary reactions were impaired, by the use of different eye drops in varying strengths, instilled locally. Observations were made over a long period of time of the findings just before the abolition of the pupillary light reflex and during the restitution phase. In addition, the effect of the Meyer and Redlich procedures were noted. For this purpose, homatropine sulphate, eserine, cocaine hydrochloride, acetyl-choline, and mecholyl chloride were used.

Homatropine sulphate acts by paralyzing the parasympathetic nerve endings, thus producing a dilatation of the pupil. Following local instillation in dilutions of one-fourth to two per cent, the first effects of the drug can be observed after about fifteen minutes. It was noted that the Redlich phenomenon was present up to the point where complete abolition of the pupillary reflex occurred. In the pupil that was showing the effect of the drug with dilatation and impairment of light reactivity, further dilatation and impairment could be obtained when the subject exerted active pressure, like squeezing some object. This phenomenon persisted in diminishing proportions until the pupils became completely fixed to light. At this point Redlich's sign could no longer be elicited. The stronger the pressure used, the more pronounced were the effects. The Redlich phenomenon reappeared during the restitution phase with increasing proportions as the effect of the homatropine wore off. The Meyer sign could be elicited only rarely during this experiment, by pressure over the abdomen.

In the same manner, eserine, in strengths varying from one-fourth to two per cent, was used on a group of patients with healthy pupils. This drug is a parasympathetic stimulant and produces constriction of the pupils. In this experiment the same results were obtained, namely, that the Redlich phenomenon on active pressure was present only as long as a pupillary reaction to light was present. When complete abolition of the light reflex occurred, the Redlich phenomenon was no longer elicited until the restitution phase had set in. Then active pressure produced more prominent effects, reaching its maximum when the pupillary reaction returned to normal. During this experiment, it was noted that the accommodation reflex was present only as long as the pupils could respond. Moreover, the Meyer sign was elicited only occasionally during the early phase, before complete fixation of the pupil and in the stage of recovery. It was never obtained when the pupils were completely fixed to light.

The effects on the pupil of varying strengths of cocaine hydrochloride were studied in another series of patients. This drug produces dilatation of the pupil by stimulating the sympathetic nerve endings. We found that the dilatation of the pupil thus obtained never reached completeness so that even when the maximum effect of the cocaine was present, a sluggish pupillary response to light could be obtained. Here also, active pressure produced further dilatation of the pupil, with an impairment of the light reflex, at times reaching complete abolition. As in the other experiments, the degree of the dilatation under active pressure depended on the extent of the mydriasis obtained with the cocaine. The greater the enlargement of the pupil, the less influence on its size could be provoked by the Redlich procedure. In this group, as in the preceding experiments, Meyer's sign was only occasionally obtained.

It is interesting to note that a greater degree of dilatation could be obtained with a drug that produces parasympathetic paralysis (homatropine sulphate) than with one which acts as a sympathetic stimulant (cocaine hydrochloride). This may lead one to suspect that the parasympathetic supply to the pupil is potentially more powerful than the sympathetic innervation, and that in order to obtain maximal mydriasis, there should be an interruption of the parasympathetic system, rather than a stimulation of the sympathetic.

In an attempt to gain further information about these pupillary abnormalities, we turned our attention to acetylcholine and its more stable derivative mecholyl chloride. Dale (1937) has shown that acetylcholine is liberated at the nerve endings of the vagus and other parasympathetic nerves. It is also manufactured at the interneuronic synapses of both the sympathetic and parasympathetic systems. The sympathetic ganglion cells receive their activating impulse from acetylcholine while the postganglionic sympathetic fibers cause the liberation of a substitute similar to adrenalin. The acetylcholine thus formed at the nerve endings of the parasympathetic on the arrival of the nervous impulse transmits the effect of the nervous impulse to the cell of the effector organ.

The evanescence of the action of acetylcholine is due to the fact that it is hydrolyzed rapidly by a choline esterase. This hydrolysis is inhibited by physostigmine. The addition of physostigmine intensifies and prolongs the effects of the acetylcholine, but does not influence its production at the nerve endings. This cholinergic drug has no effect when taken by mouth because it is quickly destroyed in the blood stream. Hall and Lucas (1937) came to the conclusion that the choline esterase is present in the body in sufficient quantities to hydrolyze any acetylcholine which may be liberated under almost any physiological or pathological condition.

Mecholyl chloride and doryl (carbaminoyl choline) are derivatives of acetylcholine and have been used because they are more stable. F. Fraser (1938) found that a .75 per cent solution of doryl when placed locally in the eye produced a strong constriction of the pupil that persisted for six hours. This action could be enhanced if one drop of a one per cent prostigmine solution were added. Meyerson and Thau (1937) reported that the local instillation of a ten-to-twenty per cent mecholyl solution in the eye produced miosis with the reaction to light preserved up to the time the pupil became pinpoint. When it was given subcutaneously, no pupillary effect could be demonstrated.

Therefore, in another group of cases fifteen per cent mecholyl and four per cent acetylcholine solutions were used as eye drops. However, we were unable to obtain the results that were reported. We could observe no pupillary effects as a result of the instillation of these drugs. The only effect produced was subconjunctival injection of the vessels, and the subjects complained of "burning of the eyes." The drugs had no effect on the elicitation of the Meyer or Redlich signs. It seems that, in order to get pupillary changes, prostigmine or eserine has to be added to the solution.

In a previous communication [see Chapter 10] pupillary changes occurring during the nitrogen inhalation therapy for schizophrenia, as conducted at Bellevue Hospital, were described. In this treatment a low oxygen and high nitrogen mixture is inhaled by the patient, in order to produce cerebral anoxia. Twenty-one patients undergoing the nitrogen inhalation therapy were studied. During each treatment it was noted that changes in the pupils occurred at about the time when restless movements of the extremities appeared. This restlessness comes on during the early part of the therapy before consciousness is lost. The first sign is usually a progressive dilatation of the pupils, not extending beyond middilatation. The reaction to light becomes progressively impaired with further anoxia. At the time consciousness is lost, the pupils are fixed to light. With the onset of decerebrate rigidity at the termination of the treatment, the pupils are maximally dilated and there is no light reaction.

In the stage where the pupils are in middilatation, and still react to light, their width changes. During this period, abdominal pressure regularly enlarges the pupil and diminishes the light reactivity even to complete stiffness. When the pressure is released, the sluggish reaction returns. The pupils return to normal almost immediately after oxygen is administered to terminate the treatment.

This is what usually happens with pupils that do not show any pre-existing abnormalities.

Of the 21 patients, fifteen had average pupils, if we disregard minor aberrations. These were cases of schizophrenia and manic-depressive psychosis. The remaining six had pupillary variations characteristic of the catatonic type. Of these, five were cases of schizophrenia and one was a psychoneurotic. They demonstrated varying degrees of sluggish reaction, sometimes more marked on one side than on the other. Active and passive pressure increased the size of the pupils and diminished their reactivity. However, in the majority of the cases these changes were not always present and could not be elicited between treatments. Two of these patients had persistently average pupils during the interval between treatments, with variations appearing only in the treatment room.

In some cases where the pupils were average in every respect just prior to the beginning of the treatment, the moment the anesthesia mask was put on, and even before the nitrogen inhalation was started, the pupils reacted very sluggishly or became fixed to light. In those cases where there were pre-existing pupillary anomalies, changes also occurred, in that the deviation became more pronounced. However, after the inhalation of the nitrogen was started, the reaction of the pupils to light improved and returned to their average state before undergoing the characteristic changes noted during the treatment. It was noted that, in some cases, after the administration of oxygen, when the pupils appeared to have assumed average character, abdominal pressure could provoke transient severe changes in reactivity.

It seems that the treatment situation brought about the semblance of a catatonic pupil with sluggishness and sensitivity to active and passive pressure. One might consider this an indication that the emotion connected with the treatment provoked a reaction. A possible interpretation is that the total situation produced this response through the medium of the conditioned reflex. Although it may be possible experimentally to condition the size of the pupils, we do not know of any investigation concerning the conditioning of the response to light.

Because a progressive decrease in the pupillary reaction occurred during the pretreatment situation in these six cases, one may consider the possibility that there is a residual impairment of the pupil which appears only under active or passive pressure. This has been true in one individual who has been taking eserine for a number of weeks to constrict his pupils. One can further speculate on the relationship between residual impairment of function and the conditioned reflex.

Usually, the characteristics of the catatonic pupil are added to the effects of anoxemia in those phases of the nitrogen treatment where only slight pupillary disturbances are ordinarily present. In these cases the pupils do not return to normal upon the administration of oxygen at the end of the treatment, but rather exhibit a more pronounced disturbance than in their ordinary catatonic state. In other words, the aftereffects of anoxemia on the catatonic pupil are more lasting than on the healthy pupil.

These findings lead to the following conclusions:

1. The anoxemic pupil in certain stages slightly resembles the catatonic pupil. There is, however, less variation in its reactivity. Both types of pupil are sensitive to abdominal pressure.

2. The treatment situation may provoke, in individuals who have had previous anoxemic therapy, pupillary changes similar to those found in catatonic pupils. This may be due to the treatment situation alone, or the conditioning process, or to residual damage to the pupils by the anoxemia.

3. The pretreatment situation may produce severe changes in patients with latent tendencies toward catatonic pupillary reactions.

4. The catatonic pupillary changes and the effects of the anoxemia reinforce each other during and after the treatment.

Similarly, the pupillary changes occurring during the intravenous administration of betaerythroidin hydrochloride were studied. Rosen, Cameron and Zeigler (1940) have shown that the severity of the therapeutic metrazol convulsion may be modified by the preliminary use of this drug. In this way, the possibility of fractures resulting from the metrazol convulsion is lessened.

Curare and erythroidin have the same effect, but the side reactions and the variability of curare render erythroidin the drug of choice. The effect of this drug is essentially peripheral in that it apparently acts on the myoneural junction, interfering with the muscular response to stimulation of the motor nerve.

The erythroidin is given intravenously at the rate of about 400 mgm. per minute. In all about 1.5 grams is generally sufficient for the average 60-kilogram patient. Usually the injection is continued until the patient develops a marked dysarthria and the pupils become almost fixed to light. At this point, metrazol is rapidly given intravenously for the convulsive effect.

Of the five cases studied who have undergone this treatment at Bellevue Hospital, two demonstrated catatonic pupillary findings previous to the initiation of the therapy. Most of these cases developed marked pupillary variation in the pretreatment stage. The pupillary reactions were very sluggish or completely absent. At times, active and passive pressure further exaggerated this response. This was exactly the same reaction as was noticed during the nitrogen inhalation treatment and was probably caused by the pre-existing anxiety.

One of the patients had average pupils before the erythroidin treatment was started. During the course of therapy, he developed pupillary anomalies, evinced only during the pretreatment stage. Another patient had healthy pupils for about ten treatments. Then she developed a severe anxiety reaction, and one pupil began to react sluggishly. At the next treatment, however, this was not obtained, although the anxiety still persisted. In one case the pupils became almost fixed to light as the patient complained of pain resulting from the insertion of the needle into the vein, before the injection started.

Shortly after the injection is started the pupils begin to react sluggishly in a changing manner. Inequality may occur with a difference in the reactivity of both pupils. Complete abolition of the light reflex comes on only toward the end of the injection. The accommodation reaction is always better than the reaction to light.

The changes due to the erythroidin and the catatonic pupil simply add to each other. In this respect the erythroidin reaction corresponds to that occurring during nitrogen inhalation. In the latter, however, the pupillary change goes one step farther and leads to a completely stiff and dilated pupil. When the pupillary changes occur under erythroidin, the patient is still conscious and is able to count and answer questions. Maximal dilatation does not appear in the catatonic pupil, the nitrogen pupil, or the erythroidin pupil. Only when the nitrogen effect becomes severe does such a change appear.

Immediately following the metrazol injection, the pupils are maximally dilated and are fixed to light. They remain so during the convulsive state. Shortly after this, the pupillary reaction returns and is sluggish. At this point, abdominal pressure tends to abolish it completely.

Pupillary anomalies of the catatonic type are found in a great variety of conditions other than schizophrenia. They can be observed in alcoholics, in both the acute and chronic states. Here, active and passive pressure produce further impairment of the light reaction. In our series of cases we have found the same type of pupil in a patient suffering from psychosis due to cerebral arteriosclerosis. In this patient there were changing pupillary reactions to light in the characteristic fashion, with a further impairment when the Redlich and the Meyer procedures were used.

Syphilis is also commonly associated with this condition. However, when the pupil is fixed to light, active and passive pressure have no effect. This was clearly demonstrated in one patient whose left pupil was dilated and fixed to light and accommodation while the right pupil reacted sluggishly. Active pressure had no effect on the fixed pupil, but produced dilatation and further sluggishness in the other. The Argyll Robertson pupil is not affected by this procedure.

One of the cases studied was a patient with Adie's syndrome. The diagnosis had been made in this case about twenty years previously, and repeated blood and spinal fluid examinations were negative. This patient had areflexia, with tonic pupils which did not react to light or accommodation. Active and passive pressure had no effect on the pupils.

The question arises of how active and passive pressure produce their pupillary effect. The impulse must be transmitted over the sympathetic or parasympathetic nerve supply to the pupil, which on stimulation evokes dilatation and constriction. Since the Redlich and the Meyer phenomena involve a dilatation of the pupil, together with impairment of the light reaction, an imbalance of the sympathetic-parasympathetic system must be present. This imbalance must be the result of either an overactivity of the sympathetic system or an inhibition of the parasympathetic.

We believe that paralysis or inhibition of the parasympathetic system accounts for these pupillary changes. Bain, Irving, and McSwiney (1935) have shown that stimulation of the central end of the divided splanchnic nerve in the abdomen causes immediate dilatation of the pupil even if the spinal cord is transected. This dilatation occurs equally well when the adrenals are tied off. They believed that the dilatation of the pupil was due to inhibition of the parasympathetic system. They produced further proof when they cut the oculomotor nerve and constricted the pupil with eserine. In either case, stimulation of the splanchnic nerves produced no pupillary response. Harper, McSwiney, and Suffolk (1935) came to the conclusion that the afferent nerves, responsible for the dilatation of the pupil, pass by way of the vagus to the medulla, by the phrenic nerves to the fifth and sixth cervical roots, and by way of the splanchnic nerves, which enter the cord as high as the third dorsal segment. Cutting the sympathetic trunk had no effect on the dilatation of the pupil produced by stimulation of the splanchnic nerves.

Possibly in the same manner, abdominal pressure produces the pupillary dilatation, with impairment of the light reaction, by stimulating the splanchnic nerves, with a resultant inhibition of the parasympathetic. As far as active pressure is concerned, it can be observed that when pressure is exerted, such as in squeezing an object or strongly flexing a group of muscles, there is a concomitant contraction of the abdominal musculature with a temporary cessation of respiration. This breath-holding increases the intra-abdominal pressure and thus stimulates the splanchnic nerves. Holzapfel (1931) has shown that intestinal diseases in children can produce dilatation of the pupil. This is probably due to the same mechanism.

Ury and Gellhorn (1939) were able to provoke a prompt dilatation of the sympathectomized pupil in rabbits by using a pain stimulus. This reaction failed to occur in the atropinized eye. They also concluded that this response was due to inhibition of the parasympathetic supply to the pupil. One occasionally sees a patient with catatonic pupils in whom active and passive pressure produce an initial constriction followed by a secondary dilatation. This may be due to early stimulation followed by inhibition of the parasympathetic.

The catatonic pupil probably occurs as an intermediate step before the parasympathetic inhibition is outspoken. Active and passive pressure, together with emotional stimuli, just tend to add to the change. In the same way, these factors may bring out latent defects in the pupils. One would expect that active pressure produces acetylcholine, which is supposed to stimulate the parasympathetic system. Nevertheless, in our experiments, acetylcholine had no effect on the pupils following instillation into the eyes.

It seems that atropine, eserine, and cocaine do not change in any fundamental way the reaction to active and passive pressure. On the other hand, the pupil already impaired in its function by any one of these agents, and still reacting to light, is further embarrassed by active or passive pressure, especially the former.

There is at least a possibility that sequelae of nitrogen and erythroidin effects on the pupils may make the individual more susceptible to active or passive pressure and psychic stimuli. Since conditioning of the pupils may occur, one must consider the possibility that the total situation connected with the pupillary changes may play a part in conditioning the pupil. However, there is no possibility of proving this assumption.

One can say that it is possible experimentally to reproduce the catatonic pupil, in that during certain stages of the erythroidin and nitrogen treatments the pupils assume catatonic features. This is likewise true in the atropinized and cocainized eye before complete abolition of the pupillary response occurs and during the restitution phase. Nevertheless, these pupils lack the characteristic changeability so common in the classical catatonic pupil.

SUMMARY

The catatonic pupil is a frequent finding in psychiatric patients and is characterized by inequality in size, inconstancy in reaction, and sluggishness or complete abolition of the light reflex. Active and passive pressure, especially the former, produce changes in both the average and catatonic pupil, consisting of dilatation and impairment of the light reaction. This is probably brought about by inhibition of the parasympathetic system through stimulation of the splanchnic nerves, by means of a rise in the intra-abdominal pressure. By means of this procedure it may be possible to bring out latent pupillary defects.

In a series of cases, solutions of varying strengths of eserine, atropine, cocaine, acetylcholine, and mecholyl chloride were instilled into the eye, and the pupils were observed. It was found that the effects of these drugs could be enhanced by using the Redlich and Meyer procedures in the stages before complete fixation of the pupil occurred. Acetylcholine and mecholyl chloride have no direct effect on the pupil when used locally without the aid of a synergist like prostigmine.

Pupillary changes occur during anoxemia produced by nitrogen inhalation, and during the injection of betaerythroidin hydrochloride. In the pretreatment stage, pupillary abnormalities are often noted. These may result from an emotional reaction to the total situation or possibly may be part of a conditioned reflex. They occur in individuals who otherwise have average pupils. The theory is advanced that the catatonic pupil is due to an imbalance of the sympathetic-parasympathetic system as the result of inhibition of the parasympathetic. The catatonic features may represent an intermediate stage before complete fixation of the pupil occurs.

CHAPTER TWENTY-FOUR

Principles of Psychotherapy in the Psychoses

Some years ago there was brought to me a 25-year-old girl who complained that men were watching her on the street. These men, she believed, were sent by her father and wanted to rape her in order to make her free of her nervous troubles. She felt depressed and wanted to kill herself. On the insistence of her family, I started with hypnotic treatment, although the diagnosis of paranoid schizophrenia was well established. The patient did not go into a deep hypnosis, but she soon felt better. During the hypnosis she trembled all over, and finally confessed her love for the physician without ever being aggressive. From that moment, her symptoms disappeared completely. She expressed insight into her symptoms. An attempt to analyze the transference to the physician was not made. The patient was dismissed with full insight, capable of working. Love for the physician remained as the only symptom. The patient remained healthy for about two years. She worked successfully in a candy store. She did not make an erotic adjustment and remained without sexual satisfaction. After two years

Appeared originally in *The Psychiatric Quarterly*, 5: 423-431, 1931.

she started to have paranoid ideas. I did not treat her at that time. The man who conducted her treatment was thoroughly competent, but psychotherapy was without any effect. I saw the patient in the clinic with a full-blown paranoid schizophrenia, full of delusions, mostly of a sadistic type. It was impossible to make contact with her.

We may ask ourselves, "What has happened?" We know that hypnosis is one of the methods by which we get transference, which is given quickly and in a great amount. The difficulty with hypnotic transference is that we never know what is going on in the patient and therefore sometimes have difficulty in handling this transference. It is an unanalyzed transference. The patient's sexual fantasies were seemingly attached to the physician in the course of the hypnotic procedure, and her psychotic activity was converted into love for the hypnotist. Generally we do not dismiss the patient from psychotherapy as long as the transference is in full strength, but I was afraid that the symptoms would come back in a case like this if I were to lessen the transference. Of course, from the beginning it was not a full recovery, otherwise the patient would have been able to find a love object for herself, but it is nevertheless astonishing that the patient not only relapsed after two years, but was also resistive to any attempt at psychotherapy.

In what way do the first and second attacks differ? Was there a greater amount of libido invested in the pathological symptoms in the second attack, or was the second attack more severe because the libido was immovably fixated in the symptoms? I am almost inclined to believe the latter was the case. At the beginning of the disease, the point of fixation, the early pathogenic events in life, already existed and libido was invested in them, but, still, this libido was movable and could be shifted to the physician. In the later development, the invested libido could not be shifted. But certainly there is also the possibility that we deal with differences in the amount of libido invested, in other words, with purely quantitative factors. Whatsoever method of psychotherapy is applied, we use the libido of the patient. The amount of libido given to us is limited, and the quantity will vary according to the object libido that can be liberated. It seems that with the progress of a disease greater amounts of libido are invested in the early points of fixation and that the amount of libido at the disposal of the psychotherapy will be less and less. The limited amount of libido we can get from a schizophrenic patient is also a barrier in the psychotherapy.

Before we try to go more deeply into the question of psychotherapy of schizophrenia, some general remarks about the psychology of schizophrenia are necessary. In schizophrenia we deal with a very deep regression to the narcissistic stage of libido. With this deep regression there is also a regression of the ego ideals and of the superego. New identifications take place. New ego ideals are built up in a more or less incomplete way. Complications in the clinical picture arise because libidinal regressions and regression in the ego ideals are not complete. The patient tries to maintain relations to the world and tries to retain an object cathexis. He defends himself against every step backward to primitive sexuality and toward narcissism. Many of the phenomena are based on the attempt at recovery from the lower regressions. The individual tries to return to reality and to fully developed sexuality of the heterosexual type. The Oedipus complex is therefore often strongly revived in the beginning of schizophrenia, sometimes as an attempt to escape homosexuality, sometimes as an attempt to escape even lower levels of regression, such as the anal or oral levels. In psychoses of the schizophrenic type there is difficulty in coming into close heterosexual contact or, in other words, the transference is insufficient.

We know that hysteria, anxiety, obsessive neurosis, and compulsive neurosis have been called transference neuroses because the transference is easily established if one uses the correct passive and analytic technique. It is true that, in the typical analysis of a neurotic, we find not only a transference starting from the fully developed Oedipus complex, but also a transference of a more primitive or pregenital type. But there is no question, however, that an analysis is finally based on transference of the genital type, that is, the Oedipus complex. Only if the analysis is based upon a transference that is a repetition of the Oedipus situation, can we expect success. Of course, the earlier types of transference—anal, oral, and sadistic—will also appear, but it is not possible to base an analysis on them. Whereas in a neurosis the free association method is sufficient to procure transference, in cases of schizophrenia we usually have to use many methods. We may be friendly, reassuring; we may even give small presents, comply with the patient's wishes, openly show our interest in him and his problems; we may evaluate delusions and hallucinations from his point of view. We may then get a transference strong enough to make the patient talk and be interested in the whole procedure of treatment. At the same time we may revive more primitive types of transference—anal, aggressive, oral—and the patient may show the transference by offering feces or urine. We do not like it if the patient hits us, showing a transference and an interest in the world of a rather primitive and aggressive type, but, still, it may be progress in comparison with the deep regression of the catatonic stupor. We would nonetheless prefer that such a transference was expressed, not in action, but only in fantasy. This is only possible if the primitive transference is counterbalanced by forces coming from an Oedipus-situation transference. The first step in the treatment is, therefore, winning the transference of the patient in a more active way than in a neurosis. Hence, we enforce the object cathexis in the beginning of the treatment.

The second phase of every psychotherapy in neurosis as well as in psychosis is using the transference. In hypnosis where we get the transference very quickly, we may use it either to find out forgotten material or to educate the patient. In psychoanalysis of a neurosis we use the transference to dig out the early infantile situations that have been of importance in the life of the patient, and, in doing so, we revive all the early situations of the patient's life. At the same time, the ego ideal is dissolved and rebuilt again. Generally we do not use any active influence in rebuilding the superego of the neurotic patient. We are convinced that the neurotic and normal patients will rebuild an ego ideal by their own efforts. We do not have to help them. We also know that the strength of the ego plus the superego system is sufficient to prevent primitive material from coming out in actions that do not fit into the social order. With the schizophrenic, we cannot be so sure about all this. If we explain to a patient that he has homicidal impulses, he may agree and, because of the weakness of the ego plus the superego system, may act accordingly.

In the second phase of psychotherapy, we have to ask ourselves how far the patient is able to stand the release of the primitive material. This is an important difference from the technique of the analysis of the neurotic. We also need to constantly reenforce the ego and superego of the patient. This is the third point in which the analysis differs from the analysis of the neurotic. In the neurotic case we hardly ever have the opportunity to order the patient to be more moral and not to let himself go too much. In the psychotic we need this principle of education. I do not believe that the ego in the psychoanalytic sense—I call it the perception ego—is primarily impaired in the schizophrenic. The difficulties of the ego in schizophrenia are the result of the breaking through of wild, primitive tendencies and the relative insufficiency in the synthetic power of the ego to correlate them, at least in the beginning. In the paranoid state there may even be an increased successful effort in this respect afterward. The ego especially lacks the help of a well-organized ego ideal. The ego is therefore impaired, and one has to help it by means of education, work, or occupational therapy. All these measures can be summarized by saying that the ego system has to be helped. Whereas in the neurosis there is a strong trend of logical thinking that we have to break into by the free association method, in schizophrenic psychoses a sharp distinction between the system of consciousness and unconsciousness will not exist. Conversation will often substitute for free association. If, instead of psychoanalysis, we use hypnosis or suggestion, no special techniques are necessary.

The third phase of psychotherapy in a neurosis is breaking the transference, and we are not satisfied with the treatment of a neurosis unless we have dissolved the transference. This is true in both psychoanalytic and hypnotic treatment. With schizophrenics we should not be so vigorous about dismissing a patient only when the transference has been broken. In many cases it will be necessary to keep the patient in some dependence on the physician and not risk taking this point of cathexis away from him. Psychotherapy that ends in an unbroken positive transference is certainly not a complete success, but in many cases we shall be glad to have a relative success, with transference remaining as the major symptom of the disease.

If we consider that in a psychosis there will usually be difficulty in the ego and ego-ideal system, we will see that what has been emphasized about schizophrenic psychosis will have some value in the treatment of psychoses in general. In the manic-depressive psychoses, besides oral regression, we deal with a change in the relation between the superego and ego. In melancholia, the superego is extremely severe toward the ego and the gap between the two is increased. In mania, ego and superego are united with each other. In melancholia, the individual is so much concerned with torturing himself that it is difficult for the therapist to get the necessary amount of libido. The severity of the superego will increase whenever new libidinal material comes to the surface. The severity of the superego has to be appeased or the individual has to be consoled, otherwise the danger of suicide will be increased. In this case we help the ego and the id against the superego. Because the danger of suicide may increase during analytic treatment, one has to watch the patient carefully in this respect. Other psychic treatment, like hypnosis and persuasion, are intended to help the ego against the superego. Whereas in melancholia it is sometimes difficult to build up the transference, it is easy to get transference in mania. It is very difficult, however, to keep it. The manic has the tendency to drop the love object. Only in cases in which the flight in ideas is not too far-going will it be possible to retain the necessary amount of transference. If psychoanalysis is done in the interval between attacks, no special technique will be necessary. In mental confusion, only psychic treatment that will lead the individual back to reality will be a help for the ego. Psychoanalysis will neither be possible nor necessary.

To summarize, we may say that the ego system (ego plus ego ideal) in a psychosis is more impaired than in a neurosis. Our methods of therapy will therefore have to help the ego plus ego-ideal system. Therefore, the methods of occupational therapy, education, and adaptation to reality will always be necessary. In persuasion and hypnosis we use specific methods in order to get the transference by which we can enforce our educational system. In psychoanalytic procedure the technique has to be different in the following points: (1) We have to enforce the transference; (2) we have to consider whether the material brought forth can be digested by the ego system; (3) we have to help the ego (melancholia) or the superego (schizophrenia) or the whole ego system; (4) we have to be very careful in the breaking of the transference. I have elsewhere (1927) emphasized these differences in the technique [see also Chapter 17]. Hinsie (1930) and Alexander (1931) have come to very similar conclusions. Waelder (1925) has rightly pointed out also that we have to direct the activities of the ego system of the schizophrenic patient in the direction in which his libidinal tendencies point, and it will be important to find out the part of reality that is easiest to reach in the patient. Since we think that the point of fixation in the schizophrenic is in the narcissistic sphere, it is not possible at the present time to reach this point of fixation with psychoanalysis. What we can do is remove conflicts belonging to the higher level of development, or, in other words, secondary points of fixation. We do not yet have statistical evidence concerning the results of psychotherapy in psychoses. But there is no question that we accomplish something in every case and that we cannot do without both direct and indirect psychotherapy.

Can we not re-enforce psychotherapy with somatic treatment? For many years I have been interested in a field I would like to call "pharmaco-psychoanalysis." Every drug that influences the central nervous system also changes the psychosexuality. If we put an individual to sleep we also change the structure of the libido and more primitive sexuality will come out. Kauders and Schilder (1923) have shown that one can help hypnosis by giving small doses of barbital or paraldehyde before one starts (see also Schilder, 1922c). The transference and the hypnosis are increased by the drug. Sedative drugs therefore have an influence on psychosexuality, bringing it nearer to the infantile sexuality of dreams and sleep, with the prevalence of a magic Oedipus complex. We know that intoxication with mescalin and cannibis indica can bring about psychic conditions that resemble narcissistic schizophrenic regression. On the other hand, acute cocaine intoxication brings a paranoid picture to the foreground. Cocaine intoxication is especially interesting because we know that after two or three months of drug addiction, heterosexuality and latent homosexuality may be converted to manifest homosexuality. On the other hand, homosexuality predisposes to drug addiction. There is at least the possibility that we could change the libidinal situation by drugs and that we can utilize this change for better transference and better education of the patient.

We know that Kläsi (1922) has inaugurated sleeping treatment of schizophrenics and excited manics. In this prolonged sleep, the individual regresses to a more infantile stage, becomes helpless, and seeks help. There is at least one psychological factor in such cures. I would not deny that something in deeper layers is going on that helps in a purely somatic sphere, too. By ether or sodium amytal, one can break the psychotic resistance for a short time and can get an increased transference. One should study the influence of opium, too, from this psychological point of view. What type of psychosexuality comes out in the opium dreams, and what is its relation to the point of fixation in melancholia? We should use drugs considering their psychosexual value. Psychotherapy and somatic treatment will not exclude each other, but will supplement each other.

Fever treatments are sometimes of effect in schizophrenic and melancholic patients. One also sees that somatic disease brings a sudden change in mental pictures. I would not like to deny that fever and somatic disease have only a somatic influence on the psychoses; fever and disease make the individual helpless. They bring the patient back to the situation in childhood in which he was craving for help and love from the parents, and this changes the whole libido situation. But disease also brings with it the fear of death, and here there may also be an important motive for the individual to strive back to reality. At any rate, if there is an artificial or natural state of weakness in the patient, psychotherapy will meet another and probably more favorable distribution of libido.

What we know about the psychotherapy of the psychoses is still in its infancy. That we have so far underrated its possibilities, there is no question. Even the ruthless forcing to occupation and work, as Simmons has done, may have considerable effect. We have not yet sufficiently utilized group treatment. We have not sufficiently utilized psychoanalysis. But whatever we do, we need psychological understanding of our patients and must evaluate the psychological implications of our procedures. Only psychoanalysis can help in this full understanding; even if we do not psychoanalyze a patient, we are better able to handle him if we know something about the deeper structure of the neuroses and the psychoses.

CHAPTER TWENTY-FIVE

The Scope of Psychotherapy
in Schizophrenia

Schizophrenia can certainly be considered an organic disease.
There are findings in the cerebral cortex which at least suggest
an organic basis. Changes in the spinal fluid have been described.
The whole course of the disease makes an organic background
at least probable. But we must not believe that an
organic disease cannot be provoked by psychic causes and
cannot be influenced in a psychic way. We can understand any
organic disease from a psychological point of view, especially
organic diseases of the central nervous system. We can explain an
intoxication with drugs by saying that psychic changes of a particular kind are taking place, describing the intoxication in purely
psychological terms. The question of whether or not schizophrenia is an organic disease has to be separated from the question of
whether or not we can understand psychologically what is going

Appeared originally in *American Journal of Psychiatry*, 11: 1181-1187, 1932.
Read at 87th Annual Meeting of American Psychiatric Association, Toronto, Canada,
June 1-5, 1931.

on in schizophrenia. Even if we believe in a pure psychogenesis of schizophrenic pictures, we have to reckon with a psychic and a somatic situation. But even if we were to suppose that schizophrenic symptoms represent a regression, this regression proceeds to such deep layers that we may even consider this very primitive psychic nucleus of schizophrenia in terms of an organic change.

Psychoanalytic investigations have so far failed to show what the fixating events and facts in schizophrenia are. This means that we do not know any specific events in the early childhood that cause schizophrenia. We are therefore justified, when going into the question of psychotherapeutic changes in schizophrenia, in asking about the general problems concerned in the psychic treatment of organic conditions. When we are dealing with a stabilized organic defect, we find that we can help the patient to help himself. Let us take the instance of a man who has lost his leg. Physical recovery may be supposed to be complete. There are many psychic problems to solve for the person who is crippled. We may help him to solve these problems by a kind of psychotherapy, but besides that we may help him by methods that help him to use his prothesis in the right way. Exercising parts of the body not directly involved will have a considerable effect. This exercise may result in hypertrophy of other parts of the body. We know that, in tabes dorsalis, exercises or any compensation therapy can be of considerable help even if the organic process as such is not touched at all. It is partly a better utilization of sensory impressions which have not been utilized correctly before. At the same time, by this therapy we influence the patient's psychic attitude. We have so far mentioned three principles of psychotherapy: (1) psychic adaptation; (2) organic utilization; (3) organic change of compensating organs.

So far, we have dealt with an unchangeable organic defect. But there certainly are diseases of a different type. In order to make the situation simpler, we shall take the example of a person who acquires epilepsy through a head injury. We know that any kind of excitement can provoke an epileptic fit. We can educate the individual to avoid such situations. There may also be some unsolved unconscious problems. By analyzing these conflicts, we can remove this source of excitement and, thus, one of the sources of the epileptic fit. It is probable that by avoiding further epileptic attacks, or at least diminishing them, the conditions for the healing of a lesion will be improved. We also have to consider that the tendency to epileptic fits probably increases with their repetition. The result of psychotherapy under such circumstances would be (4) that psychotherapy can prevent reactions in connection with the stable organic lesions; (5) psychotherapy can help by diminishing unfavorable reactions. To use a metaphor, psychotherapy takes away energies that are necessary to put pathological brain mechanisms into action. One sees, however, in the case of epilepsy, that conditions are still more complicated in that the vegetative nervous system has an influence on the genesis of the epileptic fit. Psychic influence of the vegetative nervous system has an influence on the genesis of the epileptic fit. The flow of energy we remove by psychotherapy is certainly connected with somatic changes which take place.

Psychotherapy may be used to make special efforts of an organic function possible. In Parkinsonism we see that under psychotherapy, especially hypnosis, the functions improve considerably, although only for a comparatively short time. The influence here may be either directly on the organs affected or it may work through the substituting apparatus. We would therefore have (6) the influence on the organic function in a direct way and (7) the influence on the organic function in an indirect way. One sees that these problems are more complicated when we deal with a function or an excitation instead of a simple loss, as discussed above. Thus, in the case of tabes, we deal with a problem very similar to the influence of hypnosis on Parkinsonian symptoms.

Every process in the body is dependent upon the blood vessels, which in turn can be influenced to some degree through the psyche. There is thus at least the possibility that psychotherapy can cure an organic process, either reparatory or inflammatory. The influence can even go so far as to change the conditions for a bacteriological infection. According to Heilig and Hoff (1928), it is possible to provoke a herpes by suggestion. It is, of course, very difficult to prove that an organic process has been influenced in a psychic way, and it is necessary to be very critical in any single case, but we are justified in thinking that there may be a psychic influence on organic processes. (8) Psychotherapy can create favorable circumstances for the recovery of an organic process. (9) Psychotherapy can prevent unfavorable influences. (10) Psychotherapy can have an immediate curative effect on the organic process. (11) Psychotherapy can influence the immunization processes directed against the virus.

The symptoms of carcinoma of the stomach are certainly not an immediate expression of the organic process, but are dependent on the personality of the individual, on his reactions to pain, and on his psychic state. There is a great question which symptoms in any disease are obligatory and which symptoms are not. The hysteria we so often see at the beginning of multiple sclerosis is an exaggeration of the same problem. Since the organic process does not make symptoms as such, but only changes the reactions, the symptomatology of organic processes will be largely dependent upon the psychic constellation. Acute and chronic changes will therefore bring about different symptomatologies according to the patient's various attitudes. When the patient has an opportunity of adapting himself, the actual symptomatolgy will probably be much less than in a case where there is a steady progress of organic change. We therefore have to reckon with the fact that (12) the symptomatology of an organic process will largely depend on the patient's psychic attitude.

In theory, every organic process or every organic defect can be influenced in a psychic way, but it is a matter of experience how much we can do with the limited energies we are able to manipulate by our psychotherapeutic measures. Some of the emotions of life are stronger than the emotions we can provoke and utilize in psychotherapeutic measures. There are the great conversions, the miracles done at Lourdes and, last but not least, great love. But even so, there are limits. The lost leg cannot regenerate, and there certainly are organic processes which are beyond the reach of psychic influences.

How far the psyche influences a specific organic change is an empirical question. There is at least the possibility that we could define the process of schizophrenia in a correct psychological way and proceed to cure the psychological difficulties. But we are far from this final psychological solution of the schizophrenia problem. We do not know what early events are the basis for the development of schizophrenia. We know that these events should be in very early childhood and should be specific. Although we do not hope to reach by our measure the real point of fixation in the psychoanalytic sense, we do hope to reach secondary points of fixation—events closely connected with the early traumatic scene but not identical with it. An illustration will make it clearer. We know that the increase of impulses by striopallidar nigra lesion may provoke an increase of destructive tendencies, which may lead to sadistic impulses and, when attached to the mouth, to oral sadistic impulses. Anal tendencies may also be expressed in a similar way. If we can analyze the early childhood events in such cases, we shall not change the increase of impulses immediately, but may change the flow of energy in an indirect way. The increase of impulses may finally be changed, too. It is a great question how we can apply this knowledge to our schizophrenic cases.

The difficulties in determining the success of our therapeutic measures are considerable. At first we have difficulties with the diagnosis, especially in the early or acute cases. We have to reckon with the fact that schizoid reactions are more common than we suppose. I do not think that these schizoid reactions are identical with the process of schizophrenia. At any rate, they disappear either spontaneously or under rather superficial therapeutic measures. One often meets, especially in this country, the tendency to identify the so-called schizoidia with schizophrenia, but, as far as we know, schizoidia is a comparatively stabilized reaction pattern, whereas the reaction patterns in schizophrenia are changing with the progress of something lying deeper. The schizoid patient, even if not treated, or preposterously treated, will not deteriorate. If one chooses one's material as one should, in early or acute cases, the difficulty in making a diagnosis is still greater. But even if one is assured of the diagnosis of schizophrenia, it has to be emphasized that nobody at the present time is able to give an exact prognosis in schizophrenic cases. This pertains to the scientific question whether and how far schizophrenic processes can be changed or not.

But we have to reckon that among schizophrenic cases are many in which the process of schizophrenia is mild or no longer progresses. We may deal with a scar, and especially the paranoiac symptomatology is an effort toward recovery. In those cases, even if we do not change the scar, it will often be possible to help the patient to a new adaptation. Not only paranoiac cases offer such possibilities. It will often depend on the acuity of the organic processes which one of the possibilities mentioned above will be realized in the therapeutic procedure.

Since we do not believe, as I have mentioned before, in a sharp borderline between organic and psychogenic (the organic is something psychological of a very primitive structure which we cannot understand completely), it is clear that as long as we do not have any reliable somatic therapy, we have to use our psychotherapeutic procedures. It will depend on the whole structure of the case whether we can try to come near the organic process and whether we shall use methods which lead as near as possible to the primary psychic conflicts, that is, the psychoanalytic method. Whenever the transference situation allows that, we should at least make an attempt of this kind. I will not go into the details of the psychoanalytic approach in these cases.

I have already emphasized that the technique differs in the following way. We have to reckon with a weak ideal-ego system in the schizophrenic. We have therefore to ask whether what is brought forward can be handled by the superego. Since the ideal ego is weak, we have to help the superego and the ego system. Since the transference is difficult to get, we have to try to help the transference.

But even in cases where a psychoanalytic approach is not possible, we can help the individual to adapt (according to 1, 2, and 3). Occupational therapy, fitting surroundings, milieu therapy, will be of the utmost importance here. It will also be possible to remove factors which provoke excitement and therefore pull the patient strongly back from reality (4). It is possible that even those measures will influence the process of the disease (8, 9, 10, 11). But the psychic influence may also change the appearance of the organic disorder (6, 7, 12).

One sees that psychotherapy is obligatory in every case of schizophrenia. The general principles involved concerning influencing organic changes have to be applied carefully with regard to the specific problems of schizophrenia. It is difficult to apply statistical methods to the problem of therapeutic results in schizophrenia at the present time. There is no question that one can do a great deal for the schizophrenic patient, but it cannot yet be decided whether we cure the schizophrenia or whether we help the patient to a better adaptation to reality and to his life problems.

Discussion

Dr. William A. White (Washington, D.C.)—Mr. President, Ladies and Gentlemen: I don't think Dr. Schilder's paper ought to go by without some mention. It is in a sense an epoch-making sort of presentation because Dr. Schilder has crystallized in a very clear way, and in a few moments, a process that is going on in our field of medicine and in all the rest of the fields of the biological sciences—that is, wiping out a lot of the old distinctions between mind and body and organic and functional, and so on, in order that what shall happen will be probably that we will get back to more fundamental principles and be able to come forward again to still higher levels than we were ever able to do under the old formulations.

Just as the organism as a whole has now been accepted very thoroughly, so it seems that we now must have to accept the lack of clear-cut diffentiation between organic and functional. And so long as we must accept that lack of clear-cut differentiation, we have no right to say that a therapeutic approach from the side of the psyche is incapable of affecting any changes we ordinarily call organic. We have no right to say that until we have undertaken it, tried it out, and found it to fail.

It is the same situation again that we have with reference to heredity. So long as we are willing to project all our difficulties upon heredity, we have a fatalistic philosophy which results in doing nothing. So long as we are willing to call things organic and, by that, mean that they cannot be changed, we have the fatalistic philosophy that does not admit of any kind of therapy unless it be the enucleating type of therapy of the surgeon.

So here we have really a new note of hope in conditions that are at least malignant, whether we wish to call them organic or not, and certainly there is already sufficient evidence to make us believe that this new note has not been struck in vain and that there is something in this point of view, something stimulating, something worthwhile to follow up, and that we have no right to come to any conclusions about it until it has been thoroughly worked out.

Dr. Schilder (closing)—There is one point which perhaps should be stressed, and that is that with our psychological methods today, we are able to understand much more than we did before, and even in the cases of organic destruction, like general paralysis, we see many psychological mechanisms and many psychological functions, and we are no longer right when we say that what we cannot understand is organic and what we can understand is functional. Organic diseases may make understandable symptoms. We can help better when we can understand.

This is not only an important theoretical question, but also a practical one. I was very glad when Dr. Hinsie emphasized the possibility of a somatic approach. I have experimented with ether, and there is no question that remembrances and attitudes one cannot get in psychotherapy can sometimes be obtained with the help of a narcotic. Maybe we come deeper into the psychological layers when we use the help of somatic methods.

I emphasize the somatic part in the genesis of schizophrenia because I hope that we shall gain most for our patients by approaching them from the somatic and the psychic side at the same time [see also Schilder, 1928b, 1938a].

CHAPTER TWENTY-SIX

Psychological Considerations of Insulin Treatment in Schizophrenia

The treatment of schizophrenia by insulin in doses that provoke shock has proved its value (Sakel, 1935; Sakel and Pötzl, 1938; Wortis, 1937a, 1937b). The large series of cases collected by Max Muller (1937) and the Viennese Clinic, where the method originated (Dussik, 1935), give unmistakable proof of the efficiency of the method. The European cases have been observed now for several years and the relapses are seemingly infrequent. The experiences of Bellevue Hospital about which Wortis (1936, 1937a, 1937b; Wortis et al., 1937) has reported are favorable. It seems, therefore, that, for the first time, an efficient method for the treatment of schizophrenia (Glueck, 1936) is at hand. The camphor treatment of schizophrenia, introduced by Meduna (1936), seems

Appeared originally in *The Journal of Nervous and Mental Disease*, 88: 397-412; 644-660, 1938. Leo L. Orenstein, co-author.

to be another successful pharmacological approach. It has not been as widely used as the insulin treatment, but reports published so far look promising.

When the first favorable reports of insulin treatment were published in this country, the Committee on Public Education of the American Medical Association issued a warning concerning undue optimism and protested especially against the impression presented by newspaper reports that other reliable methods for the treatment of schizophrenia were at hand (*JAMA*, 1937). "It is hoped, and may prove to be a fact," the warning said, "that the so-called insulin shock treatment for dementia praecox will find a useful place among the forms of treatment for dementia praecox, but its exact value has yet to be determined . . ."

These statements are somewhat misleading inasmuch as they convey an incorrect impression concerning the efficiency of other methods used in the treatment of schizophrenia. The leading American institutions believing in the psychogenesis of schizophrenia have never published statistics to prove their contention that psychotherapeutic methods are of a decisive value in the treatment. Whereas we do not doubt the value of psychotherapeutic procedures in schizophrenic psychosis [see Chapter 24], the number of cases in which long-lasting psychotherapeutic cures are effective is limited. Obviously, a specific constellation is necessary for the psychological influence on the organic process of schizophrenia to become decisive. The number of such cures in diagnostically clear cases is so small that it is almost impossible to find any statistical proofs for the efficiency of psychotherapy in procuring cures of schizophrenia. The New York State Hospital system can be credited with a far-going understanding of the psychological problems involved in the psychotherapy of schizophrenics. Nevertheless, the number of schizophrenics in hospitals has not changed in an appreciable way. Psychotherapy doubtless helps almost every schizophrenic patient in his adaptation to circumstances (Hinsie, 1930), but in the majority of the cases, this help is more or less symptomatic and does not lead to an adaptation to reality that makes an independent life possible.

The basic psychological conflict of the schizophrenic is obviously connected with the organic character of the disease and is only rarely accessible for the psychological methods at hand. It might be that psychological methods become more efficient when there is some preparation of the organic sphere to receive the psychological influence. The results of sleep treatment as introduced by Kläsi (1922) may be considered from this point of view. Although they are not overwhelming, the results in some cases are obviously good (Witt and Cheavens, 1936). Maybe some possibility could arise by which one could increase the psychological influence on the organic process. It is true that psychoanalysis proper has been used in only a small number of cases. Intensive group treatment has not yet been used. The question arises, to which organic layers can the psychological treatment of schizophrenia progress. The other problem, corresponding to the first, deals with the psychological changes and their meaning produced by the organic treatment. Such questions are not merely theoretical. They may sooner or later lead to changes and innovations in technique.

One obviously has to keep in mind that every organic structure, every change in the psychological structure, has a definite meaning from a psychological point of view, and that every organic change affecting the brain carries with it a definite psychological set (Schilder, 1937a).

The first psychological problem to offer itself is what is going on in insulin shock. Dussik (1935) reviews his own cases and the experiences of others by saying that, at first, slight somatic symptoms (vasomotor symptoms, tremor, slight sweating) appear. With the increase of the somatic signs, the patients move into a state of apathy which becomes more and more similar to normal sleep. Sometimes the psychotic manifestations become outspoken in this phase; sometimes they disappear. Later on, excitement may prevail or sleep may occur until the patient falls into a deep coma. Epileptic attacks sometimes take place. Epileptoid twitchings are common. In the phase of awakening after the ingestion of sugar, local symptoms like aphasia or more general symptoms like perseveration may occur (Dussik and Sakel, 1936). Such symptoms may also be present during the coma. Immediately before the awakening, states of excitement occur which are connected with violent restlessness, tossing, and, according to Dussik, with choreo-athetotic movements.

Benedek (1935) carefully studied the influence of insulin shock upon perception. He observed disturbances in the perception of movements similar to those observed by Pötzl and Redlich (1911) and Goldstein and Gelb (1920) in occipital lobe lesions. His Case 1 complained that the movements of other people had become machine-like, as if interrupted. Instead of an uninterrupted movement, the patient saw the object first in one and then in the other place. Quick movements were particularly disagreeable. After awakening, he experienced the world as very beautiful. Another of Benedek's patients saw everything turning around, people seemed to turn ten to fifteen times in the air. A third patient saw the room increased in length, with people at a great distance and appearing small. One person seemed to turn around and incline; another looked like a mirror image. Another patient saw the nurses relatively smaller, sometimes thinner and sometimes fatter, and still another patient reported about megalopsia. Primitive optic hallucinations were observed. Colors were sometimes perceived as less impressive during the shock, but appeared more saturated after the shock was over. Benedek further observed that during insulin shock the caloric reactions were changed. He also reported dysarthrias and pareses in the bulbar muscles. L. von Angyal (1937) studied the motor phenomena during the insulin shock and observed tonic phenomena, which he referred to the frontal lobe. Pisk (1936) observed a patient who experienced an acceleration in the flow of time.

A psychological theory concerning the mode of action of insulin therapy has to carefully consider what is going on during and immediately after the shock. Bychowski (1937) and Glueck (1937) reported that patients awakening from insulin shock showed great dependence on people around them. We want to emphasize that the question of the psychological theory of insulin treatment has nothing at all to do with the problem of whether the insulin acts as a physiological or as a psychological agent. The data at hand make it evident that insulin acts as an organic agent. Nevertheless, the psychological problem as such remains.

Our own investigations derive from material that belongs to the Bellevue series already mentioned, by Wortis, Bowman, Orenstein, and Rosenbaum (1937). Patients were observed carefully during the insulin shock and were examined concerning their speech faculty and their tonic and clonic phenomena, as far as the general plan of treatment allowed. Furthermore, the patients were urged to copy the gestalt figures so extensively used by Lauretta Bender (1938) in developmental psychology and in psychiatry [see Plate 1, p. 155). These are figures Wertheimer (1923) used in order to demonstrate gestalt principles. The advantage of using such figures lies in the fact that they are well known in relation to psychiatric entities as well as in child development.

Case 1. A 48-year-old paranoid schizophrenic was sometimes deeply depressed and then rather inaccessible. On June 21, 1937 he was stuporous three hours after the injection. However, he answered simple questions and was capable of naming his thumb and eyebrow. In copying the gestalt figures, he exaggerated gestalt principles. The angle was substituted by a curve, a dotted line by a straight line (see Plate 7, p. 323; figures 3, 5, 8). The disturbance was so marked that he made out of the three small circles of figure 2, a straight line which was curved and brought nearer to the vertical planes. Figure 6 underwent a particularly extensive transformation by a crossing of two approximately vertical curves. Of particular interest is his copy of figure 4 in which the open curve and the open quadrangle are closed, separated from each other and reversed in their spatial relations. A few days later the patient was given, immediately after the shock, figures 3 and 4 to copy, and very similar features occurred. The patient obviously drew with difficulty. He counted, in figure 3, how many lines he should make, but still added more lines. During another insulin shock on June 29, 1937, he merely perseverated and answered to everything with his name, and spelled the single words. It was remarkable that the patient did not show any motor phenomena in the proper sense during these shocks. He lay quietly and did not even seem to be in a deep coma or sleep. The protocol of July 1, 1937, which was taken after he got the sugar water, was particularly interesting. He found a word for nose, but called his eyebrow "handkerchief" and pencil also "nose." At this time he showed a very outspoken catalepsy in the arms. He found the names for ear and eye, but perseverated, calling a pencil a "fountain pen" and a watch "ears." In the meantime, his thumbs were brought into a position as if he would show them. He kept them motionless in this cataleptic position. Finally, he found the name for the thumb and said of a fountain pen, "Is that a pen?"; he named a watch correctly. After initial difficulties, he succeeded in copying figure 4 (see Plate 8). In figure 3, the angles were again substituted by a curve. The patient was then completely awake. He still had figure 4 before his eyes and copied it perfectly (also the motor performance was much better). He was asked to copy figure 3 from memory and, interestingly, produced a still stronger emphasis on the curve. The patient said that he recollected that he kept his thumb up, but did not know why he did it. He had no recollection of the beginning of the examination, at which time he was stuporous. On another occasion the patient said, when coming out of the stupor, "I recollect nothing, I come out groggy, I don't know where I am." Needless to say, the patient was capable of drawing the gestalt figures when fully awake; he was generally amiable on awakening from his stupor.

Many of the features of this case were typical. The following we believe were the most outstanding:

1. Difficulty in perception and naming of objects was identical in the stupor and after awakening.

2. There was a general retardation in reactions. However, there was a particular difficulty in naming objects.

3. Perseveration was outstanding.

4. Cataleptic phenomena have been observed.

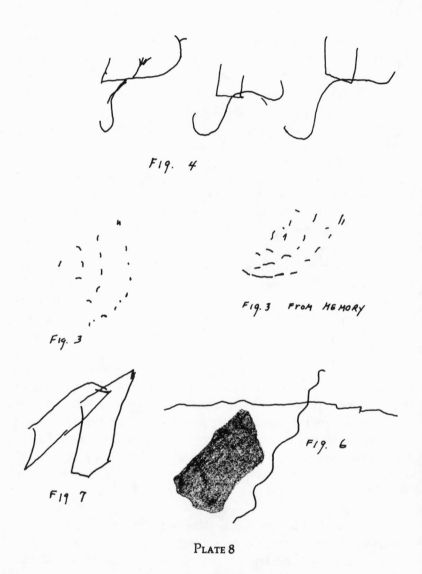

Fig. 4

Fig. 3

Fig. 3   From Memory

Fig 7

Fig. 6

PLATE 8

5. The visual motor gestalt patterns were of a particularly primitive type. Perseverative features appeared too. The difficulties in motor execution were probably due to the general motor weakness during the stupor.

6. The memory concerning the experiences during the stupor was incomplete.

7. After awakening, the patient showed generally a more friendly attachment to his surroundings.

Case 2. A nineteen-year-old hebephrenic, immediately after the interruption of the shock, was in a state of empty playfulness and agitation. He was boisterous, but it was very difficult to get him to draw. Astonishingly his drawings were then done with meticulous care and with hesitation although, in spite of his care, they showed primitive features with elimination of angles. The patient denied any memories during the stupor and the phase immediately after it. However, he was very glad to recognize the examiner. No aphasic signs have been observed in this case, which merely further illustrates the previous observations.

Case 3. A young man, age 23, a hebephrenic, had been in treatment a long time, showed marked lack of interest, and heard voices. In the beginning of the coma he was often excited, tossed around, and shouted. There was a picture of empty playfulness. He said, for instance, "Do you know what they tell me what does Christ?" "Christ, oh my, will you please shut up?" "I love you." He occasionally repeated words he heard from the examiner, found the word for nose, but called the eyebrow "nose" too. He tossed around, spit, shouted, and was manneristic. After much urging he could be prevailed upon to draw and showed primitive separation in gestalt drawings and an enormous tendency to perseverate with an almost unlimited prevalence of circles. The patient said, "I don't feel so good when I awake. I don't feel like drinking the sugar water. The time does not pass so quickly. The doctor's all right." The patient was moody and did not show any deeper attachment to the physician.

This case adds to our knowledge as follows:

8. During the state of excitement, homosexual transference, otherwise hidden, tended to come out.

9. The state of manneristic restlessness went hand in hand with deep disturbances in the perceptive functions.

Case 4. A young girl, age 24, showed problems similar to the previous case during stupor. She generally complained that she was either not alive or half dead. In the phase of excitement she shouted, "Why don't they go slow, they touch my behind. Help! Help!" She showed great interest in the physician and said, "Kiss me now, you are so nice looking." "Why don't they just touch me red?" Asked for the name of the thumb, she said, "My finger." (Nose?) "My finger. (Fountain pen?) My finger. (What do you see?) My fancies." When the magazine *Women's Home Companion* was shown to her, she read the title correctly and named the picture of a boy correctly, saying, "Faig me, oh God, faig me."

10. In this case an anal erotism, which was otherwise not present, came out during the excitement.

11. As in the other cases, there were definite aphasic signs and difficulties in perception.

It is obvious that during the excitement erotic elements of schizophrenic structure come into appearance. Whether these are merely activated by the hypoglycemic shock is difficult to determine. At any rate, in their structure, they correspond to schizophrenic manifestations.

This leads to a discussion of more complicated cases.

Case 5. A young woman, age 24, had a severe obsessional neurosis which consisted chiefly of obsessional thoughts concerning the penis and her mother's coffin. Long objects reminded her of both. When awakening from the stupor she showed the following reactions: (Nose?) "Nose (Thumb?) Straight finger, right finger. (Eyebrow?) Eye. (Eyelashes?) Eyebrow. (Pencil?) Pencil. (Eyeglass?) Eyeglass. (Thumb?) Eyeball finger. (Little finger?) Great finger. (Cigarette?) Cigarette." Patient said spontaneously, "My foot, my big toe nail feel so numb." She had great difficulty in drawing and said herself, when figure 3 was shown to her, "Dots, I can't I am so numb." Ten minutes later she was capable of drawing the figures almost correctly, although there were some primitive features still present. While drawing, she said she had less fear now; a few minutes later she found the name for nailfile without any difficulty. She explained calling the thumb "straight finger" by saying, "I am so much afraid of straight objects. I recognized you all along. My hands and feet feel numb."

This patient was very much improved when the insulin treatment was brought to an end.

11. She gave an objective description of her previous symptoms. The symptoms had lost their power. However, there was no increase in insight into the meaning of these symptoms.

The case is mentioned here chiefly in order to bring forward one more specific point:

12. Individual material may color the aphasic mistakes.

The patient gave the following description about her awakening: "When one awakens everything is queer in the room. People's faces look hazy, everything in the room is changed." She did not report any particular feelings concerning the physicians and persons around her when she awakened.

13. The patient experienced haziness of perception and a general change after awakening.

Case 6. A twenty-year-old rather empty hebephrenic girl had vague ideas of persecution. The insulin shock ended with a state of anomia. This was more outspoken in regard to parts of her body than for other objects. There were strong tendencies to perseveration. At first she called everything a key. When her nose was pointed to, she said "hold"; when her finger was touched with a pin and she was asked to name the finger, she answered "prick." After a few minutes she found the name of "nose." (Why did you call it a hole?) "Because there are the nostrils and you were holding my nose." She found the name of her thumb then. (You called it a prick?) "Because you were sticking my finger with a pin. (Why do you call all things a key?) Because you began by holding up a key. (Did you recognize me?) Yes, I know your face." A few minutes later the patient was euphoric and denied having made any mistakes. She had also forgotten her interpretation, but said, "Sometimes I make a mistake."

14. In spite of the patient's denial, it was obvious that sexual material that she otherwise repressed came out in her paraphasic mistakes. She generally did not want to talk about sex. "It is far from being interesting."

The patient was seen and interviewed often immediately after the coma. Her reactions were basically always the same. She said after awakening, "I feel a little dizzy, it was a deep sleep. (Did you have nice dreams?) No, just deep sleep. (How did you feel before you fell asleep?) I just felt a little dizzy. I know immediately where I am and what I do. Sometimes I have not chosen the correct word that I have to use. Later on I get hungry."

Toward the end of the coma the patient showed interesting tensions. The arms went into a flexion and the legs into extension; the jaws were tightly closed so that she was in danger of biting her tongue. She perspired and salivated profusely. There was extreme sensitivity in the muscles toward stretch which was answered by rigidity. Her head was mostly turned to the right. The tensions were changing. After awakening she showed lively postural reactions to turning of her head. The flexor and extensor tendencies in the legs completely disappeared. The gestalt function could not be examined immediately after awakening, but a few minutes later showed typical slight disturbances which soon cleared up completely.

These investigations are not primarily concerned with the motor phenomena discussed by Angyal (1937). However, it is important to state that we have not seen any case in which typical pyramidal spasms were present. The hypertonus has the character of rigidities one sees in cases of prefrontal lesions. Phenomena of grasping and sucking are not uncommon. Angyal is indeed inclined to refer the motor phenomena observed in the insulin shock to the frontal lobe. Such an interpretation, however, remains doubtful since similar phenomena have been observed by Bender and Schilder in alcoholic encephalopathy in which the localization of the lesion is chiefly periventricular [see Chapter 14]. There is no doubt that one deals with a general lesion of the brain in insulin coma and only with difficulty can one single out specific parts of the brain. The extrapyramidal motor system is obviously more strongly affected than the pyramidal system. However, the Babinski sign and epileptic seizures common in our observation series give proof that the motor area of the cortex is affected too. The complaint of dizziness after awakening was very common. As mentioned, Benedek has described clear symptomatology of vestibular character in and after insulin shock. He has also shown that the reaction to irrigation of the ear is fundamentally changed in many of these cases.

Case 7. A 31-year-old, artist was the first of a group of more complicated cases in our study. He felt that his soul was dead and that he was a living corpse. He reported about previous spiritual experiences which did not recur. He had given up working, but had remained generally rather amiable. The insulin treatment, which had been going on for several months, had made him a little more quiet and contented but had not changed the basic structure of his behavior. It was characteristic for him that when he approached deep coma he became wildly excited, grimaced, tossed around, and made gestures that were partially playful and partially threatening. No real attacks occurred. Soon after awakening he was bland and agreeable again. During and after the stupor it was very difficult to make him name objects or draw. After one stupor, for instance, he recognized a pencil. When eyeglasses were shown to him, he said, "Barber Seven." He named a watch "monocle," and named a handkerchief similarly. He afterward named nose and eyebrows correctly, but delayed in responding. When the thumb was shown him, he said, "That's an eye," then "finger," and then "thumb." He then recognized a handkerchief. His drawings showed the characteristic tendency to perseverate and the reversal to primitive forms of gestalt. It was particularly characteristic that he drew slanted lines that curved back instead of the small circles of figure 2, and he even failed to keep within the plane of the drawing paper (see Plate 7, p. 323). Very similar results were reached repeatedly. He never showed neurological signs in the narrower sense. He often said, while copying, "all right, all right." When somewhat more alert, he started to count the dots by little circles. Once, during such an excitement, he persistently called his nose "or," but found the name for the index finger. When he was completely awakened he did not know anything of his antics, but reported that when he awakened and looked at something, the object seemed to remain quiet. Later on, everything seemed to move slowly, "like in a slow motion picture. People move slowly, and you move slowly yourself. I want to speed it up. Also my heartbeats follow each other very slowly." By way of comparison, the patient was able to determine that he experienced time between two heartbeats as about eight seconds, "also my breathing is slow. It seems very long till movements become faster again. The space is not changed at all. The faces of the people and the colors don't show any difference."

The patient had no memory for his state of excitement, and, as far as can be determined, his state of excitement in which he made quick violent gestures corresponded to when he experienced the slowing down of time. After awakening he did not show any particular sympathy or fear concerning the people around him.

Of particular interest in this case was the time-sense disturbance. No disturbances in the spatial relations were present. We do not know whether there is any case described with such pure time-sense disturbances. In hashish intoxication, space disturbances are mostly combined with the time-sense disturbance. Pisk (1936) has reported a case in which time passed much quicker during and after insulin shock. However, the space was changed in this case. Based upon observations of Hoff and Pötzl (1934), he comes to the conclusion that one deals with a parieto-occipital *"Zeitraffer"* effect due to an insufficient interaction of the two hemispheres, and he quotes as proof pyramidal-tract signs which changed from one side to another (Babinski sign).

15. Time-sense disturbances of a different type have been observed; this case showed a "pure" time-sense disturbance consisting of a considerable decrease in the speed of the flow of time.

16. Time-sense disturbance and states of violent excitement can coincide. The memory of the excitement can be absent.

Von Pap (1937) quotes one case who felt as if his whole life had passed during the insulin shock—as if sleep had lasted several days or a week. According to our observations, many patients appreciate the time spent in the insulin shock correctly and others underrate and overrate it. It is doubtful whether the appreciation of time spent in the insulin shock and the more general time-sense disturbances are identical.

Case 8. A patient, age 32, for several years had been complaining that he did not experience things in the right way. It was as if he were more or less dead. He said that he could not concentrate and he had given up his teaching a long time before. He was clear, oriented. The diagnosis was doubtful, though it may be that one dealt here with a severe neurosis or schizophrenia. He reported about the insulin shock in the following way: "When I fall asleep, the book blurs, a white light comes and I fall asleep. I have difficulties in articulating when I awaken." He reported that before awakening he felt he had to struggle in order to come to consciousness. One protocol on the 27th of June is given here. It was taken immediately after he had sugar. He named eyeglasses correctly, but called the thumb "digit." He named the ear correctly. He picked up words like "fingernail," which he heard. He said, "What am I to distinguish from?" He got irritated and said: "I am doing the talking." He named a red pencil correctly. He called the eyebrow a "black pencil" and the same for an eyelash and wrist watch. When questioned, he said, "I do not need drink of water of." When asked to name the thumb, he said "thumb of." He moved his arms and hands in a manneristic way and said again: "Digits, digits." The next day he had a vague memory that he had talked about digits and a red pencil.

On the 30th of June, upon awakening from coma, he was in a state of great apprehension and indecision. He looked at the nurse, who was wearing street clothes, and said: "The first decision was with the lady. The decision had to do with the door, whether to get the door open or to get something to eat. I am telling you I had to decide whether the predatory instinct or the instinct of equalization is paramount." He was very circumstantial and had difficulties in formulation. (What has that to do with the lady?) "The lady was to identify. I don't know which one. Her passing was a cue, cue of getting out of the cue. She moved swiftly, passing the bed. (She had indeed passed the bed while walking through the room.) She symbolized something. I had to come to the conclusion which power is paramount. I desire the equalization force. To be powers. The colors of her dress meant something violent. Colors, colors meant the predatory instinct. I had to decide on a principle. Dr. R. was the equalization idea and the lady was the predatory instinct. I had to decide between the two, in which one to put my faith. Otherwise, I would not come out of the coma."

On the first of July, in the beginning of the insulin coma, he was found grimacing, fussing, and was manneristic. He said, "I have lost my chance." He grabbed for the examiner's eyeglasses, saying, "Are these my eyeglasses?" He repeated, "I have lost my chance." He showed great difficulties in talking. He did not name any objects or parts of the body. He was continually pouting, almost sucking. There was no grasping.

There was another patient in our series who reported that he had the feeling that he struggled in order to come back to consciousness. This patient (Case 8) combined this fear of not coming out with an ambivalence of a decidedly schizophrenic character. Is this an activation of schizophrenic trends which otherwise are not present? And is the patient in reality a schizophrenic? Such questions cannot be decided yet. Sakel (1938) has stated that when the acute phase of schizophrenic psychosis has passed and the patient is clinically better, the psychosis may be reactivated during hypoglycemia. Von Pap (1937) follows him in this opinion. Muller (1937) is doubtful about this interpretation. He thinks that the insulin provokes psychosis of its own, of a type different from the schizophrenic types. If this patient should really be a schizophrenic, it is at least possible that schizophrenic manifestations become more outspoken when the whole organism is in an upset state. The probably schizophrenic Case 4 experienced hallucinations of a schizophrenic type for the first time during the hypoglycemic state. We do not think these occurrences are very common, although it seems that there are at least some cases in which phenomena of this type occur (activation of schizophrenic symptoms).

17. States of empty, almost playful excitement and fussiness occur. They are not of schizophrenic type and are entirely due to the hypoglycemic state.

18. In some cases schizophrenic symptoms occur. Probably, but not definitely, they are an activation of the schizophrenic psychosis.

Case 9. An eighteen-year-old patient with a severe schizophrenic bewilderment heard voices and was afraid that she might be eaten up by rats. She was also afraid that her mother might be killed. Sometimes she talked about mad dogs. She showed decided negativistic attitudes mixed with fears. She was often cataleptic. When awakening from the stupor, she showed disturbances in the gestalt function as seen in the other cases. After many days of treatment, she became freer immediately after the insulin coma. In the insulin shock, there were often extrapyramidal tensions, especially in her right arm. Awakening from the coma, she often showed a great attachment to the physician who treated her.

When she was entirely free of symptoms, the following protocol was taken: (Think all right now?) "Yes. (But dogs will bite you again?) No, they won't. I don't know where I got that from. (Hear voices?) No. (Thought there was poison around?) I don't know where I got that idea either. I guess my imagination went astray. (Like your mother?) Of course. (First remembrance about your mother?) She was very good to me all the time. (How many boy friends?) Hardly any. (Masturbate?) No. (Remember I took you twice to the lecture hall?) No. I don't remember that. (Remember you were stiff?) I don't remember that. (How feel when get injections?) I don't know, they were all right. I feel swell after them. (Sometimes got excited, what about?) I guess about the mad dogs. After awhile I did, but later on after the injections it left me. (How long does time seem when get injections?) I don't know. It seems quite short. (Afraid when people moved around you?) No. (Ever want to go bed with a boy?) No. (Will you ever?) No. (Why?) I don't know. (If married?) Then it is O.K. (Anybody you want to marry?) Not yet. (Nice to be married?) I don't know. (What dream of?) I don't dream anything. (How long here?) About three months. (What do at home?) I don't know. Guess I go out, rest up, have a lot of fun."

This patient was considered recovered from a clinical point of view. It is true she had formed comparatively good attachments when awakening from coma. However, the psychosis did not help her at all in coming to an understanding of her vital problems and her symptoms. The psychodynamics of her symptoms are as little understood as in the beginning. The patient showed some degree of emptiness. The whole picture had some similarity to pictures one sometimes sees in cases of general paralysis.

19. The improvement in these cases has not been effected by an increase in insight.

Case 10. A woman, age 35, showed a classical schizophrenic paranoid picture. She felt influenced in her sex parts by remote control and experienced orgasms which she otherwise was not able to achieve. The picture was slightly improved before the insulin treatment started. Under the insulin treatment the psychosis cleared up completely. She recognized the illusional and delusional character of her experiences and recognized that she had had hallucinations. The patient was inclined to make a connection between her psychosis and her frigidity. However, no deeper-lying material was revealed by the insulin treatment. She did not experience her past psychosis as a revelation. (The voices had accused her of being bisexual.) Everything was distant afterward. "The treatments have helped me. The ideas were not entirely gone when I started. I didn't have any dreams during my sleep. I knew that the sleep lasted two or three hours. When I woke up I could not pronounce names—I could not enunciate them. I knew where I was and I was not afraid of anything."

It is remarkable that this case also did not get any deeper insight into her psychodynamics following the insulin treatment, although she was an unusually intelligent person with a good insight into psychodynamic relations in general.

20. Psychodynamic insight is not increased by hypoglycemic therapy.

Case 11. A 35-year-old woman had a schizophrenic episode in which she felt she might be under a voodoo spell and was particularly afraid that her family might be hurt. "When I imagine something, I can see it very clearly. I could see these things, and I could just see my family practically mangled. I had an idea people were aware of the things I was thinking about. It seems as if every thought I had was being broadcasted." The patient had had several love affairs, with satisfactory intercourse. "While I was under treatment I always noticed that for two hours, between eight and ten, I had a very free feeling in my head. I felt relaxed. For the remaining part I felt very miserable—very blue, very depressed, and very hungry. When I was in the coma, I had difficulties in finding words. I felt like I was going through various stages, like going through prisms and also through stages of my past life too. I was sort of semiconscious. (What did you remember particularly?) Well, about when I was working recently—my job, my home, walking around where I had been living. (Did you repeat your sex experiences too?) My mind did not seem to dwell on it especially, it was also vague. When I came to, I was always relieved about it being over. (How did the time pass?) Very slowly; it just seemed to last an awful long time. When I finally woke up, I found myself in the same room. It seemed to be like years. (Did you recognize the people around you?) No, I don't think I did. I don't think I was aware of what was going on in the room. I did at times think they seemed to come closer, the various people. Dr. O. and the nurses. I felt the doctors were trying to help me. I just had the feeling that if anything should happen they would know what to do. I always had the fear of going into the coma and dying." The patient still had some doubts whether voodooism might not harm people. This idea, however, was not of a delusional character. The patient could be considered recovered after the treatment, although she, too, was rather flat in her emotions. Her insight into psychodynamics was obviously not increased by the treatment.

21. The contents of the psychosis become pale, do not seem important, and are not considered a valuable part of her inner life.

Case 12. A woman, age 26, had a schizophrenic picture in which the delusion of being the child of rich and influential parents played the most important part. During the treatment she reported the following sensations: "It is difficult to get up. My hands are numb. They go to sleep, it is painful. I dreamt about my home town, going to a party in Petersburg, Va. It is a small town. I could not remember names and faces. It took about half an hour. Yesterday it felt as if it would have lasted several hours. When awakening it is almost as if there would be a spasticity around the mouth. The tongue is protruding. My God—I cannot swallow."

The following protocol was taken on May 21st: (How do you feel?) "Just a little dizzy. (Know immediately what is going on?) Yes. It takes a little while. A few minutes. (What happens in these few minutes, can you find the words?) No, it is hard. I think while coming out of the unconsciousness. (Recognize people immediately?) Yes, in about five minutes or so. Yes, it is just hard to talk. (Feel people want to do something to you?) Yes. It is just a sick feeling. (Time passes quickly when you get insulin?) I don't know. You mean in the coma? I don't know. (Do you know approximately how long you were in the coma?) I think about two hours. It feels like two or three hours. (Did you awaken very hungry?) Yes, that is the main thing. (Where did you feel the hunger?) In the stomach. (Anywhere else?) Maybe it is in the head, I don't know. (What about the sex feelings?) You don't have any feeling in the coma. There aren't any sex feelings. (Feel you like anyone particularly?) I don't feel hostile toward anyone. No, I never had any special sex feelings when I woke up, I have to watch for it. You are so tired and hungry."

When the treatment was finished at the end of June, the patient reported: "After awakening you feel rest and comfort. I like the nurse, but had a hostile attitude toward the doctors. I thought they treated me unjustly. I was hungry. I did not know immediately where I was. The people looked like statues and moved stiffly like automatons. I knew the persons around but I could not remember their names. This happened after every severe coma. They moved as if made of china. They might have been smaller and thinner. The bed shrank in size. A feeling of unreality. The nap of the blanket looked soft and white. The nightgowns became pajamas and vice versa. The patterns changed and there were little circles instead of squares. I felt like dying and the doctor helps to bring you back."

This patient was obviously helped in her recovery by the discussion of the family situation and of some psychological mechanisms. However, a feeling of insecurity remained. She felt inferior because of her education, which she considered inadequate. The comparatively small amount of insight into the psychodynamics was due merely to the talks she had with the physician. It is remarkable that this patient showed, in the phase of awakening, a rather typical depersonalization concerning the outside world (derealization). Time-sense disturbances were present in some degree. Her form disturbances were rather typical. She also showed difficulties in orienting herself and in finding words. Her emotional attitude after the insulin shock consisted mostly of relaxation, with an increase in friendly feelings toward the physician. This physician had also given her psychotherapeutic help. At the end of the treatment the patient still showed an emotional instability, still complained about her lack of education.

22. The positive transference after awakening is often mixed with fears, apprehensions, and a suspicious attitude.

23. After awakening, this insecurity is closely allied with a picture of depersonalization with optic disturbances in a sense of micropsia.

Case 13. A 25-year-old man gave the following protocol when he was in a remission following a course of treatment. Patient was clear and oriented. He said that he had a nervous breakdown and was brought here. When he came he had pain in his stomach and felt that he might have a child. Since his brother's marriage he has had less opportunity of seeing him, and he would like to be together with him much more. The patient said that he did not then know the difference between a man and a woman, but he knows now. He did not draw any conclusions of a psychological nature himself, and accepted with good-natured skepticism the interpretation of the physician that he wanted to be the wife of his brother: "Who said that? That is crazy. Take it away. Don't put it there. Oh, that's nuts. Take that out. Oh, you are off."

He further said that he had a million other crazy ideas. He felt that the hospital would be blown up and that there was a chain gang, but he used the term "white slavery." "The people were sent out to rob stores. (Is that right?) Yes that is what I thought. That was a long time ago. (What do you think about it now?) That is all crazy. (What did they bring home?) I don't know what it was. **(Did you think the chain gang would sell you?) No. It was** something like a chain gang. (You didn't think they would sell you as a woman?) No. I said something about a slave gang. Not a white slave. Maybe I was supposed to be the head of it. (Maybe you were supposed to be sold as a woman?) I don't know where you got the nerve, where you put it in there as my brother's wife. That is crazy. Don't mix anything in about my brother. That is absolutely crazy. (What else did you experience?) I cannot remember. (How did you feel when you got the injections?) I lay in bed as a rule and read for a while. My eyes would not concentrate anymore. I would sleep, I guess, after that. (Can you remember that you have all these ideas during the injections too?) No. (Did something move before your eyes?) No. All those dreams were during the period I probably had a relapse. (Do you like Dr. W.?) Yes, very much. I didn't at first. I didn't like his suit at first. The brown suit.

"I thought there was something wrong with my stomach. I looked at his suit, and it was all fuzzy in the back. I wondered whether my stomach is all fuzzy on the inside like his suit. (What has your stomach to do with his suit?) It was that type of suit that was all fuzzy on the back. (Did you have any ideas that maybe he was a fairy?) Who, the doctor? No. (Your stomach was fuzzy at that time because you thought a child was in it?) I got some other dreams too.

"I used to swallow a pit, and I used to think a grape vine would grow in my stomach. It just so happened, I didn't like the fuzziness on his brown suit. (Did you think the fuzziness of your stomach came from his brown suit?) No, I didn't see how a person could buy such a suit. (Did you think that something from his fuzzy suit had gone into your stomach?) No. His suit just sort of made me think of my stomach. There was really no connection, when I saw the fuzziness of his suit."

[The underlying idea is that he felt that something from the back of the physician's suit had grown into his stomach so that one deals with an anal fertilization fantasy. The fuzziness is a symbolization for the semen.]

(Has anyone else in your family a fuzzy suit, a brown suit?) "My brother has a brown one. I picked a piece off from Dr. W.'s suit. I told him his suit was falling apart. I told him it was all raggy. Dr. W. will have a fit if you talk about his suit. (What else did you imagine?) I don't know. (Afterward you started to like Dr. W.?) I liked Dr. W. He is a nice fellow. That is all. (Have any other dreams?) I get a dream every day. When I come out of the hypoglycemia. (What?) That is pretty bad. I don't know. You think you are being electrocuted as a rule. You think that there is a certain word you should probably say or something you should do to get out of it, but you don't know what it is. Sort of searching around, trying to find it. (Always have these dreams of electrocution?) No, it is just that you are limp when you come out. You feel you are rather helpless, and you realize it when you come out. I never had any dreams while I was under the hypoglycemia at all."

[During another interview the following was elicited:]

(Ever been afraid since here?) "No. (Why come here?) I was confused. (How?) In several ways. (What did the voices say?) I don't know. (Did they threaten you?) No. (What did you hear, what did they say?) I am not sure about that, whether I was hearing voices or not. I used to talk to people the same as I am talking to you now. I don't remember any particular thing that they said. (Think people hate you?) No. (Think somebody wanted to do something to you?) Yes. (What?) I don't know. I couldn't understand that. (Cut you to pieces?) No. (What did you think they wanted to do to you?) I couldn't understand that. (Threaten you?) Well nobody wanted to threaten me. No, I don't feel that the world is threatening to me. No sir."

(What else were you confused about?) "I was confused about a lot of things in general. (How feel now?) I don't feel so good right now. (Why?) I don't know. I guess the treatment. (What do you feel after you get the injection?) You get sleepy after awhile. (Fall asleep after the injection?) Sometimes after, yes. (Is it an agreeable sleep?) Sometimes it was and sometimes it was sort of dreams. You seldom can remember those dreams when you wake up. You don't know whether you are alive or asleep."

(Did you see something?) "No. (See beautiful girls or huge animals?) No. (What dream about?) I don't say that they were dreams, you see everybody moving around in the room. Then you sort of see the different people coming in and out. You are just sort of semiconscious. Like when you walked into the room. (Who did you think I was?) I thought you were a doctor. (Last time when I talked to you, you were agitated?) I don't remember being agitated. I remember waking up, and you asked me what I was afraid of, and I was not afraid of anything at that particular time. (You started praying, do you remember?) No. (You remember saying Jesus help me?) That is a short prayer. Jesus, Mary, and Joseph. (Then you clung to Dr. W. and asked him to help you?) I don't remember any of that. (Feel that you may need help when in this state?) I think so sometimes. You don't know what it is all about. (Is one afraid of something?) When you are like that sometimes you can't breathe and sometimes you feel funny. Sometimes your head feels like it is doing almost anything. The back of your head feels funny. I don't know, your head seems to be in a funny shape, when you wake up. It feels funny."

(Sometimes have feeling that people want to do something against you?) "No. Those were some of the ideas I used to have. (What?) I don't know; become suspicious of people. (Think they wanted to do something sexually to you?) I don't know if it was that or what it was. (Think they wanted to kill you, cut you?) I don't think so. I am not sure just what it was all about. (Think they wanted to make a woman out of you?) No. (You felt you were suspicious of people?) Well, suspicious as anybody would be suspicious. (I am not suspicious.) I am not suspicious, that is, the way I was. I didn't have any conclusion what might be done to me. (How do you feel now?) I feel tired."

The discussion reproduced above is very characteristic in that the patient was not prepared to consider psychoanalytical contents experienced during his psychosis, although the associations came freely. He knew that his idea of being pregnant was one that was not objectively correct, but he was not able to see the connection between his relation to his brother and his fantasies. He was also unable to see the relation of the transference situation to the brother. His attitude to the interpretation was an objective attitude and was less of an emotional resistance than an impersonal refusal to believe in these things. His attitude to the psychosis, which was past, is rather unusual in schizophrenia. One finds this more in some confusional states and particularly in organic states. The patient afterward relapsed again, but eventually recovered and was discharged.

The patients discussed so far did not experience their previous schizophrenic ideas as a part of their personality. The question remains whether this objective attitude concerning the hallucinations and delusions should be preserved in the patients or whether, sooner or later, the psychiatric and objective insight should be substituted by analytic insight.

The associations of the patient in the course of these interviews made psychoanalytic approach and interpretation easy. The homosexual love for his brother was transferred to the physician and came into the foreground. However, the patient refused the psychoanalytic insight and developed rather strong negative attitudes toward the physician who tried to give him such insight. This antipathy remained after the treatment was finished, at which time the patient showed an objective insight into his psychosis. The psychosis had lost its value completely for him. He by no means considered it as revelation. The treatment as such did not help him in an understanding of psychodynamics.

24. One almost has the impression that this insight into psychodynamics was better when he was psychotic.

25. Our cases indicated, moreover, that objective insight was not reached completely in cases that did not clear up completely.

Cases not influenced at all by the insulin treatment show, of course, a typical schizophrenic attitude concerning their symptomatology and view the insulin shock objectively without interest. Very often one can't get any description of their experiences.

The purpose of this communication is not merely descriptive. The problem arises, what does the insulin shock mean from the point of view of psychology, and, furthermore, does the psychology of the insulin shock give any hints concerning the mechanism of the recovery process in schizophrenia under insulin therapy?

The insulin hypoglycemia obviously deeply influences the whole central nervous system. It seems that its beginning is not so very different from sleep and therefore has an influence on the sleeping center in the ventricular gray area of the brain. It is obvious that when the dosage is increased, sleep is substituted by coma, and, probably, all the centers of consciousness down to the medulla oblongata are more or less involved. In motility, there is evidence of a slight impairment of the pyramidal-tract system (Babinski signs). However, the bulk of the symptoms point to lesions in the apparatuses for extrapyramidal-tract rigidities. They obviously are of a type which one sees in the lesion of the pre-frontal area and of the subcortical gray areas. However, not only is subcortical tonicity released, but there are twitchings of epilepti-form character and fits that are not different from epileptic fits. We are of the general opinion that these are irritation phenomena originating from the motor area involving also the extrapyramidal cortical and subcortical apparatus. Our investigations do not give any proof for the theory proposed that the dominant hemisphere is affected first and stays so longest. We have observed the oc-currence of paresis of pyramidal-tract character. As the coma pro-gresses, the reflexes finally disappear. It seems almost hopeless to come to an exact classification of these motor phenomena.

In addition to neurological phenomena in the narrower sense, motor phenomena frequently occur, which seem to be partially voluntary. The patients toss around, make all kinds of threatening gestures, try to jump out of bed, turn around, groan, grunt, purse their lips, move their tongues, salivate, howl, grimace, clutch, tear pillows apart, and show all kinds of more or less violent manner-isms. In some cases, patients express anxiety in connection with this state of manneristic excitement. Not all patients show such states. They may occur before, during, or even after the interrup-tion of the coma. Sometimes it appears as if they could be stopped voluntarily. One of the patients was tossing around after inter-ruption and asked, "Did I get the sugar water?" He stopped his antics when he was reassured in this respect. In patients who become quiet in the insulin coma, catalepsy may be present. Thus, for instance, in a case of catatonic excitement, whenever psycho-logical examinations are possible during the so-called excited states, they show a deep disturbance in the perceptive faculty. This will be discussed in more detail later on.

This manneristic syndrome occurs in cases which otherwise do not show any trace of it. The conclusion might be drawn that this syndrome in schizophrenia has at least an organic background, a conclusion the more probable since Parker, Schilder, and Wortis have observed a similar syndrome in severely alcoholic Negroes [see Chapter 16]. They concluded that this syndrome is an attenuated form of alcoholic encephalopathy and postulated that its pathology is to be sought especially in the subcortical extrapyramidal motility. However, it is worthwhile mentioning that the disturbances in consciousness and in the gestalt function are much more outspoken in the insulin shock than in the motility syndrome of alcoholics. The motility syndrome in schizophrenics is generally not connected with disturbances in consciousness. Here it is almost impossible to differentiate the so-called organic from the so-called psychological disturbances.

If there were any doubt that cortical apparatuses are also involved in insulin shock, one could point to the aphasic symptoms that occur so often just after awakening. The aphasia is, of course, colored by the presence of the disturbance in consciousness. However, there is a decided difficulty in naming objects. The difficulties in naming parts of the body are generally more outspoken than the difficulty in naming objects. Some patients complain about difficulties in finding individual names. A strong tendency to perseveration, which shows the typical features, is outstanding. It is astonishing how quickly this aphasia can clear up. The patients uniformly remember that they could not find words. One patient found only the Hungarian word for nose. Others substituted for "thumb" the more general term of "finger" or "digit." In some cases, complex material determines the paraphasic reaction. The aphasia is never isolated. It is connected with a deep disturbance in the gestalt function. The disturbances in the gestalt function can be characterized in the following way:

1. Tendency to perseveration.
2. Substitution of the dot by circle and loop.
3. Substitution of an angle by a curve.
4. Substitution of a dotted line by a straight line.
5. Change of angles into straight lines.
6. Bringing slanted lines nearer to the vertical.

7. Exaggeration of primitive gestalt principles and separation of gestalt units in space.

8. Transgression from one plane to another and reversals of 180 and 90 degrees.

These gestalt-function disturbances appear as a combination between gestalt disturbances observed (L. Bender, 1938) in toxic, infectious, and organic confusion and in cases of sensory aphasia. On the whole, the gestalt disturbances add another probability for a lesion of the temporal, parietal, and occipital lobes. We conclude, therefore, that the functions of large parts of the cortex are also disturbed by insulin shock.

It is difficult to understand the time-sense disturbances in these cases. Two fundamental problems have to be separated. The one is how long does the patient experience the duration of the shock. There is obviously no regularity. Some experience the duration of the shock in an appropriate way and to some it seems to last a long time, while to others it seems to last only a short time. The same variation has been found in purely psychogenic gaps in memory in amnesias (Abeles and Schilder, 1935), and the conclusion that the final appreciation of the duration of a shock is dependent upon complicated psychological factors, which are not immediately dependent upon the physiological changes provoked by the insulin shock, can be allowed.

Some patients, toward the end of the shock and at the beginning of awakening, experience either an acceleration or a retardation in the flow of time. These experiences remind us of the phenomena observed in intoxications with hashish and mescal. They obviously have an organic genesis which cannot at the present time be brought into connection with specific apparatuses. Pisk (1936), however, concluded that an occipital lesion accounted for his case of time-sense disturbance in the insulin shock, and refers to observations of Hoff and Pötzl (1934) on local lesions of the brain. The observations of Benedek (1935) also speak for such an occipital lesion. He noted disturbances in the visual perception of movement, a phenomenon which, according to Pötzl and Redlich (1911), has to be referred to the òccipital lobe. The metamorphopsias observed by Benedek and ourselves belong in the same category. It is remarkable that derealization is also observed in some of these cases. This speaks for the correctness of Schilder's assumption (1914) that the occipital-lobe lesions and depersonalization symptomatology have much in common.

After the insulin shock, most patients feel more relaxed, freer from anxieties, and ready to have a greater confidence in the persons around them. Hypomanic attitudes are not uncommon during insulin shock. Many patients feel danger and uncertainty, and they experience a struggle against the unconsciousness which means death. Phenomena of ambivalence may occur.

These are the data, and it is obvious that the psychology of insulin shock is the psychology of an individual with a severe organic disturbance of the central nervous system. Personal material taken from the individual life history appears obviously only toward the beginning and the end of the shock. The shock appears to the patient in two aspects. It is a complete escape and a complete withdrawal. It is also a threat of death and complete annihilation. It is obviously the second part that has the greatest importance. The individual struggles against this danger and rejoices when it is over. The psychology of the shock is in this respect rather similar to the psychology of the epileptic fit. It seems that the danger of the shock in its organic massiveness supercedes all the other dangers in connection with schizophrenia. The way seems to be cleared, after the shock is over, for an attitude of confidence in the person who is nearby—the physician or the nurse. "Overcoming the danger of organic destruction" would be in some way the motto of insulin shock. Psychological formulations of this type are clumsy because they give comparatively little help in differentiating this organic danger from any other organic danger.

One perhaps might compare the attitude of the schizophrenic during insulin shock with that during the epileptic attack or with the attitude of a person who suffers from fever or is under the influence of drugs. Fever and drugs have indeed been used in the treatment of schizophrenia. Even high degrees of fever do not lead to such deep disturbances in consciousness and do not show such signs of a universal impairment of brain function. The therapeutic results of fever treatment in schizophrenia have not been satisfactory. The treatment of schizophrenia with narcotics instituted by Kläsi (1922) has produced only limited results. In these patients, the disturbance in consciousness cannot be driven as deep as in insulin shock. Furthermore, the signs of an influence on the cortical apparatuses is missing. It is perhaps interesting to point to the fact that the reports about metrazol treatment of schizophrenia, in which severe epileptic attacks are produced, are very optimistic.

One would conclude that the great depth in the disturbance of consciousness and an involvement of cortical and subcortical structures are of importance for the therapeutic results on the schizophrenic process. This formulation is independent of the question whether the insulin shock acts immediately on the central nervous system or by metabolic intermediaries. In the final analysis, the central nervous system has to be influenced in order to change a disturbance that appears in the psychological field. The severity of the disturbance in the cerebral function as well as its distribution has to express itself in the psychology of the shock.

It seems reasonable to postulate that a physiological agent with a specific effect on the mental disturbance should express itself in a specific psychological picture. This, however, is not true; the effect of fever therapy on a paralytic process cannot be anticipated by the study of the general paretic under the influence of fever. Physiological curative agents can therefore express themselves in psychological terms, but do not necessarily do so.

This discussion of the psychopathology of the patient during insulin shock may help us to a deeper understanding of the patient's attitude toward his psychosis after he recovers as a result of this therapy. The attitude of the schizophrenic when his psychosis has passed without organic therapy has been studied by Mayer-Gross (1920) and Bertschinger (1910). Schizophrenics may experience their psychosis as a great revelation and an important part of their lives. They may try to push it aside as something uncanny. They may try to forget it completely, or they may see it as a symbol of a life which has to be realized. When we treat the schizophrenic psychologically, we try to give him an increased insight into his own problems and into the situation he has to face. One may characterize this procedure by saying that it gives him a deeper understanding of his emotional problems, and of the connection of the emotional problems to his symptoms, so that he is finally capable of using the psychic energies pent up in his symptoms for the purposes of everyday life. It is obvious that the insight into the psychodynamics of a symptom (we shall so designate the psychic causation of a symptom in connection with the inner life history) does not always help the schizophrenic patient. The schizophrenic often has a spontaneous insight into many psychodynamic problems. It helps him only when this spontaneous insight is directed by another person, and, even then, results are not very often obtained. When a patient is cured by psychotherapy he knows that his hallucinations and delusions were such and that he was mentally sick (objective insight). In addition, he has some knowledge of his inner life history and its connections with the symptoms (psychodynamic insight). When one has suffered from a cancer and has been successfully operated upon and cured, one may have a complete objective insight into what happened. A psychodynamic insight is neither necessary nor desired, even if it is assumed that there are psychological components in the genesis of the cancer—which is at least highly improbable.

In the cancer case and in the organic case in general, even objective insight is not indispensable. Although it is desirable that the patient should know about his having been sick, there is no absolute necessity that he should know that he had a cancer. In psychoses, of course, objective insight and the capacity to act according to one's insight is one of the criteria of recovery, and certainly the most important one. We would not expect more in general paresis. The patient knows that he has had ideas of grandeur, defects of memory and judgment. He therefore has objective insight when he is cured by malaria treatment. Psychodynamic insight is not possible concerning the majority of his symptoms and is superficial if present at all. Indeed, the attitude of the general paretic concerning the general paresis that has been cured is objective. He considers it an organic disease of no concern to the vital problems of his personality. He has not only objective insight, but also an objective attitude. It is in connection with this attitude that the patient is not very much interested in the details of his psychosis and intends not to care about it and wants to forget it.

One can venture the general statement that the schizophrenic patient does not gain psychodynamic insight by insulin therapy, but merely objective insight. His resistance against understanding his symptoms is in no way lessened by the insulin therapy. In one case the resistance against understanding was particularly strong, and the antipathy against the physician who had tried to give this insight was lasting. We may summarize by saying that the schizophrenic patient has objective but not psychodynamic insight into his psychosis when he recovers by means of insulin. Furthermore, he does not show any particular interest in the psychosis. It is not a great event in his life; does not reveal anything to him; it is merely an organic disease, something like a catastrophe coming from outside. The experiences of the psychosis become pale and unimportant. Furthermore, the patient does not change his general attitude toward life. He does not come out enriched by new insight. Indeed, one gets the impression of an emotional flatness. At least one or the other of the patients made a good social adaptation after the treatment was finished.

One is justified in saying that insulin treatment helps the patient return to his prepsychotic state. In psychoanalytic terminology, we might say it deflects libido from the symptoms and uses this libido in order to cement the forces of the ego. The dynamic forces performing this seem to come from a depth that is not merely what one usually terms psychological. It is a physiological change. The protocols clearly show the transference phenomena that played some part in this process of fortifying the ego against the id. However, as far as one can judge the quantity of such phenomena, they are far from overwhelming and are merely the reflection of deeper-lying physiological processes, the appreciation of which transgresses the psychological limits. The psychological experiences therefore speak decidedly in favor of the theory that insulin shock acts chiefly as a physiological agent. One should beware of generalizations. A suggestive treatment of any kind or a treatment that cures merely by transference also deflects libido from the symptoms and lets them appear pale, although one deals with a process we call psychological with our present nomenclature.

This psychological description contains everything we can say at the present time about the theory of insulin shock therapy. We may suspect that the enormous vital danger for the individual, experienced during the shock, provokes restitutive psychological processes. The regeneration put into motion in this way brings with it a regeneration in those spheres of the personality that seem to be less organically fixated. In other words, the shock acts on organic structures that are generally more crystallized and more rigid (psychologically in the periphery of the ego). The shock involves a regeneration of the organic sphere. The processes in these deeper-lying organic layers bring about a re-evaluation of the emotional problems that belong to a sphere nearer to the center of the personality, which is more plastic than the structuralized sphere constituting the periphery of the personality. These remarks are purely psychological. Sakel (1935) has evolved the theory that insulin therapy destroys the new faulty associations. This is not so very different from the remarks we have made.

The question remains which psychological treatment and how much psychological treatment the patients need in insulin therapy. This problem has come into the foreground through the investigations of Glueck (1936). The problem cannot be psychotherapy or no psychotherapy, since psychological factors are always present in the way we handle the patient. Reassurance and friendliness are psychotherapeutic measures, too, and there is no question that patients coming out of shock need such reassurances. The question, remains, however, how much understanding of his psychosis shall we try to give the patient. Shall we use psychoanalytic technique? It is understandable that at the height of the stress, deep-going psychotherapeutic measures will probably not be of any particular advantage and may even hinder the physiological consolidation. However, the patients who show improvement are frequently free from symptoms in the afternoons, and the possibility exists of discussing their psychosis with them. Sakel advises against such active procedure. Glueck seems to be generally more in favor of it, although he shows a high degree of cautiousness. The experiences at hand are not sufficient for a definite decision whether, and in which degree and when, active psychotherapy should be done with the patient. Sufficient evidence is present that active psychotherapy is not necessary in order to obtain the state of remission. Whether psychotherapy can prevent relapses is not known. Since insulin therapy alone does not increase the patient's insight, one feels that psychotherapeutic attempts that would better adapt the patient to the tasks of his life seem to be advisable.

Summary

A study of cases of schizophrenia treated with hypoglycemic shock was undertaken from a psychological point of view. Attention was given to the study of gestalt functions during and immediately after termination of the hypoglycemic state. Furthermore, the attitude of the patients toward their symptoms under the insulin treatment was considered. The following conclusions were reached:

1. Difficulty in perception and naming objects is identical in the stupor and after awakening.

2. There is a general retardation in reactions; particularly outstanding is the difficulty in naming objects.

3. Perseveration is outstanding.

4. Visuomotor gestalt patterns are of primitive type.

5. After awakening the patient shows a friendly attitude toward his surroundings; the memory concerning experiences during this stupor is incomplete.

6. During states of excitement, otherwise hidden sexual material, anal erotism, homosexual transference may appear. Sexual material may come out in paraphasic mistakes.

7. The state of manneristic restlessness is associated with deep disturbances in perceptive functions.

8. Time-sense disturbances occur, one case observed showed a "pure" time-sense disturbance consisting of a considerable decrease in the speed of flow of time.

9. States of empty, almost playful excitement, which are not schizophrenic in type, occur. They are due merely to the hypoglycemic state. However, in some cases schizophrenic symptoms occur, which may be an activation of the schizophrenic psychosis.

10. Recovered cases show objective insight but no understanding of psychodynamics. One frequently has the impression that the latter is better during the psychotic state. Complete objective insight is lacking in partially improved cases.

CHAPTER TWENTY-SEVEN

Notes on the Psychology of Metrazol Treatment of Schizophrenia

Meduna (1937) has introduced a treatment of schizophrenia by inducing convulsions. He first used camphor oil, which had to be given intramuscularly, and later on substituted this with metrazol, a preparation with slight chemical resemblance to camphor, and which is water soluble and can be given intravenously. The clinical results of this treatment have been satisfactory in his hands and in the hands of Friedman (1937).

Up to the present time (1939) we have treated around twenty cases in Bellevue Hospital. The number of cases and the duration of their observation are too limited to give a definite opinion about the clinical value of the procedure. However, our results in acute cases in which the disease had lasted no more than six months were uniformly excellent. One case relapsed two months

Appeared originally in *The Journal of Nervous and Mental Disease*, 89: 133-144, 1939.

after he was discharged. When the treatment was resumed, the symptoms disappeared completely after two convulsions. We do not yet know how long the other patients, who are now out of the hospital for three or four months, will remain free from symptoms. In most of these cases improvement came after the second or third convulsion. The symptoms disappeared after the fifth or sixth successful injection. In a case of three years' duration, a good remission started after the seventh convulsion. In other chronic cases and in cases previously treated with insulin the results were less satisfactory.

This communication is not concerned with clinical questions, but with problems of symptomatology and the psychology of induced convulsions and their aftereffects.

In the majority of cases the intravenous injection is followed in less than 30 seconds by the first twitchings, which are generally short cloni in the muscles of the shoulders and the hip. If the dosage has been insufficient, the short cloni (two or three) remain the only symptom. The cloni very often are preceded by cough. The patients feel as if electricity is playing all over their body. The sensation is extremely disagreeable. They may also have the feeling that they are about to be destroyed completely. Some cases experience an optic aura, and the room appears to be filled with dazzling white light. In some cases, there is a delay between this first phase and the tonic clonic phase. The time interval between the injection may go up to one minute and a half or two minutes. It is important that in this phase the patients are deeply confused. Very often they do not answer questions and have a completely empty look. The face shows the expression of deep anxiety. One of the patients always exclaimed, "Mother, mother help me." In such delayed reactions the pupils are at first mid-wide and react, but become stiff before the tonic clonic convulsion starts. In cases in which the dosage was insufficient or the injection too slow, the motor or sensory aura may remain the only effect. Some degree of confusion usually persists, which in some cases extends over several hours. The patients are moody, irritable, and negativistic and may show paranoid trends otherwise not present. One patient said, for instance, to the physician toward whom she otherwise has a rather friendly attitude: "You are nothing at all, you kill me." Such patients resist the next injection.

If the injection is successful the aura is followed by a tonic and clonic convulsion. Each phase lasts not more than 30 seconds. Very often the first sign is a tonic turning of the head and eyes to one side, the direction of which is determined particularly by the position of the head when the injection was given. The further phases of the convulsion are symmetrical. In the majority of cases, the arms are in extreme extension but extremely flexed in the wrists and in the fingers. The thumb is adducted. The legs are in extreme extension. In some cases, the extension of the legs is persistently anteceded by an extreme flexion in all the joints of the legs. They are then mildly abducted. The eyes are turned upward without any exception, mostly not straight ahead, but either to the left or to the right. During the tonic phase, without exception, the mouth is widely opened. Toward the end of the tonic phase it is vigorously clamped down and remains so, long after the clonic phase has passed. The clonic phase does not show any special features. The big toe often shows clonic dorsal flexions. During the convulsion the patients are flushed. There is obviously no regular breathing. Only rarely is the epileptic cry at the beginning of the convulsion present.

A period of complete flaccidity with diminished or absent tendon reflexes follows. At this stage a Babinski reflex cannot be elicited. Only the mouth is still clamped. Toward the end of this period, changing rigidities appear which are more outspoken in the flexors of the arm and in the extensors of the legs. At this stage it is possible to elicit foot cloni but no Babinski reflex. Isolated cloni may appear in any part of the body, and the patient may toss around. In the beginning of this phase the patient is bluish pale and his color returns, accompanied by irregular breathing. In some cases, slowing down of the pulse is present in the beginning. Without graphic methods, one mostly observes a rapid pulse up to 120. In some cases more or less severe arrhythmias have been observed. In men, emissions without erections are common.

While the patient is still deeply unconscious, a Babinski reflex appears, usually in both legs at the same time. Occasionally it is at first present only on one side. Without recognizable reason, the Babinski reflex may come or go on either side. The Rossolimo, Mendel-Bechtereff, and Oppenheim reflexes cannot be elicited as a rule. The Babinski reflex persists generally for three or four minutes. It disappears at about the same time as the clonus. During this period the complete lack of consciousness changes into deep clouding and tossing in bed.

In the majority of cases, the first reaction to the physician or nurse is a friendly one. Only one case, a deeply dissociated catatonic made threatening gestures toward the examiner. In one case with severe negativistic tension the period of flaccidity changed immediately into renewed negativistic tensions with the expression of great anxiety. In the later stages of the treatment the patient showed great friendliness toward the persons around him. The usual friendly attitude of the patient after the convulsion is at first clumsy and awkward, but later on becomes more articulate. They grab the hands of those around them, slap their arms or their back, and try to pull the person toward them. These reactions occur irrespective of sex, although heterosexual reactions are more outspoken. In some cases the friendliness increases to real advances toward the nurses and doctors of the opposite sex.

At first, the patients have difficulties in talking and speak only when urged to. Emotional phrases like "Leave me alone" are expressed comparatively fluently. One can make the patients name objects; in the majority of cases, they have much greater difficulties in naming parts of their own body than objects. Perseverations are frequent.

Of special interest are observations of a 35-year-old woman who had previously had insulin treatment, had recovered, and relapsed again. She showed considerable improvement after the second metrazol injection. After the convulsion she was asked to name objects. (Eyebrow?) "That is my back." When she was asked she showed her right hand. (Put your right hand on your left ear.)

"It's on the right, on the left side." She puts the right hand on the right ear. (Put your right hand on your left ear.) Puts her left hand on her left ear and says it's the right ear. When the order is repeated once more she again puts her right hand on her right arm, says: "no," and puts her left hand on her left ear. She is asked three more times and puts either the right hand to the right ear or the left hand to the left ear. She is asked to name more objects. (Eyebrow?) "That's my forehead. (Flashlight?) That's a powder puff. (Watch?) (Correct.) (Quarter?) (Correct.) (Clock?) (Correct.) (Candy, cigarette, money?) (Correct.) (Flashlight?) Clock. (Thumb?) Clock." Later on, "thumb." (Put your right hand on your left ear.) Puts her right hand on her right ear. Only after five demonstrations is she capable of crossing the midline and of putting her right hand on her left ear. (Flashlight?) "Fountain pen. (Flashlight?) Fountain pen. (Flashlight?) Something to test eyes. (What does one do with it?) You take your temperature with it. (Pencil?) Pencil. (Flashlight?) It is a pencil. You tell your temperature. You shine it in your eyes. They told my temperature." Repeats that several times. "You see I'm dizzy." (Crayon?) "Crayon." She repeats several times, when asked to name the flashlight, "That's a thing with which to tell your temperature. You put it in your mouth to shine in your eyes with a thermometer." At the same time she correctly names the electric light on the ceiling and a penknife.

After another convulsion she has the same difficulties in crossed movements even after they have been shown to her. She names a pen correctly. (Doctor's nose?) "My nose. (Doctor's thumb?) My thumb. (Thumb?) A thingabub. (Her thumb?) My hand. (Her eyebrow?) My forehead. (Her big toe?) My feet. (Doctor's thumb?) My thumb. (Doctor's thumb?) My little thumb. (Her big toe?) My little finger. (Doctor's little finger?) My feet. (Big toe?) My foot. (Watch?) Watch. (Big toe?) My foot. Gee, I don't know." After half an hour has passed she still complained of dizziness. She remembered that the watch was shown to her, that she couldn't find a word for toe, and that she couldn't do what she was told. When the examiner then showed her his thumb, she still said, "It's my thumb," but corrected herself immediately.

We can say that aphasic symptoms were observed after every convulsion. Paraphasias and perseverations were common. Emotional phrases were formulated better than other words. The aphasic phenomena disappeared in a quarter to half an hour. They did not impair the patient's euphoric attitude and her attachment to the people around her.

The fact that particular difficulties were present in naming parts of the body was the more remarkable since Stengel (1937) found that, in postepileptic dreamy states parts of the body can be named, as well as other objects, if they are personally meaningful to the person, whereas other objects cannot be named. It is impossible to say at the present time what this difference between the metrazol effect and the dreamy state of the epileptic means.

At the time when the aphasic disturbances are present the patients are also unable to copy simple gestalt patterns [see Plate 1, p. 155] (L. Bender, 1938). They tend to perseverate. In all cases, one can find the tendency to revert to primitive gestalt principles, as, for instance, the separation of rhomboid and circle in figure A, the separation of curve and open quadrangle in figure 4, the separation of the different configurations in figures 7 and 8. We find, furthermore, the prevalence of loops in figures 2 and 3, and the substitution of dotted lines by straight lines; the substitution of points by circles, loops, and filled-out ovals. There is, in addition, the tendency to closure in figure 5 and the substitution of simple forms by numbers. All these are criteria that prove, according to Bender, the deep organic disturbance of the form function. This is completely different from the disturbance in copying configurations otherwise observed in schizophrenia. The cases reported here were capable of copying correctly before and after the treatment. Even in cases in which disturbances in copying of configurations in the schizophrenic sense are present before the attack, configuration disturbances of the organic type can be observed immediately after the attack. The difficulties in copying the gestalt tests were parallel to the aphasic disturbances and cleared up, as did the latter, from one half hour to an hour after the convulsion. It is necessary to urge the patients to draw. Very often they are overmeticulous, try again and again, and repeat one test form several times.

It has been mentioned that patients often fear the injection. It is absolutely typical that they forget that they have received an injection in the phase of confusion. However, this amnesia does not persist, and about 45 minutes after the injection the patient remembers that he got an injection. A period of uncertainty often precedes the return of the remembrance.

Even during the period of confusion, a friendly attitude toward the persons around is prevalent, as mentioned above. Severe cases of catatonic stupor and catatonic anxiety may not show this friendly reaction after the first injections. The anxiety and the negativistic stupor return immediately after the severe neurological phenomena have passed. But in many of those cases the change to a friendly reaction after the injection becomes obvious later on. In the further course of the treatment, the favorable reaction extends over a longer time after the injection. Finally, the patient remains free from symptoms from one injection day to another. In two cases of long standing the patients became restless after the injection, wanted to leave the room and run into the corridors when allowed to do so. Even severe cases are easier to handle in the ward after the first few injections. Catatonic symptoms often disappear first. Paranoid ideas may remain. The paranoid ideas become paler immediately after the injection. Later in the course of the treatment they lose their importance in the intervals as well and finally, in the successful cases, disappear completely. This change is accompanied by considerable change in mood. The tensions disappear, the patients become amiable and friendly, even in cases in which the delusional and hallucinatory experiences do not disappear. The transference to the physician is crude and disorganized during the confusion state and consolidates into a real attachment, which becomes stronger after every injection. It does not disappear after the treatment is finished.

In the cases that came to treatment after the schizophrenia had persisted for several years and emotional deterioration had been present, the transference phenomena, although not absent, were more subdued. The patients did not form new hallucinations and delusions, they became doubtful concerning the validity of their previous experiences and finally came to an insight that they were sick, that they had had delusions and hallucinations. One patient, for instance, who had the fear that he might be crucified as punishment for not having told his friends that he was a Jew, said, "My fears were imaginative, my mind being playful, I made the story out of one or two remarks, it was all a lot of bunk in plain English. Now people look to me as they should look; before they looked threatening. (What did the voices tell you?) These voices were supposedly fellows. It was addressed to me indirectly. They spoke to each other. They were imaginations." Although the treatment gave the patient insight that he was sick and had delusions and hallucinations, he did not gain insight into his fundamental problems. The psychodynamics of his hallucinations and delusions remained unrevealed. We may say that he gained objective insight; however, he did not gain insight in the psychoanalytic sense. This was typical for the recovered cases. They did not show psychotic symptoms after the treatment was over. They knew they had had psychotic symptoms. They were sensible, were capable of planning for the future; however, they knew nothing about the problems reflected in their psychotic symptoms. They were full of interest in reality, rather elated, alert, quick in repartee. One often had the feeling of some underlying tension and rigidity. This picture was not fundamentally different from what one sees in schizophrenics who have been successfully treated with insulin shock. Those treated with metrazol seemed perhaps to be a little more elated. Even when they looked back to the treatment, they emphasized that they suffered by it. They complained that they had headaches, dizziness, and nausea. Some patients who had undergone insulin treatment as well as metrazol treatment reported that they became clearer much more quickly following the metrazol injection than following the interruption of the insulin shock. Cases unsuccessfully treated with metrazol still showed an improvement in their mood. They were more outgoing than they were before and took their hallucinations and delusions less seriously.

Summary

Whatever the psychology of schizophrenia may be, there is no question that it is different from the psychology of the epileptic attack. During metrazol treatment the patient at first feels threatened by the injection as such, but during the aura a much more fundamental threat is experienced. It is the threat of annihilation and death, and, indeed, during the convulsion and the following coma the patient comes very near to death. After the convulsion he experiences a slow revival of his interest in the world and an enormous feeling of relief, grasping for any contact offered him. The confusional state after the convulsive treatment is filled with perseverations and expresses the organic inability to come in close contact with the world, which the patient desires after his revival from psychological death. Schilder (1925), Clark (1917), and others, have previously shown that the epileptic experiences death and rebirth. Hypomanic elation, which so often follows the epileptic attack, is the joy of rebirth. The convulsion provoked by metrazol is in this respect not different from the epileptic fit due to other causes. In comparison with these experiences, other experiences lose their importance. The patient's psychic energy is free once again. The previous fixations of libido have lost their importance, and there is renewed interest in the people near the patient. The victory over the death threat, expressed in the convulsion and lingering on in the perceptual and aphasic difficulty, enables the patient to start life and relations to human beings all over again. The previous fixations of libido lying in a more personal layer of experience are washed away by the recovery from a cataclysmic catastrophe in the depth of the organism.

This is the same explanation that Jelliffe (1937) has given for the curative effect of insulin shock (Sakel, 1938). "There are innumerable death threats from without that entail increased object libido investments and many threats from within. The hypoglycemic death threat however is unique. Genetically considered it may be thought of as a very primordial, primitive and massive type of threat which strikes at the very initial stages of life's unholding" (Jelliffe, 1937, p. 577). Indeed, the psychological phenomena following insulin shock are very similar to the phenomena observed after the metrazol injection. It seems that, after insulin, perseverations are more outspoken and there is a greater variability of psychotic pictures. The phase of excitement between deep coma and consciousness is more elaborate and more grotesque. These are, however, minor differences. There are the same aphasic and gestalt disturbances in both treatments. Orenstein and Schilder [see Chapter 26] did not find any proof that insulin affects the dominant hemisphere first, or more. To be sure, the anatomic phenomena point to the left hemisphere, but the right hemisphere, even when affected, remains silent. Insulin, as well as metrazol, affects psychic structures that are fundamentally different from the psychic structures involved in the regressive process of schizophrenia. Both therapies provoke objective but not psychodynamic insight.

The patients do not know the psychic conflicts which are reflected in their symptoms and their fundamental attitude toward life problems remains unchanged. We do not know yet whether the remissions observed after metrazol treatment (and after insulin treatment) will last without the help of psychotherapy. At the same time, we also do not know whether they will last with psychotherapy. Both approaches should be tried. We may expect that, as in insulin therapy, permanent remissions may occur without psychotherapy. However, even if that were so, there is no reason why we should not treat the psychological maladaptation of the organically treated schizophrenic case as we treat any other difficulty in psychological adaptation.

It is not permissible to attribute the therapeutic success of shock therapy to the fact that amnesias occur. The amnesias after metrazol clear up completely. The psychosis and the psychotic symptoms are not forgotten, but the patient has changed his emotional attitude.

This is a psychological interpretation. The fact that we can understand the results of the treatment with the help of the tools of modern psychology is not to say that metrazol treatment acts as a psychological agent in the usual sense. Its effects are deeper than the effects of what we call psychic influence. The treatment is an organic treatment reflected in psychological attitudes. Quite in the same way as in insulin treatment, it looks as if the organic processes of regeneration that are put in action by metrazol bring with them a reorganization of the more labile organic structures that serve emotions and that are damaged by the process of schizophrenia. The forces liberated by metrazol and insulin treatment come from depths generally not accessible to the organic processes we usually call psyche.

CHAPTER TWENTY-EIGHT

The Goodenough Test in Insulin and Metrazol Treatment of Schizophrenia

Goodenough (1926) has worked out a method of measuring the intelligence of children from drawings. She gives the following instructions:

> On the papers I want you to make a picture of a man. Make the very best picture that you can. Take your time and work carefully. I want to see whether the boys and girls in_____ school can do as well as those in other schools. Try very hard and see what good pictures you can make.

Extensive experiences in Bellevue Hospital have proven her methods to be valid and of important help in determining the levels of intelligence in children (L. Bender, 1952). Earl (1933) has studied the drawings of a man by feebleminded

---

Appeared originally in the *Journal of General Psychology*, 21: 349-365, 1939. Hyman H. Fingert, M.D., and Julia Kagan, M.D., co-authors.

adults with mental ages of five to nine years. He observed that the adult feebleminded person draws a human figure in a manner different from that of a normal child of the same mental age. He tends to give a greater number of unimportant details and uses primitive and mature capacities in the same drawing, whereas the child is more interested in the body as a whole and his performance is more consistent. Earl noted that, in pathological cases, there are not only quantitative but also qualitative changes.

Lauretta Bender (1940) has studied the Goodenough test in encephalitic children and found that they scored lower on this test than on other standard intellectual tests and that, in general, details were badly handled. On this test they did less well than children of a lower mental age. Their motor execution was poor, and they often spoke of their dissatisfaction with the results. Bender concluded that the capacity to draw is not related to a simple optic gestalt, but to the visual image the child has of his own body, the formation of which is significantly determined by motility.

As yet, systematic studies of the Goodenough test in adults have not been made. Our own preliminary studies, which are only on a qualitative level, have shown us that variations occur which are greater than one would expect.

Our present study is concerned with the drawings of schizophrenics under the influence of insulin and metrazol. We have chosen this method, since we expect in this way to get a deeper insight into the mental state during these treatments. The preceding remarks show that the Goodenough test reflects not only optic perception, but also the degree to which the approach to an important part of the world, the human body, is integrated.

Schizophrenic drawings have been studied repeatedly from a more general point of view. The most elaborate attempt is the work of Prinzhorn (1922), who studied the art productions of schizophrenics in connection with their personality problems. Guttmann and Maclay (1937) find that these drawings are characterized by an indulgence in detail, meticulous elaborations, and by endurance in collecting bits and pieces. They point also to the symbolic and religious content of these pictures. Our study was different insofar as we placed the patient in a comparatively simple test situation. We gave the same direction to the patients as Goodenough did, without the reference to the schools.

We have collected 50 drawings of untreated schizophrenic patients. Because sufficient data concerning the drawings of so-called normals of a comparable social group is not available, we have refrained from making any final conclusion from scoring.

In our preliminary formulation we may say that, in many dissociated cases, one finds a return to the primitive curved lines which are very often used for a manneristic distortion of the human figure (figures 1-2, Plate 9). One gets the impression that the patient prefers the complicated manneristic form to the simpler one which he could command. In other cases there is a striking incompleteness and a disregard of the total gestalt. In striking contrast to the incompleteness, distortion, and mannerisms of the spontaneous drawings, are copies of a figure of a man which show the patients' good technical ability. However, the same characteristics can be found in these drawings to a minor degree. Sometimes the drawings of normal or neurotic subjects contain similar incompleteness and awkwardness. Therefore, we are not prepared as yet to draw any diagnostic conclusions, which must be based on much larger material.

In schizophrenic patients who were treated with insulin or metrazol we tried to get drawings before therapy was started. Some of these cases, however, were too disturbed in the beginning, so that pictures could not be obtained.

Our experience with insulin treatment was as follows. We were particularly interested in obtaining drawings after the termination of hypoglycemia. Serial drawings were gathered through the period of awakening from coma to clear consciousness. This part of our investigation seemed to promise the possibility of coming to a better understanding of the psychological processes that are taking place during the treatment. We expected that conclusions might be drawn from the re-evolution of functions after insulin coma.

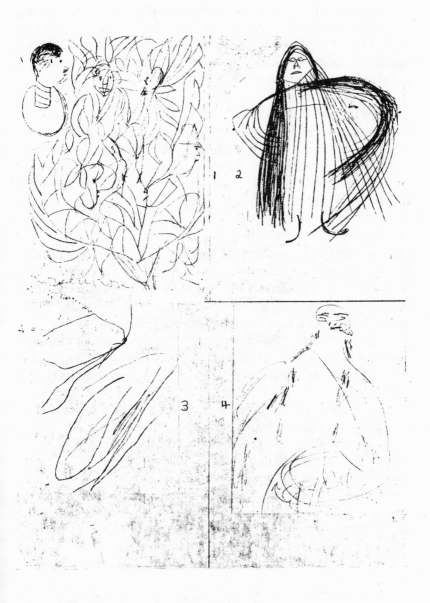

Plate 9

Immediately after awakening, the patients always had great difficulty in using the pencil. They scribbled and perseverated and had to be admonished again and again to draw. These difficulties gradually disappeared. Our series of drawings from a patient were obtained two to ten minutes apart.

F. H. was a college graduate with perplexity, fearfulness, and tenseness in connection with his paranoid delusions. A series of drawings obtained from him after awakening from insulin coma was scored, as were other drawings in our study.

Figure 3 (Plate 9)—The first effort contains only some lines drawn in a repititious fashion without any definite form. No scoring was possible.

Figure 4 (Plate 9)—This drawing shows considerable perseveration of curved lines. The very large figure with distorted features is not drawn in proportion to the size of the paper. There is absence of the extremities and incomplete indication of the torso, with some lines drawn in counterclockwise fashion. This was scored according to the Goodenough method (see Table 5).

Figure 5 (Plate 10)—This drawing shows considerable perseveration of lines with an attempt to draw the upper extremities. The features are markedly distorted. Imcompleteness is still present.

Figure 6 (Plate 10)—Here the figure is somewhat diminished in size, with considerable perseveration of lines. There is an attempt at greater detail of the face. The extremities and torso are still indefinite and less well marked than before.

We omit one drawing for the purpose of brevity.

Figure 7 (Plate 10)—We now see more definite indication of the upper and lower extremities and of the torso. A still further diminution of proportions is noted in this picture. There is an attempt at clothing by putting on a hat. We still see perseveration of lines, but not so markedly as before. There are better details of the face.

Figure 8 (Plate 10)—In this picture we see that the patient has cleared up enough to indicate definitely the proper proportions of

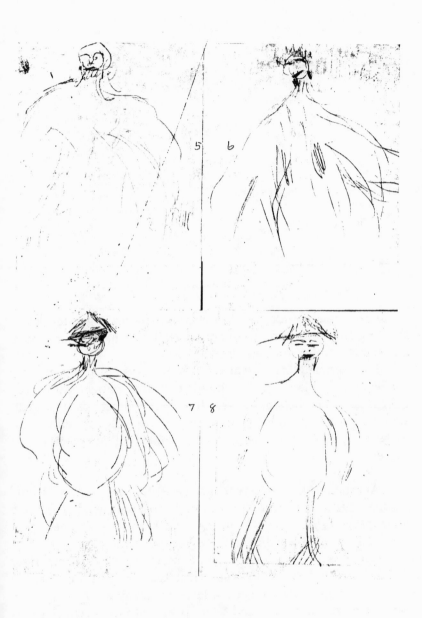

PLATE 10

TABLE 5

Figure	Points Scored	Mental Age
3	Scoring impossible	
4	5 to 6 points	4 years-3 months to 4 years-6 months
5	6 to 7 points	4 years-6 months to 4 years-9 months
6	6 points	4 years-6 months
7	13 to 14 points	6 years-3 months to 6 years-6 months
8	27 points	9 years-9 months
9	36 points	12 years

the figure. He also indicates the upper extremities in greater detail, showing five fingers on the hand. Details of the face are clear. Lower extremities are well drawn.

The complete list of scores of the series is given in Table 5.

Figure 9 (Plate 11)—A drawing of this patient during an afternoon, when he was entirely free of the effects of treatment, showed proper proportion in a figure well drawn, with slight perseveration of lines. This scored 36 points, with a mental age of 12 years.

Abraham N., a 21-year-old patient, was a high school graduate and was admitted to the hospital as a catatonic schizophrenic. A series of drawings of a man was obtained from patient as he awakened from hypoglycemic coma.

Figure 10 (Plate 11)—At first he merely scribbled some lines, then he made a drawing of a man which is out of proportion to the size of the paper. He indicates a large protruding upper lip. The ears are poorly indicated and seem to run into the neck. A hat is indicated.

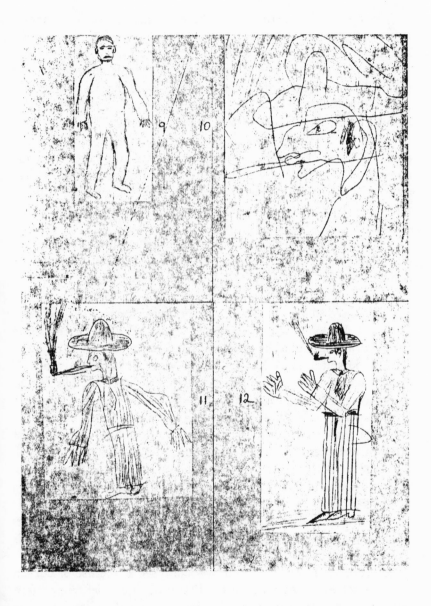

PLATE 11

In the next two drawings there is marked distortion and incompleteness. In one attempt, he wrote: "I'll be a son of a gun," instead of drawing a man.

Figure 11 (Plate 11)—Here we see a completed picture of a man. The proportions are greatly reduced, and the size of the arms and hands is distorted. We note that, in spite of an attempt at detail, the eye has no pupil. The figure is clothed.

Figure 12 (Plate 11)—A drawing made three months after the patient's discharge from treatment, with his condition noted as complete remission, shows practically the same pattern as before, although there is much better detail and proportion. We still see marked perseveration of lines and exaggeration of the size of the hands.

It is clear that in this case the functions studied, as shown in the series after coma, becomes better with a clearing of consciousness.

We have followed a similar procedure in cases treated with metrazol. We obtained drawings in series following the epileptic fit. No drawings could be obtained from Henry W. when he came into the hospital, since he was in a severe negativistic, catatonic stupor combined with a terrific fear and anxiety. He feared television machines and thought he was watched continually. We have many series of drawings made by him during his awakening from seizures. A description of one of these follows: His first attempt was merely a scribbling of lines repeatedly.

Figure 13 (Plate 12)—In this we see a series of lines drawn with a curve at the end, which we shall see later as attempts to draw eyes. This was not scored.

Figure 14 (Plate 12)—Here we see a free use of curved lines with only a very slight suggestion at some kind of pattern. There is vague indication of what we later see to be features.

Figure 15 (Plate 12)—Here we again see a free use of curved lines, which are integrated for the first time into a definite pattern with marked distortion, indicating face in some detail and a vague adjacent torso.

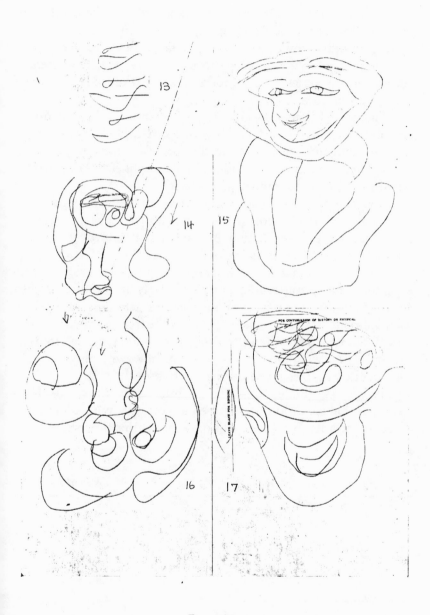

PLATE 12

Figure 16 (Plate 12)—Here we see a distortion of the figures into an almost unrecognizable group of lines, but we believe that there is an indication as to parts of the face. This is an example of the fluctuation in levels of performance that we have seen in several of our series. We note the more marked distortion and disruption of an attempt at a figure.

Figure 17 (Plate 12)—Here we see again a marked distortion and disproportion of the features with no attempt to draw a torso. Eyes are indicated repeatedly in the forehead, nose is markedly exaggerated, and there is an indication of a right ear. Also, there is repetition of lines to indicate a forehead.

The complete list of scores of the series is given in Table 6.

In the complete scoring, as noted above, it is particularly clear that there is oscillation in the gradual improvement and integration of functions as the patient awakens.

Figure 18 (Plate 13)—Drawings he made after the acute symptoms had disappeared are particularly interesting as they show, according to our opinion, the characteristic features of schizophrenic drawings: distortions and the free use of curved and wavy lines which are often effectively used and integrated into the picture. This development was possible, however, only with the therapeutic progress made during the treatment.

Figure 19 (Plate 13)—Five months after discharge from treatment his condition is described as recovery with some slight defect in the affective sphere. His drawings at this time show again

TABLE 6

Figure	Points Scored	Mental Age
First attempt	Not scored	
13	Not scored	
14	2 to 3 points	3 years-6 months to 3 years-9 months
15	9 points	5 years-3 months
16	2 points	3 years-6 months
17	3 points	3 years-9 months

PLATE 13

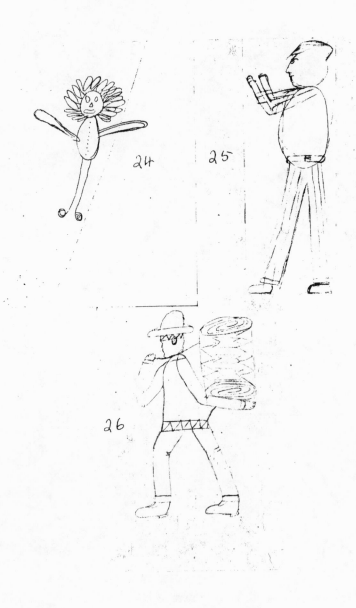

PLATE 14

the free use of curved lines, an eccentric placement of the upper extremity, and a peculiar grotesqueness of the figure, seen in all of his drawings.

Figure 20 (Plate 13)—Here is an example of a patient's, after a seizure, drawing a house instead of a torso as part of his figure.

Katherine G., a markedly dissociated schizophrenic, produced figures 21, 22, and 23 (Plate 13) and figure 24 (Plate 14) during awakening from metrazol seizure. In this series we note that the first picture is a bare outline of the body and that, as consciousness cleared, more and more details were added. In this series, we again note repetition of the pattern, incompleteness, and a tendency to distort the form of the head by the addition of excrescences. A tabulation of the scoring with the mental ages indicated by these drawings is very interesting, since we again see clearly the progression toward completeness and in scoring (Table 7).

TABLE 7

Figure	Points Scored	Mental Age
21	5	4 years-3 months
22	6	4 years-6 months
23	10	5 years-6 months
24	12	6 years

Two cases of our series were artists by profession, but their drawings were in no way different from those mentioned above. Their productions in the awakening states were not influenced by their technical abilities.

It is of interest to compare the drawings before and after final termination of treatment, both as to scoring and qualitative features. As we have already seen in the drawings of Henry W. and Abraham N., after the patients are discharged and their symptoms have disappeared, they draw pictures with a similar pattern but less rigid. The drawings of these patients are characterized by a complete stereotypy. To mention one more case in regard to this feature, John B., a fourteen-year-old catatonic schizophrenic, scored 23 points with a mental age of eight years, nine months on his drawing, figure 25 (Plate 14) before treatment began. A drawing (figure 26, Plate 14) obtained four months after discharge, after he had completed treatment and was in complete remission, scored 33 points with a mental age of eleven years, three months.

In all, 40 series of drawings of insulin and metrazol cases were carefully examined. Our findings may be characterized as follows:

1. Schizophrenic drawings of a man are characterized by: (a) incompleteness and distortion, (b) disproportion between parts of the body, (c) stereotypy, (d) disruptive addition of primitive form elements (excrescences, wavy lines, and baroque backgrounds), (e) perseveration. No diagnostic conclusions can be drawn at the present time.

2. In the beginning of insulin coma and in awakening from the coma and metrazol seizure one finds: (a) a persistence of the basic schizophrenic features as characterized above; (b) the first attempts are scribbling and sometimes awkward writings; (c) there are very outspoken perseverative tendencies; (d) the drawings start with one detail which is very often perseverated, without a tendency to completion (eye, mouth, forehead); (e) the detail may be in connection with the specific contents of the psychosis; (f) with the gradual return of consciousness, the completion of the picture in the schizophrenic sense progresses; (g) the disproportions in the figure and the disproportion between the figure and the available space diminishes with the re-evolution; (h) the progress of re-evolution does not take place in a steady, but in an oscillatory manner; (i) the formal scoring proves the gradual tendency to completion and oscillations observed qualitatively; (j) in no stage of the observation does one find merely a simple returning of infantile pattern.

3. There are no basic differences in the drawings in the hypoglycemic shock before and after final termination. There are, furthermore, no fundamental differences between the phenomena

seen in insulin shock and after metrazol convulsion. It seems that perseveration is a little more outspoken in the insulin shock cases.

4. The Goodenough drawings, before the beginning of the treatment and after recovery or improvement has been achieved, show the same basic pattern; however, the schizophrenic pattern is held to less rigidly after the treatment is finished.

In order to understand these findings, we have to keep in mind the general characteristics of the psychic phenomena observed during insulin and metrazol treatment. In insulin shock, and after metrazol treatment, definite signs are present which point to a disturbance in the organic function of the brain. Aphasic signs are the rule, and many organic phenomena are present in the motor sphere. The patients show, furthermore, a confusion of the organic type that has been studied by Orenstein and Schilder [see Chapter 26], with the Bender gestalt test. Our findings confirm that a confusion of an organic type is present. Such a confusion is not merely a return to primitive stages of development, which one would surmise if one merely looked at the quantitative score. The confusion is closely associated with perseveration. Our series shows with clearness that one deals with a re-evolution, not in the sense of a total personality pattern, but a rebuilding of part functions of the personality—those of perception and orientation. Our studies parallel in this respect the studies of Hughlings Jackson (1931) of re-evolution after the epileptic fit. Jackson has, however, overlooked that one deals merely with the re-evolution of a part function.

Engerth and Urban (1933), studying the return of artistic ability with the passing of a sensory aphasia, have seen a like development extended over a longer period of time. A similar observation can be found in a paper of Kennedy and Wolf (1936).

It is of fundamental importance to recognize that the person who regains his abilities after recovery from shock is always a schizophrenic person both before and after treatment. Distortions and disproportions as noted in the early stages of the series gradually disappear. In these drawings the arbitrary disssolution of form and elaboration characteristic of schizophrenia appear early. In the organic signs of distortion to which perseveration belongs, some apparent infantile or primitive tendencies may come out, but, in addition, the schizophrenic pattern has its way from the beginning. The pictures are organized according to the principles of schizophrenia as far as organization is possible on the general basis of difficulty in gestalt perception. Months after the completion of therapy, while the patient is in an excellent condition, we have noted that the schizophrenic tendencies seen in the drawings when the patient is sick are still present, although in a minor degree. Rymer, Benjamin, and Ebaugh (1937) have also noted: "We should add that the Rorschach test reveals some degree of schizophrenic defect in all 'recovered' cases, both insulin and untreated" (p. 1250). The schizophrenic pattern observed in our cases before treatment becomes less rigid, corresponding with the improvement, but does not disappear entirely. We noted that less rigidity of pattern and stereotypy occurred in the more improved cases. Bender (1940), in her work on the Goodenough test in children with chronic encephalitis, notes: "The drawing of the child is an experiment in the visual motor interpretation of the integrated pattern of kinesthetic motor, cutaneous, and visual impressions" (p. 278). According to this formulation, we can therefore regard the Goodenough test as an expression of total organization, which incorporates not only technical abilities, but also total tendencies.

Summary

The Goodenough drawings of schizophrenic patients during the awakening from the effects of metrazol seizure or insulin coma show decided signs of organic confusion in gestalt perception and representation. However, these apparent primitive form elements are used by the schizophrenic individuals in the schizophrenic integration, which remains incomplete in the first stages of confusion. This schizophrenic integration soon gets the upper hand when the organic confusion expressed in the drawings subsides. The treatment, therefore, introduces a completely new element, organic confusion, into the schizophrenic picture. This corresponds in clinical observation to the aphasic signs and to investigations with gestalt tests by Orenstein and Schilder [Chapter 26].

The effect of insulin and metrazol therapy does not lie, therefore, in a direct attack on the schizophrenic structures. It is an attack on the more deeply seated structures. In the process of reorganization of the organic function, a reconstruction and reorganization take place in the deeper layers. This may in the long run lead to a reorganization of the schizophrenic process, which although organic, is not of the same massive organic type as the disturbance provoked by the shock therapy. If this reorganization of the schizophrenic process takes place, it is reflected in the gradual loosening of the schizophrenic characteristics of the drawings.

IV

THE DEPRESSIVE STATES

CHAPTER TWENTY-NINE

Psychogenic Depression and Melancholia

The excellent clinical studies by Reiss (1910) on depression take the point of view that there is no sharp borderline between psychogenic depressions and depressions that belong to manic-depressive psychoses and involutional melancholia. Reiss applied the term "melancholia" to a clinical picture belonging to the manic-depressive group. So-called involutional melancholia, in my opinion, belongs to the manic-depressive group and is only tinged by involutional factors. This view was rather generally accepted in Germany. Only recently, Kurt Schneider (1920) and J. Lange (1928) have said that there is a fundamental psychological difference between psychogenic and nonpsychogenic depression insofar as the latter shows a vital depression and inhibition in the body, whereas the former does not.

I do not believe that this differentiation is justified, but it is true that from a clinical point of view there are many different types of depression. I shall first give a sketchy enumeration of these types. The psychological meaning of some of them will be

Appeared originally in the *Psychoanalytic Review*, 20: 10-18, 1933.

discussed later. (1) There is a prolonged sadness after the death of beloved persons. It is well known that depth and duration of grief after a loss of love objects varies in different individuals. (2) There are depressions with some inhibitions which follow disagreeable and depressing situations of any kind with some degree of inhibition, some complaining, and the feeling that joy has gone from life. They pass away after weeks or months. (3) This depressive attitude may continue for a very long time and may practically extend over a lifetime. Depressions of this type will be discussed in a later paper [see Chapter 30]. (4) Melancholias with severe inhibitions and a classical symptomatology may follow an upsetting event, but may show the course of a melancholia and even be followed by a manic phase. (5) Finally, there is the classic depression of the manic-depressive psychosis, coming without any apparent psychic cause.

It would be very easy to point to some other types, but we are not addressing ourselves to clinical questions; we only want to have a basis for the following discussion. To repeat, in the symptomatology of the melancholias we find severe inhibitions, self-accusations, depressing delusions, strong suicidal tendencies, and rigid sadness in the foreground. In psychogenic depressions, the inhibitions and the sadness are not so rigid and not so extensive.

My discussion will center around the case history of a prolonged psychogenic depression. I have for comparison another analysis of a patient with a psychogenic depression and two analyzed cases of melancholia very carefully studied from a psychological point of view, although not analyzed.

The patient was a woman, 39 years old, a virgin. She complained about depression, despair, and inability to work. With a few interruptions, this state had existed since she was seventeen years old. At that time she refused a proposal of marriage by a young man. The depression lasted until she was 21. By and by she improved and intended to go to college. When she felt ready, at about 28, her father became sick and soon died. She developed a terrible depression again, which abated after a few years. She felt that she was almost back to normal and finally felt ready to marry a man with whom she had gone out for many years and who had often proposed to her, but whom she had rejected because he did not seem to be the ideal lover. At this point, the man married another girl, and she fell into another deep depression, during which she came for treatment. Analysis showed that her preparedness to marry this man was due to an unconscious insight that he was turning away from her.

This sketchy life history points to a very strong Oedipus complex, and the data concerning the Oedipus complex are therefore reported first. Her first remembrance dates back to the age of two. Her mother was away. She was sick in the cradle. She was crying. There was candy covered with paper. She knew that her father was there. When she was about four years old, her mother started an affair with another man. She had a remembrance of the quarrels following this, but her father pardoned her mother. About the same time she was looking in the mirror and saw her father and mother in bed. Her father was uncovered. Her mother was playing with his penis. Her father was reading a newspaper. From then on she had a great desire for sex. She thought about a little boy who lived across the street; had fantasies about his urinating on her genitals and then pressing his penis on her organ. The idea of sex relations was always connected in her mind with urination and moisture. It went back to some remarks of her father; she could remember that he "likes it juicy." Later on she had sex play with little boys and girls. A boy even touched her genitalia with his penis. In all her later sex fantasies she imagined the male sex organ as being like the organ of a child. She had no knowledge about erection. Only about a year before she started treatment did she discover what erection actually meant. When she was six, seven, and eight years old she had many scruples. She had the feeling of having committed a sin. Her father dominated her childhood. She did not resent it when he spanked her for disobeying, which did not happen very often. She always felt that her mother was not the right wife for her father. She hated and had contempt for her mother, who was lazy and indifferent. In her childhood she felt that she would be a better wife for her father. But her father never was demonstrative. She missed it. He seemed disinterested in sex. He did not talk about it. He was not interested in whether she married or not.

Her early sex activities were also connected with an enormous interest in children. Very early she wanted to have children. At the same time she had a great interest in monkeys. She had seen monkeys while together with her father. She always wanted her mother to have more children. When her mother finally gave birth to a boy when the patient was fourteen, and to a girl when she was 23, she felt as if she was the mother of the children, and she cared for them like a mother. Her manifest sex activities stopped when she was about six years old, when another girl told her that it is a bad thing to touch another girl's genitals and to be touched. This reprimand provoked great fear. At the same time, this girl's sister died of diphtheria, and the girl talked about a death angel. Before her first communion she developed serious doubts and worried a great deal.

During a depression at about age nineteen, the patient had the opportunity again to hear something about sex relations between her father and mother. She got violently sexually excited, started masturbating, put herself in the place of the mother. Fantasies of prostitution followed. Once in a train she even thought that a man was trying to bring her into a house of prostitution. When masturbating she felt nearer to life again. When the father was sick (nine years later) he had a nurse. Some noises made the patient suspicious, and she once found her father in bed with the nurse. There was a violent outburst on her part against the nurse. She even wanted to kill her. After the death of her father, she reproached herself for having been so violent. When her mother married the second time, she again had the opportunity of hearing her mother and stepfather while they were having sex relations and got into a violent rage.

Unquestionably the patient had an active interest in the sex relations between parents and parent substitutes. Her violent hatred for the mother and those who took the place of the mother also came out in the hatred for her brother's fiancée, whom she even wanted to kill. In the analysis, the Oedipus situation was transferred into the psychoanalytic situation. I may add a technical remark: the patient not only had dreams and free associations, but visions as well. These visions often contained psychogenic material. Words also came into her mind. I do not know whether the patient's bringing so many visions and words had a special significance. Only in the analysis of a normal individual have I found similar visions. In structure, they were similar to hypnogic hallucinations, the symbolic content of which Silberer (1912) has demonstrated so well.

In one of the patient's visions she saw King Alfonso of Spain. His eyes were bright. (Association: He could have taken another wife in order not to get idiotic children.) She compared the psychoanalyst with King Alfonso. On another occasion she had the words, "If you can catch a little Canadian" in her mind. She herself felt it was a combination of alien and Canadian. Her associations were about a Canadian banker who divorced his wife. The alien was the analyst. In one of her visions she saw a nude man lying on his back, his sex organs shriveled, wasting away. (Association: The father, when caught in bed with the nurse, said, "I am only the husk of a man.") In the analysis she often complained that the analyst did not satisfy her. His wounded fingers[1] in some way became for her a symbol of his inefficiency in sex. When she felt worse, she frequently reproached the analyst very severely in the same way she reproached her father for not taking enough care of the family. The interest in sex organs and in heterosexuality prevailed. In one vision there was a big heavy metal cannon ball which was about to drop in the ocean. It was suspended. She feared it might slip off. She wanted to make a groove around the ball so that it could not slip off.

One dream toward the end of the analysis may be repro- duced: "There is a place in the city. She wanted to get away. A

[1] [Paul Schilder had two fingers of his left hand amputated in an automobile accident—Ed.]

dark man like a bandit came. She was frightened. He came in the house after a woman. He wanted to take her. He said, "I didn't know you are as old as you are. It doesn't make much difference." The analyst is in the dream. He has a moustache and beard and a lot of hair on his face. (She liked her lover's moustache, but the analyst has too much of a beard.) His hair was brown. The analyst punches her genital organs. She does not like it. He punches harder. She takes it as a test as to how she would stand married life. She decides that she cannot stand the test.

Here one sees some sadistic elements connected with the genital element. Once, she had the idea that the analyst should take her and shake her. The following vision has a similar meaning: There is a deep receptacle like a round tank reaching into the sky. She tries to get the body of a man in it. She wants to get it in upright. The body is naked. The man is dead. She feels it would be nicer if she could get it in upright.

In her attitude toward the sex organs there are not only sadistic but also oral elements. At first she had a vision of a lead pencil lying between two fingers. It fits there. Immediately before the vision, she had thought about handling a penis. When she was fifteen or sixteen she saw a man urinating. Afterward, she made a joke out of it. After this vision she saw three pictures hanging on the wall. One was hanging crooked. One was of Christ with something on his head like a headdress, like a cap. She suddenly felt a piece of roast pork in her mouth. She smacked her lips in a very realistic way. (Association: Kissing played a great part in her life. A few days before, she had been interested in the glans penis. Christ was to be interpreted as the penis. His headdress was the glans. Behind it were penilingus wishes.) There were many visions of an oral type. She saw a tray with dishes. The dishes were on one end and the butter on the other end. She put the tray on the floor. She thought a cat might come to lick up the butter. She saw a large bowl. There was soup in it. (Association: Her father especially liked soup. He liked it yellow. Association: Urine.) Or still more clearly, she saw herself with her finger in her genital organs, but it was really her mouth.

Anal elements did not play a very important part. She heard

queer words. "I was always full of contingency. I was always hateful. I was always contemptible." Her next associations were that she was always contented and happy. She played "pig Latin" with the children with whom she had sex relations. Words for buttocks were often used at that time. She dreamed that there was a yard with old flower beds. There were two or three big black bugs. She did not know what to do. Later on they were gone. The hired woman was there. (Association: The bugs are the black pubic hairs of a woman. She imagines her mother this way. As a child she was afraid of bugs. The family tradition was that she took a bug into her mouth when she was eight or nine months old. She thought that women always have black hairs on their genitals.)

There were many hints of a castration complex of a typical kind, but she never gained full insight into it. One dream may be reproduced in this connection: She was riding on a street car. Her foot got twisted. She tried to get it loose and was afraid of getting caught and losing her foot. She got it out. Her shoe came off. She was afraid of being seen with her shoe off. She got to the sidewalk. On the corner, her brother was lying with his legs stretched. She saw his penis coming out of his trousers. It looked like snakes or fangs. She felt like looking at it. She did so. She thinks she ought to tell him not to do such things.

The patient's transference was violent in the positive and negative sense. She often felt deeply disappointed with the analyst, a repetition of the continuous disappointment she had with her undemonstrative father, who always gave her away for mother and mother substitutes. I do not want to go into the technical details. The analysis is still unfinished, but the patient is clinically recovering and free from symptoms.

When we go over this case history we immediately see that the patient reached the full Oedipus level in her development. At the same time, she reached the genital level. The wish to have children by the father dominated the picture. That is a characteristic feature of psychogenic depression. In another case I analyzed, the patient was deeply attached to her father and hated her mother. At the same time she had strong heterosexual wishes, but remained dissatisified in her marriage. She was almost completely frigid. One of her fantasies was to cut off her husband's and her analyst's genitals and to introduce them into her vagina until she got complete satisfaction. Another of her fantasies was to be satisfied through every hole in her body. The genital zone predominated in both cases. The strongly developed Oedipus complex provides a strong superego, and, with the superego, strong repressions set in. I do not think that the force of the repressions comes only from the inhibition acquired with the Oedipus complex. We therefore see that in the case reported the patient runs away from heterosexual satisfaction and answers with a depression when she has denied herself heterosexual genital satisfaction. I think this is a characteristic feature of psychogenic depressions.

It is remarkable that melancholics often come to a much fuller heterosexual sex satisfaction. This is probably connected with the fact that the conflicts in these cases are on a much deeper layer. It is almost as if it were not worthwhile to repress the heterosexuality. The whole problem lies much more in the oral and sadistic spheres. It is remarkable that the same problem is met in an obsessional neurosis in which heterosexual satisfaction is very often reached. Helene Deutsch (1933) thinks that in some of these cases the vagina acts like the male sex organ. I would not deny such an interpretation, but in the obsessive neurosis, too, genitality is in some way outside of the psychic battlefield. It is true there are some melancholias in which frigidity is present. In one of my melancholia cases, not only frigidity was present, but also clear-cut kleptomania. I may mention in this connection that the first analysis of a melancholia case by Gross (1907) revealed kleptomanic impulses. The patient reported here had fantasies that someone would steal a diamond and she would buy it very cheaply. Once, a man offered her a fur on the street for a very cheap price, hinting that it was stolen goods. The patient bought it very hastily and found out later that it was a worthless imitation. But the case of kleptomania that I analyzed was one of those melancholia cases in which psychogenic factors played an enormous part. She also had a rather strongly developed Oedipus complex. Her symptomatology was in many respects hysteriform, so that this atypical melancholia confirms our point of view that the hysterical depression and the hysteriform melancholia have a strong Oedipus complex with repressions against heterosexuality. We therefore find many signs of repressions such as frigidity or the evasion of sex activities in cases of psychogenic depression.

Fenichel (1931a) has correctly pointed out that all pregenital activities tinge the Oedipus complex. We must also ask: What is the particular type of Oedipus complex of psychogenic depressions? What are the pregenital activities of these patients and what is their significance?

Our case shows, for instance, oral and urinary tendencies, both connected with her father. Her earliest memory reveals an oral attitude. The soup her father liked, meaning urine, is the connecting link between these two tendencies.

There is no question but that there were sadistic tendencies in the patient, but these sadistic tendencies were closely connected with the Oedipus complex. They were especially directed against the person of the same sex, who was a rival. In addition to these aggressive tendencies were masochistic tendencies, but they were again closely connected with the genitals, so that we can say that we had a sadomasochism of the genital and of the Oedipus level. This is in sharp contrast to the sadistic attitude of the melancholia cases. They are much more violent and much more aggressive, much more destructive and, as Abraham (1924) and Freud (1917) have pointed out, in closer connection with oral tendencies. They are therefore essentially cannibalistic. Sadomasochistic tendencies certainly have a development that parallels the development from pregenital to genital sexuality. Oral sadomasochism, anal sadomasochism, and genital sadomasochism are very different from each other. One way of explaining the development of sadomasochism is that it is a partial desire of sexuality; or one may state, according to the later formulations by Freud (1930), that the higher development of sexuality neutralizes the aggressive instinct more efficiently. I, myself, am in favor of the first formulation. I therefore believe in the development of the sadomasochism. At any rate, the sadism of psychogenic depression is milder and not as destructive as the sadism of melancholia. It is in connection with this fact that the danger of suicide is much less in psychogenic depressions. The merging of sadomasochism into the Oedipus complex protects against suicide, when sadomasochism does not remain cannibalistic, but helps the tendencies of the Oedipus situation.

I may mention that in psychogenic depressions I have found so far, illusions about time are lacking. Melancholia cases often complain that time does not pass; that there exists for them an eternity. I regard these illusions of time as the expression of an extreme sadism which, as I have said, is lacking in psychogenic cases.

In spite of the fact that oral tendencies were present in our case, they did not play the same part as in melancholia cases. They were also better merged with the Oedipus complex. I do not think that the Oedipus complex is not developed in melancholia, but the fixation in the Oedipus complex is not as strong as in the cases of psychogenic depression. In melancholia not only is the Oedipus complex saturated with sadomasochistic tendencies, but the oral and sadistic tendencies also change the structure of the superego. It is as if the oral aggressivity would use the oedipal material for its purposes.

As for the anal tendencies, they are not clearly expressed in our case. The analysis also has not made very clear so far the homosexual elements in the case, although there are many indications of it, tendencies to an identification with the father.

I would also say that in psychogenic depression we have the chief point of fixation in the oedipal stage and accessory fixation points in oral sadism. In melancholia there are the same points of fixation, but the fixation in the region of the Oedipus complex is less important. Oral-sadistic fixation is in the foreground. Generally speaking, in every neurosis and psychosis we must consider not only one point of fixation but the whole development, and there will always be accessory points of fixation in this development. The various symptomatologies of neurosis and psychosis depend upon the primary as well as the secondary points of fixation. The various symptomatologies of psychogenic depressions and melancholias depend on the relative value of the various points of fixation. We may ask why a hysteria takes the form of a depression and why hysteria takes this particular symptomatology. The preliminary answer would be that in psychogenic depression we deal, not only with the primary point of fixation in the region of the Oedipus complex, but also with secondary fixation points in the oral-sadistic sphere. The similarity with melancholia is based on a partial identity of the points of fixation, but the relative value of these fixations to the whole development and to the sexual structure is different.

This is only a very sketchy approach to a problem of some general importance. I will not go into the question of the differences in the ego and superego structures in psychogenic depressions and in melancholia. There is no question that a more severe and cruel superego corresponds to the stronger and more aggressive sadism of melancholia. The degree and quality of inhibition in melancholia and psychogenic depression varies according to the difference in the superego.

CHAPTER THIRTY

Particular Types of
Depressive Psychoses

Although the grouping of the manic-depressive psychoses into one
large entity has often been criticized, one cannot deny that each
individual has his special way of reacting to what is going on
around him. There are swings in emotions which, although they
are connected with specific situations, get their final shape and
coloring from constitutional factors. These constitutional factors
can be modified and even substituted for by the somatic influences
of certain diseases—arteriosclerosis, head injuries, endocrine disturbances, etc. There is an entity manic-depressive psychoses, but
this entity is not rigid. A constitutional factor is also present, an
individual factor due to particular somatic or psychic experiences.
These factors collaborate in different ways and can substitute for
each other in a large measure. Manic-depressive psychoses affect a

Appeared originally under the title, "Clinical Studies on Particular Types of
Depressive Psychoses—Their Differential Diagnosis from Schizophrenia Pictures and
Some Remarks on the Psychology of Depression," in the *Journal of Nervous and
Mental Disease*, 80:501-527; 558-683, 1934.

specific psychic system. Such a psychic system is, in our opinion, always connected with a specific brain apparatus, which is dependent on the whole metabolic and endocrine process. But a disease of a psychic system in the sense described here is based on a constitution that expresses itself in a specific psychic make-up. Childhood experiences will reflect this constitution; the constitution will determine the experiences. But it would be erroneous to believe that experiences have no influence on shaping what is constitutional.

In the manic-depressive psychosis, the leading psychological symptom is, according to Freud (1917), the changed relation between the ego ideal and the other parts of the self (the ego and the id). In all pictures of the depressive type we therefore find self-accusation and the feeling of guilt as an expression of self-condemnation by the ego ideal. Every self-condemnation contains a sadomasochistic element. In our cases we find, quite in a similar way to Hoch and Kirby (1919), self-accusations and aggressive tendencies against others. That is one more reason why I have brought what I call the perplexity psychosis (to be described shortly) into relation with manic-depressive psychosis.

A picture of doubt is in the center of the manic-depressive psychosis when there is hatred and when the hatred is not fulfilled. Sadism does not play the same part in depersonalization in which the individual fights against narcissistic tendencies which endanger contact with the world. The sadistic aggression in our case is of the same quality as sadomasochism in typical depressions, except that, in these, the destructive tendencies go further. In mental confusion the difficulty in the integration of perceptions brings with it the feeling that an important part of the ego is destroyed, and the individual feels threatened in the integrity of his body (dismembering motif, castration complex). These remarks are inadequate, for we do not have analyzed cases of this type and do not know enough about the infantile situation of the patient. It is remarkable that, in our cases, oral elements do not seem to play an important part.

The formal problem of these psychoses is connected to the life situation and the patient's attitude toward the world. In this respect I am in clear opposition to the point of view generally maintained in German psychiatric literature. Kurt Schneider (1920) speaks about the "vital depression" in cases belonging to the manic-depressive group. Westermann (1928) has gathered material. Both believe that the depression has nothing to do with the problems of the patients' lives; that it comes from unknown depths and is an inhibition of vital functions. For them this inhibition is meaningless. Lange (1928) has a very similar point of view. I have emphasized that the depression and inhibition of depressives is connected with their sadomasochistic tendencies. Vital depression ("Vitale Depression") is due to a specific attitude toward life and is much more understandable from a psychological point of view than Schneider and Westermann suppose.

The specific difference between psychogenic depression and depressions of the manic-depressive group is a difference in the libidinal conflicts and problems. The sadism of depressives is not as yet brought in connection with libidinal tendencies from the Oedipus complex; it is more primitive and violent than the sadism of a psychogenic depression, where the greater part of the libido is bound around the Oedipus complex.

Another purely formal attempt has been made by Straus (1928) and von Gebsattel (1928). They report the common complaints of melancholics—"time no longer changes"; "there is eternity and no progress." The inner feeling of time stops; the experiences do not come to a real end; there is no future in the life of the depressive cases (cf. F. Fischer, 1930).[1] In the case histories to follow, one can find many remarks of this sort. But if one studies a case history carefully, one sees immediately that time is not an independent unit for the patient. They want to perpetuate their own suffering and the suffering of others, their sadomasochistic tendencies. They have specific life problems which are reflected in

[1] Fischer (1930) has reported interesting findings concerning the time experiences of schizophrenics. In schizophrenics, the change in the time experience is the expression of changed attitudes to the world and has a definite meaning in the actual life of the patient.

their attitude toward time. There is no inner time experience. We experience something in time, and the time experience is closely connected with what we actually experience. One of my depressed cases stated that she had destroyed everything from the beginning of the world, an expression of her enormous sadistic tendencies. From the point of view of dynamic psychology, I generally reject the idea that the experiences of a patient come independent of his life situation. From this point of view, it is senseless to state, with Straus, that the inner time experience has stopped because of unknown "biologic-vital" reasons. We insist on asking about the patient's emotional attitude. This general principle can also be well applied to some of the newer attempts in German literature to solve the problems of schizophrenia in a merely formalistic way, as Gruhle (1922) and Kurt Schneider (1920) have done. They describe psychological phenomena, isolate them from all problems of the personality, and then call them primary symptoms.

DOUBT AND PERPLEXITY
(A SPECIFIC GROUP OF MANIC-DEPRESSIVE PSYCHOSES)

Case 1. Mrs. S. C., 39 years old, became suddenly ill September 1, 1928, with confusion and disorientation. She had not been well for several months previously. The family history showed no psychosis. The father was very energetic, the mother died at 40 of pulmonary tuberculosis; she was rather thrifty. The patient was an only child. She had a normal birth and development. Her schooling was irregular. When she was sixteen her mother died, which upset her. She often spoke about the death of her mother. She graduated at twenty, was sociable but quiet, and had a large circle of friends of both sexes. She taught in a school for feeble-minded. At 28 she had a nervous breakdown, which necessitated her giving up teaching for a year. She resumed her teaching until her marriage at 35. She was her husband's second wife. His first wife was her intimate friend. She had formerly considered marrying her husband before he went away to college. The patient remained friendly with both and often visited them. She married her husband a year after his first wife's death. She developed a strong love for her two stepchildren and was even oversolicitous of their welfare. She had no children of her own.

In May, 1928 an extremely painful attack of arthritis necessitated hospital care for ten days. Following this she was so reduced physically that she was unable to resume her household duties. While recuperating in bed, she complained that it was hard for her to plan. She dreaded preparing for the children's return to school in the fall. She said she could not go on. She became interested in Christian Science and seemed to be helped during July and August.

On September 1, while out with the family for the day, her husband noticed a forced gaiety on her part. She told him that she was afraid they were not giving the children a good time. She told the children to wake her husband up. She tried to make her husband laugh. After that, she became tense and said, "I don't know what to do, I'm all mixed up." In the middle of the night she rushed downstairs, again in a state of ecstasy. She said, "A miracle has be performed, I am perfectly well. Christian Science has cured me." Then she said, "Oh, I have said the wrong thing again." She was unable to sleep. She exclaimed, "I have got to kill S." (S. was the first name of her husband. Grace, a friend of hers, had shot her husband when in a psychotic state.) "Grace shot Arthur and I've got to kill you. I don't want to shoot you." She kept stating that her husband's first wife was dead. At times she appeared to see something in front of her. She slapped the nurse two or three times. She took down one of the children's pictures and broke the glass. She would hold up two fingers and exclaim, "There, I have it all right now." She was constantly begging someone to straighten her out mentally. On September 29 she was fairly rational. On October 13 she was again markedly confused. She entered Bloomingdale Hospital on October 21, 1928.

In the hospital the physical status and laboratory findings were negative. From time to time she showed a tendency to play on words and to pun. Her behavior was perplexed and restless.

Mostly, perplexity and fear were in the foreground. She was afraid the physician would cut her head off or harm her in some other way. She said, "If I could only reach my soul. Don't you want to save me? How is it that I can see all right sometimes? I am afraid you are going to do something to me. I am afraid you are going to kill me in some way. I don't know where I am. I feel that I am in the space between. That frightens me." When asked to write her name, she signed her maiden name.

Next day, the patient was again restless and perplexed. At times she smiled momentarily. She noticed everything the physician was doing. She objected to his writing. She picked up the paper he was writing on and glanced at it. She took his pencil out of his hand or picked one out of his pocket. She attempted to pick instruments out of his pocket, took his stethoscope, examined it, and put it down. She was resistive to any physical examination. She was neat and tidy about her person. She found out that the woman across the hall was named Mrs. Biggers, called out, "She is bigger than the other lady," and laughed. "It is something about politics. It is politics or religion that puts my mind off. I don't know what. It is all death. I am sleeping away, it is all gone. Are you trying to bring life back to my soul?" She admitted that she was confused, reached over and felt the doctor's face, to see if it was real. "You see, it is so confusing, doctor. What do you want me to say? Just confess? Well, I don't know, somebody brought me. I don't know. If I gave you some money, could I get out? Just take me home. I have had so many homes, I don't know which one to go to. I have been through hell and through heaven." At this point she picked up a book and looked at it. She said she was distressed by the nurse, bent forward, and rubbed her head on the table in front of her. She saw the doctor's wedding ring and tried to remove it. She read "Bloomingdale Hospital White Plains" on the paper and said, "At last I have got back to earth. Oh, it is something about this mental state that I am in. It is something about faith, about religion. When I do something right you always do the wrong thing. We are all crossing and criss-crossing you. There is always some confusion around here. I thought I was pretending to be a baby." She looked at herself in the mirror and said, "Oh, I am a funny-looking woman." She looked about the room and cried, "Oh, do they look up things? We are both dead, we are both in heaven. Well, we can't be in heaven and on earth. I see that. I dream of death, I am a death, I could just blow away."

On October 24 she was sometimes clear, but mostly confused and resistive, clenched her teeth, and refused to eat. On October 29, when she saw the physician, she said, "Oh, I know you, I have seen you before; lots of people here are not the doctor." She put her hand on the physician's knee and touched him repeatedly. "I like the occupation classes. I am very glad to meet you. Don't go so fast because I want to be good." She rubbed the doctor's face again. "I want to see if you are a real man and I am a woman. Are you a man? I can't see. I got religion and politics all mixed up. One day the doctor came in here and pricked my wedding-ring finger. Will you keep me until after Election Day? . . . Thank the Lord I am not alive. I don't know why I want to keep making poetry all the time. I was graduated from high school in 1907." Then she gave a rather composed report about her past. "Oh, it takes so long to take a tooth out. It seems as if something terrible had happened to me. Do you want me to pay money here to get well? In Albany (in the hospital where she was first) something snapped in my head. I dreamed somebody murdered me. A man had a pistol and shot me in the back. I was just covered with pistol marks. I never want to see a pistol again as long as I live. (Do you hear voices?) I hear them say out in the hall, old Mr. and Mrs. Confusion and Doubt. (She lay down.) I do not want to hurt my own husband or his two children. We were so very happy together before I thought I must entangle the whole world in the subject of religion and politics."

November 2. "I have to prove everything to myself. When I go to sleep I have the sensation of everybody watching me. The pain in my head is terrible. I know when I talk to you I do funny things. (She picked at the doctor's shirt, watch chain, and face.) Music always kind of bothers me. It seems as if I gave my clothes to somebody else and I am not nice. I thought I had shot my husband and was imprisoned. If I confessed to you that my husband shot or murdered me, he would be put in prison ... I had a fear of going home and talking to the children." She stated that the physician told her before she came to the hospital that she had a subconscious longing for a baby. She thought she was pregnant and had a baby. She pleaded in her subconscious mind for a baby, and they gave her a black or Jewish baby to take home. During the next week she often wondered what her name was. Sometimes she heard voices. "Life or death or things. I keep dreaming that I was running around naked. Listen, don't you hear all those noises? They should be right here."

She again touched the doctor's face. "I dreamed I don't know you. I can't go to tubs[2] or have the tubs. I am not afraid to die, but I want to see my husband before I die. Did I poison myself before I came here?" She was gaining slowly in weight. She wondered if she were herself; thought herself bad; wondered where she was. She stressed the fact repeatedly that she was Mrs. S. C. When given any physical support, she relaxed her muscles and tried to fall. She was continually sitting up and rolling about in bed. When admonished, she cooperated better for a time. "Are you a doctor? How do I know whether you are a doctor or not? How do you know whether I am a manic or not? I feel, and you felt too once. You are sitting up, and I am lying down. You can't stay with me a whole week. It would take me that long to explain. Our stateroom—yes. Our hour and there is an our hour. You have to watch in your pocket and I told you a little fib and I don't want to tell you what it is. Are you a doctor? How do I know if you are a doctor or not? A-B-C-D-E-F, it starts with the sixth letter of the alphabet. I just keep going around in a circle and it keeps getting bigger all the time." She turned and looked to the other side. "I am ashamed of myself. That tortures me. Oh, you are a male and I am a female. I think dreams put me off. I thought I was getting naked and running up and down the hall. I think you were doing the same thing. You are unkind and I am not unkind. I don't want to

---

[2] [This refers to hydrotherapy, a treatment commonly used in the 1930's—Ed.]

uncover myself before any man." She is scantily dressed in a thin nightdress, but is reluctant to place the bedclothes about her.

She did not change until December 8. In her talk there was always the same praise for her husband; and she spoke about shooting and that she was dead. In general she was a little more quiet. She mistook the physician for her husband. She pricked her neck with her sewing needle. At times she was fearful and apprehensive. "I don't want to be smothered. I thought I was coming back to life just as I was going out of it. I know where I am. When I am alone, I doubt. I lied because I could not remember."

On January 26 she smiled at Dr. A. and looked at him staringly. "You are the same Dr. A. You are my doctor. Oh, pull your sleeves over, Dr. A. (Touches him also now.) I am S. Aren't you the doctor? (Touches his cheek.) Did I say dirty words? I don't want to take off my clothes again. When I am alone, things do not look right to me. (Why do you touch him?) Because I don't know. I know faces and places, but it is hard to remember it." Says now she remembers in detail. "S. and Dr. A. you would not take your clothes off before me. I thought I had come to life as every other does. The old book is not right. I know where I am. I want to be a nice lady, a dignified nice lady. You try to help me. You're a doctor. Why do they make names? You understand these names? (Lies down, touches the physician's face, hair, and hands.) You are alive. You don't want to kill me. There is something not quite right. (Touches the physician's hair again.) I feel so lonesome. Is Dr. A. alive? S. can go to bed with me." She puts her fingers in the buttonhole of the physician's coat. "You have got your clothes pressed. Do these windows look dirty? Let us speak of the history. The history is written on my face. (Pays great attention to every little detail in the environment.) Where is the hospital for mental defectives? S. loves me, I want to speak to him. Do I hurt the nurses? That is your coat. (Touches the physician's sleeve.) Women can give birth to children. These are my own shoes. I am the doctor. I can't go home in order to get a baby by S. This is the last chance I have. Maybe I am a little peculiar. We all do the best we can."

On January 30. "I am suspicious of all these men because they are old and not my husband." She clung to Dr. A. and did not want to let him go. Anxiously, "Why do you ask so many questions? I am alive." She touched the physician's hand, hair, and face. "It is a picture of a man and I am a picture. Are you writing that? I do not know anything about the hospital. S. is a girl's name." She was very perplexed. "You count the hairs of my head. I've got teeth. I do not mean I'm a grown-up person. I could get everything when eating." She pushed the chair forward and repeated, "S. is my husband. I do not want to go to bed with any other man. I want to be a good girl."

On February 2 she stated that she had a previous breakdown when her friend broke their engagement. She confessed dreaming about this man after she had married Mr. S. C. Many times when she was with her husband she would think of this man. Recently she had thought that she had syphilis. Syphilis is a very bad thing to have, and she was about the first woman to have it. She still showed a rather marked erotic trend and asked, as if for assurance, "I am not a bad woman because I had intercourse, am I?" She was still astonished and perplexed. "Do you have hands and skin?" She touched the physician and asked, "Are you a man? Men and women help each other. Dr. A. is helping me. I don't look like a woman. I don't want my husband to take me home." She touched the physician's foot with her foot and said, "You don't want to kill me. You are not interested in me. You have a pencil in your hand. You have a white shirt. Everything is white. Your face is white. You must be completely white. Sometime I have to go home. Don't I stay long enough. I don't know whether the Physician-in-Chief is Gaynor or Raynor. Somebody could think I was in bed with a strange man. I am light. There is some girl who is wanting to try everything on me. They talk outside now."

After February 5, she became much clearer and no longer had so much doubt about reality. On February 15 she stated that formerly at night she dreamed that she was dead in bed, but now she had ceased dreaming. On February 26 she was clear and felt self-assured. She reported that in the Albany hospital she had dreamed about fire and also that she shot her husband. While in the hospital she felt locked up in a monastery and was turned into a nun. She also thought the staff officer at the other hospital was changing her and was going to shave her head like a nun's. At times she felt that she was dead and that her spirit had come to earth again. She felt compelled to see whether the people were dead. When the patients changed, she thought that she was being plotted against. The words were not spelled right in letters. She felt that many things had relation to her. She was not sure whether the physician was not her husband. She pinched herself to see whether she was alive. All things seemed unreal. She thought that she might harm children. "I must have been insane." After the end of February she was practically normal.

On March 18 she stated that she had had no menstrual period from Christmas until the middle of February. She had a strong period February 14. She had forgotten all that happened during her psychosis. She only knew that almost everybody in the hospital looked like somebody else to her.

On May 6, she gave a detailed report about the onset of her difficulties. They followed an attack of arthritis which lasted from April to May, 1928. In the Albany hospital she felt homesick and lonely. She spoke about a burglar with a revolver. He shot her and filled her full of bullet holes. There was a numbness of her ears, as if her nerves were being pinched. She thought that her husband shot his son. She confused the names of Bloomingdale and Bloomberg, and confused White Plains with Plainfield. She thought the place was a prison. She thought that she had shot her husband and he had shot one of the children and that he therefore had to leave the state. She thought she was in Sing Sing, and had the sensation of being watched. She felt she was being burned alive when she was in packs, and took the nurse for an undertaker. She felt that she went to another home to become a nun and have her head shaved and a white robe put on.

She stayed in the hospital until June 17 and was then in good health. She was seen December 17, 1929 and had remained healthy.

In this picture, doubt is the dominant factor. It is a real doubt. Touching objects has the purpose of helping her out of the doubt. It is remarkable that she touched living persons, especially those toward whom she felt sympathetic. She was aware of the erotic meaning of this behavior. Many of the problems in her life came out in the psychosis and its delusions and hallucinations. There was the marriage, which was not very satisfactory to her. Aggressive tendencies against the husband came out in connection with the fact that a friend of hers shot her husband in a psychotic state. There were self-reproaches because of sex wishes she had concerning another man. Her first nervous breakdown when she was 28 was seemingly related to the breaking of the attachment to this man. The painful attack of arthritis which preceded the psychosis may have lessened her psychic resistance.

The feeling of guilt is very remarkable in all her utterances. But all the delusional trends so closely connected with her complexes remained in the background. In the foreground was always the doubt about everything that was going on and especially the doubt about her husband. Of course, the psychological understanding of such a psychosis remains incomplete as long as we do not know more about the childhood history.

Case 2. Lavinia H., 39 years old, came into the Phipps Clinic of Johns Hopkins Hospital on June 15, 1928. Her mother had two psychotic attacks characterized by persecutory ideas. A maternal cousin has had two depressions.

Two years after an operation by Dr. Dandy, her son had an epileptic seizure again. She was profoundly disturbed by this and worried about it, crying frequently. Her husband reassured her, but she either telephoned him several times a day or drove to his office. She slept little. In April, 1927, she became very much disturbed when, on a shopping expedition, she could not get what she wanted. In a hospital at Nashville the patient was agitated, frequently noisy, and wept easily. She made repeated attempts to run away. She took a rather large amount of bromide. She was also greatly agitated while on a trip to Baltimore to enter the hospital.

The patient was the youngest of four children. She was an energetic child, enjoyed undertaking things and completing what she had started. She was social, outgoing, desired friends, and was very fond of amusements. At fourteen she went away to school, but became very unhappy and homesick so that her family permitted her to return home. Later she returned to the school and completed her work satisfactorily. She was distressed when her father lost a large amount of money in a bank failure. At 23 years of age she had a very difficult time. Her mother was in a state mental hospital, and she had to care for her mother's home and an imbecile niece. She felt very depressed because people criticized her for hospitalizing her mother and taking money from the bank for the living expenses. She became depressed, had marked insomnia, and lost weight. This period lasted about a year, then she improved and soon married. Her mother recovered from her psychosis and returned to her home. The patient's home life was unsatisfactory because her husband was a chronic drinker. Their son had epilepsy, and when she again became pregnant she had an abortion, fearing there might be epilepsy in the family. She has never forgiven herself for this.

On admission, the patient's behavior showed some degree of bewilderment and apprehension, and occasionally she became frankly fearful. She feared the physician, and would say, "I am," which meant that he was the Heavenly Father. Her movements were abrupt and somewhat aimless. She expressed fear of dying. She said she would die at two o'clock because a nurse removed two glasses on her tray at the same time. She was clearly oriented, but did not evaluate her surroundings in relation to herself. She often said to the nurse, "You are not Miss V." She saw shadows or snakes and said she was going to purgatory because she had done wrong. (She had a period of considerable excitement. She seemed terrified and repeatedly said, "Please, please," but went no further.) On July 7 she said that she was no one, had no name. She asked, when going into the garden, what one of the buildings was, then said, "It seems as if I was there once, but it can't be so." When asked later what floor of the building she stayed on with her son, she said "second," which was correct. On July 18, she said, "Everybody is happy. I would like to be like the other people. I want to live as other people do to be happy. I do not feel of any importance." There seemed to be a marked tension, as if she was under a strain. At times it seemed difficult for her to talk, as if the words were sticking in her throat. She knew the year, date, and month. At times she cried a little. On July 27 she said, "I remember the date Dick was born; no, I don't, because I am nobody." On August 6 she refused food. She insisted that the clothes in the locker were charged with electricity—"I am charged with electricity and can't get up. Everybody is somebody; I am just a speck. I am not sure whether this room is one or more. (Why don't you eat?) What is why? (Is eating a little better.) I don't want to eat, Miss L. I can't eat because food does not agree with me, it might get into my bowels and not get out." She asked the nurse, "Will you take me out on the sidewalk?" Then asked, "How can I walk on my side? Walks are so funny, they have two meanings." On August 24 when her temperature was taken, she said, "It is a lightning rod. They are trying to harm me. Why should I be nobody? I never did anyone any harm." She picked at her clothes and seemed suspicious. "You put poison in my food. I will not eat because it is harmful to someone. Why is it that things I have done do so much harm when I wouldn't harm anyone? Do you believe there is a world and there are people in it? They took my clothes away, Doctor, and they took my head along with them. Look at those pictures. They change while you are looking at them. (Seems to be afraid of being alone.) Something terrible is going to happen today."

When visited by her husband and son, she said, "What do you think, someone dressed up like Junior came in here to fool me. I thought it was he, but maybe it was someone dressed up like him. Mr. H. or the gray man in the gray suit are coming today. No, I will never see him as long as I live. Don't let anything happen! They are going to cut me in pieces." The patient was constantly more or less resistant. It was always difficult to make her eat. Her face usually had a more or less vacant expression. At times she smiled. Her facial expression and speech seemed queer, but not in a stereotyped, stiffened way. She talked whiningly, like a baby. It was impossible to focus the conversation on any special subject. She was fearful, felt ill-treated, but there were no fixed delusions. There was marked indecision, bewilderment, and apprehension. Often she did not answer questions, looking away from the physician with eyes open. One day she said that she was being killed and cut up. At the beginning of September she said, "I am not Mrs. H. I am nobody. I did not know you wanted me to go to the tub." Afterward she said the nurse had taken her shoes and so she did not have any feet. She blamed herself for happenings on the ward and always insisted that she should never have done what she did. One day she said repeatedly, "If I did not eat breakfast I would be better now. People would respect me more if I did not eat." She asked the nurse whether she, the nurse, was two persons. She was afraid of another nurse. When visited by a friend, she said she did not know her, and that she did not weigh as much as a pencil point. Pointing to the door, she said, "Is that the judgment gate?" She did not know whether the nurse was male or female, and wanted to see her undressed. She said she saw strange faces in the ward, and that someone came in through the window at night and put things in the room. There were difficulties in getting her to dress: "I am afraid to put them on." She did not think the patients slept. On September 20 she said to the nurse, "I don't believe I swallow my food do you? Where does it go?" She talked about a patient who had been put in a wet pack the night before, and said, "And yet she did not seem to have them on, did she? I don't believe she had any on, do you?" Once she said she wished she could go on the campus in order to watch a car go by so she could be sure it was a real car.

Toward the end of the month, the patient hesitated in making decisions, stayed most of the time in her room looking out of the window or lying in bed. She slept all night on top of the bedcovers. It was difficult to make contact with her. She talked continuously to the nurse, saying, "I am to blame for everything.

Why can't I be like you? Would it have been better had I not eaten?" The next day she thought the shower given her was the last of everything. "If I had not taken that shower there would not have been any last day. I know I will never be well." She often did not cover herself properly. She said, "I want to die." She was restless, without any real emotion, with a rather empty face. At times she had fits of anger and outbursts against the nurses. When visited by a friend she said, "You look like yourself in one way, in another way you look like a lot of people. Please come back." The patient was very agitated all morning, would not help the physician; later she told the nurse, "I can't dress, I am nobody. There is no eternal life for me. You know last night I was laying there and someone stood by and pushed me into the flames and I was burned. It was terrible. And I am still burning. These clothes are my burial clothes. Today at 2 p.m. the world will be in utter darkness and I will be lost and alone. Why wasn't I saved long ago?" Sometimes it was necessary to tube-feed her. Sometimes she was agitated, combative, and resistive against going to bed and getting dressed. On the 25th she lay on the bed, turned her head to the wall, sent furtive glances occasionally toward the physician, mumbled to herself, wrinkled her brow. There was anger in her facial expression. She told the ward physician, "I want him to write his name." The examiner did so. After the physician had left she told the nurse that Dr. Sch. had written his name on the paper before he entered the room. She said she would like to see him alone in her room. She seemed to doubt the reality of everything.

The following night she came out of her room and asked the nurse if there was something under her pillow. The next day she again behaved very ambivalently. First she called to the physician. When he approached her, she went back two or three steps watching attentively. She then asked him to write Alabama and Dr. Sch., and the name of the hospital, saying, "See little Dr. Sch." She came nearer to the physician, bending her trunk backward, and asked, "Why did you start to play with flowers when you came in?" She often looked curiously at the other patients and asked, "Are they dead? Are they mummies?" On one of the succeeding days she asked the physician to take off his coat, then felt his shoulders and said there seemed to be too much padding. She asked if Dr. D. was real. She asked about the patients and whether they were real, but always with a smile and a curious tenseness. She asked Dr. Sch. how long she would have to stay, and answered herself, "Three months, three keys, three months." (Physician had three keys in his hands.) Everything meant something to the patient. When the physician looked at his watch, she asked him, "Why don't you look at the clock?" She was very attentive to unimportant details and had a good memory for them. "I think Dr. Sch. thinks things and people do them."

On November 2 she was anxious to talk with Dr. D. and said that everything about her had a meaning. She asked Dr. D. whether he had ever seen a skeleton dressed up in clothes, and said that she had heard that medical men did such things. She intimated that one of the doctors might do something of that sort, but Dr. D., being very large, seemed real. "Isn't it too bad that the big people and thin people cannot get together and even things up?" She said that others would go to heaven and she would go to hell. She also said that she would like to be like other people. They all seemed to be so much happier and smarter. She felt that Dr. Sch. and Dr. Sq. were too thin to be exactly real. On November 8 she helped a catatonic patient walk. When another patient was put in a wet pack, she complained and said the packs were just like coffins. When weighed, she doubted her weight. She said she weighed just as much as her shoes and wanted to weigh them. She made incoherent remarks about the way she educated her son. She stated that something in the Bible referred to what had happened in the past, the actions of the exodus were foretold. When, on November 11, she got a letter from her son, she thought it wasn't his writing. She expressed a wish to be home with family. She talked about certain doctors being dead; also about patients, especially catatonic ones.

She complained about a terrible dream. She wanted to walk and move, and something held her and would not let her move. She thought that a catatonic patient moved very well in a familiar way. During rounds on November 21, she said, "I do not think that Dr. D.'s name is Dick (her son's name). He couldn't have grown up so quickly. I have seen him and he looks like Dick." Her general attitude did not change during the month. Everything had a meaning for her and was a sign; her husband's coughing, the knocking of the physician at the door. She said that she died when Mr. H. was here, and talked of being sure her physician was Mr. H. (her husband) because he walked like him and looked like him. "There is something peculiar about it." She told the nurse that all the people did not realize how sick she was.

At the beginning of December she was much less active, sat on the bed sucking her lips and swinging her legs, and did not speak unless interfered with. She did not wish to go for a walk—"All those people would be left." Her rapport was changing. She said that the people around her seemed to be against her; the nurses made her do things. "Well, nothing is real, but I can't think now." She complained in the next few days that nobody liked her. She said she had made faces at the doctors. Sometimes the patient did not want to dress, and retired to the bathroom. When urged by nurses to follow the routine, she was combative and vulgar. She menstruated December 16 to 18, her last menses being September 10 to 12. Toward the end of the month she was still irritable with the nurses and combative against being weighed. She had some contact with her husband and child, who visited her.

In January she refused at times to respond in any way, and merely shook her head. She believed the physician was real only after putting up her hand in order to feel his breath. She complained that the former ward physician had a queer inflection in his voice when he introduced her to the present ward physician. She did not consider her clothes her own. "There's a great deal of talking around here that means nothing. I have asked questions lots of the time when I have known the answers. That was wrong." She picked at her chin constantly. Toward the end of the month she was still definitely agitated. She was unfriendly, refused food, but after the tray was removed immediately went to the kitchen and asked the maid for bread. She shrank away from people and appeared to be apprehensive. After being touched, she said people were bringing sins on her when they touched her. She said that someone in the ward had told her that she would be killed tomorrow. "Everybody's sins in the world are laid on me. When anyone comes near me it does me harm. Right now you are doing me harm." She also said that she felt electricity when touched. She made jokes, sometimes, with clang associations.

Her attitude of doubt continued through the next month. "How can one know that Dr. Sch. is a real doctor? Could he not be a murderer who just came in? I shall talk with him and they will put the blame on me. Everybody dislikes me here (becomes more agitated) because I have been so fussy." She said she felt electricity, which meant she felt different. In the bathtub, her arms felt different—real numb—and she thought they might have electricity in the tub water. Sometimes she greeted the ward physician with, "Well, I haven't died yet, have I? Everything is against me. I know I am going to die tomorrow, but everybody has fixed up their hair. They are getting ready for the world to come to an end." In the next few days she spoke of death in the electric chair. "I used to think people could disappear, then appear. You know that is silly. You can't make yourself invisible, can you?" She continued to be negativistic. As soon as a desire was granted, she immediately said she did not wish it, and began to make excuses for not accepting it. The only time she showed cooperation was definitely to surprise the nurse. She frequently expressed a rather relieved sort of surprise—"Well, I haven't been killed yet; I am really still here. Sins are on me. I don't like this hypnosis staring at me." Toward the end of the month she moved about more at times, laughed heartily and cheerfully.

The patient had been on a trip to Annapolis and there she had seen the Navy men in drill formation. She thought the second row was a reflection of the first and not real men. She said, "I wish I hadn't said such foolish things today. Every time I take a bath, that puts me that much deeper in purgatory. I suppose I was the snake in the Garden of Eden."

In March the patient was difficult to get out of bed and to

bathe. This was only accomplished with the aid of five persons, and she became extremely combative—biting and scratching. "I won't put on that stocking; someone voided last night that committed adultery." She was angry and impudent to her special nurse, but when the nurse was away for a day she was very contrite about her bad behavior and asked to have her back. When the nurse appeared the next morning, she said she thought the nurse had gone to Washington to get a reward from the President. Later on she decided that only fat people could get rewards. "Are you a detective dressed up as a nurse?" She said to the physician, "How would you like to be in my place? I used to have a good education. I used to be able to think, now some of the time I haven't any sense to think." Menstrual period started on March 8, lasting five days. During this month she was still resistive, talking frequently of a new patient being a mulatto. The perplexity changed into suspicion. She would lie in bed brooding, revolving the idea that the patients, her nurse, and the ward physician were white mulattoes, that money was obtained by everyone and there would be more for her soon. She continued to express regrets that her behavior had been undesirable, but made no effort to correct it. She asked apprehensively, "What is it they put on you to make your feet dead?" She said that her whole body was dead, starting with her left arm and shoulder. She was afraid of being killed. She remained in bed with her clothes on. She complained that the nurses contradicted each other sometimes. She was very agitated and wrung her hands. At the beginning of April she said, "They are all devils. I saw Miss B. have two horns grow out of her head and she turned red all over. They put electricity in the chairs. It counts against me every time I get mad." She complained that everything was unreal. "The tallest people walk through the ward." After being weighed, she said, "The scales are wrong. You won't let any fat people come around me, will you?" Toward the middle of the month she showed more interest in other people, but expressed great fear of being given soiled sheets or clothes that have been worn. She expressed fear of death. She felt that she could be accused of murdering the Frank boy, and wept bitterly. At the beginning of May, her activity increased. She complained and became agitated because another patient was walking in her tracks, and walked about most of the night. She complained at times of having gotten smaller here in the hospital. She began to talk about the clothes she used to have and the various color combinations she wore. Her apprehension concerning approaching death persisted, although she joked about it occasionally. Menstruation was regular after March.

When on May 8 her husband arrived, she refused to see him, pretended not to know him, and rushed out of the ward and down the hall to a corner, where she stayed, crying loudly. She finally went with her husband, but said, "I never saw him before, I don't like him." She continued to feel that if she recognized her husband as such that, instead of putting the crime on her, they would put it on him. She slept only from two to four hours at night. In the next few days her agitation increased. After her husband's departure she grew quieter and permitted one of the other patients to touch her and her things without becoming agitated. In the following weeks she became quieter. She laughed occasionally, but was still slovenly about her appearance. She laughed occasionally, but was still slovenly about her appearance. She still picked her chin and walked about stockingless and shoeless. She blamed her husband for putting her in the hospital. The next week she said that she wished she had never come to any hospitals. Toward the end of June she broke the glass in the fire alarm when alone in the hall. She started quarrels with other patients. She often talked about being killed, but generally she improved. She had more contact with physicians and patients. She spoke about the unpardonable sin and asked what it is. She continued, "It does not matter now. My mind does not work right anyway." She complained at the beginning of July of being very depressed and felt that the doctor could read her mind, but generally she improved constantly. She wrote letters to her husband, occupied herself, read and discussed books. She thought she had a very vivid dream early in her illness. She saw a little girl and someone was gouging her eyes out by means of a very high-powered stream of water. After this they made bricks out of this girl.

On July 29 she asked if she was older than two years and four
months. She had been in the hospital that long. "But what did I do
before? I am not sure I am in D. or whether I was married and had
a child or not." She was agitated. She complained that the hospital
made her just what she was then. She was no longer a human
being, but a monkey. She saw a moving picture once where
humans were talking to monkeys, and this impressed her. The
nurses in the ward talked of monkey business, and this made her
realize she was a monkey without a soul. She wept constantly
when saying this. On August 2 she spoke of not being a person, of
having changed: "My body is all right, but my head is empty. I
have no soul and cannot understand the Bible any more. I will
never be different. I am a monkey. I am so bad maybe I am a
baboon." She laughed and then wept. She was working intelli-
gently and writing frequent and long letters to her family. She
asked the physician if he did not really think she was changed. "Of
course I am a person, see how my head has changed. It is so flat,
and there is nothing in it. It is absolutely empty. I am different. I
am not the same." She reported another dream at the beginning of
her illness: She was dead and tried to go to heaven but could not
get there. She tried harder and harder. Someone asked her if she
had ever done any good, but she thought and thought about what
she had done and could not think of anything good. Patient was
facetious and somewhat overactive. In the dream she saw an
attendant with brilliant red hair. In other dreams she was full of
red paint. She spoke more and more about her family and showed
more normal reactions to their visits. Gradually she gained some
insight. Toward the end of August her insight was increased, but
she still complained that she had not much sense. There were no
signs of depression. Her whole attitude was hypomanic. She was
discharged on August 23. She explained that in the beginning of
her illness, the physician in her home town had given her medicine
and also had made a pelvic examination. She thought she was
pregnant and believed that an abortion was performed. She felt
that all her senses had left her. When put into restraint and
struggling with her feet, she felt like a monkey. In previous days

she often jested with friends, saying it would be best to be a monkey and live in the jungle, because being a monkey she would not want to talk with a physician. It would be a disgrace for them. She chuckled to herself thinking of the humor, as it were, of a doctor shaking hands with a monkey. She felt hopeless. She resented the tube feeding. At the time of dismissal the patient was overactive, but otherwise normal. On December 24 the patient and her husband stated that the patient was active and healthy, without signs of mental illness.

Here, too, psychogenic factors were present: her only child, an epileptic; her husband, an inveterate drunkard. This patient also showed doubts, which in some instances led to punning. In the background were feelings of guilt and the fear that she would be killed. Doubt and perplexity were in the foreground. The doubt was, again, a real one and deep-seated. It sometimes changed into suspicion. There were times when she no longer doubted, but had the feeling that she was changed, especially her body. We may call this a case of perplexity. Depressive features are more obvious here than in the first case.

Psychoses characterized by distress and perplexity have been described by Hoch and Kirby (1919). We shall first try to come to a psychological understanding of this type of psychosis. Hoch and Kirby spoke about a sensory unreality complex. One of their patients said that nothing looked natural; everything looked the same. But it seems to me of importance to try to characterize this perplexity in a more detailed way.

(1) In depersonalization we find a feeling of unreality and a lack of sense of reality in the foreground. But these patients always know that the world is real; that their bodies are real. There is never any real doubt. They know that the world exists, but that they have another impression about the world and about their own bodies.

(2) We find perplexity with helplessness and the feeling of difficulty in orientation in cases of mental confusion. In all cases of mental confusion, the patient shows real doubt. But in all these

cases the patients have difficulty in perception. They cannot put together details of pictures; they cannot make a whole of them; they mix them together; in other words, there are difficulties in the integration and differentiation of perceptions. The doubt is based upon an imperfection of the perception. This is as true with respect to doubt about the outside world as about their own bodies.

(3) I have already mentioned (Hartmann and Schilder, 1923) that phenomena akin to the doubt and helplessness of mental-confusion cases can be observed in agnostic cases, but here the disturbance in the perceptive apparatus is more severe.

(4) It may be mentioned, of course, that the hysteric or schizophrenic patient who lives in another world doubts what is going on around him and his world. But we shall find in these cases that this doubt is closely related to the immediate individual complexes and, in the psychosis, plays a secondary part in comparison with the delusions, illusions, and primitive world in which the patient is living.

(5) In both of our cases the doubt is directed toward the unreality of the world and contains aggressive elements. But the patients never completely give up their belief in reality. The world still exists for them, and their doubt is only the first step on the way to the negativistic ideas that deny the existence of the world. But sometimes our patients come nearer to the depressive nihilism when their doubt is over whether they have killed somebody and whether the other person is dead and whether they are dead themselves.

These cases are therefore psychologically characterized by definite doubt which is based on neither confusion nor difficulties in perception. Some confusional elements and some delusions may be present. Case 1 started with what the patient called a dream and what in reality was a delirious episode. The second case was afraid of being killed and of death. She also complained about electricity. Depressive self-accusations were more prominent in this case.

Hoch and Kirby remarked that in all the cases they observed there was an underlying feeling of guilt, which found expression in accusatory hallucinations, and the patient may have had a feeling that he was responsible for wrong trivial incidents in the environment. Among the cases of Hoch and Kirby were also those in which real difficulties in perception were present, but most of their cases correspond rather closely to the group described here.

In our first case, psychogenic factors were certainly of importance for the outbreak of the psychosis. What predominated were dissatisfaction in the marriage and the negative feelings toward her husband and sexual feelings toward other men. A relation to the infantile history could not be determined. In the second case the psychic factors were not so specific. In the first case the sadistic aggressions were obvious. She thought she had shot her husband. Her doubt about reality had the double meaning of getting rid of the husband and substituting other love objects for him. The sadistic background of this doubt will be discussed later in another connection.

The question arises, of course, of the clinical classification of this psychosis. Both cases had previously had depressive episodes. These depressive episodes were seemingly connected with special events in both patients' lives. The family history in Case 1 seemed insignificant. In Case 2, the mother had two psychotic attacks with persecutory ideas, both of which cleared up. In Case 2 depressive ideas played an important part. In both cases, feelings of guilt were present. There was no negativism. We therefore have to classify both cases as atypical pictures of manic-depressive psychosis.

Hoch and Kirby saw this similarity too, but they denied it. They found that two or three of their cases belonged to manic-depressive families. Three of the patients had former attacks from which they recovered. One of their cases ended with an unmistakable depression.

I do not think that there is any reason to separate these cases from the manic-depressive psychosis. The diagnostic difficulties in the beginning were great in both cases. Sometimes it looked as if there was a tendency to complete withdrawal, and in Case 2, especially, some mannerisms were present. The diagnosis of schizophrenia seemed rather probable for a while, but the final analysis of the case showed that we dealt with an atypical picture of the manic-depressive group.

Lewis and Hubbard (1931) do not mention this group of cases, but they speak of manic-depressive cases with odd, distorted depersonalization features. Some of their cases and some of Greenacre's (1918) show trends similar to the cases described here. Hoch and Kirby do not consider the manic-depressive group as a unit, but as a group most frequently showing constitutional reactions in the form of an affective psychosis. We have to decide whether manic-depressive psychoses can be considered as a unit or not.

Depressive States with Hallucinations and Illusions

Abraham (1924) has shown that primitive oral, anal, and sadomasochistic tendencies are at the basis of the depressive psychosis. I have often emphasized that the psychosis or neurosis only rarely affects a single psychic system. Psychic systems have psychological relations to each other. When one system is severely damaged, the psychologically and topically related systems will often undergo changes too. Constitutional factors and life experience will determine which allied systems are affected. This holds true for organic diseases of the central nervous system as well as for those diseases whose organic background is not yet known. In general paralysis, the psychic system related to judgment is deeply affected. Speech and the gnostic functions, which have close topical and psychological relations to the functions of judgment, are also very often involved. When there are organic disturbances of judgment, we regularly find memory impairments of an organic type. The schizophrenic process will not only lead to narcissistic attitudes, but will provoke a series of other primitive attitudes which, in the developmental history, are near to narcissistic attitudes. According to the psychoanalytic scheme, oral tendencies follow the stage of primary narcissism. Therefore, we would expect that, wherever primitive oral sadism makes an appearance, the tendency to narcissistic attitudes will be increased; the same holds true for primitive sadistic tendencies. Generally speaking, we expect that the so-called projection may come into the foreground whenever a deeper regression takes place. When the regression is to such a primitive level as the oral stage, the probability that hallucinations and illusions will occur is therefore great.

Hallucinatory and projection mechanisms have indeed been observed very often in depressive states. Strecker and Appel (1931) have emphasized them, as have Lewis and Hubbard (1931). Bowman and Raymond (1931a) have studied delusions from a statistical point of view. They have also studied (1931b) the problem of hallucinations in depressions. Unquestionably, hallucinations as well as illusions are not uncommon in many depressive psychoses. One finds, according to Bowman and Raymond, delusions in 57 per cent of male and 59 per cent of female patients, hallucinations in 30 per cent of males and in 37 per cent of females. But even in cases in which hallucinations and persecutory ideas are present, the emotional life shows the characteristic features of depression. There is a superego that blames and hates the ego and the id. The problem of the depressive state is the problem of an individual with strong sadistic tendencies who wants to maintain high moral standards. The depressive patient does not dare to live out his sadistic tendencies against others, the sadistic tendency will be directed toward the ego and the id in the analytic sense. And the superego tortures the ego. I shall start with the case history of a depression with anxiety.

Case 3. Mabel, 48 years old, was admitted to Bloomingdale Hospital on July 5, 1927 from a private sanitarium where she had been for some time.

Three years before, the patient began to complain about minor ailments, tending to magnify them. On June 10 she went into the bathroom, took a razor and cut her throat, cutting through the windpipe. It was not possible to keep her in the sanitarium, and she was therefore admitted to the hospital. Her paternal grandfather came of a line of distinguished scholars— fine, strong characters. He had a cousin who died at 31 of some mental disorder. Her father, who died in 1908 at the age of 67 of pneumonia, was a minister, a brilliant preacher and scholar; he was high-strung and nervous and suffered from insomnia all his life. He had three breakdowns, the exact nature unknown. The first occurred in college, lasting one year; the second after graduation, lasting three years; and the third in 1903, lasting three and a half years. The maternal grandfather was a successful man of business. The mother was a strong, domineering character, although sweet and gentle. She had poor judgment, was very prudish, fanatical in religion, and puritanical. She had been tacitly opposed to the marriage of her sons and daughter. She had one sister who was somewhat sickly and peculiar. The patient was the eldest of five children, the only girl. The brothers were all intelligent men, but high-strung and nervous. The second one had a breakdown, a depression, lasting three years. The youngest was very temperamental, high-strung, and unbalanced. He had several nervous attacks.

The patient's birth and early development were normal so far as was known. She did well in school and graduated from college in 1902. She then took a position at school as a secretary, which she held for some years. In 1904 she started concert work and had considerable success. From 1911 to 1912 she had several attacks of laryngitis which interfered with her work, and after this she ceased to take concert engagements. In 1913 she became a musical director of a public school system, which position she held for two and a half years. In 1915 her speaking voice gave out at times, and subsequently she quite often lost her voice for a week after any extra exertion. She was always very energetic and never happy unless she was running something, starting a club, and so on, showing catholicity in her interests and having many friends, although her circle was small. For more than ten years she had wished to go to work, but this was opposed by her mother and brothers. In December 1924, she became a little peculiar, stayed in bed on several occasions saying she was ill, but, on a doctor's assurance, she would get up and act as usual. She had two abortive love affairs in her early twenties, both men dying of tuberculosis. From the age of 25 she took no interest in the opposite sex, although she was quite sociable with her brothers' friends. From 1909 she had lived at home with her mother and her eldest brother.

Her personality trends were the following: learning came easily to her; she did not have particularly good judgment, but was practical and a capable manager. She had always been social, had many friends and a wide range of interests. Her enthusiasm was somewhat extreme; she was easily offended and intensely reserved. She was overconscientious, devoted to her mother and not very upset by the death of her father. She was matter-of-fact, not imaginative, not overcritical in religious matters. She followed her own line of interests, although as a girl she was fanatic and orthodox. She had no sex instruction and was brought up to believe that anything in connection with the subject was shameful. She was very reticent about sexual matters until recently. She has masturbated occasionally from the time she was about 23 years old. She was decidedly intolerant of sexual subjects. She was meticulously neat, humble, and self-deprecatory.

The present illness started on June 9, while the patient was in New York; she suddenly felt that she was a complete failure in life and that she should make an end of herself. She went down into the subway, walked to the end of the platform, but could not summon up courage to throw herself under a train. Returning home, she went to a party, and behaved normally. The next day she had breakfast as usual, but about a half hour later was found in the bathroom with her throat cut. When found by her brother, she was conscious and, although bleeding profusely, said, "I have been a failure as a daughter and a sister. You don't know. I have done awful things, I have disgraced the family. I should have married." After her wound had been cared for she gradually became more agitated and apprehensive, thinking that people knew what she had done and were talking about it, that detectives were looking for her, and that it was in all the newspapers. She said that she was to act in a play and when they were all in costume on the stage the police would come to take her away, and that everyone would hoot in derision at her.

In the hospital, she was quite cooperative and frank in her demeanor. She showed no motor retardation, but was a little restless, constantly pulling the sheet up to as to hide the scar on her throat. She was tense and apprehensive. She felt it hard to concentrate but did fairly well on the formal tests. She told of periods when sex worries came up and she would have dreams of the kind she did not wish to talk or think about. She thought for several days that she was to be taken away in a boat. She attached special meanings to everything and identified the nurses and attendants as detectives, spies, and police.

On July 6 she did not wish to talk about her trouble. "It is too horrible." She was afraid that people were listening at the door or outside the window, that everyone would find out about her. She had a slight vaginal discharge and thought it had some terrible significance. On July 7, "Oh, doctor, you know what they are going to do with me? I am not going to stay here. They are coming sometime to take me away. Oh, my poor mother! Will you tell her as gently as you can?" She could not be persuaded that nothing was to be done with her. On July 8 she was a little more composed. In the next few days she was apprehensive and tense, looking around and listening. She heard her mother and brothers talking and seemed to believe that they were in the hospital. She was especially apprehensive about being arrested and of being sent away in a boat. On July 29 she said, "They treat me so differently now. They are very nice about it. One of the physicians thinks something terrible about me. I am sure of it by the way he spoke. Of course I can't prove anything. Only time alone will decide that, if you won't believe me." In the next weeks she still believed that she was followed by police and detectives. She thought all the other patients disliked her. On August 10 she showed acute agitation. She was restless and talkative, took her hair down, and kept running her fingers through it. She said her family was being tortured because of the things she had done, especially her two little nephews, and that only by her going to prison could they be saved.

On August 20 she heard queer things in the corridor. "I have got to get away to save them all this expense. I am sinking down."

On September 3 she believed that her family was being tortured somewhere in the building. She felt that her stay was injuring her family and that she must get home. "Do you think if I were to tell Dr. R. I was pregnant and had Negro blood in me that that would get me out?" She then began to cry, saying that somewhere the German workmen and some Negroes were torturing her mother. During the next month she felt that her brother might be arrested. She talked incoherently about animals being tortured. She had seen it under the window—"Chinese images rising back and forth, made out of human beings." She complained about a desire to masturbate.

November 27 the patient was still depressed. She always thought she was harming her family by staying here. She accused herself of being a prostitute and of having Negro blood, and also of having had five children in order that she should be sent away from the hospital. While she was accusing herself of all these things, her sense of the ridiculous was often too strong for her and she could not help laughing. On January 28 she said, "You make people colored here with an electrical instrument by putting Negro blood in people. My mother was married and they say she was not. I want to get rid of my family. No, no, I don't mean that. They want to get rid of me." She could not be persuaded that hydrotherapy was done without extra charge and refused to have it for several months. She was still worried that her family might be harmed by her. On March 28 she stated that people believed terrible things of her mother and family, reiterating that her mother was perfectly beautiful and that her brothers were only brothers and not her lovers, and that the hospital had put all these ideas into her head. She accused all the physicians of talking in puns and making play upon words. She said that everyone disliked her and would like her to go. The next few months produced no considerable change. She accused herself of masturbation. In July she thought that she was believed to be a prostitute and complained that she did wrong when attempting suicide. She felt tortured. She made play on words, for example, "Death is fine. What do you mean has to be a sign?" Toward August of this second year she quieted down, but in October she was still irritable and sarcastic. Delusions and depressions had disappeared. After January she showed no pathological trends. She wanted to give a detailed description of all that had appeared in her illness.

In the middle of February the patient was absolutely friendly and composed and gave a detailed report. Since her 23rd year she had masturbated. She said it was mostly without fantasies, but often she masturbated thinking of her brothers and of her father, but sometimes she also thought of two other men. She had dreams with the same content. After the suicidal attempt she was operated on under ether narcosis and thought she had told about these dreams. When she said that she had twelve children and Negro blood, she did not believe it. She thought she would be sent away when these things were known about her. She felt that the people did not like her, that her life was a failure, that her relatives would have to pay about one hundred million dollars for her being in this hospital. Dr. D. was the Czar. She believed that she would be tortured and her eyes would be hurt and badly damaged with sharp pencils. She believed that she was put into hot packs for her wickedness. She felt that they cut the limbs of her nephews and tied them to her. She thought that the food consisted of human flesh and so she did not want to eat it. She felt it was her nephews chopped up and given to her for food. She believed also that her brother, her mother, and her sister-in-law were to be cut into pieces because of her wickedness. She thought she was to be murdered. She heard these things partly in hallucinations, but very often it was a strong conviction without hallucinations. She never thought of genitals, only arms, eyes, vocal cords, and ears were cut out. She hated everybody. Going to occupational therapy cost a hundred dollars a day. When the brothers visited her, she felt it was a miracle that they still lived. Some people wanted to intrude and force her. The patient thought she was pregnant and feared that she might be kept as a prostitute. She has had no sex feelings since coming to the hospital. She was glad about it. Finally, she felt very happy. She was discharged in a perfectly healthy state.

The patient was readmitted on November 23. She was over-active at home, talked in the office freely, but was irrelevant and circumstantial. Her trend related chiefly to striving to gain her independence from her mother after many years. In the hospital she showed a hypomanic picture. There was considerable antago-nism toward her mother, and much attachment toward her broth-ers came up. She occasionally referred to her attempted suicide and regretted that it happened because she felt it a disgrace. She reported that at that time she was going to be put in jail and that the police were after her. In the chapel all the men were there to watch her. She thought all her family were in the hospital and that they were tied up because of her suicidal attempt. She thought Dr. F. was one of those planning to torture her family. Very frequently she thought she heard them being tortured in the middle of the night. Her mother and sister-in-law were the ones most frequently tortured. "I always had a definite reason in my mind for what I did. I thought the Pope was trying to gain control so he might rule America and I thought that a Roman Catholic nurse did me up in a pack in order to get back at me regarding my feelings against the Pope." She really believed that her family were being put out and that this was done by the Germans. She believed that the German porter was the ringleader. She thought that her mother and sister were gradually being cut up—a small slice at a time was cut off to cause more pain. She thought another patient was a witch and responsible for this. "I thought I was man crazy and that I had two children. These two children later seemed to be my nephews, and they were cut up by workmen. They were a part of the scheme and were only there to torture the family." She believed that sailors were making certain arrhythmic signs with a brush and were trying to send her messages which she found very hard to interpret. She thought they were going to take her to a house of ill fame, and she heard them discussing who was going to have her first. This was frightfully humiliating to her. People were coming from jail to take her with them. She was afraid she was going to have her eyes put out, particularly when the physician came into the room and took out pencils, which seemed to her very sharp and menacing. She was sure the boat, Maria, was coming to get her, and she didn't think she would ever get back to take her place as a human being. She believed the whole world was accusing her of being some unmentionable wild person. Every remark was ambiguous. In the following weeks her state did not change. She was hypomanic, overactive and overtalkative.

This psychosis clearly belongs to the manic-depressive group. It was not possible to doubt this diagnosis. It was a circular psychosis. The family history contained only manic-depressive elements. The patient's whole life was dominated by heterosexuality and the Oedipus complex. In her masturbation she had fantasies of having intercourse with her father and with men who are "perfectly clean men." Still, the patient lived in an abstinent way throughout her whole life. It was partly the influence of her father and partly the influence of her mother that prevented her from marrying. There were many attempts at sublimation, especially sublimation through singing, which finally failed.

One could question whether her recurring laryngitis was not the expression of the same difficulties that later on led to her attempt at suicide, which occurred at a time when the chances of sex satisfaction were almost nil. We must reckon that involution, in addition to involving physical problems, was closely connected with this urgent psychological problem. The patient tried to cut her throat, hurting the organs of the imperfect sublimation; she was aware of this connection.

In the narcosis following the suicidal attempt, the patient had the feeling that she had told about all her heterosexual desires. The heterosexuality was strong during the whole psychosis. The projection mechanism was widespread, particularly in serving her heterosexual tendencies. Her heterosexual wishes also came out in her pretense that she had Negro blood in her veins and that she had several illegitimate children. The patient herself had the feeling, although not always with the same strength, that she invented the latter story in order to be dismissed and not to be kept in the hospital, causing thereby an enormous loss of money to her relatives.

Besides these heterosexual motives, anal libidinal tendencies came out symbolically: the patient spoke about money, which
apparently was of great importance to her throughout her whole
life. Her repression was strong enough to prevent the anal tendencies from coming out undisguised. This is true in many depressive cases, thus showing the strength of the superego. Cases 4 and
5, in which anal tendencies come out only thinly veiled, are rather
atypical.

There is a remarkable difference between the symbolization
of the anal tendency and the more open breaking through of the
sadistic tendencies, which were directed against her own body.
The body is cut to pieces. In some way we deal with a continuation of the suicidal tendency, but there is a partial projection in
that the patient now feels that others want to kill and torment her.
The torture is never directed against the genitals, as such, but
against the eyes, breasts, and buttocks. Seemingly, the repressive
element is stronger concerning the genitals than the other parts of
the body.

It is remarkable that a special torture was applied to her
nephews. Her nephews were the children of the brothers who were
the objects of her sexual fantasies and they seemingly took the
place of her own children with her brothers. Hence the special
cruelty concerning her nephews. The sadism did not come out in a
direct way, but in projection as a fear concerning others. The
patient nevertheless once said that she hated everybody.

But there was also the sadomasochistic fear that her body
would be hurt. We may conclude that, in this case at least,
repressions concerning sex and anal tendencies were stronger than
those concerning the cruel tendencies. It was not possible to trace
the psychosis back to actual events of childhood.

The patient's reproaches were against herself rather than
against others, except for the manic phase following, when she
blamed her mother. There was no evidence that the self-reproaches
were primarily directed against other persons with whom the
patient identified herself.

The self-reproaches were a function of the superego, which
was severe. Where did the aggressivity of the superego come

from? Freud states that aggressive tendencies that are not lived out increase the cruelty of the superego. But there are cruel and aggressive instincts in every love relation. Whenever there is a failure in love, the aggressive tendency will increase. According to Freud (1930), it is not libido that is changed into aggressivity, but the aggressivity, which primarily was directed toward an object, treats the ego in the way that the ego would have liked to treat the love object. In our patient, the aggressivity was primarily neither an aggressivity against others nor against herself, but was neutral. Depressive cases have an increased "neutral" aggressivity.

Where this increase originates, only analyzed cases can help to say. One possible answer would be that whenever oral tendencies are increased, they bring with them aggressive tendencies. In our case there are hints at increased oral tendencies (she did not want to eat because it was human meat). But the identification with puritanical parents had also helped to form her superego. The mother's severity toward her prepared the ego for a masochistic tendency. Did she also want to treat her mother as her mother treated her? Then the identification with the mother would be twofold—in the ego (in the analytic sense) and in the superego. But had the severity of the mother not also provoked aggressive tendencies against the mother? Whenever aggressivity appears, it is always sadistic and masochistic at once. And even more multiple identifications take place in the ego and the superego as well. It is very difficult, even in fully analyzed cases, to follow this complicated series of psychic processes.

But we have still neglected an important factor. We generally feel that we have an immediate and reliable knowledge of our own body, whereas we gain knowledge of the body of others more or less by controlled experience. But my investigations on the postural model of the body (1935) (body image) have shown that we do not have an immediate knowledge of our own body and that optic perception furnishes us data about the bodies of others as well as about our own body. Here lies another reason why aggressivity against oneself and another person are not so different from each other.

Aggressivity is, as I have formulated it, a *Grenzphaenomen*—

a phenomenon on the borderline between subject and object. Neither masochism nor sadism is primary. Both are crystalizations according to the particular life situation of something that was in the wide no-man's-land between subject and object (especially love object). There may be an urge to kill. It is of secondary importance whether one kills oneself or somebody else. But there is always the problem: how did this urge originate? What is the libidinal situation? What factors determine the way in which the urge is finally attributed to either subject or object?

Violent aggressivity is one of the leading symptoms of depressions. I have called sadomasochism a *Grenzphaenomen* (borderline phenomenon). I have pointed out that this neutral zone between subject and object is larger than we suppose. In dizziness either we see the illusion of movement in the objects in the environment or we experience it in ourselves. Probably the majority of our experiences are at first neutral. In the process of psychic development, every experience is finally attributed to either the one or the other. Such an attribution is possible only when we have a primary knowledge that there is an outside as well as a body and a subject. This knowledge is a basic knowledge of the human being. It would be erroneous to think that the knowledge of one's own body precedes knowledge of a world outside. What we call projection is therefore often not projection in the proper sense, but a borderline phenomenon is attributed to the outward world where we would expect the opposite. My general conception is that the bulk of our experience at first enters no-man's-land and is incorporated in the process of psychic development either to subject or object, according to the whole constellation of desires.

We should not wonder that, when sadomasochism with its specific borderline qualities comes through, other borderline phenomena occur, and, with the uncertainty in such an important part of the psychic life, other experiences also are pushed into the borderline, remain there unshaped and less differentiated, and are finally differentiated and crystalized in a way corresponding to the desires of the subject. We shall therefore not wonder when we find a tendency to "projection" (hallucinations and delusions) in cases with violent melancholic sadomasochism. Cases 3, 4, and 5 all point in this direction.

Case 4. Pamela R., 35 years old, was admitted to the Phipps Clinic, Johns Hopkins Hospital on July 10, 1929. She had been well until November, 1928. Then she developed fear of paralysis and a host of hypochondriacal complaints. In April, 1929, she complained of fatigue and difficulties in concentration. Self-reproaches for masturbation and intercourse before her marriage followed. She talked of suicide. Patient had always been a rather energetic person, but she had two mild depressions six and seven years before. A year before, her child had an accident which worried the patient. Also moving into a new home in December caused worries. The patient's grandmother, according to a state hospital report, had cycles of depression and excitement every six months. A cousin was in a state institution for thirteen years with the diagnosis of dementia praecox. Her mother was excitable and emotional. Two brothers were high-strung. The patient had one six-year- and one four-year-old child. Both were healthy.

At the time of admission, the patient often stared, moved her hand in a queer way, showed unusual postures but no catalepsy. She had "rigid spells" in which she went into an opisthotonus position. There were transitions from laughing to crying, but the latter prevailed. At times she shouted at the examiner. She was mostly coherent, but played with words. "I feel like hell . . . there hell . . . little hell . . . hell." She said that at home neighbors threw sticks and stones at her. She thought the whole country was in commotion because of her coming to the hospital. "My husband was supposed to be dead and has risen from the dead." In the next few days the patient did not talk. She had to be tube-fed, she complained that she heard voices of many people which accused her of many things. She continued to question who she was, what everything was, what condition her family was in. "Why are they always arresting me? I was arrested with my children, but I don't know why, I want to get out of this damn place. You have tortured me enough . . . is the war still going on?" She insisted that she had wronged her family and her husband's family and said that her mother-in-law was behind it. "I think all my people are dead. People talk from all angles and say such terrible things. I have been cursed, my elder brother is dead, he is the finer." She said that people stoned her at night. "I have caused the war, I have caused the death of many people, I don't know how, but it is so. I hear people shouting at me from all sides at every minute of the day. You know, you brute, you are part of it all, why don't you kill me or let me die?" She spoke of having had a vision made by "them" in which dead souls, skeletons, unborn and real children came. She had occasional crying spells.

On July 29 she complained that doctors had disappeared in the same way as a girl at home in the theatre box office disappeared from her seat. She complained that she was not able to take care of the children. She defended herself against thousands of voices shouting at her saying there are no sins in her family. "I thought everything was killed." On August 3, the patient said, "I saw you go up into the sky. You were sitting on the steps and then rose to the sky. My grandmother who is dead came to me, but there was no place to take her to the cemetery. It is so confused. . . . They say I am cursing her but I am not." In the next few days she was sure that she had done something to cause the death of her family and to cause all living people to crumble just as the college did. She still complains, "Everything is so confused."

In September she heard people saying awful things about her mother. She struck nurses and attendants. All the people she saw seemed to change into other people, to change from one person into another without being conscious of the change. Her brother Tom did likewise. She complained that she felt "body-lust" feelings. On September 28 voices accused her and her brother Tom of having syphilis. She attacked nurses whom she believed were saying untrue things about her family. On January 7, patient stated, "I feel better. Everybody is against me. There are so many things I don't understand. I have wild filthy thoughts which I don't understand. I have sex feelings, they are horrible. People say it is a religious issue that I shall be kept here all my life. Spirits, dead people I don't understand. (What do the voices talk about?) About my father, mother, and brother. They are all over the world. They are being tortured and persecuted. I don't understand why I am being held in this place and that place. I don't know what to do about it. They say father, mother, and I steal. I don't understand a great deal of it. They are being tortured, persecuted, and damned. I am no good. I don't care to live any longer, but I don't want my family tortured. There is a religious movement on. I know about that. It is about money. They will be tortured for all time. I do not know who brought me here. (What did the neighbors say?) They say that I am no good to my husband and child. (Why do the neighbors care so much?) I don't know. Why should they say that my mother is dishonest?"

She had acoustic as well as optic hallucinations. But there were also changes in her optic experience which were not strictly hallucinatory. She complained that her neighbors called her and her mother prostitutes. She was afraid that her children might be dead. "Mother will be persecuted thousands of years—eternity . . . It is a world issue." She believed also that her brother was tormented. She complained that men made her have sex feelings. They rushed spiritually in her. They did not actually touch her. "Spirits fall, I know. . . . Am I kept here for monetary purpose, something about churches, I feel that I am being wrongly treated." The patient was not confused concerning her perceptions and thoughts. But her hallucinatory experiences were disconnected as well as her delusional ideas. She felt completely helpless and confused concerning this hallucinatory world. The contents were typically depressive, although they did not come as a conviction, but as hallucinations and as disconnected delusions.

On January 17, patient felt that she tortured the spirits of everybody, that her mother was tortured in hell. "There are very few people on earth now. A millenium or something has occurred. It has all been forced on me, these men annoying me, I am a prostitute . . . I have been here for years . . . my mother has to live for two thousand years in torment and torture, I hope that she tortures my mother-in-law. I hope that my brother will torment my husband. I don't know what I am. Whether my brother is my husband. They say my husband is married to somebody else.... My brother died and was reborn.... My brother Tom has died several times for me." On January 31, patient stated, "I have not been cruel to anybody. Is everybody dead? Everything is so mixed up. I don't know what has happened. I am afraid my mother and father are in hell with all the rest. Everybody is unhappy." On February 1 the patient was discharged to a state hospital. On March 22, she showed the picture of a typical far-going depression. She no longer had hallucinations and the delusions had gone into the background. "I am depressed, I would rather die than stay here." The patient had a very strong suicidal tendency.

The clinical diagnosis was not very simple in this case since projection played such an important part, but the content was so typically depressive (money also played an important part) that we may suppose that we dealt with a depressive case. Toward the end of the observation the patient showed, indeed, a purely depressive picture with strong suicidal tendencies. The diagnostic problem was of special interest.

What does it mean when depressive ideas come as a hallucination? Does it mean a deeper dissociation? Is there a constitutional element in it? Is there a great danger for the prognosis? At any rate, in spite of the hallucinations, there was no reason to suppose that we dealt with a case of schizophrenia. All the experiences reported in the previous cases show that projection is present in many cases of depression and under special circumstances it may appear in the foreground. Strong sadistic tendencies, which at one time are directed against one person and at another time against another person and then against the subject, blur the borderline between subject and object and make projections easier. We may say that when there is one borderline phenomenon present, other borderline phenomena may appear too. Or, in other words, even numerous hallucinations do not necessarily prove the diagnosis of schizophrenia.

It is remarkable that the patient had a feeling of perplexity concerning only her hallucinations and not her other impressions. Her ideas were chiefly of torture and self-reproaches because of sexual feelings and wishes. Husband and brother substituted for each other rather often. The hostility against her husband was obvious. Oral trends did not play an important part.

Case 5. Mrs. Edna S., 52 years old, was brought to the Phipps Clinic of Johns Hopkins Hospital on May 14, 1929. She had been increasingly depressed for a month and had threatened suicide. On Easter, 1929, patient became sleepless, restless and nervous, and was at times agitated. She thought she was losing her mind. At times she lay quietly, refusing to speak. She feared this illness was a punishment from God for having threatened suicide in a previous depression. She ate very little, lost a little weight, and talked of poverty and having lost all her money. She was afraid of disease (cancer, syphilis) and that something had happened to her friends.

Little is known of the patient's early development. She progressed well in school, completing normal school. She taught for two years, but was always worried about it. She married at 25 and was frigid for a long time after marriage, but for some time before having a baby (five years after marriage) she did derive some satisfaction. After the baby was born 22 years ago, she had a uterine and vaginal laceration and, following this, she had pain during intercourse and no longer desired to have it. Her husband never forced it in any way. At first, intercourse occurred once in four or five months; it gradually stopped, and now has not been indulged in for the past four or five years. She regrets this for her husband's sake, but he insists he does not desire it.

The first depression, lasting ten days, occurred when she was in school. She was sleepless, restless, and agitated, and very apprehensive of failing in her work without cause. She recovered suddenly. Following an operation when she was 33, she was again depressed, this time with ideas of poverty, feeling that they had lost all their money and would go to the poorhouse. This lasted a month and cleared rather abruptly. Following extra work renovating her home while her husband was away, a third depression occurred during menopause at 41. She was agitated, restless, fearful of poverty, and talked of suicide. She consulted various physicians and traveled with her husband for several months. After she returned home, she recovered almost overnight, one year after the onset. Each depression was increasingly more severe, with marked swings up and down.

She was always a cheerful person, interested in social activities, fairly ambitious, liking to lead and direct, but was sometimes timid. She was fairly sensitive to the opinions of others, but always met situations well. She enjoyed outdoor life. The father was alcoholic, the mother very nervous.

This patient had several depressions before the present psychosis started. Ideas of poverty played an important part in two of them. The patient complained in the beginning of her psychosis that she had syphilis and cancer, and infected others. Later, she felt that her disease would spread over the whole world and that she had ruined the world. She accused herself of being dirty, of behaving like a child, and not having any control over her bowel movements and urination. She developed fantastic ideas about changes in her body, which culminated in the conviction that she had to turn into an animal; that she couldn't talk any more and could only growl; and that she was mated with animals. She felt also that she was the origin of a war going on between the white and the colored races. She traced her uncleanliness back into her early childhood.

But she did not only blame herself, she blamed others who persecuted her. She heard voices, but there were also smells and tastes, which showed her that food was adulterated with feces and urine. The persecutors sent insects on her which bit; they forced her to sex acts with all kinds of animals.

Also the world of perception was completely changed for her. Persons sometimes seemed larger and sometimes smaller. Things were moving that should not have moved. Objects disappeared. There were funny shadows on the floor. The faces of other persons were distorted. Everything was blurred. There were also flashes of light. She complained about noises, but she was only hypersensitive and hyperattentive to the noises of everyday life, which she misinterpreted. There were paraesthesias in her skin. But there were clear-cut hallucinations of smell and taste. She smelled the odor of feces and urine, and had the same taste in her mouth. Changes in her own body paralleled changes she experienced in the outward world. She felt twisted, bent over, choked. The great number of queer experiences contributed to the feeling of doubt and perplexity. But her doubts were not only due to the hallucinatory experiences. She had comparatively little uncertainty concerning her perceptions. But she doubted her illusions. She doubted her past, and she doubted in many respects her hallucinations as well. Doubting was the root of her illness and unfolded itself in her attitude toward the world, toward her own body, toward herself and her past. Her doubting was very closely related to her self-condemnation and her condemnation of her parents.

We do not know enough about her personal life history. We do not know the infantile pattern according to which the psychosis is formed. But oral and anal-sadistic trends dominated the picture, and with the return of the primitive sexuality she felt turned into an animal, mated with an animal, and was definitely condemned by her superego. It was probable that her almost complete frigidity was due to this deep-lying tendency, which came to the surface in the psychosis.

This case links the cases described in the first and in the second group of this paper. The projection mechanisms play an important part. There were illusions, hallucinations, paraesthesias, and delusions. But there was also doubt and perplexity. The changes in perception this patient experienced had a deep similarity with the perceptive changes described in the first and second cases. One may raise the question whether the case was not schizophrenic. But the clinical course speaks against this diagnosis. Moreover, in the last psychosis, the patient preserved a comparatively good contact. There was never a rigid negativism. She did not lose herself completely in her imaginary world. She retained contact with the examiner even when she was strongly under the influence of her psychosis. When she turned her head away, it was not in order to withdraw, but because she feared that there might be something wrong in her looks. The psychosis centered around the feeling of guilt, and anal, oral, and urethral tendencies were persistently in the foreground. When these trends are present, one is allowed to make the diagnosis of a case of manic-depressive psychosis even when there are hallucinations and paranoid ideas. Doubt and perplexity are also rather a sign of a manic-depressive psychosis than of a schizophrenia.

SOME REMARKS ON THE PSYCHOLOGY OF DEPRESSION

We shall never fully understand the mechanism of depression unless we study cases by the psychoanalytic method. I therefore report two cases which have been analyzed. The first one, in which the analysis could only be continued for about four months, will be given briefly. In neither of these cases does the analysis give a final decision, but in both the material is interesting. They show the psychological background of the psychosis that we have so far discussed from a more descriptive point of view.

Case 6. G. T., 28 years old, came for treatment in the second attack of depression. She had her first attack more than two years earlier, was treated by individual psychology, and recovered. She had a second child and became sick again a few months after the birth. In the foreground of the picture were self-reproaches and depression. She reproached herself especially for having stolen when she was a girl, mostly between her eighteenth and 22nd year. She stole money from her aunt and uncle, but once she even took money from a maid. When she was about twelve years old, she stole a photograph from her piano teacher and tore it up, but even when smaller she stole candy from her father's shop. She also reproached herself because of her masturbation, which started very early. As a child she often had the opportunity of observing her parents having sex relations. She became sexually excited and masturbated without any special fantasies. Her masturbation continued to the age of twelve and was also occasionally indulged in later on.

In her depression, self-reproaches played the most important part, but were very strongly mixed with reproaches against her husband, who was too severe with her and not fond of her. At the same time she was jealous. The patient was anesthetic; she had an orgasm only when she concentrated very much. At the beginning of her marriage she became sexually excited when her husband fondled her nipples. Marital intercourse was almost disgusting to her. She was very self-conscious and felt that she was not good looking. She thought her breasts were ugly. Among her early remembrances was that she falsely accused her younger brother and that he was beaten severely. She could not stand any cruelty; could remember that she got very upset in her early child-wounds and blood.

One of her dreams was the following: She was in a shop. There were two aunts who sold vegetables. She took a cabbage and said, "They are bigger in our place. Our garden is five acres large." In the dream she remembered that this was not true. There were many people in the room. She looked through the window, which looked out on the garden. It was the garden of her sister-in-law. She said that the plums had been taken although they were not completely ripe. Different people took plums away without having the right to. She was angry and called a policeman. Somebody was running away. A man came into the room and washed his hands. Somebody offered her black plums and said, "They are from last year. The plums of this year are still green." She wanted to wash her hands. Her husband was coming in with a scourge and wanted to beat her. His expression seemed to indicate, "I am the boss. I can do what I want." She ran into the street, and somebody wanted to tie up her husband. He was tied by a policeman. The policeman was a girl. Her husband and the girl were sitting on a bench. She thought, "Now he is alone with this girl." She called her husband to come because she wanted to talk to him. He came and lay down on the couch. She reproached him and asked him why he wanted to beat her and why he wanted to be the boss. He must promise that he would not beat her again. He said he could not promise that. He looked at his watch. There were many watches lying around, as in a jewelry shop. He said, "I will whip you 50 times so that it will be two thousand."

The associations to the dream were as follows: In her childhood she saw her father whipping her brothers. She also remembered how much she resented it when she saw horses beaten. She could remember that she got very much upset in her early childhood when she saw a man tied down by a policeman. In her later life it upset her when her husband told her stories about prisoners who were beaten. She was very much against severe discipline, whereas her husband favored it. When she was around five years old a servant tried to beat her when she was naughty. When the maid was prevented from beating her, she pinched her secretly. She was beaten by her father up to her eighteenth year.

The domineering father and the domineering husband were identified with each other in this dream. She wanted to be the domineering woman herself.

The first part of the dream linked up with her peculiar attitude toward food. Eating and cooking played an important part in a series of her dreams. In her conscious life whether she should eat much or not played an important part. She thought she was too fat and should not eat at all. When she was depressed she often went out and had an irresistible desire to eat a great deal. She often dreamed about festivals. Sausages were distributed at wedding parties. Among the first things she stole was candy. The big cabbage symbolizes the male sex organs, the black plums the anal element. Dreams about swelling things were common with her. Once she dreamed about an enormous condum. Her husband wanted to come to her. He extended a condum which was very big. Her child was crying and had defecated in the bed.

The last part of the dream again pointed to her acts of stealing. She counted again and again how much money she had taken from her aunt and uncle. The price of a watch she presented to her husband was 50 shillings.

The first part of the dream pointed to an oral desire and the tendency to take away the male sex organ, which at the same time had anal character. In the second part of the dream she was cruelly punished. In the third part of the dream she expiated by giving back the sex symbol and giving back the money she had stolen.

In other dreams, sexual feelings in connection with her father and the analyst came out. She was afraid of her father, who was extremely fond of her. But the father was cruel to the mother and to herself.

This incomplete analysis showed strong heterosexuality almost in the foreground of the picture. There is the relation to the father and the early jealousy, which was aroused by the fact that she observed her father sexually attacking a servant girl. But earlier than this scene, which occurred in her eighth year, were observations of parental intercourse. The father was her first love object; the brothers followed. Her sexuality started with stealing candy which belonged to her father. Many dreams not reported here pointed to early experiences concerning the father's sex organ. She stole a photograph of her piano teacher's fiancé. It is of interest that she stole from the maids, who were also the love objects of her father.

Her masturbation started at the same time as her stealing. They served the same purpose. In the analysis she often said she would kill herself immediately if she stole or masturbated again. There was a strong heterosexuality in the sense of the Oedipus complex. Freud was of the opinion that kleptomania expressed the wish of the girl to get back the penis she wanted and which she thought she was entitled to. But in our case the evidence does not go farther than to show that she wanted the penis for sex satisfaction, and there was some doubt whether she wanted it as her own sex organ.

It is remarkable that in spite of her strong heterosexuality her sex feelings were very incomplete. She was almost completely frigid. Her longing for the penis was strongly oral, as the dreams I have reported show. But these oral tendencies were certainly not the only ones that prevented her from having complete sex satisfaction. There was strong sadomasochism. She falsely accused her brother, who was then beaten. Self-reproaches and the feeling of guilt followed. She was extremely sensitive concerning cruelties. The attitude of her father, who was often ill-tempered and rude toward the children (brothers), increased her sadomasochistic tendencies. She felt masochistic toward men, toward her father, and toward her husband, and protested against the masochistic position into which she was pushed by the stronger male. On the other hand, she complained very severely about her husband and father, living out her sadistic tendencies against them. But only the strong Oedipus complex, heterosexual and homosexual, makes it understandable that the heterosexuality was so strongly repressed.

The patient identified strongly with the ill-treated mother. On the other hand, as in all cases in which children have the opportunity of knowing something about parental intercourse, there was another tendency to identify with the father and with the husband. Some of her self-reproaches may have primarily been directed against her father and against her husband. But there was enough open aggressivity left against her father and husband, and a part of her self-reproaches were based upon her insight into her aggressivity.

The incompleteness of the analysis did not allow us to estimate the amount of anal tendencies, but they come out in a very open way in her dreams and tendencies. Her stealing of money and her great interest in money and the tendency to squander it are at least hints of anal tendencies.

The material in this case does not allow us to go to the basic oral and anal situations, but it shows that there are three points of fixation: in the oral and the anal spheres and in the Oedipus complex. The strong sadomasochism was in connection with all these points of fixation. I am inclined to believe that this multiplicity of points of fixation is typical of deep depressions. Only the strong Oedipus complex makes possible a strong superego, which absorbs the sadistic tendencies. The strength of the superego in depressions is based to a great extent on the fact that it is supported by heterosexuality (and less homosexuality). Individual cases vary according to the different amounts of libido fixated in the oral or in the genital phases. Cases like the one described here have a strong heterosexuality and therefore show hysteriform symptoms. The kleptomania[3] fits into the scheme. The frigidity in these cases is the expression of the strength of the superego concerning the strong heterosexuality. Of course, her sadism was still destructive, but the strong Oedipus complex prevented archaic destructive trends.

The important question arises again, of course, of what part identification mechanisms play in such cases. The identification with the mother and with the father's love objects is obvious. Her jealousy was the jealousy of the mother against the father. But her reproaches were especially directed against men and their cruelty. Some identification tendencies with them were certainly present, but remained more or less in the background.

If one goes over the material one is again in doubt whether one can, in this case, accept Freud's formulation that the self-reproaches are directed primarily against the love object with whom the individual identifies himself. One has rather the impression that she reproached herself for the sadistic attitude concerning the love object. Identification with the love object played a secondary part.

We had here strong sadistic and sadomasochistic tendencies, but it would be difficult to say which one was prior to the other. The patient seemingly at first wanted to be in the passive masochistic situation in which she saw her mother, her brother, and the servant girl in relation to her father. Her sadistic protest was more or less secondary. It is difficult to say whether taking the candy away from her father was not a punishment she inflicted upon him. But was not her sadistic protest also based on a tendency to

[3] It is remarkable that in the first case of manic-depressive psychosis in which an attempt at analysis has been made, kleptomania was also present. It is the observation of Otto Gross (1907).

identify herself with the sadistic father? It seems that the tendencies to manifold identification were increased whenever more primitive aggressivity came into play. Whether these aggressive tendencies were due only to the infantile situation concerning the father or have only constitutional components was impossible to decide. I do not think that identification with the love object in the ego played an important part in the symptomatology.

I also emphasize again the heterosexuality in depressive states. Our formulations will become clear when we study the findings in our next case.

Case 7. E. P. was a woman of 49 years. The first attack followed a disease of her child who was several months old at that time. The patient was then 38 years old. There was a mild depression which increased gradually and lasted more than fourteen months. A hypomanic phase followed. The hypomania never disappeared completely. Toward the end of 1928 a slight depression followed gradually, which increased.

The patient was analyzed during the first attack of depression, but at irregular intervals. After the depression had disappeared, the analysis was discontinued, but started again in March, 1929 and continued for several months. In the second analysis the patient especially complained about fatigue, sadness and the impossibility of undertaking anything. She felt particularly hindered in her profession. Reproaches against her husband, distrust of servants, inhibition in spending money, and self-reproaches were present in the first as well as in the second depression. The patient never showed any inhibition in speech or motility. But in the first, and in the second attack as well, she had great difficulty getting up in the morning and spent hours during the day on the couch.

The patient very often thought what would happen when her husband died; whether there would be money enough for her and for her child. She always complained that he was too rough with her; that he did not give her enough of his time and was tyrannical. She was his second wife; he was divorced from his first wife. She had already had relations with him during his first marriage. Fear of disease and death of her husband played an important part in her fantasies. She also thought of what would happen if her mother died. The patient was quarrelsome, especially with her husband's family, and had many enemies.

Her sadistic tendencies went very far back. When she was seven years old, she wet herself and was laughed at by the family. The next night she dreamed that there was a black mirror, that one member of the family after another had to go before this black mirror, and that she gave a sign and the person fell dead. She also had remembrances from her fourth year. At that time her father died. She remembered that she was with neighbors on the day of the funeral. When the funeral was passing, the neighbors made jesting remarks that it was the funeral of a gentile, until the patient realized that it was the funeral of her father. The patient had hair of a reddish color and had been very often laughed at when she was a child, which filled her with great anger and gave her desire for revenge.

One of her earliest remembrances was of an oral type. Her father kept her on his lap when she was less than four years old. It was the Day of Atonement. She was eating, and some crumbs fell on his coat. He said, laughing, "People would think that I am eating on the Day of Atonement." In her childhood she always slept with her mother's breast in her hand. In the first phase of the depression, she had a dream that she had her mother's nipples in her mouth and was sucking them. "It was like a brownish red sausage" (anal tendencies combining with oral).

In discussing a dream, early memories came out about the ritual killing of chickens. She remembered that she went with her servant to the house where the chickens of the whole village were killed by the ritual butcher. Her grandfather died when she was nine years old. He had eaten chicken the day before he died.

At the time these problems were being discussed, she dreamed that she was sitting in a coffee house and remembered that she had to buy food. She went to the butcher. There was a chicken breast. She bit into the raw meat. She came home. A quarter of the chicken was boiled. Many people were coming. There was a festival. She did not know where they wanted to go. She did not know what they had to eat.

As a child she was very curious and dissected frogs. In one of her dreams she saw dissected bodies of children lying around.

She had a wet nurse. She had been told in her childhood that this nurse killed several other children. She had a fantasy that she saw this wet nurse standing in the kitchen at the stove, and there were bones of killed and burned children. She felt it was a memory from childhood. Her uncle once hurt himself on the skull with an axe. This same uncle once made a joke, arranging his clothing as if he were hanging himself. She was very fond of this uncle, who was supposed to have many sex relations with servant maids, and she slept in his bed at about her sixth year.

In the depression, the feeling of tension and of being torn played an enormous part. She had fantasies of suicide in which she cut herself to pieces. She had the feeling that she was cut into the chest like a chicken. She was torn like a chicken. She saw in fantasy the bloody genitals of a woman and had the feeling, "I looked like that after the birth of my child." She had the feeling that she would like to look at her genitals as she had done when she was a child. Her mother had always told her about the pains she had to suffer during the birth of the patient. She felt that she always knew that her birth was painful for her mother.

She felt she would like to beat herself up. She saw herself in the bathtub, her blood running. She felt an enormous fear. She felt as though she were making somersaults and destroying the furniture; as if she were flying around the room. She was at that time under the influence of allonal. She felt a great restlessness in her whole body. Everything was flying around. She had the feeling when she was lying on the couch that she was at the same time flying around in the room in a multiplied way. At the same time she always felt tired, especially in the legs. She had the idea that it was not possible for her to get rest. She had a tendency to lie on the couch the whole day. It was difficult for her to get up and to do anything. She felt that she had a rigid face. Her greatest difficulty was to go out to buy something. At the same time, she felt she spent too much money. This is again a hint of anal tendencies, which are also otherwise outspoken. In her early sex activities, anal masturbation with another girl played a great part. Her mother talked a great deal about constipation. When there was constipation the mother, as well as the patient, took out the feces with her fingers.

It seems that the anal remembrances go still farther back. Toward the end of the analysis, it was recalled that her father brought home black figures made out of wax. These black figures were made from the by-products of a mill where her father worked. At the same time she also had recollections that her father died from an unknown disease and that people spoke about poisoning. Her mother even spoke about a crime.

At the time of the depression the patient often was hungry, but had to force herself to eat. Her hatred against her husband was increased. Her feelings toward her mother since childhood were very strongly mixed with hatred and contempt. Her mother forced her to go clothed in dresses she did not like. Her mother also had other peculiarities. Money was very scarce. She was jealous of her mother, after the death of her father, when she was out with men friends. She reproached her mother for not wanting her birth.

In her early life she masturbated with a girl cousin. This masturbation partly took place on the nipples. The nipples were brought in touch with the genitals. In her later development quarreling with an older sister and jealousy against her played an important part. The patient was regarded as very gifted. Her mother expected very much from her. She retained her virginity until she finally began the love relation with the man who became her husband.

During the first part of the analysis, the transference was rather outspoken. In the second part of the analysis, the patient very often doubted what she had said. She even got into a fury, declared that the interpretations were foolish and that the analyst had invented them. Very often she denied in the subsequent sitting what she had told in the previous one. She asked for love and again love. The analyst should pity her. She knelt down before him. Hatred followed when she felt that the analyst could not give her as much as she wanted. She often thought of what would happen if the analyst should die.

One can easily reconstruct in this case a deep early attachment to the mother. The nipples and the breast played an important part in this relation. The reported dream connected nipples-penis-feces. She learned from her mother to remove feces with her hands. In early sex relations with her girl cousin, nipples are used as a sex organ.

There were seemingly intensive relations to the father. He appeared as the possessor of a black formed stuff which is probably a cover remembrance for anal relations. The other remembrance is of an oral type. The father was not allowed to eat. It is probable that the mother played the masculine part, too, after the death of the father. She took care of the family and was a professional woman. But the patient found, around her fifth year, the way back to heterosexuality. There was a distinct relation to her uncle. All her experiences were accompanied by the fear of danger and destruction. The mother appointed as her substitute a maid who, according to the patient's belief, had killed other children. The mother hinted that the father may have been poisoned. The uncle was also in danger of death. Recollections about killed and devoured chickens play an important part. In the later psychosis she identified herself with the killed chickens. The destructive tendencies provoked by these early experiences come out in the dream of the latency period when she lets all her relatives die. Her attachments to the mother were always ambivalent and full of hatred. She still admired her and there was doubtless a strong tendency to identification present. But at the height of the psychosis, her self-reproaches were directed to her aggressivity and not against the introjected mother. She had felt the danger of destruction in her early childhood and answered it with hatred. But she also identified herself with the destructive forces around her. One may say that she had reached full object relations and had reached the Oedipus level, but her heterosexuality had been impaired by the father's early death. Strong sadistic tendencies underlined her object relations from the very beginning and made them ambivalent. She had destructive tendencies against her love objects. In her marriage she soon developed an attitude toward her husband similar to that she always had to her mother. This attitude may have been provoked by living with her mother-in-law, whom she hated. The pain suffered during the birth of her child and the child's subsequent disease may have increased her sadomasochistic tendencies. The protest against the duties connected with the household, which hurt her masculine pride, was an additional factor. She broke down when the outward difficulties were solved. She checked her sadistic activities in the first and the second depression. She became fatigued and was inactive.[4] Her activity caused her guilt. She became stingy and constipated. But she remained a strong hater. She hated her mother and her husband. In the second depression cruel fantasies were referred to her genitals and herself. Bloody genitals meant the genitals of her mother, torn by her birth, and her own genitals torn by the birth of her child. Even here, the genital adjustment that the patient had reached finds its expression. One may ask why she had reached the genital level with full orgasm, whereas the other patient did not. The deep conflicts of this patient lie in the pregenital sphere of anal and oral sadism. Her Oedipus relation was almost uncontested. In the previous case the infantile conflict as such lies on a higher level. She had a conflict concerning her father. This patient had not.

In the manic phase her hatred came out more freely, but in a less destructive form. Her hyperactivity was a partial sublimation of her destructive aggressivity. The patient had a rather considerable professional success in this phase of her disease.

The structure of this case is comparatively clear, and one sees that there are at least three points of fixation: the oral sadistic, the anal sadistic, and the Oedipus level. The oral-sadistic tendency

---

[4] The fatigue of the neurasthenic has very similar roots. The patient feels tense when she checks her tendencies to destroy the other by dismembering. She is tense because she fears that the dismembering is finally directed against herself.

here is stronger than in the other case. The difference in the different type of depression can be only partially explained by the different levels of fixations. The different amount of libido invested in the various points of fixation is of fundamental importance. The case histories do not tell us definitively whether a different ego structure in the two cases had a deciding influence on the symptomatology. Theoretically it is at least probable that this is so.

I do not intend to go into the psychoanalytic theory of depressions. Rado (1928b) has pointed out that the ego of the depressive patient humiliates itself in order to get back the love of the superego. It is true our patient wants the love of the husband, of the mother, and, especially, the love and help of the analyst.

Rado (1928a) thinks that the prototype of the pardoning mother is the giving again of the nursing breast after a period of hunger. This piece of psychology, however interesting it may be, is purely constructive, and I think it is good to remember that one part of analytic knowledge belongs to observation and actual revival of remembrances. The reconstruction of an infantile scene that cannot be remembered will have to reckon with an uncertainty, which is the greater the more one goes back. Even the continual repetition of a pattern in the transference situation is much more ambiguous than the actual remembrance of a situation with the help of the transference. But, as I have said, I do not intend to go into the psychoanalytic theories. I have only gone so far in order to help in the understanding of the psychosis I have described.

There is no question that aggressivity is in the foreground in all of our cases. It is an aggressivity that tends to complete destruction of the love object. In our first case the oral component in this destruction was not obvious; nor in the second case. I doubt whether, if one had analyzed deeper, the oral component would have come out. The manifest symptomatology reflects, always in a symbolic way, the infantile conflict. In Case 4, too, the oral component is not as obvious as in the others. But the tendency to complete destruction of the love object is an observed trend. This aggressivity is not acted out in any of those cases.

I believe, therefore, in a primary aggressivity of the manic depressive. It may be a reaction to the aggressivity of others; it may be a constitutional tendency. In both analyzed cases we found sufficient evidence that there was a tendency to revenge. There may be an identification with the torturer, which helps to this reaction. This aggressivity, not lived out, may finally be turned against their own ego as punishment. The well-developed Oedipus complex hinders the free output of sadistic activities and increases the tendency to self-punishment. The analyzed cases gave sufficient proof for the strength of the Oedipus complex. Case 3 among the unanalyzed cases pointed in the same direction. The ego was punished in the same way as the cruel parents had punished before. Maybe it was a repetition of an early suffering. I could not see here any primary death wish, as Federn (1926) has done. I also failed to discover an outstanding tendency in the ego to identify itself with the love object, as Freud (1917) has stated. This identification showed up in the cycle of identifications, but I do not think it had an outstanding dynamic value. Our patients did not choose their objects in a narcissistic way.

It is possible, as I have said, that the patients perpetuated in their self-torture an early situation in which they were tortured by their parents. But is that a primary tendency to suffering? Perhaps the question as such is erroneous. Freud (1930) has told us that instincts and drives do not have general aims, but have their meaning in connection with specific life situations. It is true he has himself tried wide generalizations. The death instinct tends, according to him, to the destruction of the individual, the life instincts (Eros) to its preservation. But he has also identified death instincts with aggressive tendencies, and aggression is for him primarily aggression toward one's own body. Let us try to come to a less schematic understanding of the problem. Suffering is one of the characteristics of human life and probably of life generally. There is either pain or physical discomfort or mental and moral suffering.

Pain, when perceived, disrupts the unity of the body image and provokes forces which try to push out the disrupting element. Reconstructive forces are dominant. Masochism does not mean that pain is substituted for pleasure. Pain also provokes displeasure in the masochistic person. The individual would flee from it unless he has more important aims for which he is ready to tolerate even the displeasure of pain. He may try to get rid of the fetters of the body, there are always destructive forces concerning the body image. One's own body is, after all, not so different from the bodies of others. There is an interrelation of body images. Destructive forces may be directed, under the influence of guilt and atonement, toward one's own body. Moral suffering is derived from physical suffering. It has an innate tendency to go back to physical suffering. If one suffers morally, one tries to inflict pain or at least discomfort on oneself. One denies oneself nourishment and sex satisfaction. The tendency to suffer finds its full expression only under the influence of the moral forces of the superego.

In the masochistic neurosis, the suffering serves to establish a deeper relation to the sex partner. Complete surrender guarantees the final grace of the sex partner. This is the concept Rado stresses. But the masochist also participates in the grandeur of the torturer, whom he has endowed with the quality of unlimited power. The superego of the depressed plays the same part. The primary oral aggressivity of the depressive case can be, because of the neutrality of the body image, directed against one's own body. The body image has in itself the tendency to its dissolution. It takes this turn when the infantile situation—punishment or fear of punishment by the parents—enforces the child's masochistic passive attitude. The masochistic attitude then becomes a means for a closer relation to the love object. But this self-destructive attitude gets its full force only by the final development of the Oedipus complex, which creates a strong superego, which binds the destructive tendencies and gives them their final direction. In typical manic-depressive cases, the ego organization is strong enough to give a more or less uniform shape to the diverse tendencies. In the cases with doubt and perplexity, the ego is helpless and has given up the task of synthesis. In the hallucinatory and delusional cases, the deep-going narcissistic regression provokes a more fundamental reconstruction in the ego.

The difference between the different types of depressions are probably due to different points of fixation and the relation between the different types of fixation. Our first two cases make it probable that perplexity is due to a sadistic tendency in which the oral components do not play as leading a part. It is a purely destructive tendency toward the world and the own body. In the delusional and hallucinatory cases, the fixation partly goes back to the narcissistic level. In the case of kleptomania, the hysteriform element plays an important part. Certainly, we should not consider only the libidinal situation, but also in what way the central personality organizes various partial drives, in other words, the ego in the psychoanalytic sense. It seems that in the cases of doubt and perplexity, this central organization is particularly inadequate.

Our general opinion is, therefore, that the variation of the pictures of depression is connected with the various points of fixation and the relative value of these different points to each other. The strong sadistic component belongs to all cases. The Oedipus component is of varied strength, but always present. Anal and oral tendencies can be in the foreground, but do not play any outstanding part in some of the cases. Narcissistic trends are present in some cases, but do not dominate the picture. The organizational power of a total personality also has a decided influence on the final picture.

CHAPTER THIRTY-ONE

Self-Consciousness and Optic Imagination in a Case of Depression

The 21-year-old medical student, Albert S., complained, "I can't talk in the past year, I do not think to say what I think. Thought and speech are not correlated. There is always something stiff in me when I talk with people. I must put them ill at ease. Most of the time nothing goes through my mind. There is only a mental activity without direction. I am manufacturing things in my mind. I often said things for the saying of them. I am afraid I shall not remember everything."

He complained that he had lost his power of imagining anatomical relations. He had particular difficulties in imagining the anatomy of the pelvic region; when he finally succeeded, it turned around and was distorted. But he had also difficulties in imagining the topical relations between stomach and liver. It was as if he

Appeared originally in the *Psychoanalytic Review*, 21:316-328, 1934.

were trying to pull up the liver so that he could look into the deeper parts. (The mother had a gall bladder operation about a year ago.)

"I feel blank—everything is futile. I never could do anything without thinking of myself. I always try to think what I am thinking. The knowledge I had was temporary. I have never had lasting knowledge."

These complaints came out in the first two weeks of the analysis. The condition had developed gradually in the course of the last four months. It had become so severe that he didn't dare go to medical school and face his colleagues. He felt that everything was futile, and he laughed at the idea that he would ever recover. He sat at home in despair, moaning and groaning. He said, "I feel like a dog! I feel like a robot or mechanical thing."

The patient was the oldest of three children; he had a sister two years younger and a brother six years younger. His parents had always bestowed a great amount of admiration and love on him. Whereas the father, a rather successful business man, showed his admiration in a restricted and indirect way, the mother was always effusive in praising him. She not only admired his physique and spoke about his royal appearance and features, she also called him a noble character. Her praise for his intellectual faculties was unlimited. She often said that he dropped pearls out of his mouth and that what he was saying was pure gold. The remembrances of this maternal attitude went far back, nor did it ever change. The family's admiration increased enormously when he proved to be gifted in school. He had failed in college twice when he was not very interested in his work, preferring to play with other boys on the street. But an unbroken series of scholastic successes followed, culminating in the second year of medical school, when he received a gold medal for his achievements in pathology. He became more and more accustomed to being admired by everybody. He was considered witty and unusual. Everybody expected a great deal from him, and he regarded himself as a superior being. He had the ambitious idea of being the best medical student in the country. At the beginning of his illness he was at the height of his outward success, but when he got the gold medal he began to doubt whether he actually deserved it. A disappointment in his love life had become definite a short time before that event. A girl with whom he had fallen in love did not return the feeling and finally married somebody else. At the same time he started to worry about the enormous strength of his sexual urges, which he felt interfered with his studies. He thought that a person of his superiority should not have feelings and tendencies that did not conform to the ideal picture his parents, his friends, and he himself had formed. We thus acquire an insight into the actual causes of his depression.

We come to a deeper understanding when we consider the material the analysis brought forward concerning his sex life. His attachment to his mother was very early mixed with feelings of disgust. She didn't close the door when she went to the toilet. These remembrances go back to a very early age. He felt there was often an unpleasant smell like feces on his mother's hands. He was very much ashamed when she came half dressed into his room. He was also very much ashamed to undress in her presence. In the course of the analysis a remembrance came into his consciousness that after a throat operation in his fifth year he was sitting on the toilet and his mother was with him and his buttocks were exposed. During the analysis he had a fantasy that he was sitting as a baby on the toilet seat and defecating. Another fantasy he reported at that time was, "How would it be if I looked under a nurse's skirt and she urinated in my face?" When he was six years old, he was lying in bed with his sister; the mother, in the next room, gave birth to his brother. She was screaming. He buried his face in the pillow and cried. There are two other important early memories, which came out in the later course of the analysis. When he was less than two years old he was riding in a carriage drawn by a Shetland pony, the mother sitting in the back. The cart had large wooden wheels. He was sitting between his mother's legs. He had an impression of the driver with a whip, riding on a road of red clay. At a slight rise of the road, the sky behind looked like a sea of rolling water, and he was afraid they would fall into water. The mother quieted him down. When he was between three and four years old, he had measles; he remembered the dark room with the green shutters. Between four and five another boy showed him a long rifle.

The two most important features of his psychosexuality came to expression in this way. The enormous interest in seeing and the disgust connected with the anal function, which probably changed his attitude toward sex. His mother's constant interest in his outer appearance increased his interest in seeing. She was interested in the size of his penis. He himself later compared his penis with those of other boys and also thought about what his father's penis might look like. He had a great curiosity concerning his sister's sex part. The mother, with justification, considered him good looking, and he had always been much concerned about his appearance. He worried because one of his teeth was missing. He wanted others to admire him. He worried, when he was ten or eleven, that he was too fat and that other boys laughed at him. In the course of the illness he felt that he was too fat and should diet. He reproached his mother for eating too much and being too fat. He had the same attitude toward his sister. During prepuberty, he had a great series of active and passive homosexual experiences in which mouth and anus were used. In his masturbation fantasies he imagined a man and a woman in intercourse. He tried in vain to take the man's place. He was very much afraid of being detected. At sixteen he had his first heterosexual experience. In the following years he had incomplete heterosexual activities until about a year before the onset of the illness. This was rather infrequent intercourse with a girl he did not care for. After the first week of the analysis he started another heterosexual relation, but he found the girl ugly and unattractive.

We are now able to better understand the symptomatology during his illness. He still had a great interest in his appearance. He felt that he was good looking, but when his general doubts started, he found that his features became common and ugly. He thought also that he smelled bad and perspired too much and that his clothes no longer fit him. We can say that his interest in his own body had been increased by the enormous attention the mother had given to it. His narcissism concerning his outer appearance was the immediate continuation of the love the mother had given to his body. He started to doubt the appearance of his body when his narcissism increased so much that he did not dare, especially under the influence of his disappointments, go to school any more. His attitude to his body was now the reversal of an extreme narcissism—a narcissism that was closely interrelated with seeing and being seen.

His attitude to his own thinking was the direct continuation of his attitude to his own body. He became narcissistic concerning his thinking because the mother had praised it so much. The same factors that wrecked his confidence in his beauty wrecked his confidence in his thinking. He viewed his own body and his own thinking with his mother's eyes. His self-consciousness concerning both was directly related to the introjection of the mother (and, to a lesser degree, of the father) into the superego. The undermining of his self-confidence, which followed the extreme expansion of his somatic and intellectual narcissism, increased self-observation and self-consciousness. He continually observed himself with the eyes of his superego, which were the eyes of the mother. But he expected the same admiration he got from his mother from everybody around him; the mother became the exponent of human society.

He wanted to be admired by all the other people, by the mother, and by himself (his superego). There was a continual interchange between his superego and those in the outside world. In patients of this kind one has the impression that the relation between the superego and the outer world has remained flexible. He despised himself and felt despised. He admired himself and felt admired. I have elsewhere (1935) shown that the knowledge of one's own body is a product of the social relations to the group. The same is true concerning the knowledge of our own thinking. We think about ourselves what the others have thought about us. Self-consciousness is a social phenomenon.

But this phenomenon would never have occurred in the same way if the patient had not had strong visual tendencies from the start. This tendency undoubtedly had, as the scattered remarks show, libidinal roots. He had an extreme curiosity concerning sex matters. He wanted to see. His visual imagination served his sex curiosity. His sex curiosity came out in his attempts to imagine his mother's pelvic region and abdomen. He looked at his thinking process with the same curiosity. He wanted to see everything. He was not satisfied with knowledge that could not be visualized. He wanted his whole knowledge experienced immediately. Self-observation is therefore based upon visual libidinal components and on the introjection of the admiring mother, a distinct part of the superego. When the patient improved in the course of the analysis, he said that he never believed he had lost all his knowledge and all his power of imagination: His continual self-depreciation provoked frantic assurances of appreciation from his mother. He depreciated himself in order to get more appreciation. He humbled himself intellectually in order to be appreciated more by his mother and by others. The self-depreciation made it unnecessary to prove his enormous narcissistic claims. He would have been the greatest man if he had not been afflicted by the illness. This mechanism is similar to that which Rado (1928b) has pointed out in depressions, where the ego depreciates itself in order to get reassurance of love from the superego and the parents from whom it is derived.

But the picture cannot be understood unless we take into consideration that sadomasochistic tendencies express themselves in the tendency of continual self-observation. The patient observes himself in order to punish himself. Self-observation, as Reik (1927) has pointed out, always has a sadistic tendency. The parents see, in order to control and to punish. The omniscience of God enables him to punish.

The phenomena of self-observation and self-consciousness therefore have the following roots: narcissism, visual libido, and sadomasochistic tendencies.

It is important to see how the patient's relations to other

people were changed by his self-observation. He thought that everybody was attentive whether he was witty, clever, successful in his work, good-looking or not. But it did not make much difference to him whom he impressed. The result of the narcissism was not the disappearance of object relations, but a quantitative increase, which was connected with a general leveling that did not acknowledge specific individuals as such.

All these tendencies found clear expression in the sex relations he started during the analysis. He found the girl ugly. He thought, why do I allow her to be so familiar with me, and got into a rage when she called him "Honey." He ordered her to go into queer postures during intercourse. He examined her vaginally. He found a uterine retroflexion and had intercourse without protective measures because he was curious whether or not his diagnosis that she could not conceive was correct. She was only a vagina for him. He felt that it did not make any difference for him with whom he had intercourse. Every girl meant the same to him. He would have liked to have intercourse with everyone. With the progress of his analysis, the personal relation to his love object awakened.

A still clearer picture of his tendency was found in the transference situation. He was curious about what the analyst thought of him. He was very proud when he said something the analyst considered witty and clever. He wanted to impress the analyst. He confessed a high appreciation for him, but he felt that the analyst was inferior to him because he had to serve him. He thought the analyst would not ask for any money. Especially in the beginning of the analysis, he often had the impression the analyst was sitting very far away on a wooden chair, which he associated with a throne and an electric chair. (When he had fever at six or seven years, people also seemed to be very far away.) Once he thought he smelled the flatus of the analyst. At another time he found that the analyst's cigarette had a very bad smell. Once, when he had to wait, he developed the fantasy that the analyst was masturbating. He also wondered whether the analyst had intercourse with his female patients.

He thus projected his own desires and concerns into the analyst and introjected the analyst into himself. If the analyst lived in the low instinctual sphere of odors, masturbation, and illicit sex relations, things couldn't be so bad. There was no reason why he could not be as good as the analyst. The discussion of money, brought out many hostile feelings about the analyst. The analyst should be glad to treat such an interesting case without any fee. After discussing the money situation with his parents, he felt they wanted to shirk their financial responsibility and started to blame himself in a similar way. A part of the reproaches he now directed against himself were primarily directed against his parents, especially his mother. It can easily be seen that he had introjected his mother twice. She was a part of the observing and praising superego, which continued in the tendency to self-observation. The analyst should admire him as much as the mother did and as he wanted to admire himself. Sometimes he said to himself, "Was it not clever, am I not witty," or "The analyst would certainly admire my clever remarks." But the mother was also a part of his ego and id. She represented the gross sexual and anal sides of his personality. Near the time of recovery he summed up in the following way: "Will I know that the obsessional preoccupation with the desire to see has left me? If so, then I shall have the natural ability back."

The analysis led to a complete recovery after six months. The process of cure went in the following way: Ego and id features were projected into the analyst, who seemingly tolerated this part of his ego. A part of the analysis was the undoing of introjections by projection. After projection had taken place, the analyst was taken back by identification into the patient. Introjections, identifications, and projections operated circularly. Two different movements, one in the ego, the other in the superego, influenced each other.

Clinically, the case belonged to the group of manic-depressive psychosis. It was a depression, but one should not think that we dealt with the emotion of grief and sadness. The patient said correctly, "I am not sad, but my thinking is paralyzed." He complained chiefly about his inability to think and to imagine visually. This inability forced him to continual self-observation. His self-observation was similar to the self-observation of depersonalization cases.

But our patient never complained that his thoughts were mechanical, automatic, and not his own thoughts. He complained about the inhibition in thinking, but reckoned his thoughts to his own personality. He also felt his body always as his own body, although he said he would like to be like a dog or like a piece of wood. In other words, the inhibition in thinking and imagination was much more in the foreground than in depersonalization cases. He also completely lacked the feelings of estrangement characteristic of depersonalization cases. His difficulties were more circumscribed than the difficulties of depersonalization cases. He withdrew less from his experiences concerning the body and concerning the personality and therefore still retained the feeling that his acts belonged to his own personality. There was no question that these descriptive differences were due to differences in libidinal development and in the structure of ego and superego. There is nevertheless no question that both pictures can belong to the manic-depressive type, in spite of the considerable differences they show from the classical type of depressions. Oral-sadistic features did not play any part in the case described here. We are far from a complete understanding of the differences in the various depressive pictures. The studies of Abraham (1911), Rado (1928b), and others are merely concerned with the classical group of depressive psychosis, and we have no right to transfer their findings to the variety of so-called depressive pictures we find in manic-depressive psychosis.

I do not think we have the right to consider the case described as merely a neurosis. I am convinced, from experience in other cases, that this patient would have recovered, although in an indefinite time, without treatment. But his personality would have remained distorted.

When I discussed this case before the New York Psychoanalytic Society (the case was at that time at the end of the third month of analysis), there was an almost unanimous opinion that this was a case of schizophrenia. The self-observation, the leveling of the object relation were considered proof for this diagnosis. I do not think there were any of the characteristic dissociations of schizophrenia in the case. The course of the case spoke very much for the diagnosis of a depression, under which I presented it. The patient had gained a fuller appreciation of his love object. He deeply felt the incompleteness of sex relations in which he had no real feeling for his love object. He assisted the girl with whom he had sex relations when she became pregnant. He made a complete adaptation in his relations to his family and to his studies.

An observation like this, incomplete as it may be from the analytic point of view, leads to important general problems. The patient continually observed his own psychic processes in a particular way. Wundt (1874) said that the *innere Sinn* is different from consciousness. Comte (in Kronfeld, 1920, pp. 370-371) said, "The thinking individual can't be divided in two, one of which is meditating whereas the other sees it meditating. The organ that observes and the organ that is observed are identical. How could an observation take place?" But there is no question that the subject observed himself. Self-observation is a fact and not a theory. Brentano's theory acknowledged that.

Brentano (1907) also believed that every psychic act includes the knowledge of this psychic act. In the act of perception, the knowledge that one perceives is included. Analytic observation shows that we observe ourselves in the same way that we have been observed by others, especially by the parents. Self-observation and self-consciousness are therefore acts of a social character and are the expression of the fact that human beings are basically social human beings. Reik (1927) has drawn the conclusion that self-observation is not based upon the primary qualities of the human mind. I would not draw such a conclusion. I think that the human mind and, especially, the function of consciousness are the expression of the essential social quality of human existence. Our individual experiences, the attitude of others to our actions and thinking as far as it expresses itself in words, belong to the very nature of our acts. I therefore think that Brentano is right when he states that the knowledge that we are perceiving is an integral part of the perception. But I would add that this knowledge of one's own action is the expression of the social character of the psyche. Our patient's particular experiences only exaggerate trends that are present in all of us.

I have said (1935) that we build up the knowledge of our own body, not only by observing ourselves, but also by observing others. Furthermore, we are interested in those parts of our body that provoke the interest and actions of others. I spoke about the socialization of the body image. Our observation shows that the same principle holds true concerning mental processes. Thinking is always socialized thinking. Here lies the importance of the word, since the word makes the socialization of the thought possible. But, from another point of view, one's own thinking has a close relation to the body image. In the construction of the body image, visual factors play an outstanding part. One may say that observation generally is to a great extent observation through the eyes. Whenever we want to observe we use optic perception and optic imagination. Curiosity is to a great extent optic curiosity and optic curiosity is closely related to the curiosity concerning sex. Not from a phenomenological point of view, but from a dynamic point of view, self-observation and optic curiosity are closely linked with each other. Here lies the explanation for the fact that depersonalization so often starts with the complaint of no longer being able to experience visual images. Optic perceptions and imaginations are basic, not only for the socialized knowledge of our own body, but also for the socialized knowledge of our own thinking. We come to the following general formulations. (1) The knowledge of one's own psychic acts belongs to the characteristics of psychic life. (2) This knowledge is the expression of the social character of human existence. (3) The differentiation of the superego out of the ego forms the basis for socialized acts. The body image and the knowledge of one's own psychic acts are closely related to each other. Visual interest and curiosity are basic for both of them.

In the course of our discussion we have come to the problem of narcissism, and we have seen that our patient's narcissism did not consist of a lack of relations to other people. On the contrary, his relations to others were, in the course of the illness, more in the foreground than they had ever been before. One could perhaps say that it was only the attempt to regain object relations and to come into a closer contact that was primarily prevented by the increase in the narcissistic tendencies. But we must refuse this interpretation since the early history tells us that the increase in his narcissistic attitude was due to the enormous investment of libido from the parents. The narcissistic attitude in this case was the result of object relations of special intensity and character. In a study on blushing and other social neuroses (1938b) I came to the conclusion that in these cases the so-called narcissism is the expression of the oversocialization of the body image. Self-consciousness concerning thinking is oversocialization of the thinking process. Narcissism in this respect means not disappearance but leveling of object relations. We come also to the general formulation: (5) Narcissism, at least in special cases, is not due to the disappearance of object relations but to an oversocialization with leveling of object relations. We may add: (6) The relation between superego and the persons outside retain a special flexibility. Federn has studied ego feeling in several interesting articles (1926, 1927, 1929). He speaks about the sense of boundaries of our ego. Whenever an impression impinges, be it somatic or psychic, it strikes a boundary of the ego normally invested with ego feeling. If no ego feeling sets in at this boundary, we sense the impression in question as alien. So long as no impression impinges upon the boundary of ego feelings, we remain unaware of the confines of the ego. But we come to much simpler and clearer formulations if we study the psychology of the body image and the investment given to the different parts of the body image in connection with the reactions of others to our body and their actions concerning our body. Federn believes also that ego feeling is the original narcissistic investment of the ego. But in studies on the body image (1935) I have shown that we do not come to a knowledge of our own body unless we have contact with other people and the outside world. It is a mistake to believe that we have an immediate knowledge of our body image. As I have mentioned, it is built up in the process of socialization and this socialization is already present at the most primitive levels. I therefore do not think that Federn (1932) is right when he says that the original narcissistic investment of the ego has at first no object. I insist that, even in the most primitive experiences, psychic acts are socialized. Psychoanalysis should give up the idea that we have an immediate and primary knowledge of our own body and should consider more what human beings actually are: socialized in their body image and socialized in their process of thinking.

A final theoretical question arises. What is the essence of a so-called conscious act? According to Brentano's formulation, perception and action are conscious in themselves. Our discussion shows that this formulation has to be enlarged by saying: The knowledge of one's own psychic act is at the same time the expression of the social character of human existence which finds its final expression in the superego, but is already based on the first construction of the body image, which needs the world, other persons, and their actions. We come therefore to the conclusion: (7) Consciousness is a social function which reflects in the superego. (8) Overconsciousness (self-consciousness) is the result of oversocialization with leveling of object relations.

I know that some of these formulations are not in accord with current psychoanalytic formulations. The chief difference lies in the denial of an objectless narcissistic stage. This denial implies a greater stress on the social character of human existence. I consider as a factual addition to psychoanalytic knowledge that the case described shows that self-observation has three specific roots: dissatisfied narcissism, sadomasochistic tendencies, and visual curiosity; and, furthermore, that the increased narcissism is the result of the self-sacrificing love of the parents.

The formulation that consciousness is a social function should be acceptable from an analytic point of view. It leads back to very early formulations of Freud concerning the nature of repressions. But it approaches the problem more from the positive side. The continual interplay of identifications and projections that take place in the ego as well as in the superego are the expressions of the primary social function already present in every psychic act, which never can be an isolated psychic act, but an act of a person who lives in a social group.

CHAPTER THIRTY-TWO

The Motility of
Manic-Depressive Psychoses

The group of manic-depressive psychoses is one in which emotions are in the foreground. Every emotion has its specific motility. We shall understand these statements better if we make clear to ourselves what an emotion is. We may say that an emotion is a response to a situation which tries to express itself in movements, but that this motoric answer is checked. According to the general rules concerning psychic and nervous energy, the energy of the motoric answer cannot disappear. Therefore it has to be discharged in a changed way. It will be discharged partly in a motor component akin to the movement primarily intended, but the psychic energy will also enforce the emotional experience concerning the situation.

Take the instance of wrath. One would like to attack the enemy with one's whole force. The hands may be used as fists, or they may seize the object. If such an attack were possible, the

Appeared originally in *Proceedings of the Association for Research in Nervous and Mental Disease*, 2:304-313, 1931.

wrath would disappear rather quickly. If the outflow of motility is not possible, the motility has to be checked by the general tension of the muscles. The clenching of the fist is partly a remainder of the aggressive tendency, partly the expression of the checking of the aggressive action, and the general tension of the muscles prevents any action. In the meantime, the vasomotor changes as well as the psychic tension increase. This is a typical instance of an emotion.

We may say that emotions are never lived out completely, and that is why we find so many expressive movements primarily intended, according to Darwin's theory, as a response to a specific situation. One can also study this when conducting experiments of conditioned reflexes in human beings. When the individual has a strong tendency to withdraw the hand before the electric shock comes, the action is very often checked. There is a general tension of the muscles, accompanied by a very disagreeable feeling of fear and expectation. One can say that this tension is the expression of this emotion, but at the same time it has the meaning of a checked motoric answer. We may generally say that every emotion has its motor expression. What comes out in the emotion comes out in the action, too.

The emotions of manic depressives express themselves in expressive movements as well as in actions. The problem of motility in manic depressives is therefore closely linked with the problem of manic-depressive emotions. Before proceeding to the discussion of specific emotions, we will make a general survey of the organic background of emotions and the actions following out of these emotions.

We have developed the general point of view that an emotion is always an answer to a situation. The apperception of the situation is therefore the basis for every emotion. We know that every apperception of a situation is concerned with cortical activities, and, in the apperception of every life situation, all sensory activities of the cortical area take part. Of course, we are not of the opinion that these activities are purely cortical. These sensory activities of the cortical region are also based on the activities of many lower levels. But cortical activities are built up in different levels, the lower of which appear, for instance, in cases of agnosia and aphasia. When the impression of a situation is received, the total personality immediately reacts. Or we could say that a feeling and an emotion are connected with every apperception of a situation. The basis for these feelings must therefore be cortical in some way. But there is no question that subcortical activities go into action at the same time, especially the thalamus opticus and the striopallidar system. We have the right to assume that the thalamus opticus is especially connected with expressive tendencies concerning the face and general motility, whereas the function of the striopallidar system, which gets its impulses chiefly by the thalamic system, is concerned with automatic motor activities. Therefore, every situation brings with it, not only many instinctive expressive impulses, but also impulses to actions.

We should never forget that emotions and impulses are very closely related to each other. We know, indeed, many cortical lesions which change the emotions as well as motor activities. One finds that patients with cortical lesions very often have a phenomenon one may call incontinence of emotions. Of course, there is always the question whether in these cases the defectiveness is not only cortical but general.

It is interesting that we find clear-cut types of changes in motility and in impulses connected with motor and sensory aphasia. The so-called motor-aphasic case is sullen, has a tendency to depression, and has neither impulses to speak nor any other kind of motor activity. We can say that there is a close relation between the motor-aphasic case and the depressive one. In the sensory-aphasic case, we find not only paraphasias, but an enormous tendency to talk. Accompanying this tendency to talk, one finds a great number of motor impulses of another kind. These patients cling to the examiner. They have a tendency to touch things and to run around. At the same time they are in high spirits. They tend to ignore their speech difficulties. They are optimistic. Their facial expression is that of happiness. Unquestionably there are close relations between the motility of these patients and manic cases. I may mention that one may find that a whole group of patients do not appreciate pain and dangerous situations as they did before. Their motility and reactions in this respect are greatly diminished.

In the last few months I have studied another type, probably due to a lesion of a region proximal to the Wernicke region, in which an aphasia of a partly motoric type is connected with greater motility concerning pain and an increase in both expression of emotions and a tendency to imitative movements. These few remarks should only point to the importance of the cortical region for emotions and impulses. It is not necessary to go into deeper detail about the thalamic and striopallidar activities concerning emotions and motility.

I may mention that in amyotrophic lateral sclerosis we find forced laughing and crying in connection with the loss of the inhibiting impulses of the pyramidal tract. We know, on the other hand, that in encephalitis cases we very often find stiff smiling which is seemingly connected with a lesion of the striopallidum and the substantia nigra. I have often emphasized the importance of the different sources of impulses. The many experiences in postencephalitis cases show that there are impulses originating in the deeper parts of the brain that are transposed to the cortical apparatus in various ways. What we know from the point of view of clinical pathology is completed by experimental findings. Cannon (1932) and his co-workers have observed that rage occurs in animals the anterior part of whose brain has been removed. They call it sham rage. It can be observed after transection through the diencephalic region, but when one cuts in the posterior part of the diencephalic region, the sham rage disappears. Sherrington (1900) and Bazett and Penfield (1922) have observed that decerebrated animals show many reactions when they are cleaned or when food is put into their mouth that look like affective movements. They show expressions of anger and aggressivity. There are also tendencies to biting, bristling of the hair, and so on. These are called pseudoaffective reactions. I may say that we do not have the right to speak of sham rage and pseudoaffective reactions in these cases. It is at least probable that something like an emotion takes place in the mutilated animal. At any rate, there is no methodical way of determining this. But these experiments show that the patterns of emotivity and emotional reactions are based on philogenetically old parts of the brain, and we suppose that the emotional and motor responses to a situation generally start with the perception of the situation through the cortical apparatus, which immediately corresponds to thalamic and strio-pallidar activities and the activities in the diencephalon, midbrain, and medulla oblongata. The cortical apparatus in some way shapes the patterns that are prepared and given by the activities of the lower levels, which are shaped and integrated by the higher levels.

The motility of psychotics can therefore be understood only if we ask, "How do they react to the situation as personalities?" We can generally say that in manic-depressive psychoses the personality acts in a more or less integrated way. One emotion predominates, and this emotion shapes the patterns. The emotivity of the manic, for instance, leads him again and again back to reality. The reality he perceives and toward which he reacts is highly developed. Therefore, we find real actions. These are characterized by the fact that they follow in the direction of the object. There will therefore be no tendency to symmetrical movements. Asymmetrical movements prevail. It is characteristic that rhythm and iteration are generally absent in the movements of manics. Since the manic has a highly developed personality, in which the individual remains isolated without the loss of the personality structure, we generally do not find a tendency to imitation in manic pictures. The hyperactivity of the manic follows the lead of the object or, in other words, the cortical impressions and the cortical motives dominate in the final integration of motor activities. Schematically, in manic pictures we see an overflow of motor energy developed in order to escape disagreeable complexes. When the overflow of psychomotor energy increases, then the movements of the manic to some degree lose the character of high development. The tendency to imitation, rhythm and iteration, symmetrical movements, may come out more or less clearly, but they are never dominating. In another formulation we may say that, at the height of manic excitement, catatonic features in motility are not unusual. Expressed differently, the emphasis is displaced partly from cortical to subcortical activities. But the emotivity will always be in some way uniform and the emotivity and motility will fit each other. We know that in manic pictures crying and depressive elements are almost always present. I agree with the formulation given by MacCurdy (1925) that every manic-depressive picture is in some way a mixed state—a mixed state not in the mechanical sense in which Kraepelin used the term, but in the sense that manic emotions need stimulation by unhappy experiences and complexes. From time to time these break through and provoke pictures that look depressive, or what is called manic stupor. But this coincidence and interrelation between depression and elation are basically different from the dissociation of emotivity one sees in schizophrenic psychoses. It is important to point out that manic motility is the motility of a restless, striving, grasping for, and seizing, and not the motility of rapture, serenity, contemplation, and ecstasy. The motility of the manic depressive is based upon an interest in the world which is renewed again and again. But we have to assume that this grasping for objects needs great help from subcortical activities; otherwise, the cortically based tendency would not find sufficient support.

What we mean becomes especially clear when we study postencephalitic children, with their hyperactivity due to subcortical release. This flow of energy in many respects resembles the manic hyperactivity, but is not guided in the same way by the tendencies of the whole personality. I remember seeing a postencephalitic child between six and seven years who offered the complete picture of a mania. I mention this in order to show that seemingly subcortical energies are used in manic activity. Here it may be mentioned that the motility of children very often reminds one of manic motility, but when we deal with younger children, we find that the tendency to symmetrical movements and to rhythm is greater than in a manic patient. I would not deny that the manic patient may show rhythmic and symmetric movements, too, especially when he dances, but this symmetry and rhythm are always related to a real or an imagined purpose. The tendency is not to move merely for the sake of moving. It is not a pleasure in muscular action as in schizophrenics, but a pleasure in acting with real or imagined objects—in acting toward the world. Moreover, the schizophrenic's pleasure has a dimly perceived, often symbolic, object, but we can ignore that in this connection.

Our formulation might help us to a better understanding of why brain injuries of children very often release subcortical motility and restlessness, whereas in the adult the same lesion may have another effect. In some way the motor hyperactivity that comes out so clearly in the postencephalitic child is one of the reaction patterns of the childhood, and we see similar activities to those the manic integrates to higher purposes. The hyperactivity of a lower degree of the choreiform and of the athetoid type observed in children and in cases with brain pathology does not belong to the material of manic overactivity. We know that the catatonic excitement very often uses these more primitive elements of action. In this connection, I must emphasize that I have never found increases in postural and righting reflexes in manic-depressive cases. As I have often emphasized (see Hoff and Schilder, 1927), in catatonic states we find an increased divergency of the arms, an increased tendency to turn, and an increased tendency to postural and righting reflexes following the position of the head. Very often, when the head is turned, a catatonic will continue to turn and will turn 180 degrees with his whole body—even more— and turn several times around his longitudinal axis. We do not see the same in manic patients.

When we consider the motor aspects of a depression, we see the lack of impulses as the outstanding feature. It is worthwhile studying the posture of a depressed case from this point of view. We see that, usually, he droops his head. He is bent forward. He does not like to be erect. His arms are bent; his elbows, wrists, and fingers flexed. We may generally say that the posture is similar in many respects to what we see in paralysis agitans. Seemingly, the lack of directing cortical impulses checked by the depressive emotions influences striopallidar activities in a special way. In one of the cases I have observed in Bellevue Hospital, the picture showed a striking resemblance to paralysis agitans, since the patient also showed some rigidity. It is not so much the lack of tone; it is the tendency not to act and the inhibition of the action that are in the foreground.

We know from a psychoanalytic point of view that the depressive in his fantasies and his wishes is active and sadistic and has wild motor activities. Therefore, one sees this sudden breaking through of homicidal and suicidal impulses. We can also understand the small movements of distress and anxiety one so often sees in depressive cases. They are in some way the breaking through of a motor activity, and it is perhaps remarkable that they break through in one of the most expressive parts of the body, a part especially suited to action. The intertwining of the hands is in some way an active inhibition of the sadistic tendency. One of my patients, while lying quietly, had the feeling that she was moving about actively in the room and breaking the furniture, or flying around and pushing against the walls. In some way the active manic tendencies were breaking through, not into motility, but into fantasy.

We can now better understand the restlessness of the melancholic as the expression of a suppressed tendency to an action the individual does not allow himself, and, at the same time, we have here a general interpretation of the motility of restlessness. These emotions also use subcortical activities to a great extent. I may remind you of the cases of acute hyperkinetic encephalitis which so often showed all the motility of anxiety and restlessness without the corresponding emotion. Apparently we again deal with subcortical energy, which is used by the emotions, and by the cortical adaptation to the emotional situation. All these remarks also pertain to anxiety states in which the motility expresses itself in movements of the fingers through which the whole body tries to find a restless escape.

The pictures of confusion and perplexity which are so

common in manic-depressive psychoses do not have a special type of motility. Generally the helpless individual will diminish his activities toward the world, and the motility of the perplexity states will show a close relation to the motility of the more mildly depressed cases. It is not worthwhile acting when we do not have the feeling that we know the world in which we are acting.

This description of manic-depressive motility is certainly schematic. We must reckon with the fact that motor integration of different individuals varies greatly and may suppose that integration under the cortical lead is more highly developed in some than in others. This would be the type Kretschmer (1921) calls the pyknic cyclothymic. In other types of motility, integration under cortical lead has not progressed so far. We then speak about the schizoid personality and schizoid tendencies of motility. Generally, we may suppose that manic-depressive psychoses are more likely to occur in those who have a great tendency to integrate their motility. But this rule has exceptions, and we know that in some manic excitements catatonic motility may come out more strongly when a less integrated motility is constitutionally present; or the actual motoric picture in the manic-depressive psychosis will depend on the individual motor constitution. I would point especially to the investigations of Homberger (1923), which show the great differences among people in the development of motility. In this respect it is also remarkable that depressive pictures in the feebleminded, whose motility is less integrated, strongly resemble catatonic pictures.

Whenever we study the motor situation, we shall ask, "What part of the emotional apparatus predominates?" and use the scheme I have given above. We may generally say that manic-depressive psychoses mostly occur in persons also well integrated from the motor point of view, and that the unbroken and undissociated emotion of the manic-depressive case finds an integrated expression in the more highly developed motor actions.

Only one question remains. Do there really exist Kleist's (1908, 1927a) so-called motility psychoses in which hyperkinetic and akinetic pictures occur periodically based on a constitutional inferiority which comes out in a periodic way? I personally cannot believe in a clinical entity of that kind. According to my experience, most of these cases turn out to be schizophrenics, and they then have a typical schizophrenic motility. In other cases we deal with the occurrence of manic-depressive emotions acting in an individual with a motor system of the nonintegrated type. We may then see pictures that are sometimes difficult to differentiate from schizophrenic and catatonic pictures. In my opinion, motility psychosis as an independent clinical entity does not exist.

We may summarize by saying that in manic-depressive psychoses the individual is directed toward the world and forms his emotions according to the situation. Every emotion is based on and liberates cortical activities, but at the same time shapes and integrates and directs subcortical activities and motor patterns. The emotions of elation, depression, and anxiety are integrated with the help of cortical apparatus, but use and shape largely subcortical activities and energies.

REFERENCES

Abeles, M. & Schilder, P. (1935), Psychogenic loss of personal identity: Amnesia. *Arch. Neur. & Psychiat.*, 34: 587-604.

Abraham, K. (1911), Notes on the psycho-analytic investigation and treatment of manic-depressive insanity. In: *Selected Papers of Karl Abraham*. New York: Basic Books, 1953, pp. 137-156.

———— (1924), A short study of the development of the libido, viewed in the light of mental disorders. In: *Selected Papers of Karl Abraham*. New York: Basic Books, 1953, pp. 418-501.

Adler, A. (1907) *Study of Organ Inferiority and Its Psychical Compensations*, New York & Washington, D.C.: Nervous & Mental Disease Publ. Co., 1917.

———— (1917) *The Neurotic Constitution: Outlines of a Comparative Individualistic Psychology and Psychotherapy*. New York: Dodd Mead, 1930.

Alexander, F. (1927), *Psychoanalysis of the Total Personality. The Application of Freud's Theory of the Ego to the Neuroses*. New York & Washington, D.C.: Nervous & Mental Disease Publ. Co., 1930.

———— (1931), Schizophrenic psychoses: Critical consideration of psychoanalytic treatment. *Arch. Neur. & Psychiat.*, 26: 815-828.

Alexander, F. A. D. & Himwich, H.E. (1939), Nitrogen inhalation therapy for schizophrenia. *Amer. J. Psychiat.*, 96: 643-655.

Allers, R. (1909), Zur Pathologie des Tonuslabyrinths. *Monatschr. Psychiat. u. Neur.*, 26:116-155.

———— (1916), *Uber Schädelschusse*. Berlin: J. Springer.

Almàsy, E. (1936), Zur Psychoanalyse amentia-ähnlicher Fälle. *Internat. Ztschr. Psychoanal.*, 22: 72-96.

André Thomas,—(1916), Syndrome de rotation autor de l'axe longitudinal dans l'homme dans les lesiones cerebelleuses. *Cpt. rend des Séances de la Soc. Biol.*, 19:89.*

Angyal, A. (1935), The perceptual basis of somatic delusions in a case of schizophrenia. *Arch. Neur. & Psychiat.*, 34:270-279.

———— (1936a), The experience of the body-self in schizophrenia. *Arch. Neur. & Psychiat.*, 35:1029-1053.

———— (1936b), Phenomena resembling Lilliputian hallucinations in schizophrenia. *Arch. Neur. & Psychiat.*, 36:34-41.

———— (1937), Disturbances of activity in a case of schizophrenia. *Arch. Neur. & Psychiat.*, 38:1047-1054.

Angyal, L. von (1936), Coincidence of the interparietal syndrome and automatic changes of posture in a case of schizophrenia. *Arch. Neur. & Psychiat.*, 37: 629-637.*

———— (1937), Uber die motorischen und tonischen Erscheinungen des Insulinshocks. *Ztschr. ges. Neurol. u. Psychiat.*, 157:35-80.

Association for Research in Nervous and Mental Disease (1928), *Schizophrenia* (Dementia Praecox). New York: Paul S. Hoeber.

Babinski, F. & Jarkowski, A. (1921), De la surréflectivité hyperalgésique. *Rev. Neurol.*, 37:433-438.

———— * The Editor was unable to verify or complete those references marked with an asterisk.

Bain, W. A., Irving, J. T. & McSwiney, B. A. (1935), Afferent fibers from the abdomen in splanchnic nerves. *J. Physiol.*, 84:323-333.

Bang, S. (1918), *Biochem. Ztschr.* 90:383. In: Wells, H. G., *Chemical Pathology*, 5th ed. Philadelphia: Saunders, 1925.

Barach, A. L. & Kagan, J. (1940), Disorders of mental functioning produced by varying the oxygen tension of the atmosphere. *Psychosom. Med.*, 2:53-67.

Bárány, R. (1907), *Physiologie und Pathologie des bogensgang apparates beim Menschen.* Leipzig: Deuticke.

Bazett, C. & Penfield, W. (1922), A study of the Sherrington decerebrate animal in the chronic as well as acute condition. *Brain*, 45:185-265.

Bechterew, W. von (1911), Uber die Anwendung der assoziativ-motorischen Reflexe als objektives Untersuchungsverfahren in der klinischen Neuropathologie und Psychiatrie. *Ztschr. ges. Neur. u. Psychiat.*, 5:299-318.

–––––– (1912), Die Anwendung der Methode der motorischen Assoziationsreflexe zur Aufdeckung der Simulation. *Ztschr. ges. Neur. u. Psychiat.*, 13:183-191.

Bender, L. (1934a), The anal component in persecutory delusions. *Psychoanal. Rev.*, 2:75-85.

–––––– (1934b), Myelopathia alcoholica associated with encephalopathia alcoholica. *Arch. Neur. & Psychiat.*, 31:310-337.

–––––– (1938), *A Visual Motor Gestalt Test and Its Clinical Use.* New York: American Orthopsychiatric Association.

–––––– (1940), The drawing of a man (Goodenough test) in chronic encephalitis in children. *J. Nerv. & Ment. Dis.*, 91:277-286.

–––––– (1952), *Child Psychiatric Techniques.* Springfield, Ill.: Charles C Thomas.

–––––– Curran, F. & Schilder, P. (1938), Organization of memory traces in Korsakoff's syndrome. *This Volume*, Chapter 18.

–––––– & Schilder, P. (1930), Unconditioned and conditioned reactions to pain in schizophrenia. *This Volume*, Chapter 21.

–––––– (1933), Alcoholic encephalopathy. *This Volume*, Chapter 14.

–––––– & Woltmann, A. G. (1937), The use of plastic material as a psychiatric approach to emotional problems in children. *Amer. J. Orthopsychiat.*, 7:283-300.

Bender, M. (1945), Synkinetic pupillary phenomena and the Argyll-Robertson pupil. *Arch. Neur. & Psychiat.*, 53:418-422.

Benedek, L. (1935), *Insulinshockwirkung auf die Wahrnehmung.* Berlin: Karger.

Berger, H. (1915), *Trauma und Psychose.* Berlin: Springer.

Beritoff, J. (1926), Uber die Individuellerworbenetätigheit des Zentralnervensystem. *Arch. ges. Physiol.*, 213:370-406.

Bertschinger, H. (1910), Process of recovery in schizophrenia. *Psychoanal. Rev.*, 3:176-188, 1916.

Betlheim, S. (1924a), Zur Frage des zwangsmässigen Greifens organischen Hirnkrankungen. *Monatschr. Neur. u. Psychiat.*, 57:141-145.*

–––––– (1924b), Säuglingsreflex bei Apraxie. *Jahrb. Psychiat. & Neur.*, 43:226-234.

Bibring, E. (1929), Klinische Beiträge zur Paranoiafrage, II: Ein Fall von Organprojektion. *Internat. Ztschr. Psychoanal.*, 15:44-66.

Blalock, J. R. (1936), Psychology of the manic phase of the manic-depressive psychoses. *Psychiat. Quart.*, 10:262-344.

Bleuler, E. (1910), *The Theory of Schizophrenic Negativism.* New York & Washington, D.C.: Nervous & Mental Disease Publ. Co., 1912.

–––––– (1911), *Dementia Praecox, or the Group of Schizophrenias.* New York: International Universities Press, 1950.

–––––– (1924), *Textbook of Psychiatry.* New York: Macmillan, 1955.

Bleuler, M. (1931), Schizophrenia: Review of the work of Professor Eugen Bleuler. *Arch. Neur. & Psychiat.*, 26:610-627.

Boggs, T. R. & Padget, P. (1932), Pellegra. *Bull. Johns Hopkins Hosp.*, 50:21-32.

Bouman, L. (1931), Hemorrhage of the brain. *Arch. Neur. & Psychiat.*, 25:255-272.

Bowman, K. M. & Raymond, A. (1931a), A statistical study of delusions in manic-depressive psychoses. *Amer. J. Psychiat.*, 11:111-121.

—————— (1931b), A statistical study of delusions in manic-depressive psychoses. *Amer. J. Psychiat.*, 11:299-309.

Brain, R. (1922), On the significance of the flexor posture of the upper limb in hemiphgia. *Brain*, 45:113-121.*

Brentano, F. (1907), *Untersuchungen zur Sinnespsychologie.* Leipzig: Dunker u. Humboldt.

Breslauer-Schück, A. (1917), Hirndruck und Schädeltrauma. *Mitteil. Grenz. Med. u. Chir.*, 29:117.*

Bromberg, W. & Schilder, P. (1933a), Death and dying: A comparative study of attitudes and mental reactions toward death and dying. *Psychoanal. Rev.*, 20:133-185.

—————— (1933b), Psychologic considerations in alcoholic hallucinations—castration and dismembering motives. *Internat. J. Psycho-Anal.*, 14:206-244.

Brunner, H. (1927), Ergebnisse der Funktionsprüfung des ohres. *Zentralb. ges. Neur.*, 37:145-161; 44:3-55.*

Bürger-Prinz, H. & Kaila, M. (1932), On the structure of the amnesic syndrome. In: *Organization and Pathology of Thought*, ed. D. Rapaport. New York: Columbia University Press, 1951, pp. 650-686.

Bychowski, G. (1937), Psychoanalyse im hypoglykämischen Zustand. *Internat. Ztschr. Psychoanal.*, 23:540-547.

Campbell, C. M. (1935), *Destiny and Disease in Mental Disorders with Specific Reference to the Schizophrenic Processes.* New York: Norton.

Canestrini, S. (1913), *Uber das Sinnesleben der Neugeborenen.* Berlin: Springer.

Cannon, W. B. (1932), *The Wisdom of the Body.* New York: Norton, 1963.

Carmichael, N. & Stern, R. (1931), Korsakoff's syndrome: Its histopathology. *Brain*, 54:189-213.

Clark, L. P. (1917), *Clinical Studies in Epilepsy.* Utica, N. Y.: State Hospital Press.

Courville, C. B. (1936), Asphyxia as a consequence of nitrous oxide anaesthesia. *Medicine*, 15:129-245.

Curran, F. J. (1937), Personality studies in alcoholic women. *J. Nerv. & Ment. Dis.*, 86:645-667.

—————— & Schilder, P. (1935), Paraphasic signs in diffuse lesions of the brain. *This Volume*, Chapter 11.

—————— (1937), Experiments in repetition and recall. *This Volume*, Chapter 12.

Dale, H. (1937), Transmissions of nervous effects by acetylcholine. In: *The Harvey Lectures*, 31:229-245.

Davis, D. B. & Currier, F. P. (1931), Forced grasping and groping. *Arch. Neur. & Psychiat.*, 26:600-607.

Deutsch, H. (1933), The psychology of manic-depressive states, with particular reference to chronic hypomania. In: *Neuroses and Character Types.* New York: International Universities Press, 1965, pp. 203-217.

Diethelm, O. (1930), Bromide intoxication. *J. Nerv. & Ment. Dis.*, 71:151-165; 278-292.

Dimitz, L. & Schilder, P. (1921), Uber die psychischen Störungen bei der Encephalitis epidemica des Jahres 1920. *Ztschr. ges. Neur. u. Psychiat.*, 68:299-340.

Dobrovizky, P. T. (1929), Fixation of alcohol in the brain cortex and subcortical ganglion of alcoholics. *Medicobiological Journal* (Russian), 4:117-125.

Duret, F. (1887), *Traumatismes Cranio-Cerebaux.* Paris.*

Dussik, K. T. (1935), Uber die Insulinschockbehandlung der Schizophrenie. *Jahres-*

kurse f. Arztl. Forbildung. Sonderdrück aus d. Maiheft. Munich: Lehrmanns Verlag.

—— & Sakel, M. (1936), Ergebnisse der Hypoglykämie Shockbehandlung der Schizophrenie. *Ztschr. ges. Neur. u. Psychiat.*, 155:351-415.

Earl, C. J. (1933), The human figure drawings of adult defectives. *J. Ment. Sci.*, 79:305-327.

Economo, C. von (1929), Schlaftheorie. *Ergeb. Physiol.*, 1:28, 312-339.

Engerth, G. & Urban, H. (1933), Zur Kenntnis der gestörten künstlerischen Leistung bei sensoricher Aphasie. *Ztschr. ges. Neur. u. Psychiat.*, 145:753-787.

Federn, P. (1926), Some variations in ego feeling. In: *Ego Psychology and the Psychoses.* New York: Basic Books, 1952, pp. 25-37.

—— (1927), Narcissism in the structure of the ego. In: *Ego Psychology and the Psychoses.* New York: Basic Books, 1952, pp. 38-59.

—— (1929), The ego as object and subject in narcissism. In: *Ego Psychology and the Psychoses.* New York: Basic Books, 1952, pp. 283-322.

—— (1932), Ego feelings in dreams. In: *Ego Psychology and the Psychoses.* New York: Basic Books, 1952, pp. 60-89.

Feigl, E. (1918), *Biochem. Ztschr.* 92:282. In: Wells, H. G., *Chemical Pathology,* 5th ed. Philadelphia: Saunders, 1925.

Fenichel, O. (1926), Identification. In: *Collected Papers of Otto Fenichel,* 1:97-112. New York: Norton, 1953.

—— (1931a), *Hysterien und Zwangsneurosen.* Vienna: Internationaler Psychoanalystiche Verlag.

—— (1931b), *Perversionen, Psychosen, Charakterstörungen.* Vienna: Internationaler Psychoanalytische Verlag.

Ferenczi, S. (1911), On the part played by homosexuality in the pathogenesis of paranoia. In: *Sex in Psychoanalysis.* New York: Basic Books, 1950, pp. 154-186.

—— (1912), On the definition of introjection. In: *Final Contributions to the Problems and Methods of Psychoanalysis.* New York: Basic Books, 1955, pp. 316-318.

—— (1913), Stages in the development of a sense of reality. In: *Sex in Psychoanalysis.* New York: Basic Books, 1950, pp. 213-239.

Fetterman, J. E. & Pritchard, W. H. (1939), Cerebral complications following ligation of the cartoid artery. *JAMA,* 112:1317-1322.

Fingert, H. H., Kagan, J. & Schilder, P. (1939), The Goodenough test in insulin and metrazol treatment of schizophrenia. *This Volume,* Chapter 28.

Fischer, F. (1930), Zeitstruktur und Schizophrenie. *Ztschr. ges. Neur. u. Psychiat.*, 121:544-576.

Fischer, M. H. & Wodak, E. (1924), Beiträge zur Physiologie die menschlichen Vestibullärapparates. *Arch. ges. Physiol.*, 202:523-553.*

Fleischhacker, H. (1930), Uber Störungen des Sprachverständnisses bei Schizophrenen. *Monatsch. Psychiat. u. Neur.*, 77:1-37.

Foerster, O. (1923), Die Topik der Hirnrinde in ihrer bedeutung für die Motilität. *Dtsch. Ztschr. Nervenh.*, 77:124-139.

—— (1927), *Die Leitungsbahnen des Schmerzgefühles.* Berlin: Urban & Schwartzenberg.

Forster, E. (1918), Die psychischen Störungen der Hirnverletzten. *Monatsch. Psychiat. u. Neur.*, 46:43-46.

Fraser, F. (1938), The clinical aspects of the transmission of the effects of nervous impulses by acetylcholine. *Brit. Med. J.*, 1:1249, 1293, 1349.

Fraser, R. & Reitmann, F. (1939), A clinical study of the effects of short periods of severe anoxia with special reference to the mechanism of action of cardiazol "shock." *J. Neur. & Psychiat.*, 2:125-136.

564   *Paul Schilder*

Freeman, W. & Crosby, P. T. (1929), Reflex grasping and groping. *JAMA*, 93:7-12.

Freud, A. (1930), Psychische Sättigung in Menstruum und Intermenstruum. *Psychol. Forsch.*, 13:198-218.

—— (1936), *The Ego and the Mechanisms of Defense. The Writings of Anna Freud*, 2. New York: International Universities Press, 1966.

Freud, S. (1891), *On Aphasia, A Clinical Study*. New York: International Universities Press, 1953.

—— (1894), The neuro-psychoses of defence. *Standard Edition*, 3:41-61. London: Hogarth Press, 1962.

—— (1896), Further remarks on the neuro-psychoses of the defence. *Standard Edition*, 3:159-185. London: Hogarth Press, 1962.

—— (1900), The interpretation of dreams. *Standard Edition*, 4 & 5. London: Hogarth Press, 1953.

—— (1911), Psycho-analytic notes upon an autobiographical account of a case of paranoia. *Standard Edition*, 12:3-80. London: Hogarth Press, 1958.

—— (1914), On narcissism: An introduction. *Standard Edition*, 14:67-105. London: Hogarth Press, 1957.

—— (1915a), A case of paranoia running counter to the psycho-analytical theory of the disease. *Standard Edition*, 14:262-272. London: Hogarth Press, 1957.

—— (1915b), Thoughts for the times on war and death. *Standard Edition*, 14:274-300. London: Hogarth Press, 1957.

—— (1915c), The unconscious. *Standard Edition*, 14:161-215. London: Hogarth Press, 1957.

—— (1917), Mourning and melancholia. *Standard Edition*, 14:239-258. London: Hogarth Press, 1957.

—— (1920), Beyond the pleasure principle. *Standard Edition*, 18:3-64. London: Hogarth Press, 1955.

—— (1921), Group psychology and the analysis of the ego. *Standard Edition*, 18:67-143. London: Hogarth Press, 1955.

—— (1922), Some neurotic mechanisms in jealousy, paranoia and homosexuality. *Standard Edition*, 18:221-232. London: Hogarth Press, 1955.

—— (1923), The ego and the id. *Standard Edition*, 19:3-66. London: Hogarth Press, 1961.

—— (1924a), The loss of reality in neurosis and psychosis. *Standard Edition*, 19:183-187. London: Hogarth Press, 1961.

—— (1924b), Neurosis and psychosis. *Standard Edition*, 19:148-153. London: Hogarth Press, 1961.

—— (1926), Inhibitions, symptoms and anxiety. *Standard Edition*, 20:77-174. London: Hogarth Press, 1959.

—— (1930), Civilization and its discontents. *Standard Edition*, 21:59-145. London: Hogarth Press, 1961.

—— (1932), New introductory lectures on psycho-analysis. *Standard Edition*, 22:3-182. London: Hogarth Press, 1964.

Friedman, E. (1937), The irritative therapy of schizophrenia. *N.Y. State J. Med.*, 37:1813-1821.

Fuchs, S. H. (1937), On introjection. *Internat. J. Psycho-Anal.*, 18:269-293.

Gamper, E. (1926), Arhinencephalie. *Ztschr. ges. Neur. u. Psychiat.*, 102:154-235; 104:49-120.

—— (1928), Zur Frage der Polioencephalitis haemorrhagica der chronischen Alkoholiker. *Dtsch. Ztschr. Nervenh.*, 102:122-129.

Gatzuk, L. & Hoff, H. (1930), Rauschgiftgewöhnung und Lagebeharbung. *Klin. Wochenschr.*, 9:1-5.

Gebsattel, V. E. von (1928), Zeitbezogenes Zwangsdenken in der Melancholie. *Nervenärzt*, 1:275-287.

Gellhorn, E. (1938), Effects of hypoglycaemia and anoxia on the central nervous system. *Arch. Neur. & Psychiat.*, 40:125-146.

Gerard, R. W. (1938), Anoxia and neural metabolism. *Arch. Neur. & Psychiat.*, 40:985-996.

Gero, G. (1936), The construction of depression. *Internat. J. Psycho-Anal.*, 17: 423-461.

Gerstmann, J. (1926), Körper-rotation um die Langsachse bei cerebellar Erkrankung. *Arch. Psychiat. u. Neur.*, 76:635-641.

—— Hoff, H. & Schilder, P. (1925), Optisch-motorisches Syndrom der Drehung um die Körperlängsachse. *Arch. f. Psychiat. u. Nervenkr.*, 76:766-784.

Gierlich, N. (1920), Uber die Beziehungen des Prädilektionstyps der hemiplegischen Lähmung zur phylogenetischen Entwicklung der Pyramidenbahnen. *Ztschr. ges. Neur. u. Psychiat.*, 60:59-76.

Glaser, A. & Shafer, F. W. (1932), Skull and brain traumas. *JAMA*, 98:271-276.

Glover, E. (1932a), On the etiology of drug-addiction. *Internat. J. Psycho-Anal.*, 13:298-328.

—— (1932b), Medico-psychological aspects of normality. *Brit. J. Psychol.*, 23: 152-166.

Glueck, B. (1936), Induced hypoglycemic state in the treatment of psychoses. *N.Y. State J. Med.*, 36:1473-1489.

—— (1937), Clinical experience with the hypoglycemic therapy of the psychoses. *J. Nerv. & Ment. Dis.*, 85:564-565.

Goldstein, K. (1927), Das Kleinhirn. *Handb. Norm. u. Path. Physiol.*, 10:222-317.*

—— (1939), *The Organism.* New York: American Book Co.

—— & Boernstein, W. (1925), Uber die Pseudospontanen Bewegungenäussernden Spasmen. *Dtsch. Ztschr. Nervenh.*, 89:234.*

—— & Gelb, A. (1920), Psychologische Analysen hirnpathologischer Fälle. Partially translated in: *Source Book of Gestalt Psychology*, ed. W. D. Ellis. New York: Harcourt Brace, 1938, pp. 26-30.

—— & Katz, S. E. (1937), The psychopathology of Pick's disease. *Arch. Neur. & Psychiat.*, 38:473-490.

—— & Riese, W. (1923), Uber induzierte Veränderungen des Tonus bei normalen Menschen. *Klin. Wochenschr.*, 2:1201-1206.

Goodenough, F. (1926), *Measurement of Intelligence by Drawings.* New York: World Book.*

Gordon, A. (1933), Delayed mental disorders following cranial traumatism. *J. Nerv. & Ment. Dis.*, 77:259-273.

Grant, F. C., Weinberger, L. M. & Gibbon, J. H. Jr. (1939), Anoxemia of the central nervous system produced by temporary complete arrest of circulation. *Trans. Amer. Neur. Assn.*, 65:66-72.

Green, W. F. & Adriani, J. (1940), Effects of anoxia induced by nitrogen inhalation in the treatment of psychoses. *Arch. Neur. & Psychiat.*, 44:1022-1030.

Greenacre, P. (1918), The content of the schizophrenic characteristics occurring in affective disorders. *Amer. J. Insanity*, 75:197-202.

Gregor, A. & Schilder, P. (1913), Beiträge zur Kenntnis der Physiologie und Pathologie der Muskelinnervation. *Ztschr. ges. Neur. u. Psychiat.*, 14:359-443.

Gross, O. (1907), Das Freudsche Idiogenitätsmoment und seine Bedeutung. In: *Manisch-depressiven Irresein Kraepelins.* Leipzig: Vogel.

Grotjahn, M. & French, T. M. (1938), Akinesia after ventriculography. *Psychoanal. Quart.*, 7:319-328.

Grünbaum, A. A. (1930), The pointing position of the hand as a pathological and primitive reflex. *Brain*, 53:267-277.

Gruenthal, E. (1923), Zur Kenntnis der Psychopathologie des Korsakoff. *Monatsch. Psychiat. u. Neur.*, 53:89-132.

Gruhle, H. W. (1922), Psychologie abnormen Seelenzuständen. In: *Die Funktionen des Abnormen Seelenlebens*, ed. G. Kafka. Munich: Reinhardt.

Gurewitch, M. (1932), Uber das interparietale Syndrom bei Geisteskrankheiten. *Ztschr. ges. Neur. u. Psychiat.*, 140:593-603.

Guttmann, E. & Maclay, W. S. (1937), Clinical observations on schizophrenic drawings. *Brit. J. Med. Psychol.*, 16:184-204.

Hall, G. E. & Lucas, C. C. (1937), Acetylcholine-choline-esterase system. *J. Pharm. & Exper. Therapy*, 61:10-20.

Hall, G. S. (1923), *Senescence*. New York: Appleton.

Halpern, F. (1928), Zur Frage der Manegebewegungen beim Menschen. *Jahrb. ges. Neur. u. Psychiat.*, 46:43-52.

Hárnik, J. (1931), Introjection and projection in the mechanism of depression. *Internat. J. Psycho-Anal.*, 13:425-432, 1932.

———— (1933), Die postnatale erste Entwicklungsstufe der Libido. *Internat. Ztschr. Psychoanal.*, 19:147-151.

Harper, A. A., McSwiney, B. A. & Suffolk, S. F. (1935), Afferent fibers from the abdomen in the vagus nerves. *J. Physiol.*, 85:267-277.

Hartmann, H. (1924), Ein Beitrag zur Frage der katatonischen Pupillenstarre. *Wien. Klin. Wochenschr.*, 37:1013-1015.

———— & Schilder, P. (1923), Zur Klinik und Psychologie der Amentia. *Monatschr. Psychiat. u. Neur.*, 55:321-326.

———— ———— (1925), Zur Psychologie Schädelverletzter. *Arch. Psychiat.*, 75:287-300.

Haven, E. (1932), *Alcohol and Man*. New York: Macmillan.*

Head, H. (1926), *Aphasia and Kindred Disorders of Speech*. New York: Macmillan.

Heilig, R. & Hoff, H. (1928), Psyche Beeinflussung von Organfunktionen. *Allg. gerstl. Ztschr. Psychother.*, 1:268-280.*

Henderson, D. K. & Gillespie, R. D. (1927), *A Textbook of Psychiatry*. London & New York: Oxford University Press, 1947.

Hiller, F. (1928), Electivity of diseases of the nervous system. *Arch. Neur. & Psychiat.*, 20:145-154.

Himwich, H. E., Alexander, F. A. & Lipetz, B. (1938), Effect of acute anoxia produced by breathing nitrogen in the course of schizophrenia. *Proc. Soc. Experim. Biol.& Med.*, 39:367-375.

———— Bowman, K. M., Wortis, J. & Fazekas, J. F. (1939), Metabolism of the brain during insulin and metrazol treatment of schizophrenia. *JAMA*, 112:1572-1573.

———— Frostig, J. P., Fazekas, J. F. & Hadidian, Z. (1939), The mechanism of the symptoms of insulin hypoglycemia. *Amer. J. Psychiat.*, 96:371-385.

Hinsie, L. (1930), *The Treatment of Schizophrenia*. Baltimore: Williams & Wilkins.

Hoch, A. & Kirby, G. H. (1919), A clinical study of psychoses characterized by distressed perplexity. *Arch. Neur. & Psychiat.*, 1:415-458.

Hoff, H. & Pötzl, O. (1934), Uber eine Zeitrafferwirkung bei homonymer linksseitiger Hemianopsie. *Ztschr. ges. Neur. u. Psychiat.*, 151:599-641.

———— & Schilder, P. (1925a), Uber Drehbewegungen um die Längsachse. *Ztschr. ges Neur. u. Psychiat.*, 96:683-697.

———— ———— (1925b), Uber Lage- und Stellreflexe beim delirium tremens. *Jahrb. Neur. u. Psychiat.*, 44:189-193.

———— ———— (1926), Uber die spontane Abweichreaktion. *Monatschr. Neur. u. Psychiat.*, 64:260-261.

——— ——— (1927), *Die Lagereflexe des Menschen.* Vienna: Springer.

Hoffman, E. P. (1935), Projektion und Ich-Entwicklung. *Internat. Ztschr. Psychoanal.*, 21:342-373.

Hollós, S. & Ferenczi, S. (1925), *Psychoanalysis and the Psychic Disorder of General Paresis.* New York & Washington, D.C.: Nervous & Mental Disease Publ. Co.

Holzapfel, W. H. (1931), Pupillary reactions in health and disease other than ocular. *N.Y. State J. Med.*, 31:765-766.

Homberger, A. (1923), Zur Gestaltung der normalen menschlichen Motorik und ihre Beurteilung. *Ztschr. ges. Neur. u. Psychiat.*, 55.*

Hoppe, F. (1933), Erfolg, Auschauer und Aktivität beim Säugling und Kreinkind. *Psychol. Forsch.*, 17:268-305.*

Horney, K. (1937), *The Neurotic Personality of our Time.* New York: Norton.

Howe (1932), Communication presented to the New York Neurological Society. Unpublished.*

Ingvar, S. (1928), On the pathogenesis of the Argyll Robertson phenomena. *Bull. Johns Hopkins Hosp.*, 43:363-396.

Isaacs, S. (1935), *The Psychological Aspects in Child Development.* London: Evans.

Isakower, O. (1938), A contribution to the pathopsychology of phenomena associated with falling asleep. *Internat. J. Psycho-Anal.*, 19:331-345.

Jackson, J. H. (1931), *Selected Writings.* London: Hodder & Stoughton.

JAMA (1937), Editorial: Insulin shock treatment for schizophrenia. 108:560.

Jekels, L. & Bergler, E. (1934), Transference and love. In: Jekels, L., *Selected Papers.* New York: International Universities Press, 1952, pp. 178-201.

Jelgersma, H. C. (1931), Die Psychoanalyse der Dementia senilis. *Ztschr. ges. Neur. u. Psychiat.*, 135:657-670.

Jelliffe, S. E. (1933a), The death instinct in somatic- and psychopathology. *Psychoanal. Rev.*, 20:121-132.

——— (1933b), Discussion of Winkelman, N. W. & Ekel, J. L., Brain trauma. *Trans. Amer. Neur. Assn.*, 59:51-52.*

——— (1937), Discussion of Glueck, Clinical experience with hypoglycaemic therapy of the psychoses. *J. Nerv. & Ment. Dis.*, 85:575-578.

Jung, C. G. (1907), *The Psychology of Dementia Praecox.* New York & Washington, D.C.: Nervous & Mental Disease Monogr., 3.

——— (1912), A criticism of Bleuler's theory of schizophrenic negativism. In: *Collected Papers on Analytic Psychology,* 4:200-205. New York: Moffat Yard, 1917.

Kahn, E. & Thompson, L. J. (1934), Concerning Pick's disease. *Amer. J. Psychiat.*, 13:937-946.

Kardiner, A. (1932), The bio-analysis of the epileptic reaction. *Psychoanal. Quart.*, 1:375-483.

Karsten, A. (1928), Psychische Sättigung. *Psychol. Forsch.*, 10:142-254.

Kauders, O. (1925), Drehbewegungen um die Körperlängsachse. *Ztschr. ges. Neur. u. Psychiat.*, 98:602-614.

——— & Schilder, P. (1923), *Hypnosis.* New York & Washington, D.C.: Nervous & Mental Disease Publ. Co., 1927.

Kehrer, F. (1923), Zur Pathologie der Pupillen. *Ztschr. ges. Neur. u. Psychiat.*, 81:345-408.

Kempf, E. J. (1918), *The Autonomic Functions and the Personality.* New York & Washington, D.C.: Nervous & Mental Disease Publ. Co.

Kennedy, F. & Wolf, A. (1936), Relationship of intellect to speech defect in aphasic patients. *J. Nerv. & Ment. Dis.*, 84:125-145, 293-311.

Kielholz, A. (1926), Analyseversuch bei Delirium tremens. *Internat. Ztschr. Psychoanal.*, 12:478-492.

Kläsi, J. (1922), Uber die therapeutische Anwendung des "Dauernarkose" mittels Somnifens bei Schizophrenie. *Ztschr. ges. Neur. u. Psychiat.*, 74:557-592.

Klauder, J. V. & Winkelman, N. W. (1928), Pellagra among chronic alcoholic addicts. *JAMA*, 90:364-371.

Klein, M. (1932), *The Psycho-analysis of Children.* New York: Grove, 1960.

―――― (1935), A contribution to the psychogenesis of manic-depressive states. *Internat. J. Psycho-Anal.*, 16:145-174.

Kleist, K. (1908), *Die psychomotorischen Störungen Geisteskranken.* Leipzig: Klinkhardt.

―――― (1913), Die Involututionsparanoia. *Allg. Ztschr. Psychiat.*, 70:1.*

―――― (1914), Aphasie und Geisteskrankheit. *Münch. Med. Wochenschr.*, 1:8-12.

―――― (1922), Die psychomotorischen Störungen und ihr Verhältnis zu den Motilitätsstörungen bei Erkrankungen der Stammganglien. *Monatschr. Neur. u. Psychiat.*, 52:253-302.

―――― (1926), *Episodische Dämmerzustände.* Leipzig: Thieme.

―――― (1927a), Bewegunsstörungen und Bewegunsleistungen der Stammganglien des Gehirns. *Naturwissensch.*, 15:973-977.

―――― (1927b), Gegenhalten (motorischer Negativismus) Zwangsgreifen und Thalamus opticus. *Monatschr. Neur. u. Psychiat.*, 65:317-396.

―――― (1934), Kriegsverletzungen des Gehirn und ihre Bedeutung für die Hirnlokalization und Hirnpathologie. *Artzlich. Erfahr. Weltkrieg.* 1914-1918. 4:345-416.*

Koester, W. (1927), Uber die Häufigkeit des Vorkommens des Spasmus mobilis. *Arch. Psychiat.*, 8:601-605.

Kovacs, S. (1912), Introjektion, Projektion und Einfühlung. *Zentralbl. Psychoanal.*, 2:253-264, 316-327.

Kraepelin, E. (1908), *Clinical Psychiatry.* New York: Macmillan, 1923.

Krapf, E. E. (1936), *Die Seelenstörungen der Blutdruckkranken.* Vienna: Deuticke.

Kretschmer, E. (1919), Psychogene Wahnbildung bei Traumatischer Hirnschwäche. *Ztschr. ges. Neur. u. Psychiat.*, 45:272-300.

―――― (1921), *Physique and Character.* New York: Harcourt Brace, 1925.

Kronfeld, A. (1920), *Das Wesen der psychiatrischen Erkenntnis.* Berlin: Springer.

Kubie, L. (1937), Modification in a schizophrenic reaction with psychoanalytic treatment. *Arch. Neur. & Psychiat.*, 37:874-880.

Kumer, L. (1931), Uber Versprangte Pellagra in Tirol. *Wien. Klin. Wochenschr.* 44:849-852.

Laforgue, R. (1926), Scotomization in schizophrenia. *Internat. J. Psycho-Anal.*, 8:473-478, 1927.

Lange, J. (1928), Die Endogenen und rektiven Gemütserkrangen. *Handb. Geisteskrankh*, ed. O. Bumke. Berlin: Springer, 6:2-37.*

Levin, M. (1932), Bromide delirium and other bromide psychoses. *Amer. J. Psychiat.*, 12:1125-1163.

Levine, A. & Schilder, P. (1940), Motor phenomena during nitrogen inhalation. *This Volume*, Chapter 10.

―――― ―――― (1942), The effect of drugs on the catatonic pupil. *This Volume*, Chapter 23.

Lewin, B. D. (1937), A type of neurotic hypomanic reaction. In: *Selected Writings.* New York: Psychoanalytic Quarterly, Inc., 1973, pp. 71-77.

Lewin, K. (1938), The conceptual representation and measurement of psychological forces. In: *Contributions to Psychological Theory.* New York: Johnson Reprint Co., 1968.

Lewis, N. D. C. & Hubbard, L. D. (1931), The mechanisms and prognostic aspects of the manic-depressive-schizophrenic combination. In: *Manic-Depressive Psychosis.* Baltimore: Williams & Wilkins, 1931, pp. 539-608.

Liddell, E. G. T. & Sherrington, C. (1924), Reflexes in response to stretch (myotatic reflexes). *Proc. Roy. Soc. Med.,* 96:212-242.

Loewenstein, O. (1927a), Uber die Natur der sogenannten Pupillenunruhe. *Monatschr. Psychiat. u. Neur.,* 66:126-147.

—— (1927b), Uber die sogenannte paradoxe Lichtreaktion der Pupille. *Monatschr. Psychiat. u. Neur.,* 66:148-167.

—— (1927c), Uber die Variations breite des Lichtreflexes und der Psychoreflexe der Pupillen. *Arch. Psychiat.,* 82:285.*

Lüthy, F. & Walthard, K. M. (1928), Uber Polioencephalitis hemorrhagica superior (Wernicke). *Ztschr. ges. Neur. u. Psychiat.,* 116:404-422.

MacCurdy, J. T. (1925), *The Psychology of Emotion.* New York: Harcourt Brace.

McFarland, R. A. (1938), *The Effects of Oxygen Deprivation [High Altitude] on the Human Organism.* Report No. 13, United States Department of Commerce, Bureau of Air Commerce.

Magnus, R. (1924), *Körperstellung.* Berlin: Springer.

—— & de Kleijn, A. (1912), Die Abhängigkeit des Extremitätenmuskeln von der Tonus der Köpfstellung. *Arch. ges. Physiol.,* 145:455-548.

Mayer-Gross, W. (1920), Uber die Stellungnahme zur abgelaufenen akuten Psychose. *Ztschr. ges. Neur. u. Psychiat.,* 60:160-212.

—— (1924), *Selbstschilderungen der Verwirrtheit.* Berlin: Springer.

—— (1938), Discussion on presenile dementias: Symptomatology, pathology, and differential diagnosis. *Proc. Royal Soc. Med.,* 31:1443-1447.

—— & Reisch, Z. (1928), Uber die Widerstandsbereitschaft des Bewegungsapparates. *Verhandl. Gesellsch. Deutsch Nervenärzt.,* 17:258.*

—— & Stein, J. (1928), Pathologie der Wahrnehmung. *Handb. Geisteskrankh,* ed. O. Bumke. Berlin: Springer, 1:1.*

Meduna, L. J. (1935), Versuche über die biologische Beeinflussing des Ablaufes der Schizophrenie. *Ztschr. ges. Neur. u. Psychiat.,* 152:235-262.

—— (1936), New methods of medical treatment of schizophrenia. *Arch. Neur. & Psychiat.,* 35:361-363.

—— (1937), *Die Konvulsionstherapie der Schizophrenie.* Halle: C. Marhold.

Menninger, K. A. (1933), Psychoanalytic aspects of suicide. *Internat. J. Psycho-Anal.,* 14:376-390.

—— (1938), *Man Against Himself.* New York: Harcourt Brace.

Menninger, W. C. (1928), Pupillary anomalies in schizophrenia. *Arch. Neur. & Psychiat.,* 20:186-192.

Meyer, Adolf (1904), The anatomical facts and clinical varieties of traumatic insanity. *Amer. J. Insanity,* 60:373-442.

—— (1906), Fundamental conceptions of dementia praecox. *Brit. Med. J.,* 11:757.

—— (1922), Constructive formulation of schizophrenia. *Amer. J. Psychiat.,* 1:355-364.

Meyer, Alfred (1927), Klinische-anatomische Erfahrungen über Kohlenoxydvergiftung des Zentralnervensystems. *Klin. Wochenschr.,* 6:145-147.

Meyer, E. (1909), Die Körperlichen Erscheinungen bei Dementia Praecox. *Ztschr. Psychiat. u. Psychisch. Med.,* 66:371.*

Meyerson, A. & Thau, W. (1937), Effect of cholinergic and adrenergic drugs on the eye. *Arch. Ophthal.,* 18:78-90.

Meynert, T. (1889-1890), Amentia, die Verwirrtheit. *Jahrb. Psychiat.,* 9:1-112.

Miles, W. R. (1935), Age and human society. In: *Handbook of Social Psychology,* ed. C. Murchison. Worcester, Mass.: Clark University Press, pp. 596-683.

Monakow, C. von (1905), *Gehirnpathologie.* Vienna: Alfred Holder.

Muller, M. (1937), Insulin- und Cardiazolschockbehandlung der Schizophrenie. *Fortschr. Neur. u. Psychiat.*, 9:131-166.

Näcke, P. (1899), Kritisches zum Kapital der normalen und pathologischen Sexualität. *Arch. Psychiat.*, 32:356.

Neuberger, K. (1931), Uber Hirnverländerungen nach Alkoholmissbrauch. *Ztschr. ges. Neur. u. Psychiat.*, 135:159-209.

Nielsen, J. M. & Stegman, L. N. (1926), Nonsyphilitic pupillary inaction. *Arch. Neur. & Psychiat.*, 16:597-604.

Nunberg, H. (1920), On the catatonic attack. In: *Practice and Theory of Psychoanalysis.* New York & Washington, D.C.: Nervous & Mental Disease Publ. Co., 1948, pp. 3-23.

────── (1921), The course of the libidinal conflict in a case of schizophrenia. In: *Practice and Theory of Psychoanalysis.* New York & Washington, D.C.: Nervous Mental Disease Publ. Co., 1948, pp. 24-59.

────── (1922), Review of *Zur Psychoanalyse der paralgtischen Geisterstörung. Internat. Ztschr. Psychoanal.*, 8:354-358.

────── (1930), The synthetic function of the ego. In: *Practice and Theory of Psychoanalysis.* New York & Washington, D.C.: Nervous & Mental Disease Publ. Co., 1948, pp. 120-136.

────── (1932), *Principles of Psychoanalysis.* New York: International Universities Press, 1955.

Oedegaard, O. & Schilder, P. (1930), Turning tendency and conjugate deviation. *This Volume,* Chapter 9.

Ogden, C. K. & Richards, I. A. (1923), *The Meaning of Meaning.* New York: Harcourt Brace, 1959.

Ohkuma, T. (1930), Zur pathologischen Anatomie des chronischen Alkoholismus. *Ztschr. ges. Neur. u. Psychiat.*, 126:94-128.

Oppenheim, H. (1923), *Lehrbuch der Nervenkrankheiten.* Berlin: Karger.

Orenstein, L. L. & Schilder, P. (1938), Psychological considerations of insulin treatment in schizophrenia. *This Volume,* Chapter 26.

Orton, S. T. & Bender, L. (1931), Lesions in the lateral horns of the spinal cord in acrodynia, pellagra, and pernicious anemia. *Bull. Neur. Inst.*, New York, 1: 506-531.

Pap, Z. von (1937), Erfahrungen mit der Insulinshocktherapie bei Schizophrenen. *Monatschr. Psychiat. u. Neur.*, 94:318-346.

Parker, S., Schilder, P. & Wortis, H. (1939), A specific motility psychosis in Negro alcoholics. *This Volume,* Chapter 16.

Pavlov, I. P. (1927), *Conditioned Reflexes.* London: Oxford University Press, 1941.

Pette, H. (1925), Klinische and anatomische Studien zum Kapitel den tonischen Hals- und Labyrinthreflexe beim Menschen. *Dtsch. Ztschr. Nervenh.*, 86:193-219.

Pfeifer, B. (1928), Die psychischen Störungen nach Hirnverletzungen. In: *Handb. Geisteskrankh,* ed. O. Bumke. Berlin: Springer, pp. 405-482.*

Pick, A. (1915), Beitrage zur Pathologie des Denkverlaufes beim Korsakoff. *Ztschr. ges. Neur. u. Psychiat.*, 28:344-383.

Pisk, G. (1936), Uber ein "Zeitraffer" Phänomen nach Insulinkoma. *Ztschr. ges. Neur. u. Psychiat.*, 156:777-786.

Pötzl, O. (1917), The relationships between experimentally induced dream images and indirect vision. In: *Preconscious Stimulation in Dreams, Associations, and Images* [*Psychological Issues,* Monogr. 7]. New York: International Universities Press, 1960.

────── & Herrmann, G. (1928), Die optische Alloaesthesie. *Abhandlung. Neur.*, 46:1.*

—— & Redlich, E. (1911), Demonstration einen Falles bilateraler Affektion der Occipitallapper. *Wien. Klin. Wochenschr.*, 24:517.*

Pratt, K. E. (1933), The neonate. In: *Handbook of Child Psychology*, ed. K. Murchison. 2nd ed. Worcester, Mass.: Clark University Press, pp. 163-208.

Prinzhorn, H. (1922), *Artistry of the Mentally Ill.* Berlin: Springer, 1972.

Rademaker, G. G. J. (1926a), *Die Bedeutung der roten Kern und des übrigen Mittelhirns für Muskeltonus, Körperstellung und Labyrinthreflexe.* Berlin: Springer.

—— (1926b), Statik und Motilitätsstörungen kleinhirnloser Tieren. *Dtsch. Ztschr. Nervenärzt*, 94:114-148.

Rado, S. (1926; 1928), The psychic effects of intoxication: Attempt at a psychoanalytic theory of drug addiction. *Internat. J. Psycho-Anal.*, 7:396-413; 9:301-317.

—— (1928a), An anxious mother. *Internat. J. Psycho-Anal.*, 9:219-226.

—— (1928b), The problem of melancholia. *Internat. J. Psycho-Anal.*, 9:420-438.

Rand, C. W. & Courville, C. B. (1932), Histologic studies of the brain in cases of fatal injury to the head. *Arch. Neur. & Psychiat.*, 27:1342-1379.

Rank, O. (1924), *The Trauma of Birth.* New York: Harcourt Brace, 1929.

—— (1927/1928), *Grundzüge einer genetischen Psychologie*, 2 vols. Leipzig: Deuticke. Abstracted by author: *Arch. Psychoanal.*, 1:1104-1140.

Rapaport, D. (1951), *Organization and Pathology of Thought.* New York: Columbia University Press.

Redlich, E. (1908), Uber ein eigenartiges Pupillenphänomen. *Dtsch. Med. Wochenschr.*, 34:313-315.

—— (1921), Zur Charakteristik des von mir beschriebenen Pupillenphänomen. *Monatschr. Psychiat. u. Neur.*, 49:1-13.

Reichardt, M. (1904), Uber akute Geissststörungen nach Hirnerschütterung. *Allg. Ztschr. Psychiat.*, 61:524-551.

Reichman, F. (1913), Uber Pupillenstörungen bei Dementia Praecox. *Arch. Psychiat. u. Nervenkr.*, 53:302-322.

Reik, T. (1927), *Wie Man Psychologe wird.* Vienna: International Psychoanalyse Verlag.

Reiss, E. (1910), Konstitutionelle Verstimmung manisch-depressives Irresein. *Ztschr. ges. Neur. u. Psychiat.*, 2:347-628.

Richter, C. P. & Bartmeier, L. H. (1926), Decerebrate rigidity in the sloth. *Brain*, 49:207-235.

Rickman, J. (1927), A survey. The development of the psycho-analytical theory of the psychoses. In: *Selected Contributions to Psycho-Analysis.* New York: Basic Books, 1957, pp. 224-383.

Riese, W. (1928), Uber die Enstehungsmechanismus der Wortneubildungen bei Amnestisch Aphasischen. *Monatschr. Neur. u. Psychiat.*, 68:507-514.

Ritterhaus, E. (1920), Die klinische Stellung des manisch-depressiven Irreseins. *Ztschr. ges. Neur. u. Psychiat.*, 47:10-93.

Riviere, J. (1936), On the genesis of psychical conflict in earliest infancy. *Internat. J. Psycho-Anal.*, 17:395-422.

Rosen, S. R., Cameron, D. E. & Zeigler, I. B. (1940), Prevention of metrazol fractures by beta-erythroidin hydrochloride. *Psychiat. Quart.*, 14:477-480.

Rosenhagen, F. (1932), Pons und Haubenblutungen als Komplikationen von Tumoren des Grosshirns. *Dtsch. Ztschr. Nervenh.*, 127:27-44.

Ross, N. (1932), The postural model of the head and face. *J. General Psychol.*, 7:144-162.

—— & Schilder, P. (1934), Tachistoscopic experiments on the perception of the human figure. *J. General Psychol.*, 10:152-172.

Rothfield, J. (1928), Der Zwang zur Bewegung ein striäres Symptom. *Ztschr. ges. Neur. u. Psychiat.*, 114:281-292.

Rothschild, D. (1937), Pathologic changes in senile psychoses and their psychobiologic significance. *Amer. J. Psychiat.*, 93:757-788.

Rymer, C. A., Benjamin, J. D. & Ebaugh, F. G. (1937), The hypoglycemic treatment of schizophrenia. *JAMA*, 109:1249-1251.

Sakel, M. (1935), Schizophreniebehandlung mittels Insulin Hypoglykämie sowie hypoglykämischer Shocks. *Wien. Med. Wochenschr.*, 84:97; 85:35.*

———— (1938), *The Pharmacological Shock Treatment of Schizophrenia*. New York & Washington, D.C.: Nervous & Mental Disease Publ. Co.

———— & Pötzl, O. (1938), *Neue Behandlungs methode der Schizophrenie*. Vienna & Leipzig: Perles.

Schaltenbrand, G. (1925), Normale Bewegungs- und Lagereaktionen bei Kindern. *Dtsch. Ztschr. Nervenh.*, 87:23-59.

———— (1929), Theorie der proprioceptiven Reaktionen. *Dtsch. Ztschr. Nervenh.*, 100:165-202.*

Schatner, M. & O'Neill, J. F. (1938), Some observations in the treatment of dementia praecox with hypoglycemia. *Psychiat. Quart.*, 12:5-41.

Scheid, K. F. (1933), Die Psychologie des erworbenen Schwachsinns. *Zentralbl. ges. Neur. u. Psychiat.*, 67:1-55.

———— (1937), Uber senile Charakterentwicklung. *Ztschr. ges. Neur. u. Psychiat.*, 148:437-468.

Schilder, P. (1914), *Selbstbewusstsein und Persönlichkeitsbewusstsein*. Berlin: Springer.

———— (1920), On the development of thought. In: *Organization and Pathology of Thought*, ed. D. Rapaport. New York: Columbia University Press, 1951, pp. 497-518.

———— (1921), Vorstudien zu einer Psychologie der Manie. *Ztschr. ges. Neur. u. Psychiat.*, 68:90-135.

———— (1922a), Bemerkungen über die Psychologie des paralytischen Grössenwahns. *Ztschr. ges. Neur. u. Psychiat.*, 74:1-14.

———— (1922b), Einige Bemerkungen zu der Problemsphäre: Cortex, Stammganglien, Psyche, Neurose. *Ztschr. ges. Neur. u. Psychiat.*, 74:454-481.

———— (1922c), *The Nature of Hypnosis*. New York: International Universities Press, 1956.

———— (1923a), *Das Körperschema*. Berlin: Springer.

———— (1923b), Zur Psychologie epileptischer Ausnahmzustände. *Ztschr. ges. Neur. u. Psychiat.*, 81:174-180.

———— (1923c), Uber eine Psychose nach Staroperation. *Internat. Ztschr. Psychoanal.*, 8:35-44.

———— (1923d), *Seele und Leben*. Berlin: Springer.

———— (1924), *Medical Psychology*. New York: International Universities Press, 1953.

———— (1925), *Introduction to a Psychoanalytic Psychiatry*. New York: International Universities Press, 1951.

———— (1927), Theorie der Psychoanalyse. *Arch. Psychiat. u. Nervenh.*, 81:431-444.

———— (1928a), Der Begriff der Demenz. *Wien. Med. Wochenschr.*, 78:936-938.

———— (1928b), *Gedanken zur Naturphilosophie*. Vienna: Springer.

———— (1928c), Kurze Bemerkung über die Mittellinie. *Nervenärzt*, 1:726-729.

———— (1929a), Conditioned reflexes. *Arch. Neur. & Psychiat.*, 22:425-443.

———— (1929b), Posture with special reference to the cerebellum. *This Volume*, Chapter 8.

———— (1930a), Convergence reactions in alcoholics. *This Volume*, Chapter 17.

—— (1930b), Problems in the technique of psychoanalysis. *Psychoanal. Rev.*, 17:1-19.

—— (1930c), Studies concerning the psychology and symptomatology of general paresis. In: *Organization and Pathology of Thought*, ed. D. Rapaport. New York: Columbia University Press, 1951, pp. 519-580.

—— (1931a), *Brain and Personality*. New York: International Universities Press, 1951.

—— (1931b), The motility of manic-depressive psychoses. *This Volume*, Chapter 32.

—— (1931c), Principles of psychotherapy in the psychoses. *This Volume*, Chapter 24.

—— (1932a), Paralysis agitans pictures in alcoholics. *This Volume*, Chapter 15.

—— (1932b), The scope of psychotherapy in schizophrenia. *This Volume*, Chapter 25.

—— (1933), Psychogenic depression and melancholia. *This Volume*, Chapter 29.

—— (1934a), Particular types of depressive psychoses. *This Volume*, Chapter 30.

—— (1934b), Psychic disturbances after head injuries. *This Volume*, Chapter 13.

—— (1934c), Self-consciousness and optic imagination in a case of depression. *This Volume*, Chapter 31.

—— (1935), *The Image and Appearance of the Human Body*. New York: International Universities Press, 1950.

—— (1937a), Health as a psychic experience. *Arch. Neur. & Psychiat.*, 37: 1322-1337.

—— (1937b), The psychological implications of motor development in children. *Proc. 4th Institute for the Exceptional Child*. Langhorne, Pa.: Research Clinic of Woods School, pp. 38-59.

—— (1938a), *Psychotherapy*, rev. by L. Bender. New York: Norton, 1951.

—— (1938b), The social neurosis. *Psychoanal. Rev.*, 25:1-19.

—— (1939a), Notes on the psychology of metrazol treatment of schizophrenia. *This Volume*, Chapter 27.

—— (1939b), The psychology of schizophrenia. *This Volume*, Chapter 20.

—— (1940), Aspects of old age and aging. *This Volume*, Chapter 19.

—— (1942a), *Goals and Desires of Man*. New York: Columbia University Press.

—— (1942b), *Mind: Perception and Thought in Their Constructive Aspects*. New York: Columbia University Press.

—— (1951), *Psychoanalysis, Man and Society*, ed. L. Bender. New York: Norton.

—— (1964), *Contributions to Developmental Neuropsychiatry*, ed. L. Bender. New York: International Universities Press.

—— & Gerstmann, J. (1920), Studien über Bewegungsstörungen. I. Eigenartiger Formen extrapyramidaler Motilitätsstörang. *Ztschr. ges. Neur. u. Psychiat.*, 58:267-275.*

—— & Parker, S. (1931), Pupillary disturbances in schizophrenic Negroes. *This Volume*, Chapter 22.

—— & Stengel, E. (1928a), Der Hirnbefund bei Schmerzasymbolie. *Klin. Wochenschr.*, 1:535-537.

—— —— (1928b), Schmerzasymbolie. *Ztschr. ges. Neur. u. Psychiat.*, 113: 143-158.

—— —— (1931), Asymbolia for pain. *This Volume*, Chapter 7.

—— & Sugar, N. (1926), Zur Lehre von den schizophrenen Sprachstörungen. *Ztschr. ges. Neur. u. Psychiat.*, 104:689-714.

—— & Weissman, M. (1927), Amente Psychose bei Hypophysengangtumor. *Ztschr. ges. Neur. u. Psychiat.*, 110:767-778.

Schmideberg, M. (1931), A contribution to the psychology of persecutory ideas and delusions. *Internat. J. Psycho-Anal.*, 12:331-367.

Schmidt, A. (1918), Homolateral Hyperaesthesia bei Hemiplegia. *Arch. Psychiat.*, 219:501.

Schneider, A. (1927), Uber die Sprachstörungen bei Schizophrenen. *Ztschr. ges. Neur. u. Psychiat.*, 108:491-524.

Schneider, C. (1925), Uber Beiträge zur Lehre von der Schizophrenie. *Ztschr. ges. Neur. u. Psychiat.'*, 96:251-274.

Schneider, K. (1920), Die Schichtung des emotionalen Lebens und der Aufbau der Depressionszustände. *Ztschr. ges. Neur. u. Psychiat.*, 59:281-286.

Schroeder, J. (1930), Alkoholica Encephalopathia. In: *Handb. Geisteskrankh*, ed. O. Bumke. Berlin: Springer, 2:793.*

Schuster, P. & Pineas, H. (1926), Weitere Böbachtungen über Zwangsgreiten und Nachgriefen. *Dtsch. Ztschr. Nervenh.*, 91:16.*

Schwab, O. (1927), Uber Stützreaktionen (Magnus) beim Menschen. *Arch. Psychiat.*, 81:702-706.

Serko, E. (1919), Die Involutionsparaphrenie. *Monatschr. Psychiat. u. Neur.*, 45:245-286.

Sharpe, J. E. (1934), Bromide intoxication. *JAMA*, 102:1462-1465.

Sherrington, C. (1900), Experiments on the value of vascular and visceral factors for the genesis of emotions. *Proc. Roy. Soc. Med.*, 66:390-403.

———— (1907), *The Integrative Action of the Nervous System*. New Haven: Yale University Press, 1948.

Silberer, H. (1912), On symbol formation. In: *Organization and Pathology of Thought*, ed. D. Rapaport. New York: Columbia University Press, 1951, pp. 208-233.

Simmel, E. (1930), Zum Problem von Zwang und Sucht. *Allgem. Arzt. Kong. Psychother.*, 5:17-23.

Simons, A. (1923), Kopfhaltung and Muskeltonus. *Ztschr. ges. Neur. u. Psychiat.*, 80:499-549.

Smith, M. I. & Lillie, R. D. (1931), The histopathology of triorthocresyl phosphate poisoning. *Arch. Neur. & Psychiat.*, 26:976-992.

Spielmeyer, W. (1912), Die Psychosen des Rückbildungs- und Greisenalters. In: Aschaffenburg, *Handb. Psychiat.*, 5:83-164.

———— (1922), *Histopathologie des Nervensystem*. Berlin: Springer.

Stärke, A. (1921), Psychoanalysis and Psychiatry. *Internat. J. Psycho-Anal.*, 2:361-415, 1921.

Stein, H. & Weizsäcker, V. von (1928), Zur Pathologie der Sensibilität. *Ergeb. Physiol.* 27.*

Stengel, E. (1927), Zur Pathologie der letalen Hirnschwellung. *Jahrb. Psychiat. u. Neur.*, 45:187-200.

———— (1937), Studien über die Beziehungen zwischen Geistesstörung und Sprachstörung. *Monatschr. Psychiat. u. Neur.*, 95:129-173.

Störring, G. E. (1931), Uber der ersten reinen Fall eines Menschen mit völligerm isoliertem Verlust der Merkfähigkeit. *Arch. ges. Psychol.*, 81:257-384.

Stransky, E. (1905), *Lehrbuch der Psychiatrie*. Leipzig: Voegel.

———— (1911), *Das Manisch-depressive Irresein*. Leipzig: Deuticke.

Straus, E. (1928), Das Zeiterlebnis in der endogenen Depression. *Monatschr. Psychiat. u. Neur.*, 68:640-656.

———— (1931), Stützreaktionen und Gegenhalten. *Nervenärzt*, 4:399.*

Strauss, I. & Savitsky, N. (1934), Head injury: Neurologic and psychiatric aspects. *Arch. Neur. & Psychiat.*, 31:893-955.

Strecker, E. A. & Appel, K. E. (1931), The prognosis in manic-depressive psychosis. *Assn. Res. Nerv. & Ment. Dis.*, 11:471-537.*

Symonds, C. P. (1932), The effects of injury on the brain. *Lancet*, 1:820-823.

Tausk, V. (1915), On the psychology of alcoholic occupation delirium. Abstracted in: *Psychoanal. Rev.*, 9:448-450, 1922.

—— (1919), On the origin of the "influencing machine" in schizophrenia. *Psychoanal. Quart.*, 2:519-556, 1933.

Titley, W. B. (1938), Prepsychotic personality of patients with agitated depression. *Arch. Neur. & Psychiat.*, 39:333-342.

Tsiminakis, G. (1931), Alcohol and the central nervous system. *Arbeit Neur. Institut Wiener Univ.*, 33:24.*

Ury, B. & Gellhorn, E. (1939), On the influence of anoxia on pupillary reflexes in the rabbit. *J. Neurophysiol.*, 2:136-141.

Van Ophuijsen, J. H. W. (1920), Uber die Quelle der Empfindung des Verfolgtwerdens. *Internat. Ztschr. Psychoanal.*, 6:68-72.

Vigotski, L. S. (1931), Thought in schizophrenia. *Arch. Neur. & Psychiat.*, 31:1063-1077.

Vogt, C. & Vogt, O. (1922), Erkrankungen der Grosshirnrinde. *J. Psychol. u. Neur.*, 28:1-171.

Vowinckel, E. (1930), Der heutige Stand der psychiatrischen Schizophrenieforschung. *Internat. Ztschr. Psychoanal.*, 16:471-491.

Waelder, R. (1925), The psychoses: Their mechanisms and accessibility to influence. *Internat. J. Psycho-Anal.*, 6:259-281.

—— (1930), The principle of multiple function. *Psychoanal. Quart.*, 5:45-62, 1936.

—— (1936), The problem of the genesis of psychical conflicts in earliest infancy. *Internat. J. Psycho-Anal.*, 18:406-473, 1937.

Wagner-Jauregg, J. (1889), Uber einege Erscheinungen im Bereiche des Zentralnervensystems. *Jahrb. Psychiat. u. Neur.*, 8:313-332.

Walshe, F. M. R. (1923), On certain tonic and postural reflexes. *Brain*, 46:1-37.

Wechsler, D. (1939), *The Measurement of Adult Intelligence*. Baltimore: Williams & Wilkins, 1944.

Wechsler, I. S. (1932), Communication before the Neurological Section of the New York Academy of Medicine.

Weiss, E. (1926), The delusion of being poisoned in the light of introjective and projective procedures. *Arch. Psychoanal.*, 1:226-228.

—— (1932), Regression and projection in the super-ego. *Internat. J. Psycho-Anal.*, 13:449-478.

Wenderowič, E. (1928), Irritatives Syndrom des architektonischen Feldes. *Arch. Psychiat.*, 84:759-767.

Wernicke, C. (1906), *Grundriss der Psychiatrie*. Leipzig: F. Barth.

Wertham, F. I. (1929), Klinische Kerngruppe des chronischen Manie. *Ztschr. ges. Neur. u. Psychiat.*, 121:770-779.

Wertheimer, M. (1923), Studies in the theory of gestalt psychology. In: *A Source Book of Gestalt Psychology*, ed. W. D. Ellis. New York: Harcourt Brace, 1938, pp. 71-88.

Westermann, J. (1922), Uber die vitale Depression. *Ztschr. ges. Neur. u. Psychiat.*, 77:391-422.

Westphal, A. (1907), Uber ein katatonischen Stupor beobachtetes Pupillenphänomen. *Dtsch. Med. Wochenschr.*, 33:1080-1084.

—— (1921), Uber Pupillenphänomene bei Katatonie, Hysterie, etc. *Monatschr. Psychiat. u. Neur.*, 68:226-240.*

—————— (1925), Zur Frage des von mir beschriebenen Pupillenphänomene bei Post-encephalitis (Spasmus mobilis). *Dtsch. Med. Wochenschr.*, 51:2101.*

White, W. A. (1926), The language of schizophrenia. *Arch. Neur. & Psychiat.*, 16:395-413.

Wilson, A. & Winkelman, N. W. (1926), Gross pontile bleeding in traumatic and nontraumatic cerebral lesions. *Arch. Neur. & Psychiat.*, 15:455-470.

Wilson, S. A. K. (1922), On decerebrate rigidity in man and the occurrence of fits. *Brain*, 45:220-268.

Winkelman, N. W. & Eckel, J. L. (1934), Brain trauma: Histopathology during early stages. *Arch. Neur. & Psychiat.*, 31:956-986.

Witt, G. F. & Cheavens, T. J. (1936), Prolonged barbiturate narcosis in the treatment of acute psychoses. *South. Med. J.*, 29:574-578.

Wortis, H. (1936), A case of cerebral degeneration with encephalographic study eight years after common carotid ligation. *Amer. J. Med. Science*, 192:517-519.

Wortis, J. (1936), On the response of schizophrenic subjects to hypoglycemic insulin shock. *J. Nerv. & Ment. Dis.*, 84:497-506.

—————— (1937a), Experience of Bellevue Hospital with hypoglycemic treatment of the psychoses. *J. Nerv. & Ment. Dis.*, 85:565-569.

—————— (1937b), Sakel's hypoglycemic insulin treatment of psychosis: History and present status. *J. Nerv. & Ment. Dis.*, 85:581-595.

—————— Bowman, K. M., Orenstein, L. L. & Rosenbaum, I. J. (1937), Further experience at Bellevue Hospital with hypoglycemic treatment of schizophrenia. *Amer. J. Psychiat.*, 94:153-158.

Wundt, W. M. (1874), *Grundzüge der physiologischen Psychologie.* Leipzig: Engelmann, 1911.

Wuth, O. (1927), Rational bromide treatment: New methods for its control. *JAMA*, 88:2013-2017.

Ziehen, T. (1910), Uber das Bild des sogenannten "moral insanity" nach Hirn-schütterung bei Kindern. *Ztschr. Jugendfürsorg.*, 11:173.*

Zilboorg, G. (1930), Affective reintegration in the schizophrenias. *Arch. Neur. & Psychiat.*, 24:335-345.

Zingerle, H. (1926), Klinische Studie über Haltungs- und Stellreflexen sowie andere automatische Körperbewegungen beim Menschen. *Ztschr. ges. Neur. u. Psychiat.*, 105:548-599.

NAME INDEX

Abeles, M., 425
Abraham, K., 25, 39, 59, 62, 65, 299, 310, 473, 501, 544
Adler, A., 27
Adrani, J., 96
Alexander, F., 10, 30, 52, 312, 322, 387
Alexander, F. A. D., 96
Allers, R., 176, 315
Almásy, E., 7, 64
André Thomas, 83, 84
Angyal, A., 315, 408-409
Angyal, L. von, 315, 401
Appel, K. E., 502

Babinski, F., 85-86, 215
Bain, W. A., 378
Bang, S., 249
Barach, A. L., 106
Bárány, R., 83, 85
Bartmeier, L. H., 77
Bazett, C., 78, 553
Bechterew, W. von, 334, 352
Bender, L., 21, 58, 76, 175, 193n, 249, 272, 282, 289-290, 294, 301, 304, 316, 319-320, 323, 330n, 402, 409, 425, 438, 444, 445, 460
Bender, M., 107, 154
Benedek, L., 328, 401, 409, 425-426
Benjamin, J. D., 459
Berger, H., 152
Bergler, E., 16
Beritoff, J., 78
Bertschinger, H., 427
Betlheim, S., 209, 210
Bibring, E., 21
Blalock, J. R., 61
Bleuler, E., 309, 310
Bleuler, M., 297, 308-309
Börnstein, W., 209
Boggs, T. R., 194, 249
Bouman, L., 251
Bowman, K. M., 105, 402, 502
Brain, R., 78

Brentano, F., 545, 546, 548
Breslauer-Schück, A., 174
Bromberg, W., 11, 65
Brunner, H., 221
Bürger-Prinz, H., 160
Bychowski, G., 55, 401

Cameron, D. E., 375
Campbell, C. M., 322
Canestrini, S., 311
Cannon, W. B., 553
Carmichael, N., 249, 253
Cheavens, T. J., 400
Clark, L. P., 441
Comte, I., 545
Courville, C. B., 102, 104, 177
Crosby, P., 209
Curran, F. J., 65-66, 109n, 133n, 289, 295
Currier, F. P., 209

Dale, H., 372
Darwin, C., 551
Davis, D. B., 209
de Kleijn, A., 78
Deutsch, H., 61, 472
Diethelm, O., 124
Dimitz, L., 124
Dobrovizky, P. T., 248
Duret, F., 177
Dussik, K. T., 398, 400, 401

Earl, C. J., 444
Ebaugh, F. G., 459
Eckel, J. L., 152
Economo, C. von, 210
Engerth, G., 459

Fazekas, J., 105
Federn, P., 10, 15, 16, 43, 533, 547, 548
Feigl, E., 249
Fenichel, O., 1, 25, 27, 45, 328, 473

577

SUBJECT INDEX

Adiodokokinesis, 86
Aggression, 54, 299, 315
  in child, 39, 48
  in depressive psychoses, 41, 57-61,
    473, 477, 511, 512, 524, 526,
    532-533
  after head injury, 282
Aging, 296-306
Agnosia, 7, 32-36, 552-553
Alcoholic encephalopathy, 175, 193-
    258, 283
  histopathology of, 177-178, 247-254,
    257-258
Alcoholic hallucinosis, 20, 64, 65, 230
Alcoholism
  convergence reaction in, 285-288
  and head injury, 160, 165, 173, 183,
    189-191
  in Negroes, 263-285
  in women, 65-66
Alloeroticism, 14
Amentia, 6-9
Amnesia, 170, 175
  after head injury, 164-165, 175, 189-
    190
  hysterical, 55, 164-165
  in shock therapy, 327, 329, 425, 439,
    442
Amyotrophic lateral sclerosis, 553
Anxiety, 30, 31, 383
  in aging, 298
  in depression, 502
  in development, 23, 28
  in schizophrenia, 46, 50-51
Aphasia
  and agnosia, 7, 552-553
  in cerebral anoxia, 102
  clinical case report of, 73-74
  in diffuse lesions of brain, 109-132
  emotional patterns in, 552-553
  after head injury, 170, 171, 173,
    190-191

in insulin treatment, 324-325, 406-
    408, 424
  in metrazol treatment, 438, 442
  in nitrogen inhalation, 204, 206, 208
  in senile psychosis, 302
  sensory, and pain asymbolia, 73-76,
    330
Appersonization, 20-22, 24, 25, 27, 39,
    299
  see also Depersonalization
Apraxia, 93, 95, 210, 302
  and pain asymbolia, 75, 330, 331
Arteriosclerosis, 7, 79, 297, 302-303,
    330
  and decerebrate rigidity, 79
  with psychoses, 7
Asymbolia for pain, 73-76, 95, 176
  see also Pain
Asynergia of trunk, 211
  in alcoholic encephalopathy, 196,
    200, 205, 207, 215, 228
Athetoid movements, 211
Autism, 310
Autoeroticism, 13
Automatic obedience in schizophrenia,
    46, 314
Autopsy reports
  in aphasia, 73-74
  in pain asymbolia, 73
  see also Alcoholic encephalopathy

Bewilderment
  in early schizophrenia, 50
  and head injuries, 163-165, 173, 176,
    189-191
Body, 20, 62, 311, 540
  and catalepsy, 45-46
  and narcissism, 11, 12
  perception of, 315, 511, 534
  and projection, 18, 21
  and reality, 12-15, 17, 512

582

Date Due